CHRISTOPHER
J. H. WRIGHT

KNOWING
G⊕D
THROUGH
the OLD
TESTAMENT

THREE VOLUMES IN ONE

IVP Academic

An imprint of InterVarsity Press
Downers Grove, Illinois

InterVarsity Press
P.O. Box 1400, Downers Grove, IL 60515-1426
ivpress.com
email@ivpress.com

*InterVarsity Press® is the book-publishing division of InterVarsity Christian Fellowship/USA®, a movement of students
and faculty active on campus at hundreds of universities, colleges, and schools of nursing in the United States of
America, and a member movement of the International Fellowship of Evangelical Students. For information about
local and regional activities, visit intervarsity.org.*

Cover design and image composite: David Fassett
Images: blue-green textured background: © enjoynz / iStock / Getty Images Plus
        creeper plant: © enviromantic / E+ / Getty Images
        Iceland River delta: © Justinreznick / E+ / Getty Images
        painted winter background: © Pobytov / DigitalVision Vectors / Getty Images

ISBN 978-0-8308-5243-7 (print)
ISBN 978-0-8308-7207-7 (digital)

Printed in the United States of America ♾
*InterVarsity Press is committed to ecological stewardship and to the conservation of natural resources in all our operations.
This book was printed using sustainably sourced paper.*

Library of Congress Cataloging-in-Publication Data
A catalog record for this book is available from the Library of Congress.

P	21	20	19	18	17	16	15	14	13	12	11	10	9	8	7	6	5	4	3	2	1
Y	37	36	35	34	33	32	31	30	29	28	27	26	25	24	23	22	21	20	19		

CONTENTS

Preface to the Anthology   vii

BOOK ONE

KNOWING JESUS
THROUGH THE OLD TESTAMENT

Preface to the Second Edition   3

Preface to the First Edition   5

1   Jesus and the Old Testament Story   9

2   Jesus and the Old Testament Promise   51

3   Jesus and His Old Testament Identity   91

4   Jesus and His Old Testament Mission   119

5   Jesus and His Old Testament Values   156

6   Jesus and His Old Testament God   214

BOOK TWO

KNOWING GOD *the* FATHER
THROUGH THE OLD TESTAMENT

Preface   241

Introduction   243

1   Knowing God as a Father in Action   251

2   Knowing God Through Experience of His Grace   266

3   Knowing God Through Exposure to His Judgement   283

4   Knowing God as the Father of His People   294

5   Knowing God Through Engaging Him in Prayer   312

6   Knowing God Through Reflecting His Justice   336

7   Knowing God Through Returning to His Love   351

8   Knowing God in Expectation of His Victory   373

9   Knowing God Through Trusting in His Sovereignty   385

   Epilogue: How Do You Know That You Know God?   404

BOOK THREE

KNOWING *the* HOLY SPIRIT
THROUGH THE OLD TESTAMENT

   Preface   411

1   The Creating Spirit   413

2   The Empowering Spirit   430

3   The Prophetic Spirit   451

4   The Anointing Spirit   469

5   The Coming Spirit   495

   Bibliography   522

   Scripture Index   527

PREFACE *to the* ANTHOLOGY

More than twenty-five years have passed since I wrote the first book in this trilogy (and four since its second edition). At the time I did not anticipate that it would be the foundation for two other books. All I had in mind back then, as the preface to Book 1 below indicates, was to help people understand Jesus better in the light of the Old Testament (the Scriptures that shaped his whole identity, life and mission), and in the process to help people also understand the Old Testament Scriptures better in the light of the One to whom they bear witness. It is encouraging to hear from time to time that readers have found that it seems to achieve both intentions.

The title of that first book, *Knowing Jesus Through the Old Testament*, was chosen (after exploring many possibilities) to express the hope that the book would be not merely a doctrinal survey, whether of Christology or Old Testament hermeneutics, but would rather strengthen and deepen readers' personal relationship with Christ by enabling them to know him with a richer and more biblically rooted understanding and appreciation. The contents of the book arose out of years of preaching and teaching, so I knew from experience that those with whom I had shared the perspectives of the book, in the course of many journeys of biblical discovery, often testified to having come to a greater love and knowledge of the authentic Jesus of the Scriptures as a whole, and in the process to a greater appreciation of the Old Testament as the "Bible of Jesus."

The same motivation underlies the other two books, even though they were written much later. As the prefaces to Books 2 and 3 indicate, they too have their origin in the labor and privilege of Bible expositions in a variety of church and conference settings. The chapters of each book considerably expand the oral preaching that lies behind most of them. But the objective and ethos remains the same—to encourage the listener or reader to know God better through deep immersion and engagement with his Word, especially in the less familiar voices of the Old Testament.

This is a voyage of biblical discovery, crossing many horizons and exploring especially the Old Testament sources of our knowledge of God the Holy Trinity—Father, Son and Holy Spirit.

For that reason, this really is the kind of book you need to read with your Bible close at hand. Many texts are quoted in full, but many more are referenced only and it will greatly add to whatever benefit this book can bring if you take the time to stop and read them as you travel along. Since the books were written at different times, there is unavoidably a certain amount of repetition of discussion of certain texts in different contexts. However, this is fairly minimal and I have not attempted to edit out all such instances.

I am grateful to the various editors and publishers who have brought each of the three books to print over the years, but most recently in particular to Vivian Doub and Claire Moore of Langham Creative Projects for editing all three books into this single trilogy, and to Elissa Schauer and Jon Boyd of InterVarsity Press for this North American edition.

Chris Wright

BOOK ONE

KNOWING
JESUS
THROUGH
the OLD
TESTAMENT

PREFACE *to the* SECOND EDITION

The convictions on which the book was first based, as expressed in the preface to the first edition, are as firm in my mind as they ever were. And they have been strengthened through ongoing teaching on the subject. Wherever I teach on this topic, there is usually a moment of eye-opening fresh insight on Jesus when he is presented in the light of how he saw himself in relation to the Old Testament. Somehow, and not surprisingly, the whole Bible comes to make much more sense when Jesus Christ, as the Bible's center of unity, is brought into focus in a way that affirms rather than overlooks all that went before him.

This edition of the book has an additional sixth chapter. When I wrote the original book with its five chapters, I had in mind readers for whom, as for myself, the deity of Jesus of Nazareth is an absolutely solid affirmation of faith and an assumption that author and readers could share. It goes without saying, I thought. Comments I have received from time to time have made it clear that it is dangerous to make that kind of assumption. If it goes without saying, it needs even more to be said! In fact, I have realized that the omission of any discussion of the way in which the Old Testament also shapes what we mean by speaking of Jesus as God was a serious defect of the original book. So I have added this sixth chapter, explaining how the Old Testament reveals the God whom Jesus embodied. Some of the content of the chapter is abbreviated and adapted from my book *The Mission of God*, chapter four.

I have added a few questions and exercises at the end of each chapter that I hope may be used either by individuals or by groups.

It is pleasing to hear from time to time that the book is being used in a number of institutions of theological education on the list of textbooks for courses in biblical theology—even though it was intended for a more popular readership. For that reason, I have included a few more items in the bibliography at the end for those who wish to study further the whole vast field of historical Jesus research and the Old Testament background to the New Testament. Of these, by far the most significant in my view have been the magisterial works of N. T. (Tom) Wright. With enormous erudition and historical scholarship, he has argued in phenomenal depth for an understanding of Jesus in relation to Israel of the Old Testament and intertestamental period, with which my own much more amateur portrait here is in broad accord. For those who need to study further, most of the books listed provide comprehensive additional bibliography.

I express my thanks to Pieter Kwant and the staff of Langham Literature who have kept encouraging me to believe that this book has an ongoing future. I am delighted that at least part of that future will be within the global fellowship of Langham Partnership.

Chris Wright
March 2014

PREFACE *to the* FIRST EDITION

My love for the Hebrew Scriptures of the Old Testament came somewhat later in life than my love for Jesus Christ. But each has reinforced the other ever since I entered the world of biblical studies. In the midst of the many intrinsically fascinating reasons why Old Testament study is so rewarding, the most exciting to me is the way it never fails to add new depths to my understanding of Jesus. I find myself aware that in reading the Hebrew Scriptures I am handling something that gives me a closer common link with Jesus than any archaeological artifact could do.

For these are the words *he* read. These were the stories he knew. These were the songs he sang. These were the depths of wisdom and revelation and prophecy that shaped his whole view of "life, the universe and everything." This is where he found his insights into the mind of his Father God. Above all, this is where he found the shape of his own identity and the goal of his own mission. In short, the deeper you go into understanding the Old Testament, the closer you come to the heart of Jesus. (After all, Jesus never actually *read* the New Testament!) That has been my conviction for a long time, and it is the conviction that underlies this book.

For it saddens me that so many Christians these days love Jesus but know so little about who he thought he was and what he had come to do. Jesus becomes a kind of photo montage composed of a random mixture of Gospel stories, topped up with whatever fashionable image of him is current, including, recently, the New Age caricatures of him. He is cut off from the historical Jewish context of his own day, and from his deep roots in the Hebrew Scriptures.

It is ironic that this widespread lack of biblically informed knowledge about Jesus is growing at the very time when there is a new impetus and enthusiasm in scholarly circles, both Christian and Jewish, for historical research on Jesus. The so-called Third Quest for the historical Jesus has already generated numbers of exciting and fascinating works of scholarship, which at times almost persuaded me I would rather be a student of the New Testament than of the Old!

That feeling usually evaporated fairly quickly as I felt my own amateur status in that field, which needs to be made clear at this point. I have been acutely aware that to write anything at all on the New Testament in general or Jesus in particular is like crawling through a minefield under crossfire. However, with the help of several friends of undoubted New Testament scholarship, I have been bold enough to crawl on, trying to take into account as much of current scholarship as was feasible. My constant comfort has been to remind myself that I am not writing for fellow scholars but for people who want to deepen their knowledge of Jesus and of the Scriptures that meant so much to him. In that sense, I found it hard to decide whether this is a book about Jesus in the light of the Old Testament, or a book about the Old Testament in the light of Jesus. Perhaps it is both.

I have also managed to fulfill one other minor life's ambition with this book, which was to write at least one book entirely without footnotes. This again was dictated by the sort of reader I had in mind. Biblical experts will detect in every paragraph the sources of so many of my ideas, but it is tedious to hang them out at the bottom of every page. My acknowledgment to all those from whose books I have learned so much is paid by the bibliographical list at the end of the book.

More personal gratitude is due to many who have helped me through the minefield in various ways. First, to my students at the Union Biblical Seminary in Pune, India, who bore my first gropings in this area, under the title "Old Testament Hermeneutics." It was while teaching that course that I came across John Goldingay's articles on "The Old Testament and Christian Faith: Jesus and the Old Testament in Matthew 1–5," in *Themelios* 8, nos. 1-2, (1982–1983). They provided an excellent framework, first for that course and then, with his kind permission, for the broad structure of this book, which is rather loosely linked to the themes of the early chapters of Matthew's Gospel. Second, to Dick France, who helped to prime the pump for my amateur New Testament research with some very helpful bibliographical suggestions that generated a flood of other discoveries. Needless to say, neither of these two friends bears any responsibility for the final content of this book.

My thanks are due also to Kiruba Easteraj and the Selvarajah family for their hospitality and kindness in Montauban Guest House, Ootacamund, India, where the first chapters were written during summer vacations.

My wife, Elizabeth, and our four children know only too well how much I depend on their love and support, and over the years they have learned to share or bear my enthusiasm for the Old Testament. They need no words to know my appreciation, but this at least puts my deep gratitude on paper.

Finally, a word of explanation for the dedication. It was Jim Punton, a man who always made me think simultaneously of Amos in his prophetic passion for justice and of Jesus in his warmth and friendship, who first sowed the seed of this book. "Chris," he said to me once, putting his arm around me like an uncle, "you must write a book on how the Old Testament influenced Jesus." That was nearly ten years ago. Sadly, Jim's untimely death means that he cannot judge whether I have achieved what he had in mind.

Chris Wright
All Nations Christian College
Ware, England
1992

JESUS *and the*
OLD TESTAMENT STORY

Judging from the selection of readings in an average Christmas service, in the consciousness of the average Christian the New Testament begins at Matthew 1:18, "This is how the birth of Jesus the Messiah came about. . . ." A natural enough assumption, we might agree, since Christianity began with the birth of Jesus and this verse proposes to tell us how it happened. What more do you need at Christmas?

If the average Christian pauses between the Christmas hymns to wonder what the previous seventeen verses are all about, his or her curiosity is probably offset by relief that at least they weren't included in the readings! And yet those verses are there, presumably because that is how Matthew wanted to begin his Gospel, and also how the minds that shaped the order of the canonical books wanted to begin what we call the New Testament. So we need to respect those intentions and ask why it is that Matthew will not allow us to join in the adoration of the Magi until we have ploughed through his list of "begettings." Why can't we just get on with the story?

Because, says Matthew, you won't understand that story—the one I am about to tell you—unless you see it in the light of a much longer story that goes back for many centuries but leads up to the Jesus you want to know about. And that longer story is the history of the Hebrew Bible, or what

Christians came to call the Old Testament. It is the story that Matthew "tells" in the form of a schematized genealogy—the ancestry of the Messiah.

His opening verse sums up the whole story: Jesus, who is the Messiah, was the son of David and the son of Abraham. These two names then become the key markers for the three main sections of his story:

from Abraham to David;
from David to the Babylonian exile;
from the exile to Jesus himself.

For any Jew who knew his Scriptures (and Matthew is usually reckoned to have been writing primarily for Jewish Christians), every name recalled stories, events, periods of history and memories of their national past. It was a long story, but Matthew compresses it into seventeen verses just as Jesus could later on compress it into a single parable about a vineyard and its tenant farmers.

What Matthew is saying to us by beginning in this way is that we will only understand Jesus properly if we see him in the light of this story, which he completes and brings to its climax. So when we turn the page from the Old to the New Testament, we find a link between the two that is more important than the attention we usually give it. It is a central historical interface binding together the two great acts of God's drama of salvation. *The Old Testament tells the story that Jesus completes.*

This means not only that we need to look at Jesus in the light of the history of the Old Testament, but also that he sheds light backward on it. You understand and appreciate a journey in the light of its destination. And certainly as you journey through the history of the Old Testament it makes a difference to know that it leads to Jesus and that he gives meaning to it. We shall look at that in more depth after we have reviewed that journey in the next section. First let us note several things as regards Jesus himself that Matthew wishes us to understand from his chosen means of opening his story.

Jesus was a real Jew. In Jewish society genealogies were an important way of establishing your right to belong within the community of God's people. First Chronicles 1–9 and Ezra 2 and 8 are examples of this. Your ancestry was your identity and your status. Jesus, then, was not just "a man." He was a particular person born within a living culture. His background, ancestry and roots were shaped and influenced, as all his contemporaries were, by the history and fortunes of his people. We need to keep this in mind, because it often happens that we can talk and think (and sing) about Jesus in such general and universal terms that he becomes virtually abstract—a kind of identikit human being. The Gospels bind us to the particularity of Jesus, and Matthew anchors him in the history of the Jewish nation.

There are (and always have been) those who do not like this Jewishness of Jesus, for a wide variety of reasons. Yet it is the very first fact about Jesus that the New Testament presents to us, and Matthew goes on to underline it in countless ways in the rest of his Gospel. And as we shall see throughout this book, it is this very Jewishness of Jesus and his deep roots in his Hebrew Scriptures that provide us with the most essential key to understanding who he was, why he came and what he taught.

Jesus was a real man. Jesus was "the son of Abraham." When Abram first makes his appearance in the Old Testament story in Genesis 12, the stage is already well set and populated. Genesis 10 portrays a world of nations—a slice of geographical and political reality. It is a world of real human beings, which we would have recognized if we'd been there—not some mythological utopia full of heroes and monsters. This is the human world whose sinful arrogance is described in the story of the tower of Babel in Genesis 11. And this is the world within which, and for which, God called Abram as the starting point of his vast project of redemption for humanity.

The main point of God's promise to Abram was not merely that he would have a son and then descendants who would be especially blessed by God. God also promised that through the people of Abram God would bring blessing to *all nations* of the earth. So although Abraham (as his name was changed to, in the light of this promise regarding the nations) stands at the head of the particular nation of Old Testament Israel and their unique history, there is a universal scope and perspective to him and them: one nation for the sake of all nations.

So when Matthew announces Jesus as the Messiah, the son of Abraham, it means not only that he belongs to that particular people (a real Jew, as we have just seen), but also that he belongs to a people whose very reason for existence was to bring blessing to the rest of humanity. Jesus shared the mission of Israel, and indeed, as the Messiah he had come to make it a reality at last. A particular man, but with a universal significance.

At several points in the most Jewish of all four Gospels, Matthew shows his interest in the universal significance of Jesus for foreign nations beyond the boundaries of Israel. It emerges for the first time here in the opening genealogy in an unexpected and easily overlooked feature. In his long list of fathers, Matthew includes just *four mothers*, all in Matthew 1:3-6: Tamar, Rahab, Ruth and Bathsheba. It may be that one reason for Matthew including them is that there were question marks and irregularities in their marriages, which may be Matthew's way of showing that there was scriptural precedent even for the "irregularity" of Jesus' birth from an unmarried mother. But probably more significant is the other thing they all have in common. They were all, from a Jewish point of view, foreigners. Tamar and Rahab were Canaanites (Gen 38; Josh 2); Ruth was a Moabitess (Ruth 1); Bathsheba was the wife of Uriah, a Hittite, so probably a Hittite herself (2 Sam 1). The implication of Jesus being the heir of Abraham and his universal promise is underlined: Jesus the Jew, and the Jewish Messiah, had Gentile blood!

Jesus was the son of David. Matthew states at the outset what he will develop and demonstrate through his Gospel: that Jesus was the expected Messiah of the royal line of David with the rightful claim to the title "King of the Jews." He establishes this further by tracing Jesus' descent through the royal line of kings descended from David who ruled over Judah (Mt 1:6-11). Probably this represents an "official" genealogy, whereas Luke (Lk 3:23-38) has recorded Jesus' actual biological parentage (or rather that of Joseph, his legal but not biological father). The two lists are not contradictory but rather trace two lines through the same "family tree" from David to Jesus.

Much more was involved in asserting that Jesus was the Davidic Messiah than mere physical ancestry. We shall look at the implications in chapters three and four. They expected that when the true son of David would arrive, God himself would intervene to establish his reign. It would mean the rule of God's justice, liberation for the oppressed, the restoration of peace among humankind and in nature itself. Furthermore, the mission of the Messiah was also connected to the ingathering of the nations. The universal scope of being the son of Abraham was not canceled out by the particular identity of being the son of David. In fact, in Old Testament expectation there was a link between the two. It would be through the son of *David* that the promise to *Abraham* himself would be fulfilled.

Psalm 72 is a good illustration of this. It is a prayer on behalf of the Davidic king, with the heading "Of Solomon." As well as looking forward to prosperity and justice, it includes this hope and expectation:

> May his name endure forever;
> > may it continue as long as the sun.
> Then all nations will be blessed through him,
> > and they will call him blessed. (Ps 72:17)

This is a very clear echo of the personal and universal promise of God to Abraham in Genesis 12:2-3. (Compare also Ps 2:7-8; Is 55:3-5.)

Jesus is the end of the time of preparation. At the end of his genealogy, Matthew 1:17, Matthew makes an observation about it before he moves on to the birth of Jesus: "Thus there were fourteen generations in all from Abraham to David, fourteen from David to the exile to Babylon, and fourteen from the exile to the Messiah."

Matthew is very fond of threes and sevens in his presentation of material in his Gospel. Both were symbolic numbers for completeness or perfection. Three double-sevens is pretty complete! His purpose is not merely statistical or just a matter of a historical curiosity. From that point of view his observation is not strictly accurate, since at several places in the genealogy biological generations are skipped over (as was quite common in Old Testament genealogy). Rather he is being deliberately schematic, with a theological intention. He is pointing out that Old Testament history falls into three approximately equal spans of time between the critical events:

> from the foundational covenant with Abraham to the establishing of the monarch under David;

> from David to the destruction and loss of the monarchy in the Babylonian exile; and

> from the exile to the coming of the Messiah himself who alone could occupy the throne of David.

Jesus is thus "the end of the line" as far as the Old Testament story goes. It has run its completed course in preparation for him, and now its goal and climax has been reached.

The Old Testament is full of future hope. It looks beyond itself to an expected end. This forward movement, or eschatological thrust (from

Greek *eschaton*, "ultimate event" or "final conclusion") is a fundamental part of the faith of Israel. It was grounded in their experience and concept of God himself. God was constantly active within history for a definite purpose, working toward his desired goal for the earth and humanity. Just as Matthew has summarized that history in the form of his genealogy, so his concluding observation in verse 17 points out that it is a history whose purpose is now achieved. The preparation is complete. The Messiah has come. In that sense, Jesus is the end. The same note is echoed throughout the Gospel in the urgency of Jesus' preaching about the kingdom of God. "The time is fulfilled; the kingdom of God is at hand."

Jesus is also a new beginning. Matthew's Gospel (and the New Testament itself) opens with the words, "An account of the *genesis* of Jesus, the Messiah . . . " (my translation). A Jewish reader would immediately be reminded of Genesis 2:4 and Genesis 5:1, where exactly the same expression is used in the Greek translation of the Hebrew Scriptures. The same word in the plural (*geneseis*, "origins," "generations") is used several more times in the book of Genesis to introduce genealogies and narratives, or to conclude them and mark off important divisions in the book.

So the use of the word *genesis* here, by a careful author like Matthew, is fairly certainly deliberate. With the echo of the book of Genesis we are meant to realize that the arrival of Jesus the Messiah marks a new beginning, indeed a new creation. God is doing his "new thing." Good news indeed. Jesus is not only (looking back) the end of the beginning; he is also (looking forward) the beginning of the end.

So much of significance is contained within Matthew's opening seventeen verses. In its own way, it is rather like the prologue of John's Gospel, pointing out dimensions of the significance of Jesus before introducing him in the flesh. We see that Jesus had a very particular context in Jewish history, and yet that he also has the universal significance that was attached to that history ever since the promise to Abraham. We see him as the messianic heir of the line of David. We see him as the end and also the beginning. Only with such understanding of the meaning of the story so far can we proceed to a full appreciation of the gospel story itself.

Returning, however, to our average Christian in a Christmas service, probably the succession of names in Matthew's genealogy will not make her quite so aware of the outline of Old Testament history as it would have done for Matthew's original readers. So at this point it may be helpful to step back and very briefly review the Old Testament story, following the three broad divisions that Matthew observes.

THE STORY SO FAR

From Abraham to David.

(1) The problem. Matthew begins with Abraham, at the point of God's promise from which Israel took its existence. Luke begins further back with Adam. And indeed we can only understand Abraham himself in the light of what goes before. Genesis 1–11 poses the question to which the rest of the Bible, from Genesis 12 to Revelation 22, is the answer.

Having created the earth and human beings to dwell with him upon it, God witnessed the rebellion of the human race against his love and authority. The earlier stories portray this at the level of individual and family life. The later ones go on to show how the whole of human society is enmeshed in a growing web of corruption and violence, which even the judgment of the flood did not eradicate from human life. The climax of this "prehistory" is reached with the story of the tower of Babel in Genesis 11. At the end of that story we find the effects of sin have reached a "global" scale, with humanity scattered in division and confusion across the face of the earth, an earth still under the curse of God. Is there any hope for the human race in such a condition? Can the nations of the earth ever be restored to the blessing and favor of God?

(2) Election. God's answer was a seventy-five-year-old man. To that man and his childless and elderly wife, God promised a son. And through that son, he promised a nation, which, in contrast to the nations since Babel, would be blessed by God. And through that nation, he promised blessing to all the nations.

No wonder Abraham and Sarah both laughed on different occasions, especially as they neared their century and God kept renewing the promise in spite of it becoming ever more remote. But the promise was kept. The laughter turned into Isaac ("he laughs"), and the family that was to become a great nation began to take shape and increase. So important was this choice that it formed part of the identity of the God of the Bible thereafter. He is known, and indeed chooses to be known, as "The God of Abraham, Isaac and Jacob." That description means he is the God of promise and fulfillment, and the God whose purpose ultimately embraced all nations.

This choice of Abraham also defined the identity of the people of Israel. Who were they? The chosen people, yes, but chosen, as Moses reminded them deflatingly and often, not because of their numerical greatness or moral superiority, but only because God had loved and chosen Abraham for his own redemptive purpose (Deut 7:7-8; 9:4-6).

(3) Redemption. Having migrated to Egypt as guests in a time of famine, the descendants of Abraham ended up as slaves—an oppressed ethnic minority in a hostile land. The book of Exodus vividly describes how they were exploited. Then it goes on to an even more vivid description of how God liberated them, through Moses. In the process of this great story of deliverance, God acquires a new name alongside this fresh dimension of his character: "Yahweh," the God who acts out of faithfulness to his promise in liberating justice for the oppressed. The exodus thus becomes the primary model of what redemption means in the Bible and gives substance to what an Israelite would have meant by calling God "Redeemer."

(4) Covenant. Three months after the exodus, God at last has Israel to himself, at the foot of Mount Sinai. There, through Moses, God gave them his law, including the Ten Commandments, and entered into a covenant with them as a nation. He would be their God and they would be his people, in a relationship of sovereignty and blessing on the one hand, and loyalty and obedience on the other.

It is important to see that this covenant was based on what God had already done for them (as they had just recently seen, Ex 19:4-6). God's grace and redemptive action came first. Their obedience to the law and covenant was to be a grateful response, and in order to enable them to be what God wanted them to be as his people in the midst of the nations. We shall explore the meaning of this in chapter five.

(5) Inheritance. The generation of the exodus, through their own failure, unbelief and rebellion, perished in the wilderness. It was the next generation who took possession of the Promised Land, fulfilling the purpose of the exodus liberation. Under the leadership of Joshua, the Israelites gained strategic control of the land. But there followed a lengthy process of settlement in which the tribes struggled—sometimes in cooperation, and sometimes in competition—to possess fully the land allotted to them.

During the centuries of the period of the judges there was much disunity caused by internal strife and external pressures. Alongside this went chronic disloyalty to the faith of Yahweh, though it was never lost altogether, and was sustained, like the people themselves, by the varied ministries and victories of the figures called "judges," culminating in the great Samuel.

The pressures eventually led to the demand for monarchy (1 Sam 8–12). This was interpreted by Samuel as a rejection of God's own rule over his people, especially since it was motivated by a desire to be like the other nations when it was precisely the vocation of Israel to be different. God, however, elevated the sinful desires of the people into a vehicle for his own purpose, and after the failure of Saul, David established the monarchy firmly and became its glorious model.

Possibly the most important achievement of David was that he at last gave to Israel complete and unified control over the whole of the land that had been promised to Abraham. Up to then it had been fragmentarily occupied by loosely federated tribes, under constant attack and invasion from their enemies. David defeated those enemies systematically, giving Israel "rest from their enemies round about," and established secure borders for the nation.

So there is a kind of natural historical arc from Abraham to David. With David the covenant with Abraham had come to a measure of fulfillment: Abraham's offspring had become a great nation; they had taken possession of the land promised to Abraham; they were living in a special relationship of blessing and protection under Yahweh.

But then, as often happens in the Old Testament, no sooner has the promise "come to rest," so to speak, than it takes off again in a renewed form as history moves forward (we shall look at this characteristic of the Old Testament in the next chapter). And so, in a personal covenant with David, God tied his purpose for Israel to his promise to the house of David himself. As in the covenant with Abraham, the promise to David included a son and heir, a great name and a special relationship (2 Sam 7). So then, with this new royal dimension, the story of God's people moves forward to its next phase.

From David to the exile.

(1) *Division of the kingdoms.* Solomon glorified and consolidated the empire that David had built, and built the temple his father had desired and planned. That temple then became the focal point of God's presence with

his people for the next half-millennium, until it was destroyed along with Jerusalem at the time of the exile in 587 B.C.

Solomon also introduced Israel to foreign trade, foreign culture, foreign wealth and foreign influences. The golden age of Solomon's wealth and wisdom, however, had its dark side in the increasing burden of the cost of an empire—a burden that fell on the ordinary population. Samuel had warned the Israelites when they asked for a king that having a king would eventually mean forced labor, taxation, conscription and confiscation (1 Sam 8:10-18). Solomon's later reign proved all these things painfully true. All of this was totally contrary to the authentic Israelite tradition of covenant equality and freedom, and it produced increasing discontent among the people, especially in the northern tribes, who seemed to suffer more than the royal tribe of Judah.

When Rehoboam, Solomon's son, refused the people's request and his elders' advice to lighten the load and instead deliberately chose the way of oppression and exploitation as state policy, the discontent boiled over into rebellion. Led by Jeroboam, the ten northern tribes seceded from the house of David and formed a rival kingdom, taking the name of Israel, leaving Rehoboam and his Davidic successors with the remnant—the kingdom of Judah. The date was in the second half of the tenth century B.C., about 931 B.C. From then on the story of Israel is one of the divided kingdoms, Israel in the north and Judah in the south.

(2) The ninth century B.C. The northern kingdom of Israel, as with many states founded by revolution, went through a period of instability, with successive coups d'état after the death of Jeroboam and four kings in twenty-five years.

Eventually in the ninth century B.C., Omri established a dynasty and built up the political and military strength of the country. This was sustained by his son Ahab, whose wife Jezebel had been chosen for him as a marriage alliance with powerful Phoenicia, the maritime trading nation to the north of Israel. Jezebel's influence, however, was more than political and economic. She set about converting her adoptive kingdom to the religion of her native Tyre. She imposed the cult of Baal and systematically tried to extinguish the worship of Yahweh.

This produced a crisis. God called Elijah to be his prophet to the northern kingdom of Israel in the mid-ninth century. Elijah courageously brought about a (temporary) revival and reconversion of the people to their ancestral faith through the judgment of drought followed by the fiery climax of Mount Carmel (1 Kings 18). Elijah also addressed the anger of God against the economic and social evil that was threatening the material structure of Israel's faith, as typified in Ahab and Jezebel's treatment of Naboth (1 Kings 21). Elijah was followed by Elisha, whose long ministry lasted throughout the rest of the ninth century and influenced both national and international politics.

In the southern kingdom of Judah, the ninth century was a quieter affair. With its established capital, court, bureaucracy and dynasty, Judah proved much more stable than the northern state. The first fifty years saw the reigns of only two kings: Asa and Jehoshaphat. Both were strong and comparatively godly and preserved the faith of Yahweh. Jehoshaphat also introduced a major judicial reform.

The second half of the ninth century saw an attempt by Athaliah, of the house of Omri, who had been married to Jehoshaphat's son Jehoram (as another of Omri's marriage alliances), to capture the throne of David for the house of Israel after her husband's death. Her reign only lasted five years, however, before she was removed in a counterrevolution and the Davidic succession was restored in the person of seven-year-old Joash.

(3) The eighth century B.C. Meanwhile, in northern Israel, the dynasty of Omri had been overthrown in a bloody revolution led by Jehu, a fanatical Yahwist who considered it his mission to remove all traces of Baal, his prophets and his worshipers, by fair means or foul—mostly foul. His blood purge weakened the kingdom and lost him his allies. But by the second quarter of the eighth century his great-grandson, Jeroboam II, restored Israel to a degree of political, military and material prosperity that it had not seen since the days of Solomon.

But, as in the days of Solomon, the prosperity was not enjoyed by all. Underneath the upper and external extravagance, and in spite of the thriving and popular religious cult, lay an increasing poverty gap and a world of exploitation and oppression. There were economic problems of debt and bondage, corruption of the markets and the courts, and the nation was divided between rich and poor. God sent prophets to express his anger at the situation.

Amos and Hosea both prophesied in the northern kingdom of Israel in the mid- to late-eighth century. Amos fiercely denounced the social injustices that he observed on all sides, defending the poor and exploited as "the righteous" (i.e., those with right on their side in the situation), and attacking the wealthy, luxury-loving class, especially in Samaria, as "the wicked." This was a total and very surprising reversal of popular religious understanding of the day. At the same time Amos claimed that the thriving religious practices at Bethel and Gilgal were not only *not* pleasing in the sight of God as the people believed but actually stank in his nostrils. The rampant injustice and oppression in the nation was not only a complete betrayal of all their history as God's covenant people (a history Amos recounts accusingly), but also turned their pretended worship into a mockery and an abomination.

Hosea, through the bitter experience of his own marriage to an unfaithful and adulterous wife, saw more of the internal spiritual reality of the people's condition. He saw the syncretistic Baal worship with the sexual perversions that went along with it, including ritual prostitution. So he accused the people of being infected with a "spirit of prostitution." Amos had predicted that the kingdom would be destroyed and king and people exiled. It must have seemed laughable in the prosperous days of Jeroboam II, but within twenty-five years of his death, it happened and Hosea probably witnessed it.

By the middle of the eighth century B.C., Assyria had become the dominant world power and was rapidly expanding westward to the Palestinian states. After several rebellions, Israel was attacked by Assyria in 725 B.C. Samaria was besieged and eventually fell in 721 B.C. The bulk of the Israelite population (the ten northern tribes) was deported and scattered throughout other parts of Assyria's empire, while populations of foreigners from other parts were brought into Israel's territories. In this act of Assyria—an example of its policy of imperial subjugation—lies the origins of the mixed race of "Samaritans." So the northern kingdom of Israel ceased to exist. Its territory became nothing more than a province under the paw of the Assyrian lion—a paw now poised and threatening very close to Judah.

In Judah, the eighth century began, as in Israel, with half a century of prosperity and stability, mainly under the strong king Uzziah. His successor Jotham was also a good king, but all was not well among the people who, according to the chronicler "continued their corrupt practices" (2 Chron

27:2). Apparently the same social and economic evils had penetrated Judah as were blatant in Israel. This provides the background for the ministries of two great eighth-century prophets in Judah—Isaiah and Micah—who began during the reign of Jotham.

The Assyrian threat loomed over Judah also in the last third of the eighth century. King Ahaz, in 735 B.C., in an attempt to protect himself from threatened invasions from Israel and Syria, appealed to Assyria for assistance against these more local enemies. The Assyrians readily came "to help." They first smashed Syria, Israel and Philistia, and then turned to demand of Judah a heavy tribute for the favor. Ahaz's action, which had been directly opposed by Isaiah, proved politically and religiously disastrous, since Judah became virtually a vassal state of Assyria and was forced to absorb much of its religious practices as well.

Ahaz's successor, Hezekiah, reversed that policy. He linked major religious reforms to a renewed bid for freedom from Assyrian domination. His rebellion brought Assyrian invasions of devastating force, and indeed he surrendered and paid up. But Jerusalem itself was remarkably delivered, in fulfillment of a prophetic encouragement from Isaiah. But instead of producing national repentance and return to Yahweh and the demands of the covenant, as preached by Isaiah, this miraculous deliverance only made the people complacent. They began to think that Jerusalem and its temple were indestructible. God would never, ever, allow them to be destroyed. But they were wrong. Terribly wrong.

(4) The seventh century B.C. The seventh century in Judah was like a seesaw. The reforming, anti-Assyrian policies of Hezekiah were completely reversed by Manasseh. His long, half-century reign became a time of unprecedented apostasy, religious decay, corruption and a return even to ancient Canaanite practices long abominated and forbidden in Israel, such as child sacrifice. His reign was violent, oppressive and pagan (compare 2 Kings 21 and 2 Chron 33), and as far as can be seen, no voice of prophecy penetrated the darkness.

His grandson Josiah, however (Amon the son only reigned two years), brought in yet another reversal of state policy. Josiah both resisted Assyria and reformed Judah's religion. In fact the reformation of Josiah, lasting about a decade from 629 B.C. and including the discovery of a book of the law (probably Deuteronomy) during repairs to the temple, was the most thorough and severe in its effects of any in Judah's history. Jeremiah, who was only slightly younger than Josiah, was called to be a prophet in the early flush of Josiah's reformation. But Jeremiah saw that its effects were largely external and didn't purge the idolatry from the hearts of the people or the corruption from their hands.

In the passion of his youth, Jeremiah denounced the religious, moral and social evils of Jerusalem society, from top to bottom. But he also appealed movingly for repentance, believing that God's threatened judgment could thereby be averted. As Jeremiah's ministry wore on into his middle age, God told Jeremiah that the people had become so hardened in their rebellion that he should stop even praying for them. From then on, Jeremiah foretold nothing but calamity for his own generation at the hands of their enemies. Their disbelief turned to outrage when he predicted even the destruction of the very temple itself, against the popular mythology which, since Isaiah's day, believed it to be safe forever under Yahweh's protection, like Jerusalem itself. He suffered arrest, beatings and imprisonment for so unpopular a message. Unpopular, but accurate.

In the later seventh century the weakening Assyrian empire quite rapidly collapsed and was replaced by the resurgent power of Babylon under an energetic commander, Nebuchadnezzar. Irritated by repeated rebellions in Judah, which after the death of Josiah in 609 B.C. was ruled by a succession of weak and vacillating kings, Nebuchadnezzar finally besieged Jerusalem in 588 B.C. Jerusalem was captured in 587 B.C. and the exile began. The destruction was total: the city, the temple and everything in them went up in smoke. The bulk of the population, except for the poorest in the land, were carried off in captivity to Babylon. The unthinkable had happened. God's people were evicted from God's land. The exile had begun and engulfed a whole generation. The monarchy was ended. The exile of Jehoiachin ("Jeconiah") and his brother Zedekiah, the last two kings of Judah, brings to an end the second section of Matthew's genealogy.

(5) Some lessons of history. We saw some of the important features of the first period of Israel's history (Abraham to David). It showed the nature of Yahweh as a God of faithfulness to covenant promise and of liberating justice for the oppressed. It also showed the nature of God's people (Old Testament Israel). They were called into existence for the sake of God's redemptive purpose for all the nations. They experienced God's redeeming

grace. They lived in covenant relationship with him, in the inheritance of the land he had given to them.

The central section (from David to the exile) also had its vital lessons, which the historical books and the books of the prophets made clear.

One affirmation was that Yahweh, the God of Israel, was in sovereign control of world history—not merely the affairs of Israel. The prophets had asserted this with incredible boldness. They looked out on the vast empires that impinged on the life of Israel and at times appeared to threaten its existence, and regarded them as mere sticks and tools in the hands of Yahweh, the God of little, divided Israel. Those who edited the historical books of Israel, from Joshua to Kings, did so most probably during the exile itself, when Israel was in captivity to one of those empires. Yet they continued to make the same affirmation of faith: Yahweh has done this. God is still in control, as he always has been.

A second vital truth that permeates this period is the moral character and demand of Yahweh. The God who acted for justice at the exodus remained committed to maintaining it among his own people. The law had expressed this commitment constitutionally. The prophets gave it voice directly, each to his contemporary generation and context. God's moral concern is not only individual (though the masses of individual stories show that it certainly does claim every individual) but also social. God evaluates the moral health of society as a whole, from international treaties to market economies, from military strategy to local court procedures, from national politics to the local harvest. This dimension of the message of the Old Testament would reverberate from Matthew's list of kings, since so many of them heard the unforgettable rhetoric of the great prophets of the monarchy period.

A third unmistakable dimension of this era was the realization that God did not want external religious rituals without practical social justice. This was all the more surprising in the light of the strong Pentateuchal tradition that ascribed the religion of Israel—its festivals, sacrifices and priesthood—to the gift and commandment of Yahweh himself. Of course, even in the law itself the essential covenant requirements of loyalty and obedience had come before the detailed sacrificial regulations. And since the days of Samuel there had been the awareness that "to obey is better than sacrifice" (1 Sam 15:22). Nevertheless there was still something radically shocking when Amos and Isaiah told the people that Yahweh hated and despised their worship, and was fed up and sickened by the very sacrifices they thought he wanted. Jeremiah told them that they could mix up all their rituals the wrong way around for all that God cared (Amos 5:21-24; Is 1:11-16; Jer 7:21-26). God will not be worshiped and cannot be known apart from commitment to righteousness and justice, faithfulness and love, the things that define God's own character and are his delight (Jer 9:23-24; 22:15-17).

All three of these prominent features of the message of the Old Testament in the period of the monarchy are to be found in the teaching of Jesus, son of David: the sovereignty (kingship) of God, the essentially moral demand of God's rule and the priority of practical obedience over all religious observances. In these, as in so many ways as we shall see, especially in chapter five, Jesus recaptured and amplified the authentic voice of the Scriptures.

From the exile to the Messiah.

(1) The exile. The exile lasted fifty years (that is, from 587 B.C. to the first return of some Jews to Jerusalem in 538 B.C.). The period from the destruction of the temple to the completion of its rebuilding was approximately seventy years.

It is remarkable that Israel and its faith survived at all. That they did survive was largely due to the message of the prophets—particularly of Jeremiah up to, and of Ezekiel after, the fall of Jerusalem. They consistently interpreted the terrifying events as the judgment of Yahweh, punishment for the persistently evil ways of his people. From that perspective, the exile could be seen as a punishment that was *logical* (it showed God's consistency in terms of his covenant threats as well as his promises). But it was a judgment that was also *limited* (so there could be hope for the future). Both Jeremiah and Ezekiel foretold a return to the land and a restoration of the relationship between God and his people. Jeremiah portrayed it in terms of a new covenant (Jer 31:31-34). Ezekiel had visions of nothing short of national resurrection (Ezek 37), with reunified tribes of Israel living once again in God's land, surrounding God's temple and enjoying God's presence (Ezek 40–48).

Nevertheless, by the later years of the exile it seemed that many had abandoned hope. The Israelites accused Yahweh of having forgotten and forsaken them (e.g., Is 40:27; 49:14)—a rich irony in view of the fact that it was they who for centuries had treated him that way! Into this lethargic despair came the message of Isaiah 40–55 addressing the exiles. At a time when all they could see was the threatening rise of yet another empire (the Persians), these chapters of the book of Isaiah called on them to lift up their eyes and hearts once more to see their God on the move, bringing liberation at last.

The ringing affirmation of Isaiah 40–55 is that Yahweh is not only still the sovereign Lord of all creation and all history (and is utterly, uniquely so), but also that he is about to act again on behalf of his oppressed people with a deliverance that will recall the original exodus but dwarf it in significance. The clouds the people so much dread—the sudden rise of Cyrus, ruler of the new, expanding Persian Empire—would burst in blessings on their head. Babylon would be destroyed and they would be released, free to return to Jerusalem, which, sings the prophet, was already exulting in joy at the sight of God leading his captives home.

In the midst of all this directly historical prediction, the prophet also perceives the true ministry and mission of Israel as the servant of God, destined to bring his blessing to all nations—a destiny in which they are manifestly failing. The task will be accomplished, however, through a true Servant of Yahweh, whose mission of justice, teaching, suffering, death and vindication will ultimately bring God's salvation to the ends of the earth. The *particular* story of tiny Israel and the *universal* purposes of God are again linked together.

(2) The restoration. The historical predictions were fulfilled. Cyrus defeated Babylon in 539 B.C. and granted freedom to the captive peoples of the Babylonian empire to take up their gods and go home—under his "supervision," of course. In 538 B.C. the first return of some of the exiled Jews began. They were a tiny community facing enormous problems. Jerusalem and Judah were in ruins after half a century of neglect. They experienced intense opposition and a campaign of political and physical obstruction from the Samaritans. Their early harvests were disappointing, creating further problems. Not surprisingly, after a start was made and the foundations laid, work on the rebuilding of the temple was soon neglected. However, as a result of the encouragement of two of the postexilic prophets, Haggai and Zechariah, it was eventually completed in 515 B.C.

Throughout this period Judah had no independence, of course. It formed just a small subprovince of the vast Persian Empire, which stretched from the shore of the Aegean Sea to the borders of India and lasted for two centuries. In the fifth century it appears that disillusionment and depression set in again, partly as a result of the apparent failure of the hopes raised by Haggai and Zechariah. And this led to a growing laxity in religious and moral life. This was challenged by the last of the Old Testament prophets, Malachi, probably about the middle of the fifth century. He was concerned about the slovenliness of the sacrifices, the spread of divorce and the widespread failure of the people to honor God in practical life.

The same kind of situation was addressed a little later by Ezra and Nehemiah, whose terms of office overlapped somewhat in Jerusalem. Ezra's achievement was the teaching of the law and the reordering of the community around it, consolidated by a ceremony of covenant renewal. Nehemiah's achievements included the rebuilding of the walls of Jerusalem, giving its inhabitants not only physical safety but also a sense of unity and dignity. As the officially appointed Persian governor, Nehemiah was able to give the needed political patronage and authority to the reforms of Ezra, as well as engaging in some social and economic reforms of his own.

(3) The intertestamental period. The canonical history of the Old Testament comes to an end in the mid-fifth century with Malachi, Ezra and Nehemiah. But of course, the Jewish community went on, as does Matthew's genealogy. The Jews lived through two more changes of imperial power before Christ.

Twice during the early fifth century Persia tried, and failed, to conquer the Greek mainland and spread its power to Europe. It was heroically beaten back by the Spartans and Athenians—who then fell to fighting with each other. Not until the mid-fourth century were the Greek states forced into unity by the power of Macedon, which then turned its attention east to the wealth of the Persian Empire just across the Aegean Sea. Under Alexander the Great, Greek armies sliced through the Persian Empire like a knife through butter, with amazing speed. The whole vast area once ruled by Persia, including Judah, then came under Greek rule. This was the beginning of the "Hellenistic" (Greek) era, when the Greek language and culture spread throughout the whole Near East and Middle Eastern world.

After the premature death of Alexander in 323 B.C., his empire was split up among his generals. Ptolemy established a dynasty in Egypt, and for more or less the whole of the third century, Palestine and the Jews were under the political control of the Ptolemies. From about 200 B.C. onward, however, control of Palestine passed into the hands of the Seleucid kings of Syria, who ruled from Antioch over the northern part of the old Alexandrian empire. Their rule was much more aggressively Greek, and Jews faced increasing pressure to conform religiously and culturally to Hellenism. Those who refused faced persecution. The supreme insult was when Antiochus Epiphanes IV in 167 B.C. set up a statue of Zeus, the supreme god of Greek mythology, in the temple itself.

This sacrilege sparked off a major revolt when Jews under the leadership of Judas Maccabeus took up arms. It ended with a successful struggle for independence, climaxing in the cleansing of the temple in 164 B.C. For the next century, the Jews more or less governed themselves under the leadership of the Hasmonean priestly dynasty. This lasted until the power of Greece was replaced by that of Rome, which had been gradually expanding its sphere of influence throughout the whole Mediterranean basin during the second and first centuries B.C. In 63 B.C. Roman legions under Pompey (also, but less deservedly than Alexander, known as "the Great") entered Palestine. Thus began the long period of Roman supremacy over the Jews. And so it was that, when the Roman emperor Caesar Augustus decided that he wanted a census of the whole Roman Empire so that he could get maximum taxes from all the subject populations, a virgin from Nazareth gave birth to her firstborn son in Bethlehem of Judea, the city of David, and brought Matthew's genealogy to an end.

Two features of this intertestamental period are worth noting in view of their influence on the world into which Jesus arrived. The first was an increasing devotion to the law, the Torah. This became the supreme mark of faithful Jews. It eventually developed into a somewhat fanatical cause, supported by a systematic building of a whole structure of theology and exposition and application around the law itself. There were professional experts, called scribes, involved in this. There were also lay movements devoted to wholehearted obedience to the law—such as the Pharisees. We may be tempted to dismiss all this as legalism. Doubtless it tended in that direction, and Jesus, with his unique insight and authority, exposed some of the failure and misguidedness of his contemporary devotees of the law and tradition. But we should also be aware of the positive and worthy motives that lay behind this emphasis on keeping God's law. Had not the exile, the greatest catastrophe in their history, been the direct judgment of God on the failure of his people precisely to keep his law? Was that not also the message of the great prophets? Surely then they should learn the lesson of history and make every effort to live as God required? In that way they would not only avoid a repetition of such judgment but also hasten the day when God would finally deliver them from their present enemies. The pursuit of holiness was serious and purposeful. It was a total social program— not just a fringe of hyperreligious piety.

The second feature was the upsurge of apocalyptic, messianic hope. As persecution continued and as the nation experienced martyrdoms and great suffering, it began to hope for a final, climactic intervention by God himself, as the prophets had foretold. God would establish his kingdom forever by destroying his (and Israel's) enemies. He would vindicate and uplift the righteous oppressed and put an end to their suffering. In varied ways these hopes included the expectation of a coming figure who would bring about this intervention of God and lead the people. These expectations were not all linked together or attached to one single figure. They included terms like messiah (anointed one), son of man, a new David, the return of Elijah, or the Prophet, the branch, etc. We shall look at some of these in chapters three and four. The coming of this figure would herald the end of the present age, the arrival of the kingdom of God, the restoration of Israel and the judgment of the wicked.

So just imagine the stirring of hearts and quickening of pulses in Jewish homes and communities when, into this mixture of aspirations and hopes, dropped the message of John the Baptist, and then of Jesus himself: "The time is fulfilled! [what you have been waiting for as something future is now here and present]; the kingdom of God is at hand! [God is now acting to establish his reign in the midst of you]; so repent and believe the good news [urgent action is required of you now]."

Light on the story. This, then, is the story that Matthew condenses into seventeen verses of genealogy, the story that leads up to Jesus the Messiah, the story that he completes. It is the story from which Jesus acquired his identity and mission. It is also the story to which he gave significance and authority. The very form of the genealogy shows the direct continuity between the Old Testament and Jesus himself. This continuity is based on the action of God. The God who is manifestly involved in the events described in the second half of Matthew 1 was also active in the events implied in the first half. In Jesus, God brought to completion what he himself had prepared for. This means that it is Jesus who gives meaning and validity to the events of Israel's Old Testament history. So when we accept the claims of this chapter about Jesus (that he is indeed the promised Messiah, that he was conceived by the Holy Spirit of God, that he is uniquely God's Son, that in him the saving God has truly come among us), we also accept the claim that the same chapter makes about the history that leads up to him—the Old Testament.

It is important to remember that we are still talking about *history* here, and not only about *promises* being fulfilled (which is the subject of the next chapter). We know that, as Paul put it, all the promises of God "are 'Yes' in Christ" (2 Cor 1:20). But in a sense all the acts of God are "yes" in Christ also. For the Old Testament is much more than a promise box full of blessed predictions about Jesus. It is primarily a story—the story of the acts of God in human history out of which those promises arose. The promises only make sense in relation to that history.

If we think of the Old Testament only in terms of promises that are fulfilled, we may fall into the trap of regarding the historical content of the Old Testament as of little value in itself. If it is all "fulfilled," is it worth anything now? Now that we have the "reality" of Christ, do we need to pay any attention to the "shadows" (as the author of Hebrews puts it, Heb 8:5)? But the events of the Old Testament story were themselves reality— sometimes life-and-death reality—for those who lived through them. And through them there was a real relationship between God and his people, and a real revelation of God to his people, and through them to us. It is the same God. The God who in these last days has spoken to us by his Son (as the author of Hebrews puts it, Heb 1:2), also and truly spoke through the prophets. And those prophets were rooted in the earthy specifics of their own historical contexts. They spoke into history, and their words come to us out of that history. We cannot, must not, simply throw that history away, like a discarded ticket when you reach your destination at the end of a journey.

Light on the old. When we look at events in the history of the Old Testament, then, with these points in mind, it has several effects. First of all, we must affirm whatever significance a particular event had in terms of Israel's own experience of God and faith in him. "What it meant for Israel" does not just evaporate in a haze of spiritualization when we reach the New Testament. Second, however, we may legitimately see in the Old Testament event additional levels of significance in the light of the end of the story—that is, in the light of Christ. And third, the Old Testament event may provide levels of significance to our full understanding of all that Christ was and said and did.

Take for example that foundational event in Israel's history—the exodus. The event itself and the lengthy texts that describe it leave no doubt that God is characterized by care for the oppressed and is motivated to action for justice on their behalf. So prominent is this aspect of the significance of the story in the Hebrew Bible that it became permanently definitive of the nature of Yahweh, Israel's God. The exodus also defined what Israel meant by the terms *redemption* and *salvation*. That dimension of the exodus event remains true, as a permanently valid part of God's revelation, after the coming of Christ. His coming in no way alters or removes the truth of the Old Testament story in itself and in its meaning for Israel—namely, that God is concerned for the poor and suffering and desires justice for the exploited. On the contrary, it underlines and endorses it. What the Old Testament saw in that event remains true.

Looking back on the event, however, in the light of the fullness of God's redemptive achievement in Jesus Christ, we can see that even the original exodus was not merely concerned with the political, economic and social aspects of Israel's predicament. There was also a level of spiritual oppression in Israel's subjection to the gods of Egypt. "Let my people go *that they may worship/serve me*" was God's demand on Pharaoh. And the explicit purpose of the deliverance was that they would *know* Yahweh in the grace of redemption and covenant relationship. So the exodus, for all the comprehensiveness of what it achieved for Israel, points beyond itself to a greater need for deliverance from the totality of evil and restoration to relationship with God than it achieved by itself. Such a deliverance was accomplished by Jesus Christ in his death and resurrection. It was the reality of that accomplishment that Moses and Elijah discussed with him on the mount of transfiguration, as, in Luke's words, they talked about "the exodus he would accomplish in Jerusalem" (Lk 9:31, my translation). And indeed when the Hebrew prophets themselves looked hopefully into the future, they pictured God's final and complete salvation in terms of a new and greater exodus, as a result of which salvation would reach to the ends of the earth. So, when we look back on the original historical exodus in the light of the end of the story in Christ, it is filled with rich significance in view of what it points to.

Light on the new. But it is equally important to look at the other end of the story, the achievement of Christ, in the light of all that the exodus was as an act of God's redemption, as it is understood in the Old Testament. The New Testament affirms that the gospel of the cross and resurrection of Christ is God's complete answer to the totality of evil and all its effects within his creation. But it is the Old Testament that shows us the nature and extent of sin and evil—primarily in the narratives of Genesis 4–11, and then also in the history of Israel and the nations, such as their oppression in the first chapters of Exodus. It shows us that while evil has its origins outside the human race, human beings are morally accountable to God for our own sin. It shows us that sin and evil have a corporate as well as an individual dimension, that is, they affect and shape the patterns of social life within which we live, as well as the personal lives we lead. It shows us that sin and evil affect history itself through inescapable cause and effect and a kind of cumulative process through the generations of humanity. It shows us that there is no area of life on earth in which we are free from the influence of our own sin and the sin of others. In short, the Old Testament portrays to us a very big problem to which there needs to be a very big answer, if there is one at all.

Now, in the New Testament, of course, as Christians we believe we see God's big and final answer to the problem. But in the Old Testament God had already begun to sketch in the dimensions of his answer through successive acts of redemption in history, with the exodus as the prime model. Here we come back to the importance of treating the Old Testament as real history. Christians tend to say something like "the Old Testament is a foreshadowing of Jesus Christ." Carefully explained, this is true. But it can lead to the prejudice that dispenses with the Old Testament itself as little more than shadows, or a kind of children's picture book, of no significance in itself but only for what it foreshadowed. And then we can spiritualize and individualize our interpretation of the work of Christ in such a way that it loses all touch with the earlier dimensions of God's first works of redemption in the history of Israel.

But the exodus was *real* redemption. It was a real act of the living God, for real people who were in real slavery, and it really liberated them. They were liberated from political oppression as an immigrant community into independent nation status. They were liberated from economic exploitation as a slave labor force into the freedom and sufficiency of a land of their own. They were liberated from social violation of basic human rights as a victimized ethnic minority into an unprecedented opportunity to create a new kind of community based on equality and social justice. They were liberated from spiritual bondage to Pharaoh and the other gods of Egypt into undeniable knowledge of and covenant relationship with the living God.

Such was the meaning and scope of redemption in the Hebrew Bible. The very word *redemption* took its substantial meaning from this event. Ask any Israelite what he meant by saying that YHWH their God was a Redeemer, or that he himself was redeemed, and he (or she, if you had asked the likes of Deborah or Hannah) would have told you this story of the exodus and said, "That is what redemption is. That is how I know I belong to a redeemed people."

That is exactly what some of the psalms do. They celebrate redemption by telling this story. They knew the scale of the problem, and they had experienced the scale of God's answer.

Now of course, the exodus was not yet God's last word or act in redemption. Yes, a greater "exodus" and a complete redemption still lay in their future. But within the limits of history and revelation up to that point, the exodus was a real act of the Redeemer God, and it demonstrated unmistakably the comprehensive scale and scope of his redemptive purpose. The exodus was *God's* idea of redemption. How big, then, is our "New Testament gospel"? It should not fall short of, or be narrower than, its Old Testament foundation, for God is the same God and his ultimate purpose is the same.

This means that it is inadequate also merely to explain it like this (this is how I was taught as young Christian): "In the exodus, God rescued Israel from bondage to Pharaoh, and through the cross God rescues me from bondage to sin." That is true, of course. But the mighty act of the exodus was more than just a parable to illustrate personal salvation. Furthermore, the nature of the bondage is not quite so parallel as that. Gloriously it is true that the cross breaks the bondage of my personal sin and releases me from its effects. But the exodus was a release from bondage to the *sin of others*. The Israelites were in Egypt and in slavery, but not because of their own sins or God's judgment. Their sufferings were the direct result of the oppression, cruelty, exploitation and victimization of the Egyptians. They were suffering most from the sin of others. Their liberation therefore was a release from bondage, not to their own sin, but to the evil of others who had enslaved them.

This is not for a moment to imply that the Israelites were not themselves also sinners. They were as much in need of God's mercy and grace as the rest of the human race. The subsequent story of their behavior in the wilderness proved that beyond a doubt, just as that story also proved God's infinite patience and forgiving grace toward their sinful and rebellious ways. The sacrificial system, indeed, was designed precisely to cope with the reality of sin on the part of the people of God and to provide a means of atoning for it. The point here is that atonement and forgiveness for one's own sin is not what the exodus redemption was about. It was rather a *deliverance from an external evil* and the suffering and injustice it caused, by means of a shattering defeat of the evil power and an irrevocable breaking of its hold over Israel, in all the dimensions mentioned above—political, economic, social and spiritual.

If, then, God's climactic work of redemption through the cross transcends, but also embodies and includes, the scope of all his redemptive activity as previously laid bare in Old Testament history, our gospel must include the exodus model of liberation, as well as the sacrificial model of atonement, or the restoration model of God's forgiving grace (as after the exile). The New Testament does, in fact, affirm the death and resurrection of Jesus as a cosmic victory over all authorities and powers "in heaven and on earth." At the cross Jesus defeated all the evil forces that bind and enslave human beings, corrupt and distort human life, and warp, pollute and frustrate the very creation itself. That victory is an essential part of the biblical "good news." And applying that victory to every dimension of human life on earth is the task of Christian mission.

So then we can see that when we take Old Testament history seriously in relation to its completion in Jesus Christ, a two-way process is at work, yielding a double benefit in our understanding of the whole Bible. On the one hand, we are able to see the full significance of the Old Testament story in the light of where it leads—the climactic achievement of Christ; on the other hand, we are able to appreciate the full dimensions of what God did through Christ in the light of his historical declarations and demonstrations of intent in the Old Testament.

We have concentrated on the exodus so far. But the same principles could be applied to other major dimensions of Israel's story, such as the land—the story of its promise, gift and inheritance, and all the theology, laws, institutions and ethical imperatives that surrounded it.

The story of the monarchy, with the accompanying ministry and message of the prophets, would be equally illuminating, handled in both directions, as we have tried to do.

Matthew's opening genealogy, then, points us to one major way for us as Christians to take account of the Hebrew Bible in relation to Jesus and the New Testament, and that is as story—*the* story, with a multidimensional relevance culminating in the story of Jesus himself. Taken together, both Testaments record the history of God's saving work for humanity. *Salvation history* is a term that has been used by many scholars to refer to this, and some would regard it as the primary point of continuity or relationship between the two testaments of the Christian Bible. As with most scholarly positions, this has been argued over, but it does seem unquestionable that history is one important aspect of the link between Old and New, and that Matthew's genealogy, with all its explicit and implicit levels of meaning, points to this very clearly.

A UNIQUE STORY

We have used the expression "salvation history" about the Old Testament. This affirms that in the history of Israel, God was acting for salvation in a way that was not true elsewhere. Now this claim is an embarrassment for some. Not everyone likes the idea of one single chosen people of God enjoying a unique history of salvation, over against all the rest of the nations who seem to get a rather poor deal on the whole. Surely, some people say, if we believe in one God who is and always has been the one universal God of all humanity, then we need to see all the varied histories of different nations and cultures as being also part of his work on the earth. And can those extrabiblical histories not also function as valid preparations for the fullness of his saving work in Jesus Christ? Obviously, the history of the Old Testament represents *one* way to Jesus—the history of his own people. But, it is said, we need not stress that particular history as far as other peoples are concerned who do not stand within the stream of the Judeo-Christian historical heritage. Rather, we should look within worldwide history for other preparatory routes to the knowledge of the gospel of Christ. When taken to the logical conclusion, this train of thought leads to the view that we may in fact dispense with the Old Testament (at least as far as any canonical authority is concerned) for people who have their own religious and cultural history and scriptural traditions. What are we to say to such arguments?

Clearly, if we believe that the Christian church has been right all through the ages to hold on to the Hebrew Scriptures of the Old Testament as a vital and integral part of the canon of Christian Scripture, then we must say something about this problem of the relationship between *Israel's* history, or salvation history, and the rest of *human* history. Otherwise we might as well go on pretending that the New Testament really does start at Matthew 1:18 and forget all that Matthew was trying to tell us in his unique prologue. But, as we shall see, if we were to throw away the Old Testament, we would lose most of the meaning of Jesus himself. For the uniqueness of Jesus is built on the foundation of the uniqueness of the story that prepared the way for him to come.

Unfortunately, this is a link that is not often preserved in the current debate about the relationship between Christianity and other faiths. Many discussions about the significance of Jesus Christ within the context of world religions virtually cut him off from his historical and scriptural roots. People speak of Jesus as if he were the founder of a new religion. Now, of course, if by that is meant merely that Christianity has historically become a separate religion from Judaism, that may be superficially true. But certainly Jesus had no intention of starting another "religion" as such. He came to fulfill the faith of Israel. Who Jesus was and what he had come to do were both already long prepared for through God's dealings with the people Jesus belonged to. We really must understand the distinctive claims of the Hebrew Scriptures if we are to get our understanding of Christ's uniqueness straight also.

*A **universal goal**.* The proper place to begin our discussion of this issue is to repeat a point made earlier: the Old Testament itself quite clearly intends us to see Israel's history not as an end in itself or for the sake of Israel alone, but rather for the sake of the rest of the nations of humanity. The order of the biblical story itself makes this clear. Just as the New Testament withholds our introduction to Jesus until we have been reminded of what went before, so the Old Testament brings Israel on stage (in the loins of Abraham) in Genesis 12, only after an extensive introduction to the dilemma of the whole human race. Genesis 1–11 is entirely occupied with humanity as a whole, the world of all nations, and with the apparently insoluble problem of their corporate evil. So the story of *Israel*, which begins at chapter 12, is actually God's answer to the problem of *humanity*. All God's dealings with Israel in particular are to be seen as the pursuit of God's unfinished business with all nations. Old Testament Israel existed for the sake of all nations.

This, as we have seen, was the explicit purpose of God's covenant promise to Abraham, first expressed in Genesis 12:3 and repeated several times throughout the book: "All peoples on earth will be blessed through you."

It is then echoed in many various ways in other parts of the Old Testament. At Mount Sinai, for example, at the very point where God is impressing on Israel their unique identity and role in the midst of the nations, he leaves no doubt that he is far from being a minor local deity or even your average national god. The scope of his concern and his sovereignty is universal: "the whole earth is mine" (Ex 19:5). He had already tried, with less success, to establish the same point with Pharaoh, whose resistance afforded the opportunity for a display of God's power and a proclamation of his name "in all the earth." The purpose of the plagues and the liberation to follow was:

> so you may know that there is no one like me in all the earth . . .
> that my name might be proclaimed in all the earth . . .
> so that you may know that the earth is the Lord's. (Ex 9:14, 16, 29)

The same universal dimension of Israel's role is alluded to by the prophets at times. Jeremiah, for example, looking back nostalgically to Israel's comparative faithfulness to God in the wilderness (compared, that is, with their apostasy in his own day), says:

> Israel was holy to the Lord,
>   the firstfruits of his harvest. (Jer 2:3)

What harvest? Presumably his harvest among the nations. Israel was not the sum and limit of God's interest, precious though it was, as the context emphasizes. It was rather the firstfruits that guaranteed a much larger ingathering. Later the same prophet envisages what would happen if only Israel could be brought to true repentance:

> and if in a truthful, just and righteous way
>   you swear, "As surely as the LORD lives,"
> then the nations will invoke blessings by him
>   and in him they will boast. (Jer 4:2)

This is not only an echo of the universal promise to Abraham in Genesis 12:3, but also of its expansion in Genesis 18:18-19, where God says:

> Abraham will surely become a great and powerful nation, and all nations on earth will be blessed through him. For I have chosen him, so that he will direct his children and his household after him to keep the way of the LORD by doing what is right and just, so that the LORD will bring about for Abraham what he has promised him.

God's promise—the blessing of all nations—is here linked to the ethical demand on Abraham's descendants. They were to be a community committed to the way of Yahweh—namely, to righteousness and justice. Only in that way could their mission of being a blessing to the nations be fulfilled. Jeremiah picks up this condition to the promise and builds it into his plea for genuine repentance. If Israel would only come back to living as it was created to, with social life and public worship both grounded in "truth, justice and righteousness," then God could get on with his wider and greater purpose—blessing the rest of humanity. Jeremiah, who had been called to be a "prophet to the nations" (not merely Israel), was aware of the universal dimension of his mission. Much more was at stake concerning whether Israel would or would not change its ways than the fate of Israel alone. Israel's response to God had implications for the rest of the world.

So we need to keep this perspective in our minds at all times when reading the Old Testament and its very particular history. It is like keeping a wide-angle lens viewpoint alongside the more close-up picture. Israel's history is a *particular means for a universal goal.* So we should not be tempted to give in to the accusation that by holding on to the Old Testament and its history as vitally and indispensably linked to the New

Testament (as Matthew's genealogy requires us to), we are somehow being narrow and exclusivist in our theology or our attitudes. Quite the opposite is the case. The rest of the world was not absent from the mind and purpose of God in all his dealings with Old Testament Israel. Indeed, to borrow a not unfamiliar phrase from John's Gospel: God so loved the *world* that he chose *Israel*.

A *unique experience*. Having made the point above, it still has to be maintained that according to the Old Testament, no other nation experienced what Israel did of the grace and power of God. God's action in and through Israel was unique. The story of election, redemption, covenant and inheritance, outlined in the historical survey above, was a story shared by no other people.

Now this does *not* mean that God was in no way active in the histories of other peoples. The Old Testament explicitly asserts that he was, and we shall look at that below. It *does* mean that only in Israel did God work within the terms of a covenant of redemption, initiated and sustained by his saving grace. Deuteronomy presents the events of Israel's previous history as unparalleled in all of time and space.

> Ask now about the former days, long before your time, from the day God created human beings on the earth; ask from one end of the heavens to the other. Has anything so great as this ever happened, or has anything like it ever been heard of? Has any other people heard the voice of God speaking out of fire, as you have, and lived? Has any god ever tried to take for himself one nation out of another nation, by testings, by signs and wonders, by war, by a mighty hand and an outstretched arm, or by great and awesome deeds, like all the things the LORD your God did for you in Egypt before your very eyes? . . . Because he loved your ancestors and chose their descendants after them, he brought you out of Egypt by his Presence and his great strength, to drive out before you nations greater and stronger than you and to bring you into their land to give it to you for your inheritance, as it is today. (Deut 4:32-34, 37-38)

This passage includes all four elements of the redemptive history referred to above: election, redemption, covenant and inheritance. The passage then goes on to draw a theological implication, namely, that the uniqueness of Israel's historical experience points to the uniqueness of Yahweh himself as God: "You were shown these things so that you might know that the LORD is God; besides him there is no other" (Deut 4:35).

Thus the revelation of the character of God and the nature of his redeeming work for humanity are bound together with the history of Israel. Israel's uniqueness is tied to God's uniqueness. To put it simply, God did things in and for Israel that he did not do in the history of any other nation. And that was how Israel knew that Yahweh alone was the true God.

This uniqueness of Israel's historical experience, however, was because of its special role and function in the world. It was to facilitate God's promise of blessing to the nations. It was to be his priesthood in the midst of the nations (Ex 19:6)—representing him to the rest of humankind and being the means of bringing the nations to saving knowledge of the living God. To fulfill that destiny it was to be a holy nation (different from the rest), characterized by walking in the way of Yahweh in justice and righteousness (as we saw in Gen 18:19). That is why the text from Deuteronomy above draws out not only a *theological* implication about God but also a *moral* implication about what is required of Israel in the light of their unique experience: "Acknowledge and take to heart this day that the LORD is God in heaven above and on the earth below. There is no other. Keep his decrees and commands, which I am giving you today, so that it may go well with you" (Deut 4:39-40).

So Israel's unique historical experience was not a ticket to a cozy state of privileged favoritism. Rather it laid upon the people a missionary task and a moral responsibility. If they failed in these, then in a sense they fell back to the level of any other nation. They stood, like all nations and all humanity, before the bar of God's judgment, and their history by itself gave them no guaranteed protection.

Amos was a prophet who perceived very clearly how Israel's unique history, like a double-edged sword, cut both ways. He recounts the critical stages of Israel's redemptive history from the exodus, through the wilderness, victoriously into the land, up to the rise of the prophets. But he uses it not in order to congratulate Israel on its blessings and privilege but as a stark contrast to its present behavior. By rampant injustice and social corruption it was denying all that its history was meant to have made it. Its unique experience of God's salvation thus exposed it to even more severe penalty for their rebellion (Amos 2:6-16; 3:2).

So Amos predicted the unthinkable: Israel would be destroyed and its land left deserted. But surely, his hearers must have protested, God cannot treat his own people so! Are we not those whom he brought up out of Egypt? Yes indeed, came the reply. But so what, if you have reduced your moral standards of social life to the lowest common denominator of the rest of humanity? Your history by itself gives you neither excuse nor protection.

> "Are not you Israelites the same to me as the Cushites?"
>   declares the LORD.
> "Did I not bring Israel up from Egypt, the Philistines from Caphtor and the
>   Arameans from Kir?" (Amos 9:7)

This devastating word must have rocked Israel to the core, even more than the fierce words of destructive doom that surround it on both sides. What? Israel, the same to God as remote foreigners on the very edge of the known world (Cush was roughly Sudan/Ethiopia)?! God, as sovereign in the movements of Israel's traditional enemies as of Israel itself?! Precisely, says God through Amos, if by your disobedience you forfeit all that your own history entitled and prepared you for.

We ought to be careful in handling this verse not to make it say more than it does. It has been used by some scholars to argue that other nations stood on a level with Israel in God's sight and that he had been *savingly* active in their history also. This then can be used as part of an argument for various forms of religious universalism or pluralism. But Amos did not say that other nations were like Israel but that Israel had become like them, in God's sight, because of their sinfulness and his imminent judgment.

Similarly, the fact that Amos affirms the sovereignty of Yahweh over the national histories of other peoples—including their "exoduses" and migrations—cannot mean that he believed that God had "redeemed" those nations through those events, or that they stood in the same covenant relationship with God as Israel did. Such a view flatly contradicts what Amos himself had very emphatically stated a few chapters earlier:

> Hear this word, people of Israel, the word the LORD has spoken against you—
> against the whole family I brought up out of Egypt:

> "You only have I chosen
>   of all the families of the earth;
> therefore I will punish you
>   for all your sins." (Amos 3:1-2)

God had indeed chosen Israel and made a covenant relationship with it. As far as *that* is concerned, the text says, Israel alone had experienced it, whatever God may have done in the histories of other peoples. But as the verse also says in its last line, with that brilliant twist of the unexpected so characteristic of the rhetorical skill of Amos, this very uniqueness was no comfortable privilege but the reason why they were facing God's judgment.

So then, the Old Testament clearly teaches that Israel's history was unique. It is the history of the redemptive acts of God in his dealings with a people in covenant relationship with himself. Amos's unambiguous affirmation of it in 3:1-2 is even sharper when we notice that he knew that Yahweh the God of Israel *was* certainly active in the histories of other nations and was also morally sovereign over the activities of all nations (Amos 1:2–2:3).

To remember and stress this truth about Israel (that it was unique) does not take away from the other truth, namely, that God's purpose was ultimately universal in scope. Israel existed only because of God's desire to redeem people from every nation. But in his sovereign freedom God chose to do so by *this* particular and historical means. The tension between the universal goal and the particular means is found throughout the Bible and cannot be reduced to either pole alone. What it comes down to is that, while God has every nation in view in his redemptive purpose, in no other nation did he act as he did in Israel, for the sake of the nations. That was its uniqueness, which can be seen to be both exclusive (in the sense that no other nation experienced what it did of God's revelation and redemption) and inclusive (in the sense that it was created, called and set in the midst of the nations for the sake of ultimately bringing salvation to the nations).

Now when we consider Jesus in the light of this, the vitally important fact is that the New Testament presents him to us as the *Messiah*, Jesus the *Christ*. And the Messiah "was" Israel. That is, the Messiah was Israel representatively and personified. The Messiah was the completion of all that Israel had been put in the world for (i.e., God's self-revelation and his work of human redemption). For this reason, Jesus shares in the uniqueness of Israel. What God had been doing *through no other nation* he now completed *through no other person* than the Messiah Jesus.

The paradox is that precisely through the narrowing down of his redemptive work to the unique particularity of the single man, Jesus, God opened the way to offering his redemptive grace to all nations. Israel was unique because God had a universal goal through it. Jesus embodied that uniqueness and achieved that universal goal. As the Messiah of Israel he could be the Savior of the world. Or as Paul reflected, going further back, by fulfilling God's purpose in choosing Abraham, Jesus became a second Adam, the head of a new humanity (Rom 4–5; Gal 3).

ISRAEL AND OTHER STORIES

God in control of all history. Although the history of Old Testament Israel is the unique story of God's saving acts, the Bible also clearly affirms that Yahweh was in control of the histories of all other peoples as well. Sometimes this was a control exercised in direct relationship to how those other nations impinged on Israel. But in other cases it was not directly so. The migration of the Philistines from the Aegean, or of the Syrians from northern Mesopotamia, had no connection with the Israelites at the time; however, says Amos 9:7, it was Yahweh who "brought them up." And whoever the Emites were, or the Horites, or the Avites, not to mention the dreaded Zamzummites, they had nothing to do with the Israelites! Yet their movements and destinies were under the disposition of Yahweh just as much as Israel's own historic migration, according to some fascinating bits of ancient geography and history in Deuteronomy 2:10-12, 20-23.

Mostly, however, it is the case that other nations are said to be under Yahweh's control in relation to how their history interacts with Israel's. That is to say, God fits them into his purpose for his own people Israel— sometimes for Israel's benefit, sometimes as agents of God's punishment on his own people. But then, God's purpose for Israel was ultimately the blessing and redemption of humanity as a whole. So it can be said that God's activity in the history of other nations also fits into that wider redemptive purpose.

In other words, we can make a theological distinction, but not a complete separation, between the history of Israel and other histories. Salvation history is real history. It must be seen as having happened within the flow of universal world history, all of which was under God's control. It is not some kind of extraterrestrial, sacred or religious history, just because "it's in the Bible."

Some examples of God's activity in the historical affairs of nations other than Israel will help to illustrate this point. Some of these have been touched on already.

Egypt   God's activity there had the whole world in view (Ex 9:13-16).

Assyria   The dominant world power for a century and a half, but to the prophetic eye, a mere stick in the hands of Yahweh (Is 10:5-19).

Babylon   Jeremiah owed much of his unpopularity in later life precisely to his conviction that Nebuchadnezzar had been raised up by Yahweh and entrusted with world dominion. He even went so far as to call him "my servant" (Jer 27:5-7). Habbakuk was dumbfounded by the same revelation (Hab 1). According to the book of Daniel, this interpretation of current events was relayed even to Nebuchadnezzar himself (Dan 2:37-38; 4:17, 25, 32).

Persia   The central theme of Isaiah 40–48 was that the most burning topic of international alarm of the day—the sudden rise of Cyrus, king of the united Medes and Persians—was directly the work of Israel's God and no other. Such was God's involvement with the unwitting Cyrus that he could scandalize his own people by referring to him as "my shepherd" and "my anointed one" and by picturing him as led by God's own hand in all his victories (Is 44:28–45:13).

The saving acts of God within or on behalf of Israel, then, most certainly did not take place in sterile, vacuum-sealed isolation, but within the turbulent crosscurrents of international politics and the historical rise and fall of empires whose destinies Yahweh himself controlled.

The nations share in Israel's history. In the Old Testament it often seems as if the nations are the intended audience of what God is actually doing in Israel. They are presented almost as the spectators of the drama he is engaged in with his people. The nations will tremble, sings Moses, when they hear what Yahweh has done to the Egyptians on behalf of his people (Ex 15:14-16). But, on the other hand, what would the Egyptians think of Yahweh if he were to turn and destroy his rebellious people, as he threatened to do (Ex 32:11-12)? Moses' intercession on their behalf at the time of the golden calf incident made much of God's reputation among the nations.

God had put Israel on an open stage. So if Israel would keep the laws God had given it, its national life would be so conspicuously righteous that other nations would notice and ask questions about its laws and its God (Deut 4:6-8). But on the other hand, if it failed to do so and if God then kept his threat and acted in judgment upon his own people, destroying his own city, land and temple, then the nations would ask why such an incredible thing could have happened. The answer was ready in advance (Deut 29:22-28).

But even if that judgment was fully deserved, such a state of affairs was a disgrace to God's own name. So when God acted to restore his people to their land, that too was for the purpose of reinstating his reputation among the nations (Ezek 36:16-23).

More than this, however, there is in some of the psalms a sense that the history of Israel is in some way actually available for the nations to appropriate for themselves. In the psalms celebrating the kingship of Yahweh, the nations (plural) or the whole earth are repeatedly called on to rejoice and praise God for his mighty acts in Israel. Read, for example, Psalms 47; 96:1-3; 98:1-3. Now if Israel's salvation history (which is referred to in these psalms as the "marvelous deeds," "righteous acts," etc., of Yahweh) is to be a cause of *rejoicing* among the nations, then it must be that they in some sense benefit from it, or are included within the scope of its purpose, even though they have not personally experienced it.

How this could be so remains a mystery in the Old Testament. Indeed, I sometimes wonder what went on in the mind of the Israelites when they wrote some of the amazingly universal words in the Psalms. What did they think when they sang words like:

> Clap your hands, *all you nations*;
> > shout to God with cries of joy.
> For the LORD Most High is awesome,
> > the great King over all the earth.
> He subdued nations under *us*,
> > peoples under our feet.
> He chose our inheritance for us,
> > the pride of Jacob, whom he loved. (Ps 47:1-4, my italics)

or this:

> Sing to the LORD a new song;
>   sing to the LORD, *all the earth.*
> Sing to the LORD, praise his name;
>   proclaim his salvation day after day.
> Declare his glory among the nations,
>   his marvelous deeds among all peoples. (Ps 96:1-3, my italics)

For the Israelites, Yahweh's *name, salvation, glory* and *marvelous deeds* meant only one thing—the incomparable history of his own people and everything that God had done for them. Yet in this hymn they are heartily inviting all nations, all peoples, all the earth no less, to join in the celebration and proclamation of those unique events. Mysterious as it may be, this universal and inclusive element in the worship of Israel is unmistakably there. And it is very important to set it alongside the call for exclusive worship and loyalty to Yahweh alone, and the abhorrence of the religious practices of other nations, especially their idolatry, which is denounced in these very same psalms. Israel was to worship Yahweh only. But Yahweh was not God of Israel only. He was to be worshiped as the God of all nations and the whole earth.

The nations share in Israel's future. The Old Testament, however, goes further in its program for the nations than casting them in the role of spectators, even clapping spectators. Psalm 47, which is really quite breathtaking in its vista, moves the nations out of the audience in verse 1, right onto the center of the stage in verse 9:

> God reigns over the nations;
>   God is seated on his holy throne.
> The nobles of the nations assemble
>   *as the people of the God of Abraham,*
> for the kings of the earth belong to God;
>   he is greatly exalted. (Ps 47:8-9, my italics)

The nations before God's throne are there not behind the people of God, nor even just alongside them, but *as the people of the God of Abraham*— the God whose promise to Abraham had the nations in mind from the beginning. It must have stretched the imagination of the Israelites when they sang such psalms as to when and how the words they had just sung could ever be a reality. Yet there they are, to be sung with enthusiastic faith and hope.

The prophets stretched the imagination even further. Amos, in the same chapter that we read his devastating likening of Israel to the other nations because of their sin and its deserved doom, speaks of a future restoration of the house of David, such that it will include "nations that bear my name" (Amos 9:11-12). This indeed is the very passage quoted by James as scriptural authority for the inclusion of the Gentiles in the young Christian church (Acts 15:13-19). We shall look at the significance of that event in chapter four.

James could easily have chosen several other prophetic texts to support his understanding of the event. Isaiah 19, for example, concludes with an amazing vision of both Egypt and Assyria gathering to worship God alongside Israel, being blessed by God and becoming a blessing on the earth. They will be transformed from enemies into "my people" by a process of healing and restoration, which has deliberate echoes of the very exodus itself. A saving exodus for the Egyptians?! (Is 19:19-25).

Jeremiah holds out to the nations the same hope, in virtually the same terms that he had held out to his own people. They stand under God's judgment, and he will punish them for what they do to Israel, but for those nations also repentance could be the road to restoration—*and inclusion*:

> After I uproot them [the nations], I will again have compassion and will bring each of them back to their own inheritance and their own country. And if they learn well the ways of my people and swear by my name, saying, "As surely as the LORD lives" [notice the echo of 4:2]—even as they once taught my people to swear by Baal—then they will be established *among my people*. (Jer 12:15-16, my italics)

The link between belonging to the people of God and acknowledging the name of Yahweh as the one true and living God is even more clearly forged in a beautiful picture of the conversion of outsiders as the result of the outpouring of God's spirit and blessing, like fertilizing, life-giving water, in Isaiah 44:5 (my italics):

> Some will say, "I belong to *the* LORD";
>> others will call themselves by the name of *Jacob*;
> still others will write on their hand, "*The* LORD*'s*,"
>> and will take the name *Israel*.

The same prophet moves far beyond this individual picture to a climactic vision of the saving work of God extending to all nations on earth. The same saving, liberating justice that God had shown on Israel's behalf will be activated for the nations:

> Listen to me, my people;
>> hear me, my nation:
> Instruction will go out from me;
>> my justice will become a light to the nations.
> My righteousness draws near speedily,
>> my salvation is on the way,
>> and my arm will bring justice to the nations. (Is 51:4-5)

God is the speaker in that passage, but the mission is elsewhere committed to the servant of Yahweh, who, in the power of the Spirit, "will bring justice to the nations" and establish "justice on earth" (Is 42:1, 4).

In view of his mission, which God lays upon him,

> I will also make you a light for the Gentiles,
>> that my salvation may reach to the ends of the earth. (Is 49:6)

The appeal can go out universally:

> Turn to me and be saved,
>> all you ends of the earth. (Is 45:22)

In chapter four we shall look at how these particular texts and the figure of the servant of the Lord are taken up into the identity and mission of Jesus.

This, then, is the "end of the story" to which the Old Testament points but which is never reached within its pages, and indeed still awaits us. The eschatological future hope of Israel saw its own history ultimately flowing into the universal history of the nations, in order that people from all nations could be granted salvation and included within the people of God.

This confluence was achieved, as we have seen, without abandoning the uniqueness of the history of Israel as a history of saving acts of God unparalleled in any other history, but equally without denying the activity and interest of God within all human history. On the contrary, the eschatological vision sees the achievements of the nations being brought into the new age and new creation. The economic and cultural history of the nations, coming as it does within the creation mandate to all humanity to use and steward the resources of the earth, is seen eventually to flow into the substance of the people of God. Isaiah 23:18, for example, after the declaration of historical judgment on the economic oppressions of Tyre, foresees all the profits of the great trading empire as ultimately destined for the people of God. Haggai 2:6-9 envisages the wealth of the nations returning to its rightful owner—the Lord himself, in his temple. This expectation is endorsed in the vision of Revelation 21:24. In other words, human history "beyond" salvation history, the history of the rest of humanity who live by God's grace on the face of God's earth, also has its meaning and value and will ultimately contribute in some way to the glory of the kingdom of God as he rules over his redeemed humanity in the new creation.

A unique history, then, with universal effects. This is where the story that underlies Matthew's genealogy leads. We shall look further at the theme of the ingathering of the nations in chapter four, but it is fitting to conclude this chapter by noticing how Paul, so conscious of his unique mission to the nations, binds together the two dimensions of history.

It had indeed been a "mystery" (to use Paul's own word) all through the ages of Old Testament Israel as to *how* God could bring about for Abraham what he had promised him—namely, blessing for all nations. But Paul saw very clearly how that mystery had been revealed through the tremendous achievement of God in Christ. He saw that it was paradoxically through the narrowing down of God's redemptive acts to the unique particularity of one single man—the Messiah, Jesus—that God had opened the way to the universal offering of the grace of his gospel to all nations. In Galatians 3 and Ephesians 2–3, Paul explains that what the Gentiles had not had before (because it was at that time limited to the nation of Israel) is now available to them in the Messiah (and nowhere else—either for them or for the Jews). The great Old Testament hope that the nations would come to be part of Israel is then already being fulfilled through Jesus the Messiah.

But in Romans 9–11, Paul wrestles with the fact that it is happening in an unexpected and (from his own point of view as a Jew) undesirable way. The majority of his contemporary Jews had in fact rejected Jesus as Messiah. But as a result of that rejection, the Gentile nations were being "grafted in." However, the Gentiles did not constitute a separate "olive tree." For Paul there was only one people of God—then, now or ever. No, the Gentiles were being grafted into the original stock. In other words, as in the Old Testament worship and prophecy, the nations were now participating in the saving work of God, which he had initiated through the history of Israel. These were Gentiles from every conceivable background. But they now shared the root and sap of Israel's sonship, glory, covenants, law, temple worship, promises, patriarchs—and . . . "the human ancestry of the Messiah" (Rom 9:5). The Gentile Christian, therefore, is a person of two histories: on the one hand, his or her own national and cultural background, ancestry and heritage, which as we have seen is by no means to be despised, and on the other hand, his or her new spiritual, "ingrafted" history—that of God's people descended from Abraham, which the Christian inherits through inclusion in Christ.

So ultimately the Christian believer singing hymns at Christmas and the Israelite believer singing psalms in the temple are as much brothers and sisters in the Messiah as the rest of the church congregation is brothers and sisters in Christ. The genealogy of Jesus conceals a story that led up to Jesus but that, as Luke also perceived, led up to a new beginning with him (Acts 1:1). The story goes on, until the promise to Abraham will finally be fulfilled, in a great multitude from every nation, tribe, people and language. That is the goal of all history, as it was of Israel's history. And in the church of the Messiah that goal is already being brought about in anticipation: "There is neither Jew nor Gentile, neither slave nor free, nor is there male and female, for you are all one in Christ Jesus" (Gal 3:28).

One people, one story. The fact is that whether we read Matthew 1:1-17 in our Christmas service or not, that story of Old Testament Israel is our story as much as it is the story of Jesus. For through him, we have come to be the spiritual descendants of Abraham. "If you belong to Christ, then you are Abraham's seed, and heirs according to the promise" (Gal 3:29).

CHAPTER 1 QUESTIONS AND EXERCISES

1. Many people ignore or skip over Matthew 1:1-17 as a boring genealogy. How would you explain to someone else why it is important?

2. Read Psalm 96. How is Israel's story of God's salvation something that the other nations of the world would benefit from and therefore rejoice in?

3. Select ten Old Testament texts that would give an outline of the Old Testament story, showing how it leads up to Christ. This should consist mainly of texts that describe significant events (such as creation, fall, call of Abraham, exodus and so on), and not just texts containing promises or predictions. Give a one- or two-sentence explanation of why you selected each of the ten Old Testament passages.

4. Study Psalms 105–107. Make notes connecting the different events that are mentioned in those psalms to the historical texts in the Old Testament that first described them. What is the overall message of those psalms, and why do you think Israel thought so much about its own history and included it in worship? What does Psalm 107 finally promise?

5. Study the transfiguration of Jesus in Luke 9:28-36 and make appropriate connections to the Old Testament. Explain why it was Moses and Elijah who came to talk with Jesus. Explain what Luke meant when he said that they were talking about "the exodus" that Jesus would accomplish in Jerusalem (v. 31).

JESUS *and the* OLD TESTAMENT PROMISE

E ven if Matthew's genealogy is understandably omitted from the readings at our Christmas services, the list will undoubtedly include other portions from the rest of Matthew 1–2, for they are among the most familiar of Jesus' infancy stories. Matthew weaves together five scenes from the conception, birth and early childhood of Jesus. And then, perhaps for the benefit of those who missed the point of his genealogy (or more likely skipped it altogether), he ties each of those five scenes to a quotation from the Hebrew Scriptures that, he claims, has been "fulfilled" by the event described.

Five scenes from Jesus' childhood. The five scenes and their scriptural links are as follows:

1. The assurance to Joseph concerning the child conceived in Mary: Matthew 1:18-25 "to fulfill" Isaiah 7:14, which was the Immanuel sign given by Isaiah to King Ahaz.

2. The fact that Jesus was born in Bethlehem: Matthew 2:1-12 "to fulfill" Micah 5:2, in which it is prophesied that a ruler of Israel will come from Bethlehem.

3. The escape to Egypt, and then the return from there: Matthew 2:13-15 "to fulfill" Hosea 11:1, which is a reference to God having brought Israel, his son, out of Egypt at the exodus.

4. The murder by Herod of the boys in Bethlehem: Matthew 2:16-18 "to fulfill" Jeremiah 31:15, which is a lament for the Israelites who were going into exile.

5. The settlement of Jesus' family in Nazareth: Matthew 2:19-23 "to fulfill" "the prophets," which is a bit of a puzzle because there is no text that says exactly what Matthew records here. It seems to be a reflection of several possible allusions, which needn't detain us here.

The five scenes thus cover the early life of Jesus, from conception through his birth in Bethlehem and his temporary stay in Egypt up to his settling in Nazareth. And in all of it Matthew sees Old Testament reflections. By repeated use of the fulfillment phrase, Matthew clearly wants his readers to see that Jesus was not only the *completion* of the Old Testament story at a historical level, as his genealogy portrays, but also that he was in a deeper sense its *fulfillment*. This gives us another way of looking at the Old Testament in relation to Jesus. Not only does the Old Testament *tell the story that Jesus completes*, it also *declares the promise that Jesus fulfills*.

A destination is not just the end of a journey; it is also the point of a journey. We can ask about any journey not only the question, "Where are you going?" but also, "Why are you going there?" The journey is undertaken because of some purpose or commitment, which is fulfilled when the journey reaches its destination. Or the journey may be undertaken because of some invitation and promise that the person on the journey had received earlier. In the Old Testament journey, God had declared his purpose and made his promise. He had made them known in all kinds of ways to and through Israel—especially in the prophets. God's purpose or commitment was then fulfilled in the arrival of this child, Jesus. And through his five Old Testament quotations in quick succession, Matthew makes sure we don't miss the point.

Now some people get a bit suspicious over what Matthew does here. Is he not just "prooftexting"?—that is, just matching up a few Old Testament predictions with some stories that seem to fit them. Or is it even worse: according to some, that Matthew has *invented* stories about Jesus to make the Old Testament predictions "come true"? This idea that the infancy narratives are pious fiction, produced by a Scripture-fired imagination, has become quite popular in some quarters, but it really does not stand up to the evidence. There are two solid objections.

First of all, why did Matthew pick such obscure texts? If his purpose was to start from Messianic prophecies and create stories to fulfill them, there are any number of texts that, already in Matthew's day, were far better known and much more detailed regarding the coming Messiah. Any of them could have produced good narratives, if the "facts" could simply be invented.

Second, it is clearly mistaken to say that the narratives Matthew tells are fulfillments of Old Testament *predictions*, because only one of the texts he quotes is in fact a recognized Messianic prediction at all, and that is Micah 5:2, predicting that the future king would be born in Bethlehem. The others were not primarily predictions at all. The "Immanuel" prophecy was a sign given to King Ahaz in his own historical context, not (originally) a long-range prediction. In any case it would be odd as a straight prediction, since the child was actually given the name Jesus, not Immanuel—a fact that hardly escaped Matthew's notice, so he cannot have regarded his story as a neat prediction-fulfillment. Hosea 11:1 was not a prediction but a *past* reference to the exodus, when God had brought his son Israel out of Egypt. Jeremiah 31:15 is a figurative picture of the mourning of Rachel at the time of the exile of her descendants in 587 B.C. after the fall of Jerusalem. It was not predictive and had nothing to do with the Messiah in its context. The concluding comment related to Nazareth is so obscure that no one is completely sure what texts Matthew had in mind. That is hardly compatible with the view that Matthew was making up stories to fulfill well-known Messianic predictions.

It seems altogether much more probable that Matthew is doing exactly what he says—working back from actual events that happened in the early life of Jesus to certain Hebrew Scriptures in which he now sees a deeper significance than they could have had before. It was the events in the life of infant Jesus that suggested the Scriptures, not the other way around. And since the Scriptures are not obvious predictions of the events recorded, Matthew must have meant more by his affirmation that the Scriptures were being fulfilled by Jesus than just that predictions had come true. But then, a *promise* is much more than a *prediction*, as we shall discuss shortly.

Geography and history. So then, what *was* Matthew's intention in his choice of Scriptures to punctuate his narrative? Probably there is more than one level of meaning in his mind. On the surface, the passages "accompany" Jesus in a geographical sense. That is, they are linked up to the fact that the Messiah, born in *Bethlehem*, ended up in *Nazareth* after a stay in *Egypt*. This in itself was probably a form of explanation as to why the person whom Christians claimed was the Messiah had come from Nazareth (not a good place to come from). This was a point of conflict between Christians and Jews that went back to the days of Jesus himself (cf. Jn 1:46; 7:41-43). Matthew is pointing out that Jesus was actually born in Bethlehem and that this fact fitted in with the Scriptures. So his point is that the prophet Jesus of Nazareth could legitimately be claimed as the Messiah because not only had he actually been born in Bethlehem (as the Scriptures foretold), but also the movements by which he ended up a resident of Galilee were also consistent with the fulfillment of Scripture. This Scripture-fulfillment motif in the infancy narratives serves the same purpose as the genealogy in Matthew 1:1-17. They both portray Jesus as the Messiah, the completion of a *story* and the fulfillment of a *promise*.

But even in this geographical dimension there lies a deeper significance to be picked up by those with a little more awareness of the Scriptures. There is, in fact, rather a lot of geography in Matthew 2–4. Either by his travels or by his reputation Jesus had an effective ministry that spans the whole of the classical area of ancient Israel—particularly the boundaries of the old Davidic kingdom (note especially the places referred to in Dan 4:24-25). The one who was the son of King David has a ministry as wide as the kingdom of David itself. The focal point of that ministry in the region of Galilee is further vindicated by Scripture when Matthew quotes from Isaiah 9:1-2 (Mt 4:13-16). Isaiah 9:1-7 is one of the outstanding Messianic and Davidic prophecies in the whole Old Testament. And it begins with referring to Galilee:

> In the past he humbled the land of Zebulun and the land of Naphtali, but in the future he will honor Galilee of the nations, by the Way of the Sea, beyond the Jordan—
>
> The people walking in darkness
>   have seen a great light;
> on those living in the land of deep darkness
>   a light has dawned. (Is 9:1-2)

So, the point of the *history* lesson in the genealogy of chapter 1 is corroborated by the *geography* lesson in chapters 2–4. "Great David's greater Son" is claiming his kingdom.

The genealogy, however, has a wider scope than David, as we saw in our first chapter. There is the universal scope connected with Abraham, and the inclusion of Gentiles among the female ancestors of Jesus. This historical dimension also has its geographical counterpart in what follows. Foreigners enter the story.

After the birth of Jesus, the first story Matthew recounts is the visit of "Magi *from the east*"; and the second is the visit of Jesus himself to *Egypt*, in the west. The stories thus embrace both extremes of the biblical world—especially in Old Testament times—east and west. Furthermore, both regions are included within various Old Testament prophecies concerning the extent of God's work of salvation (most notably Is 19:23-25). God's purpose for Israel, and for the Messiah who would embody Israel, was the blessing of all nations.

Matthew then, though he wrote the most Jewish of the Gospels, wastes no time at all before getting to the point that when the Messiah came he had visitors, gifts and worship from the east, and was personally, if temporarily, resident in Egypt in the west. Furthermore, the worship of the Magi is almost certainly intended as an echo of Psalm 72:10, which in turn echoes the visit of the Queen of Sheba to Solomon, while the gifts of gold and frankincense recall Isaiah 60:1-6, where they are brought by kings from Arabia to greet the dawning of God's new light in Zion. So the geographical ripples spread even wider in Matthew's allusive and suggestive narrative. By showing Jesus in relation to the wider Gentile world so early in his Gospel, Matthew clearly wants us to see him as more than merely Israel's Messiah, as the fulfillment of God's saving purpose for the nations beyond Israel. And that is a fundamental part of what the Old Testament is all about.

There is yet another level of meaning in the Scriptures linked to these stories. Talking about Egypt on the one hand and Mesopotamia (Assyria, Babylon, "the East") on the other would never leave any Jew thinking only of geography. He or she would inevitably revert to history, as Jews characteristically do. As we saw in the first chapter, the bulk of the history recorded in the Old Testament is slung like a great hammock between the two poles of Egypt and Babylon, more specifically between the exodus from oppression in Egypt, and the exile to Babylon and the return. And that indeed is what is in the mind of Matthew as he reflects on the infancy of the Messiah, for he puts together two quotations from the Scriptures, one of which refers to the exodus from Egypt and the other to the exile to Babylon.

Hosea 11:1, quoted in Matthew 2:15, looks back to the exodus. Jesus has been taken to Egypt, but he will return, and so Matthew sees a correspondence with the exodus experience of Israel itself: "Out of Egypt I called my son" (meaning Israel, cf. Ex 4:22). He is not suggesting that the Hosea text was a prediction. His point is simply that what God had done for his people Israel—in fact the greatest thing God had done for them—had its counterpart, even in a purely physical sense, in the life of Jesus.

Then Matthew records Herod's slaughter of boys under two years old in Bethlehem. This he links to Jeremiah 31:15 about Rachel weeping and mourning for her children. You don't need a biblical chapter and verse to prove that parents whose children are killed will mourn and grieve. So the meaning of Matthew's quotation from Jeremiah lies a bit deeper than that. The verse in fact refers to the events immediately after the fall of Jerusalem to the armies of Nebuchadnezzar in 587 B.C., when the defeated Israelites had been marshaled at Ramah for their long trudge into exile in Babylon. This was the cause of Rachel's "mourning," since there was a tradition that Rachel was buried at Ramah (cf. Jer 40:1). So Matthew observes that Jesus' "exile" to Egypt was followed by an outburst of grief and mourning, and he likens it to the grief that accompanied Israel's exile to Babylon. But the context of his quotation puts it in a more positive light. For all the rest of Jeremiah 31 is in fact a message of hope that out of the tragedy and grief would come future blessing. The very next words after Matthew's quotation run on:

> Restrain your voice from weeping
>   and your eyes from tears . . .
>   They will return . . .
> So there is hope for your descendants. (Jer 31:16-17)

So then, in his reflection on the single event of Jesus' going to Egypt and returning (and the linked massacre at Bethlehem), Matthew sees a double historical analogy, which he brings out by the use of two Scriptures, one referring to the exodus, the other referring to the exile, key points in the history and theology of Israel in the Old Testament.

But of course, the exodus and the return from exile were key points in the Old Testament precisely because they were indeed much more than mere history. Both events were utterly saturated in *promise*. And that is what makes them especially significant for Matthew, who is here presenting Jesus as the fulfillment of Old Testament promise. The exodus is described from the very beginning as the result of God acting in faithfulness to his own promise (cf. Ex 2:24; 3:16-17; 6:5-8, etc.). Even the text Matthew quotes from Hosea, with its designation of Israel as God's son, implies this, for God could not allow his son and heir to languish further in slavery. The exodus proved God's commitment to his people and his purpose for them.

Likewise, the prophets predicted the exile for two centuries. But they also predicted that there would be a return from exile and a future hope for the people. In the prophecies of Jeremiah, Ezekiel and Isaiah 40–55, that note of promise and hope became a symphony of expectation. Significantly, the original exodus itself was used as a pattern for God's future action. There would be a "new exodus." In the same way, Matthew uses both exodus and return from exile as patterns for what he sees in the life of Jesus.

Furthermore, by taking a text that describes *Israel* as God's son (as was fairly common in the Old Testament), and applying it to *Jesus*, Matthew is obviously also setting up a Jesus-Israel correspondence, which is even more suggestive for the thoughtful reader. After all, the Old Testament Israelites were the people of promise. They existed as the fruit of a promise to Abraham miraculously fulfilled. They were inheritors of a promised land. And they were bearers of a universal promise for the human race.

What a legacy Matthew pins on this little toddler being hurriedly carried off to Egypt by his anxious parents!

Now we could go deeper still. These early chapters of Matthew are so full of direct and indirect allusions to the Old Testament that scholars never tire of finding more and more of them—some more plausible than others. Certainly there is a clear intention to echo the Moses story: the hostile king, the threat to the child's life, the flight amid the suffering of others, the death of the hostile king, the return (cf. Ex 4:19-31). And this only adds to the picture of imminent salvation, for Moses was the liberator *par excellence*, and "Jesus" (the same name as "Joshua" in Hebrew) has already been explained as the one who will deliver his people.

Our purpose here, however, is not primarily to expound Matthew's Gospel but rather to see from it how Matthew (and of course the other Gospel writers) saw Jesus in relation to the Old Testament. And it stands out clearly that the Old Testament had declared a promise that Jesus fulfills. What Matthew does in these opening chapters about the childhood of Jesus is programmatic for the rest of his Gospel. He repeatedly comes back to this note of fulfillment, whether in some action or some teaching of Jesus, and supremely of course in his suffering and death.

But it is not just, as we have observed, a matter of predictions coming true. Rather Matthew sees the whole Old Testament as the embodiment of promise—in the sense of presenting to us a God of gracious and saving purpose, liberating action and covenant faithfulness to his people. That generates a tremendous sense of expectation and hope, reflected in all parts of the Hebrew canon. Hence, all kinds of Old Testament writing (not just prophecies) can be drawn in relating that promise to Jesus.

In order to explain Jesus, the New Testament connects him to a whole range of Old Testament Scriptures that are all perceived as expressing God's promise—whether directly or by implication. For Matthew, as for other New Testament authors, their Hebrew Scriptures stood before them rather like the words of a song I once heard a child sing, a song composed presumably by understandably optimistic parents:

> I am a promise, I am a possibility,
> I am a promise with a capital "P,"
> I am a great big bundle of potentiality . . .
> (written by Bill and Gloria Gaither)

THE PROMISE DECLARED

Now that we have reached some understanding of what is meant by saying that Jesus fulfills the Old Testament promise, we can move on to explore how the concept of promise helps us gain a better understanding of the Old Testament itself, which is part of our overall purpose in this book. A good starting point for that will be to point out in more detail the difference between promise and mere prediction. Even in everyday life, promise is a much deeper and more significant thing than prediction. It is one thing to predict a marriage between two people. It is quite another thing to promise to marry a particular person! That is a good illustration of the first major difference, which is very clear in the Bible.

Promise involves commitment to a relationship. A promise is made between two people, as an "I-you" matter. It presupposes a relationship between them; indeed it may cement or forward that relationship, or depend on it. A prediction, on the other hand, may be quite impersonal, or "third-personal," and does not require any relationship between the predictor and the person or persons about whom the prediction is made. A promise may involve some degree of prediction (or expectation), but a prediction need not have anything to do with a promise. A promise is made *to* someone, whereas a prediction is made *about* someone.

Now in the Old Testament there are plenty of predictions involving the nations beyond Israel. Some of them are surprisingly detailed and even more surprisingly fulfilled in the course of ancient history. But they do not indicate a relationship or any commitment between God and those nations in terms of those predictions. In most cases the nations concerned were most probably unaware of the predictions. So in those cases predictions could be made and fulfilled without any ongoing relationship involved.

It was totally different in the case of the promises God made concerning Israel. There the very existence of Israel was the substance of the promise as it had been first declared to Abraham. And that promise was the immoveable foundation on which the relationship between God and Israel survived in spite of all that threatened it. To say that the Old Testament declares God's promise is another way of saying that at a particular time in history God *entered into a commitment* to a particular man and his descendants. It was a commitment to a relationship between himself and them that involved growth, blessing and protection.

But it involved something else as well, of course—namely, the universal goal of bringing blessing to all nations through the descendants of Abraham. Indeed, sometimes this is emphasized as the very thing that God had promised Abraham. For example, in Genesis 18 the immediate promise that Abraham and Sarah would have a son within a year is quickly subsumed under the much more long-term and ultimate promise that God would bless all nations through the community that had not yet even begun (cf. Gen 18:19).

In that sense, God's promise to Abraham is in fact a commitment to *humanity*, not just to *Israel*. So although, as has just been said, the predictions concerning the other nations in the Old Testament period do not

entail any promise or relationship with those nations *at that time*, the
promise of God to Abraham does ultimately encompass humanity, precisely
by envisaging people from all nations entering into the same saving and
covenant relationship with God that Israel currently enjoyed. Israel enjoyed its relationship with God for the purpose of enabling other nations
eventually to share in it. So it is perfectly appropriate that when the New
Testament authors speak of Jesus as the fulfillment of the promise of the
Old Testament, they think not just of Israel but also see Jesus as the Savior
of the world, or rather see God saving the world through Jesus.

Think of the apostle Paul here. Paul's whole theology of mission was
founded on his understanding of the crucial importance of the promise to
Abraham and its universal significance. Galatians 3 is a clear witness to this.
For Paul, the gospel itself began not with Jesus but with Abraham. For what,
after all, *was* the good news? Nothing other than God's commitment to
bring blessing to all nations of humanity, as announced to Abraham.
"Scripture foresaw that God would justify the Gentiles by faith, and announced the gospel in advance to Abraham: 'All nations will be blessed
through you'" (Gal 3:8).

The redeeming work of the Messiah Jesus was therefore "in order that
the blessing given to Abraham might come to the Gentiles through Christ
Jesus, so that by faith we might receive the promise of the Spirit" (Gal 3:14).

Then after further discussion of the relationship between this fundamental promise based on grace and other aspects of the Old Testament,
specifically the law, Paul concludes his words to these Gentile believers: "If
you belong to Christ [the Messiah], then you are Abraham's seed, and heirs
according to the promise" (Gal 3:29, my italics).

Today, just as much as back in the days of the apostle Paul, every
Gentile believer who enjoys a *relationship* of sonship to God as Father does
so as a living proof of the fulfillment of the Old Testament *promise* in Jesus
the Messiah.

Promise requires a response of acceptance. A prediction needs no response. It can be made and fulfilled without the persons concerned knowing
anything about it, let alone doing anything about it. There are examples
of this in the Old Testament also.

There is no evidence, for example, that Cyrus ever acknowledged
Yahweh (Is 45:4, "you do not acknowledge me," seems to rule it out). And

although it is possible, it seems unlikely that he ever heard of the predictions concerning him made in Isaiah 40–45. Nevertheless, he fulfilled them remarkably. Without knowing it, he submitted to the sovereignty of God, who used him for his redemptive plans involving Israel. Cyrus proclaimed liberty to the exiles after their generation in Babylonian captivity.

This is an interesting example because in this case the prediction concerning Cyrus was *part* of a *promise* concerning Israel, and it helps to point out the difference between prediction and promise. In fulfilling the prediction made concerning him, Cyrus was instrumental in fulfilling a promise concerning Israel, but he himself did not participate in it. His part in enabling the promise to be fulfilled did not require him personally to make any response to God. He simply acted in the exercise of his own ambitions, thereby in the mystery of providence also carrying out God's promise.

But his action carved out the historical and political space within which the promise of God for the future of Israel could operate, and *that* most definitely called for *its* response. Indeed, the whole burden of the prophetic word of Isaiah 40–55 is to stir up that response among a people who had come to fear that they were finished forever. There was no point in God having promised a return from exile if nobody actually got up and returned! They had to respond. And that meant exercising faith in God's word, uprooting from two generations of settled life in Babylon, and setting out on the long journey back to Jerusalem. Without that faith and action on Israel's part, God's promise would have gotten nowhere.

This, of course, is the pattern we find from the start. The promise to Abraham was effective because he believed it and acted upon it, and went on trusting and obeying long after it had become humanly impossible. The exodus was promised by God, but it would not have happened if the Israelites had not responded to the leading of Moses to get out of Egypt, and even then some of them did so reluctantly. The same people received the promise of the land, but because their faith and obedience failed at the crucial point, they never received it and perished in the wilderness. And so it goes on all the way through Scripture. The promise comes as the initiative of God's grace and always depends on God's grace. But God's grace has to be accepted and responded to by faith and obedience.

This way of regarding the Old Testament, as *promise*, thus has two effects. First, it helps us realize that salvation is, and always was, a matter of God's grace and promise. Some people have the idea that the difference between the Old and New Testaments is that in the Old salvation is by obeying the law whereas in the New it is by grace. But that sets up a totally false contrast. In the Old as in the New, it is God who takes the initiative of grace and calls people to faith and obedient response. In the book of Exodus, there are eighteen chapters describing God's mighty act of redemption, in fulfillment of his own love and promise, *before* the giving of the law to the people he had already redeemed. Israel, in the psalms and elsewhere, regarded the law itself as a further gift of grace to those already redeemed by grace. Far from setting aside the promise, the law was given to enable those who received the promise to live as they should in response to God's redeeming grace. Paul saw this clearly and argued it strongly against those who wished to build everything on Moses and the law. Don't forget, he points out that Abraham and the promise came *first*—chronologically and theologically, and that is what our "inheritance" of blessing and salvation depends on (Gal 3:16-22).

The second effect of regarding the Old Testament as *promise* is that it reminds us that there is a conditional element to the promise. The response of faith and obedience from those who received the promise is required in order for the promise to be fulfilled. The prophets ruthlessly demolished Israel's confidence in the very things that had promises of God attached to them whenever that confidence was not linked to moral response. Here are some examples:

Amos, faced with a people who were living in blatant disobedience to God's social demands, turned the fundamental promises upside down. Neither election by itself (Amos 3:2), nor the exodus by itself (Amos 9:7), nor the land by itself (Amos 2:10-16; 5:2) was any guarantee of immunity from God's judgment. They could not claim the mere *fact* of having received those promises as if it excused them from living in obedience to God. A century later in Jerusalem, Jeremiah condemned those who were showing complacent trust in the promises concerning the temple on Mount Zion but at the same time were living in contempt of the law of Mount Sinai (Jer 7:1-15). That temple was indeed destroyed, but in the courts of the one that replaced it, Jesus himself fought the same battle with those who were proud of their election in Abraham but failed to "*do* as Abraham *did*" (Jn 8:31-41). And the author of Hebrews, who had the highest possible understanding of the eternity and assurance of God's promise, nevertheless has the sternest warnings in the New Testament about the danger of not responding to that promise by faith and obedient action—using Old Testament Israel for his object lessons (Heb 3:7–4:11; 10:19-39). Both of these two points will receive some fuller discussion in chapter five.

The message is clear and consistent throughout the Bible. The covenant promise of God is axiomatic and fundamental, and all our hope of salvation hangs upon it. But no doctrine of election, no covenant theology, no personal testimony of redemption, can take away the imperative necessity of faith proving itself in active obedience.

So when we talk about the Old Testament declaring the promise that Jesus fulfills, it does *not* mean that the Old Testament is declared redundant because Jesus fulfilled it. (If the Old Testament were merely a book of predictions, that would be so, because once a prediction comes true, it has no further useful function.) Rather, what it *does* mean is that in the Old Testament God has both proclaimed and proved his purpose of redemption. And that initiative of God's grace (God's promise) calls for a response of obedient faith, just as much from us as from the Israelites.

Promise involves ongoing levels of fulfillment. A prediction is a fairly flat affair. Either it comes true or it doesn't. If it does, that's the end of it. If it doesn't, you can either say the prediction was mistaken or try to say it wasn't properly understood and may yet come true in some redefined way. That is why the biggest prediction industry of all—astrology—is so notoriously vague or ambiguous in its pronouncements. The kind of things that astrologers predict for you can hardly fail to come true! By the same token, that is why it is so remarkable that so many Bible predictions, which sometimes include specific detail, did in fact come true.

A promise is different. Because it involves personal relationship and commitment, a promise has a dynamic quality that goes beyond the external details. Even something that may seem quite trivial like, "I promise to give you back the book I borrowed," goes beyond just the book itself. Once that promise has been made, something of my character is invested in it. Can I be trusted? Will I keep my word? Am I the kind of person who keeps a promise or just forgets to? So even very simple promises can reveal something about the person who makes them. But of course the more long-term and demanding a promise is, the more it can grow and develop in significance as time goes by.

When a young man and woman commit themselves to get married, a promise is involved in the betrothal or engagement, often with the sign of an engagement ring. At one level, that specific engagement promise at the time of betrothal is fulfilled on the day of the wedding itself. But it is then taken up and surpassed by a fresh exchange of promises (sometimes with more rings!), which launches their married life. In those promises, words such as "for better, for worse; for richer, for poorer; in sickness and in health" are included. This is because the promise "to have and to hold, to love and to cherish" looks far beyond the honeymoon. Fulfilling that wedding-day promise will take different forms and make different demands and call for different responses as life and circumstances proceed. The promise remains. The words don't need to be changed or added to. From here on it is the relationship that dictates how the promise will be fulfilled in any given situation.

Now, because it is the relationship behind the promise that really matters, and because the intention of the promise is to sustain and nurture that relationship, the material form in which the promise gets fulfilled may be quite different from the literal form of words in which it was originally made, and yet everybody knows that the promise has been truly kept.

Imagine a father who, in the days before mechanized transport, promises his son, age five, that when he is twenty-one he will give him a horse of his very own so that he can ride around and be independent. Meanwhile, in the years in between, the motorcar is invented. So on his twenty-first birthday the son wakes up to find a motorcar parked outside, "with love from Dad." It would be a strange son who would accuse his father of breaking his promise just because there was no horse. And it would be even stranger if, in spite of having received the even better gift of a motorcar, the son insisted that the promise would only be fulfilled if a horse *also* arrived, since that was the literal promise. It is obvious that with the change in circumstances, unknown at the time the promise was made, the father has *fully* kept his promise. In fact he has done so in a way that *surpasses* the original words of the promise. When the promise was made, the only independent means of transport was a horse. But now four legs have been replaced by four wheels. So the promise is fulfilled in a different *form* but with the same *intention*. The promise was made in terms that were understood at the time. But the promise was fulfilled in the light of new historical events and the possibilities they create.

Coming back to the Old Testament promise, I hope the relevance of these illustrations can be seen. God's promise went on being kept through the many ages of the Old Testament. And also, even though the New Testament fulfillments may look different from the literal words used in some Old Testament prophecies, they are still true fulfillments. God has kept his promise, even if it looks like he gave four wheels instead of four legs. In Christ, God has given us all he promised.

God's relationship with Israel through all the centuries was founded on the specific promise to Abraham. But in the Old Testament itself that promise is seen in different levels of fulfillment. In one sense, the promise to Abraham of "seed" was fulfilled the moment Isaac was born. But of course it went further than that. A major theme of Genesis is how from such small and threatened beginnings the posterity of Abraham grows to a community of seventy people—hardly yet a great nation. But the book of Exodus opens with those seventy having been "exceedingly fruitful; they multiplied greatly, increased in numbers and became so numerous" (Ex 1:7), thus fulfilling the promise at another level. The New Testament can see yet another level of fulfillment in referring to Jesus, as the "seed" (singular) of Abraham (Gal 3:16, 19), and still another in regarding the believing Gentiles of all nations as the sons of Abraham, in fulfillment of the same promise. One promise, but with several levels of fulfillment as history proceeds.

Another dimension of the Old Testament promise is the way it leads to a recurring pattern of promise-fulfillment-fresh promise-fresh fulfillment, repeating and amplifying itself through history. Like some science-fiction, time-traveling rocket, the promise is launched, returning to earth at some later point of history in a partial fulfillment, only to be relaunched with a fresh load of fuel and cargo for yet another historical destination, and so on.

Launched at the time of Abraham, God's promise receives its first specific fulfillment at the time of the exodus. The references back to the patriarchs in the exodus narratives are frequent. At that point the promise of posterity is indeed kept, for Israel is not only a great nation, but also it has been freed to live as such.

But the promise also included a special relationship between God and this people, and that becomes the focal point at Mount Sinai. "Let my people go that they may serve me," God challenged Pharaoh, and when at last they reached Sinai, as God had promised Moses, they would when he commissioned him there (Ex 3:12). God says that he had brought them to himself for the purpose of entering into a covenant with them (Ex 19:4-6).

Launched from Mount Sinai, the people of the promise head for its next stage of fulfillment—the gift of the land. After the failure initially at Kadesh Barnea, the next generation realizes the promise under Joshua's leadership. But, as Hebrews observes, even Joshua did not give them "rest" in the land. That is, they were in the land but not yet fully in possession and control of it. The promise lurches precariously forward during the two centuries of tribal federation and infighting and judges, until at last under David there emerges a unified Israel in possession of the whole of the land as promised to Abraham.

At that point the promise receives a fresh launch with the promise to David that God would give him an heir (deliberately echoing the Isaac promise) and that his descendants would reign over Israel forever. That promise appeared to have crashed to earth amid the ruins of Jerusalem, which ended the Davidic monarchy in 587 B.C. But already it had been given a fresh impetus, which survived and transcended that catastrophe, by the prophetic vision of a future true son of David who would reign over his people in an age of justice and peace. And additionally, out of the wreckage of the exile arose the promise of future redemption, still fueled by the original ingredients of the promise—a new *exodus*, a new *covenant*, a fresh appropriation of the *land* under the blessing and presence of God himself.

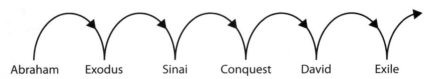

Abraham   Exodus   Sinai   Conquest   David   Exile

The historical flight path of the promise looks a bit like this:

There is, then, a clear pattern of promise-fulfillment-fresh promise in the Old Testament. It was built into the ongoing historical relationship between God and Israel over the centuries. This means that when the New Testament talks about Jesus fulfilling the Old Testament promise it is not doing something new or unprecedented. Rather it sees Jesus as the final destination of an already well-recognized pattern of promise-fulfillment. By the end of the Old Testament, we are left *expecting* God to do again what he has done so often before.

The repeated "refueling" of the promise for fresh application also prepares us to expect that the final fulfillment will not be in exactly the same terms of the literal details of the original promise, like the horse and motorcar analogy. The New Testament delights to portray Jesus as the one in whom the reality of the Scripture promises is found, even in surprising ways. Even Jesus played on that surprise element. He teased the learned teachers of the law with questions about who the Messiah could be if David called him lord, though he would actually be David's son. He puzzled them with claims to be the Son of Man—did he mean that term with all the meaning that Daniel 7 implied? Even those who believed in him had difficulty recognizing the fulfillment of promises in his person and ministry. John the Baptist was baffled. His disciples took offense. If Jesus really was the Messiah king, where was his kingdom? When would it really be seen in power?

It was only as the church reflected on its experience of Jesus in the light of the resurrection that they came to see, as Paul put it, that *all* the promises of God "are 'Yes' in Christ" (2 Cor 1:20). "We tell you the good news," Paul said. "What God promised our ancestors he has fulfilled for us, their children, by raising up Jesus" (Acts 13:32-33). These are some of the things they saw were now true about Jesus:

- He was the singular seed of Abraham, through whom that seed would become universal and multinational.

- He was the one through whom people of all nations would be blessed. For anyone anywhere, to be "in Christ" was to be "in Abraham" and therefore to share in the inheritance of God's people.

- He was the Passover Lamb protecting God's people from his wrath.

- His death and resurrection had achieved a new exodus.

- He was the mediator of a new covenant. His sacrificial death and risen life fulfilled and surpassed all that were signified in the tabernacle, the sacrifices and the priesthood.

- He was the One in whom we now have an inheritance, greater even than Israel's Old Testament inheritance of the land—an inheritance that cannot be robbed or lost.

- He was the temple not made with hands.
- Indeed he was Mount Zion itself, the place of the name and presence of God.
- He was the son of David, but his Messianic kingship was concealed behind the basin and towel of servanthood and obedience unto death.

In the next two chapters we shall look further at the meaning of some of these pictures and patterns, which the New Testament uses to portray all that Jesus meant. Our point here is simply that all these features of the *original* promises of God in the Old Testament were quite naturally literal or physical, in relation to the historical nationhood of Israel. So promises concerning God's actions in the future *had to be made* in terms already within the experience and comprehension of those who received them (just as a five-year-old boy before mechanization could understand the reality and the usefulness of a horse as a means of transport). But the *fulfillment* of the promise, with all these varied forms, through what God actually did in Christ, is at a different level of reality. It was fulfilled at a different level but still with continuity of meaning and purpose in line with the original promise (just as a motorcar is a quite different "level of reality" from a horse but has the same function and purpose as a means of transport).

Of course, even in the age of motorcars, there are those who would prefer horses. The writer to the Hebrews addresses those who, although they had certainly come to faith in Jesus as Messiah, had not fully understood what that meant in terms of the complete fulfillment of all that their scriptural Old Testament faith had meant to them as Jews. So Hebrews sets out to demonstrate that because we have Christ we actually *have* all that the great institutions of Israel signified, only "better." He wanted Jewish believers in Jesus to recognize that they had not *lost* anything of their Jewish scriptural inheritance by putting their faith in Jesus as Messiah. In Christ they *have* it all still, but even better—enriched, enhanced and fulfilled. So much so that to want to go back to the previous era would be not merely retrograde but would actually be a denial of what they now already possessed in reality in Christ. To hang on to the original forms of the promise would be like preferring shadows to real objects. Or like wanting four legs when you've been given four wheels.

In our own day, there are those who look for future fulfillments of Old Testament promises in a manner as literal as the original terms themselves. They expect to see things happening literally in the land of Israel, with a tribal division like Ezekiel describes. From the same prophet, they look for a rebuilding of the temple and reconstitution of the priesthood and sacrificial system. Or a battle between biblically identifiable enemies. Or Gentile nations on actual pilgrimage to the present, physical Jerusalem. Or a revival of the throne of David.

There is a wide variety of such interpretations of prophecy held by many sincere Christian people. However, such expectations seem quite wide of the mark. Sometimes they simply make the mistake of taking literally what the Bible *always* intended figuratively even in its original form. But at other times they fail to see the living and "transformable" quality of promises that were probably understood quite literally at the time of their giving. Just because the gift turns out to be a motorcar doesn't mean we should try to argue that the original promise of a horse was only meant figuratively. A horse was meant, a horse was what the child understood, and a horse was expected. But the changed circumstances and the progress of history enabled the promises to be fulfilled in a different and far superior way, without emptying the promise either of its purpose (to give a means of transport) or of its basis in a relationship of fatherly love. The father kept his promise in a way that was even better than when he made it.

To expect that all the details of Old Testament prophecies have to be literally fulfilled is to classify them all in the category of flat *predictions* which have to "come true" or be judged to have failed. Certainly, as we saw at the beginning of the chapter, the Old Testament *did* make predictions, and they were fulfilled with remarkable accuracy—as in the case of Jesus' birth in Bethlehem. But as we also saw, Matthew's understanding of promise and fulfillment goes way beyond mere prediction. To insist on literal fulfillment of prophecies can be to overlook their actual nature as *promises*—promises that had built into them the potential for different and progressively superior levels of fulfillment. To look for direct and literal fulfillments of, say, Ezekiel in the twenty-first-century Middle East is to bypass and short-circuit the reality and the finality of what we already have in Christ as the fulfillment of those great assurances. It is like taking delivery of the motorcar but still expecting to receive a horse. Or even worse—just ignoring the motorcar and de-manding to get a horse.

THE PROMISE GUARANTEED

To speak of "the Old Testament promise" is almost a repetition. The word *testament* would actually be better called *covenant*, for that is the word used in the Hebrew Bible, and it is the word used by the New Testament when referring to the Old. And the idea of promise is very much at the heart of the word *covenant*.

The features of biblical covenants. In the world of ancient Israel, cov-enants of all kinds were common in secular life. There were international treaties between a superior, imperial power and its vassal states, in which the "benefits," protection and services of the conqueror were granted in exchange for political and military loyalty and allegiance. Such treaty cov-enants were sanctioned by threats of dire punishment from the gods or men or both. In everyday life there were simple covenantal oaths in which promises were elevated to a very solemn and binding form. There were "parity" covenants, entered into by equal partners who swore mutual obliga-tions and responsibilities to each other, similar to what we call contracts.

When the term *covenant* is used in the Old Testament as a means of describing the relationship between God and human beings, it is somewhat flexible—that is, it does not conform wholly or neatly to any of the existing secular models but draws from different features of them, some more than others. Among the "standard" features of covenants made between God and people, the following are important:

(1) *God's initiative*. It is God who takes the initiative in making the cov-enant. Sometimes this may come "out of the blue," as with Abraham; some-times as a sequel to what God himself has done, as at Sinai after the exodus; sometimes in response to some human action or attitude, as in the case of Noah's righteous obedience, or David's desire to build a house for God. In all cases, it is God himself who says, "I will make a covenant with you." To that extent, although there is a human response and obligation, the biblical covenants involving God are not "parity" ones—that is, between equal partners. God is the sovereign initiator—the Lord of the covenant.

(2) *God's promises*. In declaring his initiation of a covenant, God under-takes some specific commitment, which constitutes the substance of the

covenant. God, of course, remains sovereign and free (he is not "bound" in the sense of being under constraint to any authority higher than himself). But God *chooses* to bind himself to his own word, and bases the security of that word on his own name and character—"by myself have I sworn . . ." The effect of the covenant, therefore, is to put the promises of God under guarantee, since they come from the truthfulness and eternity of God himself.

(3) *Human response.* In all of the divine-human covenants in the Bible, there is a required response. We saw this already in the last section. Sometimes theologians argue about whether certain covenants are "unconditional" or "conditional." Actually, in my view, the words aren't really adequate either way. The covenants are all "unconditional" in the sense that they issue from the redemptive intention of God to act in blessing for human beings, who neither deserve such action nor could fulfill any condition to deserve it. They *call* for human response, but they are neither *based* on it nor motivated by it. God simply acts of his own accord and on his own initiative.

Yet in another sense they are all "conditional" in that some clear stipulations are laid down for those who are to benefit from the covenant relationship. This is clearly so in the Sinai covenant, with the commandments and laws written into it. But the continuance of the covenant itself is not conditional on those laws. If the survival of the covenant had *depended* on Israel's obedience, the people would never have left Sinai, let alone have made it into the Promised Land, for they broke the most fundamental commandments within weeks of receiving them. Exodus 32–34 is the story of the golden calf, Moses' intercession and the renewal of the covenant. That story makes it very clear that the covenant was not only initiated by God's grace, it was also sustained by God's grace. It can be called "conditional" if one thinks of any given generation of Israelites, for whom the blessings of the covenant were indeed dependent on their obedience. Many a generation suffered the curses and threats of the covenant by their disobedience. But the *covenant itself* continued, grounded as it was in the grace of God's redemptive purpose for humanity, not just the obedience or blessing of Israel.

In our first chapter we did a rapid survey of Old Testament history along the three-section analysis of Matthew's genealogy. Earlier in this chapter, we reviewed it again as the "flight path" of God's promise, in its constant pattern of fulfillment and reinterpretation. It is worth surveying the route one last time, through a brief summary of the successive major covenants in the Old Testament, seeing how each is related to the others, and how all eventually lead toward the New Covenant inaugurated by Jesus himself.

Some books talk about an Adamic or an Edenic covenant, between God and Adam and Eve in the Garden of Eden. Certainly there were instructions, permissions and warnings in the narrative of creation and the Garden of Eden, but the text itself never speaks of a covenant, and it is not described that way anywhere else in the Old or New Testament. Even after the fall, there are certainly marks of God's grace: the provision of skins for clothing; the naming of Eve (mother of living—life would go on, in spite of the disobedience); and the prediction that the seed of the woman would ultimately crush the head of the serpent. This verse (Gen 3:15), sometimes called the *proto-evangelium*—or "first gospel"—is taken in some quarters as the first messianic prophecy in the Old Testament. Looked at retrospectively, of course, it is possible to see that Jesus did indeed crush Satan and will finally destroy him. But it is reading a lot into the verse in its own context to regard it as "messianic." It simply predicts that there will be unceasing conflict between the serpent and the human race, but that in the end, it will be humanity that wins—as indeed it was, in the man Jesus, representative of new humanity. So there are rays of hope in the engulfing darkness of the fall and the curse. But there is no reference to any covenant as such in Eden, either before or after the fall.

In each of the following covenants in the Old Testament we shall think about the scope of each one, then the substance (content) of it and then the response that God required.

The covenant with Noah (Genesis 6:18-21; 8:21–9:17). The scope of this covenant is universal. It is explicitly a commitment by God to the whole of his creation, to all life on earth—not just the human race but every living creature. It comes in two parts—first of all God's promise to preserve Noah in the midst of the judgment of the flood, and then, after the flood, God's commitment is extended to all humans and all creatures.

The substance of the promise is both negative and positive. Negatively, God promises never again to destroy the earth with a flood, in spite of the continuing wickedness of humanity. There will be no destructive global judgment in the course of human history itself (this does not of course rule out the reality of a final, universal and destructive judgment. Peter uses the flood as a prototype of that, 2 Pet 3:3-7). Positively, God promises to preserve the conditions necessary for life on earth—the seasons, the regularity of nature, the provision of harvests.

The ongoing history of the human race is based on the endurance of this Noahic covenant. As all development agencies point out, the hunger of so many of the human race is not because of an overall shortage of food on the earth, or the inability of the earth to produce food for its current (or future) population. The productive resources of the earth's crust and the oceans seem almost limitless in their resilient renewability. God has kept his covenant. It is *human* incompetence, greed, injustice and aggression that deny the benefits of it to so many. God gives us the means to live and let live. Humanity chooses to live and let die.

The response stipulated with this covenant is very appropriate to its substance. God promises to *preserve* life. He calls on humanity to *respect* life. Though animals may be eaten, their "lifeblood" is exempt. And the lifeblood of human beings is to be held in highest sanctity, because God made human beings in his own image (Gen 9:3-6).

The Noahic covenant teaches us God's providence. It is not limited to a particular people or a particular place. It emphatically includes all life in the whole earth. It also illustrates quite well the inadequacy of asking whether it is unconditional or conditional. On the one hand, God has clearly continued to keep this covenant in spite of humanity's failure to maintain the sanctity of life. But on the other hand, where human beings have shown utter disregard for life, human and animal, they tend to reap consequences of great severity in the natural world also—eventually. Not all deserts, famines and droughts are the result of purely "natural" causes. There is a close connection between human behavior and ecological health or disaster. Hosea observed this long before twentieth-century environmentalists when he complained about the degraded human behavior that accompanies ignorance of God:

> There is only cursing, lying and murder,
>   stealing and adultery;
> they break all bounds,
>   and bloodshed follows bloodshed.
> Because of this the land dries up,
>   and all who live in it waste away;

the beasts of the field, the birds in the sky
   and the fish in the sea are swept away. (Hos 4:2-3)

The covenant with Abraham (Genesis 12:1-3; 15:1-21; 17:1-27).
The scope of this covenant is also universal, but in a different sense from
the Noahic covenant. The earlier covenant is the basis of God's *providential*
preservation of all life throughout the span of human history. That is sometimes referred to as God's "common grace"—the indiscriminate good will
of the Creator by which "He causes his sun to rise on the evil and the good,
and sends rain on the righteous and the unrighteous" (Mt 5:45).

The covenant with Abraham, on the other hand, is the basis of God's
redemptive work within human history. The universal goal of this covenant
is to bring God's redemptive blessing to all nations. The "all" clearly does
not mean every human being who ever lived but has a representative
sense. God's redemptive purpose will ultimately be as global in its scope
as the current sinfulness of the human race, as typified in the nations at
Babel. People of every nation will share in the blessing covenanted to and
through Abraham.

The substance of the covenant is seen in what was specifically promised
to Abraham and his descendants, in pursuance of that ultimate, universal
goal. It was threefold:

Posterity: From Abraham would come descendants who would be a great
nation.

Relationship: With them God would have a special relationship of blessing
and protection: "I will be their God; they will be my people."

Land: To them God would give the land of Abraham's own wanderings as an
inheritance that would prove his faithfulness and their relationship to him.

The response required by God is first specified as circumcision, in Genesis
17. Superficially this might seem a rather undemanding sort of response.
But that would be just that—superficial. Even in its own context, the
command to circumcise comes after the summons to Abraham to "walk
before me and be blameless"—an obviously ethical injunction. Chapter 17
then describes how Abraham circumcised his whole household. Immediately following, in Genesis 18:19, God affirms that the purpose for which
he had chosen Abraham was so that he will direct his children and his

household after him (that is, the precise ones he had circumcised) to keep the way of the Lord by doing what is right and just.

The expressions "the way of the LORD" and "righteousness and justice" would come in the top five most significant and content-rich ethical expressions in the Hebrew Bible. Here they occur as the very purpose of the election of Abraham, and as the means by which the promise will be fulfilled (see the last expression of purpose in the same verse, "so that the LORD will bring about for Abraham what he has promised him"). The ethical nature of the response required from Abraham is very clear and stands out in stark contrast to the context of this section of Genesis, which describes the wickedness of Sodom and Gomorrah and God's judgment upon them. In the midst of a world going the *way of Sodom*, God wants a community characterized by the *way of the Lord*. That is the response he is looking for in Abraham and the covenant community yet to emerge.

Circumcision was more than just an outward ritual. It involved the commitment of the heart to practical obedience. That was a truth well perceived in the Old Testament itself. It did not need Paul to point it out for the first time (Rom 2:25-29). Moses had done so emphatically before the people even reached the land of promise. In Deuteronomy 10:12-22, the command "circumcise *your hearts*" is preceded by reference to the ancestors of Israel, and is therefore clearly intended to recall the fact that circumcision was essentially the sign of the covenant with Abraham. And it is followed by specific ethical instruction to imitate God in his compassion and justice, since that is what it means to "walk in his ways."

So we can see a strong connection between the universal, missional goal of the covenant with Abraham ("blessing to all nations"), and this practical, socioethical response required of Abraham and his descendants ("walking in the way of the Lord"). Israel could only fulfill its role in the mission of God if it lived in obedience to the covenant with God. We shall develop this further in the next chapters.

The Sinai covenant (Exodus 19:3-6, 24, and Deuteronomy). The scope of this covenant was national. God initiated it between himself and the national community of Israel after its deliverance from Egypt. But the explicit links with the Abrahamic covenant prevent it from being national in an exclusive or narrow sense. First of all, the whole sequence of events from Egypt to Sinai is repeatedly said to be in fulfillment of God's promise to Abraham. God will act in redemption for this people because he is the God of Abraham, Isaac and Jacob, whose descendants they are. So Israel is the people through whom God's promise of blessing to all nations will be forwarded. The initiation of a new and covenanted relationship with Israel is not an end in itself. It is simply the next step on the road of God's ultimate purpose in history for all nations.

Second, in his "preface" to the making of the covenant, recorded in the key verses of Exodus 19:3-6, God gave Israel an identity and role that was explicitly related to the rest of the nations. In the midst of "all the nations" in the "whole earth," which belongs to God (Ex 19:5), Israel was to be a priestly people and a holy nation. The function of priesthood in Israel itself was to stand between God and the rest of the people—representing God to the people (by their teaching function) and representing and bringing the people to God (by their sacrificial function). Through the priesthood, God was made known to the people, and the people could come into acceptable relationship to God. So God assigns to his people as a whole community the role of priesthood for the nations. As their priests stood in relation to God and the rest of *Israel*, so they as a whole community were to stand in relation to God and the rest of the *nations*.

There is, therefore, a missional dimension to the Sinai covenant also, linked to the ultimate goal of the Abrahamic covenant. It is not greatly stressed in the covenant arrangements and the laws, but it is unmistakably there (cf. Deut 4:5-8). It comes into focus again in some prophetic passages that reflect on Israel's failure to keep the covenant as being a failure in their mission to the nations.

The substance of the Sinai covenant filled out what had been promised to Abraham for the sake of the nation as a whole. A useful summary is given in the "program" God sets before Moses just before the onslaught of the plagues, in Exodus 6:6-8. God promises to accomplish four things:

- The *redemption* of Israel from its oppressors (v. 6);

- the special *relationship* between God and Israel: "I will take you as my own people, and I will be your God" (v. 7a);

- the *knowledge of Yahweh*: "You will know that I am the LORD your God" (v. 7b); and

- the gift of the promised *land:* "I will bring you to the land I swore with uplifted hand to give to Abraham, to Isaac and to Jacob" (v. 8).

As these themes are developed in the rest of the Pentateuch, we can see that:

- God achieved that promised redemption in the exodus, proving his faithfulness, love and grace;

- the special relationship included God's promise to continue to bless and protect Israel, provided it continued in its commitment to live in obedience to his ways;

- the knowledge of Yahweh as the unique and living God was a responsibility as well as a privilege entrusted to Israel through its unique experience of his saving power (Deut 4:32-39); and

- the land was not a gift to be taken for granted and squandered in forgetful complacency but a place to live responsibly before God with a lifestyle that would ensure prolonged enjoyment of the gift itself (Deut 8).

The response stipulated within this covenant is total and exclusive loyalty to Yahweh. This involves not only the worship of Yahweh alone, to the exclusion of all other gods, but also moral commitment to the values and character of Yahweh. The commandments and laws stress both—to worship God alone and to live in God's ways. That is reflected in the way Jesus selected love for the Lord God (Deut 6:5) and love for one's neighbor (Lev 19:18) as the heart of the law, or the hook from which it all was suspended. We can see the same double point negatively when we notice that the law constantly emphasized two primary evils—idolatry and injustice.

Covenant obligation, then, can be pictured as two perpendicular lines. There is the vertical line of loyalty and obedience to God alone. And there is the horizontal line of love, compassion, justice and brotherhood to other human beings. The two directions of obligation are inseparable. In the law this is sometimes seen in the way social legislation is motivated by gratitude and loyalty to the God who delivered them. Since God had acted in justice and compassion on behalf of Israel, it was required to show the same things toward the weak, poor or vulnerable in its own society. This feature of Hebrew law was very influential on Jesus, as we shall examine in chapter five.

Looking again, then, at the relationship between the Sinai covenant and the covenant with Abraham, we can see a definite link between the required *response* to the Sinai covenant and the ultimate *goal* of the Abrahamic covenant. That is, Israel's loyalty to Yahweh and obedience to the law were the major means by which it would enable God to fulfill his goal of bringing blessing to the nations. The Sinai covenant was not an end in itself, to make Israel into a separate nation for its own exclusive sake and benefit. It was a means toward the achievement of God's ultimately universal purpose for humanity. The prophets perceived this in passages such as Jeremiah 4:1-2 and Isaiah 48:17-19. In the Old Testament, ethics is linked to mission, as means is to end. There is no biblical mission without biblical living.

The covenant with David (2 Samuel 7; 23:1-7; Psalm 89; 132). The scope of the covenant with David was primarily the house of David itself—and that indeed was the substance of the covenant also (i.e., that there *would be* a house of David to continue on the throne of Israel).

As we saw in the historical survey in chapter one, the arrival of a monarchy was a major change in the nature of Israel as a people. After the loose federation of tribes with their internal fragmentation, and the external pressures from Canaanites and other enemies, the Israelites were finally bound together into a single state not only occupying the territory promised to Abraham but also controlling a number of subject states on their borders. And so at that point of change in the nation's life, even though it was initiated by human desires and compromises that God himself through Samuel disapproved of, God renewed his commitment to its future by pledging yet another covenant with the king he had given it. So although the scope of the promise was the house of David itself, it was in fact a covenant for the whole nation, because the promise that David's line would continue permanently was by implication a promise of a future for the people of Israel also.

The context in which the covenant with David is recorded also makes this link clear. The chapter immediately before it (2 Sam 6) records how David brought the ark of the covenant into Jerusalem. David had recently captured Jerusalem and made it his capital city. From Jerusalem he reigned over all the tribes of Israel, having previously reigned for seven years over the tribe of Judah alone at Hebron. The ark, more than anything else, symbolized the ancient historical tradition and faith of Israel as the people of Yahweh. It was constructed at Sinai and represented all that the Sinai covenant meant to Israel—the law, the holiness of Yahweh, his approachability only through the blood of sacrifice at the mercy seat and his presence in the midst of his people. David's action in bringing the ark of the covenant into Jerusalem, therefore, was clearly a deliberate move to demonstrate his allegiance to the ancient traditions of Israel's historical faith in Yahweh and to show that his understanding of his kingship was founded on the same covenantal basis as the old tribal federation.

In God's oracle to David through the prophet Nathan, we likewise find that the substance of God's promise was both for the house of David and also for Israel. God promised Israel continued security and "rest" (i.e., peace from enemies, 2 Sam 7:10-16). And in the prayer of response, which David offered after hearing God's promise through Nathan, the editor of the books of Samuel obviously wishes his readers to hear clear echoes of the exodus-Sinai theme. (Read 2 Samuel 7:22-24 and compare it with Deuteronomy 4:32-38.) So the covenant with David is presented not as something utterly new or as a break with the past but as an extension of God's covenant relationship with his people to the line of Davidic kings who would now reign over them. The covenant with David does not remove the covenant at Sinai but assumes it and builds on it.

The Davidic covenant not only has these explicit links with the Sinai covenant but also seems deliberately framed in such a way as to recall the Abrahamic covenant. We have already seen that it was David, in fact, who first achieved for Israel the possession of all the territory promised to Abraham. Other parallels between Abraham and David include the promise to make David great, to make his *name* great, to maintain a special *relationship of blessing* with him and his offspring, and especially the promise of a *son* and heir.

These echoes of the Abraham tradition in the historical books are greatly amplified in the poetic materials concerning the link between the throne of David and God's purpose for the nations beyond Israel. There are some psalms, for example, known as "royal psalms," that celebrate different features of the Davidic kingship and its base in Zion. Characteristic of these royal psalms is the idea that David, or his descendant on the throne, rules over all the nations of the earth! Now, whoever wrote hymns like that (e.g., Ps 2:8-11; 72:8-11; 110:6) knew perfectly well that such worldwide dominion had never been the privilege of any historical king of David's line. And as the history of the monarchy dragged onward and downward, it would have been absurd to imagine that it ever would be. Yet they wrote such hymns, and people sang them, and presumably meant something by them.

Now we might be tempted to say that that kind of language was just typical flattery of monarchs making grossly exaggerated claims for their imperial ambitions, and that maybe nobody took it seriously (or literally at least). But there are times when it is clear that the psalmists had more in mind than just the historical or geographical statistics of the Davidic kingdom itself. Rather they saw that behind the throne of David stood *the throne of Yahweh himself.* This is clearest in Psalm 2. So God's purpose for Israel's king was the same as his purpose for Israel itself (i.e., to be the vehicle of God's intentions for all nations). Psalm 72, one of the most notable of the royal psalms, has this to say about the son of David:

> May his name endure forever;
>> may it continue as long as the sun.
> *Then all nations will be blessed through him,*
>> *and they will call him blessed.* (Ps 72:17, my italics)

The echo of the promise to Abraham could scarcely be more loud and clear.

When we observe the response that is written into the Davidic covenant, it reinforces the links that we have already pointed out between the Davidic covenant and the Sinai and Abrahamic covenants. It is the same fundamental demand for loyalty and obedience. In this case that demand is grounded on the relationship of son to father, which God grants to David and his descendants on the throne. The son-father relationship of the Davidic king to God is recorded both in the historical record (2 Sam 7:14) and also in the poetic celebration (e.g., Ps 2:7; 89:26-37).

The king in a sense "embodied" Israel, since Israel was also designated Yahweh's "firstborn son" (Ex 4:22). So to speak of the king as God's son had a double purpose—just as it did for Israel: to emphasize God's love (i.e., his unbreakable commitment) on the one hand, and the requirement of obedience (the primary duty of sonship) on the other. We shall see in the next chapter how both of these were fundamental to Jesus' self-consciousness as the Son of God.

The moral response expected of the Davidic king existed, in a sense, before there even was one. The Deuteronomic law of the king (Deut 17:14-20) very carefully makes the point that the king is not to consider himself above his fellows or above the law. On the contrary, he is to be exemplary in paying heed to the law and obeying it. The king was not to be a super-Israelite but a model Israelite. Psalm 72, written by or for a Davidic king, with the covenant much in mind, goes to the heart of the law's concern and expects the king to act for the special interest of the poor and needy:

> May he defend the afflicted among the people
> and save the children of the needy;
> may he crush the oppressor. (Ps 72:4; cf. vv. 12-14)

This standard was not forgotten, even (especially, perhaps) in later days when the monarchy in Jerusalem had become a matter of royal wealth and power, exercised on behalf of the wealthy and powerful elite in society, not on behalf of the "afflicted and needy." Jeremiah saw some of the worst of that kind of kingship, and he placarded the neglected duties of Davidic kings in the very gates of the palace itself.

> Hear the word of the LORD to you, king of Judah, you who sit on David's throne. . . . This is what the LORD says: Do what is just and right. [cf. Gen 18:19] Rescue from the hand of the oppressor the one who has been robbed. Do no wrong or violence to the foreigner, the fatherless or the widow, and do not shed innocent blood in this place. (Jer 22:2-3)

Even though these words were addressed to *the kings in Jerusalem*, they are very clearly the language of the Sinai covenant law. It shows that even after the inauguration of the Davidic covenant and all its accompanying theology about Mount Zion, the prophets still gave priority to the fundamental moral demands of the Sinai covenant. On these scales Jeremiah weighed King Jehoiakim and found him wanting on all points (Jer 23:13, 17), especially as compared with his godly father, the great reforming king Josiah (vv. 15-17).

So once again we find the same combination: the universal, missiological dimension of the covenant, in its ultimate scope, for the blessing of all nations through Israel, and the explicit moral conditions of obedience and practical, social justice, which are here laid as a duty not solely on the nation as a whole as in the Sinai covenant but also on those who were entrusted with leadership and authority within it.

The new covenant. Ceremonies of covenant renewal are scattered through the history of Israel in the Hebrew Bible. The first happened less than two months after the Sinai covenant was made, while Israel was still at Mount Sinai (Ex 34). After that we could mention occasions of renewal by Moses on the plains of Moab (Deuteronomy), by Joshua after the conquest (Josh 23–24), by Samuel at the institution of the monarchy (1 Sam 12), by Hezekiah (2 Chron 29–31) and by Josiah (2 Kings 22–23).

The last of these, at the time of Josiah, was the greatest of them all. It involved a major religious, social and political reformation that radically reversed the direction of Judah's life as it had proceeded for the previous half-century. And Jeremiah witnessed it. In fact, Jeremiah's call to be a prophet as a youth came when the reforms of Josiah had been going for about two years. About five years later, the book of the law (probably Deuteronomy) was discovered in the temple during repairs, and that led to an even more stringent reformation. And then Josiah had a ceremony of covenant renewal.

It was all very impressive, externally. But Jeremiah saw beneath the surface and observed that the heart of the people was not really changed. The religious purges had not purged the deep-seated idolatry or the rampant social corruption (see especially Jeremiah 2; 5, and his comments, probably, on Josiah's covenant renewal in Jeremiah 11). Something much more transforming was needed, not so much a renewal of the covenant as a new covenant altogether. For his own generation, Jeremiah could see that nothing but judgment lay ahead. For them, there would come the fulfillment of the curses and threats inherent in the Sinai covenant. But beyond that judgment, Jeremiah had a vision for the future of his people. And part of that future vision was his portrait of a new covenant (Jer 31:31-34).

Because Jeremiah is quoted twice in the letter to the Hebrews (Heb 8:9-13; 10:15-18), it is Jeremiah's picture of the new covenant that is commonly meant when people speak about the "new covenant." However, the idea of a new covenant was not unique to Jeremiah, though it may have originated with him. Ezekiel was a prophet among the exiles, and he also held out hope of a new covenant. And the idea is also found in the rousing words of encouragement to the exiles in Isaiah 40–55.

This breadth of material about a new covenant makes it more difficult to analyze in quite the same way as we did for the previous historical covenants, especially since this one is in the realm of visionary expectation, not precise historical detail. But it is well worth the attempt. Please take the time to look up the passages as we go along. It's the only way to get a grasp of the rich content the prophets were talking about. What we will clearly see is that the prophets made use of items from all the earlier historical covenants in their rich and allusive portrayal of the new covenant of their future hope.

The scope of the new covenant is at first very clearly national. In both Jeremiah and Ezekiel, the major thrust is the hope of the restoration of Israel itself. Jeremiah's new covenant saying comes in the midst of two chapters (Jeremiah 30–31) wholly taken up with this comforting hope (these chapters are sometimes called "The Book of Consolation," in contrast to the bulk of Jeremiah's oracles of doom and judgment). God says he plans "to build and plant" his people. Accordingly, the new covenant will be one that God will make with "the house of Israel and the house of Judah."

Ezekiel's vision of the future restoration of Israel, with a new covenant relationship between God and his people, is spread mainly over Ezekiel 34; 36–37. Again, the scope is predominantly national in the terms described. God promises a restoration of the theocracy. God himself will be their true "shepherd," that is, the true king of Israel. But at the same time, "David" will be prince over them (Ezek 34:11-24). In Ezekiel 36 the restoration of Israel will be a marvel in the sight of the nations, which will vindicate the reputation of Yahweh, their God. The reunification of the nation is the theme in Ezekiel 37:15-28 (following hard on the resurrection of the nation in the first part of the chapter). Again, "David" will be king of the unified nation.

In Ezekiel's vision, the nations are referred to rather in the role of spectators. When God acts to restore Israel, then the nations will see and hear and know who really is God. So there is a universal dimension, but it is not integrated into the covenant itself.

In Isaiah, however, the universal inclusion of the nations is worked into the covenant idea from the start. The scope of the new covenant in Isaiah

40–55 is as wide as the scope of salvation itself in those chapters, and that is "to the ends of the earth." The identity of the "servant of God" figure in these chapters is much debated (and we shall add to the debate in chapter four), but it is clear that he is sometimes identical with Israel (cf. Is 41:8; 42:19, etc.) and sometimes apparently distinct from Israel. In the so-called servant songs, it appears that an individual, called and anointed by God, will fulfill the role and mission of Israel—enduring great suffering as he does so. His mission, as it was Israel's mission in terms of the Abrahamic covenant, will be to bring God's salvation to all nations. And this idea is first expressed in Isaiah 42:6, using covenant language:

> I will keep you and will make you
> to be a covenant for the people
> and a light for the Gentiles.

The creation-wide context of the immediately preceding verse (Is 42:5) shows who is in the prophet's mind—all those who breathe and walk on the earth. The same point is made in Isaiah 49:6 (a verse used by Paul to authorize his own decision to take the gospel to the Gentiles, in Acts 13:47) and Isaiah 49:8. In Isaiah 54:9-10, the "covenant of peace" (an expression also favored by Ezekiel) is primarily again made with a restored Israel. But the explicit comparison with the Noahic covenant shows that the universal aspect is not lost from sight. It comes back into full view in Isaiah 55, the great "evangelistic" conclusion to this section of prophecy. There the "everlasting covenant" is equated with God's "unfailing kindness promised to David" (his covenant commitment). And that in turn is filled out by envisaging peoples and nations coming to Israel and to their God (Is 55:3-5), which is a link between the Davidic and the Abrahamic covenants that we noticed before.

The echoes of all four historical covenants should have been audible in that brief survey, but here is a replay in case you missed any of the notes.

Noah gets his explicit mention in Isaiah 54:9. But there are other places where the idea of all creation being involved in God's future covenant blessing is present. Ezekiel's covenant of peace included God's promise to restrain the ravages of nature and instead to give his people such an abundance of harvest that it would be like Eden itself (Ezek 34:25-27, 29; 36:30, 33-35). Jeremiah also uses the regularity and unfailing consistency of nature (which was a feature of the Noahic covenant) as a way of guaranteeing God's own intention to maintain his covenant with his people (Jer 31:35-37; 33:19-26).

Abraham can be heard in the resounding universalism of Isaiah 40–55 and the extension of God's salvation to the ends of the earth through one who will be a covenant and a light for the nations.

Sinai can be heard in almost all the passages: Jeremiah's emphasis on the law being written in the heart and on the knowledge of God; Ezekiel's emphasis on the cleansing of sin and the dwelling of God among his people; Isaiah's expectation of a new exodus, liberation from all kinds of bondage and the administration of justice for the nations.

David can also be found in all three prophetic visions of the new covenant: Jeremiah's "Righteous Branch" who will "do righteousness and justice" as the Davidic king was supposed to (Jer 23:1-6; 33:15-18); Ezekiel's true shepherd, ruling again over a united Israel of God (Ezek 34); and Isaiah's witness, leader and commander for the peoples (Is 55:3-4).

The substance of the new covenant is also complex, and ideally we should analyze each of the prophetic passages separately in its own context. But for the sake of gaining an overall view, we can isolate several key themes common to all of them.

(1) A new relationship with God. "You will be my people and I will be your God." These words formed the very essence of the covenant relationship between God and Israel from the beginning. The new covenant would reaffirm that central, warm and possessive relationship. One people, one God, forever (Jer 31:33; 32:38-40; Ezek 37:23, 27). Isaiah expresses it in terms of a restored marriage (Is 54:5-10).

(2) A new experience of forgiveness. So much of the prophets' message had been accusation of the people for their accumulating sins. Judgment was inevitable. But they also saw that God's capacity for forgiveness was not bounded by the people's capacity for sin. It was his divine desire and intention to "solve the sin problem" for good. He would remember it no more (Jer 31:34). Characteristic of his priestly imagery, Ezekiel envisages it as a complete cleansing (Ezek 36:25; 37:23). Isaiah invites the sinner to an abundant pardon that surpasses human reasoning (Is 55:6-9).

(3) A new obedience to the law. If even the reform of Josiah, in which the law was read and publicly assented to, brought little change in the people's

behavior, then more than external pledges of obedience were needed. So Jeremiah writes into his new covenant God's intention:

> I will put my law in their minds
>> and write it on their hearts. (Jer 31:33)

The result will be that knowledge of God will no longer need to be "taught" because it will be an inner characteristic.

> They will all know me,
>> from the least of them to the greatest. (Jer 31:34)

This is sometimes regarded as a picture of the individualizing and personalizing of the knowledge of God, with the assumption that previously it had only been thought of in corporate or national terms. Certainly it does imply that every person will know him. But on the other occasions that Jeremiah uses the phrase "from the least of them to the greatest," it is a way of portraying a whole community by a single common characteristic (Jer 6:13; 8:10). That is probably its intention here also. The people of God *as a whole* will be characterized as a community who knows him.

Now if we go on to ask what it means to know God, Jeremiah allows us no sentimental feelings of private spiritual piety. He is absolutely clear. To know God is to delight in faithful love, justice and righteousness, as God himself does (Jer 9:24). More than that, it means not only to *delight* in such things but actually to *do* righteousness and justice by defending the rights of the poor and needy—that is to know God. Jeremiah defines the knowledge of God in one of the most challenging verses in the Bible.

> "He [Josiah] did what was right and just,
>> so all went well with him.
> He defended the cause of the poor and needy,
>> and so all went well.
> Is that not what it means to know me?"
>> declares the LORD. (Jer 22:15-16)

These things were the heart of the law, the law that would now, in the new covenant, be written in the heart.

"The law written on the heart" means much more than a new upsurge of sincerity in keeping it. We have already seen that the Old Testament from the beginning had called for obedience from the heart. The popular parody of the Old Testament as a religion of external legalism is far from the truth. The heart, as the seat of the will and intelligence (not just emotions), was of great importance in the law, in the psalms and in the book of Proverbs. Ezekiel goes further in emphasizing that such obedience of the heart involves not just a new law but a new heart itself—a spiritual heart transplant performed by the Spirit of God. Only such a spiritual miracle will produce the obedience called for (Ezek 36:26-32). True obedience would be the gift of the same Spirit who could turn dead bones into a living army in the mighty act of resurrection pictured in Ezekiel 37:1-14.

The book of Isaiah does not include this dimension in its sayings about the covenant itself, but there is a strong emphasis on the full acceptance of the law and the reign of justice in its visions of the mission of the servant to the nations as the agent of God's purpose for humanity (Is 42:1-4; 51:4-8). This is very similar to the prophecies of the messianic age under the future anointed son of David found in the earlier chapters of Isaiah (cf. Is 9:7; 11:1-5). It will be an age ruled by a new David but ruled according the law and justice of God.

(4) *A new Davidic king.* Jeremiah includes this element in his future hope as we saw (Jer 23:5-6; 33:15-26), and Ezekiel looks to a future "David" as the agent of theocracy and of the unity of the people (Ezek 34:23-24). It is possible that the "David" referred to in Isaiah 55:3-4 is actually an identity for the servant figure, previously anonymous and mysterious. If that were so, it would certainly link up the expectations associated with the coming "David" with the mission of bringing God's law and justice to the nations.

(5) *A new abundance of nature.* Abundance and fruitfulness were part of the promised blessings for obedience to the Sinai covenant (Lev 26:3-13 contains language that recalls the bounty of Genesis 2; Deut 28:1-14). If the covenant were to be restored on the farther side of the fulfillment of its curses in God's judgment, then it is not surprising that we find as part of that hope the expectation of return to the land, secure settlement on it, freedom from the traditional perils of wild beasts and human enemies and abundant fertility of crops and herds. Creation itself would be part of the renewal of God's covenant.

Old Testament hope was not merely the hope of some mysterious paradise after death but the living reality of God's blessing on his creation here and now for his renewed and obedient people. The recollection of Eden is also not out of place, because the hope of humanity since the fall, so poignantly expressed by Lamech at the birth of his son Noah, was that God would lift the curse from the earth and return to dwell once more with humanity in the earth (Gen 5:28-29). This is also the hope that brings the whole Bible to a close, with a vision of its fulfillment in a new heaven and new earth (Rev 21:1-3). A foretaste of that new creation is seen in the otherwise extravagant language with which the prophets look forward to the renewal of the land of Israel itself (Jer 31:11-14; Ezek 34:26-29; 36:8-12). As elsewhere in the Bible, the land of Israel functions in part as a token of the future new creation, as the place of God's presence and unhindered blessing.

So then there are several distinct "horizons" of future vision in these combined Old Testament pictures of God's new covenant. At horizon one, within the Old Testament period itself, there was a fulfillment of God's immediate promise to restore Israel to its land and continue his purpose with it as a people. That happened when Cyrus of Persia defeated Babylon and gave freedom to captive peoples to return to their homelands in 538 B.C. The national dimensions of God's promise were fulfilled.

But at horizon two, the New Testament clearly saw the fulfillment of the new covenant promises in Jesus Christ, and specifically in his death and resurrection. Jesus himself interpreted his death in those terms, and the apostles likewise preached that in the coming of the Messiah Jesus, the new age of the new covenant and the outpouring of the Spirit had now begun.

Finally, at horizon three, the eschatological vision reaches right to the end of the Bible story. For the Bible concludes with the perfect fulfillment of the new covenant vision: God dwelling with his people in the earth, redeemed and restored to its beauty and fruitfulness, in a perfect relationship of love and obedience, with all sin, evil and curse removed forever, and all ruled over by the Lord Jesus Christ, the Lion of Judah and the Lamb who was slain but now reigns on the throne of God.

CONCLUSION

We have made a long journey through the historical span of the Old Testament and its rich array of promise. We need to finish off by stepping back for a moment to survey the way we have come.

To change metaphors yet again, the Old Testament, considered as promise, is like a great river. Along the way several streams flow into it from different starting points and with different individual courses. These are the different streams of tradition, law, narratives, poetry, prophecy, wisdom and so on. But in the end, they all combine into a single current, flowing deep and strong—the ongoing, irresistible promise of God.

Scholars can map each stream of tradition, indicating its distinctiveness, the route it takes through the Old Testament literature and the individuals or groups responsible for preserving its flow. Our survey has been only a very roughly sketched map, because our aim has not been the minute details of Old Testament history and literature but to feel the full force of the great current of promise, fed by all its many streams.

The overwhelming impression through all this study of promise and covenant is *God's unwavering intention to bless*. God's covenant with Noah proclaims his blessing through the promise to preserve the conditions of life for all his creation. God's covenant with Abraham proclaims his purpose of blessing all humanity in and through the descendants of Abraham. And that remains the constant background to all God's subsequent dealings and promises involving Israel. God's commitment to that intention for humanity is what motivates and sustains his commitment to Israel in the midst of all the ups and downs of their checkered historical relationship.

So when the writers of the New Testament witnessed God's climactic discharge of that commitment to humanity in the life, death and resurrection of Jesus of Nazareth, they checked what they had seen in Jesus with what they already knew through their Hebrew Scriptures. They looked at all the events surrounding Jesus, and they understood them, illuminated them, explained and finally recorded them, all in the light of the whole sweep of Old Testament promise. God had made a commitment. And God had kept his word.

The Old Testament declared the promise that Jesus fulfilled.

CHAPTER 2 QUESTIONS AND EXERCISES

1. Study the fulfillment texts in Matthew 1 and 2. How does Matthew see the childhood of Jesus against the background of the story of Old Testament Israel and the promises of God—not just certain predictions coming true? How do these two chapters encourage people's faith in God and in the great story of the Bible, which centers on Christ?

2. Read Isaiah 7, the "Immanuel sign." What did it mean at horizon one (for Ahaz and the people of Judah at that time)? How did Matthew reuse it at horizon two (in relation to the conception and birth of Jesus)? How does it reach right to horizon three, when God promises in Revelation 21–22 that he will "dwell with us" forever?

3. Discuss and explain the difference between prediction and promise. Think of examples in your own culture that would help to illustrate the difference between them in the Bible.

4. Read Acts 13:13-52. Take notes on how Paul uses the story of Old Testament Israel to lead his listeners to understand how God had kept his promises through Christ.

5. How would you explain to someone the sequence of covenants in the Old Testament? Select at least one text for each of God's promises to Noah, Abraham, Israel (at Sinai through Moses), David and the new covenant. Aim to show the links between them and how together they provide a route through the whole Bible story and lead ultimately to Christ. Do not forget to notice that all of them required some response from people, and ask what that means for our response to God today, standing in the new covenant relationship through Christ.

JESUS *and* HIS OLD TESTAMENT IDENTITY

So Jesus came as the completion of the story that the Old Testament had told, and as the fulfillment of the promise that the Old Testament had declared. That much has been made abundantly clear by the way Matthew uses his Hebrew Bible even before we have gotten beyond chapter 2 of his Gospel.

But who was Jesus?

Mark, whose Gospel gets us into the action of Jesus' ministry faster than any of the others, punctuates his narrative with a whole series of questions that were raised by the impact of Jesus.

The demons started it: "What do you want with us . . . ? Have you come to destroy us?" (Mk 1:24). Too true!

Then the crowds took it up: "What is this? A new teaching—and with authority!" (Mk 1:27). True again!

The religious leaders took offense: "Why does this fellow talk like that? . . . Who can forgive sins but God alone?" (Mk 2:7). Truer than they realized.

"Why does he eat with tax collectors and sinners?" (Mk 2:16).

"Why are they doing what is unlawful on the Sabbath?" (Mk 2:24).

"Where did this man get these things?" (Mk 6:2).

"Isn't this the carpenter?" (Mk 6:3).

Finally, his disciples got to the real point, as they sat trembling in a gently rocking boat that a few moments before had been tossing and on the brink of swamping in a storm, which Jesus had simply snuffed out with a word.

"Who is this?" (Mk 4:41). That was the real issue. Who was *he?*

Coming back to Matthew's Gospel, we remember that Matthew 2 ended with Jesus growing up as a child in Nazareth. Nazareth the insignificant. Nazareth in Galilee of the Gentiles. Nazareth from which no good thing was expected to come. How could a local boy from such a background have the kind of significance that Matthew's first two chapters have prepared the reader to expect? This very question dogged Jesus in his own lifetime. It has been suggested that the word *Nazarene*, the mystery term of Matthew's list of fulfillments in chapter 2, may actually be a nickname meaning some thing like "the insignificant." Not the most promising identity for one born to be the very pivot of history.

"THIS IS MY SON"

Perhaps that is why Matthew's next chapter leads up to a climax with a very different assessment of the identity of Jesus. Matthew 3 describes the ministry of John the Baptist and how he was persuaded, reluctantly, to baptize Jesus. This event, the baptism of Jesus, was so important that it is included in all four Gospels. And when the apostles preached the gospel in Acts, they often started with John the Baptist. It was obviously important to God as well, because here we have God the Holy Spirit coming down visibly on God the Son, and the voice of God the Father: "This is my Son, whom I love; with him I am well pleased" (Mt 3:17).

And it was important to Satan, since the three Synoptic Gospels all record that immediately after this event, Satan threw all his effort into getting Jesus to exploit his identity as the Son of God in ways that would divert him from his real mission. For Satan saw that if Jesus were to fulfill his mission it would mean defeat and destruction for Satan. So Satan began all his temptations with the challenging, questioning words, "*If* you are the Son of God . . ."

And clearly his baptism was important to Jesus himself. As a boy Jesus had been aware of the special relationship that he had with God as his Father (which Luke, not Matthew, tells us about in Lk 2:49). But through his baptism, in his adult maturity at the age of about thirty, he receives full divine confirmation of his true identity and mission from the mouth of his

Father himself. So awesome was this sense of identity and the implications it carried that it led to a period of intense struggle, alone in the desert. But immediately after he had survived that and proved his loyalty to his Father by resisting Satan with the very Scriptures Satan cunningly used, Jesus entered into his ministry with immediate, stunning effect.

So there is a contrast between what other people thought of Jesus (at least in the beginning) and what God his Father thought of him. Luke brings this out in a rather clever way by putting his version of the genealogy of Jesus immediately after his baptism. So just after we have read that God declared "You are *my* Son," Luke begins his next paragraph: "Now Jesus himself was about thirty years old when he began his ministry. He was the son, *so it was thought*, of Joseph . . . " (Lk 3:23, my italics).

In other words, to human eyes, Jesus was the son of an unimportant carpenter in insignificant Nazareth. In God's sight, however, he was "my beloved Son in whom I delight." That was his real identity. God knew it. Jesus knew it, and in the course of his ministry others would come to know and believe it.

For such an important occasion as the baptism of his Son, you might have thought that God would have come up with something wholly new. Words never heard before by human ears. A fresh burst of divine speech, such as launched the ministry of Moses or Isaiah. But no. Whether history repeats itself or not, God certainly does. The words that meant so much to Jesus at this critical moment in his life were actually echoes of at least two and probably three different passages in the Old Testament. Presumably, God the Father knew that his incarnate Son, by age thirty, was so steeped in his Hebrew Scriptures that he would not only recognize the texts but also understand all that they meant for his own self-identity. The words themselves were not new. What was new was the way the three passages are brought together and related to a single person with a unique identity and mission. The three texts echoed here are Psalm 2:7, Isaiah 42:1 and Genesis 22:2.

"This is / You are my Son." This is an echo of Psalm 2:7, which was originally a psalm about King David and any king descended from him. He need not fear the posturing and antagonism of his enemies because it is God himself who has anointed him king and who protects him. The declaration "You are my son; today I have become your father," was probably

said at the coronation or enthronement of Davidic kings as God's way of endorsing their legitimacy and authority. However, the fall of Jerusalem and the exile in 587 B.C. was the end of the line for the Davidic kings. So this psalm was given a future look. People began to apply it to the expected, messianic son of David who would reign when God would restore Israel. The heavenly voice at his baptism identified Jesus as that very one.

"My loved one, in whom I delight." This is an echo of Isaiah 42:1, the opening verse of a series of "songs" in Isaiah 40–55 about one called the servant of the Lord. He is introduced rather like a king, but as the songs develop (Is 42:1-9; 49:1-6; 50:4-10; 52:13–53:12) it becomes clear that this servant will accomplish his calling not by kingly power as we know it but through frustration, suffering, rejection and death. By willingly paying that cost, however, the servant will not only bring restoration to Israel but also be the instrument of bringing God's salvation to the ends of the earth. God the Father identifies Jesus as that One—the Servant of the Lord.

"My son, my beloved one." This is very probably a third echo from the Hebrew Bible, Genesis 22:2, where God told Abraham, "Take your son, your only son, whom you love—Isaac," and sacrifice him to the Lord. In the end, Isaac was spared, but Abraham was commended for his willingness to trust and obey God even to that ultimate extent. The story, known in later Jewish lore as "The Binding of Isaac," was deeply studied and reflected on for its double theme of Abraham's willingness as a father to sacrifice his son and Isaac's willingness as a son to be sacrificed (for Isaac was not a young child but at least a strong teenager/young adult by that time who could have resisted his hundred-year-old father and run away if he had wanted to).

Paul probably had this story in mind when he wrote Romans 8:32, "He who did not spare his own Son, but gave him up for us all—how will he not also, along with him, graciously give us all things?" And almost certainly it was in the mind of God the Father as he identified Jesus at his baptism as his only Son whom he loved, but whom he was willing to sacrifice for the salvation of the world. Only this time it would be for real. There would be no ram to substitute at the last minute. Was Jesus, like Isaac, willing for that? No wonder Jesus, fully aware in his adult manhood of the identity that he carried, went from this experience of baptism and God's voice straight into a time of intense and prolonged personal struggle and testing (which we shall look at more closely in chapter five). What was it going to mean for him to carry out the mission of being the Son of God in the light of all those Scriptures? What would it mean to *be* who he *was?*

OLD TESTAMENT PICTURES AND PATTERNS

Later in this chapter and the next, we shall look at these various terms that were used about Jesus in more depth. The point to observe for the moment is how the Old Testament is being used here in relation to him. This moment of baptism, as we have seen, was of immense significance for Jesus. At the threshold of his public ministry he experiences divine confirmation and complete certainty about who he was and what he had come to do. Both his identity and his mission were involved in the way he took the initiative in asking to be baptized by the prophetic herald of the coming kingdom of God—John the Baptist. And how did his Father declare and confirm that identity? By quoting the Scriptures. By using figures, events and prophecies from the Old Testament as a way of filling in the content of who Jesus truly was.

Matthew has shown us how the Old Testament tells the story that Jesus completed. Then he showed us how the Old Testament declares the promise that Jesus fulfilled. Now Matthew shows us how the Old Testament described the identity that Jesus had. He opens up the Old Testament as a storehouse that provides images, precedents, patterns and ideas to help us understand who Jesus was.

Indeed, to step further back, it was the Old Testament that helped *Jesus* to understand Jesus. Now we might immediately think, "Surely Jesus knew everything about himself from the start—he was God!" Well, yes, of course he was God, and we will think a lot more about exactly what that means in chapter six below. But Jesus was fully human too, and we should not minimize that. I don't think we should imagine that Jesus as a baby or as a little toddler was "omniscient"—knowing everything in some supernatural way. In fact, Luke quite explicitly tells us that he was not. Luke makes a point of saying that Jesus grew up like any other human child, both in physical size and in intellectual capacity: he "increased in wisdom and stature," as the King James Version puts it in Luke 1:80; 2:52. Jesus grew up! Luke means that Jesus had a normal human development, from baby to toddler, child, boy, youth and adult. I am sure that Jesus grew up with increasing awareness of his special relationship with God as his Father from an early age—the story of Jesus in the temple as a twelve-year-old boy shows that. But at the same time, if he was truly human, then he must also have thought deeply about himself, his own people, what God wanted him to do and so on. He would have reflected on these things in the light of the Scriptures, which clearly filled his mind and heart.

So then, in his humanity as a growing young man and at the point when he entered his public ministry, who did Jesus think he was? What did he think he was destined by God to do? The answers came from his Bible, the Hebrew Scriptures. Jesus would have studied them very thoroughly as a Jewish boy of his generation. He would have learned large sections by heart, as the rest did. And in those Scriptures Jesus found a rich tapestry of figures, historical persons, sequences of historical events, prophetic pictures and symbols. And in this tapestry, where others saw only a fragmented collection of various figures and hopes, Jesus saw his own face. His Scriptures provided the shape of his own identity.

By pointing this out to us in connection with Jesus' baptism, Matthew shows that this was not some arbitrary, fanciful use of the Bible by later romantic admirers of Jesus. Rather, it was God's own way of declaring the identity of his Son. Jesus' self-identity was confirmed by his Father's explicit identification of him. And that in turn was based on the Hebrew Scriptures of our Old Testament.

This point has brought us a step further in our purpose in this book. Our conviction has been that the more you understand the Old Testament, the closer you will come to the heart of Jesus. In our first two chapters we were seeing that fact "externally," so to speak. They described how the observers and interpreters of Jesus understood and explained him in relation to the Old Testament story and promise. But here we are reaching into the "internal" self-identity of Jesus himself. We are no longer talking about a newborn baby or a migrant child, or even about an abstract concept of messiahship. Here we have an adult man, at one level indistinguishable among the crowds of those who flocked to John for baptism and in any case otherwise unknown except as a carpenter's son from Nazareth, who knows his own identity with awesome personal consequences. And his Father's voice affirms that identity through three Old Testament figures—Abraham, David and the Servant of the Lord.

He has the authority of the Davidic king, with a special relationship of sonship to God, the divine King. This means that from the beginning of his ministry Jesus was conscious of his identity as the Son of God and Davidic Messiah, even though later on he sought to play it down among his followers because of its political misunderstandings. Jesus chose rather to emphasize a dimension of Davidic sonship, which we looked at in the last chapter—namely *obedience to his Father God*. Obedience to God was required from the Davidic king (2 Sam 7:14-16; Jer 22:1-5). How much more then for the Son of God himself, who later affirmed that obedience to his Father's will was his very meat and drink (Jn 4:34).

Obedience was also the link between being the Son in the line of King David and being the Servant of the Lord. These two ideas were not closely linked in the popular mind of Jesus' day, as far as we can tell. It seems to have been an insight of Jesus himself to see the messianic role of the Davidic king in the light of the suffering, obedient Servant of the Lord. Similarly, obedience was the link with the allusion to Isaac, as the one willing to be sacrificed, even as the only son of a loving father. Isaac was obedient unto death (almost).

Kingship, servanthood, sacrifice. All three are built into the calling of Jesus. All three are given depth and meaning by the Old Testament characters whose identities are merged in Jesus. His personal identity, the shape of his mission and the pattern of his life are all, so to speak, programmed by the intricate spiral patterns of a genetic code provided by the Old Testament Scriptures.

That "genetic" metaphor is not meant to suggest that somehow Jesus himself was "programmed." Of course not. He chose his course and acted with careful deliberation and prayer. Nor does it mean that it was possible simply to "read off" from the Old Testament the "genetic fingerprints" of Jesus of Nazareth. In the Gospels, it was those who knew their Hebrew Scriptures best who did not or would not recognize him as the Messiah. And Jesus' own use of the Scriptures in relation to himself was creative and sometimes surprising. As we have already seen in chapter two, it was no simple matter of matching predictions to fulfillments in a kind of messianic identity parade.

However, what the genetic metaphor is trying to emphasize is that Jesus was not some new and exotic species. Especially Jesus was not, as so many people think, the "founder of a new religion." Yes, of course, he was unique in so many ways, which we shall discover as we go on. But for those with eyes and ears and memories, the Hebrew Scriptures had already provided the patterns and models by which Jesus could be understood, and by which he understood and explained himself and his goals to others.

Before going on to think further about what it meant for Jesus to be the Son of God, we need to give just a bit more attention to how the Old Testament is being used here.

"That's just typical." The word *typology* is sometimes used to describe this way of viewing the relationship between the Old Testament and Jesus. The images, patterns and models that the Old Testament provides for understanding him are called *types*. The New Testament equivalents or parallels are then called *antitypes*. This used to be a very popular way of handling the Old Testament in former generations, but it has fallen into disfavor among many scholars recently. Typological interpretation remains a traditional way of using the Old Testament, however, in some quarters of the Christian church. It is worth explaining a bit about it, for the benefit of those who have never heard of it, and also for the sake of those who may have been exposed to unbalanced or fanciful uses of it.

(1) Biblically, typology is not a theological or technical term. The English word *type* comes directly from the Greek word *typos*, which means an example, pattern or model. It is found in the New Testament with a loose range of meaning, sometimes applied to Christ but often to others. For example, Paul uses the word when he speaks of the events in the history of Israel as "warnings" or "examples" for us (1 Cor 10:6, 11). In several places, the word means an example to be followed, either by the apostles themselves, or certain churches, or pastors for their flock (Phil 3:17; 1 Thess 1:7; 2 Thess 3:9; Titus 2:7; 1 Pet 5:3). In Romans 5:14, we find Adam described as a pattern for Christ. In 1 Peter 3:21, we find an analogy being drawn between the flood and the ark on the one hand and Christian baptism on the other. So typology, then, is not a hard-and-fast method of tying the Old to the New Testament. Biblically, it still just means a *range of examples*, models and patterns of correspondence. It is not a major interpretive key to unlock the mysteries of the Old Testament.

(2) Typology is a normal and common way of knowing and understanding things. There is really nothing fanciful about typology. We use it every day

when trying to learn or teach something new or as yet unknown. Any teacher knows that in introducing new ideas or skills, you have to work by analogy or correspondence from what is already known and familiar— either past events, or experience, or preunderstandings. Even at the most advanced level, scientific knowledge progresses within what are called "paradigms" in the trade (i.e., accepted models or patterns of how physical reality is believed to function). Often one proven scientific result will act as a "type" or model for attacking as yet unsolved puzzles. And in the whole world of law and law courts, we build steadily on the power of "precedents"— a judgment that was made in one specific case will function as a model or "type" in future cases in which corresponding issues are at stake. And even in everyday speech, when we exclaim "That's just typical!" about somebody's action, what we mean is that we are not really surprised by it because it fits in with *a pattern of behavior* that we have come to expect from previous experience of that person.

(3) *Typology was already a feature of the Old Testament itself.* Already, in our survey of the Old Testament in the last two chapters, we have seen how the Old Testament itself has a kind of internal typology. Many events and persons are picked out and seen as "typical." That is, they illustrate something characteristic about the way God does things. So those particular cases can then be used to help understand when God does something new— either in promise or threat. *Sodom and Gomorrah* become proverbial for God's judgment against human sin. What God had done in destroying *Shiloh* is used by Jeremiah as a graphic type of what he intends to do to Jerusalem (Jer 7:12-15). Hosea and Jeremiah use the *wilderness* period as a picture for the future purification of Israel (Hos 2:16-23; Jer 32:2). The *exodus* is repeatedly used as a model for subsequent historical acts of deliverance. Even individuals can take on this "typical" dimension—*David*, of course, as the ideal king, but also *Abraham* as the model of faith and obedience (Gen 15:6), and *Moses* as the model prophet (Deut 18:15, 18). So the use of "types" in the sense of examples or models is commonly found within the Old Testament.

(4) *Typology is a matter of analogy.* I said that the word *typos* itself is not used in a technical or formal sense in the New Testament. But there are many ways in which the writers of the New Testament draw our attention to analogies between the Old and the New where the word *typos* may or may not

be used. In the midst of the obvious differences between the Testaments, there are also real points of correspondence.

We find, for example, correspondence between the word of God in creation in Genesis and the beginning of the new creation with Jesus, the Word, in John 1. The birth of Jesus as the beginning of the gospel of redemption in the New Testament is paralleled to the birth of Isaac as the child of promise in the Old (Gal 3–4, Rom 4). The shedding of the blood of Jesus can be understood by analogy with the exodus, the Passover Lamb and the crossing of the Red Sea all rolled into one! There are definite analogies between the community that Jesus gathered around him as the Messiah and a restored Israel, which we shall look at later. Paul draws heavily on the analogy of land and kinship to describe the new status of the formerly excluded Gentiles once they have been reconciled to God through Christ (Eph 2:11-22). The same passage makes comparisons between the temple and the church (meaning people, not a building, of course). Peter has the same combination of ideas in 1 Peter 2:4-12. There are other analogies, some of which we have noted already, such as between the new covenant in Christ and all the previous covenants in the Hebrew Bible, between the kingship of Yahweh and of Israel's kings and the kingdom of God, between God's concern for all nations and the whole world in the primal history of Genesis 1–11 and the scope of the Gentile mission and our future hope of all creation being redeemed and united in Christ.

So there is good biblical justification for seeing *analogy* as a valid feature of biblical interpretation, because the Bible itself uses it. The Old Testament uses analogy to speak of what was as yet future. "*That* (the future) will be like *this* (the present)." And the New Testament uses analogy to explain present events by reference to the past. When Peter stood up to preach on the day of Pentecost, the sun was not darkened and the moon was not blood, but he could confidently relate the significance of what was happening at that moment to Joel's famous vision in Joel 2:28-32 and assert, "*This* is *that* . . . " (Acts 2:16-21).

(5) Typology is a matter of history. The correspondence between the Old and New Testament also points to the repeating patterns of God's actual activity in history. "Salvation history" is a shorthand expression for the belief that God has acted through specific events in history to accomplish salvation. In the last two chapters we saw in some detail how that action

followed patterns of promise and fulfillment and then fresh promise. This helps us to grasp both God's sovereign control over history and his consistency in action.

God behaves typically as God. That is, there is something characteristic, something predictable, about what God does, once you know his previous actions. As I once heard a new Christian put it, in sheer wonder at her fresh experience of God's constant and consistent action, "God is always Godding!"

Now, of course, this is not at all saying that God is bound to a boring repetition of the past. God is also the master of surprise and could even exclaim triumphantly through Isaiah, "Forget the former things; . . . See, I am doing a new thing!" (Is 43:18-19). But even then, his "new thing" could be described in terms of the original thing—new exodus or new creation or new covenant. So when the New Testament witnesses saw who Jesus was and what he had achieved, they said in effect, "That's just typical of God! What God has done in Jesus Christ is just like all the things that God actually did in the past, though of course it surpasses and completes all God has ever done before."

(6) *Typology is not merely prefiguring or foreshadowing.* The older view of typology fell into disfavor because it was solely concerned with finding "prefigurations" of Christ all over the Old Testament. The idea was that the central feature of a "type" was that it prefigured Christ. But this was handled not as something observed *afterward* in the light of Christ but rather as the very reason for existence of whatever was being regarded as a "type." So a "type," in this view, was any event, institution or person in the Old Testament that had been arranged by God for the *primary purpose* of foreshadowing Christ. This had two unfortunate side effects.

First, it usually meant that the interpreter of the Old Testament failed to find much reality and meaning in the events and persons of the Old Testament in themselves. There was no need to spend time understanding and interpreting the texts *in their own Israelite historical context and background* or to ask what they meant to those people at that time. You could just jump straight to Christ, because that is where you would find the supposed "real" meaning. This ends up with a very "Platonic" view of the Old Testament. That is, it is really only a collection of "shadows" of something else. Such a way of reading the Bible devalues the historical reality and validity of Old Testament Israel and all that God did in and through and for them.

Second, this kind of typology had a tendency to indulge in fanciful attempts to interpret every detail of an Old Testament "type" as in some way a foreshadowing of some other obscure detail about Jesus. Once you had severed the event, institution or person from its actual historical roots in Israel, then the details would no longer be seen as simply part of the story as the Old Testament narrator told it. Since the "real meaning" was actually to be found in Jesus and the New Testament, all the details must have some *hidden* significance that could be applied to Christ. It was up to the skill or imagination of the writer or preacher to bring such meanings out, like a magician bringing rabbits out of a hat to the astonished gasps of admiring readers or listeners. All the colored threads of the tabernacle could signify something about Jesus. The five stones that David picked up represent the five wounds of Christ, or the five loaves he used to feed the crowd, or the five ministries that Christ has given to the church. He took them out of a stream, which was the Holy Spirit. And so on. This way of handling the Hebrew text is quite rightly now regarded as invalid and subjective. Unfortunately it is still around, and some preachers love that kind of clever speculation—which is usually all it is.

Typology, then, to sum up, properly handled, is a way of understanding Christ and the various events and experiences surrounding him in the New Testament by analogy or correspondence with the historical realities of the Old Testament seen as patterns or models. It is based on the consistency of God in salvation history. It has the backing of Christ himself who, on the authority of his Father, saw himself in this way.

But typology is not *the only* or *primary* way of interpreting the Old Testament for itself. This is partly because it is selective in the texts it uses from the Old Testament (i.e., those that particularly help us to understand Christ), whereas the New Testament itself tells us emphatically that the *whole* of the Scriptures are written for our profit (2 Tim 3:16-17), and partly because it is limited in the meaning it extracts from those selected texts (again, meanings that specifically relate to Christ). To come back to our three texts in the declaration at Jesus' baptism, it is clear that each of them helps us to understand great truths about the identity and mission of Jesus. But when we go back and read the whole of Psalm 2, Isaiah 42 and Genesis 22, it is equally true that they have enormous depths of truth and meaning for us to explore that are not directly related to Jesus himself. Typology is a way of helping us understand Jesus in the light of the Old Testament. It is not the exclusive way to understand the full meaning of the Old Testament itself.

JESUS AS THE SON OF GOD

Having come back, then, to Jesus and his baptism after our detour through the meaning of typology, let us look more closely at the sense of identity and purpose that Jesus derived from his baptismal experience. We shall check out the Old Testament background a bit more thoroughly and see how it influenced the way Jesus thought of himself. But we shall also discover that Jesus was not just an identikit figure pasted together from bits of the Old Testament. He transcended and transformed the ancient models. He filled them with fresh meaning in relation to his own unique person, example, teaching and experience of God. So for his followers what began as a moment of recognizing and understanding *Jesus* in the light of their Scriptures ended up as a deepening and surprising new understanding of their *Scriptures* in the light of Jesus. That was certainly the experience of the disciples on the Emmaus road in Luke 24.

So we go back to the baptismal voice and its first phrase, "You are my son." The awareness of God being his Father and himself being God's Son is probably the deepest foundation of Jesus' selfhood. This is something on which most New Testament scholars would agree. Even those who sift the texts of the Gospels with rigorous suspicion as to what may be regarded as authentically from Jesus himself agree that the Father-Son language regarding God and himself survives the most acid skepticism. And they would also point out that for Jesus, God's fatherhood and his own sonship were not merely concepts or titles. Nor were they merely part of his teaching curriculum. They were living realities in his own life. Jesus *experienced* a relationship with God of such personal intimacy and dependence that only the language of Father and Son could describe it. It was deepest in his prayer life, and that was also where his closest friends observed it, as they heard him habitually use *"Abba,"* the intimate Jewish family word for father, in personal address to God. This was something new and unprecedented that Jesus brought to the meaning of being children of God.

Let us then turn back to the Scriptures from which Jesus would have soaked up his preliminary understanding of what it meant to call God Father and to think of himself as God's Son.

And the first point we need to make is that Israel also called God Father and God called Israel his son.

GOD AS FATHER—ISRAEL AS SON

In order to understand Jesus we have to look at more than just the titles by which he was addressed or that he used for himself. In fact, Jesus tended to avoid titles, with the single exception of the "Son of Man." And even if we take those titles that we find in the New Testament and go back to the Hebrew Scriptures, we have to do more than just look up a concordance and check out the phrases there. This is especially so of this expression "Son of God" as it was used in the Old Testament.

If we only look it up in the concordance, we may end up very confused, for the expression has a bewildering elasticity. It can, for example, refer to angels (probably, Gen 6:2, 4; Ps 89:6). Even Satan is called one of the sons of God (Job 1:6; 2:1). It can be used to describe human rulers and judges (Ps 82:6). Even the pagan king Nebuchadnezzar used it to describe the mysterious fourth man in his fiery furnace (Dan 3:25). And, of course, we have already seen that it was applied especially to the Davidic king.

Rather, what we must do is look at the whole range of material that was associated with sonship in relation to God as father in the Hebrew Bible. The idea was not, of course, anywhere near as dominant as the idea of covenant relationship between God and Israel, but it is much more extensive than many Christians think. And it also began early.

It is found in Deuteronomy 32, the Song of Moses, which is one of the oldest of the poetic texts in the Hebrew Bible. This poem is therefore a very ancient witness to the faith of Israel and rules out the idea that the fatherhood of God was a late development in Israel's history, or that it was a brand-new teaching by Jesus. Actually in Deuteronomy 32 it would be better to talk about the parenthood of God, since it uses the imagery of mother as well as father to describe God. This parenthood of God is linked to his creation of his people (Deut 32:6), Yahweh's own uniqueness as God (Deut 32:15-18, 39) and his corrective discipline of his people (Deut 32:19-20).

We shall look at the parental metaphor in four ways. First, we shall check up what the parent-child relationship actually meant in Israel's society, since that will clarify what it meant when transferred to God and Israel. Second, we shall see how the metaphor undergirded the covenant concept, which we already studied in some depth in chapter two. Third, we shall see how sonship was a relationship that generated hope and expectation. Fourth, we shall see how the idea was broadened and given a universal and eschatological flavor. In each case we shall find significant links with Christ that help us to understand more deeply his sense of identity and destiny.

Fathers and sons in Israelite society. Obviously, to use the language of father and son is to draw from the human experience of family life, and then to apply the parent-child experience metaphorically to God and to human relationship to him. (This is to look at the matter from the human perspective. Ultimately, our own human experience of parenthood and family is a reflection of God, for we are made in his image. That is probably what Paul is getting at in Eph 3:14-19.)

In Israel we find evidence of the metaphor in common life in the use of the Hebrew word *Ab* (father) in *"theophoric"* names (i.e., personal names that include all or part of the name of God; my own name, Christopher, is "theophoric"—it means "Christ-bearing"). In Hebrew names, translated into English, *jah, jo, jeho* were all abbreviations of Yahweh. And *el* was the general word for God. These syllables could be combined with other words, so that names were like statements. "Elijah" puts them together—"Yahweh is my God." "Jonathan" and "Nathaniel" mean "Yahweh/God has given." "Johanan" (John) and "Hananiah" mean "Yahweh is gracious." "Jehoshaphat" means "Yahweh is judge." And so on.

Names such as Joab, Abijah, Eliab, etc., mean "Yahweh (or God) is father," or "my God is father" or "Yahweh is my father." The person who had such a name, and the parent who gave it to them, were making a statement about God in relationship to the named person, or possibly to the whole people. This shows clearly that the idea of God as father was common enough in the popular life of Israel, even if it did not achieve a prominent place in their major theology. There were plenty of people with names like that walking around in Israel at any time.

The metaphor has two fairly well-defined, complementary meanings.

(1) The attitude of God as Father toward Israel. This is one of concern, love, pity and patience with the son, but it is also a desire for the son's best interests, which therefore includes discipline.

The LORD your God carried you, as a father carries his son. (Deut 1:31)

> Know then in your heart that as a man disciplines his son, so the LORD
> your God disciplines you. (Deut 8:5)

Other examples of this would include Psalm 103:13, Proverbs 3:12 and 2 Samuel 7:14.

(2) The expectation of God as Father from Israel. God, in the same way as a worthy human father, is to be viewed as a trustworthy, protective authority to be respected and obeyed. This aspect can be seen negatively when God complains or grieves that his fatherly care is being scorned, abused or ignored. Texts such as Deuteronomy 14:1, Isaiah 1:2-4; Jeremiah 3:19 and Hosea 11:1-4 show how God felt toward his son, Israel, and what was expected of his son in return. The best expression of God's heart on this point is: "'A son honors his father, and a slave his master. If I am a father, where is the honor due me? If I am a master, where is the respect due me?' says the LORD Almighty" (Mal 1:6).

At the human level these dimensions are seen clearly in the laws related to parental authority, which were unusually strict in Israel because of the vital importance of the stability of the family within the covenant basis of the nation (e.g., Ex 20:12; 21:15, 17; Deut 21:18-21; 27:16; Prov 30:17). In Old Testament Israelite society, the father was the head of the household ("head of a father's house" was his technical title in Hebrew). That is, he had domestic, judicial, educational, spiritual and even military authority over a quite sizeable community of people, including his adult sons and their families and all dependent persons (the extended family, which might have been up to forty or fifty people). He was, in short, a figure of considerable power, social importance and protective responsibility.

The important status of these heads of households is illustrated positively in Joash's protection of his adult son, Gideon, in Judges 6, and negatively in Job's lament of what he had lost as a result of the calamity that had deprived him of family and substance in Job 29–30. It was almost certainly these heads of households who consulted, decided and acted together as "the elders" whom we read of in many Hebrew stories.

The fatherhood of Yahweh was not, then, primarily an emotional metaphor. Rather it was a matter of authority on the one hand and obedience on the other, within the framework of a trusting, providing and protective relationship. Already we can see the matching outline shape of Jesus' personal awareness of God as his Father. For authority, willing obedience and complete trust were the hallmarks of that intimate relationship as Jesus enjoyed and expressed it.

Israel's sonship and the covenant. Although the idea of the fatherhood of Yahweh is overshadowed by the covenant concept in the Hebrew Bible, there is a close link between the two. When you analyze the texts where father-son language is used for God and Israel, they show an interesting dual aspect that is quite similar to the dual nature of the covenant itself. On the one hand, the relationship between Israel and God was a given fact that God had achieved, and on the other hand, it also contained a demand that Israel must fulfill. The covenant was both a statement and a claim, both an indicative and an imperative. As regards Israel's sonship, this same dual aspect emerges when we notice the difference between passages where Israel is referred to as "son" in the *singular* (which tends to emphasize the givenness of the relationship) and those where Israelites are addressed as "sons" or "children" in the *plural* (which tends to emphasize the expectations of the relationship).

(1) National level. There are some passages where Israel as a whole is called Yahweh's son, or Yahweh is portrayed as father of the whole nation. These would include Exodus 4:22; Deuteronomy 32:6, 18; Hosea 11:1; Jeremiah 31:9 and Isaiah 63:15-16; 64:8.

The point here is that Israel owes its national existence to the creative or "procreative" action of Yahweh. Yahweh was father and Israel was his son because he had brought Israel into existence. He had "fathered and mothered" the nation as "the Rock who fathered you . . . the God who gave you birth" (Deut 32:18; "you" is singular). So it was not by Israel's choice or action or merits that it enjoyed the status of being Yahweh's son any more than we earned the right to be born. In this respect, Israel's sonship is a *given* that corresponds with the unconditional *givenness* of Israel's election and the covenant. It was entirely a matter of divine initiative. Israel was the "firstborn son of Yahweh" for no other reason than that he had brought it into existence as a nation, just as it was the "people of Yahweh" for no other reason than that he had "set his affection on" them and chosen them for himself (Deut 7:6-8). Sonship here is very much a matter of privilege.

(2) The personal level. There are other passages where Israelites are addressed as sons/children of Yahweh in the plural. These would include Deuteronomy 14:1; 32:19; Isaiah 1:2; 30:9 and Jeremiah 3:22.

Here the focus is on the Israelites' responsibility before Yahweh to show the loyalty and obedience required of sons. Thus Deuteronomy 14:1 argues that the "sons of Yahweh," a holy God, must themselves be holy. Most of the prophetic passages that use the metaphor are in this plural category, accusing Israelites of failing in their duty as sons to live in ethical obedience to God. In the texts above, for example, they are "rebellious sons," "faithless sons" or "lying sons." This second aspect of Israel's sonship thus clearly corresponds to the other side of the covenant relationship, namely the imperative demand for obedience—a demand that applied to all individual members of the nation.

So what we find, then, is that both poles of the covenant (God's initiative and Israel's obedience) are held together within the same relational metaphor of father and son.

Deuteronomy adds two other ideas to enrich the metaphor still farther. First, there is its use of *inheritance* language. This is a prominent feature of Deuteronomy. It repeatedly describes the whole land as Israel's inheritance. This is another way of expressing and reinforcing the point that Israel is Yahweh's son, for it is the firstborn son who inherits. This inheritance image corresponds precisely with the first aspect of Israel's sonship, namely, that it is something unconditional and simply given, for that is exactly what Deuteronomy stresses again and again as regards the gift of the land to Israel.

Second, there is Deuteronomy's use of *love* language. Deuteronomy is very fond of love! It highlights Yahweh's love for Israel (Deut 7:7-9 and elsewhere). And it was Deuteronomy that Jesus quoted when asked what was the greatest commandment in the law: "Love the LORD your God with all your heart and with all your soul and with all your strength" (Deut 6:5; cf. Deut 10:12). Now "love" in Deuteronomy is a love that can be commanded and therefore means much more than just the emotion or affection that father and son share. It is rather a matter of faithfulness and obedience within the discipline of the father-son relationship. In fact, some scholars have argued that in Deuteronomy filial love is synonymous with covenant obedience. That is, to love God as son to father is the same thing as to obey God and keep the covenant.

When we turn back to the New Testament, we can detect some of these covenantal patterns in the ways it speaks of Jesus as Son of God.

We saw in the last chapter that the successive covenants of the Old Testament all come together in Jesus as the inaugurator of the new covenant. In several ways Jesus was aware of being the one who represented Israel. In referring to himself, for example, as "the true vine" (Jn 15:1-8) he was drawing on the Old Testament imagery of Israel as Yahweh's vine or vineyard. In a related image, he described himself as the heir (Mk 12:7), and the language of inheritance entered into Christian vocabulary to describe aspects of Christian experience through Jesus Christ, who is "heir of all things" (Heb 1:2).

On the shoulders of Jesus as the Son of God lay the responsibility of being God's *true son*. Jesus would succeed where Israel had failed, submitting to God's will where it had rebelled, obeying where it had disobeyed. This was certainly a dimension of Christ's temptations in the wilderness after his baptism, which we shall look at more fully in the next chapter.

The author of Hebrews who, more than any other New Testament writer, glories in the exalted status of Jesus as the unique Son of God, also links his sonship with his suffering and obedience. "Son though he was, he learned obedience from what he suffered" (Heb 5:8). This of course does not mean that Jesus had to be compelled by suffering to be obedient after being previously disobedient. Not at all. It is simply underlining that sonship for Jesus, as for Israel, was tied to obedience and that for Jesus obedience to his Father's will involved suffering. The fact that he was willing to suffer proved the depth of his obedience. Perhaps the author of Hebrews had Christ's temptations in mind, or perhaps more particularly the final great spiritual battle in Gethsemane. There, as Jesus faced the extremity of what obedience would cost him, he chose finally and fully to submit his own will to that of his Father, as he had done all his life to this point. There, too, we find on his lips the intimate word *Abba*, as he struggled to hold together his lifelong experience of his Father's loving presence and protective care on the one hand with the immediate prospect of abandonment to death on the cross as the price of obedience on the other (Mk 14:36).

Sonship as the foundation for hope. Gethsemane shows us that Jesus shrank back from suffering and death like any other human being would. Yet the Gospels also tell us that he went to his death with complete confidence that God would raise him from the dead. Earlier, during his ministry, as soon as his disciples had begun to grasp who he truly was and to affirm that he was the Messiah, Jesus immediately began to prepare them for his rejection, suffering and death (Mt 16:21). He did this repeatedly. But all the Gospel accounts add that he also said he would be raised again on the third day. Apparently this made little impression on the disciples in their shock and bewilderment over a suffering Messiah, but after it happened, they remembered that Jesus had indeed said it.

We must not think, of course, that having this confidence concerning his resurrection in any way lessened the horror of the cross for Jesus. Gethsemane itself wipes out any facile idea that the expectation of resurrection somehow neutralized the depths of pain and suffering he endured in bearing the sin of the world, as does the agonized cry of dereliction and abandonment from the cross. However, the question arises, how and why could Jesus have been so sure of his resurrection? Why did he tell his disciples again and again (even if they couldn't "hear" it) that he would rise again?

One clue in the Caesarea Philippi passages is that Jesus, while accepting Peter's recognition that he was the *Messiah*, redirected his teaching in terms of the *Son of Man* (Mk 8:31). As we shall see in the next chapter, "the Son of Man" was a term Jesus used for himself that was derived from Daniel 7. And one marked feature of the imagery in that text is that the Son of Man figure apparently is vindicated and endowed with great glory and authority. Another clue is that Jesus identified himself with the suffering servant figure of Isaiah 40–55. We saw that that was part of the identity he had confirmed for him at his baptism. And again, the servant was a figure who, beyond suffering and death, would see vindication, victory and the positive achievements of his ministry (Is 52:12; 53:10-12).

But in my view the strongest reason for Jesus' confidence in the face of death lies in his self-conscious identity as the Son of God. As such he embodied and represented Israel, the son of God in the Scriptures. And the father-son relationship between Yahweh and Israel was a ground for hope and permanence, even when Israel stood among the wreckage of a broken covenant—a covenant that it had broken by its own disobedience. The sonship relationship was something that survived the greatest disaster. Even as a covenant-breaking, rebellious nation, Israel remained God's son. A rebel son but still a son. A "prodigal son" but still a son who could return from death to life.

In the narrative texts, the declaration that Israel was Yahweh's firstborn son came *before* the exodus and the making of the Sinai covenant (Ex 4:22). And in the prophetic texts, the relationship of sonship not only survived even *after* the judgment of exile had fallen on the nation but also could be appealed to as the basis for a fresh act of redemption and a restored relationship. So, in Isaiah 63–64, Israel cries to God as its Father in the expectation of his loving care after discipline, and his forgiving, restoring power. As Father, he will be its champion, defender and redeemer, even if he has had to exercise parental discipline on it also.

> Yet you, LORD, are our Father.
>> We are the clay, you are the potter;
>> we are all the work of your hand. (Is 64:8)
>
> You, LORD, are our Father,
>> our Redeemer from of old is your name. (Is 63:16)

The same combination of ideas is found in Jeremiah 31:18-20.

The father-son relationship between God and Israel, therefore, contained within itself an element of permanence, which injected hope into an otherwise hopeless situation amid the ruins of the Sinai covenant. Israel's relationship to Yahweh could continue to be affirmed in spite of alienation from the land and in spite of the experienced wrath of God. Yahweh still had a future for his people. He could not abandon them. The Father could not ultimately disown his son.

If this had been so for Israel as the *rebellious* son of Yahweh, then how much more must it be true for the *sinless* Son of God himself? If God would not abandon or utterly destroy his son Israel, whose sufferings were the result of its own sin and God's judgment upon it, then he would certainly not abandon the Son whose sufferings were not for his own sin but for the sin of the world, including Israel itself (cf. Acts 2:24-26). Jesus went to his death confident in his Father, because he knew his *history* (God had always proved his covenant faithfulness to his son Israel) and because he knew his *identity* (as Son of God he embodied Israel and would therefore prove that faithfulness of God, even in death).

Another small clue to this understanding of Jesus' confidence lies in his prediction of resurrection on "the third day." The texts in which he told his disciples that he would be rejected and put to death add that he would rise again "on the third day" (Mt 16:21; Mk 8:31; Lk 9:22). He repeated this detail when explaining the whole event to the disciples after his Emmaus encounter (Lk 24:46). It even entered into the Christian tradition, since Paul summarizes the gospel as he had received it with the phrases: "that Christ died for our sins according to the Scriptures, that he was buried, that he was raised on the third day according to the Scriptures" (1 Cor 15:3-4).

Now the only Scripture that makes any reference to a third day in relation to resurrection is Hosea 6:1-2.

> Come, let us return to the LORD.
> He has torn us to pieces
>   but he will heal us;
> he has injured us
>   but he will bind up our wounds.
> After two days he will revive us;
>   on the third day he will restore us
>   that we may live in his presence.

The meaning here is unquestionably national. That is to say, it is the people of Israel who, in the midst of God's judgment, look forward in repentance to him raising them up again. By taking up that detail of the prophecy, Jesus links his own expected resurrection to Israel's. In *his* resurrection lay *its* restoration. We shall examine that point in the next chapter. For the moment we recall from chapter one that Matthew has already made the connection between Jesus as the Son of God and Hosea's description of Israel as God's son (Hos 11:1). The Father who brought his son out of Egypt, in the face of threat and death, would not abandon the same son to the power of death forever (cf. Acts 2:24-28). Sonship meant hope and confidence.

Israel's sonship and God's universal purpose. This inextinguishable hope that Israel always maintained was based on the unique relationship that it had with God, a relationship pictured on the one hand as a father-son relationship and on the other hand as a covenant that bound them both together. But Israel's hope was also linked to its understanding of its role in the fulfillment of God's great purpose for all the nations and the world. There was a future for Israel because, by God's grace and promise, there was a future for the world.

We saw already, in the first two chapters, that from the start Israel was aware that its very existence was for the sake of the rest of humanity. This had been explicit in the covenant with Abraham (Gen 12:3; 18:18, etc.). It had been recalled in the prelude to Sinai, when Israel was given its identity and mission as God's priesthood in the midst of the whole earth, which belongs to Yahweh (Ex 19:4-6). All God's dealings with Israel were simply carrying forward God's unfinished business with the nations.

So when you examine key Old Testament concepts, which in their immediate contexts seem to apply only to Israel, you find that they also have this universal dimension or vision. *Election* obviously meant the choice of Israel, but not to status, rather for servanthood and for the sake of the nations, as Isaiah 40–55 points out. *Covenant*, likewise, indicated God's unique relationship to Israel, but that too was to enable it to be a "covenant to the nations" and to bring the knowledge of Yahweh's law and justice to the ends of the earth (Is 42:4-6; 51:4-5). *The kingship of Yahweh* was acknowledged in Israel, but in the Psalms, which celebrate it, it is also clearly universal: God is and will be king over all nations (Ps 47:7-9; 96; 98).

It is worth asking, then, whether the idea of Israel as son and Yahweh as Father also had led to a more universal, eschatological dimension. Because if it did, this would clearly be another important thing to include as we explore what sonship meant for Jesus.

"Israel is my firstborn son," declared God (Ex 4:22; cf. Jer 31:9). The expression *firstborn son* implies the existence or the expectation of other sons. This cannot mean that Yahweh was somehow the father of all other nations or of their gods at that time. The earliest use of Yahweh as Father of Israel in Deuteronomy 32 actually distinguishes between Israel and the rest of the nations on the grounds of Israel's unique relationship to "the Rock who fathered you." Nevertheless, the idea of Israel being Yahweh's *firstborn* son certainly envisages the possibility, indeed the definite expectation, that other nations *will become sons*. But that expectation in turn depended on Israel fulfilling the demands of its *own* sonship (i.e., that it should live in loyalty and obedience to Yahweh). From this point of view, the sonship of Israel can be understood as a missional concept. If Israel, as Yahweh's firstborn son, would live by God's standards and obey his laws, then God could pursue his goal of bringing blessing to the nations— "bringing many sons to glory," as Hebrews puts it.

We have seen the very strong link between Israel's ethical obedience (especially social righteousness and justice) and God's fulfillment of his promise to Abraham to bless all nations. In Genesis 18:18-20, especially verse 19, we saw that the very purpose of election is that Abraham and his descendants should keep the way of the Lord in righteousness and justice in order that God would be able to keep his promise—that is, blessing all nations. Ethical obedience stands as the middle term between election and mission. But, as we have seen, ethical obedience was the primary significance of the son-father relationship of Israel to Yahweh.

Jeremiah 3–4 gives us an interesting combination of these ideas. The overall thrust of the passage is an appeal for true repentance, a genuine turning back to God with practical evidence and not mere words. The father-son motif is used several times (as well as Jeremiah's more familiar husband-wife motif). In Jeremiah 3:4, Jeremiah pictures Israel appealing to Yahweh as father to let it off and not be angry any more. But it is clear that it is just superficial talk and not a true ethical repentance. "This is how you *talk*," says God, "but you do all the evil you can" (Jer 3:5).

Later we find God himself yearning for a real father-son relationship between himself and Israel—with an inheritance gift from him and obedience from them. There is a real pathos in his words.

> How gladly would I treat you like my children
>   and give you a pleasant land,
>   the most beautiful inheritance of any nation.
> I thought you would call me "Father"
>   and not turn away from following me. (Jer 3:19)

Finally, God appeals for a genuine repentance from Israel, and goes on to point out what will happen if it does as he asks.

> "If you, Israel, will return,
>   then return to me,"
>   declares the LORD.
> "If you put your detestable idols out of my sight
>   and no longer go astray,
> and if in a truthful, just and righteous way
>   you swear 'As surely as the LORD lives,'
> *then the nations will invoke blessings* by him
>   and in him they will boast." (Jer 4:1-2, my italics)

Here we find a clear allusion to the universal promise of the Abrahamic covenant, and it is linked to the requirement of ethical obedience on the part of Israel, using three of the "biggest" ethical words in the Old Testament vocabulary: truth, justice and righteousness. If Israel, as the Son of God, would turn back to living in the way God wanted them to, then the consequences would be wider than just the forgiveness of Israel itself. God would be able to get on with his ultimate purpose of bringing blessing to the nations. Similar thinking lies behind Isaiah 43:6-7; 48:1, 18-19.

"IF YOU ARE THE SON OF GOD . . . "

We can see what an awesome responsibility lay on the shoulders of Jesus as he faced up to the task of being the Son of God. As the representative or embodiment of Israel, he was called to obedience. But what was at stake in that obedience was not merely Jesus' own conscience and his relationship with God his Father, vital though that was. Nor was it even just a matter of proving, in his own person, that Israel could be obedient after all and thus satisfy the longing of God's heart as expressed in the prophecies above.

More than both of these, the obedience of Jesus as Son of God opened the way for the fulfillment of God's universal purpose for all humanity, the purpose for which he had called Israel his firstborn son. Christ's obedient sonship fulfilled the mission that Israel's sonship had prepared for but had failed in disobedience. The saying attributed to David Livingstone, "God had only one Son and he made him a missionary," has more depths of truth than perhaps the old explorer himself appreciated.

For that reason, because so much was at stake—no less than the salvation of the world—the devil's onslaught on Jesus' sonship tried so desperately to deflect him from obedience to his Father's will. Aware that Jesus, through his obedience, would win the world for God, the devil offered him the world in advance if he would sell out to him. But Jesus resisted and set himself deliberately on the path of loyal obedience to his Father in full awareness that it would lead to suffering and death. There was no other way. But it was the way by which he, the firstborn Son, would "bring many sons to glory." Very probably it was this combination of Jesus' sonship, obedience, suffering, humanity, temptation and victory that underlies the profound meditation of Hebrews 2:10-18; 5:8-9.

The apostle Paul was appointed as "apostle to the Gentiles [the nations]" and thus had a special, personal interest in the effect for all nations of what God had done through his Son. At the beginning of his letter to the Romans he summarizes the gospel in an interesting way that combines the human and divine sonship of Jesus with the opening up of salvation to all the nations:

> The gospel he promised beforehand through his prophets in the Holy Scrip-
> tures regarding his Son, who as to his earthly life was a descendant of David,
> and who through the Spirit of holiness was appointed the Son of God in
> power by his resurrection from the dead: Jesus Christ our Lord. Through him
> we received grace and apostleship to call all the Gentiles to the obedience
> that comes from faith for his name's sake. (Rom 1:2-5)

Later on, when he is exploring the mystery of how the current rejection of Jesus by most (but not all) Jews had led to the ingathering of the non-Jewish, Gentile believers, he picks up a prophecy of Hosea that talked about the sons of God (one of Hosea's favorite metaphors, as we have already seen): "Yet the Israelites will be like the sand on the seashore, which cannot be measured or counted. In the place where it was said to them, 'You are not my people,' they will be called 'children of the living God'" (Hos 1:10).

Hosea was talking about the restoration of Israel after judgment and envisaged it in the language of the father-son relationship. But in the first part of the verse he alludes to the Abraham promise of the expansion of Israel into a great nation beyond the possibility of numbering (Gen 13:16; 15:5). This allusion to Abraham, as we have seen so often already, "opens up" the prophecy to a wider future scope than the restoration of Israel alone. It breathes in the air of God's universal promise of blessing.

So although Hosea undoubtedly had *Israel* alone in mind, Paul, when he quotes the verse in Romans 9:26, picks out the wider implication and applies it to the fruit of his own missionary work. It is the *Gentiles* who are now becoming "sons of the living God" through their believing response to Jesus. The expression "not my people" had originally, in Hosea's prophecy, been a term of judgment on Israel. But Paul uses it here to describe those who previously had no share in the blessings of Israel (i.e., the Gentiles). It is *they* who have now been called to belong to the people of God. It is *they* who thereby enter into a relationship of sonship to God as Father. Paul has taken the Old Testament terminology for Israel as God's people and God's son and transposed it into his own missionary vocabulary and applied the terms to people from the Gentile nations, in order to explain what was going on as a result of his own evangelistic work.

What he says there in Romans is the theological expansion of what he had much earlier written to the Galatians—a church of Gentile believers. First of all he emphasizes that through the Messiah, Jesus, they are one with the Jews in relation to God—using the language of sonship.

> So in Christ Jesus you are all children [sons] of God through faith, for all of you who were baptized into Christ have clothed yourselves with Christ. There is neither Jew nor Gentile, neither slave nor free, nor is there male and female, for you are all one in Christ Jesus. If you belong to Christ, then you are Abraham's seed, and heirs according to the promise. (Gal 3:26-29)

Then he goes on to show how this has come about through the work of God's own Son.

> When the set time had fully come, God sent his Son, born of a woman, born under law, to redeem those under the law, that we might receive adoption to sonship. Because you are sons, God sent the Spirit of his Son into our hearts, the Spirit who calls out "*Abba*, Father." So you are no longer a slave, but a son; and since you are a son, God has made you also an heir. (Gal 4:4-7, my translation)

We have come a long way from our starting point, the baptism of Jesus, and have already begun to jump ahead to the missionary theology of Paul and the early church. I hope it is clear from what we have surveyed in this chapter that New Testament missionary theology was based on the identity of Jesus, and that in turn was based on a deep understanding of the Hebrew Scriptures. In the next chapter we shall look at Jesus' own sense of mission and how it both derived from his Hebrew Scriptures on the one hand and shaped the mission of the New Testament church on the other.

What we have seen in this chapter is that the Old Testament provided the models, pictures and patterns by which Jesus understood his own essential identity and especially gave depth and color to his primary self-awareness as the Son of his Father God. In an eternal sense, of course, Jesus always was, is and always will be God the Son, the second person of the Trinity. But we have seen how in his earthly life and historical context he embodied and fulfilled the identity and mission of Old Testament Israel, the "firstborn son" of God.

CHAPTER 3 QUESTIONS AND EXERCISES

1. Make a list of all the points you have learned in this chapter that have filled out from the Old Testament your understanding of what it means that Jesus Christ is the Son of God.

2. What else have you learned about what it means for us as Christian believers to be children of God, having received "adoption to sonship" through Christ? What does it say about (a) our status in Christ before God and (b) how we ought to live?

3. How would you explain the significance of Jesus' baptism to someone? Examine the Old Testament background to the words of God the Father and their significance for Jesus. Use those Scriptures to help explain who Jesus was and what he had come to do.

4. Select five or six Old Testament texts (from the ones we surveyed in this chapter) that speak about Israel as God's son and God as its Father. Take notes for each text on what it says about this concept for Old Testament Israel and what it would have meant for Jesus to know that he was the Son of God. How should these texts speak to the church today if we claim to be God's children?

5. Study Romans 1:1-5. It is often neglected or rushed over when people want to study Romans. How does Paul link together Jesus as the son of David and as the Son of God, and connect these ideas to the resurrection? Why are these links important to the way Paul will then present the gospel in Romans, as God's faithfulness to his promises to Israel? Why does he link these truths about Jesus to his missionary task of calling people from all nations to "the obedience of faith" (something he repeats in Romans 16:26)?

6. Muslims reject the whole idea that Jesus was "the Son of God"— which they often misunderstand in physical or sexual terms. Are there any ways that your deeper understanding of what the Bible means by "Son of God"—especially connecting Jesus to Old Testament Israel—could be helpful in explaining the concept to Muslims?

JESUS *and* HIS OLD TESTAMENT MISSION

One thing that is very clear about Jesus is that he knew he had been sent. He was no self-appointed savior, no popularly elected leader. He had not just arrived. He was sent. This awareness of a purpose and a mission seems to have developed alongside his consciousness of being the Son of his Father, even from a young age, as Luke tells us (Lk 2:49). But it became crystal clear, as we have seen, at his baptism. Knowing what his mission would entail led him into that time of struggle and testing in the wilderness.

No sooner, however, had he returned from that costly victory over the testings of Satan than he declared the manifesto of his program in the Nazareth synagogue with a word from the prophets, "The Lord has anointed (commissioned) me." From then on his driving purpose startled his friends and enemies alike. Nothing could stand in the way of what he was conscious of having been sent to do. To do his Father's will was his very meat and drink (Jn 4:34).

What then was his mission? What did Jesus himself believe he was sent to achieve? What were his personal aims and objectives? What did he think he was doing?

Much scholarly ink has been used up answering these questions! There are two ways of approaching the problem. One way is to look at the kind of expectations that surrounded Jesus in the Jewish society of his day. If the Messiah were to come, what did people think would happen? Of course, as the Gospels make plain, Jesus did not fit all these expectations precisely. Nevertheless, he was as much aware of them as any of his contemporary Jews would have been. And insofar as they had scriptural roots, he must have been deeply influenced by those expectations and would have sought to interpret his own ministry and mission in relation to them.

The other way to find out what Jesus' aims were is to look at the sayings and actions of Jesus himself. How did Jesus speak about his own mission? Here again we will find that it is Jesus' creative and original way of handling his Hebrew Scriptures that gives us the clearest clues to his mission. These two ways of approach, of course, interlock and overlap in many ways. But we shall take each in turn and see how they reinforce what we have been discovering already.

JEWISH EXPECTATIONS AT THE TIME OF JESUS

The sources for knowing what Jewish expectations were at the time of Jesus are found in what is known as the intertestamental literature. This includes a great variety of materials—poetic, narrative, apocalyptic and so on—from the centuries that lie between the end of the Old Testament era and the emergence of the Christian church. These writings come from many different ages and sources and are not at all homogeneous. But they are of very great importance in understanding the world of Jesus and the first disciples and therefore as background to the New Testament. Great amounts of scholarship, both Jewish and Christian, have been devoted to studying this literature.

By the time of Jesus the strongest strand of expectation among Jewish people, widely evident in these writings, was a looking forward with desperate hope to the *restoration of Israel*. It was expected that God would intervene in world affairs to vindicate his people, liberate them from their oppressors and restore them to their rightful place as his redeemed people.

They described their current situation as similar to still being in exile. Even though the Jews had come back to their land after the Babylonian exile in the sixth century B.C., many believed that in a sense the exile had not ended as long as they were still an oppressed people in their own land. In fact, Rome was regarded as the new Babylon, and "Babylon" was used as a code name for Rome among resistance movements. So the hopes of restoration, originally expressed by the prophets in terms of return to the land after the exile, were reapplied to the hope of ultimate freedom from their all enemies. This hope was sometimes based on God's direct action; sometimes linked with the arrival of the Messiah—though that was not a clearly or unanimously defined figure; sometimes linked to the expectation of a new Jerusalem and/or a new temple. Whatever the accompanying details, the core of the hope was clear—Israel would be restored.

A second expectation in these writings was that after the restoration of Israel there would be an *ingathering of the nations* to become part of the people of God with Israel.

The fate of the nations was rather ambiguous in Jewish expectations. On the one hand there were many predictions that they would be judged and destroyed as the enemies of God and his people. Yet on the other hand there was the belief that the judgment of the nations, like the judgment of Israel itself, would be a purging judgment after which salvation would be extended to the nations, and some from among them would be gathered in to the future people of God.

Both of these aspects of Jewish expectation at the time of Jesus—the restoration of Israel and the ingathering of the nations—had deep roots, of course, in the Old Testament itself. As regards *Israel*, even the prophets with the sternest words of judgment on Israel held out the hope of restoration beyond that judgment. And from the exile onward, that hope grew stronger and clearer. It can be seen in Jeremiah's "Book of Consolation" (Jer 30–34), in Ezekiel's vision of the new land and temple (Ezek 40–48) and in the soaring vistas of new creation and redemption in Isaiah 40–55. And as regards the *nations*, we saw in chapter one that God's purpose for them was ultimately that they would be included within God's restored people. The coming of the king to Jerusalem would mean peace and universal rule for the nations (Zech 9:9-13). When God would act to restore Zion and reveal his glory, then the nations would also gather to worship him.

> You will arise and have compassion on Zion,
>> for it is time to show favor to her;
>> the appointed time has come.
> For her stones are dear to your servants;
>> her very dust moves them to pity.
> The nations will fear the name of the LORD,
>> all the kings of the earth will revere your glory.

For the LORD will rebuild Zion
    and appear in his glory.
He will respond to the prayer of the destitute;
    he will not despise their plea.
Let this be written for a future generation,
    that a people not yet created may praise the LORD:
"The LORD looked down from his sanctuary on high,
    from heaven he viewed the earth,
to hear the groans of the prisoners
    and release those condemned to death."
So the name of the LORD will be declared in Zion
    and his praise in Jerusalem
when the peoples and the kingdoms
    assemble to worship the LORD. (Ps 102:13-22; cf. also Is 49:5-6; 56:1-8;
    60:10-14; 66:18-24)

So Old Testament prophecies concerning the future of Israel are interwoven with prophecies about the future of the nations also. There is even a comparable "ambiguity" of judgment and hope. Israel is to be sifted in judgment virtually to extinction, yet Israel will be redeemed and restored (e.g., Is 26:9; 35; Jer 16; 25:15-33; Amos 9; Mic 2–3). Likewise, the nations are to be judged and destroyed as enemies of God, yet the nations are to be gathered in to share in the salvation and inheritance of the people of God (e.g., Is 24; 34; Mic 4; Joel 3). In Zephaniah, the punishment of the nations is set parallel to the judgment on Jerusalem, and so, in Zephaniah 3, the restoration of Jerusalem (Zeph 3:14-17) has universal overtones for the nations (Zeph 3:9).

In other words, the dividing line between judgment and salvation is not a line that runs simply *between* the nations and Israel but *through* both of them. Just as there will be a "remnant of Israel," so there will be "survivors of the nations" (Is 45:20-23; 66:19-24; Zech 14:16-19). And the Old Testament sees *both together* (the purified and believing, obedient remnant of Israel together with those of the nations who respond to the appeal to identify with Yahweh and his people) as the eschatological future people of God.

So Jewish hopes at the time of Jesus, then, focused primarily on the restoration of Israel, with the closely attached implications for the nations. The restoration of Israel and the ingathering of the nations were seen in eschatological terms as the final great act of God, the Day of the Lord. The two things would be part of the same final event that would usher in the new age, but the restoration of Israel was logically and chronologically expected first. Only when Israel was redeemed could the nations enjoy the blessing promised to Abraham (Gal 3:14).

JOHN THE BAPTIST

Into this charged atmosphere of eschatological hopes, "there was a man sent from God whose name was John" (Jn 1:6). It is indeed this framework of restoration hope that provides the context for understanding the ministry and message of John the Baptist. As the records of his preaching show, John regarded his mission as one of winnowing and sifting the nation by his call to repentance so that it would be prepared for God's imminent purging and restoration. John consciously stood on the threshold of the fulfillment of Israel's hope.

But not every child of Abraham by birth would enter into the fulfillment of that hope. Only those who produced the "fruit of repentance" in radically changed lives (Lk 3:8-9) would escape the purging judgment and belong to the renewed people of God. John's mission was to identify, through his call for repentance and baptism, the remnant of Israel who, by responding, was destined for cleansing and restoration as the true, eschatological people of God. His ministry would thus prepare the ground for the imminent intervention and arrival of God himself, as the quotations from Malachi 3:1 and Isaiah 40:3 make clear (Mk 1:2-3). That, indeed, was how the angel who announced his conception to his astonished father, Zechariah, summed up in advance John's life's work: "He will bring back many of the people of Israel to the Lord their God. And he will go on before the Lord, in the spirit and power of Elijah, to turn the hearts of the parents to their children and the disobedient to the wisdom of the righteous—to make ready a people prepared for the Lord" (Lk 1:16-17). And the Lord, when he came, submitted himself to be baptized by John!

So we come back to the baptism of Jesus, but now we can see it from a different perspective. We can see how Jesus, by accepting John's baptism, accepted and agreed with John's message and recognized his significance for the fulfillment of the hope of Israel. Jesus queued up with the crowds of those coming to the Jordan. Jesus himself had no need of personal repentance or cleansing, but nevertheless he identified himself with those who wanted to express their longing to be right with God, to be obedient to God's will and to see the coming of God's kingdom. Jesus joined those who were longing for the restoration of Israel, for that was his hope too. Indeed, it was his personal mission.

All the Gospels begin their accounts of Jesus' ministry with his baptism by John. It was also a key point in the preaching of the apostles about Jesus among Jews in the book of Acts. Scholars who have researched the aims of Jesus regard this as a vital piece of evidence. The fact that Jesus accepted and endorsed the ministry of John the Baptist and launched his own ministry on the foundation of John's shows that Jesus also saw his own mission in terms of the fulfillment of the great expectations of the restoration of Israel. If John was the one who had been sent to *prepare* Israel for its eschatological restoration by God himself, then Jesus was the one who had been sent to *accomplish* it.

THE MESSIAH

We need to look again at the baptismal voice and the identity it conferred on Jesus. We saw that the first part of what the voice from heaven said identified Jesus as the Son of God in the sense of the Davidic king, whose rule was celebrated in Psalm 2. And we have noted that Psalm 2 was already interpreted messianically in the time of Jesus. Among the many varied ideas about who or what the Messiah would be and do, it was popularly agreed that the Messiah would be the son of David, so much so that Jesus could use that belief as the basis for a characteristic piece of brain teasing that challenged people to think through the consequences of their beliefs in the light of Scripture (Mt 22:41-46).

We are so used to calling Jesus "Christ" (which is simply the Greek form of the Hebrew "messiah") that it comes as something of a shock to realize that the word itself as a title is actually hardly ever found in the Old Testament. It is in fact ironic that we talk so much about "messianic" ideas and hopes when not only is the word not common in the Old Testament, but also Jesus himself rarely used the word, told others not to use it and preferred other titles. What can account for this?

The term *messiah* (*mashiah* in Hebrew) occurs in Daniel 9:25-26. It is part of Daniel's visionary prophecy of the long-term future for his people.

An "anointed one" will come and will bring a climax to God's purpose, which is summed up in the words "to finish transgression, to put an end to sin, to atone for wickedness, to bring in everlasting righteousness, to seal up vision and prophecy and to anoint the Most Holy Place" (Dan 9:24). The idea of fulfillment and completion is very strong.

Before this, the word is not used in a predictive sense in the Old Testament. That is, there are no texts specifically predicting a future "messiah" in so many words. But the idea of *anointing* certain people for specific tasks was common enough in Israel. There were "anointed" people in the community. The word *anointed one*, then, was not originally *predictive* but simply *descriptive*.

To anoint someone with oil was symbolic of setting him or her apart for a particular role or duty with appropriate authorization for it. Priests were anointed with very special sacred oil. Kings were anointed at their accession (or beforehand in some cases, as for example David himself as a lad). Prophets were also regarded as anointed ones, which may have been literal in some cases, or perhaps metaphorical. The basic idea was that the anointed person was set aside and equipped by God and for God, so that whatever he or she did was done in God's name, with the help of God's Spirit, under God's protection and with God's authority.

A most interesting use of the word for "anointed one" that is not predictive but historical occurs in Isaiah 45:1. There, to everyone's surprise, God himself uses it to describe the pagan king, Cyrus, the newly rising star of the Persian Empire. "This is what the LORD says to *his anointed*, to Cyrus, whose right hand I take hold of."

Now Cyrus was not an Israelite, certainly not a king in the line of David. Nor was he "the Messiah" in the later technical sense of the term. But God's description of Cyrus as "his messiah" at this point in history tells us a lot about what the term meant at the time. And that in turn sheds light on what it later meant when applied to the expected "coming one."

First of all it was God who *chose* Cyrus and raised him up for the appointed task (Is 41:2-4, 25). Second, therefore, Cyrus's accomplishments were really God's, for it was God who was acting through him as *God's agent* (Is 44:28; 45:1-5). Third, Cyrus's specific task was the *redemption and restoration of Israel* from the hands of its enemies (Is 44:28; 45:13) so that, fourth, all his worldwide victories and dominion actually were for the purpose of delivering and establishing the people of God (Is 41:2-4; 45:1-4). And fifth, beyond that Israelite context, his work would ultimately be a step on the way to the extension of *God's salvation to the ends of the earth* (Is 45:21-25).

All of these were features in the developing messianic concept in post-Old Testament times, particularly as associated with the expectation of a coming son of David. The messiah would be God's agent to deliver and restore Israel, not a pagan king this time but a true Israelite, the true son of David. And in delivering Israel, the Messiah would bring salvation to the world.

Why, then, did Jesus soft-pedal the "Messiah" idea? It was certainly not because he rejected it. His own Father's voice had confirmed his identity as the messianic son of David. Jesus claimed, from his earliest preaching, to be anointed by the Spirit of God (Lk 4:18-21, quoting Is 61). He accepted Peter's half-understood confession of faith at Caesarea Philippi. He identified himself as such to the woman by the well in Samaria (Jn 4:25-26). And when challenged on the point in his trial he did not deny that he was the Messiah but went on to add further definition to it (Mk 14:61-62).

Nevertheless it is striking that on several occasions when those he had healed or blessed in some way acknowledged that he was the Messiah, he urged them not to spread the rumor around—which most of them promptly did, of course—such is human nature. And it is equally striking that, of all the figures and titles in the Old Testament relating to the coming eschatological deliverer of Israel, the one that Jesus used *least* was that of the Davidic, kingly Messiah. Indeed, although others used it about him, he never used it about himself in his own teaching.

So why this reticence? The most probable reason is that the term *Messiah* had become so loaded with the hopes of a national, political and even violent Jewish restoration that it could not carry the understanding of his messiahship that Jesus had derived from a deeper reading of his Scriptures. If he had stood up and claimed to be the Messiah it would have been "heard" by his contemporaries with a load of associations that were not part of Jesus' concept of his mission.

Jesus lived in the midst of a highly charged political atmosphere. In spite of the return from Babylon centuries before, the Jews had never known real freedom and independent sovereignty—apart from a relatively short period after the successful Maccabean revolt. Under the Persians, and then the Greeks and now the Romans, the Jews were still in a kind of exile, even in their own land. The longings for national freedom, the murmurs of revolt and the apocalyptic, messianic hopes all bubbled close to the surface of national life.

There were others who claimed to be messiahs before and after Jesus. They all ended up as tragic, failed heroes. And it would unquestionably have been within that potent mixture of hopes and angry aspirations that any messianic claims (by Jesus or anyone else) would have been interpreted and evaluated. If Jesus really were the Messiah, then his Jewish contemporaries knew exactly what *they* expected of him. The trouble was that what *they* expected of a messiah and what Jesus intended in being the Messiah did not match. Jesus had no intention of being a conquering king, militarily or politically. Which is not to say that he was not a king or indeed not a conqueror, but of a very different sort from popular expectations.

Now at this point we need to be very careful to understand what is *not* being said here. It is *not* being said that Jesus disassociated himself from Jewish hopes of restoration. We have seen that the whole thrust of both Old Testament and post-Old Testament expectation was that God would act to restore Israel. If Jesus had tried to opt out of that he would never have gone to the Jordan for baptism in the first place and he would have found no followers of his own either. We shall see shortly other features of his teaching and actions that clearly show that he believed *passionately* in the scriptural promises of the restoration of Israel and his own part in it. No, the difference between Jesus and his contemporaries was not *that* Israel must be restored, but *how* it would happen and what it would mean.

Nor is it being said that just because Jesus did not initiate a political movement or a revolt against Rome he therefore had no interest in politics or that his message had no political implications. In the next chapter we shall look more fully at the ethical teaching of Jesus and take note of its political dimensions. But for the present it will be enough to say that if Jesus had intended *only* to talk about a purely *spiritual* revival in an other-worldly framework with no relevance to the seething politics of his day, then he went about it in a very strange way. So many of the words and actions of Jesus were so challenging to the political authorities that they executed him as a political threat.

Jesus did not, of course, advocate violent revolution against Rome. But to argue that because he did not preach *violent* politics he was therefore

uninterested in politics at all is absurd. Nonviolent is not simply nonpolitical—now or then. No, the difference between Jesus and his contemporaries was not that he was purely spiritual while they were political (a
modern kind of dichotomy that would probably not have made much sense
in Jesus' world anyway). The problem was that his announcement of the
arrival of the kingdom of God in the present did have profound political
and national consequences for the old order of Jewish society that were too
radical and final for its leaders to tolerate.

The Messiah came to usher in the new age. But the new age meant the
death of the old age. He came to achieve the restoration of Israel. But that
could only come about after the fires of judgment and purging. As Jesus
looked at his own society, he saw it heading for that terrifying judgment—
just as the prophets before him, like Jeremiah, had done. So much of his
preaching has that urgent note of warning and impending disaster. Like
John he saw a "wrath to come": the wrath of Rome as well as the wrath of
God. But the deeper awareness of his own messiahship lay in this: Jesus
believed he was called to take Israel's judgment on himself at another level.
For the Messiah was a representative figure. He *was* Israel. Their destiny
was therefore his, and his destiny was theirs. Yes, at one level, national and
political Israel was heading for destruction. But at another level Israel, *in
the Messiah*, would suffer judgment and then the restoration that *God*, not
the politicians or the guerrillas, planned. Jesus would redeem Israel by dying
its death and accomplishing its resurrection as its representative, its embodiment, its king, its Messiah.

That was why as soon as the disciples came to accept that Jesus was the
Messiah he *immediately* began to teach them of his impending violent death
and third-day resurrection. *That* was how the Messiah they now haltingly
recognized intended to accomplish the restoration they expected of him. It
is not really surprising that they could not grasp his meaning until after the
events of the cross and resurrection. Even then, it took a seven-mile walk
from Jerusalem to Emmaus to spell out to two of them what it all meant.
Like everybody else in Palestine (except, presumably, the Romans), those
two disciples were hoping for the redemption of Israel, as they dolefully told
him. In Jesus they thought they had the answer to their dreams. Jesus told
them that actually they had indeed gotten that answer—in him, the
Messiah. But, just as Israel's restoration lay on the other side of judgment,

so, in his person, it was necessary for "the Messiah to suffer these things *and then* enter his glory" (Lk 24:26). The Messiah's resurrection was Israel's redemption. God had done for Jesus the Messiah what they were expecting God to do for Israel. But in Jesus *as* the Messiah, God had at a deeper level actually done it for Israel. As Paul would later put it, "We tell you the good news: What God promised our ancestors he has fulfilled for us, their children, by raising up Jesus" (Acts 13:32-33). The new age of redemption and restoration had dawned.

So it is not surprising either, therefore, that whereas during his earthly ministry Jesus had muted his messiahship (because of misunderstanding among even those who believed in it), *after* the resurrection the disciples went about enthusiastically proclaiming that Jesus was truly the Messiah, with a new understanding of what that meant—an understanding that was exciting, surprising, joyful—but still just as threatening to the Jewish establishment, as the early chapters of Acts show.

THE SON OF MAN

Jesus, then, saw that for him to be the Messiah meant taking on himself the identity and destiny of Israel. This is confirmed by his favorite term for himself, "the Son of Man." If Jesus was reticent about using the name of Messiah, then the reverse was true of this expression. He sprinkled it so freely into his conversations and teachings that people inquired in genuine puzzlement, "Who is this Son of Man?" (Jn 12:34). Scholars have filled libraries asking and answering the same question!

In fact it was not really a title at all. In the Hebrew Bible it is an expression (*ben-adam*) used frequently as a poetic alternative to the word *man* in the general sense (e.g., Ps 8:4; 80:17; Is 51:12, etc.). It simply means "a human being," with an emphasis on human weakness and mortality often implied. It is a bit like the word *Mister*. Just any ordinary man. In Ezekiel it is used ninety-three times as a way of addressing the prophet. It may be to suggest humility before the glory of God, or it may be in some sense a representative term—he as the individual prophet representing his people as a whole.

In the Galilean Aramaic that Jesus spoke, the equivalent expression (*bar nash*, or *bar nasha*) had a similar sort of meaning and could also be used as a way of speaking of oneself, rather like the English use of *one* instead of *I* or *me* (a modest English speaker might say, "One likes to think," rather than the stronger, "I think"). It probably had a self-effacing tone as an alternative for *I*. Thus Matthew quite often changes the phrase "Son of Man" in a passage in Mark into "I" or "he" in his own Gospel when referring to Jesus.

Most scholars are agreed that the "Son of Man" was not a messianic title or figure in the intertestamental Jewish writings. That is, the people of Jesus' day, whatever else they were hoping for in the way of a messiah, they were not on the lookout for a "Son of Man." This meant that by using it of himself Jesus could avoid the package of misunderstandings surrounding other familiar messianic titles and instead fill this term with meaning that was based on his own true perception of who he was and what he had come for.

On the other hand, because it did not have a fixed meaning already, people got confused! They asked Jesus about the Christ and he answered about the Son of Man! As we have seen, it was really only after the cross and resurrection that his messiahship could be fully understood. From then on, Jesus as the *Christ* and as the *Son of God* dominated the preaching of the church, and the term Son of Man was scarcely heard again. In fact in the whole New Testament it is found almost exclusively on the lips of Jesus alone, the only exceptions being Stephen's vision at the point of his martyrdom (which echoes Jesus, Acts 7:56), Hebrews 2:6 (which quotes Ps 8:4) and Revelation 1:13 and 14:14 (which are allusions to Daniel 7:13).

So what meaning then did Jesus fill into this unusual self-designation? Scholars have studied in great depth all the sayings of Jesus in which the term "Son of Man" occurs. There are plenty of them—thirty in Matthew, fourteen in Mark, twenty-five in Luke and thirteen in John. There is general agreement that, apart from some distinctive uses in John, the Son of Man sayings fall into three broad categories.

First, there are those where Jesus uses it when he is talking about his then present, earthly ministry. These sayings tend to speak of his authority over sin, sickness or even nature (e.g., Mk 2:10, 28).

Second, there is a larger group of Son of Man sayings that speak of the Son of Man suffering rejection, dying and rising again, which significantly come after the disciples begin to recognize Jesus as Messiah (e.g., Mk 8:31; 9:31; Lk 9:44, etc.).

And third, the largest group of all, there are sayings that talk about the Son of Man coming in eschatological glory, sometimes with the clouds (which represent deity) and sometimes to act as judge on God's behalf (e.g., Mk 14:62; Mt 13:41-42; 19:28, etc.).

Taken together, these three categories are remarkably comprehensive as a way of encapsulating how Jesus saw his own identity, as well as how he envisaged his immediate and more long-term destiny. He was the one, first, entrusted with authority in his ministry, which he exercised over sin, disease, death, nature and even such fundamental ordinances of the law as the Sabbath. It was a startling and unique authority, which raised eyebrows, questions and hackles all around him. But as he exercised that "unauthorized authority" it led him into conflict with the existing authorities. That conflict eventually ended up with his rejection and death. We have already seen how he understood the mission of the Messiah in terms of suffering and also, in the last chapter, how he recognized that suffering would be the price of his obedience as the Son of God. However, beyond suffering and death, Jesus spoke about being vindicated in resurrection and then exercising the heavenly authority of God himself.

Where did he get all this? (Another question Jesus himself had to answer!) There is no doubt that the third of the categories above, the idea of future vindication and glory, comes from the description of "one like a son of man" in Daniel 7, and it seems clear that the figure described in Daniel is what substantially lay behind Jesus' choice of the Son of Man as a self-designation. So we need to look at that chapter.

In Daniel 7, Daniel sees the kingdoms of this earth, portrayed as ravaging beasts from the sea, given controlled freedom to oppress and harass the people of God. The people of God, described as "the saints of the Most High," are attacked and devoured almost to the point of extinction. But then the visionary scene changes dramatically in verse 9. Instead of a picture of human history at ground level, we are transported into the presence of God ("the Ancient of Days") seated on his throne. There, through the presence of a human figure described as "one like a son of man," the tables are turned. This son of man comes into the presence of the Ancient of Days, the beasts are stripped of authority and destroyed, and dominion, kingdom and authority are given to the son of man and the saints forever.

This "son of man" figure in Daniel 7 has a curiously double point of reference. On the one hand, he appears to represent *the saints*—that is, the human people of God in history. The parallelism between Daniel 7:14 (where authority and kingdom are given to the son of man) and Daniel 7:18 (where the kingdom is given to the saints) shows this. The son of man, in the vision, represents or symbolizes the saints. It has been suggested that he may be an angelic figure, since in Daniel nations can be represented in the spiritual domain by angels (e.g., Dan 10:13, 20-21). Or perhaps he is simply a kind of corporate, representative human figure, embodying, in the vision, the people of God as a whole. From this point of view, the figure fitted in very well with Jesus' identification of himself with Israel. As the Son of Man he represented them. He shared their experience. His destiny was theirs and vice versa.

But on the other hand the son of man in Daniel 7 is closely associated with God himself. Daniel sees him "coming with the clouds of heaven" (Dan 7:13). That was very much part of the "ambiance" of deity in the Old Testament. Furthermore, he is given authority, glory, power and worship and his kingdom is eternal (Dan 7:14)—all rather more than the normal lot of any son of Adam. In fact, there are Greek versions of the text that translate Daniel 7:13 in such a way as to *identify* the son of man with the Ancient of Days. And this tradition finds a strong echo in Revelation, where the description of Jesus in glory is a combination of the reference to the son of man and a virtual direct quotation of the description of the Ancient of Days in Daniel 7:9-10 (Rev 1:7, 12-16). The two descriptions are conflated into one picture.

So there was an air of deity about the son of man figure also. Indeed, it may have been this aspect of the Danielic figure that clinched the verdict against Jesus on the grounds of blasphemy at his trial. When the high priest asked Jesus whether he was the Messiah, Jesus did not deny it. But immediately he went on to claim that his accusers would see the Son of Man in divine glory "coming on the clouds of heaven" (that is, in the presence of God, Mt 26:63-64). The shift from Messiah to Son of Man must be deliberate and the language comes from Daniel.

Even if this saying of Jesus in the context of his trial was not heard as a claim to a fully divine status, it was still a horrendously conflictual thing to claim. By casting himself in the role of the Son of Man in the sense of Daniel 7, Jesus was claiming to represent the true people of God, the saints of the Most High. But he was standing in the presence of the high priest, Caiaphas, who occupied that role. He was before the Sanhedrin, the representative court of Israel, in Jerusalem its holy city, near the temple, its most holy place. And in the midst of all these people and places, dripping with holiness and the very essence of Israel, Jesus calmly claims to be the Son of Man in full Danielic symbolism, the one whom God would vindicate and entrust with supreme authority. He was claiming to be the one who would be presented on behalf of the saints of God to the Ancient of Days. He was the one who would receive eternal dominion and authority to act in judgment (an impression strengthened by the other Old Testament echo in what Jesus said, namely, Psalm 110:1).

This was strong stuff from one who had just been arrested at dead of night and was himself on trial for his life. But there was worse. For in Daniel 7 the enemies of the son of man/saints of God were the beasts. Who then were these enemies of Jesus? As so often, Jesus did not need to spell out the implications of what he said to the Jewish authorities. His meaning and its implied threat were clear and quite intolerable. Chief priest or chief beast? No wonder Caiaphas tore his robes, cried blasphemy, called for the death penalty and permitted the spitting and beating. The claims of Jesus were enough to burst old blood vessels as well as old wineskins.

THE SERVANT OF THE LORD

To find Jesus talking about himself as the Son of Man at the very start of his suffering is in one sense to be expected by any attentive reader of the Gospels. Ever since Caesarea Philippi he had repeatedly emphasized that "The Son of Man must suffer many things and be killed" (Lk 9:22). Yet in another sense this whole emphasis on the suffering of the Son of Man is strange because it is not clearly part of the picture of the son of man in Daniel 7. Some would say that suffering was no part of the Danielic son of man at all. Others would say that it is only there by implication, inasmuch as he is a representative figure of the saints who certainly do suffer all the ravages of the beasts. Yet Jesus, who used this expression for himself more than any other, linked it repeatedly to his expectation of suffering, rejection and death. Why did he do so?

The answer is that Jesus drew on yet another figure from his Hebrew Bible, and that was the Servant of the Lord. We saw in the last chapter that the voice of his Father at Jesus' baptism identified Jesus as the Servant by alluding to Isaiah 42:1. The "suffering servant" in the book of Isaiah was understood messianically in Jesus' day. But it was not explicitly connected or identified with the Son of Man. It seems that it was Jesus himself who brought these two portraits together. That is, he called himself the Son of Man (which pointed to future vindication and authority, as Daniel 7 said), but he insisted that the Son of Man "must suffer" and he portrayed his coming death as fulfilling a mission that has its roots in the description of the Servant in Isaiah.

These two ideas, suffering and servanthood, come together in a key saying of Jesus in Mark 10:45: "For even the Son of Man did not come to be served, but to serve, and to give his life as a ransom for many."

The saying comes as the climax of a lesson on servanthood, which Jesus gave to his disciples in the wake of the request of James and John for privileged positions in Jesus' kingdom. To reinforce his point, he uses his own example of voluntary servanthood, proved through his self-sacrificial coming death. It is the last phrase ("give his life as a ransom for many") that lifts the saying from talking about serving in general to showing clearly that Jesus had in mind the very special ministry of the Servant of the Lord. For it is clear from Isaiah 53 that the Servant would not only suffer, but he would also die—or rather be brutally killed—and his death would be as a sacrifice for the sin of many (Is 53:10-11).

Later on Jesus makes an even clearer reference to Isaiah 53, in Luke 22:37. On the night of his arrest, Jesus warns the disciples of dangers ahead. Incidentally, in my view the reference to buying a sword was probably proverbial rather than literal. Jesus was warning his disciples what to expect, not telling them to fight, since he later prevented them from doing so. As so often, they misunderstood him (Lk 22:36). They were all going to face danger because Jesus was about to be treated like a criminal, for he says, "It is written: 'And he was numbered with the transgressors' [Is 53:12]; and I tell you that this must be fulfilled in me. Yes, what is written about me is reaching its fulfillment" (Lk 22:37).

The emphatic repetition about fulfillment shows that this was not just a casual quotation for effect. Jesus here claims to be the one whom Isaiah 53 was written about—the Servant of the Lord who would give his life for the sake of others.

In fact, finding words from Isaiah 53 on the lips of Jesus as he and his disciples were leaving for the Mount of Olives is not surprising, because that part of Isaiah seems to have been much on his mind that night. Just a little while earlier, with the disciples arguing again about their competing claims for greatness (what a time to be obsessed with that question!), Jesus had to repeat his lesson on servanthood with the words, "I am among you as one who serves" (Lk 22:27). And at the most solemn moment of all, at the end of the Passover meal, he took the fourth cup of blessing with the words: "This cup is the new covenant in my blood" (1 Cor 11:25), "which is poured out" (Lk 22:20) "for many" (Mk 14:24) "for the forgiveness of sins" (Mt 26:28).

Scholars argue over the precise reconstruction of the exact words of Jesus at that moment. What is very clear is that Jesus referred to the shedding of his own blood (about to happen in a few hours) as a *covenantal* act and a *sacrificial* act, and that it was for the benefit of others.

Several Old Testament passages seem to be combined in his meaning. The blood of the covenant recalls Exodus 24, where sacrificial blood sealed the covenant between God and Israel at Mount Sinai. But the "new covenant" recalls Jeremiah 31:31-34, which, as we saw in chapter two, was promised by God for his people and included complete forgiveness of sin. Then again, the expressions "poured out" and "for many" recall Isaiah 53:12 and the work of the Servant in his death. And finally, God told the Servant in Isaiah 42:6 and 49:8 that he would be "a covenant for the nations."

It may well be that the reason for the variations in the different accounts of the words of Jesus on this solemn occasion of the Last Supper is simply that Jesus did not just speak one sentence and move on, as if he were reciting a liturgy at a church service. He had in fact interrupted the Passover liturgy with his own startling declaration, and he quite probably explained his words from different Scriptures to make sure his disciples didn't miss his full meaning this time.

So there are good grounds for believing that Jesus saw himself as the Servant figure of Isaiah and interpreted his mission and especially his suffering and death in terms of Isaiah 53. Certainly the early church made this identification, and it seems much more likely that they got the idea from Jesus than that they invented it themselves. One of the earliest terms for referring to Jesus among his followers in the book of Acts was "God's holy servant" (Acts 3:13, 26; 4:27, 30). Peter, one of those who shared most closely in the private thoughts of Jesus, also found his own mind turning to Isaiah 53 when reflecting on how Jesus set an example of suffering without retaliation (1 Pet 1:21-25). Matthew links Jesus with the Servant very clearly, not just in his record of the baptismal voice with its allusion to Isaiah 42:1 but by his full-length quotation of Isaiah 42:1-4 (Mt 12:15-21) and of Isaiah 53:4 (Mt 8:17). Both of these are in the context of Jesus' healing ministry.

If Jesus' mind was absorbed with Isaiah 53 in relation to his coming suffering and death, it seems that he thought of his prior ministry of teaching and healing in terms drawn from the other servant songs and related passages in Isaiah. In his famous "sermon" at Nazareth right at the beginning of his public ministry, he read from Isaiah 61:1-2 and applied the words to himself as now fulfilled.

> The Spirit of the LORD is on me,
>> because he has anointed me
>> to proclaim good news to the poor.
> He has sent me to proclaim freedom for the prisoners
>> and recovery of sight for the blind,
> to set the oppressed free,
>> to proclaim the year of the Lord's favor. (Lk 4:18-19)

The passage has many similarities with the mission of the Servant as described in Isaiah 42:7. Later, when answering John's disciples, he points to the visible effects of his healing and preaching ministry in words that echo both Isaiah 35:5-6 and Isaiah 61:1. "Go back and report to John what you hear and see: The blind receive sight, the lame walk, those who have leprosy are cleansed, the deaf hear, the dead are raised, and the good news is proclaimed to the poor" (Mt 11:4-5).

So, then, it is clear from his baptism, through his public ministry, and especially in his suffering and death, that Jesus saw himself as fulfilling the mission of the Servant of God. In order to get the full value of this insight into the mind of Jesus, however, we must do the same as we did for the other figures that Jesus found in his Hebrew Scriptures and applied to himself. That is, we must look back into the Old Testament and find out how the identity and mission of the Servant was described there. For, as we have said

before, the more deeply we understand the Scriptures Jesus used, the closer
we shall come to the heart of Jesus himself. And what is more, we shall have
a sharper understanding of our own mission in the light of his. So who was
the Servant of the Lord in Isaiah, and what was he called to do?

THE MISSION OF THE SERVANT IN THE OLD TESTAMENT

In the book of Isaiah, before we are introduced to the mysterious figure of
the Servant of the Lord as an individual, the prophet first applies the term
to *Israel as a nation*. Israel was God's servant.

> But you, Israel, *my servant*,
>> Jacob, whom I have chosen,
>> you descendants of Abraham my friend,
> I took you from the ends of the earth,
>> from its farthest corners I called you.
> I said, "You are *my servant*";
>> I have chosen you and have not rejected you.
> So do not fear, for I am with you;
>> do not be dismayed, for I am your God.
> I will strengthen you and help you;
>> I will uphold you with my righteous right hand. (Is 41:8-10,
>> my italics)

This means that when God introduces his Servant in Isaiah 42:1, in
terms that appear to describe an individual, there must be some connection
with the identity of Israel already mentioned. The Servant figure is never
in fact given any actual name in these chapters *except* Israel or Jacob (cf.
also Is 44:1-2; 45:4). More significantly, many of the things that are said
about the Servant figure as an individual are also said or implied about
Israel as God's servant in a corporate sense. So, for example, we immediately notice that being chosen by God and upheld by God's right hand is
said of both (see Is 42:1, 6). Both the individual and the nation are called
to be witnesses to God in the midst of and to the nations (Is 42:6; 43:10,
21; 49:3, 6).

So there is definite *continuity* between Israel as the servant and the Servant
figure who appears to be an individual. So much so, in fact, that some
scholars interpret all the passages about the servant as being corporate—that
is, as referring to Israel. Now it is true that Israel is sometimes personified

in the Hebrew Bible as an individual—for example, as a wife or a son. But in those cases the metaphorical intention is clear. Some of the passages in Isaiah that describe the commission, experiences, words and feelings of the Servant, however, are so graphic and personal that most scholars believe that the prophet must have meant them to refer to an individual person. In any case, it is not uncommon in the Hebrew Bible for writers like prophets and poets to move back and forth between corporate and individual categories. The nation as a whole could be spoken of in the collective singular, and particular individuals could represent or embody the wider community. So there is nothing impossible about the prophet in these chapters using the same idea—servant—to describe both the nation of Israel and also a particular individual.

At this point, however, things get somewhat more complex! Not everything that the prophet has to say about Israel as the servant is as warm and positive as the verses quoted above. The historical context in which these prophecies of Isaiah 40–55 were heard was the exile. The whole section is a tremendous word of challenge and encouragement to the Jews who had survived the destruction of Jerusalem in 587 B.C. and were now into the second generation of captivity in Babylon. And they were there because of the judgment of God upon the sin, disobedience and failure of the nation, which had been denounced by the preexilic prophets. Israel, the servant of God, in spite of all the blessings and privileges it had experienced from God, was at that moment of history paralyzed and useless as far as the fulfillment of its mission was concerned. This is how Isaiah describes Israel, in the present reality of its sin and failure:

> Hear, you deaf;
>   look, you blind, and see!
> Who is blind but my servant,
>   and deaf like the messenger I send?
> Who is blind like the one in covenant with me,
>   blind like the servant of the Lord?
> You have seen many things, but you pay no attention;
>   your ears are open, but you do not listen."
> It pleased the Lord
>   for the sake of his righteousness
>   to make his law great and glorious.

But this is a people plundered and looted,
    all of them trapped in pits
    or hidden away in prisons. . . .
Who handed Jacob over to become loot,
    and Israel to the plunderers?
Was it not the LORD,
    against whom we have sinned?
For they would not follow his ways;
    they did not obey his law. (Is 42:18-22, 24)

Those words are familiar enough to anyone who has read the prophets
(and they are reinforced in Is 43:22-28). But they are very significant here
because this prophet calls Israel God's servant and puts this word of
rebuke almost immediately after his ringing description of the character
and mission of the servant in Is 42:1-9. So although there is clearly a
measure of continuity and identity between the individual Servant and
the nation of Israel, we find here that there is a definite discontinuity and
distinction between them as well. The nation of Israel, far from fulfilling
its mission as the servant of God to bring him glory among the nations
as his witness, actually stands under his judgment. They were far from
God spiritually (as well as, in a sense, geographically), and it is as if they
are blind, deaf and incapacitated. They need to be brought *back to God*,
not just *back to Jerusalem*.

Cyrus will serve God's purpose by providing the political liberation that
will bring them back to Jerusalem. But who then will restore them spiritually? Who else but the Servant figure? That is probably what is implied
by Isaiah 42:3, 7. The bruised reed and smoldering wick, the blind captives
sitting in darkness, probably meant Israel in exile. The Servant would have
a mission of compassionate restoration. Listen to his own testimony in the
second "Servant Song":

And now the LORD says—
    he who formed me in the womb to be his servant
to bring Jacob back to him
    and gather Israel to himself. (Is 49:5)

The Servant, then, has a mission *to* Israel. It is the Servant of God who will
accomplish the restoration of the servant Israel to God. But for what

purpose? Another twist in the developing picture of the Servant reveals the answer. In Isaiah 49, the Servant faces apparent failure.

> But I said, "I have labored in vain;
>> I have spent my strength for nothing at all." (Is 49:4)

This is amplified in Isaiah 50:5-9, where the Servant experiences rejection and physical abuse. It seems that the Servant's mission is failing, with frustration and opposition.

God's answer to the Servant's depression is startling. God now entrusts the Servant with an even *wider mission*—not just Israel but the world!

> And now the LORD says [vv. 5-6 are God's answer to v. 4] . . .

> It is too small a thing for you to be my servant
>> to restore the tribes of Jacob
>> and bring back those of Israel I have kept.
> *I will also make you a light to the Gentiles,*
>> *that my salvation may reach to the ends of the earth.* (Is 49:6,
>>> my italics)

The Servant, then, also has a mission to the world. But we should be careful to note that this is indeed "*also.*" That is, the universal mission of the Servant expands but does not replace or cancel the mission of restoring Israel. In fact, this particular "Servant Song" is actually addressed to the nations in Isaiah 49:1. It is as if the Servant wishes to explain to the nations how it has come about that he, who had been commissioned to restore *Israel,* has become the means of bringing salvation to *them*—the foreign nations (Is 49:6). The reason is that God himself had redirected and expanded his mission: not Israel only but the world, as well.

To sum up what we have found so far, then: Israel, as a people, was the servant of God, chosen and upheld by him with the purpose of being a light to the nations, as was the original intention of the election of Abraham. But historically Israel was failing in that role and mission. Israel as the servant of God was "blind and deaf" and under God's judgment. The individual Servant is thus at one level *distinct* from Israel because he has a mission *to* Israel, to challenge it and call it back to God. The restoration of Israel, God's servant, is the task of the Servant himself. Yet at another level, the Servant is *identified* with Israel, and similar language is used of both.

This is because, in the surprising purposes of God, the Servant will actually fulfill the original mission of Israel. That is, through the Servant, God's justice, liberation and salvation will be extended to the nations. The universal purpose of the election of Israel is to be achieved through the mission of the Servant.

THE SERVANT AND THE MISSION TO THE GENTILES

Returning now to the New Testament, we can begin to see not only how Jesus understood his own mission, but also how *his* mission to Israel is related to the later *apostolic* mission to the Gentiles (the nations).

We saw in the opening sections of this chapter that Jesus saw his own mission in terms of the hopes of the restoration and redemption of Israel. This was clear from the way he endorsed the ministry of John the Baptist and launched his own ministry from John's.

Several other actions of Jesus have to be interpreted in this light, that is, as pointing to his mission as the restoration of Israel. His choice of twelve disciples, for example, was intentionally symbolic of an embryonic restored Israel. He called them a "little flock" (Lk 12:32), which was a term for the remnant of Israel, and envisages them judging the twelve tribes of Israel (Mt 19:28). There was his entry into Jerusalem, which, without a word of explanation from him, was for all to see a claim to fulfill the promised royal restoration of Zechariah 9:9-10. There was his action in the temple shortly afterward. This was more than just a "cleansing" of the temple from traders. It was almost certainly a prophetic sign, pointing to the destruction of the temple, which he also explicitly predicted. But the only reason why the temple would be destroyed, in current Jewish expectation, was if and when the new age of Israel's restoration dawned, at which point a new temple was expected. The disciples later realized that Jesus meant exactly that. He was the new temple. A few nights later, as we saw above, he was claiming to inaugurate the new covenant in the context of a Passover meal that pointed to his own death as the sacrificial lamb. And three days after that, he was explaining to two disciples on the road to Emmaus that the redemption of Israel that they were hoping for had indeed been accomplished through his resurrection on the third day. A messianic king, a new temple, a new covenant, a new Passover, a redeemed Israel—and all in the space of a week between Palm Sunday and Easter Day!

There can be no doubt, then, that Jesus saw himself and his mission as directed primarily to Israel. Thus far we can see him fitting the role of the Servant. But what then of those texts in Isaiah that spoke of the mission of the Servant to the nations?

There are some signs even during his earthly ministry that Jesus did have a universal vision of the ultimately worldwide effect of the gospel, embracing foreign nations as well as Israel. Indeed, sometimes he gave great offense by referring to foreigners. His own townspeople in Nazareth were not at all pleased when he picked out two foreigners, Naaman the Syrian and the widow of Zarephath, as models of response to God in his synagogue address (Lk 4:24-30). Only rarely did Jesus himself deal directly with Gentiles, but his reaction to their faith was very significant. Marveling at the faith of the Roman centurion in Matthew 8:5-13, Jesus used it as a springboard for a remarkable vision of a great ingathering of the Gentile nations. But what is most interesting is that he used language drawn from Old Testament texts, which had referred to the ingathering of the exiles of Israel. "I say to you that many will come from the east and the west, and will take their places at the feast with Abraham, Isaac and Jacob in the kingdom of heaven. But the subjects of the kingdom will be thrown outside" (Mt 8:11-12).

The Old Testament background to this ingathering from different points of the compass comes from passages like Isaiah 43:5 and 49:12 and Psalm 107:3. Just as Paul used Hosea 1:10 and 2:23 (which referred to Israel) to refer to the ingrafted Gentiles (Rom 9:24-26), Jesus was redefining and extending the meaning of the restoration of Israel to include Gentiles.

However, it is clear that the dominant burden of Jesus' mission *in his own lifetime* was to Israel. "I was sent only to the lost sheep of Israel," he said (Mt 15:24). And he confined his disciples to the borders of Israel also: "Do not go among the Gentiles or enter any town of the Samaritans. Go rather to the lost sheep of Israel" (Mt 10:5-6).

After his resurrection, however, we hear the familiar words releasing the disciples from any such limits and commissioning them instead to "go and make disciples of all nations" (Mt 28:19). Luke's record of the "Great Commission" emphasizes the idea of *witness*, which has interesting roots in the servant passages of the Old Testament. He ends his Gospel with these words of Jesus, "This is what is written: The Messiah will suffer and rise from the dead on the third day, and repentance for the forgiveness of sins will be preached in his name to all nations, beginning at Jerusalem. *You are witnesses* of these things" (Lk 24:46-48, my italics).

And he begins the book of Acts in the same way. The disciples, still puzzled by events, inquire of the risen Jesus whether the time has now come for the restoration of Israel. Jesus in a sense deflects their question by redirecting their mission in exactly the way God had done for the servant in Isaiah 49. "But you will receive power when the Holy Spirit comes on you; and *you will be my witnesses* in Jerusalem, and in all Judea and Samaria, and to the ends of the earth" (Acts 1:8, my italics).

"You will be my witnesses" is a deliberate echo of Isaiah 43. In that chapter God promised that he would redeem, gather and restore Israel (Is 43:1-7) and then immediately declares twice "you are my witnesses" (Is 43:10, 12). The people of Israel were to bear witness among the nations that Yahweh is the true and living God, the only one who had revealed and saved. Now Jesus uses exactly the same words to tell the disciples that they must bear witness to the nations that Jesus alone is Lord and Savior.

As we have seen, this "witness" in the servant passages of Isaiah is to go "to the ends of the earth"—one of the favorite phrases of the prophet. So the shape of the mission of the Servant in Isaiah not only explains the primary mission of Jesus to Israel but also provides the key to the launching of the mission to the nations after his resurrection.

The Gentile mission of the early church is another important clue to an understanding of the aims of Jesus. Scholars who have researched the question we started with in this chapter, "What were Jesus' aims and intentions?" point out that at least part of the answer is found by noticing what immediately *preceded* and what very quickly *followed* his ministry. John the Baptist came first. And all the New Testament traditions stress that Jesus began his ministry from John. Jesus shared John's vision that the expected restoration of Israel was being accomplished. Then, very soon after his death, we find that the little group Jesus left behind had become a dynamic movement committed to taking the good news to the Gentile nations, willing to face all the problems that it caused—practical, geographical, cultural and theological. The first followers of Jesus were committed to world mission!

Jesus was launched by a revival movement for the restoration of *Israel*. He himself launched a movement for the blessing of the *nations*. Jesus, therefore, was the hinge, the vital link between the two great movements. He was the climax and fulfillment of the hope of Israel and the beginning of the hope of the nations. And that was precisely the role of the Servant of God.

How perceptive indeed was the prophetic word of old Simeon, when he held the infant Jesus in his arms and saw in him not only the fulfillment of all his hopes for Israel but also of God's promise for the nations.

> Sovereign Lord, as you have promised,
>> you may now dismiss your servant in peace.
> For my eyes have seen your salvation,
>> which you have prepared in the sight of all nations:
> a light for revelation *to the Gentiles*,
>> and the glory of *your people Israel*. (Lk 2:29-32, my italics)

If all this is now clear to us, as it became clear to New Testament writers like Luke, we may be puzzled as to why it was that the Gentile mission of the early church actually got off to a rather slow and shaky start. Its mission to the world did not start all at once. Remember that Luke wrote his Gospel and Acts long after those early days and in the light of his theological and scriptural reflection. Why did it take angels and rooftop visions, persecution and scattering, not to mention blinding lights on the Damascus road, to drag the early Jewish Christian church into a mission to the Gentiles, and even then not without some theological kicking and screaming?

Well, we are not told explicitly. But my own feeling is that it had something to do with the remaining ambivalence and misunderstanding about the restoration of Israel that we hear in Acts 1:6. I think there is a comparison with Jesus' teaching about the kingdom of God, which he declared had already come and was present in reality through himself, and yet was still to come in its fullness in the future. *Already, but not yet.* Likewise, the restoration of Israel had indeed already happened through the resurrection of the Messiah. And yet in another sense it still lay ahead. At least, it was not very obvious to the naked eye on the streets of Jerusalem even after Pentecost.

Imagine the reasoning of the disciples. According to their Jewish expectation, if the ingathering of the Gentiles were to take place, Israel had to be restored first. Both events were part of the great eschatological scenario. They couldn't happen separately. Yet even after the resurrection of Jesus, and in spite of their eager and enthusiastic witnessing to it, Israel had not yet responded to the good news. Or rather, those who had responded were still a tiny minority, even if they began to number thousands instead of dozens. Peter's preaching in Acts 3 passionately appeals to his fellow Jews to turn and believe his witness to Jesus, so that "the times of refreshing may come"—the redemption of Israel. The events have reached that point. The Servant has been sent first to Israel so that God can fulfill his promise to Abraham and bless the nations. If only Israel would respond to him even now. Notice how his sermon follows exactly the pattern we have seen so far: *Israel first, then the nations.* "You are heirs of the prophets and of the covenant God made with your fathers. He said to Abraham, 'Through your offspring all peoples on earth will be blessed.' When God raised up his servant, he sent him first to you to bless you by turning each of you from your wicked ways" (Acts 3:25-26). But they wouldn't turn. So the apostles may have thought, "If Israel has not yet been visibly restored, the ingathering of the Gentiles can hardly begin yet, can it?"

But then God surprised them. Here was Cornelius, a Roman centurion who respected the Jewish God but knew nothing about Jesus. Here was Peter, who knew Jesus but wanted nothing to do with unclean Gentiles. An angel. A strange vision on an empty stomach. A knock on the door. And God brings them together in an encounter so important that Luke spares two precious chapters of parchment to tell it twice (Acts 10; 11). The conversion of Cornelius astonished Peter and his friends and then the rest of the church. They had to recognize it as nothing less than an act of God (Acts 10:44-48; 11:15-18): "So then, even to the Gentiles God has granted repentance that leads to life!"

Then at Antioch the gospel showed its remarkable crosscultural power as large numbers of Greek-speaking Gentiles "believed and turned to the Lord" (Acts 11:21). Once again the church was compelled to recognize the hand of God (Acts 12:21) and the grace of God (Acts 12:23). The Gentile mission was an act of God before it ever became a strategy of the church.

So what could have happened? Nothing less than that in some sense the promised restoration of Israel must already have happened, or be happening, and was being demonstrated precisely in the ingathering of the Gentiles. If God was doing the one (gathering the Gentiles), he must be doing the other (restoring Israel). The two were inseparably linked. And this was exactly how

James interpreted events in the wake of the even more remarkable results of the first missionary journey of Paul and Barnabas. Listen to what James said at the council of Jerusalem.

> The whole assembly became silent as they listened to Barnabas and Paul telling about the signs and wonders that God had done among the Gentiles through them. When they finished, James spoke up. "Brothers," he said, "listen to me. Simon has described to us how God first intervened to choose a people for his name from the Gentiles. The words of the prophets are in agreement with this, as it is written:
>
> 'After this I will return
> > and rebuild David's fallen tent.
> Its ruins I will rebuild,
> > and I will restore it,
> that the rest of mankind may seek the Lord,
> > even all the Gentiles who bear my name,
> says the Lord, who does these things'—
> > things known from long ago." (Acts 15:12-18; quotation from Amos 9:11-12)

We should not miss the tremendous significance of this judgment. At a council of the church, convened specifically to resolve this issue, the considered apostolic interpretation of events was that the inclusion of the Gentiles into the new messianic community was an eschatological act of God. And the important point is this. James insists that this turn of events not only fulfilled prophecy concerning *the nations* but also demonstrated that the prophesied *restoration of Israel and its Davidic kingdom* was being fulfilled. If God was gathering the nations, then Israel too was being restored.

Now, Paul was at that council. Doubtless he agreed with its theological interpretation. But he was faced with reality on the ground in his missionary work. And that reality, which broke his heart, was that while some Jews did accept the message of Jesus the Messiah, most did not. He met with rejection and resistance at every turn, even though he deliberately went to Jewish synagogues first in all his travels. How could this be squared with the idea that Israel was restored? Did it not rather show that God had simply abandoned Israel, forgotten his promises and turned instead to the

Gentiles? Such an alternative possibility was faced by Paul in Romans 9–11 and decisively rejected. God had *not* been unfaithful to his promises to Israel. Quite the contrary. The inclusion of the Gentiles was God's paradoxical fulfillment of those promises.

Unfortunately many modern Christians find Romans 9–11 difficult and obscure and treat that section as a mere parenthesis or afterthought. Romans 1–8 seems to say all we think we need to know about the riches of the gospel. But in fact these later chapters are critical in understanding Paul's whole theology of history and mission.

In Romans 1–8 Paul demonstrates that our salvation depends entirely on God and not ourselves. Specifically, it depends on God's grace and God's promise, as the Hebrew Scriptures so clearly proved.

But then the question arises—How can we trust God's promise to us (Gentiles) if God has failed to fulfill his promise to Israel? If it were true, as appearances suggested, that God had just abandoned Israel in spite of all his covenants and promises, then why on earth should the Gentiles have any confidence in the promises of such a God? Unless Paul can show that God had *not* failed Israel, all his talk about salvation for the Gentiles would be hollow and baseless.

So Paul sets out to prove two affirmations: that God's promise had *not* failed (Rom 9:6) and that God had *not* rejected Israel (Rom 11:1-2). He does so by pointing out that even in the Old Testament not all ethnic Israelites truly responded to God (Rom 9:6). The prophets spoke of a faithful remnant through whom and to whom God would fulfill his promises. That remnant, to which Paul himself belonged, now included both Gentiles and Jews who believed in the Messiah Jesus and received God's righteousness by faith. Gentile believers, therefore, were not some new people to whom God had transferred his favors. The Gentiles had not *replaced* the Jews. Rather they were like wild olive shoots that had been grafted on to the original stock. They had in fact become part of Israel. And that grafting in of the Gentile nations was nothing less than the original purpose of God in calling Israel in the first place. It was by *that* means, in *that* way, that "all Israel will be saved" (Rom 11:26). What had happened was *not* the replacement of Jews by Gentiles but *the expansion of Israel* to include Gentiles, people from all nations now united by faith in the Messiah Jesus.

So, Paul argued, the salvation of the Gentiles, far from proving that God had rejected Israel, in fact proved the opposite. God was still in the business of saving and restoring Israel. The restoration of Israel had already taken place (in the resurrection) and yet still lay ahead in its fullness when all Israel would be saved. The mission to accomplish the ingathering of the nations fills the gap and tension between the two poles of Paul's thinking.

All this was Paul's mature reflection. But it is evident that even in the earliest days of his missionary work he had a rationale for his strategy of going first to the Jews and then to the Gentiles. And it was based explicitly on the Servant pattern, which shaped the ministry of Jesus. In Pisidian Antioch, Paul and Barnabas were invited to bring a message to the Jewish synagogue after the reading of the Law and the Prophets. After briefly reviewing the biblical story, Paul affirms his fundamental conviction that the resurrection of Christ was God's means of achieving the restoration of Israel. "We tell you the good news: what God promised our ancestors he has fulfilled for us, their children, by raising up Jesus" (Acts 13:32-33).

Many Jews believed on that occasion. But when opposition was aroused the following week, Paul solemnly redirected his mission to the Gentiles, using a very significant biblical text as his warrant for doing so.

> Then Paul and Barnabas answered them boldly: "We had to speak the word of God to you first. Since you reject it and do not consider yourselves worthy of eternal life, we now turn to the Gentiles. For *this is what the Lord has commanded us*:
>
> 'I have made you a light for the Gentiles,
>   that you may bring salvation to the ends of the earth.'"
>   (Acts 13:46-47, my italics)

This is a direct quotation from Isaiah 49:6, where it was the word of God to the Servant in response to his struggles and depression in Isaiah 49:4. We have already seen how deeply the pattern of the Servant influenced Jesus. Here we see that Paul also found in it the pattern of his own mission. He takes words originally addressed to the Servant of the Lord and affirms that they were God's command to himself and his missionary team. The twofold mission of the single Servant in the prophetic vision has actually been divided between two persons in its historical outworking—Jesus, the restorer of Israel, and Paul, the apostle to the nations.

Paul has sometimes been accused of distorting the simple teachings of Jesus. It seems to me, on the contrary, that there is a fundamental oneness of understanding between them at this point, which derives from the profound reflection on their Hebrew Scriptures that both of them engaged in. Both Jesus and Paul saw the prime importance of God's people Israel. Both saw God's purpose for Israel being fulfilled in and through the Messiah. Both saw the mission of the Servant as the hinge between God's promise to Israel and God's promise through Israel for the nations. Jesus wept over Jerusalem. Paul sorrowed and agonized over the hardness of heart of his own people. Jesus envisaged a great ingathering of the nations to the Lord's banquet. Paul gave his life to distributing the invitations for the banquet.

It is perhaps to Luke that we owe the observation of such a degree of agreement between Paul and Jesus. After all, he had the unique opportunity of living with the one for much of his mission to the nations and of researching the other in his mission to Israel. Luke has provided us with more of the New Testament than any other single writer in it. So in some ways we owe the very shape of the New Testament to him, not just externally, in the ordering of the books, with Acts standing between the Gospels and the Epistles, but also theologically.

For Luke begins his Gospel with the most extended emphasis on the fulfillment of all Israel's hopes for redemption and restoration. The songs and prayers and Scriptures that are festooned around the births of John the Baptist and Jesus in Luke 1–2 are saturated with the motif of fulfillment of Old Testament prophecies about Israel: John's mission is to bring Israel back to God (Lk 1:16-17); Jesus would possess the throne of David forever (Lk 1:32); God has been faithful to Israel as against the powerful of the earth (Lk 1:52-55); their salvation is now being accomplished (Lk 1:68-79); the arrival of Jesus fulfills the hope of Israel and the nations (Lk 2:29-32); and thus arouses thanksgiving among those "who were looking for the redemption of Jerusalem" (Lk 2:36-38).

Luke then ends his Gospel and begins Acts with the note of fulfillment overflowing into mission to the nations (Lk 24:44-47; Acts 1:1-8). Finally, he concludes his whole work with Paul in Rome, still hard at work summarizing for Jewish visitors his whole ministry as having been "because of the hope of Israel" and proving from the Scriptures that that hope had been fulfilled by the coming of the kingdom of God in the person of Jesus the

Messiah. But at the same time we find him more confident than ever, in view of where he was, that "God's salvation has been sent to the Gentiles" (Acts 28:23-28).

From the temple in Jerusalem to a guesthouse in Rome—that is the span of Luke's great story. From the heart of Israel to the hub of the nations—that is the dynamic thrust of the New Testament geographically, historically and theologically. It was a story shaped by the mission of God himself as Jesus and his apostles discerned it in their Hebrew Scriptures.

OUR MISSION IN THE LIGHT OF CHRIST'S

What, then, does all this say to us? It is, I hope, illuminating to reach a deeper understanding of how Jesus understood his own identity and mission through his reflection on his Scriptures, as we have strolled or stumbled our way through the last two chapters. We have dug over a lot of the soil in which the roots of his consciousness spread and drew their nourishment. And we have finished up seeing how influential his Servant identity was on the perception and shape of the mission of the early Christian church. But I want to conclude this chapter with four points where these biblical insights must have an impact on our view of how we as modern Christians must live out our own mission.

The unity and continuity of mission. First of all, we should by now be impressed with the continuity and integration of the mission of God's people from ancient Israel right through to our own day. We saw the link between the whole people of Israel as the servant of God and the individual Servant figure. And we saw how Jesus the Messiah saw himself in relation to both— embodying Israel and yet also having a ministry to Israel. And then we saw how Paul identifies the mission of the Servant with the mission of the church in reaching out to bring the gospel to the nations, just as the Servant was commissioned to bring salvation to the ends of the earth. The continuity of mission and witness to the nations thus runs through Israel, the Servant, Jesus and the church—connecting Old and New Testaments on a single trajectory.

So we ought to realize, then, that missional commitment is not some kind of optional extra for the extra-enthusiastic. Nor was it just a new idea, hastily invented by Jesus on the Mount of Ascension to give his disciples something to do with the rest of their lives after he left. Still less was it a merely modern movement of the church that coincided with colonial expansionism. *Mission lies at the very heart of all God's historical action in the Bible.* The whole Bible bears witness to the mission of God to the fallen, suffering, sinful human race, and indeed ultimately to his whole creation as well. That is why God called Abraham, sent Jesus and commissioned his apostles. For there is one servant people, one Servant King and one servant mission.

"To the Jew first." Second, we must take seriously the order of the servant mission as expressed both in Jesus' ministry and in Paul's repeated aphorism, "To the Jew first." Paul insisted that even though many Jews rejected Jesus as their Messiah, God had not rejected Israel. Israel would be saved. They would be saved along with Gentiles, both through Jesus Christ. And since the Christ had come through Israel and been sent to Israel, he must be offered first to Jews. So Paul's expression "To the Jew first" was not only a matter of missionary strategy that he followed as he moved from city to city; it was also a theological conviction.

The church was not a new Gentile phenomenon, even if it looked like that as its membership became increasingly Gentile. The community of Jesus followers was a new *humanity*, composed of both believing Jews and Gentiles. But it was also organically and spiritually continuous with the original people of God, as Paul's olive tree picture in Romans 11 shows. Israel had been redefined and extended, but the Jewish roots and trunk were not replaced or uprooted just because unbelieving branches had been lopped off.

Evangelism among Jews is a matter of considerable controversy today. There are powerful voices arguing that it is historically offensive because of the atrocities of Christians against Jews, culturally inappropriate and theologically mistaken.

One particular theological viewpoint rejects the need for evangelism among Jews. Jews, it is said, are already in covenant relationship with God and have no need of "conversion" to Christianity. Jesus, as the founder of what is now predominantly Gentile Christianity, is the Christian Savior. He is simply unneeded by Jews. This is the view of the so-called two covenant theory. The new covenant through Jesus is for Gentile Christians. Jews are saved through their own original covenant. Evangelism in the name of Jesus is therefore rejected.

There are three reasons why I cannot accept this view and regard it as fundamentally unbiblical.

First, it ignores not only the Jewishness of Jesus but also his whole conscious identity and mission that we have been exploring all through this book. Jesus came within Israel, to Israel and for Israel. To say that Jews don't need Jesus is to undermine everything Jesus believed about himself and about God's purpose in sending him to his people. It is ultimately to betray the gospel itself by excluding from it the very people among whom it was birthed and to whom it was announced.

Second, it fails altogether to see the integral link between Jesus' mission to Israel and God's purpose of extending salvation to the Gentiles. This, we have seen, is the essence of the Servant identity of Jesus. This was not only the historical interpretation of the earliest church but also is fully scriptural, that is, in accordance with the Hebrew Bible. Jesus is the Savior of the world *because* he is the Messiah of Israel. He cannot be one and not the other. If he is not the Messiah for the Jews, then he cannot be the Savior of the Gentiles. So if evangelism among Jews (in the sense of graciously calling them to see in Jesus the Messiah who fulfills their historic, scriptural faith) is disallowed, it cuts the nerve of all other evangelism. The gospel has to be good news for the Jews if it is to be good news for anyone else. And if it *is* good news for them, then to fail to share it with them is the worst form of anti-Semitism.

Third, the "two covenant theory" utterly subverts Paul's claim that the very heart of the gospel was that in it God had created *one* new people. It simply cannot be squared with Ephesians 2–3. Or even Romans 9–11. For Jesus was not just the Messiah of Israel. He was also the new Adam. In him God's purpose for humanity as a whole was achieved, precisely *not* through two separate covenant arrangements but by a single new people in Christ. "His purpose was to create in himself one new humanity out of the two, [Jew and Gentile], thus making peace, and in one body to reconcile both of them to God through the cross, by which he put to death their hostility" (Eph 2:15-16).

This mystery is that through the gospel the Gentiles are heirs *together* with Israel, members *together* of *one* body and sharers *together* in the promise in the Messiah Jesus (Eph 3:6).

Mission in servanthood. My third reflection on the depth of the influence of the Servant figure on Jesus and the church is that it ought to be the model and pattern for all Christian mission in the name of Jesus. One of the most astonishing things about Jesus is that whereas his contemporaries looked for a Messiah who would come in triumphant power, he came in humility and initial obscurity and devoted his life to compassionate service to those whom society scorned, oppressed, excluded or overlooked. And having made the point that he himself had not come to be served but to serve, he modeled it unforgettably in washing the disciples' feet *and then explicitly setting that as the example of how we should act.*

The spirit of servanthood, written into the prophetic vision of the Servant, lived out in the ministry of Jesus, should be the motive and the method of all Christian mission. First of all, of course, it ought to be characteristic of relationships *within* the church. Paul never strayed far from its influence. After a lengthy exhortation to Gentile and Jewish Christians at Rome to be tolerant of each other's conscientious scruples, he points to the example of Christ—as the Servant! "Accept one another, then, just as Christ accepted you, in order to bring praise to God. For I tell you that Christ has become a servant of the Jews on behalf of God's truth, so that the promises made to the patriarchs might be confirmed and, moreover, that the Gentiles might glorify God for his mercy" (Rom 15:7-9). For Paul the gospel is as ethical as it is missional!

With such an example before us in both Old and New Testaments, and with the explicit command of Jesus, it is one of the great tragedies of history that the Christian church has so often fallen back into the triumphalistic domination patterns of the world and then baptized them and called them "mission." We have imagined that the best way to save the world is to rule the world, with the tragically ironic result that Christian mission in the name of the Servant has been indelibly associated in the minds of many with power—military, cultural, economic and political. It is an image that is hard to live down. But the historical abuse of mission is no reason to abandon it altogether. For the mandate of the Servant King still stands. He still calls for servants, for those who will serve him by serving the world.

Mission in its wholeness. My fourth and final point, which draws this chapter to its conclusion and also prepares the way for the next chapter, takes us back once more to those Servant Songs in the book of Isaiah. The "career" of the Servant is described with a tantalizing mixture of explicit detail and reserve. The climax, of course, comes with his violent suffering and death and triumphant vindication in Isaiah 53.

But it is in Isaiah 42 that we find the greatest detail regarding the actual purpose, character and goal of the Servant's mission. The strongest emphasis in the opening verses is on his mission of *bringing justice to the nations*. In fact the nations are described as waiting for him to bring the law (*Torah*) and justice (*mishpat*) of God to them. In other words, the Servant has the task of making real to the rest of humanity the whole package of ethical values and social priorities that God had entrusted to Israel. Being a "light to the nations" includes this moral teaching dimension as well as the extending of the saving light of the covenant. The same picture, though with a different movement (the nations come to Zion, rather than the Servant going to the nations) is found in Isaiah 2:2-5. As the song in Isaiah 42:1-9 continues, this fundamental mission of justice is augmented by *compassion, enlightenment and liberation*. Justice and gentleness. Healing and wholeness. The picture is very rich indeed.

Now, if we accept the unity and continuity of the servant mission—from Israel, through the prophetic Servant, in the life and death of Jesus and then on to the mission of the church—then we have to see these as important dimensions of our mission as a whole. Christian mission, if it is true to the whole biblical pattern, cannot be confined to verbal proclamation alone. The mission of the Servant included justice, compassion, enlightenment and liberation. Jesus included these objectives in his self-definition in Luke 4:18-21.

Yet it is clear that in his own lifetime he did not complete the task entrusted to the Servant of bringing the law and justice of God to the nations. Is it not then surely the case that these are aspects of the mission that he has entrusted to his servant church—those who, being "in Christ," are commanded to carry forward "all that he began to do and to teach"? Essential to the Great Commission are Jesus' words, "teaching them to *obey* all that I have commanded you." He did not merely say "teach them all that I have taught you," as if discipleship were purely cerebral—all the stuff we need to teach and learn about the Christian faith. It is a matter of *obeying* what Christ *commanded* (which included plenty about mercy, compassion, justice, love, practical service, care for the needy, forgiveness, etc.), and then discipling others into the same pattern of practical obedience.

But what did Jesus himself understand by these words? What were the moral values and priorities of Jesus? That is what we shall turn to in the next chapter. What we have seen in this one is that the Old Testament set forth a mission—a mission Jesus accepted as the driving aim of his own life and then entrusted to his followers.

CHAPTER 4 QUESTIONS AND EXERCISES

1. Think about the ministries of John the Baptist and Jesus. List points of similarity and contrast. In what ways did Old Testament expectations influence their preaching and teaching?

2. In the light of the Old Testament, how would you answer the question, What was Jesus aiming to do in his life and ministry?

3. How would you explain to someone what it means to call Jesus "Messiah," "Son of Man" and "Servant of the LORD?" For each of these three concepts, which Old Testament and New Testament texts would you connect? What are the practical implications for each of these titles for us as we follow Jesus? Particularly, when we think about the mission of Jesus, what does it mean for our mission today?

4. Study Luke's account of Paul in the synagogue in Pisidian Antioch in Acts 13:13-52. Pay particular attention to Paul's sermon in Acts 13:16-41. What would you say is its main point? How would you describe Paul's understanding of Jesus in the light of the Old Testament Scriptures?

JESUS *and* HIS
OLD TESTAMENT VALUES

Matthew 3 ends with Jesus, still dripping from his baptism in the Jordan, basking under an open heaven in the loving approval of his Father, sealed by the visible sign of the Holy Spirit.

Matthew 4 is an abrupt contrast. The chapter divisions in our Bible were not originally part of Matthew's writing, so he just went straight on from the words in Matthew 3:17, "This is my Son, whom I love; with him I am well pleased," to say, "Then Jesus was led by the Spirit into the wilderness to be tempted by the devil. After fasting for forty days and forty nights, he was hungry. The tempter came to him and said, 'If you are the Son of God, tell these stones to become bread'" (Mt 4:1-3).

JESUS TESTED IN THE WILDERNESS

"If you are the Son of God . . ." The very words show the force of the struggle Jesus went through in the wilderness. Was he really sure who he was? Shouldn't he just prove it to himself before testing it out on others? And if he really was the Son of God, then the mission and responsibility that now lay on his shoulders were immense. Could he face up to the implications?

What did it mean to be the Son of God? Jesus had, in a sense, taken on the *identity* of Israel as the Davidic messianic king. And he had, in another sense, taken on the *mission* of Israel as the Servant of God. And therefore he had also taken on the *responsibility* of Israel—the obligations and commitment of covenant loyalty to God himself. *Jesus* must live as God had wanted *Israel* to live. He must obey where it had rebelled. He must succeed where it had failed. His identity was not to be just a matter of labels or titles or honors. It was to be lived out in the total orientation of his life toward God through his values, priorities, convictions, teaching, actions and relationships. It is those values and teachings that we want to explore in this chapter.

Where did he turn for the resources to face such a challenge? Where else but to his Bible? Jesus met and deflected each of Satan's temptations with a word of Scripture. However, this was far from any superficial "rent-a-reference" technique. The intense struggles with the meaning of his personal identity and future mission could not be evaded with a casual quote. It is clear that Jesus was meditating deeply on his Bible. In fact, the struggle he was enduring in the wilderness was partly created, partly solved, by what he found there. In this chapter we shall be looking at how Jesus was molded and formed in his values and in the priorities and principles of his life and teaching by the Hebrew Scriptures. We shall look particularly at how the teaching of Jesus reflected the Old Testament Law, the Prophets and the Psalms. Let's begin, however, with the Scriptures Jesus quoted in reply to the devil during his struggle in the wilderness.

One particular section of the Old Testament seems to have been the focus of Jesus' attention during those forty days of solitude. All three of his replies to the devil are drawn from two chapters in the first part of Deuteronomy (Deut 8:3; 6:13, 16). What special significance did Jesus find there?

The book of Deuteronomy presents itself to us as four great speeches of Moses to the Israelites. They had reached the eastern side of the River Jordan after the forty years of wandering in the wilderness, immediately before they would cross over the Jordan to conquer the land of Canaan. It was a critical moment for them—the end of one period and the beginning of the next.

For Jesus, too, the obscure safety of life as a village carpenter had come to an end. He had crossed his Jordan, leaving the wilderness of being unknown and setting out on a public and costly mission. The same crowds with whom he had mingled anonymously around John the Baptist would soon be surging around Jesus, hungry for his bread and then for his blood. The Israelites had heard from Moses a rallying call to uncompromising loyalty to God. Forty years of testing in the wilderness were brought to an end with a rousing word of encouragement to face the challenge ahead. No wonder Jesus turned to those words of Moses as he wrestled with the cost of obedience. Imagine him, the Son of God, hungry and exhausted after forty days of struggle in the desert, reading or recalling these words:

> Remember how the LORD your God led you all the way in the wilderness these forty years, to humble and test you in order to know what was in your heart, whether or not you would keep his commands. He humbled you, causing you to hunger and then feeding you with manna, which neither you nor your ancestors had known, to teach you that man does not live on bread alone but on every word that comes from the mouth of the LORD. Your clothes did not wear out and your feet did not swell during these forty years. Know then in your heart that as a man disciplines his son, so the LORD your God disciplines you. (Deut 8:2-5)

"This is my beloved Son . . . "
"As a son, the LORD your God disciplines you . . . "
"*If you are the Son of God* . . . ," then why be hungry?
" . . . feeding you with manna . . . "
If God fed Israel, why not ask him to feed you . . . *if* you're his Son?

Was this the whirling confusion of thought in the mind of Jesus within which he recognized the testing, seductive voice of the enemy who would dog his steps all the way to Gethsemane?

But the thrust of the ancient word of Scripture cleared away the fog. *Why* had God let Israel be hungry and then fed them? To teach the people dependence, not on bread but on God himself and on God's promise. God gave Israel food to show it there was something more important than food— namely, faith in God's word. Later on, Jesus would do the same for the crowds, though even his disciples would be slow to grasp the point (Jn 6). But for the present, he had the word that came from the mouth of his Father; bread could wait.

The Father God can be trusted to know the needs of his people and meet them. Jesus found this truth in his Scriptures, proved it in the testing of his own experience and was very soon teaching it to his followers. A life oriented toward God is free from anxiety and faithless worry, not because food and clothes don't matter, but because (a) there are things that matter more and (b) God knows we need them. The radical earthiness of Jesus' teaching in Matthew 6:25-34 shifts the whole life perspective of the children of God. It comes as a shaft of light out of Deuteronomy, refracted through the personal testimony of Jesus himself.

The devil learns fast. He is not very original, but he picks up the game. If Scripture is to be quoted, he can join in. And if the identity and mission of Christ is the issue, he can even show his hermeneutical skills by applying Scripture in a Christ-centered way. If Jesus believes he is called to a mission to Israel (and *if*, of course, he is the Son of God), then let him try the miracle option. Jump from the temple, the place where God is and the crowds are. Better even than the charity option of bread for the masses, a spectacular demonstration of his superpowers and of God's special protection of his person from harm would surely convince the crowds of his credentials. You need a verse? Try Psalm 91:11-12. Soft landings guaranteed.

Again, Jesus replies with a Scripture, which goes to the heart of proper response to God and exposes the superficiality of Satan's suggestions. The promise of God's protection in Psalm 91 was for the humble and obedient worshiper, not for the stuntman. The right attitude to God was to trust in that protection when it would be needed, not to test it out beforehand, to see whether God really meant it. There are circumstances when a desire for something spectacular or for a miracle is a sign of unbelief, not faith, and Jesus spotted such a trap here. So he parries Satan's misapplication of a Scripture with a direct command given by Moses in the light of Israel's complaints: "Do not put the LORD your God to the test" (Deut 6:16). And in any case, as we saw so clearly in the last chapter, Jesus saw that the path ahead of him led through rejection, suffering, physical crushing and finally death. He held no certificate of immunity from the laws of God or the laws of gravity. And he certainly would not buy Satan's spurious promise, even signed with a psalm.

Finally (for the moment), Satan tries the political option. No record of a prooftext this time, but maybe he was using the thought implanted from the Father's voice with its echo of Psalm 2:7. "You are my Son; today I have become your father."

And how does the Psalm go on?

> Ask me,
>   and I will make the nations your inheritance,
>   the ends of the earth your possession. (Ps 2:8)

"Ask of *whom*, Jesus?" whispered Satan. "If the world is your mission, why take the slow road, the hard road, the Servant's road, the Father's road? There is a much quicker route to the messianic kingdom, surely, and the crowds back there will help you take it—make you take it, even. Why disappoint them and destroy yourself? Do as I say and you will have the world at your feet."

This time Jesus' reply went right to the roots of the faith of Israel: "Fear the LORD your God, serve him only." That text (Deut 6:13-14) goes on, "Do not follow other gods, the gods of the peoples around you; for the LORD your God, who is among you, is a jealous God." Popularity is no proof of deity. Since there is only one living God, he is to be loved and obeyed exclusively, no matter how many or how attractive are the apparent alternatives. Jesus' Jewish "creed" would have been echoing in his heart, since it comes just a few verses before the one he used to dismiss Satan. "Hear, O Israel: The LORD our God, the LORD is one. Love the LORD your God with all your heart and with all your soul and with all your strength" (Deut 6:4-5).

Monotheism is a fighting faith. One Lord, one love, one loyalty. That was supposed to have been the defining characteristic of God's people, Israel. But for centuries the virus of endemic human idolatry had lain in its bloodstream and erupted with a regularity that astonished prophets and historians. Jesus took up the fight again, with an uncompromising affirmation of the faith of Moses as his own. When he was tested in the wilderness like Israel (God's firstborn son, Ex 4:22), Jesus the Son of God committed his human life to the full personal and moral consequences of Israel's monotheistic faith and worship. In his humanity, Jesus would bow down to nobody and nothing else.

So then, in the temptation narrative we see Jesus using his Hebrew Scriptures to define and affirm the whole orientation of his life toward God. He was meditating on those chapters of Deuteronomy, which preach the fundamental attitudes and commitments that God expects from his people as their side of the covenant relationship (Deut 4–11). These chapters of basic orientation come *before* the details of the laws themselves. God was concerned not about mere conformity to laws but about the whole shape of a person and society, the inner drives of the heart, the direction of the walk of life. And in wrestling with the future direction of his own calling, Jesus accepts that the values, priorities and convictions of his life on earth must be shaped by the words of Moses to Israel, words in which he heard the voice of his Father God as surely as he did when he stepped out of the Jordan.

So let us think about those chapters that meant so much to Jesus.

The basic orientation of life before God: Deuteronomy 4–11. It would be well worth taking a pause to read Deuteronomy 4–11. As you do, try to imagine its impact on Jesus as he meditated on it alone in the wilderness. Notice some of the key themes that occur again and again as Moses preaches from the heart to the heart. The repeated command is to obey God's laws wholeheartedly, since that is the way to life and blessing for a people who have already experienced God's redemption. Grace comes first, and obedience is the right response.

Notice the stress on the uniqueness of Israel's historical experience, and how it was designed to impress on it the uniqueness of its God, Yahweh, and so lead it to healthy living before him (Deut 4:32-40). Notice the scale of values and priorities embedded in the Ten Commandments (Deut 5:1-22), a sense of what matters most that influenced the teaching of Jesus greatly. We shall look at this later.

There are warnings about how dangerous it would be when the people would move from the years of manna in the wilderness to the plentiful bounty of the land. Wealth can lead people to forget God even while they are enjoying the blessings of God, especially material abundance (Deut 6:10-12; 8:6-18). One of the sharpest edges of the teaching of Jesus was precisely on the dangers of wealth. The parable of the rich fool immortalizes the challenging teaching of Deuteronomy 8:17-18. But then these warnings about the danger of wealth are balanced with warnings about the danger of forgetting or doubting God in times of need and hardship (Deut 6:16; 8:1-5), which likewise find an echo in Jesus' teaching about positive faith in God's providence.

Flattery is the mark of a false prophet. Neither Moses nor Jesus had any time for it. On the contrary, both made a point of popping the balloons of arrogance that Israel blew up for itself when they boasted about how God had chosen it and redeemed it. Three times in three chapters Moses disillusioned Israel of any idea that it could claim some credit for its remarkable history. It was not because of *numerical* superiority, as if it were some great nation. Far from it. "The LORD did not set his affection on you and choose you because you were more numerous than other peoples, for you were the fewest of all peoples. But it was because the LORD loved you and kept the oath he swore to your ancestors that he brought you out with a mighty hand and redeemed you" (Deut 7:7-8).

It was not because of *economic* superiority, as if Israel could boast of its own productive abilities. Any such ability came from God in the first place. "You may say to yourself, 'My power and the strength of my hands have produced this wealth for me.' But remember the LORD your God, for it is he who gives you the ability to produce wealth" (Deut 8:17-18).

And it was not because of any *moral* superiority, as if Israel could boast of its own righteousness over against the wickedness of their enemies. "Do not say to yourself, 'The LORD has brought me here to take possession of this land because of my righteousness.' No, it is on account of the wickedness of these nations that the LORD is going to drive them out before you. It is not because of your righteousness or your integrity . . . for you are a stiff-necked people" (Deut 9:4-6).

The fact was that if any nation had deserved to be destroyed it was Israel, and on at least two occasions only the intercession of Moses had stood between it and such a fate (Deut 9:7-29). No, the historical report card of Israel was nothing to take home with pride. The devastating use that Jesus made of Israel's history in some of his parables (e.g., the tenants of the vineyard), along with the threat of impending destruction, was one of the most controversial elements in his teaching, which led directly to the official plot on his life.

Many of the parables of Jesus are about the sharpness of choice and decision. Wheat or weeds, sheep or goats, wise or foolish, rock or sand, God or money. They are full of contrasts between one kind of behavior or attitude and another. Jesus leaves no middle ground for the apathetic. You could not just shrug your shoulders or "sit on the fence," as the English proverb puts it. You either followed him or you walked away. The same kind of moral and spiritual stark choices characterize Deuteronomy. You either love God or you hate him (Deut 7:9-10). You prove any profession of love in practical obedience. Any other way of life is to hate him. Indifference is practical hatred. And so too the consequences of our choices are simple: blessing or curse. Moses lays it out before the people with literally monumental clarity. He identifies whole mountains with one or the other (Deut

11:26-32; 27:1-26)! The closing chapters of Deuteronomy portray this choice with evangelistic zeal:

> See, I set before you today life and prosperity, death and destruction. For I command you today to love the LORD your God, to walk in obedience to him, and to keep his commands, decrees and laws; then you will live. . . .
>
> This day I call the heavens and the earth as witnesses against you that I have set before you life and death, blessings and curses. Now choose life, so that you and your children may live and that you may love the LORD your God, listen to his voice, and hold fast to him. For the LORD is your life. (Deut 30:15-16, 19-20)

Simple obedience. There is a basic simplicity about the moral teaching of Jesus that reflects the same kind of simplicity that we find in the Old Testament. I do not mean, of course, that obedience is *easy*. There is a commitment, a cost, a challenge. There is precisely the struggle against tempting alternatives that Jesus himself faced and recognized as idolatrous and satanic. What I *do* mean is that obedience ought not to be *complicated*, either by the competing claims of other gods (the moral maze of polytheism) or by the confusing rules of human experts (the moral bondage of legalism). When you read the Gospels you can see that the common people heard Jesus gladly and responded to his invitation to enter the kingdom of God not because he made things *easy* (quite the opposite) but because he made them *simple*.

Matthew found that he could summarize the preaching of Jesus in four terse phrases: "The time is fulfilled," "the kingdom of God is at hand," "repent" and "believe the good news." Each of them, of course, like the label on a filing cabinet drawer, points to a whole array of content inside. But there is a memorable simplicity. Jesus himself could summarize the whole law in two fundamental commandments—to love God and to love one's neighbor. His so-called Golden Rule—"Do to others as you would have them do to you"—was not a revolutionary bright idea of his own. He clearly says that it sums up the Law and the Prophets. It expresses the simple essence of the Old Testament.

Jesus treated his Scriptures not as a maze in which every alley has to be explored whether it leads anywhere or not, but as a map on which every feature is there to help you plan a journey with a clear sense of direction and a single destination.

It is important that we hold on to that essential simplicity, because one of the complaints many folk have about the Old Testament law is that it appears so complicated and detailed that any serious attention to it seems bound to land you in legalism. However, once you get your *orientation* right, as Jesus did through his testing in the wilderness and his meditation on the challenge of Deuteronomy, it is possible to have a clarity and simplicity in the fundamental values and priorities of the law.

That is what we find in the teaching of Jesus. It was not just a *repetition* of all the laws, like a shopping list. Nor was it a *new* law that replaced the original. Rather, he restored the true perspective and essential *point* of the law. He brought back the urgent appeal of Moses for a single-minded, uncomplicated loyalty to God himself. "And now, Israel, what does the LORD your God ask of you but to fear the LORD your God, to walk in obedience to him, to love him, to serve the LORD your God with all your heart and with all your soul, and to observe the LORD's commands and decrees that I am giving you today for your own good?" (Deut 10:12-13).

So let us turn to see some of the values in the Old Testament law that are then reflected in the teaching of Jesus.

JESUS AND THE LAW

Jesus said very emphatically that he had not come to abolish the law but to fulfill it (Mt 5:17-20). So we shall survey some of the major features of the law and see how they are reflected in the values and teaching of Jesus.

The law as response to grace. The very first thing we must do in looking for an understanding of the law in the Old Testament is to observe where it comes from. As we saw in chapter one, it comes in the context of a story. Before we face the Ten Commandments in Exodus 20, we have had a book and a half of narrative. And we have also seen in chapter one how it is a story of God's relationship with his people, through the family of Abraham and then with the nation in Egypt. It is a story of constant blessing, protection, promise and fulfillment, reaching its climax in the great act of liberation— the exodus. It is the story, in other words, of God's grace in action.

Before God gave Israel his law, he gave them himself as their redeemer. So when he finally gets them to the foot of Mount Sinai, he opens the whole proceedings of law and covenant with the words, "You yourselves have seen *what I did to Egypt*, and how I carried you on eagles' wings and

brought you to myself. Now if you obey me fully and keep my covenant . . . "
(Ex 19:4-5, my italics).

That was true. Only three months before, the people had been making
bricks as slaves in Egypt. Now they were free. The long trudge through the
wilderness might have raised some objections over the idea that they had
been carried on "eagles' wings," but they were certainly out of Egypt, liberated from "the house of bondage." And it was God who had taken the
initiative in getting them out. In God's grace and in faithfulness to his
covenant promise, he had acted first and redeemed them. He had not sent
Moses with the Ten Commandments under his cloak to tell Israel that if it
would keep the law, God would save it. Precisely the other way around. He
saved it and then asked it to keep his law in response.

So the law was given to Israel in the context of a redemptive relationship
that had already been established by God's grace. The law was never intended as a means of *achieving* salvation but rather as guidance for *responding*
to salvation by living in a way that pleased the God who had saved you.
That is why the Ten Commandments begin with a statement, not a
command. "I am the LORD your God, who brought you out of Egypt, out of
the land of slavery" (Ex 20:2).

That is why, when an Israelite son asked his father what the law *meant*,
the answer was a story—the old, old story of God's saving love and deliverance. The very meaning of the law was to be found in the gospel.

> In the future, when your son asks you, "What is the meaning of the stipula-
> tions, decrees and laws the LORD our God has commanded you?" tell him:
> "We were slaves of Pharaoh in Egypt, but the LORD brought us out of Egypt
> with a mighty hand. . . . He brought us out from there to bring us in and give
> us the land he promised on oath to our ancestors. The LORD commanded us
> to obey all these decrees and to fear the LORD our God, so that we might
> always prosper and be kept alive, as is the case today. And if we are careful
> to obey all this law before the LORD our God, as he has commanded us, that
> will be our righteousness." (Deut 6:20-25)

"*Our* righteousness," indeed—but only in response to God's righteousness.
God's righteousness was demonstrated in the exodus. Israel's righteousness
was their "right" response. Obedience flows from grace; it does not buy it.
Obedience is the fruit and proof and sustenance of a relationship with the
God you already know.

The same priority of relationship with God over the details of behavior is found in the teaching of Jesus. When Matthew introduces us to Jesus as teacher in his great Sermon on the Mount in Matthew 5–7, he shows how before Jesus got down to detailed questions about actual behavior, he sketched a portrait of the happiness that comes from a character oriented to God. The beatitudes (Mt 5:3-12) are not laws; they are *descriptions* of a quality of life lived in relation to God, life within the kingdom of God, life as a disciple of Jesus himself. The beatitudes deal with a person's attitudes, stance, commitments, relationships, priorities and loyalties. Blessedness flows from having all these dimensions of our lives centered on God. The good deeds that will then *follow* will result in praise, not for oneself but for God the Father from whom such "light" comes (Mt 5:16).

Jesus' urgent announcement of the arrival of the kingdom of God (which we shall look at later) and his call to people to enter it also point to this priority of getting one's life into a right relationship with God in order to be able to please him. His portrayals of God as the generous father, the waiting and forgiving father, the generous vineyard owner, the creditor who releases an enormous debt, all speak of the priority of grace. He taught that obedience flows from love. That was true for himself (Jn 14:31) and for his followers (Jn 14:15; 15:9-17). And he taught, in our case, that such love flows from the grace of being forgiven (Lk 7:36-50). With characteristic simplicity he stated the fundamental priority: "Seek first his kingdom and his righteousness, and all these things will be given to you as well" (Mt 6:33).

Jesus' attitude to the law, then, was explicitly not to reject it but to show that keeping the law was not the only thing that mattered; the real priority was knowing God himself. There is much in the life and teaching of Jesus that reflects the ethos of Psalm 119. The writer of that psalm rejoices in the law, certainly, but rejoices more in the richness of relationship with God and sees that relationship expressed and enjoyed through diligent obedience to God's word. In fact, the psalmist swings back and forth between his wonder at the promise, the grace, the goodness, love and salvation of God and his determination to live according to God's law. He delights in the law because it enables him to please the God he loves. Obedience to God flows from gratitude for grace—in both Old and New Testaments.

> *You* are my portion, LORD;
> > I have promised to obey *your words.*
> I have sought *your face* with all my heart;
> > be gracious to me according to *your promise.*
> I have considered my ways
> > and have turned my steps to *your statutes.*
> I will hasten and not delay
> > to obey *your commands.* . . .
> The earth is filled with *your love,* LORD
> > teach me *your decrees.* (Ps 119:57-60, 64, my italics)

Motivations for obedience. A distinctive feature of Old Testament law is the common "motive clause." These are phrases that are added to particular laws giving reasons or motives why people should keep those laws. Such motive clauses are particularly common in Deuteronomy, because that book has a preaching style in which encouragement and motivation are natural. But they are not confined to that book and can be found in Exodus and Leviticus also. The effect of them is to show that God was not merely concerned with external or mechanical obedience to rules for their own sake but wanted to instill an ethos of intelligent and willing moral behavior in Israel.

Some of the characteristic motivations and incentives that we find in Old Testament law are also reflected in the teachings of Jesus, showing how authentically he recaptured the ethos and point of the Torah. The following four points of motivation in Old Testament law should sound familiar to us when we remember the sayings of Jesus.

(1) Gratitude for what God has done. This follows naturally from our previous point about the law being set in the context of the story of God's redemption of his people. In the light of all that God had done for his people, how should they respond? Sheer gratitude should trigger obedience out of a desire to please the God of such faithfulness and salvation. The God who loved Israel's forefathers enough to rescue their descendants from slavery is the God who should be loved in return, with a covenant love expressed in obedience. "We love because he first loved us" is not an Old Testament text, but it echoes the heartbeat of Old Testament ethics—as does its sequel that if we love God we must love our brother (1 Jn 4:17-21).

This motive of gratitude for what God had actually done in liberating his people from oppression surfaces most often, as might be expected, when the law is dealing with how Israelites were to treat vulnerable people in their own society—the poor, the stranger, the debtor, the slave. These were the very conditions from which God had rescued Israel, so its behavior toward such people should, in gratitude, be correspondingly generous. Notice in each of the following examples how the command to compassionate and generous behavior is based on Israel's own past experience.

> Do not mistreat or oppress a foreigner, for you were foreigners in Egypt. (Ex 22:21)

> Do not oppress a foreigner; you yourselves know how it feels to be foreigners, because you were foreigners in Egypt. (Ex 23:9)

> When a foreigner resides among you in your land, do not mistreat them. The foreigner residing among you must be treated as your native-born. Love them as yourself, for you were foreigners in Egypt. I am the LORD your God . . . who brought you out of Egypt. (Lev 19:33-36)

> If any of your fellow Israelites become poor and are unable to support themselves among you, help them as you would a foreigner and stranger, so that they can continue to live among you. . . . You must not lend them money at interest or sell them food at a profit. I am the LORD your God, who brought you out of Egypt to give you the land of Canaan and to be your God. (Lev 25:35, 37-38)

> Because the Israelites are my servants, whom I brought out of Egypt, they must not be sold as slaves. (Lev 25:42)

> If anyone is poor among your fellow Israelites . . . do not be hardhearted or tightfisted toward them. Rather, be openhanded and freely lend them whatever they need. . . . When you release them [the debtor-slave after six years], do not send them away empty-handed. Supply them liberally from your flock, your threshing floor and your winepress. Give to them as the LORD your God has blessed you. Remember that you were slaves in Egypt and the LORD your God redeemed you. That is why I give you this command today. (Deut 15:7-8, 13-15)

The clearest example of this motivation in the teaching of Jesus comes in the parable of the ungrateful debtor (Mt 18:21-35). The mercy displayed by the king in forgiving an enormous debt ought to have generated a grateful response in the forgiven servant. He then ought to have shown his gratitude by forgiving the trivial debt owed to him. Mercy received should lead to mercy offered. Israel, of all people, should have known this. As can be seen from the laws above, a people whose very historical existence and survival proved the merciful grace and favor of God should know how to act toward the needy out of gratitude for what God had done for them.

The parable of Jesus ends on a sober note of warning, which also reflects the influence of the law. For the passages about generosity and behavior based on gratitude were not just cheerful recommendations—"It would be really rather nice if you could all be kind to each other." They were an integral part of a whole covenant law that was sanctioned by God's threatened judgment of disobedience. It is a feature of the Torah that *love is commanded*. In other words, while it certainly has an emotional dimension, love is not merely an emotion. Love is an act of the will, which is demonstrated in obeying God's commands. The same is true with gratitude. Of course it has an emotional dimension—the book of Psalms overflows with the emotion of thanksgiving. But the behavior that gratitude motivates is commanded. It is not just an optional preference for the more sensitive souls.

So Jesus portrays the painful destiny of the unmerciful debtor to make the point that mutual forgiveness is not a nice thing for the soft-hearted but an essential mandate of the King on those who submit to the reign of God. Their behavior to one another must prove the genuineness of their gratitude to the God of incredible, unbounded forgiveness.

There is an interesting reflection of this feature of the law in the teaching of the Wisdom literature. In the book of Proverbs there is a lot about compassionate attitudes and actions toward *the poor*. These sayings are linked to our response *to God*. In this case, it is not so much God as redeemer to whom we should prove our gratitude by generosity to others but rather God as Creator, to whom we are accountable for our treatment of any human being made in his image. Some characteristic texts include:

Whoever oppresses the poor shows contempt for their Maker,
    but whoever is kind to the needy honors God. (Prov 14:31)

Whoever mocks the poor shows contempt for their Maker. (Prov 17:5)

Whoever is kind to the poor lends to the Lord,
    and he will reward them for what they have done. (Prov 19:17)

Whoever shuts their ears to the cry of the poor
>   will also cry out and not be answered. (Prov 21:13)

The righteous care about justice for the poor,
>   but the wicked have no such concern. (Prov 29:7)

It seems that Jesus had imbibed this flavor of the Wisdom tradition in some of his teaching specifically about the poor: "Whatever you did for one of the least of these brothers and sisters of mine, you did for me" (Mt 25:31-46).

(2) Imitation of what God is like. The way God had acted on behalf of Israel was to provide not merely the motive for ethical obedience but also the model for it. The law was meant to enable Israel to be like Yahweh, its God. His character and behavior were to be its moral example.

A favorite expression in the Old Testament for how one ought to live is "walking in the way of the LORD." Israel was called to walk in God's way, as distinct from the ways of other gods, or of other nations (2 Kings 17:15), or one's own way (Is 53:6), or the way of sinners (Ps 1:1). Right at the start, God had chosen Abraham for the explicit purpose that he and his descendants should "walk in the way of the LORD by doing righteousness and justice" (Gen 18:19). The idea of imitation is strong. You observe what God characteristically does and then follow suit. As John Bode's hymn ("Oh Jesus, I Have Promised") puts it, "O let me see thy footsteps and in them plant my own."

We saw above how Moses includes among his fundamental requirements of God that Israel should "walk in obedience to him" (Deut 10:12). The literal Hebrew is: "walk in all his ways." Almost as if someone had asked him what "the ways of the LORD" are, he goes on to explain:

> The LORD your God is God of gods and Lord of lords, the great God, mighty and awesome, who shows no partiality and accepts no bribes. He defends the cause of the fatherless and the widow, and loves the foreigner residing among you, giving them food and clothing. And *you are to love those who are foreigners*, for you yourselves were foreigners in Egypt. (Deut 10:17-19, my italics)

Israel's social behavior was to be modeled on the character of God in all its richness. It must love others as God had loved it, when it was needy foreigners in a strange land or homeless wanderers in the wilderness. It must do for others what God had done for it.

This principle is expressed at its simplest at the beginning of Leviticus 19. "Be holy because I, the LORD your God, am holy" (Lev 19:2).

We might think that "holiness" in the Old Testament was only a matter of ritual practices, food laws and all the symbolic details of Israel's religion. But read the rest of Leviticus 19. It is quite clear that being holy did not mean what we might call being extra-specially religious. In fact only very few of the laws in the chapter are about religious rituals. Rather, it shows that the kind of holiness God has in mind, the kind that reflects God's own holiness, is thoroughly practical and down to earth. Look at the details of Leviticus 19. Holiness means:

- generosity to the poor when you get returns on your agricultural investments (Lev 19:9-10; cf. Deut 24:19);

- fair treatment and payment of employees (Lev 19:13; cf. Deut 24:14);

- practical compassion for the disabled and respect for the elderly (Lev 19:14, 32; cf. Deut 27:18);

- the integrity of the judicial process (Lev 19:15; cf. Deut 16:18-20);

- safety precautions to prevent endangering life (Lev 19:16; cf. Deut 22:8);

- ecological sensitivity (Lev 19:23-25; cf. Deut 20:19-20);

- equality before the law for ethnic minorities (Lev 19:33-34; cf. Deut 24:17); and

- honesty in trade and business (Lev 19:35-36; cf. Deut 25:13-16).

We call such matters "social ethics" or "human rights" and think we are very modern and civilized for doing so. We go to great lengths to get them written pompously into declarations for this and charters for that and codes for something else. God just calls them "holiness." All through this chapter runs the refrain, "I am the LORD," as if to say, "You must behave this way because this is what I would do. Imitate me."

In short, to "love your neighbor as yourself" (Lev 19:18, 34) is not a revolutionary new love ethic invented by Jesus. It was the fundamental ethical demand of Old Testament holiness, which Jesus reaffirmed and sharpened in some cases.

Leviticus 19, in fact, appears to have had a major influence on the teaching of Jesus (and is incidentally also strongly formative in the ethics of the letter of James). But whereas Jesus' contemporaries thought that holiness required strict religious purity and a protective separateness in national life, Jesus chose to emphasize its ethical thrust, particularly as regards compassionate and caring relationships.

Scholars who have studied most closely the conflicts between Jesus and the Pharisees in particular point out that the clash was not merely about sincerity and hypocrisy, or about internal and external obedience, or anything so simple. Jesus utterly shared with the Pharisees the consuming desire that God's people should be holy. He shared with them a deep love for the Torah and the assumption that the way to holiness was to be found there in God's revelation. He also shared the dominant motivation of imitation of God as the energizing force for moral behavior.

But whereas they pursued a program of holiness that demanded *performance* of the ritual requirements of the law to near perfection, a holiness that was characterized by *exclusion*—whether of Jews who failed or refused to live that way or of the Gentile nations in general and the Romans in particular—Jesus introduced a complete paradigm shift in the meaning of holiness itself. Imitation of God for him pointed primarily to the other characteristics of God he found in the Torah: the God who was the benevolent Creator and provider for all humanity and even for the creatures; the God of merciful deliverance and incredible grace in forgiveness; the God whose love embraced especially the outcasts and whose covenant with Abraham was specifically for the blessing of the nations. In other words, Jesus defined holiness more in terms of God's mercy and called for an imitative mercy on the part of all who would submit to his reign.

The transforming power and radical shift of behavior patterns that Jesus brought with this teaching are clearly seen in his famous "love your enemies" challenge. Notice how the motivation Jesus uses is indeed the imitation of God—the God of grace and mercy. Notice also how Jesus echoes Leviticus 19:2 but understands holiness as the perfection of loving mercy in the most earthy and practical ways.

> But to you who are listening I say: Love your enemies, do good to those who hate you, bless those who curse you, pray for those who mistreat you [that you may be children of your Father in heaven. He causes his sun to rise on the evil and the good, and sends rain on the righteous and the unrighteous, Mt 5:45]. If someone slaps you on one cheek, turn to them the other also. If

someone takes your coat, do not withhold your shirt from them. Give to everyone who asks you, and if anyone takes what belongs to you, do not demand it back. Do to others as you would have them do to you.

If you love those who love you, what credit is that to you? Even sinners love those who love them. . . . And if you lend to those from whom you expect repayment, what credit is that to you? Even sinners lend to sinners, expecting to be repaid in full. But love your enemies, do good to them, and lend to them without expecting to get anything back. Then your reward will be great, and you will be children of the Most High, because he is kind to the ungrateful and wicked. [Be perfect, therefore, as your heavenly Father is perfect, Mt 5:48.] *Be merciful, just as your Father is merciful.* (Lk 6:27-32, 34-36 my italics)

(3) Being different. The word holy, then, does not mean especially and rigorously religious. What it actually does mean, essentially, is "different." It speaks of something or someone being distinctive, set apart and separate. It is the fundamental description of God himself precisely because he is different—utterly "other" than anything or anyone in the created world. In many contexts in the Old Testament, the holiness of Yahweh is contrasted with the idols of the nations. Yahweh is the living God, the *Holy One* of Israel, the God who is utterly different. For Israel, then, being the people of Yahweh meant being different too. When God said "You shall be holy because I, the LORD your God, am holy," what it meant, colloquially, was "You must be a different kind of people because I am a different kind of God."

When God got Israel to Mount Sinai, the first thing he impressed on it, as we saw above, was *his own* initiative in delivering it from Egypt. The second thing he stressed was what he had in mind for *it*. "Although the whole earth is mine, you will be for me a kingdom of priests and a holy nation" (Ex 19:5-6).

Israel would be a nation among other nations, but they were to be holy— different from the rest of the nations. This had very practical implications, whether they looked back to where they had left or looked forward to where they were going.

You must not do as they do in Egypt, where you used to live, and you must not do as they do in the land of Canaan, where I am bringing you. (Lev 18:3)

> You are to be holy to me because I, the LORD, am holy, and I have set you
> apart from the nations to be my own. (Lev 20:26)

Even the foreigner Balaam recognized this conscious sense of distinctiveness about Israel:

> I see a people who live apart
>   and do not consider themselves one of the nations. (Num 23:9)

This could sound like the most awful snobbishness. But that would be
to misunderstand it entirely. Israel was not to regard itself as better than
the nations out of self-righteous pride (as we saw above). Rather, by
reflecting the character of their God, it was to be a light to the nations—a
light witnessing to the moral values of God himself. Switching on the light
in a dark place is not arrogant. It's common sense. God created Israel to be
a light in a dark world. But a light is only seen if it shines, and in the same
way, Israel would only be seen through its practical obedience to God's law.
Then its visibility would raise questions about the God it worshiped and
about the social quality of life it exhibited. This is exactly what is in mind
in the motivational words of Deuteronomy 4:6-8:

> Observe [these laws] carefully, for this will show your wisdom and under-
> standing *to the nations*, who will hear about all these decrees and say, "Surely
> this great nation is a wise and understanding people." What other nation is
> so great as to have their gods near them the way the LORD our God is near us
> whenever we pray to him? And what other nation is so great as to have such
> righteous decrees and laws as this body of laws I am setting before you today?

If Israel would live by God's standards of social justice and compassion,
then it would indeed be "light" to the nations (Is 58:6-10, where "light" is
mentioned twice and linked to "righteousness").

It is a short step to the familiar words of Jesus to his disciples about the
exemplary quality of their lives and its effect on the observers around us:
"You are the light of the world. . . . Let your light shine before others, that
they may see your good deeds and glorify your Father in heaven" (Mt
5:14-16; cf. 1 Pet 2:12).

And there is also a clear call from Jesus to be different. He pointed to
the familiar patterns of relationship and ambition in pagan society and
said, "You are not to be like that" (Lk 22:25-30; Mt 5:46-48; 6:31-34). He

also pointed to the very best of religious uprightness among their fellow Jews and told his disciples they must be and do differently even from that (Mt 5:20; 6:1-8).

(4) For our own good. In the Old Testament, obedience to the law was not just an arbitrary duty, "because rules is rules." A frequent motivation is the encouraging assurance that it is for our own good. This is the thrust of the exhortations in Deuteronomy. "The LORD commanded us to obey all these decrees and to fear the LORD our God, *so that we might always prosper and be kept alive*" (Deut 6:24, and see also Deut 4:40; 5:33; 30:15-20, etc.).

The assumption behind this kind of motivation is that God, as the creator of human beings, knows best what kind of social patterns will contribute to human well-being. His laws were not meant to be negatively restricting but rather to provide the conditions in which life can be most truly humane and beneficial—in that culture and at that time. Obedience therefore brings blessing not as a reward but as an intrinsic, natural result, just as physical health is not some kind of bonus or reward for good behavior. Good health is simply the natural product of sensible living the way our bodies were designed to.

Another way of looking at this, and in any case an illuminating exercise, is to apply the question "Who benefits?" to the range of social legislation in the Torah. Whose interests are being protected? What kind of vulnerability is being cared for? The answer so often is found to be that the law is benefiting the weaker, poorer, defenseless categories of people in Israel's community: the debtor, the slave, the homeless widow or orphan, the landless worker, prisoners of war, women and children, refugees.

It is very important to see that the law was given for people's sake, not for God's sake. Of course it is true that our obedience makes God happy. But the purpose of the law was not to make *him* happy, but *us*. That is what the psalmists recognized when they exclaim things like "O how I love your law," or say they prefer it to gold or honey. They could see that obedience to God's law, far from being the dry crust of stale legalism we might imagine, was actually the surest route to personal fulfillment and satisfaction, genuine freedom, and social harmony and prosperity. The law was a gift of grace, a blessing, a treasure, one of the many great privileges God had entrusted to Israel—for its own good and then for the blessing of the rest of humanity.

Jesus, in tune with this whole ethos of the Torah, was enraged by the way the legal experts of his day had turned the law from its prime purpose of being a blessing and a benefit into being a burden on ordinary people. We must note carefully that Jesus did not condemn or reject the law itself. Nor did he condemn the scribes and Pharisees for their love and passion for the law. In fact, he said that insofar as they taught what Moses taught, they were to be obeyed, but not imitated (Mt 23:2-3). What his penetrating observations exposed, however, was the way that detailed passion had robbed the law of its whole point.

What was the point of having a law for the benefit of parents, if the regulations built on top of it worked in the opposite direction (Mk 7:9-13)? What was the point of having laws about tithing, whose prime purpose was to provide justice and compassionate welfare for the poor (Deut 14:28-29), if they became so meticulous in detail that the major issues of justice and mercy were neglected (Mt 23:23)? Above all, what was the point of having a Sabbath law explicitly for human need, if it was turned into a reason for neglecting or postponing human need?

The Sabbath controversy is most interesting, partly because it was clearly a major and long-running issue between Jesus and those who opposed him, but mainly, for our purpose here, because it illustrates beautifully how Jesus "saw the point" of the law in a way which his opponents so often seemed to miss.

The Sabbath law in the Ten Commandments is given in two different forms. In Exodus 20:8-11, its theological basis is the creation account in Genesis 1 and God's own Sabbath rest after creation. In Deuteronomy 5:12-15 it is based on the fact of God's redemption of Israel from Egypt. But in both cases the *beneficiaries* of the law are listed carefully and include all domestic workers, male and female slaves, foreign workers in the community and even working domestic animals. Yes, the Sabbath was a holy day *for the Lord*. But it was also social legislation *for the benefit of the whole of society*, with particular emphasis on those most easily exploited. Indeed, Deuteronomy adds the revealing touch "so that they may rest as you do." The Sabbath was not to be a day for the leisure of a few supported by the continuing toil of the many. I believe it was Harold Macmillan, former British prime minister, who described the Old Testament Sabbath law as "the greatest piece of workers' protection legislation in history." Exodus, likewise, puts the Sabbath law as the climax of a series of laws for the benefit of the poor—in the law courts, in social life generally and in agricultural practice (Ex 23:1-12).

Jesus, then, when the Pharisees objected to his disciples in satisfying their hunger on the Sabbath or protested at his own deliberate acts of healing on the Sabbath, very pointedly makes it clear that the Sabbath, far from being the day for avoiding such things, was precisely the best day for them (Mt 12:1-14; Mk 2:23-28). It was the day above all days for bringing blessing and healing. Yes, it was God's day—but it was given for human benefit.

So when Jesus summed it all up, in another of those sayings full of potent, memorable simplicity, "The Sabbath was made for man, not man for the Sabbath" (Mk 2:27), he was not propounding some new idea— even though it was radical and shocking in the atmosphere of disapproval and misunderstanding into which he spoke it. Rather, as in so much of what he said and did, he was recapturing the *original, authentic point and thrust of the law*. The priorities and values Jesus taught were the true heart of the law. The irony and tragedy of his conflict with the scribes and Pharisees was that it was precisely they who prided themselves on being the true guardians and teachers of the law in all its glory. So they thought. But in Jesus' estimation they had not only perverted the true purpose of the law but were also preventing it from benefiting the very people it was given for (Mt 23:4, 13-14).

The law's scale of values. When one of the teachers of the law asked Jesus what was the greatest commandment in the law, it was a significant question. The rabbis of his day debated it (along with also debating which was the *least* important commandment in the law). For them, it was a somewhat academic question. The whole law in every detail was binding, so it didn't ultimately matter which detail was given pride of place. It must all be obeyed. When Jesus answered the question, however, with his famous double commandment, to love God with all one's heart and to love one's neighbor as oneself, he gave his answer a new twist at the end. "All the Law and the Prophets *hang* on these two commandments" (Mt 22:34-40, my italics). In other words, they are like the hook from which the rest of the Scriptures are suspended. They have a fundamental priority. They are the scale or criteria by which the rest should be ordered. They show you what really matters. Everything else is subordinate to these crucial two laws.

In Mark's account, the man responded to Jesus' answer with considerable insight about the scale of values in the law. "You are right in saying that God is one and there is no other but him. To love him with all your heart, with all your understanding and with all your strength, and to love your neighbor as yourself *is more important than* all burnt offerings and sacrifices" (Mk 12:32-33, my italics).

Jesus commended him by saying he was "not far from the kingdom of God." In other words, this inquirer's appreciation of priorities coincided with the way God himself operates. He shared the same value system that Jesus himself had discerned in the Hebrew Bible. For once again we have to be clear that this perception, expressed by both Jesus and this thoughtful teacher of the law, was not a clever new theory about Israel's law. It was only drawing out with clarity something the Old Testament itself had declared. So let us examine the priority scale we find there. In what ways does Old Testament law show what things are of greater or lesser importance?

(1) *God comes first.* It would be hard to miss this! The Ten Commandments make it very obvious by putting the three commandments related directly to God at the head of the list. In fact the order of the commandments in the Decalogue is revealing in itself as a clue to the priorities of God's law. They begin with God and end with the inner thoughts of the heart. And yet in a sense, the first and the tenth correspond with each other, since covetousness puts other things or people in the place that God should occupy: "covetousness which is idolatry," as Paul said more than once (Eph 5:5; Col 3:5; cf. Lk 12:15-21).

After God and God's name comes the Sabbath, which, as we have seen, was for the benefit of the whole community, especially for workers. Then comes the family (respect for parents), individual life (no murder), marriage (no adultery), property (no theft) and the integrity of the judicial process (no perjury). God, society, family, individuals, sex, property. It is an order of values that Western culture has more or less completely reversed. The idolatry of consumerism puts material things, sexual freedom and selfish individualism way above the blessing and protection of family, or commitment to the common good of society, and has no place for God at all, other than in mockery or swearing.

The demand of putting God before all else could be costly. There is a sharp edge to biblical faith. Deuteronomy 13 is an interesting example of this. The chapter warns Israel against various subtle temptations to be drawn away from total loyalty to God into other forms of idolatry. Among the sources of such temptation it cites miracle-working religious leaders (Deut 13:1-5)—a modern enough phenomenon.

Then it goes on to an area that can produce the greatest tension of all—one's own family (Deut 13:6-11). The tension in these verses is all the more sharp when you remember how central the family was in Israel's life. The whole social structure of the nation was organized around kinship. The extended family unit (the household, or "father's house") was the basis of economic life as well as fundamental in the covenant relationship with God. In the law, every effort was made to protect the household and to preserve its economic well-being. Individuals got their primary sense of identity from the wider family, owed it loyalty and could face serious sanctions for spurning its authority.

But what do you do if your loyalty to God conflicts with your loyalty and love for your own closest family circle? What if the family itself becomes the source of idolatry? What if the family becomes a stumbling block in the way of complete loyalty to God? The dilemma is one that believers have faced all through the ages and is still very real for some people today. Deuteronomy's answer was uncompromising.

So was Jesus. We can feel something of the starkness of this Old Testament text in the words of Jesus, warning his disciples that the claims of the reign of God must come before the family—and even one's own life. "If anyone comes to me and does not hate father and mother, wife and children, brothers and sisters—yes, even their own life—such a person cannot be my disciple" (Lk 14:26). Jesus uses the word *hate* here, not in an emotional sense. He was not calling people to "hate" their families in the way that English word sounds. Rather he was saying that loyalty to Christ must come above all other loyalties—including love for one's own life.

Jesus himself had to resist the attempts of his own family to deflect him from obeying his calling (Mt 12:46-50), and he gave his famously abrupt answer to the one who wanted to fulfill family commitments before following Jesus (Mt 8:21-22).

Remember, all this comes from the same Jesus who berated the Pharisees for the way they nullified the law about honoring parents; the same Jesus who made arrangements for the care of his mother in the midst of his own death agonies. Jesus was *not* (as has sometimes been alleged) *anti-family*. He was *anti-idolatry*. And the family, when it takes the place of ultimate value in a person's life, when it stands in the way of a person's submission to the reign of God, when it hinders God's mission, becomes just as much an idol as any stone statue. God must come first. That can be painful and terribly costly. But many down the centuries have proved it is the way of true discipleship.

(2) *Persons matter more than things*. One of the most fundamental principles of Old Testament law is the sanctity of human life. Nothing (in the literal sense of *no thing*) is worth more than a person. This is not contradicted by the fact that a number of offenses were sanctioned by the death penalty. The reasons behind the death penalty in the Old Testament are complex but understandable. It was not just an indication of a vengeful, primitive society where life was cheap.

Broadly speaking the death penalty applied to two kinds of offense: those that directly offended God himself and those that threatened the stability of Israel as a covenant society. The first were "vertical" offences—issues like idolatry, blasphemy, prophesying falsely in God's name and so on. The second were "horizontal"—affecting other persons, such as Sabbath breaking, intentional murder and acts that threatened the viability of families (rejection of parental authority, fracture of the sexual integrity of marriage and so on). All these capital offenses were connected in some way with the Ten Commandments. In fact, most (but not all) of the Ten Commandments were sanctioned by the death penalty through the details of other laws based on them. This shows the central place of the Decalogue in Israel's law—even though there is very little evidence that execution actually ever happened for many of the offenses listed as capital. It is possible that in some cases execution was the "maximum penalty," frequently reduced to other penalties in practice.

However, what is more interesting, but not often noticed, is what the death penalty did *not* apply to. In Israelite law no offense involving *property* carried a death penalty. This is referring to ordinary judicial procedure. Exceptional cases like Achan had to do with fundamental violations of the covenant in the context of war, not ordinary theft. Theft was, of course, treated seriously—as is clear from it being included in the Ten Commandments. But you could not be put to death for stealing in ancient Israel, which makes it a lot more "civilized" than most Western countries until fairly recently. The reason? No amount of material property was worth a human life. Life and property could not be measured against each other. However, *kidnapping*, the theft of a *person* (usually then sold into slavery), *was* a capital offense (Ex 21:16).

The other side of this coin is that deliberate murder was not to be punished by a mere fine. If someone stole another person's *life*, he could not "get off" by paying any amount of *money*. Life and money could not be matched. The fact that the law specifies this point (in Num 35:31-34) in relation to the single issue of *intentional* murder makes it possible that the death penalty may have been commuted in other capital cases sometimes where life was not directly involved.

(3) Needs matter more than claims. The law of Israel, however, went further than showing the absolute value of human life in comparison with material things. It also puts human needs before claims and apparent legal rights. There is an ethos in the Torah that calls for an attitude of consideration for the needs and sensitivities of others, even in situations where you may have a legally legitimate claim. Here are a few examples.

(a) The runaway slave: We might feel that slaves, captives, debtors and poor people ought not to exist at all in an ideal society, and we'd be right. But given that human society is fallen and sinful, and that even in Israel such results of evil did in fact exist, it is very noticeable how Old Testament law tries to restrain the claims of the stronger party and attend to the needs of the weaker party in each case. "If a slave has taken refuge with you, do not hand them over to their master. Let them live among you wherever they like and in whatever town they choose. Do not oppress them" (Deut 23:15-16).

This is an astonishing law. It cuts right across the whole grain of slave legislation in the ancient world (and indeed in modern times). The almost universal rule in societies that have had slaves is that runaway slaves were to be returned, under stiff penalties for them or anyone who sheltered them. Old Testament law swims against the stream and puts the needs of the slave above any legal "property" rights of his owner. In fact, this law undermines the whole institution of slavery. It is one of several places in the Old Testament where slaves are given human rights and dignity beyond anything in the world of that age (e.g., Ex 21:26-27; Deut 15:12-18; Job 31:13-15).

(b) The female captive: There was no Geneva Convention in the ancient world governing the treatment of prisoners of war. Little mercy was given or expected. Victorious armies especially prized women and girls. Once again, we find that the Old Testament law, on the one hand, starts with the realities of life. It acknowledges the harsh reality that prisoners are taken in wartime and some of them will be women. But on the other hand, the law tries to mitigate that harsh reality for such women, who are the most vulnerable and the most abused.

> When you go to war against your enemies and the LORD your God delivers them into your hands and you take captives, if you notice among the captives a beautiful woman and are attracted to her, you may take her *as your wife*. Bring her into your home and have her shave her head, trim her nails and put aside the clothes she was wearing when captured. After she has lived in your house and *mourned* her father and mother *for a full month*, then you may go to her and be her husband and she shall be your wife. If you are not pleased with her, let her go wherever she wishes. *You must not sell her* or treat her as a slave, since you have dishonored her. (Deut 21:10-14, my italics)

Notice how the law carefully restricts the "rights" of the victorious soldier. Rape is not an option at all. Nor can he just take the woman for temporary sexual pleasure. If he wants her, he must take the full responsibility and commitment of giving her the status of wife, with all the legal and social benefits that go with that. And even then he is not to invade her privacy immediately, as the right of a husband might allow. She is to have a full month to adjust to the grief and loss she has already suffered. And if in the end the man regrets his action, the woman is not to be further debased as if she were slave property but given the normal, though tragic, freedom of a divorced wife. The law seems designed to offer some human compassion and protection to the woman in the context of the horrible reality of the aftermath of battle.

The last line of the law is an implicit criticism of the whole practice. As we know from Jesus' comments on the divorce law, the Law of Moses *permitted* some things that it did not wholly *approve* of. God took account of human "hardness of heart." The same thing goes for slavery, polygamy and even, we might add, monarchy. The important thing, it seems to me, is not to criticize the Old Testament law for failing to eradicate all social evils (especially the ones we struggle most with ourselves, such as the oppression and abuse of women), but rather to observe the ways it tried to mitigate their worst effects by attending to the needs of the most vulnerable party in any situation. The basic human needs of the victim take priority over the rights or claims of the victor.

(c) The debtor's pledge:

> Do not take a pair of millstones—not even the upper one—as security for a debt, because that would be taking a person's livelihood as security. . . .
>
> When you make a loan of any kind to your neighbor, do not go into their house to get what is offered to you as a pledge. Stay outside and let the neighbor to whom you are making the loan bring the pledge out to you. If the neighbor is poor, do not go to sleep with their pledge in your possession. Return their cloak by sunset so that your neighbor may sleep in it. (Deut 24:6, 10-13)

Debt is degrading. It can even become dehumanizing. Debtors become the victims of practices so brutal that it is not surprising the word *shark* is often applied to those who exploit human poverty by sucking the needy into bondage and fear through unscrupulous loaning tactics.

Old Testament law recognizes reality by permitting, indeed commanding, loans to those who need them. Lending to the poor is a righteous act. But the law prohibited the taking of interest, which was one of the most radical dimensions of biblical economics. However, it did permit the taking of pledges as security for a loan. The lender needs some security for his loan. However, even this creditor's right to take a pledge is limited in the interests of the debtor. The law protected the debtor's life and needs on the one hand and his privacy and dignity on the other. The millstones ground the flour for daily bread. The cloak gave warmth for nightly sleep. To take *those* things was to rob someone of basic human necessities. No legal right justified such behavior. Needs come before claims.

(d) The gleanings of the harvest: "When you reap the harvest of your land, do not reap to the very edges of your field or gather the gleanings of your harvest. Do not go over your vineyard a second time or pick up the grapes that have fallen. Leave them for the poor and the foreigner" (Lev 19:9-10; cf. Deut 24:19-22).

Surely a landowner has the right to enjoy the full return on his investment of effort, plowing and sowing on his own property? Not so, says the law. The needs of the poor come before the claims of ownership. He must deliberately *not* take all the produce for himself. This law of gleanings was in addition to the triennial tithe, which was also available for the sustenance of the landless poor (Deut 14:28-29). Property rights are never the bottom line of a moral argument. In any case, as God rather bluntly pointed out, "The land is mine and you reside in my land as foreigners and strangers" (Lev 25:23). Tenants have no absolute right of disposal of what is the landowner's property. The owner of a property dictates how it may be used. Here the divine landlord (God) instructs the tenants (Israel) to make sure that adequate provision is made for the needs of the poor.

When we survey the life and teaching of Jesus, there is a strong echo of this dimension of the Torah. Human life and human needs take precedence over all other personal claims or rights, as well as over rules and regulations. Jesus' parables paint situations where a person could have felt justified in acting in one way but chooses to act instead with mercy or generosity. The Samaritan had good cause to ignore the Jewish casualty but didn't. In fact, by loving the Jew as his neighbor, he obeyed the law in a way that the custodians of the law (the priest and Levite) failed to. The father of the prodigal son could have rejected and disowned him but chose instead to welcome and reinstate him. The owner of the vineyard could have paid the latest workers just a fraction of the daily wage but chose generously to meet their needs rather than satisfy the jealous justice claims of the earlier hired hands.

Or, conversely, when the "rich fool" had far more harvest than he needed for himself, he could have followed the thrust of Old Testament law and shared his blessing with the needy. He knew what he should have done. But his self-centered greed cost him his life. More explicitly, at the end of the parable about the rich man and Lazarus, "Abraham" condemns the rich man because his utter failure to meet the obvious need of Lazarus was a failure precisely to heed the law and the prophets (Lk 16:29-31).

Again, the Sabbath controversy illustrates this most clearly. Human hunger comes before human regulations. Jesus backs that up with an interesting quotation from the prophet Hosea, showing that *in the Old Testament itself* there was a strong awareness that the moral values of mercy and justice have priority in God's mind over the ritual laws: "If you had known what these words mean, 'I desire mercy, not sacrifice,' you would not have condemned the innocent" (Mt 12:7; Hos 6:6).

Jesus used the same text on another occasion to answer criticism of his social intercourse with those whom society marginalized (Mt 9:10-13). Clearly it provided a significant priority guide for his own life. Likewise the healing and saving of human life matters more than Sabbath laws, with an obvious comparison with animal welfare (Mt 12:9-14).

Jesus taught the uncomfortable message about putting even the unreasonable demands of others above the legal limits of one's own responsibility (Mt 5:38-48). In the parable of the sheep and the goats, response to human need is presented as the criterion of final judgment (Mt 25:31-46). He put the need of a distraught woman for the loving assurance of forgiveness above the social etiquette of table manners (Lk 7:36-50). He put the need of a sick woman above the ritual defilement of menstrual uncleanness (Mk 5:25-34). He went about among those to whom official society gave no *rights* and met their *needs*—for food, friendship, forgiveness, love, healing, acceptance, dignity.

The authority of Jesus. "Do not think," said Jesus, "that I have come to abolish the Law or the Prophets." The radical and shocking nature of some of what Jesus said and did must have led some people to think that was what he was doing. But as we survey the whole range of his life and teaching in relation to the law we can see what he meant. "I have not come to abolish them," he went on, "but to fulfill them" (Mt 5:17).

Exactly what he meant by "fulfill" here has been much disputed among scholars. My own view, which does not deny the various technical meanings of the word given in the commentaries, is more in line what I've been saying above. Jesus was bringing into full clarity the inherent *values and priorities* of the Torah. His own teaching certainly built on and surpassed the law itself. But it was facing in the same direction. His whole life was oriented by a deep reflection on the fundamental demands of the law, since he found in it the mind of his Father God. To a people who had become so obsessed with the details of the law that they had forgotten its original purpose, he brought back a sense of what really mattered first in God's sight. Jesus was "filling out" all that God intended through the priorities that the law itself contains.

Jesus was not imposing on the Torah an arbitrary selection of his own favorite texts. Rather, the Torah itself, carefully read and understood, makes very clear its own scale of values and sense of priorities. Jesus brought back to light the simplicity and clarity of the *point* of the Torah from the layers of well-meant regulations that had been intended to protect it but had in effect buried it.

No wonder, then, that "the crowds were amazed at his teaching, because he taught as one who had authority, and not as their teachers of the law" (Mt 7:28-29). For that was indeed the point. Jesus was actually *not* just a teacher of the law. For although he shaped his own life and values by it, and restored its great central thrust in his teaching, Jesus claimed that he, himself, took precedence. Response to *him* became determinative, as once the law had been. Life and security were to be found in *him* rather than in the law. "Take *my* yoke upon you" (Mt 11:29), he said, when his contemporaries would speak only of the "yoke of the law."

When Jesus replied to the rich young man's inquiry about the source of eternal life, his answer was authentically scriptural. "If you want to enter life, keep the commandments" (Mt 19:17), he said. He certainly did not mean that obedience to the law *deserved* life in a meritorious way but rather that obedience *proved* the relationship with God from which life flowed. This was precisely the point underlined by Moses in Leviticus 18:5 (which Jesus and Paul both quote) and Deuteronomy 30:16. But when Jesus went on to invite the man to a costly discipleship, in which *Jesus himself* became the key to the life of the kingdom of God and everything else had to be renounced, the man turned away. The law in and of itself gave no life. Life came from the *source* of the law, God himself. That source confronted the man, but he walked away. Another rich fool, only in real life, not in a parable.

Fool was not my choice of word for him but Jesus' own. Not that Jesus called him a fool there and then, of course. On the contrary, we sense the sad longing in the heart of Jesus at the man's decision, when Mark tells us that "Jesus looked at him and loved him" (Mk 10:21). But he had heard the words of Jesus and chose not to do them. And that, said Jesus on another occasion, is the action of a foolish person. For it is on our active response to Jesus' words that our eternal security and destiny depend.

The immediate cause of the crowd's astonishment after the Sermon on the Mount was the way it ended, with Jesus' story of the two house builders (Mt 7:24-27). The critical difference between the wise man and the fool was not over their obedience to *the law* (as would have been expected from, say, the book of Psalms or Proverbs), but their response to *Jesus*. The word of Jesus now occupies the seat of judgment. To do or not to do, that is the question, once you have heard. One way leads to life and safety, the other way, collapse and death.

If Jesus *had* been only a teacher of the law he might have caused a stir with his radical exposure of its priorities and the way he challenged the additions that had been made over the centuries. He might have carved out a name as a great and original thinker. He might even have had a school of interpretation named after him. But they would not have set out to *kill* him. The experts in the law had some fairly serious disagreements and major disputes in Jesus' day, and indeed they tried to get Jesus to take sides in some of them. But they did not kill each other over disputed legal teaching.

Yet surely we gasp with astonishment when we read as early as Mark 3:6 that the Pharisees were plotting to kill Jesus. Why? Because he did not merely act and teach in a way that contravened their understanding of the law but actually set himself up as having even greater authority than the law. He claimed authority over the Sabbath. He took it on himself to forgive sins—a prerogative only for legally constituted authorities. He invited people to take *his* yoke upon themselves, rather than the yoke of the law. He asserted that "sinners" were entering the kingdom of God through their response to *him* (not their observance of the law), and conversely that those who rejected him had excluded themselves. Such claims not only seemed to be intolerably arrogant, but they also called in question the whole constitution of Israel as a community whose claim to God was based on covenant loyalty to the law. By putting himself in that place of central authority, Jesus threatened the whole existing system. There was ultimately only one way to deal with that, and it was not by polite rabbinical counterargument.

So they set out to kill him and be rid of the threat.

That was how they had dealt with the prophets, as Jesus pointed out. And so we turn next to think of Jesus as a prophet and in the light of the great prophets of the Old Testament.

JESUS AND THE PROPHETS

At Caesarea Philippi Jesus asked his disciples what the popular opinion was about him. Who did people think he was? The answer they gave is interesting. Some people thought he was John the Baptist revived and reunited with his severed head. Others thought he was Elijah, who was supposed to

be sent before the great Day of the Lord. Others thought he was Jeremiah—
or one of the prophets anyway. A prophet, at the very least, was how the
crowds saw Jesus. Why? What was it about Jesus that led to these rumors
and perceptions? There must have been something in the behavior and
teaching of Jesus that brought to mind memories of the great prophets of old.

"The Prophets" make up an enormous chunk of the Hebrew canon, of
course. The Latter Prophets include the three major prophets—Isaiah,
Jeremiah and Ezekiel, and the twelve minor prophets—Hosea to Malachi.
(In the Hebrew canon the Latter Prophets are distinguished from the
Former Prophets, which is what they called the history books from Joshua
to 2 Kings). These books of the Prophets (from Isaiah to Malachi) are all
different and cover nearly four hundred years of Israel's history, as we saw
in chapter one. Yet we can isolate a few central themes that dominate
their messages over the generations. Obviously, this is to simplify things
enormously, and you really have to study each prophet on his own terms
and in his own context to understand them fully. Nevertheless, it is helpful
to have a broad overview of prophetic concerns with which we can
compare Jesus to see how and where he fits and why he was reckoned
among the prophets.

Three major areas of life occupied the energies of the prophets a lot of
the time. First, there was the *spiritual* aspect, concerned with the people's
relationship with God, the threat of idolatry and the hypocrisy of worship
that was unrelated to practical moral living. Second, there was the *social
and economic* aspect, concerned with the processes in Israel's society that
were causing poverty, exploitation, debt and corruption. And third, there
was the *political* aspect, concerned with the use and abuse of power by those
who wielded it—in the palace, the temple, the courts, etc. The crowd's idea
that Jesus might be Elijah or Jeremiah is helpful at this point, because those
two prophets between them illustrate all three areas very well.

Spiritual loyalty to God. Elijah stood on Mount Carmel as the great
champion of the faith of Yahweh against Baal (1 Kings 18). He presented
the people with the starkness of choice: "If Yahweh is God, serve him; but
if Baal is God, serve him." In other words, you can't go on trying to serve
both. We have already seen earlier in this chapter how Jesus reiterated this
ultimate choice, echoing the great Old Testament prophetic challenge.
"You cannot serve God and money," he said. To submit to the reign of God

means rejecting all competitors. And just as the prophets of old had exposed the hypocrisy of Israel in claiming to worship God while ignoring his covenant law, so Jesus displays full prophetic stature in his condemnation of the claims and postures of the religious elite of his day. His use of the expression "Woe to you" was a clear echo of the prophetic word of judgment. It was not a term of polite disagreement but a solemn pronouncement of God's wrath upon someone. Isaiah 5 is a graphic illustration and background for a chapter like Matthew 23.

Like the prophets, Jesus was consumed by a spiritual jealousy for the honor of God. Like them, he attacked those who imagined that God was impressed by religion divorced from the moral and social values of God himself. Like them, he suffered for doing so. We saw in chapter one that this was a significant theme in the prophetic message in the preexilic period. On more than one occasion Jesus quoted Hosea 6:6,

> For I desire mercy, not sacrifice,
>> and acknowledgment of God rather than burnt offerings.

He quoted the verse to stress the fundamental priority of moral obedience to God over the ritual expression of religious commitments. That verse is only one of many that he could have quoted that make the same point even more graphically. It would be worth pausing again to read the following passages, reflecting on the impact they would have had on Jesus' sense of values and priorities: Isaiah 1:11-20; 58:1-7; Jeremiah 7:1-11; and Amos 5:21-24. God matters more than religion.

Economic issues. The same Elijah who stood on Mount Carmel to defend the name of Yahweh from idolatry also confronted Ahab over the illegal seizure of a vineyard. The story of Naboth in 1 Kings 21 is a graphic illustration of the second main area of prophetic concern—the economic realm.

Two things about the land of Israel stand out very clearly in the Old Testament:

On the one hand, the land was God's gift to Israel. He had promised it to Abraham and then kept that promise in the great historical events of exodus and conquest. But it was a gift that was meant for the enjoyment of *all* Israelites. So there are clear instructions that it was to be divided up fairly and as widely as possible, across the whole kinship network, with every family receiving a share—an inheritance from God himself.

On the other hand, the land still belonged to God. He was its true owner (Lev 25:23). And so this divine ownership of the land was the foundation for Israel's economic system. God was the real landlord; Israel was the tenant. God held Israel accountable to himself for everything it did on and with the land. This is what lies behind the detailed laws in the Torah concerning use of the land, preservation of people's share in it, justice and compassion in sharing its produce, protection of those who work on it, special provision for those who become poor and have to sell it, and all the other specific economic mechanisms designed to sustain an equitable distribution and enjoyment of the resources God had given to his people.

From the time of Solomon onward, this system came under increasing pressure and dissolution. Fewer and fewer wealthy families accumulated more and more land, while poorer families became dispossessed or were driven into debt bondage. The courts, far from defending the oppressed, increased the oppression through bribery and corruption. Kings, far from acting with the justice required of them, instead perpetrated the kind of high-handed tactics that the story of Naboth illustrates. As we saw in chapter one, this process aroused the anger of prophet after prophet. In fact, socioeconomic issues loom larger in the preaching of the prophets than any other, with the possible exception of idolatry itself. And of course, the two were closely linked. The faith of Yahweh underpinned a system of economic and social justice. Baal was the god of a society of stratified wealth and power. To abandon Yahweh for Baal was no mere spiritual affair, but it opened the way to rampant injustice in the socioeconomic sphere also, which is very precisely illustrated by the Naboth story, since Jezebel was actively trying to replace the faith of Yahweh with that of Baal. Idolatry and injustice went together. They still do.

Coming back to the New Testament and the Palestine of Jesus' day, we need to recognize that the country faced very similar economic problems, but they were made even worse by the imposition of the Roman imperial government. Much scholarly study has been given to the social and economic situation in first-century Palestine, and it does not make pleasant reading. There was intensive exploitation of the agrarian peasant farmers, the majority of whom were tenants, since the ownership of land was concentrated in the hands of a few wealthy families. Tenant farmers were hard-pressed trying to meet a variety of demands on what they could produce—rents, taxes, tithes, debt repayments. And all this before they could think of what they could afford to consume for themselves to stay alive and have something to invest in the next year's sowing.

Since many of the landowners lived in Jerusalem, there was antagonism between town and country. Villagers suffered many hardships and discriminations, and there was much discontent. There were clashes between Jewish peasantry and Gentile settlers in Galilee and the eastern parts of the land who were perceived as an economic threat. The pressures of poverty, debt and dispossession drove some people into the extreme revolutionary camp of the Zealots, who attacked both the Roman power and the Jewish aristocratic collaborators. It was a tense and sometimes violent agrarian scene in which Jesus grew up. The message of the Old Testament prophets would have sounded very relevant to the social and economic situation.

Jesus was a carpenter. The trade he pursued was not merely joinery. The word used to describe him, *tekton*, meant somebody skilled in practical small engineering jobs—mostly in wood but frequently also in stone or other building materials. The *tekton* was a versatile person, making or mending agricultural implements, domestic furniture, boats and other large constructions, and also frequently employed for contract work in public building works. They would have a village home base and workshop, but often they would travel around with the tools of their trade, seeking employment from private or public employers—on the farms, with the fishing fleets, in the cities on new building projects and so on.

It is very possible that Jesus, during his twenties, traveled extensively around Palestine working as a *tekton* before he eventually laid that trade aside to embark on his public ministry. Some scholars suggest this on the evidence of the wide range of social contacts that Jesus had both in Galilee and in the Jerusalem region, as well as the breadth of familiarity with so many aspects of everyday life that emerges in his parables. Jesus knew what he was talking about. He had seen life at every level, as itinerant workers certainly do. He was probably a familiar figure, using his skills among the fishing fleets around the shores of the Sea of Galilee, mending furniture and farm implements for local people, long before he called some of his friends to become his followers in a new venture. It is quite possible that he helped to build the boat he preached from. Who knows?

So, like the prophets before him, Jesus spoke from a position of close observation of the realities of the situation in which he lived. He grew up and lived within his own culture and its tensions. He would have listened to countless conversations among fellow workers, hammering away together on some construction project. He would have seen the hard slog of life on the farms and in the vineyards. He would have heard the struggles of those who had crippling debts. He would have listened to the murderous mutterings against absentee landlords by aggrieved tenants, the bitterness against tax collectors. He would have felt the pain of fathers whose sons chose to escape and go far away to what they imagined would be a good life. He would have met mothers whose daughters ended up in prostitution to pay debts that never seemed to shrink. He would have witnessed violent incidents on the roads, fatal accidents on building projects. He would have seen crucified rebels and criminals . . .

So one Sabbath, he attended the synagogue somewhere near his family's carpentry shop in Nazareth, read from the scroll of the prophet Isaiah and launched his new ministry on the basis of it. "*Today*," he said, "this Scripture is fulfilled in your hearing" (Lk 4:21). In view of the whole social context in which he lived and worked, he could hardly have chosen a more significant text:

> The Spirit of the Lord is on me,
> > because he has anointed me
> > to proclaim good news to the poor.
> He has sent me to proclaim freedom for the prisoners
> > and recovery of sight for the blind,
> to set the oppressed free,
> > to proclaim the year of the Lord's favor. (Lk 4:18-19; from Is 61:1-2)

His mission, he declared, was to be among the poor and for the sake of the poor, and the rest of his life—the places and the people where he spent most of his time—endorsed that policy statement.

The prophecy in Isaiah 61 draws on ideas connected with the jubilee year in ancient Israel. That is almost certainly what is meant by "the year of the Lord's favor." The original law of the jubilee is in Leviticus 25. It was intended to be a year when Israelites who had been compelled to sell land or dependent members of their family into slavery because of mounting debts would have their debts canceled and be able to return to full pos-session of their ancestral family land. It was to occur every fiftieth year. It was thus designed to alleviate the worst effects of continuing indebtedness. One generation's hard times should not condemn all future generations of a family to bondage. A jubilee would occur approximately every other gen-eration and give a fresh start. Its twin pillars were *release* from debt and *restoration* to one's rightful inheritance.

Some scholars suggest that Jesus was calling for an actual jubilee year to be put into operation, that is, a radical program of debt cancellation and re-distribution of land. In the context of Roman Palestine, however, that would have been essentially a call for revolution—and Jesus certainly rejected and resisted that option. Most scholars, however, point out that Jesus did not call for a literal operation of the law in Leviticus but rather quoted from the prophetic use of jubilary ideas as a way of characterizing his own ministry.

In other words, Jesus was deeply concerned about the economic realities that the jubilee had tried to remedy, but his answer was not a straight return to that ancient legislation. Jesus did not announce a jubilee and hope it would lead to the arrival the kingdom of God (by a political revolution). Rather, he announced the arrival of the kingdom of God and then used the jubilee as a picture of what it was all about. Like the prophets, Jesus took the themes of release and restoration and applied them both in the *eco-nomic* sense in which they originally functioned and also with "value-added" *spiritual* dimensions. Release from bondages of all sorts and restoration to fullness of life and harmony in relation with God and other human beings were part of the prophetic vision of the age to come and part of Jesus' vision of the inbreaking kingdom of God.

Jesus was not a revolutionary, in the usual sense of that word. There is no evidence that he sided with those who advocated violent seizure of land from absentee landowners and redistribution of it to tenant farmers. However, he was very much aware of the problem and the anger it gen-erated. The parable of the so-called wicked husbandmen (or parable of the tenants) in Mark 12:1-9 shows that he knew all about the murderous bit-terness of tenant farmers and their desire for ownership of vineyards for themselves. But he shows no sympathy with their actions or intentions, and rather uses the story (which may well have had a basis in incidents he himself witnessed) as a means of condemning the religious and political leaders of his people. That is whom Jesus was talking to (Mk 11:27; cf. Mt 21:45). The parable should not be construed as a rejection of the whole Jewish people.

On another occasion, Jesus refused to get involved in a dispute over land, using the occasion instead as an opportunity to hammer home the dangers of greed that possession of land can engender (Lk 12:13-21). In a more famous incident, he would not be trapped into siding with the Zealots who were calling on people to refuse to pay imperial taxes to Rome. Instead, Jesus put the whole issue under the higher demand of what belongs to God (Mt 22:15-22).

On the issue of debt, however, Jesus had plenty to say. As in the days of the great prophets (cf. Amos 2:6; 5:11-12; Neh 5), debt poverty was one of the major social evils. It was a source of exploitation and oppression, the prime mechanism by which the rich got richer and the poor got poorer. The jubilary hope of *release* from the chains of indebtedness was as deep as it seemed forlorn. The interesting thing is that the word for "release" in both Greek and the underlying Aramaic and Hebrew that Jesus spoke was used of both literal financial remission of debts (as in Deut 15:1-2) and also the moral or spiritual forgiveness of sins, about which Jesus was passionately concerned. So we find that a number of the parables of Jesus use stories about the release of debt to illustrate the meaning of forgiveness—and its personal, relational implications.

A king's merciful release of a debtor from an enormous debt is contrasted with the man's subsequent behavior as a minor creditor (Mt 18:12-35). A similar but shorter story illustrates forgiveness in Luke 7:41-43. The story of the so-called unjust steward in Luke 16:1-8 portrays the role of the middleman in the polarized structure of creditor and debtor. His action was not so much to cheat his master by reducing the debt but rather to remove from the debt the illegal element of interest, which had been concealed in the document. It is known that interest, which was technically illegal, was charged at frequently very high rates by simply stating that the debtor had borrowed an amount that was actually the loan plus interest. The interest did not appear on the loan document, but the amount that had to be repaid included the interest as well. The steward deleted that hidden interest from the documents, and the master could not condemn him without exposing himself as the one who had charged interest secretly in the first place. The "unjust" steward was actually restoring some justice in the sphere he could maneuver in, and by his generous action he was opening up the possibility of new relationships with those who would otherwise have rejected him.

Zacchaeus, likewise, after a meal with Jesus, which transformed his life's priorities, came back to obeying the law by promising to restore any stolen goods fourfold (as the Old Testament law required). But then he went on to offer a generosity far beyond legal requirements in giving half of his goods to the poor (Lk 19:1-9).

"Release for us our debts, as we also have released our debtors" (Mt 6:12, my translation). The well-known petition in the Lord's Prayer is of course traditionally understood as a request for forgiveness of sins, and indeed is expressed that way in Luke's version (Lk 11:4) and in Matthew's record of Jesus' own further comments. But most scholars believe that Matthew has preserved a form of the petition that shows that Jesus had financial debts in mind also. Since his parables linked debt and forgiveness, it is very likely that Jesus had both concrete and spiritual dimensions in mind. There is no reason why we should have to choose one or the other exclusively, between literal debt and spiritual sins. We do not need to spiritualize "Give us this day our daily bread" as if it has nothing to with actual physical hunger, even though we know that elsewhere Jesus could use literal bread to symbolize spiritual nourishment. For Jesus debt was a real problem, and so was sin. Both need to be fixed.

Jesus taught a prayer that, like the Beatitudes, engaged with earthly as well as spiritual realities. To pray that God's reign should come, that God's will should be done on earth as in heaven, would certainly include the longing that God should act to change the social conditions that crushed the life out of people by indebtedness. Especially since it was indebtedness that most seriously threatened the availability of daily bread. The two petitions are closely linked. The radical challenge of the prayer, however, was not just in the plea that God would intervene to relieve the burden of debt, but that those who sought such benefit of the reign of God must respond by themselves acting in generosity and forgiveness. It was authentically prophetic to insist that the vertical blessing must have horizontal effects, in the economic as well as in the spiritual sphere.

Jesus' critique of wealth was another way in which he strongly reflected the prophetic ethos on economic matters. Now Jesus was no ascetic. He did not glorify poverty. He did not live in rigid austerity. On the contrary, he was willing to be served (in life and in death) by the relatively wealthy, and his enjoyment of food and drink and company gained him a reputation as a friend of sinners (which was meant as an insult but taken as a compliment; Lk 7:34). But in word and act Jesus portrayed the dangers of wealth in terms of which the prophet Amos would have approved. He saw the insidious idolatry that wealth generates and warned against its utter incompatibility with serving God (Mt 6:24; Lk 16:13). It was not so much wealth in and of itself that Jesus condemned but rather its tendency to produce an attitude of complacent self-sufficiency (Lk 12:15-21). Self-sufficiency is the diametric opposite of the prime quality needed for entrance to the kingdom of God—humble dependence on God in faith (Mt 6:19-34).

And so, to the utter amazement of his disciples, Jesus was prepared to let a rich man who had inquired about eternal life turn and walk away because he was unwilling to meet Jesus' demands in relation to his wealth. Jesus loved the man. But Jesus also saw his heart. In his case, while he held on to his wealth, he was not free to do what the righteousness of the reign of God required. Costly discipleship was not for him. However, while Jesus stood among the prophets in his critique of wealth, he went much further than the prophets in advocating an alternative strategy. On the one hand, he taught and modeled a carefree (though not careless) attitude to material things, born of confidence in God's provision. And on the other hand, he called for a radical generosity that cut right across expected norms of behavior. These were his twin policies. Trust in God and generosity to others.

Generosity can be upsetting. Jesus himself, for example, caused great offense by generously offering his own presence and the forgiving grace of God to those whom society regarded as ill-deserving of any such things. But he reinforced his action by parables that portrayed God the Father as incomprehensibly generous. The story of the landowner who hired workers for his vineyard and then paid those who had worked only a few hours a whole day's wage (Mt 20:1-16) must have been as irritating to the real hearers as to the fictional workers. For it not only described the generosity of God that transcended human norms of fair play but also challenged them about real-life economic relationships. Anyone who acted like the farmer in Jesus' parable would actually be in trouble with neighboring landowners, and probably also with the best of the labor force as well. Generosity would actually be perceived as injustice. Justice preserved the status quo. Generosity undermined it.

Other stories have a similar double edge—both pointing to the way God does things as King and also offering models for human imitation. Jesus told the story of the rich man who is snubbed by his own associates but then goes on to give a feast for all the outcasts of society (Lk 14:16-24) not just to answer a comment about the heavenly banquet of the kingdom of God. It was followed by his specific recommendation that people should actually demonstrate that kind of unrepayable generosity in their own social lives (Lk 14:12-14). Such action is an investment in the reality of the new order of God's kingdom (Lk 12:32-34). Whether it was two whole days' wages (as the Good Samaritan gave to care for his "enemy" to whom he acted as neighbor) or two small coins (as the widow gave to God out of her poverty), Jesus observed generosity wherever he saw it and commended it. But at the same time he pointed out that to give up anything, or to give away everything, for the sake of following Christ and living under the reign of God was no loss—in this age or the age to come (Mk 10:23-31). In the end, as Jesus said, though it is not recorded in the Gospels, it is more blessed to give than to receive (Acts 20:35).

Political conflict. Some people compared Jesus to Jeremiah. Why Jeremiah? Perhaps it was because both Jeremiah and Jesus suffered abuse and rejection. It is also true that Jesus, like Jeremiah, expressed great compassion and sorrow for his own people, both in their immediate "lostness" and in their impending future disaster. The "weeping prophet" foreshadowed the weeping Messiah.

But there is another, sharper, reason for the comparison, which lies in the *reason* why Jeremiah suffered such rejection. And that was that Jeremiah brought an uncompromising warning of judgment to come upon his nation (Jer 4:5-9). He voiced and acted out prophetic threats against the very heart of the nation—the temple itself (Jer 7:15; 19:1-15). And as the external threat against Judah grew in intensity from the world power of Babylon, Jeremiah urged his national leaders to accept and submit to Babylon and not embark on futile plots of rebellion (Jer 27).

In other words, Jeremiah stood out against the whole political direction of Judah's government during its last two decades up to the destruction of Jerusalem by Nebuchadnezzar. For his words and actions Jeremiah was branded a traitor (Jer 37:11-15). He was imprisoned more than once, physically assaulted (Jer 20:1-2) and very nearly lynched on one occasion (Jer 26). Jeremiah was not just laughed at as a crank. He was hated as a serious critic and threat. His words and actions were politically intolerable. Two kings and various religious officials tried to silence him permanently.

So if the crowds saw Jeremiah in Jesus, it presumably wasn't a "gentle Jesus meek and mild" that caught their attention or provoked their historical memory. The crowds were witnesses to the gathering storm of conflict between Jesus and the religious and political authorities. The Gospels show us that, again and again, the same word or action of Jesus that led the crowds to marvel at his authority provoked opposition, censure or plotting from the religiopolitical leaders. Almost everything he said and did collided with the official line. And a major reason for that was that Jesus, like Jeremiah, declared that *Israel itself* was on a collision course with the judgment of God, and the collision was urgently, horrifyingly, inescapably close. His stance on this was authentically prophetic. He brought words of sharp warning as well as words of wonderful salvation. That was very like the Old Testament prophets.

Three features of his words and actions illustrate the seriousness of this aspect of Jesus' prophetic significance: his attitude to the Romans, his rejection of the Pharisaic agenda and his words and actions in the temple.

(1) The Romans. First of all, there was his attitude to the Romans. It is sometimes said that since Jesus did not preach revolution against Rome he must have been nonpolitical. We have already said that this is very shortsighted because it suggests that revolutionary violence is the only *political* option even in a situation of oppression. But we can go much further, because Jesus himself did. Not only did he *not* preach violent revolution, he actually advocated *positive acts of love* toward the occupying forces. This was swimming against the whole tide of Jewish political sentiment at the time. In that sense it was radical and even more truly revolutionary.

> And if anyone wants to sue you and take your shirt, hand over your coat as well. If anyone forces you to go one mile, go with them two miles. . . . You have heard that it was said, "Love your neighbor and hate your enemy." But I tell you, love your enemies and pray for those who persecute you, that you may be children of your Father in heaven. (Mt 5:40-45)

The command to love your enemies was radical enough, but Jesus was not content to leave it general like that—even though it would be unmistakable whom he was referring to in the context of his day. The confiscation of clothing and conscription of labor for baggage carrying were common features of the Roman occupation. Jesus urged that people, *in love*, should go beyond the limits of what could be demanded by those whose laws they only obeyed reluctantly and at the point of a sword.

Such teaching would not have endeared him to the Zealot movement, the armed resistance fighters. Yet it must be realized that by commanding love toward the Roman enemy, Jesus was not adopting a pro-Roman political stance, as though to condone the oppression itself, any more than God's sending rain on the unjust condones their injustice. He was even less endearing to the Sadducees, the party who collaborated with the Roman colonial government. For Jesus, the reign of God was supreme over *all* human authority, as he reminded Pontius Pilate at his trial. He could not be bought by either side in the major political conflict of his day. His radical agenda undermined both.

(2) The Pharisees. Second, there was Jesus' conflict with the Pharisees over their definition and practice of holiness. This was much more than just a matter of sincerity versus hypocrisy. The Pharisees' program needs to be seen as a comprehensive, sociopolitical theology and ethic. They, like the vast majority of Israel, longed for the overthrow of the oppressor and the establishment of Israel as God's people in freedom in their own land. And they believed that the way to achieve that goal was neither ascetic withdrawal and waiting (the way of the Essene sect) nor revolutionary armed violence (the way of the Zealots). Rather they sought to achieve a society totally shaped by the Torah. That meant fastidious observance of every detail. It meant being absolutely clear who was holy and who was not. It meant scrupulous observance of the Sabbath as the clearest badge of Israel's covenant identity.

And Jesus threatened their whole ideology and program from the roots. We have seen how he operated with a different understanding of the key values of the law and effectively devalued some of the things they emphasized most. But more seriously, like the prophets before him, Jesus engaged in activities that were symbolic of his message—or rather, actually embodied it. Among those prophetic sign-actions (actions that most infuriated the Pharisees because they undermined and radically criticized their whole system) were his table fellowship and his actions on the Sabbath.

Jesus ate with tax collectors and sinners. In so doing he broke through one of the major social and religious barriers of his society. The matter of who ate with whom was of great significance. The Pharisees operated carefully controlled table fellowships that excluded those who would not or could not fit in with their pursuit of holiness. Even when Jesus was invited to and attended meals with Pharisees, he created embarrassment by what he said and did (Lk 7:36-50; 14:1-24). But what was worse was that he deliberately cultivated close social relationships with precisely those groups of people whom the Pharisaic program excluded: "sinners," tax collectors, prostitutes. By *eating* with them, Jesus was *including* them in his vision of God's kingdom and showing that the kingdom of God was all about grace and mercy and forgiveness, not about purity and exclusion.

Jesus also went out of his way to behave in extraordinary ways toward those whom society marginalized for other reasons: the sick (especially leprosy sufferers), women (including the ritually unclean) and children. We must not underestimate the disturbing force of Jesus' actions in this area. He was deliberately flouting the religious and social status conventions that undergirded his society's perception of itself. People thought that it was essential to preserve these fundamental distinctions in the quest for the kind of society that would please God and persuade him to cast off the Roman yoke. Jesus showed his rejection of that whole philosophy by his habitual social intercourse. It was not an *occasional gesture* toward the poor and the outcast. It was not a matter of a few token photo opportunities. Jesus gained a *reputation* as the "friend of sinners." His disciples were asked critically about his table manners. It was a persistent, intentional policy, and it cut right across the dominant theology and ethos of the spiritual leaders of Israel. Jesus habitually had meals with people that the Pharisees would never have eaten with. He *included* those whom they *excluded*. It was a provocative habit.

And Jesus healed on the Sabbath. Deliberately. In fact, if you look at the healings of Jesus, it is interesting that whereas most of them happened at the request of sick persons who approached Jesus, in the case of the healings on Sabbaths, it was Jesus who took the initiative, unasked. People asked for healing at almost any time *except* the Sabbath (as the synagogue superintendent said was proper, Lk 13:14). Jesus *chose* to heal on the Sabbath. He took the initiative to do it at precisely the time when people would have been reluctant to ask. Again, there is something of a prophetic symbolic action about this. It was public, noticeable, deliberate, controversial and pointed. And it aroused his opponents to anger because he appeared to be trampling on something they considered a prime mark of a faithful, distinctive people. Once again, Jesus' understanding of what constituted the people of God and what was pleasing to God differed radically from theirs. They saw Sabbath observance as necessary to avoid God's judgment. Jesus saw it as the day above all days to demonstrate God's salvation.

(3) *The temple.* Third, there were his words and actions in and about the temple. The fact that Jesus threatened the destruction of the temple, in word and in symbolic action, was one of the most remembered things about him, which is not surprising since it was just about the most scandalous and provocative of all his actions. It featured prominently in his trial. Scholars who sift the Gospel narratives for what they are prepared to consider authentic and historical are all agreed that the so-called cleansing of the temple is firmly grounded in fact, and indeed some regard it as a major clue to understanding the aims and intentions of Jesus (Mt 21:12-13; Mk 11:15-17; Lk 19:45-46).

However, *cleansing* is no longer regarded as an adequate term for what Jesus did and what he meant. The word *cleansing* suggests that the only thing Jesus objected to was the commercial trading in the temple courts. But the exchange and purchase of animals and currency was an integral part of the whole sacrificial system for the many pilgrims from near and far. It was not regarded as "unspiritual." There may well have been an element of profiteering involved, but Jesus' action does not seem to have been directed against merely that but rather at the whole temple machinery.

Much more probably, Jesus' temple action was a prophetic sign, signifying nothing less than the coming destruction of the temple and its whole sacrificial system. This fits in with Jewish apocalyptic expectations that when the Messiah would come, there would be an end to the old temple and the arrival of a new temple, fit for the new age of God's reign over Israel and the nations. Jesus believed that he was initiating this new age in his own person. So his prophetic act in the temple (like his riding into Jerusalem on a donkey the previous day, pointing to Zechariah 9:9) was a dramatic way of announcing its arrival. This would fit also with the prophecy of Malachi 3:1-3.

We also need to understand the role of the temple as the very heart of Israel and the heartbeat of Israel's nationalism. The temple was the nerve center where Israel could most truly be itself—holy, distinct, separate, undefiled, exclusive. It was the navel of Jerusalem, the navel of the earth. It was the pinnacle of Mount Zion, the city of God. Not for nothing, therefore, did the Romans keep a garrison of soldiers right next door, since the temple was the scene of occasional unrest and the hatching of anti-Roman riots. So Jesus was also denouncing the role of the temple as the focus of nationalistic pride and antagonism to the Gentiles. It had become the symbol of an Israel at odds with the world rather than an Israel for the nations. It had become a perversion of the very mission of Israel itself. This interpretation fits well with the words that accompanied Jesus' prophetic action.

"Is it not written 'My house will be called a house of prayer for all nations'? But you have made it 'a den of robbers'" (Mk 11:17). The direct quotation is from Isaiah 56:7, which is a chapter saturated with God's universal desire for outsiders to come and enjoy the blessings of his salvation. Foreigners and eunuchs are promised inclusion and acceptance and joy in the house of God. This echoes but surpasses the prayer of Solomon at the dedication of the original temple in 1 Kings 8:41-43. Instead of being a fortress to keep Israel safe and the nations out, the temple should have been the beacon of Israel as God's light to bring the nations in. And for those who had ears to hear and scriptural memories, the donkey ride on the day before would have recalled Zechariah's prophecy that when the Messiah came he would take away the hardware of warfare and "he will proclaim *peace to the nations*" (Zech 9:10).

And that last phrase of Jesus' scathing words ("a den of robbers") brings us right back to Jeremiah. For that is exactly what Jeremiah said to the people of Jerusalem in the temple itself at a previous time of great national peril when the enemy was Babylon (Jer 7). At that time also the temple was the heart of Israel's nationalism and resistance. Then too the people believed that so long as the temple stood, they were safe, protected by the God who could never destroy his own temple. Safe, said Jeremiah, like robbers in a den; but not at all safe from the coming judgment of God, which would destroy Jerusalem and temple together.

Jesus gave the words an extra twist, because the word translated "robber," *lestes*, did not just mean a thief but was the current word for the anti-Roman resistance fighters—terrorists, in our language. Such was the perversion of the whole ethos of the temple. But it could not last. Jesus saw in the near future not (as the Jewish leaders hoped) an act of judgment by God on the Gentiles that would finally exclude them entirely from the temple, Jerusalem and the land, but rather an act of God's judgment on the temple itself as the center of such exclusiveness and the beginning of a new extension of blessing and salvation to the nations. This was a thorough and politically intolerable reversal of the temple ideology of his day. That is why it was a major factor in his trial as far as the Jews were concerned. To threaten the temple was to threaten the very foundation of the state as they understood it. Nothing but the death penalty would do.

So, like Jeremiah, Jesus uttered prophetic words of judgment on the temple, and along with it the city and nation. There is no doubt that in this respect Jesus adopted fully the stance of the great prophets of divine judgment on Israel—even though, again like Jeremiah, he did so with intense grief and compassion. There are at least eight clear predictions of the destruction of the temple or Jerusalem in the Gospels and Acts (Mt 23:37-39; Mk 13:2; 14:58; 15:29; Lk 13:34-35; 19:42-44; 21:20-24; Jn 2:19; Acts 6:14). And this is only part of a very strong strand of judgment language in the wider teaching of Jesus. One scholar has counted some sixty-seven passages where Jesus issues a warning or threat, coupled with some explanation or call to repentance or other action.

Clearly, Jesus drank deeply from the profound seriousness of the great prophets of the Hebrew Scriptures. Like them, he allowed no special immunity from the wrath of God to a people who were denying or perverting the reason for their existence. Like them, he knew that judgment begins at the house of God. Like them, he knew he would suffer for his message. Unlike them, however, as the Messiah he would in a deeper sense take that judgment upon himself.

JESUS, THE PSALMS AND THE REIGN OF GOD

Jesus came to a people who knew how to pray and how to sing. The rich heritage of worship in Israel was part of the very fabric and furniture of the mind of Jesus. So it is not at all surprising to find him often quoting from the Psalms, even with his dying breath. Nor is it surprising to find that the values and concerns that have occupied our attention in this chapter already are deeply embedded in the Psalms, because the Psalms reflect like a thousand mirrors the great themes of the law and the prophets.

There are many ways in which we could show links between the Psalms and Jesus. We could trace the pervasive contrast between the character, actions and fate of the good, the wise and the godly, on the one hand, and the wicked, the foolish and the ungodly on the other. It sets the whole tone for the Psalter from the very first psalm and surfaces in the sharp edges of the parables of Jesus. We could list the repeated ethical concerns of the Psalms and see them shared by Jesus—like the importance of truth and the damage of falsehood; the high premium placed on humility and walking in personal communion with God; the warmth of generosity and kindness that marks the righteous person in imitation of the ways of God himself; the anger at injustice, hypocrisy and perverted behavior; the celebration of the abundance of God's good gifts in nature and providence and the matching exhortations to trustfulness and freedom from anxiety; and the gratitude that overflows into a commitment to obedience to God's law.

But we shall focus on one major theme in the Psalms that provides an important background for the central pillar of the preaching of Jesus—the kingship of God. Nothing is better known about Jesus than that he came proclaiming that "the kingdom of God is at hand" and spent a great deal of time explaining what it meant.

It might be somewhat surprising that we have only come to look at the subject of the kingdom of God at this late stage in the book. Should it not have featured in a prime position of honor near the start? Well, it could have, but my strategy was deliberate. Our whole purpose has been to see how much Jesus was shaped in his identity, mission and teaching by his Hebrew Scriptures. And this was as true of this central theme in his agenda as of everything else. The kingdom of God meant the reign of *this* God—the God revealed in the history, law, prophecy and worship of his own people, recorded in the Scriptures he knew and loved. The spiritual and moral content of the expression "kingdom of God" was already shaped by the great teaching and challenges of the Torah and the Prophets and the Psalms. And so it has been important for us to work our way through that material before we ask what Jesus meant by the kingdom of God. Jesus preached about the kingship of God to people who already knew that their God was king. But he preached it in ways that certainly surprised them.

It is a common misunderstanding that the idea of the kingdom of God was something *introduced* by Jesus. Certainly there was a freshness and an urgency about his announcement of its arrival (or its imminence, depending on how one interprets "the kingdom of God is at *hand*"). He was clearly proclaiming that something new was bursting on the scene through his ministry, something that demanded attention and urgent action. But he was not putting a totally new concept before a bewildered audience. His Jewish listeners knew very well that God was king. Their Scriptures stated it often enough, and they sang words to that effect regularly from the Psalms in their synagogue worship. In other words, and in our terms, *the kingship of God is an Old Testament concept.*

In chapter one we looked at a group of psalms that celebrate the kingship of Yahweh, with an eye especially on the remarkable way in which they envisage all the nations praising the God of Israel for his saving acts. We now turn back to that same group of psalms to take note of some other themes that run through them, which would have been part of Jewish understanding of the expression "kingdom of God" as Jesus used it.

Another pause for Bible reading would be in order! Read through Psalms 24; 29; 47; 93; 95; 96; 97; 98; 99; 145 and 146. All of these include references to Yahweh as king or expressions such as "the LORD reigns" or "sits enthroned" or "rules over the nations." Apart from that common proclamation, there is considerable variety in the moods and themes of these psalms. We shall pick out just three major aspects that between them are a fairly good summary of how the idea of the reign of God was understood in the Old Testament.

The universal dimension. The widest aspect of the reign of Yahweh expressed in these psalms is the affirmation that he rules over the whole earth. The LORD is king of all nations and all creation. This universal reign of Yahweh was actually first expressed in a song of praise that is not in the book of Psalms but in the book of Exodus. It is the song of Moses in Exodus 15, which in the context of the story was sung on the far shore of the Sea of Reeds after the Israelites had safely crossed and the pursuing Egyptian army was washed away. The song ends with the climactic words "The LORD reigns, for ever and ever" (Ex 15:18). One can almost hear, under the breath, the implication "and not Pharaoh." For the whole sequence of events that had just come to its climax at the sea had been to prove exactly who was the real king, who had the real sovereign power. Moses kept pointing it out to Pharaoh, but Pharaoh never learned the lesson. Yahweh's conflict with Pharaoh demonstrated not only that it was Yahweh, not Pharaoh, who was king in Egypt, but also that his rule extended over the whole earth (see Ex 8:22; 9:14, 16, 29). Daniel conveyed the same message at the opposite end of Old Testament history to Nebuchadnezzar in words that echo the Psalms (Dan 4:3, 17, 25, 32, 34-35; cf. Ps 145:11-13).

The widest and most basic sense of the kingship of God in the Old Testament, then, is this universal sovereignty. The LORD God of Israel is God of everything and everybody in all creation.

The earthly dimension. The Psalms celebrate the kingship of Yahweh over all the earth as an act of faith. It was certainly not something evident to the naked eye. Clearly God's kingship is not in fact acknowledged by all the nations. However, Israel, through the covenant relationship, had accepted the rule of God over itself as a nation. God was the acknowledged king in Israel—so much so that for several centuries this belief prevented it from having a human king over them. And when at length the pressure for a monarchy became irresistible, the narrative presents it very ambiguously— as a definite step away from real theocracy and yet as a vehicle that God could use to express and locate his own kingship. Israel did not need to have a king at all. But once it had one, God "embodies" his own divine rule in the person of the Israelite king (a very imperfect embodiment, to be sure, but the link is made nevertheless, as in Psalm 2).

So, as well as the universal dimension of God's kingship, the Old Testament has this very particular dimension. God's covenant relationship with Israel was in a sense the relation of a king to his subjects. Indeed, the idea of a "covenant" made use of the political model of the treaties of that era between imperial kingdoms and their vassal states. That is what lies behind the description of Yahweh as "the Great King."

In the ancient world, the prime job of a king was to protect his people from their enemies and to give them laws and good government (the same basic priorities that we expect from our own governments). The two other texts in the Torah (apart from the one in Ex 15:18) in which Yahweh is portrayed as king interestingly pick up each of these. In Numbers 23:21-23,

Yahweh as king is the protector of his people. In Deuteronomy 33:3-5, his kingship is linked to the giving of the law.

So the kingship of God in Israel had very *practical, earthy effects*. It was not just a theological item of belief. It was the authority of God as king, which lay behind the specific details of Israel's law—with all its characteristics that we surveyed above. There was, therefore, a powerfully *ethical* thrust to the acknowledgment of Yahweh's kingship. His reign was one of *righteousness and justice*, earthed in the real world of social, economic and political relationships. And this is what we find in some of the psalms that celebrate it.

If the King of glory dwells on his holy hill, then Psalm 24 asks who can stand there—who can worship God acceptably? The answer is clear and ethical. "The one who has clean hands and a pure heart" (Ps 24:4). A fuller version of what these phrases mean, spelled out in social reality, is found in Psalm 15. Later kingship psalms emphasize the justice of God's reign.

Righteousness and justice are the foundation of his throne. (Ps 97:2)

The King is mighty, he loves justice—
  you have established equity;
in Jacob you have done
  what is just and right. (Ps 99:4)

Again, this is spelled out in social detail in other psalms, in terms of practical compassion on all the needy of the earth—man and beast.

The LORD is gracious and compassionate,
  slow to anger and rich in love.
The LORD is good to all;
  he has compassion on all he has made. (Ps 145:8-9, cf. 14-20)

He upholds the cause of the oppressed
  and gives food to the hungry.
The LORD sets prisoners free,
  the LORD gives sight to the blind,
the LORD lifts up those who are bowed down,
  the LORD loves the righteous.
The LORD watches over the foreigner
  and sustains the fatherless and the widow,
  but he frustrates the ways of the wicked.

The LORD reigns forever,

>your God, O Zion, for all generations.

Praise the LORD. (Ps 146:7-10)

The kingdom of God, then, meant the reign of *Yahweh*, and where Yahweh is king, justice and compassion must reign too. As we saw above, one of the very core features of the law was the imitation of Yahweh. If God chooses to behave in the ways described in Psalm 146, then his people must demonstrate the same qualities in their own social structures and relationships. That is precisely the duty laid on the king in particular, as the embodiment of God's kingship in Psalm 72.

So when Jesus came proclaiming the kingdom of God, he was not talking about a faraway place or an ideal or an attitude. It was not just pie in the sky or joy in the heart. The reality of God's rule cannot be spiritualized into heaven (now or later) or privatized into individuals. Of course, it does have spiritual and personal dimensions, which are fundamental also. We are called to submit to God's reign in our individual lives. But the term itself speaks of the aligning of human life on earth, in all its dimensions, with the will of the divine government of God. To pray "may your kingdom come" is to pray "may your will be done on earth as in heaven." The one must produce the other.

"Heaven rules," said Daniel—on earth. And the rule of the God of heaven demands a repentance that puts things right in the social realm as much as in personal humility (Dan 4:26-27). Jesus cannot have meant any less. Especially since his declared agenda, taken as we saw in its precise wording from Isaiah 61, could easily have been taken from the psalm quoted above—a psalm celebrating Yahweh's kingship in specific terms related to human needs and social evils.

To enter the kingdom of God means to submit oneself to the rule of God, and that means a fundamental reorientation of one's ethical commitments and values into line with the priorities and character of the God revealed in the Scriptures. The point of being Israel and living as the people of Yahweh was to make the universal reign of God local and visible in its whole structure of religious, social, economic and political life. It was to manifest in practical reality what it meant to live, as well as to sing, "the LORD reigns."

The eschatological dimension. So in the Old Testament the kingship of God was in one sense a universal sovereignty over all nations, nature and history. But in another sense it meant the specific rule of Yahweh over Israel within the covenant relationship where his kingship was acknowledged, and where it was supposed to be lived out in practical social and economic justice, love and compassion. But God's kingship, third, came to be thought of in a future perspective also because neither of the first two senses was being realized in full.

On the one hand it was obvious that the *nations* did not acknowledge Yahweh as king, and on the other hand it became increasingly and painfully obvious that even *Israel*, who acknowledged him as king, did not demonstrate it. He was king in name and title but not obeyed in reality in the actual life of the nation. This credibility gap between the professions of worship and the practicalities of life was the spot where the anger of the prophets was most seen and heard. That anger was directed especially at the human kings of Israel, who not only failed to reflect God's kingship in its social and ethical demands but rather perverted and denied it.

So as the Old Testament era went on, there developed the hope and expectation that at some time in the future God himself would intervene to establish his reign in its fullness over his people and over the world. God would come as king and put things right. This hope is found in the prophets. Jeremiah, after a chapter that surveys the failures of several human kings (Jer 22), announces that God himself will "shepherd" his people through a true descendant of David (Jer 23:1-6). Ezekiel, using similar language but in greater depth and detail, combines God's own future kingship with a coming true son of David (Ezek 34; it would be worthwhile to read this whole chapter, thinking about the impact it would have had on Jesus). Shepherds and shepherding were common metaphors for kings in the Old Testament. (Which incidentally shows that when Jesus referred to himself as the good, or model, shepherd, it was a claim to be the rightful king of Israel, the embodiment of God's kingship over his people. "Good shepherd" is not just a picture of cuddly compassion.)

Isaiah 52:7-10 is the basis for the familiar modern hymn "Our God Reigns." In its context it was a word of rejoicing for Israel itself at the time of the restoration from exile (Is 52:7—"say to Zion"), but it also envisages "all the ends of the earth" joining in the song of praise to God's royal salvation. It is a magnificent eschatological and missional song.

The same message of future hope and blessing in Isaiah 33:20-24 is linked to the point that God as king will also be lawgiver and judge.

> For the LORD is our judge,
>   the LORD is our lawgiver,
> the LORD is our king;
>   it is he who will save us.

Similarly, Isaiah 2:2-5 envisages all nations accepting the law and the rule of Yahweh in such a way that there will be an end to war between nations. The same prophecy in Micah 4:2-5 is followed by an even more explicit reference to Yahweh as king (Mic 4:6-9), and by the familiar word that it would be from Bethlehem that the ruler of God's people would arise (Mic 5:1-5).

So much, then, for the coming kingdom of God as envisaged by the prophets. Returning to the Psalms, the note of rejoicing on which some of them end is a celebration of the hope of God's coming. The God who reigns *now* in the affirmations of faith and worship will *one day* come to reign in reality, and when he does it will be to put all things right for his whole creation. "Putting things right" is probably the best way to catch what the Hebrew means by "he comes to judge." It does not just mean "to condemn"—though it will certainly mean the destruction of wickedness. But since the coming of God is made the subject of universal rejoicing of all creation, it must also include the idea of God reestablishing his original desire and design for his world, in which the liberation of the peoples will spell joy for nature also (cf. Rom 8:19-25).

> Shout for joy before the LORD, the King.
> Let the sea resound, and everything in it,
>   the world, and all who live in it.
> Let the rivers clap their hands,
>   let the mountains sing together for joy;
> let them sing before the LORD,
>   *for he comes* to judge the earth.
> He will judge the world in righteousness
>   and the peoples with equity. (Ps 98:6-9, my italics)

So when Jesus came announcing "The time is fulfilled, the reign of God is at hand," he was making a sensational claim. He was saying, "What you have been longing for as something in the future is now bursting into the present." What they sang about as a matter of hope in worship was now among them as a matter of reality in person—the person of Jesus. The eschatological was breaking into history. God was coming to reign.

The teaching of Jesus about the kingdom of God does show that there was still a *future* dimension even from the perspective of his earthly ministry. That is, it was not yet fully manifest in what he came and did. He likened it to a process that would be at work, even in hidden ways (like seed growing or yeast rising or net fishing).

But the point was, the reign of God had definitely arrived. It was inaugurated. It was present and at work right there in the midst of the people, said Jesus. It gave them an opportunity they must not miss. And it made demands they could not evade—demands that they already knew about from the riches of their Scriptures and all the moral depths of Old Testament faith.

For Jesus did not come to teach people *new* ideas about some new moral philosophy that he called the kingdom of God. Of course he sharpened and provoked their thinking with his questions and parables, transforming their perspectives. Of course he helped them gain a fresh, God's-eye view of how things were meant to be under his rule. Of course he drove his points right home to the inner recesses of the heart, searching our motives as well as our actions. Of course he brought a new urgency, a new power, a new motivation for the obedience of personal discipleship. But in its major features the kingdom of God already had its *essential ethical* content from the Old Testament. The kingdom of God was already filled with the whole range of ethical values, priorities and demands that we have surveyed in the law and the prophets. If Yahweh God has come to reign, then the Scriptures had already shown clearly what that would mean for God's people and for the world.

There was no ambiguity at all about what was required of the people of God under his kingship. No ambiguity about what it would mean for the world when God would establish his rule. The dynamic power of the message of Jesus lay not so much in *what* the kingdom of God meant as in *the fact that it had arrived.* The gospel that Jesus preached was good news of a present reality. Good news of the kingdom of God. Good news, at least, for those who were prepared to receive it in repentant hearts and a radical new agenda for living.

And this is also the note on which we need to end this chapter—gospel! We have spent a lot of time looking at the ethical values, priorities and principles that we find in the Old Testament—in the Law, the Prophets and the Psalms. And we have seen how they are reflected in the life and teaching of Jesus in so many ways. This is not surprising. After all, Jesus lived a life of perfect obedience, modeling what a faithful Israelite should be like.

But we must immediately be careful not to imagine that he taught that the kingdom of God was all about keeping the rules and somehow proving that you were among the righteous who would stand upright and vindicated on the day God came to establish his kingdom. No—from first to last, Jesus preached the *gospel* of the kingdom. It was a matter of grace and promise, through and through. It was to be received, not earned. You entered it through repentance and faith in him. And then, having entered, having submitted to God as king through submitting to Jesus as Lord and Savior, then and only then you would learn to walk in his ways and live under his rule—in other words, be a disciple of Jesus. That could well be a road of suffering, persecution and death, as it was for Jesus himself. But it was the road of blessing and joy.

And that note of joy—the joy of the kingdom of God—is what the Psalms most celebrate about God's kingship. Isaac Watts captured the mood of Psalm 96 and Psalm 98 in his famous hymn, which really should be sung much more often than just at Christmas! Notice how he echoes the ecstasy of those psalms and the way they include all humanity and all nature, and anticipate the universal rule of God's saving justice and love. And even without *naming* Jesus, we sing the hymn knowing that Jesus is indeed the Lord, King and Savior who Isaac Watts meant. Our final chapter will show how the God of the psalmists is indeed the God who has walked among us in the person of Jesus of Nazareth.

> Joy to the world! the Lord has come;
> Let earth receive her king!
> Let every heart prepare him room,
> And heaven and nature sing.
>
> Joy to the world! the Savior reigns;
> Let men their songs employ;
> While fields and flocks, rocks, hills and plains
> Repeat the sounding joy.

No more let sins and sorrows grow,
Nor thorns infest the ground;
He comes to make his blessings flow
Far as the curse is found.

He rules the world with truth and grace,
and makes the nations prove
The glories of his righteousness
And wonders of his love.

CHAPTER 5 QUESTIONS AND EXERCISES

1. Some people think that the coming and teaching of Jesus make the Old Testament irrelevant. Or they make a big contrast between the "violent god" of the Old Testament and the "kind and loving" teaching of Jesus. Consider or discuss how you would respond to those views in the light of the content of this chapter. What passages would you use to support your answer?

2. Study the story of the temptations/testing of Jesus in the wilderness in Matthew 4:1-11. What do Jesus' three quotes from Deuteronomy 6 and 8 tell us about how Jesus saw himself and his ministry?

3. Read Deuteronomy 4–11, imagining yourself as Jesus reading it. In what ways did those chapters influence the way Jesus thought and taught?

4. Make a list of the things Jesus taught where you can see principles or priorities that reflect the Old Testament. Build two columns—one for references in the Gospels and the other for passages in the Old Testament that you think are reflected in some way in the Gospel text. How could this list help people see how much the teaching of Jesus was rooted in the Scriptures of the Old Testament?

5. Read Luke 4:14-21, which concludes with Jesus saying, "Today this Scripture is fulfilled in your hearing." In what ways is it possible and right to apply the message of the Old Testament prophets about social and economic justice to our world today?

6. Read Psalms 93–99 and make a study of what they mean by saying "The LORD reigns." How does your study affect the way you understand the kingdom of God? How is each psalm reflected in the teaching of Jesus about the kingdom of God?

JESUS *and* HIS
OLD TESTAMENT GOD

In his opening verse, Matthew tells us that Jesus was "the Christ," or Messiah. We saw in chapter three that "messiah" was not a divine title in itself. The Messiah was the human person whom God would anoint to carry out the plan and purpose of God. That was not the same thing as saying that the Messiah would actually be God. People believed that God would act in and through the Messiah, not necessarily that the Messiah would *be* God.

So today people sometimes say, "Jesus never claimed to be God. He never directly said the words, 'I am God.'" Rather, they say, Jesus was just a particularly good, loving and humble man. It was only the church hundreds of years later that elevated Jesus to divine status and started worshiping him. The idea that Jesus is God, or a god, is nothing more than a religious myth invented by people who had to find ways to increase his importance in order to sustain their own power.

But this simply won't do. It just doesn't stand up to the facts. It certainly doesn't square with what we read all over the New Testament about how Jesus spoke about himself and how his very first followers came to understand him within his own lifetime and theirs.

Let's start again, as we did in the previous chapters, with Matthew as our guide. From the beginning he insists that, in Jesus of Nazareth, Yahweh the LORD God of Israel—the God of the Old Testament Scriptures—had kept his promise to come to his people. Then we shall look more widely at the way the rest of the New Testament portrays the identity of Jesus using words that the Old Testament had used only for God. And finally we shall see that four of the greatest functions of Yahweh in the Old Testament are calmly attributed to Jesus in the New. Jesus does, or will do, things that only God has the right to do, according to the Bible.

JESUS AND THE ARRIVAL OF GOD

At the time of Jesus, whom were people expecting to turn up? They longed, of course, for God to send somebody to lead them out of their oppression and the feeling of being exiles in their own land. That's what their hopes of a messiah mostly focused on—which (as we saw earlier) was probably the main reason Jesus tended to stop people using that title about him. The word *messiah* carried popular assumptions that Jesus did not agree with. But more important than whatever *human* figure they hoped for, the longing of the Jews was that God *himself* would come to their aid. There are many promises in the Old Testament that speak about God himself intervening to save his people, to shepherd them, to gather them back to himself, to dwell among them again.

So when Matthew introduces John the Baptist, who in turn will introduce Jesus, it is very significant how Matthew chooses to explain and interpret the arrival of John through a text from Isaiah. Matthew applies to John the Baptist the following description:

> A voice of one calling in the wilderness,
> "Prepare the way for the LORD,
>   make straight paths for him." (Mt 3:3; cf. Is 40:3)

The implication is clear: John was preparing the way not just for the arrival of Jesus but for the arrival of the Lord himself—which in Old Testament terms, of course, meant the LORD, Yahweh, the God of Israel. God himself was on the way! Get the place ready!

The difficulty was that Jesus did not appear to be doing all the things that people probably expected to happen when God showed up. Jesus spoke about the kingdom of God coming in hidden and unexpected ways, so much so that even John himself began to have questions later on. Had he announced the wrong messiah? So in Matthew 11 we read how John, after he'd been in prison for some time, sent some of his own disciples to get a straight answer out of Jesus.

"Are you the one who was to come, or should we expect someone else?" they asked. And how did Jesus reply? He did not get angry and point to his lapel badge: *"Jesus—The Messiah You've Always Wanted!"* The whole messiah thing was too confused anyway. Nor did he rebuff them with, "Look, don't you know that it's *God* you're talking to? Can't you see my halo?"

No, Jesus simply told them to look around and see what was happening in his ministry, and then lay their observations alongside another familiar passage from Isaiah. "Jesus replied, 'Go back and report to John what you hear and see: the blind receive sight, the lame walk, those who have leprosy are cleansed, the deaf hear, the dead are raised, and the good news is proclaimed to the poor'" (Mt 11:4-5).

With such a list Jesus was undoubtedly echoing Isaiah 35, a passage that was written for people like John who were discouraged and doubting that God would ever come to the rescue. To them, the prophet said:

> Strengthen the feeble hands,
>> steady the knees that give way;
> say to those with fearful hearts,
>> "Be strong, do not fear;
> your God will come,
>> he will come with vengeance;
> with divine retribution
>> he will come to save you."
> *Then* will the eyes of the blind be opened
>> and the ears of the deaf unstopped
> *Then* will the lame leap like a deer,
>> and the mute tongue shout for joy. (Is 35:3-6, my italics)

Notice the repeated word *then*. *When?* When would such things happen? When "your God will come." So if these things were clearly happening around Jesus, then the big question was: Who had come? Who was Jesus? By adding "and the good news is preached to the poor," Jesus was alluding also to Isaiah 61:1 (as he had done in his exposition of that text in the synagogue in Nazareth in Luke 4:16-21). So Jesus was claiming to be the *anointed one of* God prophesied in that text. But he was more. He was doing what the Scriptures said would be the signs that *God himself* had come.

Matthew then tells us that as John the Baptist's disciples were leaving to take that word back to John, Jesus continued to speak to his own disciples about John. Yet again he sets everything in the light of the Scriptures. Who was John? How should the crowds understand the significance of his arrival and ministry? Jesus reminds them of Malachi.

> This is the one [i.e., John the Baptist] about whom it is written:
> "I will send my messenger ahead of you,
> who will prepare your way before you." (Mt 11:10)

What Malachi had said was this: "I will send my messenger, who will prepare the way before me. Then suddenly the Lord you are seeking will come to his temple" (Mal 3:1). The *me* in Malachi's text is God himself. But Jesus hears the words as addressed to himself—*you*. That is, Jesus clearly identified himself with God in Malachi's text. God had made that promise, and now he had kept it by sending John as the messenger ahead of God's own arrival in the person of Jesus. Such an interpretation of the combined ministries of John and Jesus must have been very hard to grasp when you were living in the midst of it all.

If John and his disciples were puzzled and questioning, so were the disciples of Jesus. So Jesus took them up a mountain for a life-changing demonstration of his divine glory. If they could not grasp who he truly was, then he would show them. Here is Matthew's account of the transfiguration, slightly abbreviated.

> After six days Jesus took with him Peter, James and John the brother of James, and led them up a high mountain by themselves. There he was transfigured before them. His face shone like the sun, and his clothes became as white as the light. Just then there appeared before them Moses and Elijah, talking with Jesus. . . .
>
> A bright cloud covered them, and a voice from the cloud said, "This is my Son, whom I love; with him I am well pleased. Listen to him!"
>
> When the disciples heard this, they fell facedown to the ground, terrified. But Jesus came and touched them. "Get up," he said. "Don't be afraid." When they looked up, they saw no one except Jesus.
>
> As they were coming down the mountain . . . the disciples asked him, "Why then do the teachers of the law say that Elijah must come first?"
>
> Jesus replied, "To be sure, Elijah comes and will restore all things. But I

tell you, Elijah has already come, and they did not recognize him, but have
done to him everything they wished. In the same way the Son of Man is
going to suffer at their hands." Then the disciples understood that he was
talking to them about John the Baptist. (Mt 17:1-13)

What an experience! Peter and John never forgot it (see Jn 1:14; 2 Pet 1:16-
18). They knew they had been in the presence of God. They recognized the
signs that often accompanied a manifestation of God in the Old Testament:
extreme shining brightness, a cloud and a voice. Seeing Moses and Elijah
there too, the awestruck disciples must have wondered whether they had been
transported to Mount Sinai or Mount Carmel. They reacted as people did in
the Old Testament when God appeared or spoke: "they fell facedown to the
ground, terrified." Not surprising, really.

And once again, in the conversation afterward, Jesus helps them to understand the significance of John the Baptist. They knew the accepted
teaching of the experts—Elijah must first come before God arrives. The
staggering challenge lay in the implications. Here is the logic:

- *Elijah* comes first, then *God* will come (drawn from Mal 4:5).

- You know that *John* has already come first, and then *Jesus* came.

- So if *John* was *Elijah*, who is *Jesus*?

- Get it?

In ways like this Matthew shows that Jesus used Scriptures that spoke about
God in ways that pointed to himself. He did not stand up with a banner
proclaiming, "I am God." He did not need to. The people around him knew
their Scriptures. Jesus pointed to those texts, pointed to himself and in effect
told them to draw their own conclusions.

The most climactic moment when Matthew shows us that Jesus was the
personal embodiment of Yahweh, the God of Old Testament Israel, comes
at the very end of his Gospel in what has become known as the Great
Commission.

Then the eleven disciples went to Galilee, to the mountain where Jesus had
told them to go. When they saw him, they worshiped him; but some doubted.
Then Jesus came to them and said, "All authority in heaven and on earth has
been given to me. Therefore go and make disciples of all nations, baptizing
them in the name of the Father and of the Son and of the Holy Spirit, and

teaching them to obey everything I have commanded you. And surely I am
with you always, to the very end of the age." (Mt 28:16-20)

For those who "when they saw him" immediately "worshiped him," their
conviction had already become crystal clear. Seeing Jesus of Nazareth, crucified and risen, they knew they were in the presence of the Lord God who
alone was worthy of their worship. For some others who "doubted," Jesus yet
again echoes the Scriptures they knew so well.

In the book of Deuteronomy, exalted affirmations are made about
Yahweh. In Deuteronomy 10:14, 17, for example, we are told that he is the
God who owns the whole universe ("the heavens, even the highest heavens,
the earth and everything in it"), and exercises authority over all cosmic
powers and authorities as "God of gods and Lord of lords." Yahweh is the
one single, sovereign, cosmic God. And in Deuteronomy 4 we read this:
"Acknowledge and take to heart this day that the Lord is God in *heaven
above and on the earth below*. There is no other" (Deut 4:39, my italics).

These scriptural phrases would have been familiar to all those on that
mountain as words that could only be spoken by, or about, the living God.
But these are precisely the words that Jesus echoes when he stands there and
calmly utters the breathtaking affirmation: "All authority *in heaven and on
earth* has been given to me." Jesus meant (and Matthew wants us to understand that Jesus meant) that he shares the "Yahweh identity." Jesus adopts
the Yahweh position and uses scriptural Yahweh texts about himself. Everything that his disciples knew to be true about the God of their Scriptures,
their history and their people, they must now understand to be true of Jesus.
If they had not realized it when he first came to earth, they must now be
convinced of it before he leaves the earth: in Jesus of Nazareth, the Lord
God, the Holy One of Israel, had come among them. And those who understood this responded in the only proper way—they worshiped him.

JESUS AND THE IDENTITY OF GOD

What we have been seeing in Matthew's Gospel can be seen in the other
Gospels as well, of course. John's Gospel, written after the other three,
plunges straight in with its preface affirming the divine identity of Jesus,
the Word made flesh at his incarnation. And at its climax, Thomas declares
to the risen Jesus, "My Lord and my God." And Jesus did not contradict
Thomas. In between, John shows Jesus identifying himself in a range of "I

am" sayings, climaxing in the unequivocal claim in John 8:58 that he is none other than the one who declared to Moses, "I am who I am."

However, we do not have to wait until texts as late as John's Gospel to find clear evidence that the followers of Jesus knew and affirmed his identity as the embodiment of the LORD God of the Old Testament. The New Testament contains evidence of the prayer and worship of the earliest communities of believers, reaching back probably even to the time before they were nicknamed "Christians," and certainly back before most of the New Testament itself was written. From the very earliest days, followers of Jesus were addressing him in prayer and worshiping him as Lord—things that Jewish men and women would never have dreamt of doing unless they were absolutely convinced that Jesus was truly God and that it was right and proper to call on him in worship and prayer. Otherwise, they were guilty of blasphemy and idolatry.

We need to look at two phrases, one in Aramaic, the other in Greek. One is a prayer, the other is an affirmation of faith.

Marana tha! At the end of his first letter to Corinth, Paul concludes with an expression in the Aramaic language—*Marana tha!* (1 Cor 16:22). Since he leaves it untranslated, the words must have been familiar even to Greek-speaking Christians. The phrase means "O Lord, come!" Since Paul quotes it in its original language, it must have been a well-known, familiar part of the worship of the original Aramaic-speaking followers of Jesus. That is, it would have been an established part of the worship of the first followers of Jesus who lived in Palestine and spoke the same language as Jesus and other Jews in that part of the world. So this is a piece of the worship language of the earliest followers of Jesus long before they were even called Christians, and long before the missionary journeys of Paul into the Gentile world of Asia Minor and Europe. The phrase must have traveled with Paul and the other early missionaries as a regular part of Christian worship even when the language was Greek (just as *hallelujah* has become a universal and un-translated word in Christian worship in many languages, even though it is originally a Hebrew phrase meaning "Praise Yahweh").

Marana tha! Paul exclaims, writing it with his own hand (1 Cor 16:21) and expecting his readers to understand it and echo it themselves. *Mar* or *Maran* was the Aramaic word for "Lord." It is clear that the "Lord" Paul is referring to is Jesus, since the immediately following verse speaks of "the grace of the Lord Jesus." So here is a word that the earliest Aramaic-speaking Christian communities must have used to refer to Jesus. But we also know that the Aramaic *Mar* (*Marah, Maran*) was used among Aramaic-speaking *Jews* as a term for the God of the Old Testament Scriptures—that is, for Yahweh, the God of Israel. The word could also be used (and indeed it is still used in the Greek Orthodox tradition) for human beings in positions of authority (just like the Greek *kyrios* can be used as a human title as well as for God). But there are plenty of occasions in Aramaic texts of the period (including the Qumran scrolls) where the term is used as a title of God.

It is important to understand that the expression is a *prayer addressed to* Jesus (asking him to come), not just a *hope expressed about* Jesus (stating that he will come). So, by directing their invocation to *Mar Jesus*, the earliest Aramaic-speaking believers were addressing their prayer to the only one who can legitimately be invoked in prayer—the LORD God. They were calling on Jesus, their Lord, to come.

Kyrios Iēsous! The second piece of early evidence for the content of the faith of the first believers is the simple affirmation *kyrios Iēsous*, "Jesus is Lord." When the two words come together like this with *kyrios* first, it is not just a title (Lord Jesus) but a sentence with the word "is" understood: "Jesus is Lord."

Paul uses the term *kyrios* 275 times, almost always with reference to Jesus. But he was by no means the first to do that. As with the early Aramaic expression *marana tha*, Paul inherited this Greek confession from those who were followers of Jesus before him. Indeed he probably heard Christians using the expression *and hated it*, in the days when he was persecuting those who dared to claim that this crucified carpenter from Nazareth was (God forbid!) the Messiah and (even worse!) that he was Lord. It was Paul's encounter with the risen Jesus on the road to Damascus that made him blindingly aware that the phrase was not the heinous blasphemy he would initially have thought. Rather, it was the simple truth. Luke's account of that event stresses this point—that Paul came to recognize not just that Jesus was indeed risen and alive, but also that he was Lord (Acts 9:5, 17).

When Paul uses the two-word phrase in his own writings, it is clearly already a christological formula. That is, it was a frequently repeated phrase in Christian worship. It needed no explanation because it was already universally accepted as the standard and defining confession of Christian identity. It occurs in this formulaic way in Romans 10:9; 1 Corinthians 12:3 and with slight expansion (to Jesus Christ) in Philippians 2:11.

Now the Greek word *kyrios*, like the Aramaic word *mar*, could be used as an honorific title for human beings (just as the word *lord* can be in English, or *seigneur* in French). But long before the word *kyrios* was ever applied to Jesus, it was probably being used by those who had translated the Hebrew Scriptures of the Old Testament into the Greek texts that we know as the Septuagint as a way of rendering the personal divine name Yahweh. I say "probably" because we do not have many manuscripts of the Greek versions of Old Testament books that go back before the New Testament era. But even in them it is interesting that the scribes did not attempt to transliterate the Hebrew name Yahweh into equivalent Greek letters. Rather, they chose to indicate in Greek a custom that was already well established when Hebrew speakers read the Old Testament text aloud. Whenever Hebrew readers came to the four letters YHWH in the written text, they substituted the Hebrew word *adonay* (meaning "Lord" in Hebrew) in their oral reading (a practice that Jews still follow to this day). So the Greek translators followed this tradition, and in the earliest manuscripts they either left the four Hebrew letters blank with dots (to warn the reader) or they put in four very ancient Hebrew symbols (indicating that the Name should not be spoken aloud but another word substituted). In view of the fact that later Greek manuscripts universally inserted *kyrios* at these points (more than six thousand times), it is most likely that scribes and readers were already using that word as the Greek equivalent of *adonay* whenever the Hebrew "Yahweh" occurred.

Any Greek-speaking Jew of the first century would have been entirely familiar with this custom. So when they read their Old Testament Scriptures in Greek, it was second nature for them to read *kyrios* and think *adonay*—knowing that *adonay* was a substitute for the personal name of God in the original Hebrew. So they read *kyrios*, and they thought "the covenant God of Israel." It is altogether remarkable, then, that even before Paul was writing his letters—that is, within the first two decades after Jesus' resurrection—this same term was already being applied to Jesus. And it was being applied not merely as a term of honor for a respected human being (as would have been natural), but with the fully freighted significance of its Old Testament reference to Yahweh the God of Israel.

We know this from Philippians 2:6-11. Paul may have composed this well-known passage just as it is in his letter. But it is much more likely, as many scholars think, that these are the lines of an early Christian hymn, which Paul is quoting here because it so strongly supports the point he is making at that point in his letter. Not only does the hymn celebrate the "super-exaltation" of Jesus (Phil 2:9a); not only does it say that God has given to Jesus "the name above every name" (Phil 2:9b, which can mean only one name—Yahweh); but on top of all that the hymn clinches its point by quoting one of the most monotheistic texts in the Old Testament about Yahweh and applying it to Jesus:

> that at the name of Jesus every knee should bow,
>> in heaven and on earth and under the earth,
> and every tongue confess that Jesus Christ is Lord
>> to the glory of God the Father. (Phil 2:10-11)

This is a partial quotation of words that were originally spoken *by Yahweh about himself* in Isaiah 45:22-23. And in that context the point of the words was to underline Yahweh's uniqueness as God and his unique ability to save.

> "There is no God apart from me,
> a righteous God and a Savior;
>> There is none but me.
>
> "Turn to me and be saved,
>> all you ends of the earth;
>> for I am God, and there is no other.
> By myself I have sworn,
>> my mouth has uttered in all integrity
>> a word that will not be revoked:
> Before me every knee will bow;
>> by me every tongue will swear.
> They will say of me, 'In the LORD alone
>> are deliverance [salvation] and strength.'" (Is 45:21-24)

Those magnificent prophecies of Isaiah 40–55 assert again and again that Yahweh is utterly unique as the only living God in his sovereign power over all creation, all nations and all history, and in his sole power to save. This was a core Jewish belief about God.

So here we have an early Christian hymn in Philippians 2 that deliberately selects a Scripture from such a context and applies it to Jesus. This early Christian hymn writer and all who sang or recited his words were affirming that Jesus shares the identity and uniqueness of Yahweh as sovereign God and Savior. They were so sure of this that they did not hesitate to insert the name of *Jesus* where the name *Yahweh* had occurred in the biblical text itself.

And then Paul, by quoting this hymn as part of his argument, calmly "gives to Jesus a God-title, applies to Jesus a God-text and anticipates for Jesus God-worship" (a little triplet of phrases that John Stott often used when expounding this text in Philippians).

Philippians 2 is the most notable example of this practice of quoting Old Testament texts about Yahweh and referring them to Jesus. Paul does it quite deliberately and often. Look at the New Testament texts in the left column, and then compare them with the Old Testament texts in the right column. In each case, an Old Testament word about Yahweh God of Israel has been applied to Jesus.

Rom 10:13	Joel 2:32
Rom 14:11	Is 45:23
1 Cor 1:31; 2 Cor 10:17	Jer 9:24
1 Cor 2:16	Is 40:13
2 Tim 2:19	Num 16:5

Even more powerfully, the author of Hebrews launches his epistle with a whole salvo of God texts applied to Jesus.

This habit of taking Old Testament texts that applied to Yahweh, God of Israel, and calmly using them in contexts that clearly apply them to Jesus, is so "normal," so almost "casual," that we might miss how significant it really is. For Jewish believers to do this with their Scriptures, to apply God texts to a man who was their own contemporary, must mean that they were utterly and fully convinced that Jesus of Nazareth was none other than the Lord God whom they loved, worshiped and served.

JESUS AND THE ACTIONS OF GOD

Many of these Scriptures that were applied to Jesus are *functional* texts. That is, they speak of things that Yahweh does, provides or accomplishes.

By such scriptural quotation, those functions of Yahweh are then attributed to, or closely associated with, Jesus. In other words, in the New Testament we find that they spoke about Jesus doing things that the Old Testament had said only God could do.

Actually, this is in some ways even more important than merely saying something like "Jesus is God." Such a bald statement leaves far too much unsaid. It is too abstract and undefined. The word *god*, in English or other languages, can be used with all kinds of meanings and assumptions that are not necessarily biblical at all. What the New Testament does is far more specific. It picks up some of the most essential actions of Yahweh God in the Old Testament—things that were at the heart of what it meant to say that "the LORD is (the) God and there is no other"—and makes Jesus the subject of those actions. Jesus does what only God can do. Let's take the four most outstanding things the Old Testament says about Yahweh. The Old Testament affirms that Yahweh alone is the universal *Creator, ruler, judge and Savior*. According to the New Testament, Jesus performs those exact same roles and functions.

Creator. The new Christian believers in Corinth had a question for Paul. Could they buy and eat meat in the marketplace, knowing that the animal had been earlier sacrificed to idols in a pagan temple? The question occupies Paul's pastoral and theological attention for three whole chapters (1 Cor 8–10). Two issues are intertwined: the status of idols (are they "real"?) and the state of the meat (is it somehow "contaminated" by having been sacrificed to an idol?). Paul tackles the first issue head-on at the beginning of his argument (1 Cor 8:4-6) and the second toward the end (1 Cor 10:25-26). And significantly he applies a strong creation theology to both questions.

In 1 Corinthians 8:4-6 Paul reminds these new believers of something he must have taught them from the strong monotheistic texts of the Old Testament—especially Deuteronomy 6:4. That famous verse is known as the *shema* (because its opening word in Hebrew is *shema*, which means "Hear!"). "Hear, O Israel: the LORD our God, the LORD is one." In fact, Paul not only recalls that text but expands it, both by emphasizing God as the Creator of all things and by including Jesus in that role. "Yet for us there is but one God, the Father, from whom all things came and for whom we live; and there is but one Lord, Jesus Christ, through whom all things came and through whom we live" (1 Cor 8:6).

All things came *from one God*, the Father, and all things came *through one Lord*, Jesus Christ. So if Jesus is Lord of all creation, these other so-called gods and idols have no real *divine* existence in the universe. It is truly remarkable that Paul has identified Jesus with the word *Lord* in the Hebrew text. "One God, one Lord" is the essence of Jewish monotheism, and Paul affirms it just as strongly as any of his contemporaries. Paul was not *adding* Jesus as another "Lord" to the one God of the text. No, he was *identifying* Jesus as that "one Lord" who is the "one God." And he is saying that Jesus is one with God in the creation of all things, including the human race.

Moving to the other end of his argument, what about the meat then? Should Christians not buy and eat it because it had been sacrificed to idols? Paul's answer is that Christians are free to eat whatever they like because all food comes from the good hand of God the Creator. And to make that point, he quotes Psalm 24—"The earth is the Lord's, and everything in it" (1 Cor 10:26). In the Hebrew text, of course, "The LORD" was Yahweh, the personal name of God. But for Paul, "The Lord" is clearly Jesus, since a few verses earlier he has been speaking of "the cup of the Lord," and "the Lord's table." The whole earth, claims Paul, belongs to Jesus as its Lord, in the same way that the psalmist claimed that the whole earth belongs to Yahweh and not the gods of any other nation. Jesus is one with God the Creator.

The most outstanding text affirming the role of Christ in creation comes in Colossians 1:15-20. Five times Paul uses the phrase *ta panta*, "all things," and makes it clear he is referring to the whole created universe—all things physical and spiritual other than God himself. And it is all created, sustained and redeemed by Christ.

> The Son is the image of the invisible God, the firstborn over all creation. For in him all things were created: things in heaven and on earth, visible and invisible, whether thrones or powers or rulers or authorities; all things have been created through him and for him. He is before all things, and in him all things hold together. And he is the head of the body, the church; he is the beginning and the firstborn from among the dead, so that in everything he might have the supremacy. For God was pleased to have all his fullness dwell in him, and through him to reconcile to himself all things, whether things on earth or things in heaven, by making peace through his blood, shed on the cross.

Paul places Jesus in the same relationship to creation as the Old Testament affirms about Yahweh, the one living Creator God. The whole creation belongs to Christ by right of creation, inheritance and redemption. Christ is the source, sustainer and redeemer of all that exists. The same claims are made more briefly in Hebrews describing Jesus as God's Son, "whom he appointed heir of all things, and through whom he made the universe" (Heb 1:2), and by John describing Jesus as the Word "through him all things were made; without him nothing was made that has been made" (Jn 1:3).

Those are the most explicit places in the New Testament where Jesus is identified as the Creator, but there are plenty of hints elsewhere. When the disciples, sitting in a boat on a calm sea that seconds earlier had been a raging storm, asked the question, "Who is this? He commands even the winds and the water, and they obey him" (Lk 8:25), the Psalms had already given the only possible answer—the God who had created them (Ps 65:7; 89:9; and especially 107:23-32).

Jesus said, "Heaven and earth will pass away, but my words will never pass away" (Mk 13:31). He was claiming that his own word had a status and durability greater than the whole creation. And that meant that his word was on the same level as the creative word of God himself (Is 40:8).

On another occasion, some children were shouting his praises in the temple, and his opponents were indignant. Jesus responded by pointedly asking,

> Have you never read,
>   "From the lips of children and infants,
>   you, Lord, have called forth your praise"? (Mt 21:16)

He was quoting Psalm 8:2. That psalm, of course, was talking about praise offered to the LORD, Yahweh, for his creation of the heavens. Yet Jesus calmly claims that such praise from children is appropriate for himself.

So then, the Old Testament repeatedly affirms that Yahweh the God of Israel alone is the *sole creator of all that exists*. And we have now seen that the New Testament includes Jesus in that role.

Ruler. The Old Testament affirms this uniqueness of Yahweh, second, through the equally robust affirmation that he alone is the *sovereign ruler of all that happens*. Yahweh reigns as the governor of all history. As Psalm 33 expresses it, the LORD calls the world into existence through his word, runs the world according to his plans and calls the world to account before his watching eye. And as Isaiah 40–55 proclaims, he does all these things utterly unaided and unrivaled. Yahweh alone is ruler of all. Where, then, could Jesus the carpenter's son from Nazareth possibly fit in such a view of things?

The answer came from Jesus himself. In a bold stroke he applied to himself the words of Psalm 110. This psalm went on to become the most quoted text in the New Testament. In fact the Jews had already understood that this psalm was about the coming Messiah even before the time of Jesus.

> The LORD says to my lord:
> "Sit at my right hand
>   until I make your enemies
>   a footstool for your feet." (Ps 110:1)

The first time Jesus quotes this text it was in a question to make people think (Mk 12:35-37). If David, the author of the psalm, called the expected Messiah "Lord," surely the Messiah must be *more* than just a "son of David"?

But the second time he quoted it was in a much more dramatic and expanded way. It was at his trial when the high priest asked him directly "Are you the Messiah, the Son of the blessed One?" "'I am,' said Jesus. 'And you will see the Son of Man sitting at the right hand of the Mighty One and coming on the clouds of heaven'" (Mk 14:61-62).

The phrase "sitting at the right hand of the Mighty One" is a clear echo of Psalm 110:1, and it linked Jesus with the rule and government of God. For in the Old Testament "the right hand of God" was a powerful symbol for Yahweh's power in action. By his right hand Yahweh accomplished the work of creation (Is 48:13). By his right hand he defeated his enemies (Ex 15:6, 12). And by his right hand he saved those who took refuge in him (Ps 17:7; 20:7; 60:5; 118:15-16). For Jesus to claim that his accusers would see him occupying *that* position at the right hand of God was astonishing—indeed it was laughably grandiose at a time when he was under arrest and facing execution.

But Jesus made his startling point even more dramatically by combining this echo of Psalm 110 with an echo of Daniel 7:13-14, which spoke about the Son of Man coming on the clouds of heaven into the presence of the Ancient of Days. This was a very explicit connection to the universal power, glory, dominion and kingdom of God. The high priest knew exactly what Jesus was claiming and immediately accused him of blasphemy.

Jesus' earliest followers took their cue from Jesus himself and used the imagery of Psalm 110:1 to describe the present "location" of the risen and ascended Jesus. *Where was Jesus*, now that he was no longer walking around in Galilee? Jesus was not just "absent." Jesus was now already *"seated at the right hand of God."* That is, they were affirming that Jesus is now sharing in the exercise of universal governance that belonged uniquely to Yahweh.

Peter was the first to make this connection and affirmation on the day of Pentecost. He links Psalm 110 to the resurrection of Jesus and then draws the cosmic conclusion about the Lordship of Jesus.

> God has raised this Jesus to life, and we are all witnesses of it. Exalted to *the right hand of God*, he has received from the Father the promised Holy Spirit and has poured out what you now see and hear. For David did not ascend to heaven, and yet he said,
>
> "The LORD said to my Lord:
> 'Sit at my right hand
> until I make your enemies
> a footstool for your feet.'"
>
> Therefore let all Israel be assured of this: God has made this Jesus, whom you crucified, both Lord and Messiah. (Acts 2:32-36, my italics)

Paul was fond of using the double imagery of Psalm 110 (the right hand of God; enemies beneath the feet). It gave him the language to talk about the authority of the risen Christ and how Christ now shared the universal rule that belonged to Yahweh. And he then applied that truth in various ways. Here are some texts that echo Psalm 110. In Romans 8:34 he uses Christ's position of risen authority at God's right hand as the guarantee that no other power in the universe can separate us from the love of God. In 1 Corinthians 15:24-28 he looks forward to seeing all God's enemies, including eventually death itself, under the feet of the reigning Christ. In Colossians 3:1 he urges Christians to live their lives from the perspective of Christ's risen and ascended position at the right hand of God. And in Ephesians 1:20-23 he clearly echoes Psalm 110 in affirming Christ as Lord and ruler of all things, for the sake of the church.

> That power is the same as the mighty strength he exerted when he raised Christ from the dead and *seated him at his right hand* in the heavenly realms,

far above all rule and authority, power and dominion, and every name that is invoked, not only in the present age but also in the one to come. And God placed *all things under his feet* and appointed him to be head over everything for the church, which is his body, the fullness of him who fills everything in every way. (Eph 1:19-23, my italics, showing the echoes of Psalm 110)

Revelation climactically affirms that Jesus shares the governing rule of God over the whole universe. He is "ruler of the kings of the earth" (Rev 1:5) and "ruler [or beginning] of God's creation" (Rev 3:14). In terms of Old Testament monotheism, such things could only ever be said about Yahweh. Yet here both statements are explicitly made about Jesus. Then in his vision John sees "the Lamb that was slain" (the crucified Jesus) standing at the center of the throne, along with the One who sits on it, and he hears the worship of the vast choir of the whole creation singing praise simultaneously:

To him who sits on the throne *and* to the Lamb
    be praise and honor and glory and power,
for ever and ever! (Rev 5:13)

So it is clear that the New Testament speaks of Jesus Christ exercising the same sovereign rule that the Old Testament ascribed to the LORD God of Israel. The song of the psalmist, "*The LORD is king,*" becomes the faith of the believer, "*Jesus is Lord.*"

Judge. One of the core functions of Yahweh in the Old Testament as a dimension of his sovereign rule is that he judges the whole earth. This conviction is found in the mouth of Abraham (Gen 18:25) and echoes through the Old Testament. Israel believed it, and the whole creation would one day celebrate it. Yahweh God is the universal judge of all creation.

Let the heavens rejoice, let the earth be glad;
    let the sea resound, and all that is in it.
Let the fields be jubilant, and everything in them;
    let all the trees of the forest sing for joy.
Let all creation rejoice before the LORD, for he comes,
    he comes to judge the earth.
He will judge the world in righteousness
    and the peoples in his faithfulness. (Ps 96:11-13)

Now if Jesus shares in the rule of God "at his right hand," then that must include sharing in the exercise of God's judgment. And that is indeed what the New Testament affirms. In fact, Jesus claimed it. His parable about the sheep and the goats places himself, as Son of Man, on the seat of judgment. "When the Son of Man comes in his glory, and all the angels with him, he will sit on his glorious throne. All the nations will be gathered before him, and he will separate the people one from another as a shepherd separates the sheep from the goats" (Mt 25:31-32).

Paul picks up the Old Testament expectation of "the Day of the LORD," which several prophets used to speak about the future day of God's combined judgment and salvation, and transformed the phrase into "the day of Christ" (Phil 2:16). That will be "the day when God judges people's secrets through Jesus Christ, as my gospel declares" (Rom 2:16; cf. 2 Thess 1:5-10). And just as the Old Testament looked forward to the day when all nations would be summoned before Yahweh as the judge of all the earth, so Paul can affirm that "we must all appear before the judgment seat *of Christ*" (2 Cor 5:10), which means exactly the same as "we will all stand before *God's* judgment seat" (Rom 14:10).

Indeed, just as the Old Testament prophets warned people about the future judgment of God in order to motivate them to better behavior in the present, so Paul writes to Christian believers from Jewish and Gentile backgrounds that they must learn to accept one another and not treat each other with condemnation or contempt. And to motivate such behavior he appeals (among other things) to the fact that we all stand before Christ as judge. Once again, we find that Paul takes Scriptures that spoke about the LORD God and calmly applies them to Jesus Christ.

> For this very reason, Christ died and returned to life so that he might be the Lord of both the dead and the living.
>
> You, then, why do you judge your brother or sister? Or why do you treat them with contempt? For we will all stand before God's judgment seat. It is written:
>
> "'As surely as I live,' says the Lord,
> 'every knee will bow before me;
>   every tongue will acknowledge God.'"
>
> So then, each of us will give an account of ourselves to God. (Rom 14:9-12)

The New Testament, then, reaffirms what the Old Testament had said about the final judgment of the living God but sees it now embodied in the one whom God has appointed to that seat of final authority—Jesus Christ. The psalmist's song of joy, "*He comes to judge the earth,*" is echoed by Christ's own promise, "*Behold, I am coming soon.*"

Savior. Among the songs of the redeemed in Revelation is this great affirmation:

> Salvation belongs to our God,
> who sits on the throne,
> and to the Lamb. (Rev 7:10)

Every Old Testament Israelite could have sung the first two lines of that song. It was one of the strongest beliefs they had—that Yahweh the God of Israel was the only God who could save anybody or any nation. Saving people is his speciality. Salvation virtually defines the *identity* of Yahweh God. "Our God is a God who saves" (Ps 68:20).

One of the earliest celebrations of salvation comes from Moses in the wake of the crossing of the sea at the exodus. Moses sings, "the LORD is my strength and my defense; *he has become my salvation*" (Ex 15:2, my italics). One of the oldest poetic metaphors for Yahweh describes him as "the Rock their Savior" (Deut 32:15). In the Psalms Yahweh is above all else the God who saves, simply because that is who he is and what he does most consistently, most often, and best. The 136 occurrences of the Hebrew root *yasha* ("to save") in the Psalms account for 40 percent of all the uses of that root in the Old Testament. "LORD, you are the God who saves me" (Ps 88:1), "the horn of my salvation" (Ps 18:2), "the Rock of our salvation" (Ps 95:1), "my salvation and my honor" (Ps 62:7), "my Savior and my God" (Ps 42:5). And not just mine, and not even just of humans, for this God saves "both people and animals" (Ps 36:6). So when Israel hit rock bottom in the exile, the prophet needed to remind them who its God was: "I am the LORD your God, the Holy One of Israel, your Savior" (Is 43:3).

So yes, Israelites would have cheerfully sung, "Salvation belongs to our God, who sits on the throne." But the third line of the song in Revelation includes Jesus within the saving work of God—Jesus the Lamb who was slain, Jesus the crucified and risen Savior. Salvation belongs as much to Jesus as to the God of Old Testament faith, for the two are really one in identity and function.

The name Jehoshua (Joshua, Jeshua, Jesus) means "Yahweh is salvation." Matthew records the angel explaining the name: "because he will save his people from their sins" (Mt 1:21). Luke festoons the arrival of Jesus with the language of salvation. He uses salvation terms seven times in his first three chapters: Luke 1:47, 69, 71, 77; 2:11, 30; and 3:6.

Jesus and his contemporaries know that the power to forgive sins, a central (though not exclusive) part of what salvation means in the Bible, belonged to God alone. And God had established approved mechanisms for such forgiveness to be available in the sacrificial system in the temple. So when Jesus astonishingly declared to a paralyzed man not only that he was healed but also forgiven (and that he was forgiven simply because Jesus said so, without going to the temple), he faced the indignant question, "Why does this fellow talk like that? He's blaspheming! Who can forgive sins but God alone?" (Mk 2:7). Exactly right. So what was Jesus claiming for himself then, by claiming to do what only God could do? He was claiming the power to forgive—the saving power that belonged to God alone.

When Jesus rode a donkey into Jerusalem, it wasn't because he was tired. He had walked all the way from Galilee. He didn't *need* a donkey for the last mile or two. No, Jesus was acting out in a very deliberate and public way the fulfillment of a Scripture that everybody knew.

> Rejoice greatly, Daughter Zion!
>   Shout, Daughter Jerusalem!
> See, your king comes to you,
>   righteous and victorious, [*or, bringing salvation*]
> lowly and riding on a donkey,
>   on a colt, the foal of a donkey. (Zech 9:9, my italics)

No wonder the crowds called out "Hosanna," which is an urgent cry meaning, "Save us, now." And they cried it to the one they hailed as "coming in the name of the Lord." They may not have understood that the kind of salvation they wanted (freedom from Roman occupation) was not the salvation they actually needed. But what they did understand was that only someone who would act in the power of Yahweh could save them in any sense at all. They needed *God* to fulfill his promise that the LORD would come to Zion and to his temple—and that is exactly what God was doing that day in the person of Jesus of Nazareth.

In the rest of the New Testament, Jesus is called Savior again and again, and God's salvation comes to sinners only through Jesus Christ. But we should not get so familiar with this that we don't see how surprising it is that they could speak about Jesus in this way. The Greek word *soter* ("savior") was a fairly common term in the classical world. It was applied as an honorific title to both human kings and military conquerors, and also to the great gods and heroes of mythology. Roman emperors could be addressed as "our great god and savior." There were plenty of "saviors" in the pagan world. But not in New Testament Christianity. The word "savior" in the New Testament is applied to God eight times and to Jesus sixteen times, *and to nobody else at all ever.* "Salvation belongs to our God . . . and to the Lamb." Nobody else merits even a mention. No other Savior but God in Christ reconciling the world to himself.

The earliest followers of Jesus were Jews. They knew that Yahweh alone is God and there is no other source of salvation among the gods or on the earth. They believed this passionately because their Scriptures affirmed it with unmistakable clarity:

> There is no God apart from me,
> a righteous God and a Savior;
>   there is none but me.
> Turn to me and be saved,
>   all you ends of the earth;
>   for I am God, and there is no other. (Is 45:21-22)

Yet now they were so utterly convinced that Jesus of Nazareth shared the very identity of Yahweh their God that they could speak about Jesus in exactly the same way. Peter declares, "Salvation is found in no one else, for there is no other name under heaven given to mankind by which we must be saved" (Acts 4:12; the same point is made in Acts 2:38; 5:31; 13:38; 15:11). The writer to the Hebrews describes Jesus as the author or pioneer of salvation (Heb 2:10), the source of our eternal salvation (Heb 5:9) and the mediator of complete salvation for all who come to God through him (Heb 7:25). Paul piles up the phrases "God our Savior" or "Christ our Savior" seven times in the tiny letter to Titus alone (sometimes he even uses both together: "our great God and Savior, Jesus Christ"; Titus 2:13). And in typical fashion, he takes a text from the Old Testament that spoke about calling on the name of the LORD for salvation (Joel 2:32) and simply applies it to Christ. "If you declare with your mouth, 'Jesus is Lord,' and believe in your heart that God raised him from the dead, you will be saved. . . . for, 'Everyone who calls on the name of the Lord will be saved'" (Rom 10:9, 13).

Salvation in the New Testament is as completely Christ shaped as salvation in the Old Testament is Yahweh shaped. And so the psalmist's confident trust in *Yahweh, God of our salvation* is echoed by Paul's joyful longing for the appearing of *our great God and Savior, Jesus Christ* (Tit 2:13).

CONCLUSION

So what have we seen in this final chapter?

First of all we have seen a negative but very important point. There is one idea that we simply have to reject as impossible. That is the idea that Jesus was just a good man who gave us some rather splendid teaching about God and how we should all be more loving and kind but who only was elevated to divine status centuries later by power-hungry Christians. That idea is simply impossible to square with the earliest evidence we have from the New Testament itself, evidence that comes from before those earliest documents were written.

Then, positively, we have seen that as the earliest followers of Jesus sought to understand who he was, they naturally turned to their sacred Scriptures—what we call the Old Testament. And as they did so, they found again and again that the God of their historical faith, Yahweh God himself, had come among them in the person of Jesus of Nazareth. Jesus himself made astonishing claims to fulfill Scriptures that spoke about God coming to save his people. And with total conviction (for which they were willing to suffer and die), his earliest followers addressed Jesus in worship and prayer, using language drawn straight from passages of the Old Testament that had been written about Yahweh and sometimes spoken by Yahweh. And above all, both Jesus himself and his earliest followers attributed to Jesus functions and actions that were uniquely and exclusively things that God alone could do as Creator, ruler, judge and Savior. Jesus did, does, and will do what only God can do.

In our first five chapters we have seen that the Old Testament tells the story that Jesus completed. It declares the promise that he fulfilled. It provides the pictures and models that shaped his identity. It programs a mission that he accepted and passed on. It teaches a moral orientation to God and the world that he endorsed, sharpened and laid as the foundation for obedient discipleship. We have seen also that the Old Testament reveals to us the God who, in Jesus of Nazareth, "became flesh and made his dwelling among us" (Jn 1:14).

So when we read the Old Testament, we do not need to look for forced hints in every text that "Jesus must be in here somewhere." Rather we should be aware as Christian readers that the God who presents himself to us in these pages of the Old Testament as Yahweh is the God whom we know and see in the face of Jesus in the New Testament.

We have come to the end of a long journey in this book! I hope it has been a journey of biblical discovery that you will want to make again and again, to explore all the rich and wonderful scenery along the way. How can we summarize what we have seen? What kind of relationship exists between Jesus Christ and the Old Testament? How does it relate to him and how does he relate to it? We can summarize our six chapters like this:

- The relationship between the Old Testament and Jesus is *historical*, because the story of God with his people links them together with Christ as the climax.

- The relationship between the Old Testament and Jesus is *covenantal*, because the promise of God in the Old is fulfilled through Christ in the New.

- The relationship between the Old Testament and Jesus is *representational*, because the identity of Israel is embodied in Jesus as its Messiah King.

- The relationship between the Old Testament and Jesus is *missional*, because Jesus accomplished the great purpose of God for all nations and all creation that the Old Testament declared.

- The relationship between the Old Testament and Jesus is *ethical*, because the way of justice and compassion that the Old Testament holds up as pleasing to God is endorsed and amplified by Jesus in the New.

- And above all, the relationship between the Old Testament and Jesus is *incarnational*, because in Jesus of Nazareth, the Lord God, the Holy One of Israel, has walked among us.

As we love, worship and obey him as our Savior and Lord, may we love, honor, read and understand the Scriptures that were so precious and formative in his heart and mind.

CHAPTER 6 QUESTIONS AND EXERCISES

1. If someone challenged you with the opinion that Jesus was just a good man who never claimed to be God, how would you respond, and what Bible texts would you use?

2. Why is it inadequate simply to say "Jesus was God"? What does the word *God* actually mean to most people in your culture? What Old Testament texts would you use to make clear that the person, character and actions of the God who was revealed in the Old Testament were then embodied in Jesus?

3. Study Philippians 2:5-11, Colossians 1:15-20 and 1 Corinthians 8:4-6. In each case explain what Paul meant—and the Old Testament background to what Paul says—about Jesus.

4. From the final section of this chapter, choose a New Testament text for each of the affirmations that Jesus Christ is Creator, Ruler, Judge and Savior. How would you show from the Old Testament that each of these functions is a sovereign prerogative of the LORD God alone?

5. Think about the journey of this whole book. Choose a New Testament text and an Old Testament text that summarize the main point of each of the six chapter headings. How would you explain to someone the purpose of this book?

BOOK TWO

KNOWING GOD *the* FATHER THROUGH *the* OLD TESTAMENT

PREFACE

Years ago, teaching the Old Testament at the Union Biblical Seminary in Pune, India, I used to set as a research topic, 'The Knowledge of God in the Book of Hosea'—or in some other specified part of the Old Testament. It was always fascinating to observe the sense of excitement that students had as they returned from a voyage of considerable discovery and reported what they had found. I told myself that some day I would speak or write on the same subject in greater depth myself.

So when I was asked to give the Bible expositions at the annual conference of the European Christian Mission (ECM) in April 2002, I chose 'Knowing God' as my theme. So it was that five expositions which underlie several of the chapters of this book were first delivered next to the beautiful Lake Bled in Slovenia. I am grateful to ECM and the conference organizers for that invitation.

It had long seemed to me that the theme of knowing God had tended to be handled either in a systematic or thematic way (as in the brilliant classic with that title by J. I. Packer), or in a purely personal and devotional way, largely devoid of Old Testament content. And yet it is clear (or I hope it will be by the end of this book) that knowing God is a theme that could claim to be one of the more major concerns of the Bible, and particularly of the Old Testament.

Having written *Knowing Jesus through the Old Testament* some years ago, and then having followed it more recently with *Knowing the Holy Spirit through the Old Testament*, it seemed natural to complete the series with this volume, incorporating the Old Testament's teaching about God as Father within the wider theme of knowing God as such. At least one can be confident that no further additions to such a series will be called for.

I owe my thanks to all who have helped and encouraged me along the way, including as always my family. I am especially grateful to the Langham Partnership International for insisting in my contract that I take some time for writing each year—which is why I am delighted to assign all royalties to Langham Literature. With great affection and gratitude I dedicate the book to Rev Dr John Stott, at whose cottage in Wales (the Hookses) most of it was written, and whose friendship, encouragement and prayers in relation to all my ministry are as precious beyond words as he himself is.

Chris Wright

INTRODUCTION

When you pray, say, 'Our Father in heaven . . .'
With these words Jesus introduced his disciples to a whole new
dimension of prayer. Not that they did not already know how to pray—
even though we might think that from their request, 'Lord, teach us to pray'
(Luke 11:1). The faith of Israel was a praying faith, and the disciples of Jesus
belonged to a people for whom the prayers and praises of the Psalms were
woven into the fabric of their daily lives as much as their everyday food
(which never passed their lips without prayer). The point of their request
seems to have been, 'Lord, teach us to pray *like you do*'. For clearly the
prayer life of Jesus went beyond anything they knew themselves, or even
anything they had observed among the professional prayer experts (about
whom Jesus had some less-than-flattering things to say).

One major dimension of that prayer life of Jesus (something that probably
surprised, puzzled and perhaps shocked them) was the familiarity with which
Jesus addressed God as Father. They could see that Jesus had a unique, intimate relation with God as *his* Father, whom he addressed in the family
language of 'Abba'. But could such a way of relating and speaking to God in
prayer be available also to his followers? With his classic template of prayer,
Jesus says that it is not only possible, but it is to be normal and standard. And
so ever since then followers of Jesus have entered effortlessly (though sometimes routinely and without thought) into the limitless relational richness
of calling God 'Father'.

Calling God 'Father' in prayer is second nature to *Christian* believers, but it seems that it was surprising to Jesus's first disciples. Why was that? The simple reason is that it was not the common way of addressing God within the worshipping life of Israel. Now this is not because the ancient Israelites did not know of God as Father—both the concept and the terminology are most definitely there in the Scriptures of Israel that we call the Old Testament, and we shall explore them further below. But 'Father' is not the common or normal form of address to God in the Old Testament. It is not used, for example, in the book of Israelite hymns and prayers[1]—the Book of Psalms—even though that book abounds in other ways of speaking about God and to God.

So the question must arise then in the mind of anybody contemplating the title of this book: how can so many pages be filled with a theme that is so apparently slender in the Old Testament itself? Is it not somewhat forced or anachronistic to talk about 'knowing God the Father *through the Old Testament*'? Surely this is something that we can really only discuss as Christians in the light of the New Testament and that fuller revelation of God through his Son Jesus Christ. Indeed, it is in knowing Jesus as the *Son of God* that we know more clearly about the *Father* (as Jesus himself told his disciples). And then from that point we move toward the more developed understanding of the Trinitarian nature of God as Father, Son and Holy Spirit.

Well, of course all this is true, to a point. But we are still left with the biblical fact that Old Testament Israel did know a thing or two about the living God, and they *did* on occasions call their God 'Father'—even if other titles and forms of address are much more common. And they certainly used the role, expectations and responsibilities of human fathers as a way of speaking about certain aspects of God. That is to say, there are fatherly portraits and metaphors for God, even when he is not directly called Father.

So another way of putting our question would be this: Is the God of the Old Testament revelation—the God whom Israel knew as Yahweh— (though by the time of Jesus they had probably already ceased to pronounce this name, and substituted for it either *Adonai*—'the Lord', or *Ha Shem*— 'the Name')[2]—is that God the same as the God we call Father? In other

---

[1] Except once as a form of address by the Davidic king (Ps 89:26) and in a few metaphorical verses that we shall look at in chapter 1.

[2] The earliest Greek translations of the Hebrew Scriptures (made well over a hundred years before

words, can we equate Yahweh of Old Testament faith and affirmation with God the Father in our Trinitarian understanding of God? I believe we can say yes, with some careful qualifications, for the following reasons.

THE UNITY OF THE TRINITY

Christians do not believe in three Gods. It is of the very essence of Trinitarian confession that God is One. We believe that truth just as strongly as Israelite believers did when they recited the *shema*, 'Hear, O Israel: the LORD our God, the LORD is one' (Deut 6:4). So on the assumption that the God revealed in the Old Testament is the one true living God whom we also now know in the fullness of his final revelation through his incarnation in Jesus of Nazareth and the outpouring of his Holy Spirit at Pentecost, we must also affirm that all three persons of the Godhead (as we now call them), are 'contained' within the singular, integrated personal identity of the God who chose to be known as Yahweh in the Old Testament.

The great affirmation of Deuteronomy 4:35 and 39 affirms not only the uniqueness but also the universality and completeness of Yahweh as God.

> The LORD is God in heaven above and on the earth below. There is no other.
> (Deut 4:39)

This means not only that Yahweh is the *only* God there is, but Yahweh is also *all* the God there is, or to put it another way, Yahweh is all there is to God. There is no higher deity above or behind him, or a better one to come after him. Yahweh is not just the penultimate name for some more ultimate divine reality. Deity as such—in every sense that can be affirmed within and beyond the universe—is defined by Yahweh. God *is* as he is revealed to be in the person of *this* God and no other. This being so, then all that we would now strive to express about God through our doctrine of the Trinity is already encapsulated in the transcendent, unique, and universal God Yahweh. The Israelites may not have known all that just yet, but that does not mean it was not the objective reality and truth about God.[3] This

---

Christ), followed this practice, and rendered the divine name Yahweh as *ho kyrios*—'the Lord'. In the same tradition, English translations use the capitalized form 'the LORD' to render the personal name of God in the Old Testament. It is worth remembering, when we read this term, that it represents a personal name, not just a title.

[3] That is to say, if you like this kind of language and you can forget it if you don't, that we can make a distinction between the epistemological dimension (what Israel at any given point in their

means that it is usually rather pointless (in my view) to ask which person of the Trinity is being referred to by any Old Testament verse that speaks about Yahweh. There are some places where the Spirit of Yahweh is clearly indicated (as I survey in *Knowing the Holy Spirit through the Old Testament*), and there are certainly messianic texts (in intention, or in later canonical reading) in which we can identify the pre-incarnate second person of the Trinity whom we now know through Jesus of Nazareth. Furthermore, it is also clear that in the New Testament, the most remarkable thing that happened in the faith of the earliest followers of Jesus is that they came to identify *him, Jesus*, with Yahweh, in calling him Lord, and in many other ways.[4] So yes, it is certainly true from a whole-Bible perspective, that the God Yahweh of the Old Testament 'embodies' (if that is not too human a word) the Son and the Holy Spirit. But on the whole it is probably more appropriate in most cases that when we read about Yahweh, we should have God the Father in mind.

THE PRIMARY FUNCTIONS OF YAHWEH

When Old Testament Israelites made their great affirmation about the transcendent uniqueness of Yahweh, they frequently associated it with major roles or functions that were attributed to him. The most outstanding was that Yahweh alone is the Creator of everything else that exists apart from himself (e.g. Jer 10:11–12). A second was that Yahweh alone is king. He is supreme ruler, not only over Israel, but over all nations, and the whole of creation (e.g. Deut 10:14, 17). And a third was that Yahweh is the ultimate judge of all human behaviour—from the smallest individual thought and action to the macrocosm of international relations in the ebb and flow of history (e.g. Ps 33:13–15). Creator, king and judge: in all these spheres the sovereign universality of Yahweh was affirmed again and again. And these are typically the roles that are commonly associated with the person of God the Father. 'I believe in God the Father Almighty, Creator of heaven and earth' we recite, in the Apostles' Creed, for example.

Now of course, we have to agree that one of the major ways in which the New Testament affirms the identity of *Jesus* with Yahweh (and thereby

---

history *knew* about God through his action and revelation to that point), and the ontological dimension (all that God actually *is*, and always has been, in his own divine reality).

[4]See Christopher J. H. Wright, *The Mission of God: Unlocking the Bible's Grand Narrative* (Downers Grove, IL: InterVarsity, 2006), ch. 4, 'The Living God Makes Himself Known in Jesus Christ.'

implying his deity), is through attributing all of these primary divine roles to the Lord Jesus Christ as well—and adding another, the role of Saviour (which was another major defining characteristic of Yahweh). In the New Testament, *Jesus* is portrayed as Creator, king, Saviour and judge.[5] All this goes to demonstrate the unity of the Godhead in all the ways in which God acts. Paul combines both the Father and Jesus in his remarkable expansion of the *shema* in 1 Corinthians:

> There is but one God, the Father, from whom all things came and for whom we live; and there is but one Lord, Jesus Christ, through whom all things came and through whom we live. (1 Cor 8:6)

Nevertheless, the more common way of differentiating at a conceptual level between the persons of God is to associate the roles of creating, sustaining, ordering, ruling and judging the earth and all its inhabitants with God the Father. For this reason, again, it is natural to associate the name and character of Yahweh in the Old Testament primarily (though not, as we have said, exclusively) with the Father.

THE GOD TO WHOM JESUS PRAYED

Jesus was fully human. He grew up in a devout and believing Jewish home, and was without doubt a worshipping, praying child, young man and adult. The daily habit of prayer that we read of in the Gospels must have been ingrained in him from childhood. So when Jesus worshipped and prayed, in his home or in the synagogue in Nazareth, to whom was his worship directed? Who was the God whose name he read, in all the Scriptures he recited, and all the songs he sang? To whom did Jesus pray as a child, taught by his mother Mary, and then through all his life? The answer is, of course, to the Lord, Yahweh (though he would have said *Adonai*). Jesus would have recited the *shema* daily with his fellow Jews, and he knew the 'Lord our God' of that text to be the God of his people, his human parents and himself. So Jesus's whole perception of God was entirely shaped by the Scriptures we call the Old Testament. When Jesus thought of God, spoke of God, reflected on the words and will of God, set out to obey God—it was *this* God, Yahweh God, that was in his mind. 'God' for Jesus was the named, biographied, character-rich, self-revealed God Yahweh, the Holy

---

[5]Ibid.

One of Israel. When Jesus and his disciples talked together of God, this is the name they would have used (or would have known but piously avoided pronouncing). When Jesus read Isaiah 61 in the synagogue in Nazareth, he claimed that the Spirit of the LORD was upon him 'today'—the Spirit of Yahweh, God of the Old Testament prophets.

But of course, Jesus also knew this God of his Scriptures in the depth of his self-consciousness as *Abba*, as his own intimate personal Father. Luke tells us that this awareness was developing even in his childhood, and it was sealed at his baptism, when he heard the voice of his Father, accompanied by the Holy Spirit, confirming his identity as God's beloved Son. So in the consciousness of Jesus the *scriptural* identity of God as Yahweh and his *personal* intimacy with God as his Father must have blended together. The God he knew from his Bible as Yahweh was the God he knew in prayer as his Father. When Jesus took the Psalms on his lips on the cross, the God he was calling out to in the agony of abandonment was the God addressed in Psalm 22:1 as Elohim, but throughout the psalm as Yahweh. The psalmist was calling out to Yahweh. Jesus uses his words to call out to his Father.

Now since all our understanding of God as Father must start out from knowing Jesus, it makes sense for us also to think of Yahweh, the God of Old Testament Israel and the God of the one true faithful Israelite Jesus, as God the Father, for that is who Yahweh primarily was in the consciousness of Jesus himself.

So then, an important foundational assumption for the rest of this book is just this, that knowing God as Father in the Old Testament is really a dimension of simply *knowing God*—that is, of knowing Yahweh as God. And that perception opens up for us a horizon of great breadth and vistas of rich biblical content. *Knowing God*, or the knowledge of God, is one of the truly immense themes of the Old Testament. It is challenging, frightening and encouraging. It can be intimate and devotional, but it is also deeply practical and ethical. It applies to individuals and to nations. It looks to the past and fills the intentions of God for the future. This will be a voyage of exciting and challenging biblical discovery.

However, as I said, the Israelites did sometimes actually speak of God as Father, even though we have to recognize that it was not a prominent or common dimension of their language of worship (not anything like the extent of its prominence in the New Testament). So we shall certainly also explore this theme of the fatherhood of God in the faith of Israel, and this too should lead us in a journey around some texts and concepts that are rather off the usual tourist routes of the Old Testament. So then, we shall weave our way in the chapters that follow through a twin theme. Sometimes the main emphasis will be on 'knowing God' as we look at texts where that theme is in the foreground. Sometimes the main emphasis will be on God as Father in texts where that is a dominant metaphor. Our hope is that the combination and interaction of these themes and texts will enrich and deepen our personal understanding of, and relationship with, the biblical God.

One final observation before we set forth. Our title is obviously framed from the common Trinitarian formulation—'God the Father'. This in itself, as we have seen, is not a term that the Old Testament uses in quite that form. And it would be unfortunate if our reflections in the course of this book on the fatherhood of God were misinterpreted to imply some kind of harsh patriarchal authoritarianism. Certainly the metaphor of human fatherhood is used as a way of speaking about certain key characteristics of God. But so is the metaphor of motherhood. In fact, the language of parenthood, in both genders, is explicitly used in relation to God as early as Deuteronomy 32:18. Likewise, should human parenthood fail (whether father or mother), the psalmist looks to God to fulfil their dual role in caring for him (Ps 27:10). Another psalmist compares his attentive dependence on God to a maid looking to her mistress. And God himself draws remarkable self-comparisons to a pregnant mother in labour (Is 42:14) and a nursing mother breastfeeding her child (Is 49:15). Apart from these explicitly motherly metaphors for God in the Old Testament, we shall observe (especially in chapter 1), that the language of fatherhood, while it certainly includes appropriate exercise and expectations of authority, is commonly also associated with love, care, compassion, provision, protection and sustenance.

CHAPTER ONE

KNOWING GOD
as a FATHER *in* ACTION

When I arrived in my first parish as a newly ordained curate (assistant pastor), I was responsible for coordinating the team of youth leaders. One of the other curates, who had done this job for the previous two years, was commending a young married couple who were part of the team. 'They are pure gold,' he said to me. I had not even met them yet, but he knew them very well, and that was the metaphor he chose to explain to me their high quality and great value. The better we know someone, the more we find metaphors that sum up what they are like and what they mean to us. 'She's a pillar of the community.' 'He's the life and soul of the party.' 'She's like a rock for her whole family.' 'He's a walking volcano.' 'She's an oasis of common sense.' 'He's a loose cannon.' 'She's a bit of a butterfly.'

The Bible is rich in metaphors for God, and for the same reason. We are invited to know God as deeply and intimately as is humanly possible. And the more we know God, the more we will find ways of expressing who he is and what he means to us. Knowing God is one of the richest themes in the Old Testament. It is something that takes many different shapes, and happens in many different contexts. Not surprisingly, then, the Old Testament is rich in metaphors that people of faith used to describe the God they had come to know in all these ways.

We are familiar with the commonest of these, since they dominate the landscape of Old Testament faith, worship and theology. Yahweh is king, judge and redeemer. Those are human images. There are other less common human analogies, like Yahweh as shepherd, teacher, soldier, and farmer. And of course there are many non-human metaphors also: Yahweh is a rock, a shelter, a shield, a hiding place, a lion, fire, a spring of water, etc.

Surprisingly, the metaphor of God as Father is not as common as we might have expected. As we shall see in a moment, the Israelites certainly did not overlook the rich store of metaphorical meaning in thinking of Yahweh their God in relation to the common human experience of fatherhood. But they were reticent with the concept of Yahweh as Father at one level (in worship), while quite free with it at another (in personal names).

Only rather rarely do Old Testament texts speak about, or speak to, Yahweh as Father in contexts of worship or devotion. In the book of Psalms, for example, God is only once referred to as 'my Father' (by the king, in Psalm 89:26, and never directly by any psalmist), and God is compared to a human father only three times (see below). The most likely reason for this is that Israel chose to reject the pagan and mythological notions of divine parenthood that were common in surrounding religions. In the polytheistic environment, gods and goddesses engaged in sexual congress and gave birth to all kinds of phenomena, including some nations. The monotheistic faith of Israel rejected such a view of the relationship between Yahweh and Israel. Israel had not been literally conceived and birthed by Yahweh, or by any female goddess with whom Yahweh had consorted to produce offspring. So while they certainly made use of familial metaphors (husband-wife, conception and birth, parent-child) to portray the relationship, they did not elevate them into primary forms of address to God or of discourse about God. And when they did use them, they were very careful to rule out the pagan mythical conceptions.

So, for example, Jeremiah parodies the sexual fertility cult of the Canaanites, which had badly infected Israel in his day. They used a standing stone to symbolize the phallic sacred male, and a tree or a wooden pole to symbolize the sacred female. Jeremiah mocks the worship of this sexual pairing that was credited with some kind of divine parenthood by the worshipper—reversing the polarity.

> They say to wood, 'You are my father,'
>   and to stone, 'You gave me birth.' (Jer 2:27)

If this was the way people used 'my father' in worship, it's no wonder the orthodox Old Testament faith tended to avoid it.

And yet, while somewhat reticent to address God as Father in the context of worship, Israel was quite free in using the idea of Yahweh as Father in another way—and that is in the area of personal names. The word *theophoric* is used to describe human names that include part or all of the name of a god. My own name, for example, Christopher (which is Greek, meaning, 'Christ-bearer') is theophoric. So are Theodore, or Dorothy (gift of God), and Timothy (honoured by God). Most cultures are rich in theophoric names. The names of the Babylonian gods, Bel and Nebo, for example, are found in Belshazzar and Nebuchadnezzar. In India, names compounded from Ram and Krishna are very common. Abdulla (servant of Allah) is common in Arabic speaking nations. And so on.

El is one of the commonest names for God (the high God across the whole ancient Near East). And Yahweh was often shortened to *Yah*, or *Yeho*, or *Yo*. Thus, the wide range of Israelite names that begin or end with El (Eliezer, Elimelech, Nathaniel, etc.); or that begin with Jeho-, or Jo- (Jehoshaphat, Joshua, Jonathan); or end in -iah, or –ijah (Obadiah, Elijah, Azariah, Adonijah)—are all theophoric. They are little phrases, or affirmations about God or Yahweh, built into a personal name.

Now in Hebrew, the word for father is *ab*. 'My father' is *abi*. So when *ab* or *abi* is put together with *el* or one of the abbreviations of Yahweh, then the name becomes a statement about God as Father, or as 'my Father'. So, we have the following possibilities, all attested in the names of the Old Testament.

Abiel	God is my father (1 Sam 9:1)
Eliab	My God is father (1 Sam 16:6)
Joab	Yahweh is father (2 Sam 8:16)
Abijah	Yahweh is my father (this can be a man or woman's name—see 2 Chron 29:1)
Abimelech	My father is king (where 'king' probably refers to God, Judg 9:1)

The common occurrence of these names shows that the idea of God, or Yahweh, as father was well known and accepted. After all, a person called Abijah walking around the place was making a theological statement—

'Yahweh is my father'—every time he gave his name, or was greeted by others. Parents who decided to call their son 'Joab',—'Yahweh is Father'—had some metaphoric understanding of his and their relationship to Yahweh as father. So even if the term was not on the lips of Israelites in regular worship, it was on their lips in everyday speech as they used their own common names.

What message, then, did the metaphor contain? In this chapter we shall look at some general aspects of what it meant to call God Father, or to compare him with human fathers. In the next chapter we shall look more particularly at how the relationship between God and Israel as a nation (which was much more commonly described as a covenant, of course), could be seen in father-son terms, and what that implied.

So let us open up some rather warm-hearted Old Testament texts in which we will discover that God can be portrayed as:

- the Father who carries his children, in whom we can trust

- the Father who disciplines his children, to whom we should submit

- the Father who pities his children, to whom we should be grateful

- the Father who adopts the homeless or fatherless, in whom we find security

GOD—THE FATHER WHO CARRIES

> The LORD your God, who is going before you, will fight for you, as he did for you in Egypt, before your very eyes, and in the wilderness. There you saw how *the Lord your God carried you, as a father carries his son*, all the way you went until you reached this place. (Deut 1:30–31)

We have all seen a father pick up and carry a child in his arms, on his back or shoulders. Usually it is because the child is tired, or the terrain is difficult or dangerous—and sometimes it is because the child is being fractious and disobedient. There's something of all these in the picture Moses paints here.

Moses's memoirs of Israel's journeying since leaving Egypt fill Deuteronomy 1–3. By the start of Deuteronomy, Israel had reached the plains of Moab, just across the Jordan from the Promised Land. But it had been a long and convoluted journey. In fact, as Deuteronomy 1:2–3 laconically points out, a journey that should have taken eleven days had lasted forty years! And the reason for that was Israel's refusal to go in and take the land when the opportunity and command to do so was given them by God.

Deuteronomy 1:19–46 recalls the events at Kadesh Barnea, first described in Numbers 13–14. The bad report of ten of the spies sent out to reconnoitre the land sent the people into a tailspin of grumbling rebellion and inferiority complex. In a panic, they refused to go any further. It is in this context that Moses spoke the words quoted above. He appealed to their experience of God's provision so far, how God had rescued them from Egypt and then protected and provided for them in the wilderness. And in this, says Moses, the LORD carried you, just like a father carrying his son. Perhaps he has in mind the image of carrying that God himself had used:

> You yourselves have seen what I did to Egypt, and how I carried you on eagles' wings and brought you to myself. (Ex 19:4)

Moses simply transfers the transport from parent birds to parent humans. The point is the same—caring, strong, parental protection and support.

Unfortunately, our text goes on to say that even this was not enough to persuade the people. 'In spite of this',—that is, in spite of all their eyes had seen and all they had experienced of God's fatherly support—'you did not trust in the LORD your God' (Deut 1:32). And so they ended up in the wilderness for a whole generation, where they continued to experience God's fatherly action, though in a somewhat different way (as we shall see in a moment).

Another text uses the picture of God as the parental porter to great effect. In Isaiah 46, the prophet first pours scorn on the gods of Babylon. When their city falls, far from these gods being able to come down to rescue their *worshippers*, they can't even stoop down to rescue their own *statues*! So these 'gods' have to be carried out of the city on oxcarts. What kind of god is that? is the implied question. By contrast, God says,

> Listen to me, you descendants of Jacob,
>   all the remnant of the people of Israel,
> you whom I have upheld since your birth,
>   and have carried since you were born.
> Even to your old age and grey hairs
>   I am he, I am he who will sustain you.

I have made you and I will carry you;

I will sustain you and I will rescue you. (Is 46:3–4)

The text does not actually name God as Father, but it certainly has that picture in mind, since it speaks of God carrying Israel from birth. This is not, however, like a human father who at some point has to give up carrying his children—usually when they grow bigger than he is! God carries his people from the cradle to the grave. He is our maker, carrier, sustainer and rescuer (Is 46:4)—all supremely fatherly qualities.

The point of Moses's reference to God as the carrying Father was to urge the people to trust him in the future, since he had not failed them in the past. The point of Isaiah's similar language was to urge the people not to be intimidated by the dazzling gods of Babylon, which would soon have to be carted away by the very people they were supposed to protect. Rather they should trust in the God of their history, who had carried them all this way and would do so to the very end. Which would you prefer—a god you have to carry yourself when you most need him, or the God who carries you from start to finish? God the Fraud, or God the Father?

GOD—THE FATHER WHO DISCIPLINES

Remember how the Lord your God led you all the way in the wilderness these forty years, to humble and test you in order to know what was in your heart, whether or not you would keep his commands. He humbled you, causing you to hunger and then feeding you with manna, which neither you nor your ancestors had known, to teach you that man does not live on bread alone but on every word that comes from the mouth of the Lord. Your clothes did not wear out and your feet did not swell during these forty years. Know then in your heart that *as a man disciplines his son, so the Lord your God disciplines you*. (Deut 8:2–5)

Moses is still writing his memoirs. The wilderness had not been entirely wasted time. It had been an education. In fact, it was a learning experience for God as well as for Israel. What God wanted to know was what was in the hearts of his people, and whether or not they would learn to obey him. Our text sounds somewhat like an experimental laboratory in which various tests are carried out to examine a new product. So the privations of the wilderness journey functioned to test and to teach. In that sense, they were disciplinary.

The word 'discipline' does not simply mean punishment—even though there were occasions of that in the wilderness. Rather it means the necessary strictness, constraints, limitation and rigour that are essential for any kind of effective learning. In modern times we associate such discipline with the school or college environment, or any place of disciplined training. In Israel, education took place in the household and was the primary responsibility of the father. So, once again, God is compared to a father—a father who will allow his children to experience tough times and even severe challenges, precisely in order that they will learn from them, and a father who will not shrink from exercising all necessary dimensions of discipline to ensure that the learning takes place. Discipline, in this sense, is a very positive word, because of the results and blessings that flow from exercising it (on oneself), or being the willing object of it (on the part of God or one's father or teacher).

Such discipline is a function of parental love, and quite different of course from arbitrary domestic violence and excessive punishment that arises from sheer anger or brutality and produces alienation and despair. That is why the wise father figure depicted in Proverbs not only urges the younger learner repeatedly to respect the wisdom and authority of his earthly father and mother, but even more so, to welcome the loving discipline of the LORD.

> My son, do not despise the LORD's discipline,
>   and do not resent his rebuke,
> because *the Lord disciplines those he loves*,
>   *as a father the son he delights in*. (Prov 3:11–12)

Jesus of course never received his Father's rebuke. But he was certainly the Son whom his Father loved and delighted in. And yet the New Testament makes it clear that Jesus too went through the disciplinary and testing dimension of suffering, and that his obedience was, in that sense, 'learned'. As Hebrews puts it:

> Son though he was, he learned obedience from what he suffered. (Heb 5:8)

This does not mean that he had been disobedient before, but only that, for Jesus as well as for us, sonship, discipline and obedience were all linked together in his relationship with his Father.

In fact, it is hard to read Moses's account of Israel's forty years in the wilderness in Deuteronomy 8 (above), without thinking of Jesus's forty days in the wilderness. Try reading those verses from within the mind of Jesus as a way of understanding how he, Jesus, not only recognized the nature of the testing he was experiencing, but also found the scriptural resources to fight back against the devil's attempt to undermine his commitment to the costly way his Father planned for him. Jesus submitted to his Father's discipline in life, just as he willingly submitted to his Father's will in death, and in Gethsemane beforehand. In this, as in all else, Jesus models for us the true response to our heavenly Father—one of submission to his loving discipline. And it is a response which, as in so much of his life and teaching, Jesus learned from his Scriptures, the Old Testament, where this fatherly character of God is so effectively painted.

Hebrews, similarly soaked in scriptural teaching, draws the verses from Proverbs into a moving exhortation that builds on the metaphorical transference to God of human fatherly functions and points to the positive results if only we recognize and submit to our Father in such times.

In your struggle against sin, you have not yet resisted to the point of shedding your blood. And have you completely forgotten this word of encouragement that addresses you as a father addresses his sons? It says,

'My son, do not make light of the Lord's discipline,
    and do not lose heart when he rebukes you,
because the Lord disciplines those he loves,
    and he chastens everyone he accepts as his son.'

Endure hardship as discipline; God is treating you as his children. For what children are not disciplined by their father? If you are not disciplined—and everyone undergoes discipline,—then you are not legitimate, not true sons and daughters at all. Moreover, we have all had human fathers who disciplined us and we respected them for it. How much more should we submit to the Father of our spirits and live! They disciplined us for a little while as they thought best; but God disciplines us for our good, in order that we may share in his holiness. No discipline seems pleasant at the time, but painful. Later on, however, it produces a harvest of righteousness and peace for those who have been trained by it. (Heb 12:4–11)

GOD—THE FATHER WHO PITIES

The LORD is compassionate and gracious,
    slow to anger, abounding in love.
He will not always accuse,
    nor will he harbour his anger for ever;
he does not treat us as our sins deserve
    or repay us according to our iniquities.
For as high as the heavens are above the earth,
    so great is his love for those who fear him;
as far as the east is from the west,
    so far has he removed our transgressions from us.
As a father has compassion on his children,
    so the Lord has compassion on those who fear him;
for he knows how we are formed,
    he remembers that we are dust. (Ps 103:8–14)

The best worship songs are those that are soaked in Scripture. The best sermons are those that expound the biblical text. Here we have a psalm that turns scriptural exposition into exquisite poetry. The psalmist's basic text is Exodus 34:6–7. This was God's declaration of his self-identity, given to Moses in the wake of the great apostasy of Israel at Mount Sinai with the golden calf (in Exodus 32–34, which we will study in chapter 3). It is a powerful statement of the character of God that echoes throughout the Bible in many forms.[1]

The psalmist, along with many Old Testament writers, marvels at the imbalance between the love and the anger of God. He does not of course minimize God's wrath—how could he with all the narratives of the Old Testament to reflect on?—but he does put it into a minor key compared with God's grace and compassion. God's love is abounding; his anger is slow—that is, it is often delayed in operation. His love, as so many Scriptures affirm, is eternal; his anger will not last forever. God fully recognizes our sins, iniquities and transgressions, but does not instantly treat us as they deserve. This is the quality of grace that the psalm as a whole celebrates.

The psalmist not only revels in the affirmation of Exodus 34:6 (in Ps 103:8):

---

[1] It would be worth pausing to read the following texts to feel the force of these affirmations in many different moments of the life of God's people: Num 14:18; Deut 5:9–10; 1 Kings 3:6; Neh 9:17; Ps 86:15; 103:8, 17; 145:8; Jer 32:18–19; Lam 3:32; Dan 9:4; Jonah 4:2; Nahum 1:3.

> The LORD, the LORD, the compassionate and gracious God, slow to anger,
> abounding in love and faithfulness (Ex 34:6);

He also reflects on the first half of Exodus 34:7 (in Ps 103:10, 12):

> maintaining love to thousands, and *forgiving wickedness, rebellion and sin*
> (Ex 34:7)

For those last three words ('wickedness, rebellion and sin') are exactly the
same three Hebrew words that the psalmist lists in Psalm 103:10 and 12.
These are the things that deserve God's wrath, but God chooses *not* to 'treat
us according to them' (Ps 103:10, literally), but rather to 'remove' them
from us altogether (Ps 103:12).

Psalm 103 does not tell us why or how God can do this—only that he does,
and is to be eternally thanked and praised for doing so. Exodus 34:7 actually
says that God '*carries*' wickedness, rebellion and sin. He bears it (which the
NIV translates as 'forgiving'). Now this is interesting. Not only is this the
same Hebrew word (*nasa*) as is used in the section above for God 'carrying'
his people, it is also the same word that Isaiah uses about the Servant of the
Lord in Isaiah 53. Whereas 'we' (the unnamed observers) thought that the
Servant of the Lord was undergoing all his sufferings because God was pun-
ishing him for his own sin, what we now realize, to our great surprise, is that
it was actually *our* sins that he was '*carrying*'—and that he carried right
through his flagrantly unjust trial and horrendously violent death.

> Surely he took up our pain
>   and *bore [carried]* our suffering,
> yet we considered him punished by God,
>   stricken by him, and afflicted.
> But he was pierced for our transgressions,
>   he was crushed for our iniquities;
> the punishment that brought us peace was on him,
>   and by his wounds we are healed.
> We all, like sheep, have gone astray,
>   each of us has turned to his own way;
> and the Lord has *laid on him*
>   the iniquity of us all.
> Therefore I will give him a portion among the great,
>   and he will divide the spoils with the strong,

because he poured out his life unto death,
>and was numbered with the transgressors.
For he *bore [carried]* the sin of many,
>and made intercession for the transgressors. (Is 53:4–6, 12)

The author of Psalm 103 exalts the forgiving grace of God, in that God does not deal with us as our sins deserve, but he is careful to point out (though without further explanation) that this can happen only because God himself has 'removed our transgressions from us'. It is other Scriptures that show us how God did the removal: by carrying them himself, in the person of his Servant. Or as Peter would later express it, unquestionably reflecting on Isaiah 53 as he wrote the words:

He [Christ] himself bore our sins in his body on the cross, so that we might die to sins and live for righteousness; by his wounds you have been healed (1 Pet 2:24)

Poets and preachers expand their root themes with richly suggestive metaphors. So here, the psalmist colours in the compassionate grace of God in dealing with our sins by means of three metaphors. The first two are spatial—height and breadth. God's love is as high as the heavens are above the earth. God's moving van has transported our sins as far away as the East is from the West. And the third is relational. In behaving thus, God is like a human father who feels pity and compassion (the Hebrew word contains both emotions) for his children in their small size and physical limitations. A good father does not expect his children to have the strength of adults, and he makes allowances for their frailty. God does not expect of us more than is humanly possible. This is not to say of course that our sin is excusable, or that God is not grieved and angered by our wickedness and rebellion. No Old Testament psalmist could have entertained such a thought. Rather it means, simply, that God is no less understanding of all our human limitations than any good father is of his children's vulnerability.

One might have expected the psalmist to illustrate his general point by reference back to the historical act of forgiveness that his main text comes from—the episode of the golden calf in Exodus 32–34. But instead, the fatherly comparison in Psalm 103:13 leads him right back to creation, and another text:

The LORD God *formed* a man from the *dust* of the ground. (Gen 2:7)

As we have said earlier, the Old Testament resists any idea that the fatherhood of God implied any physical, sexual or biological parenting of the human race by God. Humans are not the offspring of the gods in any literal sense. Nevertheless, God is as surely the 'progenitor' of humanity, by having 'formed' us, as any human father is of his children. And just as a father knows when his children were born, so God 'knows our forming and remembers that dust is what we are' (a literal rendering of the Hebrew in Ps 103:14). And in that remembering, lies God's understanding of us and his fatherly compassion for us.

And in response to such fatherly factors in the character of God and in his attitude and action toward us, it is indeed right that we should summon up 'all that is within us' to bless the Lord, and forget not all his benefits (Ps 103:1–2, my translation).

GOD—THE FATHER WHO ADOPTS

> Do not hide your face from me,
>> do not turn your servant away in anger;
>> you have been my helper.
> Do not reject me or forsake me,
>> God my Saviour.
> *Though my father and mother forsake me,*
>> *the* LORD *will receive me.* (Ps 27:9–10)

> Sing to God, sing in praise to his name,
>> extol him who rides on the clouds;
>> rejoice before him—his name is the LORD.
> *A father to the fatherless, a defender of widows,*
>> *is God in his holy dwelling.*
> God sets the lonely in families,
>> he leads out the prisoners with singing;
>> but the rebellious live in a sun-scorched land. (Ps 68:4–6)

These are the only other references to God in comparison with a human father in the book of Psalms (apart from the direct address to God as 'my Father', in the mouth of the Davidic king, in Ps 89:26). They have in common the idea that God will step in as an adoptive father in circumstances where human parents have either disowned their child, or have left him orphaned. God, as Father, takes over where human fatherhood fails for one reason or another.

Psalm 27 begins with strong notes of faith in God and the courage it generates in the face of enemies. And it is clear that the author is indeed surrounded by enemies and stands in great need of God's protection and provision. Psalm 27:7–9 suggests that under the pressure of the danger that surrounds him, the author is desperate for some reassurance from God that he will indeed be there for him and deliver on his promises. It is unlikely that Psalm 27:10 means that the writer has actually been literally disowned by his human parents. Rather, he probably contemplates the pain of such a devastating disgrace hypothetically as the worst possible exacerbation of his feeling of standing alone against the world—if even his parents should turn against him! But in turning to God, as he does through the whole psalm, he knows he is turning to the one whose loving commitment to him is stronger even than the strongest human bond of parent and child. God is the Father whose protection will never be withdrawn, whose commitment will outlast all earthly fatherhood. God is the Father who, if ever the believer should be left effectively fatherless, will adopt him as his own and take him in (NIV 'receive' is rather weak; the word means to take up, take in, gather in, or gather up).

Psalm 68, overall, is a psalm celebrating the mighty power of Yahweh as the victorious God of Israel's history. So Psalm 68:5–6 is a kind of counterpoint, celebrating the compassionate and relational nature of God alongside his enormous and triumphant strength.

God's special concern for the orphan and widow is well documented of course throughout the Law and the Prophets, in the wisdom tradition (as for example in Job's echo of this text in Job 29:12–16), and in narratives such as Elijah's temporary accommodation with the widow of Zarephath or the story of Ruth. But here the concept is expressed not merely in the form of commands to human action (to care for the orphan and widows), but in picturing Yahweh himself as the adoptive father who takes care of the orphan, and the defending advocate who represents the widow in court and sees that she gets justice.

It is striking that in one of the very few Old Testament texts that actually speak directly of God as 'father', the prime focus is on God's loving, protecting and defending stance toward the weak and vulnerable in human society as typified in the most vulnerable of all—orphaned children. God is Father to those who have lost the natural bonds of human protection, whether because of rejection, or because of natural bereavement.

These are texts which surely speak with powerful and moving relevance into our world, where many people who come to faith in Christ find themselves disowned and expelled by their human families—even sometimes killed by their own fathers, and where HIV-AIDS is generating orphans and widows at a staggering rate. Loss of family is a terrible and terrifying thing in any era. The knowledge of the fatherhood of God is a biblical truth that cannot be lightly or glibly substituted as a panacea, but certainly provides a framework of ultimate and eternal security for those who come to know and trust in their heavenly Father through saving faith in his Son.

CONCLUSION

For Israel then, knowing God included knowing certain dimensions of his character and actions that could best be expressed and reflected upon by comparison with human fatherhood (or in some cases, parenthood). The idea of God as Father was not allowed to degenerate into the kind of pagan mythology that distorted the good gift of human sexuality into a lurid parody of divine sexual antics as the origin of the human race. God had not 'fathered' humans by any such means. And perhaps, as we said, this is the reason why in Old Testament times they were reluctant to refer to God simply as 'God the Father', as a title. Nevertheless, having said that, it is clear that God had acted, and could be asked to act, in ways that found analogies in the behaviour of the best human fathers.

Here is God, the Father who carries his people, protecting them through all dangers, and whom we can trust like a child in his father's arms.

Here is God, the Father who disciplines his people, but does so for their benefit and learning. The wise child will submit to such discipline, recognizing the love that motivates it.

Here is God, the Father who pities his people, remembering the simple fact of their dusty humanity from the day he formed them, and acts to carry away their sin so that it can be forgiven. Such fatherly compassion calls for our gratitude and praise.

Here is God, the Father who takes over where human fathers fail or fall, adopting those who trust in him so that they are fatherless no longer. And in that lies our eternal security.

Here is God, we can now add in the light of the New Testament, the One whom we can rightly come to know as God the Father through the fuller revelation of his Son, Jesus Christ.

There are many more dimensions to the full biblical doctrine of the Fatherhood of God, but I hope it is clear by now that, in knowing Yahweh their God, these Old Testament believers had a remarkably profound understanding of some of what it means to know God as Father.

CHAPTER TWO

KNOWING GOD
THROUGH EXPERIENCE
of HIS GRACE

Knowing God starts with knowing what God has done for us out of his love and grace. Certainly that is where Israelites would have begun. If you had asked any devout Israelite, 'How do you know God?' he or she would have sat down with you to tell you a long story—the story of God in action on behalf of his people, especially the story of the exodus. And at the end they would have said, 'And that's how we know the LORD our God. That is who he is, and that is how we know him.'

And in doing so, your Israelite friend would have been doing exactly what Moses did in the text we shall unpack in this chapter. For the whole point of their history, says Moses, was precisely so that Israel should indeed *know* the truth and reality of their God. As Moses urges the people of Israel to be faithful to God as they move forward into a challenging future, he reminds them of their remarkable past. It is a past filled with the grace of God in action. Just think of all that God had done for Israel . . .

> Ask now about the former days, long before your time, from the day God created human beings on the earth; ask from one end of the heavens to the other. Has anything so great as this ever happened, or has anything like it ever been heard of? Has any other people heard the voice of God speaking out of fire, as you have, and lived? Has any god ever tried to take for himself one nation out of another nation, by testings, by signs and wonders, by war, by a

mighty hand and an outstretched arm, or by great and awesome deeds, like all the things the LORD your God did for you in Egypt before your very eyes?

You were shown these things so that you might know that the Lord is God; besides him there is no other. From heaven he made you hear his voice to discipline you. On earth he showed you his great fire, and you heard his words from out of the fire. Because he loved your ancestors and chose their descendants after them, he brought you out of Egypt by his Presence and his great strength, to drive out before you nations greater and stronger than you and to bring you into their land to give it to you for your inheritance, as it is today.

Acknowledge and take to heart this day that the Lord is God in heaven above and on the earth below. There is no other. Keep his decrees and commands, which I am giving you today, so that it may go well with you and your children after you and that you may live long in the land the LORD your God gives you for all time. (Deut 4:32–40)

I have highlighted Deuteronomy 4:35 and 39 because they provide the focal point of the passage. Why had God done all that he had done for Israel? So that they should *know* him as the only God (Deut 4:35). What should they do then? *Know* him in their hearts (Deut 4:39)! 'Acknowledge' is simply a variation in English on what is exactly the same verb in Hebrew, 'know'.

For Israel, knowing Yahweh as God was founded on their experience of his action in history. They knew something in their heads as the truth because of something they had experienced in their lives as a reality. Knowledge and experience go together here—combined around the person and action of God. It is important that we always keep the two together, since some people tend to go to extremes in emphasizing one or the other.

'Never mind doctrine,' say some people, 'just feel the presence and power of God in your experience.'

'No, we must teach the truth that people should know and believe,' others assert; 'Experience is subjective and suspicious.'

But we should not divide the two like this. In the Bible God gives his people unmistakable *experiential* proof of his presence; but then he immediately goes on to teach them the *truth* that they need to learn in their heads from such experience.

Let's think, then, about four things from this passage. Each of them is an aspect of Israel's experience of God's grace and each of them relates to what it means to know God.

- the uniqueness of the experience
- the content of the experience
- the transmission of the experience
- the purpose of the experience

THE UNIQUENESS OF THE EXPERIENCE

Moses challenges the listening Israelites to reflect on their actual experience up to this point in their history. It is important also to recall that he is talking to people for whom this was actual historical experience. He is talking to the generation who were the children of those who had come out of Egypt in the exodus. They had been there with their parents at Mount Sinai. These were recent events in living memory. So Moses is not asking if they remember some ancient myths and legends, or if they can repeat the religious speculations of some great ancestor. He is asking them to recall things that had happened 'before your very eyes' (Deut 4:34). This is historical reality, not religious mythology. That is where our knowledge of God is rooted.

Moses asks some grand questions in Deuteronomy 4:32–34. They are rhetorical questions—that is to say, he is not asking for information, but making an emphatic point. He imagines a research project of cosmic scale in Deuteronomy 4:32 taking in the whole universe of space and the whole history of time. Even in such a vast field of enquiry, will anybody come up with anything that could be compared with what God had just done for Israel through the exodus and at Sinai? The answer expected of course is, 'No', there is nothing like these things. Nothing like them has ever happened. What God did in bringing Israel out of slavery in Egypt and in speaking to them at Sinai was unique. And it was unique in two ways: it was unprecedented (God had never done such a thing at any other time), and it was unparalleled (God had never done such a thing anywhere else for any other nation).

Now we need to say at once that this does not imply that God was not interested in, or not involved in, the histories of other peoples. The Old Testament affirms again and again that Yahweh is the sovereign Lord of all nations on the planet and is active in all human history—not just the story of Israel. In fact, just a couple of chapters earlier this book of Deuteronomy has already made that point, in affirming that it was Yahweh who had moved many of the other nations around the lands of the Middle East in the same way that he was now moving Israel into possession of Canaan (Deut 2 as a whole, but see especially Deut 2:5, 9, 10–12, 19, 20–23). But in Israel alone God had been working for his unique purposes of salvation and covenant, and within his overall mission of bringing blessing ultimately to all nations, in fulfilment of his promise to Abraham. In this sense, God did in the history of Israel what he did nowhere else and 'no-when' else.

So there is a uniqueness about Israel's experience of God that is being very powerfully affirmed here. Yahweh their God had redeemed them in a way that no other people had known (cf. Amos 3:1–2). And Yahweh had spoken to them in a way that no other people had ever heard (cf. Ps 147:19–20). And in both dimensions, God acted in his grace. The story of the exodus is presented as monumental proof of God's loving concern for his oppressed people and his faithfulness to his promise to Abraham. Love and faithfulness are both dimensions of God's grace. And the story of Sinai is presented as God, in all his awesome holiness, graciously entering into a covenant relationship with people who repeatedly prove themselves utterly unworthy of it. These were unique moments in all human history, and those who experienced them were experiencing the grace of the living God in action, grace that saved them out of slavery, grace that invited them into relationship. To know God through such experience was to know the God of grace.

THE CONTENT OF THE EXPERIENCE

We need to look in somewhat greater depth at these two aspects of Israel's experience that Moses highlights here. In fact he refers to each of them twice over in our passage, clearly intending to underline them by such repetition. They are:

- The revelation at Mount Sinai (Deut 4:33, 36)
- The redemption out of Egypt (Deut 4:34, 37—with the conquest also in view in Deut 4:38)

Both of these were primary experiences through which Israel came to know God. And both of them also have New Testament counterparts which relate to us and *our* experience of God, through which we too come to know him.

Revelation

(1) The revelation of God at Sinai. The primary account of what happened at Sinai is found in Exodus 19 and would be worth reading at this point, along with the interesting recollection of it in Deuteronomy 5. It was a staggeringly awesome audio-visual experience of the presence and power of God, and it burned itself into the collective memory of Israel for ever after. When you really needed to invoke the power of God, calling on him as the God of Sinai was the way to do it (Ps 68:8). Sinai was the greatest of all the Old Testament theophanies. *Theophany* means the appearing of God. At Sinai, God was heard (in the sound of thunder, the trumpet and the voice), felt (in an earthquake) and seen (in smoke and fire). He was not seen literally as Deuteronomy 4 has already carefully pointed out.

> Then the LORD spoke to you out of the fire. You heard the sound of words
> but saw no form; there was only a voice. (Deut 4:12)

> On earth he showed you his great fire, and you heard his words from out of
> the fire. (Deut 4:36)

But this was precisely the point. God encountered Israel at Sinai, not just to dazzle them with some spectacular cosmic fireworks, but to address them. He spoke words to them. That is, Sinai was an experience of intelligible, meaningful communication. God had things to say. Israel had things to understand. 'The words' meant first of all the so-called Ten Words (i.e. the Ten Commandments, the Decalogue). But that was certainly not the limit of God's communication at Sinai.

Already, at the burning bush encounter on Mount Sinai, God had revealed his personal name, Yahweh, to Moses, and this now becomes the focal point of all his revelation to the Israelites when they get there, too. 'I am the LORD your God', is how the Ten Words begin (Deut 5:6). So at Sinai God revealed his own *identity*. At Sinai too he revealed his *character* as the God of grace and compassion, even in the teeth of Israel's rebellion.

> And he passed in front of Moses, proclaiming, 'The LORD, the LORD, the
> compassionate and gracious God, slow to anger, abounding in love and faith-
> fulness, maintaining love to thousands, and forgiving wickedness, rebellion
> and sin. Yet he does not leave the guilty unpunished; he punishes the
> children and their children for the sin of the fathers to the third and fourth
> generation.' (Ex 34:6–7)

At Sinai, God revealed his *law*, his *covenant*, his *expectations* of Israel's worship—everything in fact that was needed to initiate and foster the relationship between God and this people that was so critical to God's ultimate plans for the world. All this God revealed at Sinai.

It only makes sense to talk about 'knowing God' if it is actually possible for God to be known. There are religions and philosophies which do not accept such a possibility. In the Hindu worldview, for example, the transcendent divine being is ultimately unknowable. The Bible insists throughout that the living God of whom it speaks not only *can* be known, but *wills* to be known. And far from leaving it up to us to get to know him through some game of religious hide and seek, this God takes the initiative in revealing himself to us. God can be known because God has spoken.

Now of course we realize that we cannot *grasp* all there is to God. We cannot, in that sense, comprehend God fully. But to say that we, as finite creatures, cannot know *everything* in the infinity of God, is not to say that there is *nothing* we can confidently claim to know about God. It does not reduce everything about God to mystery, ambiguity or just a matter of opinion. We can truly know what God has said about himself.

It is also true that God has chosen not to reveal everything to us—there are some things he has kept to himself, as Deuteronomy 29 says.

> The secret things belong to the LORD our God, but the things revealed belong to us and to our children for ever, that we may follow all the words of this law. (Deut 29:29)

What God *has* chosen to reveal to us of himself, however, is clear and intelligible, for he has spoken in words of human language for that very purpose.

> For this is what the LORD says—
> he who created the heavens,
>   he is God;
> he who fashioned and made the earth,
>   he founded it;
> he did not create it to be empty,
>   but formed it to be inhabited—
> he says:

'I am the LORD,
   and there is no other.
I have not spoken in secret,
   from somewhere in a land of darkness;
I have not said to Jacob's descendants,
   "Seek me in vain."
I, the LORD, speak the truth;
   I declare what is right.' (Is 45:18–19)

So it is not arrogant to claim that we know God, in relation to what he has revealed through his word. God has made himself known. God wills to be known. Indeed, Israel had been told that one of the underlying purposes for which God was acting to deliver them from oppression in Egypt was that they *would* know him (Ex 6:6–8).

(2) The revelation of God in Christ. For us, however, living on this side of the coming of Jesus Christ and the New Testament, the opportunity and scope for knowing God through his revelation is vastly greater than anything available to the Israelites even in the wake of their experience at Sinai. The words they heard came from the Living God, and in that sense also from the living Word of God. But in Jesus,

> the Word became flesh and made his dwelling among us. We have seen his glory, the glory of the one and only Son, who came from the Father, full of grace and truth. (John 1:14)

Or as the writer to the Hebrews put it,

> In the past God spoke to our ancestors through the prophets at many times and in various ways, but in these last days he has spoken to us by his Son, whom he appointed heir of all things, and through whom he made the universe. (Heb 1:1–2)

Once again we notice the emphasis in these New Testament texts on historical facts, experienced and witnessed by those who knew Jesus. The God who spoke at Sinai delivered his final word in Bethlehem, in Galilee and in Jerusalem—in the person of his own Son, Jesus of Nazareth. And Jesus then entrusted his own words to his disciples, and through the gift of his Holy Spirit of truth, commissioned them to teach that truth with apostolic authority to the church for all coming generations including our own.

So, just as knowing God meant for Israel first knowing his revealed word given to them at Sinai, similarly for us, knowing God means knowing the revealed Word of God through Christ. Knowing God is a process that starts from God's side, from what God has done and said to make himself known. Our responsibility is to hear and heed.

To know God is to know him as Revealer.

Redemption

(1) The exodus. The events that Moses speaks of in Deuteronomy 4:34 and 37 are those referred to in the first fifteen chapters of the book of Exodus. He does not explicitly describe them as 'redemption' here, but he certainly did in the Song of Moses immediately after the event. In fact, Exodus 15 is the first time God is described as 'redeeming' his people.

> In your unfailing love you will lead
> > the people you have redeemed.
> In your strength you will guide them
> > to your holy dwelling. (Ex 15:13)

The exodus is the first great act of God's redemption in the Old Testament, and the second greatest in the whole Bible—second only to the cross of Christ, which is spoken of in the New Testament as the 'exodus he accomplished in Jerusalem' (Luke 9:31, my translation). It was also an utterly comprehensive act in which God demonstrated the full extent of his redeeming love and power. Think of all the dimensions of Israel's bondage in Egypt.

- They were *politically* oppressed as an ethnic immigrant minority, vulnerable to the host state's manufactured hostility against them.

- They were *economically* exploited as a convenient source of cheap labour in the host state's agricultural and construction sectors.

- They were *socially* victimized through intolerable interference in their family life and then through a programme of state-sponsored genocide. The description of their plight in Exodus 1 has some very modern echoes.

- On top of all that, they were *spiritually* oppressed in servitude to the Pharaoh—one of the claimed gods of Egypt—when they should have been free to serve and worship Yahweh.

In the chain of events we call the exodus, God accomplished deliverance for them in all four areas. They were released from political injustice, from economic exploitation and from social violence. And they were released into covenant relationship with Yahweh their God at Sinai. The exodus, in other words, was an act of holistic redemption that transformed every dimension of Israel's holistic need. As such it stands as a prime biblical model of what God means by redemption, and what our missional response needs to take into account.[1]

In our text here, Moses picks out two major items in the catalogue of what the exodus proved about God (we shall think of some more in the next chapter).

- On the one hand, his immense *power* that was demonstrated in his *victory* over his enemy (Deut 4:34).

- And on the other hand, his great *love and faithfulness* in fulfilling the promise he made to Israel's ancestors (Deut 4:37).

His great power and love are combined in his 'Presence' (Deut 4:37), which is literally, his 'Face'. Israel's experience of the exodus was, in other words, an experience of the Face of God—even though they did not see his face in a literal sense. His actions of power and love on their behalf proved his personal presence in their midst. In these things therefore they had come to know him, to recognize him—just as we know someone through their face. It is another highly personal metaphor for knowing God.

(2) The cross. Just as we have the revealing word of God embodied for us in the person of Jesus, so we have the great redeeming work of God achieved for us by Jesus, through his atoning death on the cross. And amidst all the volumes we could now say about what we know of God because of the cross, we can simply pick out the same two features that match what Moses said about the exodus. For the New Testament likewise emphasizes the cross as the climactic demonstration of *God's power and his final victory* over all his enemies and over all that wrecks and spoils human life. The cross is the power of God in action.

Having disarmed the powers and authorities, he made a public spectacle of them, triumphing over them by the cross. (Col 2:15)

---

[1] I have discussed the exodus as a model of redemption and its significance for holistic mission more fully in *The Mission of God* (Downers Grove, IL: InterVarsity, 2006), ch. 8.

And the cross is the ultimate proof of God's *love and faithfulness*.

> God demonstrates his own love for us in this: while we were still sinners, Christ died for us. (Rom 5:8)

To know God, then, is to know him as Redeemer, as Saviour and Deliverer. It is to know the exodus God, Yahweh, the great I AM. It is to know the Calvary God, Jesus, 'the Son of God, who loved me and gave himself for me', as Paul delighted to say (Gal 2:20).

All of this, then, happened in history, in reality, in experience. These were unique and unrepeatable events, in which God acted in revelation and redemption. This is how God has made himself known; and therefore this is how we are to know God. This is the claim and affirmation that Moses is making in our text, and that we rightly appropriate through our wider knowledge of the revealing and redeeming God from the New Testament. We come to know God through experience of his grace in action.

But this raises a question. Moses is here describing a unique historical experience that happened to a particular group of people in one generation, and could be recalled as a living experience at the most only by the younger generation—the children whom he now addresses as adults. How could later generations come to know God if they could not have that same experience? Moses says that the Israelites know God because these things happened before their very eyes. So what about later generations who weren't there to see it with their eyes? This leads us to reflect on our next point.

THE TRANSMISSION OF THE EXPERIENCE

The same question could be asked about Jesus and the cross as well, of course. It was all very well for those who were privileged to know him, who heard his teaching and watched his life, who witnessed his death and resurrection. Of course *they* knew him, and knew God through him. But what about all those who came later? Clearly Jesus himself pondered this issue, prepared for it (John 14:15–18, 25–26; 16:12–16), prayed about it (John 17:20), and promised even greater blessing to those who would believe without having 'been there' to see what the disciples saw (John 20:29).

We have been saying that we come to know God through the experience of his grace. How does that happen? Well, for two generations in history, it happened by actually being there and witnessing God's grace in action (the

Israelites who experienced the exodus; and the disciples who saw Jesus's life, death and resurrection). For the rest of us (whether subsequent generations of Israelites in the Old Testament, or generations of Christian believers ever since the first century), there are three ways at least in which that primary historical experience also becomes ours, and thereby becomes the means of our knowing God: through telling the story and teaching the faith; through the inspired Scriptures; and through the sacramental re-enactment of the events themselves.

Telling and teaching. Again and again in Deuteronomy Moses urges the Israelites to make sure that the story was regularly told and its significance thoroughly taught to all subsequent generations.

> Only be careful, and watch yourselves closely so that you do not forget the things your eyes have seen or let them slip from your heart as long as you live. Teach them to your children and to their children after them. (Deut 4:9; cf. 6:4–9, 20–25)

Israel was a community of memory. They were to preserve the knowledge of God by constantly re-telling the story of the acts of God. Conversely, if they failed to do so, they both 'forgot God', and lost their knowledge of God—with disastrous results, as the prophets testify.

The Scriptures. The oral re-telling of the story was essential, and was to form part of every family's instruction so as to enable each generation to relive the events and enter into the experience of God's grace that they contained. But God's purpose was also to have a written record that would supplement and where necessary correct human memory, and provide a permanent witness of all that he had said and done. And so we have the Scriptures—breathed out by God, as Paul said (2 Tim 3:16), while at the same time entirely written by human authors.

Deuteronomy, yet again, sees the need for this written record alongside the oral telling and teaching, and makes clear provision for it. The book of Deuteronomy itself of course is one example of the very thing it is talking about.

> So Moses wrote down this law and gave it to the Levitical priests, who carried the ark of the covenant of the LORD, and to all the elders of Israel. Then Moses commanded them: 'At the end of every seven years, in the year for cancelling debts, during the Festival of Tabernacles, when all Israel comes

to appear before the LORD your God at the place he will choose, you shall read this law before them in their hearing. Assemble the people—men, women and children, and the foreigners living in your towns—so they can listen and learn to fear the LORD your God and follow carefully all the words of this law. Their children, who do not know this law, must hear it and learn to fear the LORD your God as long as you live in the land you are crossing the Jordan to possess.' (Deut 31:9–13)

If we look at some of the great revivals of faith that took place in the course of Israel's history, they included this element of the reading of the written Word of God, so that people could enter again into that experience of God which would lead them to repentance, but also to rejoicing and obedience (e.g. Josiah in 2 Kings 22–23, and Ezra in Neh 8). Likewise for Timothy, Paul observes that it was the faithful reading and teaching of the Scriptures that had led Timothy to saving faith in Christ and ethical instruction (2 Tim 3:14–16).

We can never stress too much the importance of the Scriptures in knowing God, even when we rightly talk about knowing God being a matter of experience. For when we say that we know God through experience of his grace, we are not talking merely about some subjective, inward or mystical personal experience. The emphasis is not just on experience for its own sake, without regard for content or control. Knowing God means entering into a *biblically informed* experience. It means entering into *this* story, as it is told in the Bible. It means engaging with the scriptural interpretation of what the story means, and what it reveals of the words and works of God. If we cut loose from the Scriptures and allow any so-called experience of God to be treated as valid knowledge of God, then we can end up in dangerous waters without a rudder or an anchor.

This affects our mission and evangelism also. We long to bring people to know God. That is surely one of our primary evangelistic goals. But we must make sure that it is the God of the Bible they are coming to know. So at some point in the whole process of bringing people to faith, and then to discipleship, we must lead them to the Scriptures, so that their own personal experience of God's grace will be biblically informed and authenticated. They need to know this story—the grand narrative of the whole Bible (not in every detail at first, of course, but in its over-arching structural unity). Here is the story of God and the world, of humanity's dignity and depravity, of where we are and who we are, of what's gone wrong and what God has done to put things right, of where it will all end and where we are headed for. Only within this grand narrative can we know God truly, through experiencing his grace in action through these great events.

If people are to come to know God, then they must know these great biblical realities, enshrined in the great biblical story. This is clear in both the Old and New Testaments. So, for example, when the psalmists contemplated how the nations would eventually come to know and worship Yahweh—the God of Israel but also the only true and living God—they saw it as a matter of proclaiming among the nations the great story of God's mighty acts in Israel through which the name, salvation and glory of Yahweh God had been revealed.

> Sing to the LORD a new song;
>> sing to the LORD, all the earth.
> Sing to the LORD, praise his *name*;
>> proclaim his *salvation* day after day.
> Declare his *glory* among the nations,
>> his *marvellous deeds* among all peoples. (Ps 96:1–3)

And among the key tasks that Jesus laid upon his apostles in their task of making disciples of all nations was 'teaching them to obey everything I have commanded you' (Mt 28:20).

The sacraments. So the story is to be told and taught; the Scriptures are to be read and taught. But in addition, and in both Testaments, God provided for a practical re-enactment of the historical events in which his redeeming grace had been so powerfully operating, so that by engaging in these regular actions the people of God would not only preserve the memory of the original events but continue to enter into the experience of grace that they embodied. We are talking about the Passover and the Lord's Supper.

Both of these are 'memorials'. That is to say, they function as reminders of the events they celebrate: the exodus and the death of Christ respectively. And that, as we have seen, is an important thing in itself. The people of God must remember, remember, remember, in order to know God through his great acts. But they are more than just memorials. When Jews and Christians celebrate the Passover and the Lord's Supper, it is as if they enter a kind of two-way time machine in relation to those events.

(1) The sacraments locate us 'as if we were there'. Every generation of Israelites recited the words of Deuteronomy 6:21, 'We were slaves of Pharaoh in Egypt, but the LORD brought *us* out of Egypt with a mighty hand.' They put themselves in the shoes of the oppressed Hebrews, and in the Passover meal they enter again into the experience of the slavery, the plagues and the night-time deliverance. They relive the story as if it were their own—which by faith and corporate identification, it is. Likewise, at every Holy Communion service, the Christian hears the words of Christ, spoken first to the disciples, but now addressed to him or her, 'This is my body given for *you*; this is the cup of the new covenant in my blood, which is shed for *you*, and for many.' The story, the actions, the words, put us in that room with Jesus on the night he was betrayed. There is an old spiritual that asks the repeated question, 'Were you there when they crucified my Lord?' Spiritually speaking, by faith and in sacramental action, the answer is 'Yes'. Of course, this is not implying that the actions of the Holy Communion are in any sense a repetition of the sacrifice of Christ. As the Anglican liturgy makes clear, we celebrate his one, perfect and sufficient sacrifice, made once for all on the cross. But it does mean that we see ourselves as witnesses and beneficiaries of what Christ did. We were there. It was for us. The cross was a unique historical event, but the sacrament connects us to it by the sanctified imagination of faith and gratitude.

(2) The sacraments present the events 'as if now'. If, on the one hand, participation in the sacrament puts us back in time to the original historical events, so, on the other hand, such participation brings the event right up into our present, as if it were happening for us now. The Israelites celebrate again the saving power of the God who is always present with them in times of need and oppression—or indeed cry out to him to do again what he did for them in delivering them from Egypt. The Christian receives once again the grace and forgiveness that flow from the cross, the cleansing power of the blood of Christ. And as the bread is broken and eaten and the wine poured out and drunk, as it was on that night two thousand years ago, we 'feed on him in our hearts by faith, with thanksgiving', here and now in the present. The *act* of grace was that unrepeatable historical event. The *means* of grace is the repeated experience of receiving it by faith and absorbing its benefits in our whole lives.

Knowing God, then, is a matter of experiencing God's grace—for Israel and for us. And of course, for each individual that has to be a personal, inward and unique experience. Each one of us must know God for ourselves as the unique person God has made us to be. Nobody's testimony of their knowledge of God is identical to anyone else's. And yet it is important to stress on the basis of the last three points, that knowing God is also a shared and collective experience. To know God I must join myself with those who experienced the original events of God's revelation and salvation. I put myself alongside them by faith and so join the great historical 'communion of saints' of every generation. And at the same time, I join the great company of those around me in the present who also share this experience, reflect upon it in the light of Scripture, and celebrate it in the presence of God.

Knowing God, then, to amplify a point made above, is not some private, esoteric devotional state of mind or heart. Nor is it 'whatever I make of it'—just so long as 'me and God' get along fine together. There are some kinds of popular 'spiritualities', and some kinds of devotional literature, which pander to this form of self-obsession. For that is really what it is. 'Knowing God' can become just another handy item in my inventory of self-fulfilment techniques. God becomes adjectival to my persona, an accessory to my self-esteem. As against all such narcissism, the Bible insists that knowing God starts out from who God is and what God has done— meaning what he did a very long time before we ever came along. To know him we must join ourselves to that great heritage of historical faith and memory, enter into these stories, and experience the grace of God in them, along with the company of all God's people.

Knowing God is not an exercise in getting God to fit into my life. Knowing God is an exercise in humbly fitting my life into God's great historical story of redemptive grace.

But for what purpose? Why did these great unique historical events take place at all, and what was it that Israel was to learn in particular in the experience of knowing God through them. That leads us, then, fourth, to:

THE PURPOSE OF THE EXPERIENCE
Our two key verses come back into sharp focus at this point.

> You were shown these things so that you might know that the LORD is God; besides him there is no other. (Deut 4:35)

Acknowledge and take to heart this day that the LORD is God in heaven above and on the earth below. There is no other. (Deut 4:39)

'So that you might know . . .' Israel's experience of the revealing and redeeming grace of God was intended to be educational. They were to learn something from it about Yahweh as God. What was that? Well, obviously, they were to learn all that had already been said in the previous verses about Yahweh. Look at those verses again and see in them some of the rudiments of Israel's knowledge of God. They now know that Yahweh is the God who speaks, who disciplines, who loves, who keeps his promises, who is a miraculous deliverer and powerful victor over his enemies. In the next chapter we shall look at some of these and more in Israel's curriculum of knowing their God.

But what verses 35 and 39 stress above and beyond all these truths is the universality and uniqueness of Yahweh as God. He is God 'in heaven above and on the earth below'—that is, he fills the whole cosmos. There is no-where else to be God in. Yahweh is the universal God, not just the national god of little Israel. And 'there is no other'. He is unique because he is the only. This is affirming much more than that Yahweh was the only God that Israel was to worship (while allowing for the existence of other gods of other nations). It is hard to read it as anything other than a statement of the transcendent uniqueness of Yahweh as the only living God in the universe.

So here we have an uncompromisingly monotheistic affirmation. But it is not expressed in the way we might expect, as if monotheism per se were all that the Israelites were supposed to deduce from their experience. Moses did not say, 'You were shown these things so that you would know that there is only one God.' If he had, one might imagine James muttering back, 'You believe that there is one God. Good! Even the demons believe that—and shudder' (Jas 2:19). Monotheism as mere arithmetic doesn't get you very far. No, the point is not so much the singularity of deity (as it is in Deut 6:4–5), but the identity of deity. The question is 'Who is God? Who is Lord?' This text answers, Yahweh alone is God. And the New Testament adds, Jesus alone is Lord—and (in both cases), 'there is no other'. No other God than Yahweh. No other name by which we must be saved, than the name of Jesus. God is as he is revealed in Yahweh. God is as he is revealed in Jesus. The only God who saves is Yahweh. The only one through whom God saves is Jesus.

These are the great affirmations that are involved in knowing God, in the way that this text and those that echo it demand. This is what we must 'acknowledge and take to heart', in the task of knowing God through the experience of his grace. To know God is to know the living, biblical God of revelation and redemption, experienced through these events—not some figment of our own imagination, or the myths of our culture, or the masquerading gods of the idolatries that surround us.

And as we choose to know this God in this way, then the final command of this passage swims across the horizon into sharp focus.

> Keep his decrees and commands, which I am giving you today, so that it may go well with you and your children after you. (Deut 4:40)

If this is the God we are called to know, then he is also the God we are called to obey. Indeed, as we shall see in chapter 4, to know God is to obey him.

CHAPTER THREE

KNOWING GOD
THROUGH EXPOSURE
to HIS JUDGEMENT

Grace comes first. In chapter 2 we saw that for us to know God at all is a matter of the grace of God. But more than that, we come to know him as we witness his grace in action and experience it for ourselves. And that is what God wants, since he told the Israelites that the purpose for which they had experienced the great redeeming and revealing work of God in their history was so that they would know him to be the only living God. And we saw that the same principle holds good for us as Christian believers also. We know God when we experience God in action.

But 'God in action' cuts more than one way. The exodus was a great deliverance for the Israelites. But it was at the same time a great judgement upon the Egyptians who had oppressed them. It is presented as the paradigmatic act of God's justice, so celebrated in the Bible, by which he vindicates and liberates the downtrodden, and condemns the oppressor. So in the exodus, the release of the Hebrew slaves required the overthrow of the power that held them captive—the Pharaoh. It did not have to be that way, as the story tells how God through Moses asked Pharaoh voluntarily to do justice, stop the oppression and let the Israelites go. But he refused. Not once, but again. And again and again. And again and again and again, as the narrative piles up the pressure of the conflict of wills between Yahweh and Pharaoh. In the end, however, the outcome is inevitable.

And apart from the obvious outcome that the *Israelites* were released, and thereby came to know the God they were dealing with, the story is at pains to make the balancing point that *Pharaoh* too came to know God. Or to be more precise, Pharaoh came to know that Yahweh, the God he refused to acknowledge, was indeed God—more powerful than himself, his magicians or any of the gods of Egypt. Knowing God, then, is not a sweet and cosy inner feeling. It is an encounter with the supreme governor of history, and its outcome depends entirely on the stance you adopt in relation to him. Israel came to know God as Saviour. Pharaoh came to know God as judge. In this chapter we will look at the content of this dual educational encounter, starting with Pharaoh.

THE GOD PHARAOH CAME TO KNOW

The pupil—a man who refused to know God. The trigger for the great power encounter between Yahweh and Pharaoh begins with Pharaoh's refusal to even recognize the name of the God in whose name Moses was making his request.

> Afterwards Moses and Aaron went to Pharaoh and said, 'This is what the Lord the God of Israel, says: "Let my people go, so that they may hold a festival to me in the wilderness."' Pharaoh said, 'Who is the Lord, that I should obey him and let Israel go? I do not know the Lord and I will not let Israel go.' (Ex 5:1–2)

Remember, 'the Lord' means the personal name of Yahweh. Pharaoh's astonishingly foolhardy answer says, in effect, 'Excuse me? Who did you say? Who is this god you are talking of? "Yahweh"—who is that? I do not recognize any god by that name in this realm. We have our own gods in Egypt, and I am one of them. I am under no obligation to take instructions from whatever god you are claiming to represent.'

You can almost hear the sharp intake of breath among the angels. 'You don't want to say that, friend. You will know who this God is by the time he has finished with you.'

And that indeed becomes a major theme in the chapters that follow. It's easy to see that the chapters of Exodus 1–15 are all about the exodus. But the subplot underneath is that this story is all about knowing God. It is about a man who claimed he did not and would not 'know' this God and how he was brought to exactly that knowledge, but only when it was too late.

The curriculum—what Pharaoh had to learn. After the encounter between Pharaoh, Moses and Aaron had gone so disastrously wrong in Exodus 5, God renews his promise that he will, without any doubt, bring the Israelites out. And he pointedly emphasizes that in the process *they* will know who he is, even if Pharaoh refuses to (Ex 6:2–8). Unfortunately, the Israelites were almost as unimpressed as Pharaoh at that stage, and even Moses thinks God needs to be more realistic (Ex 6:12). There is a lot of learning to be done on all sides in this narrative.

As the story resumes in Exodus 7, the phrase 'then you (or they) will know', or a variant of it, occurs in every chapter from Exodus 7–11 and then again in Exodus 14. All of them except two (Ex 10:2; 11:7) refer to Pharaoh or the Egyptians. Altogether the phrase comes thirteen times in these chapters. That is why it is right to include this whole episode in our study of 'knowing God through the Old Testament'. It may not be quite the kind of knowing God that we envisaged, or that we would like to add to our devotional checklist, but it is clearly an emphatic theme in the whole narrative. God intends that, like it or not, Pharaoh will *know* him and know a significant quantity of theological truth about him, even if he hardens his heart against the knowledge he accumulates so painfully, to his own final destruction. This is a portion of the Bible that has a major interest in what it means to know God.

What then was on the curriculum for Pharaoh? Let's survey the sequence of lessons.

(1) That Yahweh is truly God.

> And the Egyptians will know that I am the LORD when I stretch out my hand against Egypt and bring the Israelites out of it. . . . This is what the LORD says: By this you will know that I am the LORD: With the staff that is in my hand I will strike the water of the Nile, and it will be changed into blood. (Ex 7:5, 17)

This is the simplest starting point. Pharaoh had refused to acknowledge that Yahweh was a god at all, or at any rate one that he needed to take any notice of, let alone obey. The first two plagues demonstrate the reality of Yahweh's existence and divine power. God starts with the easier things first, as it were, since Pharaoh's magicians manage to replicate the trick with the staff and turning the Nile to blood (though I have often thought they would have served their king better if they had found a spell in their books marked, 'Blood, how to turn back to water').

(2) That Yahweh has no rivals.

> Moses replied, 'It will be as you say, so that you may know there is no one like the LORD our God. The frogs will leave you and your houses, your officials and your people; they will remain only in the Nile.' (Ex 8:10–11)

Here the point is not merely that Yahweh is to be counted among the gods (from Pharaoh's perspective), but that he is in fact unique among them (if Pharaoh wants to be comparative). There is no God like Yahweh. He has no rivals or peers. This is language that will reverberate throughout the Old Testament in many other contexts. We shall return to it as part of Israel's learning curriculum below.

By this time, Pharaoh's magicians have run out of steam. Not only can they not keep up with the demonstrations of Yahweh's power, they are now very keen to acknowledge for themselves that a pretty powerful God is at work here—even if they failed to persuade Pharaoh to agree (Ex 8:19).

(3) That Yahweh is God in Egypt.

> On that day I will deal differently with the land of Goshen, where my people live; no swarms of flies will be there, so that you will know that I, the LORD, am in this land. I will make a distinction between my people and your people. This sign will occur tomorrow. (Ex 8:22–23)

The land of Goshen had been given to the Israelites by a previous Pharaoh several generations earlier. The gift of land to a group of famine refugees at that time had been an act of the Pharaoh's sovereign authority over the land as a whole. But if the present Pharaoh thought that he was really god in the land of Egypt he was about to learn another lesson. This Yahweh was not merely the god of the despised ethnic minority Pharaoh was so mercilessly exploiting; he was in fact God throughout the whole land of Egypt and had the power to distinguish one part of it from another. Yahweh is not just in Goshen. He is 'in this land' (i.e. this land of Egypt, this domain of Pharaoh, as a whole).

(4)   That Yahweh is God of all the earth.

> Let my people go, so that they may worship me, or this time I will send the full force of my plagues against you and against your officials and your people,

so you may know that there is no one like me in all the earth. For by now I
could have stretched out my hand and struck you and your people with a
plague that would have wiped you off the earth. But I have raised you up for
this very purpose, that I might show you my power and that my name might
be proclaimed in all the earth. (Ex 9:13–16)

This is clearly an expansion on the previous statement. Yahweh is not
only God in the land of Egypt, but he is beyond compare 'in all the earth'.
This passage is also the central climax of all these 'knowing' statements in
the context. Not only does it reaffirm what God has been repeatedly trying
to get Pharaoh to acknowledge—namely that Yahweh is God, that he has
enormous power, and that he has no equals; it also affirms for the first time
God's wider educational purpose in this whole sequence of events. And
that is not confined to a demonstration of his power to this pigheaded king.
No, there is a universal intent. God wills to be known 'in all the earth', and
this event will be one of the means by which that will happen. As indeed
it has. For the exodus story is but one part of the whole Bible narrative of
the saving acts of God, culminating in the cross and resurrection of his Son,
Jesus Christ. So wherever that greater story is told, the name of the living
God of the exodus is proclaimed.

The irony here is also very stark. This Pharaoh refused to acknowledge
the name of Yahweh as God. But we do not even know for sure what *his*
name was! The word 'Pharaoh' is not a personal name; it is a title, like
'King'. And historians still dispute exactly which of the many Pharaohs of
Egypt was the Pharaoh of the exodus (depending on which century the
exodus is dated, and there are various theories). But God says to him, 'I have
raised you up' (as God does for all kings), 'not so that everybody will know
who *you* were when you've gone, but so that everybody will know who *I* am.
Your name will be lost to history. *My name* will be known in all the earth.'

(5) That Yahweh is judge of all supposed gods.

On that same night I will pass through Egypt and strike down every firstborn
of both people and animals, and I will bring judgement on all the gods of
Egypt. I am the LORD. (Ex 12:12)

This is not strictly in the sequence of 'then you will know' texts. But it
certainly adds to the knowledge of God contained in this narrative. The
climactic tenth plague that will finally bring Pharaoh and all his people to

beg the Israelites to leave is about to be unleashed. But this verse gives us one of several clues that this contest has not been merely between Yahweh and the human king of Egypt. It has been a spiritual power encounter too. Pharaoh claimed to be a god. Egypt had many gods. The plagues had already demonstrated Yahweh's superiority over some of them—as for example the attack on the Nile, the alleged divine source of Egypt's great fertility; or the darkening of the sun, the most powerful god of all in Egypt's pantheon. In this text, Yahweh makes it comprehensive. Whatever gods may be claimed in Egypt, Yahweh will act in judgement against them all.

Whatever gods and idols may actually be,[1] Yahweh the living God will have none of them. They must fall before him, as much the target of his judgement as the fallen human beings who make them and worship them.

(6) *That Yahweh is the protector of his people and victor over his enemies.*

> But I will gain glory for myself through Pharaoh and all his army, and the Egyptians will know that I am the LORD. . . . The Egyptians will know that I am the LORD when I gain glory through Pharaoh, his chariots and his horsemen. (Ex 14:4, 18)

The learning spreads from Pharaoh alone to the whole nation of Egypt, who had been involved in the genocidal oppression. The climactic finale of the story unfolds in Exodus 14 with Pharaoh's army pursuing the fleeing Hebrews, who seem helplessly trapped between their enemy and the sea. But God has it under control (in fact Isaiah 43:16–17 interprets the events as Yahweh himself leading the Egyptian army to its own destruction). Even at this last moment, as had happened before (e.g. Ex 9:20; 11:3), those around Pharaoh recognize what he doggedly resisted right to the end—that the hand of Yahweh is in action. This time it is Pharaoh's own charioteers who know the truth of what is going on:

> [Yahweh] jammed the wheels of their chariots so that they had difficulty driving [well, as you would!]. And the Egyptians said, 'Let's get away from the Israelites! The LORD is fighting for them against Egypt.' (Ex 14:25)

What a curriculum! This was a steep learning curve, which eventually ended in Pharaoh's own destruction. He certainly came to know God, but

---

[1] On the subject of gods and idols, whether they are 'something' or 'nothing', and what the Bible teaches in relation to them, see *The Mission of God*, ch. 5 (Downers Grove, IL: InterVarsity, 2006).

it did him no good in the end because he hardened his heart against the truth that was staring him in the face. Instead, he wriggled, rejected, resisted, repented, repented of his repentance, and in the end wrecked himself, his army and his country.[2]

God is not mocked. Those who will not know him in submission to his authority will know him as the rock on which they stumble to destruction. Pharaoh chose this route and repeated his choice, against all appeals to change his mind—from Moses, from his own advisors, from God himself—until God accepted and reinforced the refusal he was determined to sustain.

Exodus 14 is the last word on that Pharaoh and his army. But we can be glad that it was not God's last word on Egypt in the Old Testament. For that we turn to Isaiah 19.

Isaiah 19 is a remarkable chapter, which begins by recording God's imminent judgement on the historical Egyptian empire of Isaiah's own day. But then, Isaiah 19:18–25 looks to the unspecific future and sees there a most breathtaking reversal of fortunes for Egypt. There is a deliberate reloading of the exodus narrative, with all the elements of deliverance and salvation now applied to the Egyptians themselves. The saving grace of God was never intended to be confined to the Israelites alone. Ultimately God's salvation turns even former enemies into his own people. It is well worth pausing to read Isaiah 19:18–25 to feel something of the amazement at this prophecy.

THE GOD ISRAEL CAME TO KNOW

Israel was not very far behind Pharaoh in their reluctance to know God, at the start of this narrative. That was one of the reasons Moses himself tried to opt out of the task of getting Israel out of Egypt. Would they believe him? Would they know the name of the God he was talking about? (Ex 3:13).

---

[2]The fact that the text says sometimes that God hardened Pharaoh's heart causes difficulty for some. It is important to note that while the whole narrative is certainly set within the outer framework of God's sovereignty, the prime responsibility for Pharaoh's stubborn resistance lies with Pharaoh himself. The dual fact of Pharaoh hardening his own heart and Yahweh hardening it, is referred to at the very beginning and end of the sequence (Ex 7:3–4; 11:9–10). In between, we are told that Pharaoh hardened his heart eight times before we read of God's involvement again. In other words, the sequence is clearly Pharaoh's own stiffening resolve to reject the requests of Moses and the advice of his own counsellors. Altogether we read that Pharaoh hardened his heart twelve times, whereas God is the subject six times, and five of these are towards the end of the story when Pharaoh's resistance has become irrevocable.

And in the event, his fears were justified. No matter what God said or promised, the Israelites just didn't want to know, such was their cruel suffering (Ex 6:9).

On the other side of the Red Sea things looked rather different however. God's prediction that they would come to know him when he brought them out (Ex 6:6–8) had now been triumphantly fulfilled. They had witnessed not only his judgement on their enemies, but his amazing grace toward their plight.

Exodus 15 records the first reaction to this great event, a reaction of joyful praise and thanksgiving, celebrating not only the event itself, but also all that it proved about Yahweh. In fact, so much of Israel's knowledge of God is expressed in their songs of worship (as is true of us too, of course— which is why we need to be careful about the words we actually sing). What then, is particularly affirmed in this first song of Moses ('first', because there is another one in Deuteronomy 32)?

What was on the curriculum for Israel's knowing God at this stage of their journey with him?

That Yahweh is incomparable as God

> Who among the gods
>   is like you, LORD?
> Who is like you—
>   majestic in holiness,
> awesome in glory,
>   working wonders? (Ex 15:11)

'Who is like you?' The question is rhetorical of course. Moses is not asking for answers to be sent in with a list of candidates for comparison with Yahweh. The rhetorical question is actually a passionately strong affirmation: 'There is *no god* that is anything like Yahweh at all!' Yahweh had proved himself supreme over 'all the gods of Egypt' (Ex 12:12) in the massive demonstration of power that constitutes the story of the plagues. Some people argue over whether this text (Ex 15:11) and others like it affirm 'monotheism' in the strictest sense, but that is not really the focal point right here. All that matters is that Israel's God is clearly the most powerful God around. Yahweh is beyond comparison when it comes to a conflict of wills and power. Whoever or whatever the gods of Egypt may be (and Moses's song does not even trouble to name them, any more than he names the Pharaoh who claimed to be one of them), the God of Israel is more than a match for all of them.

The same kind of language is used elsewhere in the Old Testament to express wonder and admiration for Yahweh as the God without equal. When the Israelites said that 'there is no God like Yahweh', they meant that no other god could ever compare with him. The God of Israel was beyond all comparison, for example,

- in keeping promises and fulfilling his word (2 Sam 7:22)
- in power and wisdom, especially as seen in creation (Jer 10:6–7, 11–12)
- in the heavenly assembly (Ps 89:6–8)
- in ruling over the nations (Jer 49:19; 50:44)
- in pardoning sin and forgiving transgression (Mic 7:18)
- in saving his people (Is 64:4)

And because there is no god like Yahweh, all nations will eventually come and worship *him* as the only true God (Ps 86:8–9; 96:4–9). This is the missional dimension of this great truth. Those who know the only true and living God must be committed to the vision of bringing all people to know him, too.

Of course, as we saw in chapter 1, from Deuteronomy, this affirmation that there is no God like Yahweh quickly shades over into the stronger monotheistic affirmation that there is no other God at all. The reason why Yahweh is incomparable is because he actually *is* unique—he is utterly in a category of his own. There may be other things that human beings call gods and worship, but in reality they are not God—they do not have any divine being or substance. In fact, as the Old Testament repeatedly says, they are nothing more than the work of human hands. That too is something that 'knowing God' means. It means knowing what is *not God*, and being able to distinguish between the two.

That Yahweh is sovereign as King

The LORD reigns for ever and ever. (Ex 15:18)

This is the triumphant acclamation that comes at the climax of the song of Moses. It makes a very comprehensive claim. The form of the Hebrew verb has the flexibility of meaning 'he has now demonstrated that he is king, he is now reigning, and he will go on reigning forever'. Now here we have the first significant time the kingdom of God is mentioned in the Bible, and it is important to notice the context. Yahweh is proclaimed as king because of his victory over those who have oppressed his people and refused to know him. So there is a confrontational dimension to this affirmation of Yahweh as king. Because *Yahweh* is king, all *other* kings (Egyptian or Canaanite) tremble, since they know what happened to the kings and gods of Egypt.

Israel, however, need not tremble but rejoice. For as a result of this great event, Israel now knows a great truth about their God, Yahweh. And that truth is that the enemies of Yahweh (whether human or claimed deities), are no match for his victorious kingship. 'The Lord is king,' sings Moses, with the unspoken but clear implication, 'and not Pharaoh, or any other of the claimed gods of Egypt or of Canaan.'

The nature of Yahweh's kingship, however (that is, the way Yahweh actually functions as king) is unexpected. He exercises his kingship on behalf of the weak and oppressed. This is implied already in the song of Moses at the sea; what is being celebrated is precisely the liberation of an ethnic minority community who had been undergoing economic exploitation, political oppression and eventually a state-sponsored campaign of terrorizing genocide. But into the empire of Pharaoh steps the reign of Yahweh, the God who hears the cry of the oppressed, the God who hears, sees, remembers and is concerned (Ex 2:23–25).

Yahweh is incomparable as God and sovereign as king. These were the things Israel came to know as they watched in horrified awe the destruction of the enemy that had been crushing the life out of them. Here was the God to be reckoned with. Here was the God they needed to know in the dark years ahead of struggle in the land they were headed for. Sadly, they all too quickly forgot and ended up knowing God in the same way that the Egyptians did (i.e. through suffering his judgement). But that's another story.

The story of the exodus, then, shows us two groups of people who were exposed to God's judgement: Pharaoh and the Egyptians on the one hand, and the Israelites on the other. The former experienced it in action against themselves. The latter witnessed it in action on their behalf. In both cases, it was a profound experience of coming to know God in ways that neither side was quite prepared for when the whole exercise began.

CONCLUSION

What then, for us?

In chapter 2, we stressed how knowing God includes knowing the stories in which God came to be known. So the first thing to say is that for us, knowing God must include knowing the things that Pharaoh and Israel came to know through this great demonstration of God in action. This is indeed the God we need to know in our own struggles. The Christian life involves the realities of suffering and persecution. It also involves spiritual warfare against our unseen enemy, the 'roaring lion' who seeks to devour us, as Peter put it (1 Pet 5:8). And for many Christians in our world it involves endurance of the kind of hardship that is not unlike the experience of the Israelites in Egypt. We may not always expect deliverance on the spectacular scale of the exodus, but it is still the God of the exodus whom we are privileged to know. This is the God who rules in our land and throughout the earth; the God who will ultimately call to account all human authorities whom he has raised up for his own purpose. He is the God of Calvary and the empty tomb; the God above all gods; the God who reigns eternally but to whom we pray that his kingdom should come and his will be done on earth as in heaven. To know him is to cry out in praise, 'Who is a God like you?'

Who indeed!

CHAPTER FOUR

KNOWING GOD
as the FATHER *of* HIS PEOPLE

Then say to Pharaoh, 'This is what the LORD says: Israel is my firstborn son, and I told you, "Let my son go, so he may worship me."' (Ex 4:22–23)

I am Israel's father, and Ephraim is my firstborn son. (Jer 31:9)

You, LORD, are our Father, our Redeemer from of old is your name. (Is 63:16)

The Israelites may have been reluctant to address God routinely as Father in worship (as the absence of such language from the book of Psalms shows), but the concept of Yahweh as the father of his people Israel was far from lacking in their theological repertoire, as the texts above illustrate. We have already considered a possible reason for the former reticence—namely the fact that Israel avoided the sexual myths of other nations in which nations were birthed through the sexual exploits of various gods and goddesses. Yahweh had not fathered Israel in any literal or polytheistic sense like that. Nevertheless, in reflecting on how God behaved toward them, Israel found it natural to use the imagery of human parenthood as a way of describing the character and actions of God. God's protective, supportive, compassionate and forgiving stance toward human beings could readily be portrayed by analogy with the best of human fathers. Yahweh God is fatherly, or father-like; and indeed, as we also saw at the end of the Introduction, motherly and mother-like too.

In this chapter, however, we go beyond those parental portraits to more direct texts that affirm a relationship of sonship and fatherhood between Israel and God. In many ways this is simply another way of speaking about the covenant relationship, but we shall notice ways in which it extends even beyond that.

The Old Testament speaks of Israel (and Israel's king) as Yahweh's son. Inevitably, therefore, this forms a rich and profound context within which Jesus considered himself to be the Son of God. Certainly Jesus's own consciousness of God as his Father, and the rest of the New Testament's portrayal of his divine sonship, has deep roots in this Old Testament affirmation of the filial dimension of Israel's relationship to Yahweh. I have explored all this much more fully above, in the first book in our trilogy, *Knowing Jesus through the Old Testament.* So in this chapter we shall concentrate primarily on the Old Testament understanding of this dynamic relationship, but it is impossible as a Christian to do so for long without recognizing where and to whom the trajectories of fatherhood and sonship eventually lead.

GOD AS FATHER AND ISRAEL AS SON

When we assemble and analyse all the texts in the Old Testament that speak about Yahweh as father of Israel, or Israel as the son (or the sons) of Yahweh, we can detect two main ways in which the terms are used.[1] On the one hand there are texts which use the singular 'son' as a description of Israel collectively as a nation. These are mostly positive affirmations about Israel's status before God. On the other hand there are texts which use the plural 'sons' (often translated as 'children' in the NIV) as a description of the Israelites. These are mostly negative comments on how the Israelites were behaving in anything but the way that sons ought to behave. But then beyond these two categories, we find a third—namely that if God is Israel's Father then there can be grounds for hope even beyond a broken covenant and inevitable judgement. So we turn to these three aspects of our theme.

A given status. The concept of Yahweh as father and Israel as son goes back very early. The song of Moses in Deuteronomy 32 is reckoned by most scholars to be among the earliest poetic texts in the Bible, and it clearly

---

[1]It would be worth pausing to scan through the list which includes: Ex 4:22; Deut 14:1; 32:6, 18–19; Is 1:2; 30:1, 9; 43:6; 63:16; 64:8; Jer 3:4, 19; 4:22; 31:9, 20; Hos 11:1; Mal 1:6; 2:10.

uses this concept. Indeed, it applies the combined parental roles of both father and mother to God.

> Is he not your Father, your Creator,
>> who made you and formed you? (Deut 32:6)

> You deserted the Rock, who fathered you;
>> you forgot the God who gave you birth. (Deut 32:18)

And in the narrative historical texts, the assertion that Israel is Yahweh's firstborn son comes even before the exodus, and as part of the justification for it (Ex 4:22–23, quoted above). This is a tradition that Hosea clearly knew and quoted. The exodus involved God bringing his own son out of Egypt:

> When Israel was a child, I loved him,
>> and out of Egypt I called my son. (Hos 11:1)

In these verses, 'you' and 'son' are in the singular. The whole nation is viewed as a single entity. This is true also in Jeremiah 31.

> I am Israel's father,
>> and Ephraim is my firstborn son. (Jer 31:9)

> Is not Ephraim my dear son,
>> The child in whom I delight? (Jer 31:20)

The point here is that Israel as a whole nation owed its existence to Yahweh. He is the God who had created them and called them onto the stage of history. The metaphor of sonship, in this respect, is another way of picturing the theological affirmation of Israel's election (i.e. that God had chosen Israel to be his people for the sake of bringing blessing to the nations). But it takes it back a step further by suggesting that it was not the case that Israel was an already existing nation whom God then subsequently decided to choose and use. Rather, Israel was brought into existence for this chosen purpose. This was what they were born for. Their creation, election and calling were 'simultaneous' realities, theologically, even if the story from the call of Abraham to the existence of the redeemed people of Israel after the exodus took several centuries.

Furthermore, the metaphor of sonship excludes any merits or conditions. You don't choose to be born or deserve to be born. You just are. You exist because your parents chose to conceive and birth you. The choice was theirs not yours. In that sense, sonship is an objective *given* status, independent of what you may think of it or how you respond to it. In the same way,

> What is clear is that it was not by Israel's choice or action that they are Yahweh's son, nor does the status and privilege involved derive in any sense from Israel's own action or merits. In this respect, Israel's sonship is a *given* which corresponds entirely with the unconditional, indicative *given* of their election. Israel is the firstborn son of Yahweh for no other reason than that Yahweh brought them as a nation into existence, just as they are the people of Yahweh for no other reason than that he 'set his love upon' them and chose them for himself. (Deut 7:6–7)[2]

Grounds for rebuke. When the language of sonship is used in the plural it is mostly (though not exclusively) in a negative context of accusation. The Israelites are addressed as sons of Yahweh, but then rebuked for failing to fulfil the normal expectations of sons to fathers—namely respect and obedience within a relationship of trust and gratitude. So, whereas the use of 'son' in the singular tends to express the indicative reality of Israel's status before God, the use of 'sons' in the plural tends to express the imperative expectation of obedience.

The first use of the plural in Deuteronomy sets the expectation. If Israel as a whole people is holy, then all individual Israelites, as sons, must manifest that practical holiness before him.

> Sons, that is what you [plural] are, belonging to Yahweh your God. So do not cut yourselves or shave the front of your heads for the dead. For a holy people, that is what you [singular] are, belonging to Yahweh your God. You [singular] are the one Yahweh chose to be his people, his treasured possession out of all the peoples that are on the face of the earth. (Deut 14:1–2, my translation)

Such expectations were repeatedly dashed, however, by the history of Israel in the land, so much so that prophets use the picture of sonship not as an assurance but as an accusation. What kind of way was this for sons to behave? Even earthly fathers received better treatment from their sons than Yahweh was getting from his Israelite sons.

---

[2]Christopher J. H. Wright, *God's People in God's Land: Family, Land and Property in the Old Testament* (Grand Rapids, MI: Eerdmans; Carlisle: Paternoster, 1990), 17–18.

(1) They were rebellious and corrupt.

Hear me, you heavens! Listen, earth!
    For the LORD has spoken:
'I reared children [sons] and brought them up,
    but they have rebelled against me.
The ox knows its master,
    the donkey its owner's manger,
but Israel does not know,
    my people do not understand.'
Woe to the sinful nation,
    a people whose guilt is great,
a brood of evildoers,
    children [sons] given to corruption!
They have forsaken the LORD;
    they have spurned the Holy One of Israel
    and turned their backs on him. (Is 1:2–4)

(2) They were faithless and hypocritically treacherous. In spite of all God's desire to show generous parental affection, and in spite of all their rhetorical appeals to his paternal indulgence:

Have you not just called to me:
    'My Father, my friend from my youth,
will you always be angry?
    Will your wrath continue for ever?'
This is how you talk,
    but you do all the evil you can. . . .
'I myself said,
"How gladly would I treat you like my children [sons]
    and give you a pleasant land,
    the most beautiful inheritance of any nation."
I thought you would call me "Father"
    and not turn away from following me.
But like a woman unfaithful to her husband,
    so you, Israel, have been unfaithful to me,'
    declares the LORD. (Jer 3:4–5, 19–20)

3) They were obstinate, contrary, deceitful and incorrigible.

'Woe to the obstinate children [sons],'
>   declares the Lord,
'to those who carry out plans that are not mine,
>   forming an alliance, but not by my Spirit,
>   heaping sin upon sin.' . . .
These are rebellious people, deceitful children [sons],
>   children unwilling to listen to the Lord's instruction. (Is 30:1, 9)

Not surprisingly, even at the end of the Old Testament period, God was still lamenting the lack of honour and respect that he, Israel's father, was receiving from such feckless progeny.

'A son honours his father, and a slave his master. If I am a father, where is the honour due me? If I am a master, where is the respect due me?' says the Lord Almighty. (Mal 1:6)

So as we put both of the above sections together, we can clearly discern the same duality that is inherent in the covenant relationship. That is to say, the balance and tension between the unconditional givenness of the relationship on the one hand (Israel had done nothing to initiate or deserve it), and the imperative dimension of the response expected from Israel, on the other hand (the response of love, trust and obedience). The father-son relationship embodies the same dynamic tension.

This understanding of the relationship between Yahweh and Israel provided a rich source for the New Testament's understanding of the relationship between God the Father and those who are believers in his Son Jesus Christ. For there too, on the one hand, we are brought into a relationship of adoption and election, by God's unconditional and unmerited grace, while on the other hand we are called into a life of responsive and trusting obedience, as befits the children of our heavenly Father.

Grounds for hope. We have drawn parallels between the language of sonship and the covenant. And in the broad sweep of biblical teaching that is correct. To know God as Father through becoming a child of God through faith in his Son is the same thing as being brought into the new covenant relationship with God through the blood of Christ, and is equally eternal. However, in the specific context of the Old Testament, the two can be distinguished somewhat, inasmuch as the relationship of son to father has an enduring permanence that survived even the broken Sinai covenant. You can break a covenant, but you can't stop being a son of your father. Likewise, though Israel knew the shattering reality of a broken covenant as they languished in exile, they could still turn to God in hope. After all, God's assertion that Israel was his firstborn son had been made even before the exodus, before Sinai (Ex 4:22). And it was still there even amid the wreckage of that covenant. Thus, Jeremiah, who could anticipate the profound and permanent joy of a new covenant, finds a more emotional foundation for hope in God's inability, as father, to cast off his errant son forever. The One who brought his firstborn out of Egypt would bring the same son back from exile.

> They will come with weeping;
>   they will pray as I bring them back.
> I will lead them beside streams of water
>   on a level path where they will not stumble,
> because I am Israel's father,
>   and Ephraim is my firstborn son.
> 'Hear the word of the LORD, you nations;
>   proclaim it in distant coastlands:
> "He who scattered Israel will gather them
>   and will watch over his flock like a shepherd."' (Jer 31:9–10)

> 'Is not Ephraim my dear son,
>   the child in whom I delight?
> Though I often speak against him,
>   I still remember him.
> Therefore my heart yearns for him;
>   I have great compassion for him,'
>   declares the LORD. (Jer 31:20)

Isaiah celebrates the same hope for God's children. Those who are the sons and daughters of the living God cannot languish forever in exile.

> I will say to the north, 'Give them up!'
>   and to the south, 'Do not hold them back.'
> Bring my sons from afar
>   and my daughters from the ends of the earth—
> everyone who is called by my name,
>   whom I created for my glory,
>   whom I formed and made. (Is 43:6–7)

And in the time of waiting and longing, the people of Israel themselves knew that, while lamenting their own covenant-breaking unfaithfulness, they could still appeal to the father heart of God for restorative compassion and mercy. The fatherhood of God provided grounds for hope for a contrite people.

> Look down from heaven and see
>> from your lofty throne, holy and glorious.
> Where are your zeal and your might?
>> Your tenderness and compassion are withheld from us.
> But you are our Father,
>> though Abraham does not know us
>> or Israel acknowledge us;
> you, LORD, are our Father,
>> our Redeemer from of old is your name. (Is 63:15–16)

> No one calls on your name
>> or strives to lay hold of you;
> for you have hidden your face from us
>> and have given us over to our sins.
> Yet you, LORD, are our Father.
>> We are the clay, you are the potter;
>> we are all the work of your hand.
> Do not be angry beyond measure, LORD;
>> do not remember our sins for ever.
> Oh, look upon us, we pray,
>> For we are all your people. (Is 64:7–9)

In *Knowing Jesus through the Old Testament* I suggested that this dimension of assured permanence in the relationship of son to father in Old Testament Israel's relationship with God was one of the factors that nourished the confidence of Jesus in his own guaranteed future. Why did Jesus repeatedly affirm the certainty of his own resurrection? How could he be so sure? Because he knew his identity and his Scriptures. His identity as the Son of God meant that he was the messianic embodiment of Israel, God's son. And from the Scriptures he knew that God had always remained faithful to his firstborn son, Israel, even in their unfaithfulness to him; how much more would he preserve and vindicate his faithful, obedient and sinless Son?[3]

---

[3]See *Knowing Jesus*, 109–112.

But we can go further than the way the Old Testament concept of God's fatherhood strengthened *Jesus* as God's Son. For clearly it also underpins *our* eternal security in Christ, as Paul so richly taught. We cannot expound here all the texts in the New Testament concerning what it means to be children of God, knowing him as Father with the same intimacy that Jesus called on him as *Abba*. A glimpse at Romans 8 will have to suffice. Sonship and security are gloriously intertwined in this climax to Paul's argument in the first part of his letter.

First of all we need to remind ourselves of Paul's central point in the previous chapters of Romans. Jews and Gentiles stand on the same footing before God in regard to sin, and equally they stand on the same footing in regard to salvation. For Jew and Gentile alike, the only way into right relationship with God and membership of his redeemed and covenant people, is through the Messiah, Jesus. But that one way is open to all—Jew or Gentile. Therefore the promises of God to Israel are now available, through Christ and the gospel, to people of all nations. The privilege of being sons of God is no longer confined to one ethnic group—the Jews; rather, people of any nation can enjoy that status in Christ and effectively become part of the expanded Israel of God. To be in Christ is to be in Abraham. And to be in Christ is to share in the sonship that God's Spirit grants us. And to share in that sonship means to have an inheritance that is eternal and glorious.

> The Spirit you received does not make you slaves, so that you live in fear
> again; rather, the Spirit you received brought about your adoption to sonship.
> And by him we cry, 'Abba, Father.' The Spirit himself testifies with our spirit
> that we are God's children. Now if we are children, then we are heirs—heirs
> of God and co-heirs with Christ, if indeed we share in his sufferings in order
> that we may also share in his glory. (Rom 8:15–17)

From that foundation, Paul goes on to draw breathtaking cosmic implications—for the whole creation also looks forward to what our redeemed sonship will eventually entail, even if it groans along with us and the Holy Spirit in the meantime.

> The creation waits in eager expectation for the children of God to be re-
> vealed. For the creation was subjected to frustration, not by its own choice,
> but by the will of the one who subjected it, in hope that the creation itself

will be liberated from its bondage to decay and brought into the glorious freedom of the children of God. (Rom 8:19–21)

And if the will of the Creator is our ultimate glorification in the likeness of his own Son (Rom 8:28–30), and if the whole of creation is the object of his redemptive purpose, then there is nobody and nothing 'in all creation' that can threaten our eternal security as the children of God (Rom 8:31–39).

For I am convinced that neither death nor life, neither angels nor demons, neither the present nor the future, nor any powers, neither height nor depth, nor anything else in all creation, will be able to separate us from the love of God that is in Christ Jesus our Lord. (Rom 8:38–39)

In this wonderful passage, Paul has transformed and expanded the faith of Israel, which of course was in his bloodstream and the very foundation of his whole worldview. Israel knew what it was to call God Father and to turn to him as sons. It was a relationship that was founded on the gracious initiative of God's election. And it was a relationship that had demanded of them an obedience they so often failed to deliver. But in Jesus of Nazareth, Israel's Messiah, that relationship had been seen in its perfection. Now it was available in Christ to people of any and every nation, just as God had promised Abraham. And so, for us, as in so many other ways, what we have in Christ is not a denial or rejection of the faith of Old Testament Israel, but rather its enriched and expanded fulfilment and the eternal security of what it had pointed toward in Christ.

GOD AS FATHER OF ISRAEL'S KING

Having focused briefly on Christ for a moment, we are drawn back to another dimension of the father-son relationship in the Old Testament which undoubtedly also impacted Jesus's sense of identity and mission. That is, the way God addressed not just Israel in general, but Israelite kings in particular, as 'my son'.

The historical kings. In the ancient world human rulers and judges could commonly be called 'sons of God' (or the son of a particular god). This did not necessarily mean they were regarded as gods, or divine incarnations—though certainly some did claim that for themselves. It was simply a way of saying that their authority derived from God (or the national god) and that in some way, their decisions and actions reflected what God (or the gods in polytheistic contexts) wanted to accomplish. Thus, for example in Psalm 82 the target of God's anger is actually human judges who were failing to deliver justice as God demanded it. But God says to them, contrasting the high calling he had given them with their actual practice and dismal destiny:

'I said, "You are 'gods';
    you are all sons of the Most High."
But you will die like mere mortals;
    you will fall like every other ruler.' (Ps 82:6–7)

So it is not unusual that when God made his very specific covenant promise to David and his household after him, that he and his sons would reign over Israel forever, he used the language of sonship to frame the relationship that David and his successors would have with God. God would be father to the king, just as he was ultimately father to the people.

However, what is more unusual is the strong emphasis in the Old Testament texts on the requirement of *obedience* that this royal sonship involved. Israel's king, as a son of Yahweh, was subject to the same filial discipline as the rest of the Israelites. He was certainly not above punishment. And so we find, even in the inaugural promise to David, the same combination of unconditional promise ('forever'), and necessary ethical sanctions (punishment for wrongdoing), that we saw in the case of Israel's status and responsibilities as son (or sons) of God. Here is how God put it to David:

When your days are over and you rest with your ancestors, I will raise up your offspring to succeed you, your own flesh and blood, and I will establish his kingdom. He is the one who will build a house for my Name, and I will establish the throne of his kingdom for ever. *I will be his father, and he shall be my son.* When he does wrong, I will punish him with a rod wielded by men, with floggings inflicted by human hands. But my love will never be taken away from him, as I took it away from Saul, whom I removed from before you. Your house and your kingdom shall endure for ever before me; your throne shall be established for ever. (2 Sam 7:12–16)

Even before David, when Samuel had (with considerable reluctance) appointed Saul as Israel's first king, he made it very clear that the standards of obedience God required from Israel as a nation applied just as much to their king. The king was not above the law.

> Now here is the king you have chosen, the one you asked for; see, the LORD has set a king over you. If you fear the LORD and serve and obey him and do not rebel against his commands, and if *both you and the king* who reigns over you follow the LORD your God—good! But if you do not obey the LORD, and if you rebel against his commands, his hand will be against you, as it was against your ancestors . . . Yet if you persist in doing evil, *both you and your king* will perish. (1 Sam 12:13–15, 25)

This was entirely consistent with the law in Deuteronomy that had permitted Israel to appoint a king, if they chose to do so. Along with various criteria for selection there is a clear instruction to faithful covenant obedience, demonstrated in knowing and practicing God's law.

> When he takes the throne of his kingdom, he is to write for himself on a scroll a copy of this law, taken from that of the Levitical priests. It is to be with him, and he is to read it all the days of his life so that he may learn to revere the LORD his God and follow carefully all the words of this law and these decrees and not consider himself better than his fellow Israelites and turn from the law to the right or to the left. Then he and his descendants will reign a long time over his kingdom in Israel. (Deut 17:18–20)

In other words, Israel's king was not to be a *super-Israelite,* lording it over his subjects, but a *model Israelite,* setting them an example of what it meant to be an obedient son of Yahweh.

If only . . .

The fact is that almost every historical king, both in the line of David and in the separated northern kingdom of Israel after Solomon, failed to be such a model. God's sons, the kings, failed in their duty of obedience just as much as God's son, the nation of Israel did in theirs. In fact the nation's moral state usually reflected the monarch's lead—for good or ill.

What then would become of the promise God had made to the sons of David? This is where the historical tradition of frustrated expectations flows over into the eschatological tradition of messianic hope. There would come such a king, great David's greater son, the royal Son himself.

The messianic king. In some of the psalms we find affirmation of the king as a son of God. The most well known comes right near the beginning of the book of Psalms—in a pair of psalms that were probably quite deliberately put side by side here as a key note for the whole book. Psalm 1 holds up a picture of the model Israelite—walking in the way of the LORD, studying and obeying his law, avoiding the paths of wickedness. It is a plausible suggestion that the opening psalm is intentionally a portrait not only of the model Israelite, but also of the model king—who should have been living like this, according to Deuteronomy 17. But we also know, from Deuteronomy 4:6–8, that if Israel were to live in faithful obedience to God's law, this would make them a visible model to other nations, who would be drawn to the quality of spiritual and ethical life demonstrated in Israel.[4]

Psalm 2, however, portrays the nations, far from submitting in willing obedience to Yahweh, in continuing rebellion against him and his anointed king. The psalm begins with the fundamental question 'Why?' which is not explicitly answered in the psalm itself. One suggested answer is that the historical kings of Israel have so radically failed to live in the light of Psalm 1 that Israel itself has joined the ranks of the rebels. There would then be a tension between the 'coronation' words of Psalm 2:7 and the historical reality of persistently disobedient kings. All the kings in the line of David would have heard the words:

> I will proclaim the LORD's decree:
>> He said to me, 'You are my Son;
>>> today I have become your Father.' (Ps 2:7)

And all of them would have known the ethical content of the prayer for the king in Psalm 72:

> Endow the king with your justice, O God,
>> the *royal son* with your righteousness.
> May he judge your people in righteousness,
>> your afflicted ones with justice. (Ps 72:1–2)

Psalm 72 goes on to spell out the expectations of the king—care for the poor and needy, purging oppression, compassion for the weak, rescue from bloodshed and violence. But the fact is that the reigns of almost all the kings turned these things upside down, neglecting the weak and contributing to

---

[4] I owe this thought and the suggestion in the following paragraphs to the conversations with John Wigfield during his doctoral research.

a steady escalation of injustice, bloodshed and oppression. So how can Psalm 72 be read except either as an idealized hope, or as a hollow critique of the present?

So Psalm 89 cries out with the starkest possible tension between the original hope and the actual reality. There is a screaming contradiction. The psalm first celebrates the original promise to David, including the status and responsibilities of sonship:

> He will call out to me, 'You are my Father,
>> my God, the Rock my Saviour.'
> And I will appoint him to be my firstborn,
>> the most exalted of the kings of the earth.
> I will maintain my love to him for ever,
>> and my covenant with him will never fail.
> I will establish his line for ever,
>> his throne as long as the heavens endure.
> 'If his sons forsake my law
>> and do not follow my statutes,
> if they violate my decrees
>> and fail to keep my commands,
> I will punish their sin with the rod,
>> their iniquity with flogging;
> but I will not take my love from him,
>> nor will I ever betray my faithfulness.
> I will not violate my covenant
>> or alter what my lips have uttered.
> Once for all, I have sworn by my holiness—
>> and I will not lie to David—
> that his line will continue for ever
>> and his throne endure before me like the sun;
> it will be established for ever like the moon,
>> the faithful witness in the sky.' (Ps 89:26–37)

But then the psalm goes on abruptly to acknowledge the historical abyss into which all this seemed to have fallen, with the collapse of the kingdom of Judah, the destruction of Jerusalem, the exile of the people, and the end of David's royal line (at least in terms of reigning kings).

> But you [God] have rejected, you have spurned,

you have been very angry with your anointed one.

You have renounced the covenant with your servant
    and have defiled his crown in the dust. (Ps 89:38–39)

But had he?

Who, exactly, had rejected and spurned whom? Was it not the repeated and incorrigible wickedness of Israel's kings and people that had led to the fracture of the covenant and the punishment of exile? Indeed so. But what then could become of the promises to David? Who then would reign on his throne forever?

There is no doubt that psalms like Psalm 2, 72 and 89 were already being interpreted messianically even within Old Testament times, and certainly by the time of the New Testament. That is to say, they were understood not only as having originally applied to David and the historical kings that followed him, but also as having a prophetic dimension. They pointed forward to One who would come, as a son of David and (like David but more so) as the Son of God; One who would fulfil the expectations of reigning in justice, fruitfulness and peace, not only over Israel but over the nations.

And these of course were precisely the expectations that the New Testament affirms were realized in Jesus of Nazareth, though their complete fulfilment lies ahead of us in our expectation of his return to reign in glory. The identity of Jesus as the messianic son of David, the royal Son of God, was affirmed to him in the words of his Father at his baptism, clearly echoing Psalm 2:7: 'You are my Son, whom I love; with you I am well pleased' (Mark 1:11).[5]

Many of the prophets pointed forward in a similar way, using different figures and pictures to express this hope, including the coming of a true son of David. But one mysterious, though extremely well known, prophetic text combines sonship and fatherhood in a tantalizing way.

Among all Isaiah's great prophetic visions of the messianic era to come, perhaps the most well known (through its repeated reading at Christmas) is Isaiah 9:1–7. The future era that will bring light, hope, joy, justice and peace will be inaugurated through the gift of a son—a gift of God himself as the passive verb ('is given') implies.

---

[5]The words of the Father at Jesus's baptism probably also echo Isaiah 42:1 and Genesis 22:2. For further reflection on these connections, see *Knowing Jesus through the Old Testament*, ch. 3.

For to us a child is born,
  to us *a son* is given,
  and the government will be on his shoulders.
And he will be called
  Wonderful Counsellor, Mighty God,
  Everlasting Father, Prince of Peace.
Of the greatness of his government and peace
  there will be no end.
He will reign on David's throne
  and over his kingdom,
establishing and upholding it
  with justice and righteousness
  from that time on and for ever.
The zeal of the LORD Almighty
  will accomplish this. (Is 9:6–7)

The most remarkable and mysterious phrase in this wonderful text is the third of the four titles given to this divine son: 'Everlasting Father'. What can it mean for one who is a son to be named as father? In terms of Old Testament concepts, it must refer to the governance dimension of his role. Fathers were expected to rule their households. God as Father was the true Lord and King of his people, exercising his government (or seeking to) through human kings. This given Son, then, will be the one on whose shoulders the government of the Father will rest. The rule of this coming one will reflect the fatherly qualities of God himself. So he can even be given that name and title with astonishing boldness—a boldness matched only by the preceding title—'Mighty God'.

> Christians will see what God did in Jesus as guaranteeing the vision's fulfilment. In Jesus we see the evidence that the Mighty God really will bring to effect a wonderful purpose and that the Everlasting Father will act effectively as a commander, for the sake of the people's spiritual and physical wellbeing. . . . The passage is a vision of what God is committed to achieving through David's line. It receives partial fulfilment in the achievements of kings such as Hezekiah and Josiah, and then a fulfilment in Jesus that is potentially final even if its potentiality remains unrealized. It thus still indicates the agenda to which God has made a commitment and gives human beings grounds for hope.[6]

---

[6]John Goldingay, *Isaiah*, New International Biblical Commentary (Peabody, MA: Hendrickson; Carlisle: Paternoster, 2001), 72.

In New Testament fulfilment, it is reflected in the unity of Father and Son, so profoundly articulated by Jesus himself on various occasions. His will was to do his Father's will. 'I and the Father are one' (John 10:30). And it is further reflected in the apostolic teaching that the rule of the Messiah is effectively the rule of the Father—now and for all eternity. To know God the Son is to know God the Father. The lordship of Christ and the sovereignty of God the Father are one. And to submit in loving obedience to God's Son is to do the will of the Father.

CONCLUSION

What, then, have we learned in this chapter about knowing God the Father through the Old Testament?

Possibly the most significant contribution this chapter will have made to our understanding will be as a counterbalance to our tendency to think of the fatherhood of God in primarily personal and spiritual terms. Now of course it is entirely proper to enjoy a personal relationship with God as Father. This was modeled, promised and taught by Jesus himself; it is the gift and witness of the Holy Spirit in our hearts; it is the birthright of every child of God. We thank God profoundly for this intimate relationship and for his fatherly love, provision, guidance and protection. And as we shall see in the next chapter, such intimacy with God was not at all foreign to the faith of Old Testament Israel.

However, we need to expand our horizons beyond our personal enjoyment of God's fatherhood and build into our Christian thinking those dimensions of it that we have explored here. For we have seen that the primary way the Old Testament speaks of God as Father is corporate—that is, as Father of his people Israel. This powerful metaphor for the collective relationship between God and his people connects several key truths.

It speaks of the given status and security that we enjoy by belonging to this people. God has chosen to make us part of the people whom he has 'brought to birth' and of whom he rejoices to be called Father. That is why, for example, the Lord's Prayer begins, '*Our* Father'.

But it also speaks of the responsibility that rests upon us as children of our Father. As we saw, the prime duty of Israel toward God, as son to father, was that of obedience within the covenant. The use of the parental metaphor preserves the relational dimension. Obedience in the Old Testament was never intended to be (as it is often caricatured), a blind or slavish adherence to impersonal external regulations. The warmth and profoundly personal language of psalms like 19 and 119 rule out that kind of misconception. Rather, the whole relationship between God's people and God as Father should indeed be one of authority on the one hand and obedience on the other, but set within a framework of love, provision, security and trust.

And finally, we have noted that the father-son imagery was used in relation to Israel's kings, in such a way that it eventually flows over into the messianic kingship of Jesus, the true Son of God. This means that we must always include within our understanding of God as Father the reality of his governance of history, his rule over the nations, exercised in and through his Son, our Lord Jesus Christ. That is also why the Lord's Prayer, addressed to 'Our Father', begins with the prayer that his sovereign will be done on earth and ends with the acknowledgment of his kingdom, power and glory.

CHAPTER FIVE

KNOWING GOD THROUGH ENGAGING HIM *in* PRAYER

It may have come as some surprise that the theme of knowing God in earlier chapters has largely been a matter of corporate or national knowing. Whether through the collective experience of God's redeeming grace, or through being the objects or witnesses of God's judgement, Israel and Egypt as whole nations came to know Yahweh as God in ways they had not done before. We can't dismiss or diminish such examples of our theme, since the language of knowing God is used repeatedly by the Bible itself in these contexts, as we have seen. Nevertheless, we may be wondering, surely 'knowing God' is a personal and intimate matter, more to do with the devotional life of prayer and spiritual engagement with God. Is there nothing of that dimension of knowing God in the Old Testament? There is, of course, and we would immediately think of the close relationship between God and Joseph, Hannah, Samuel, David, many anonymous psalmists, Jeremiah, Nehemiah, Daniel and others.

In this chapter we shall consider the two most outstanding examples of a personal relationship of knowing God in the Old Testament—Abraham and Moses. Particularly we shall focus on an incident of intercessory prayer in the life of each, and see what it has to tell us about the way they knew God. Both are described as men whom *God* claimed to 'know', though the text itself is more explicit about Moses specifically wanting to know God than in Abraham's case, where it is more inferential, but equally clear. In both cases they have an enormous amount to teach us about what it means to know the living God and engage with him in the meaningful, personal and challenging dialogue of prayer.

ABRAHAM—GOD'S FRIEND

Three times in the Bible, Abraham is described as 'God's friend' (2 Chron 20:7; Is 41:8; Jas 2:23). The word literally means 'loved one'. When we read the story of Genesis 18, it is not hard to see why. Jesus once said that a man may not tell his servants what he is doing, but he will share his plans with his friends (John 15:14–15). His Father had taken the same stance with Abraham, feeling almost obliged to share his plans with him—a sign of intimate friendship (Gen 18:17). So let's look at the story and detect the marks of this divine-human intimacy. It is a story that takes two chapters, beginning at Genesis 18:1 and concluding at Genesis 19:29, yet it covers less than 24 hours in the life of Abraham—from one afternoon to the next daybreak. But what a day!

Abraham's intimacy with God

> The LORD appeared to Abraham near the great trees of Mamre while he was sitting at the entrance to his tent in the heat of the day. Abraham looked up and saw three men standing nearby. When he saw them, he hurried from the entrance of his tent to meet them and bowed low to the ground.
>
> He said, 'If I have found favour in your eyes, my lord, do not pass your servant by. Let a little water be brought, and then you may all wash your feet and rest under this tree. Let me get you something to eat, so you can be refreshed and then go on your way—now that you have come to your servant.'
>
> 'Very well,' they answered, 'do as you say.'
>
> So Abraham hurried into the tent to Sarah. 'Quick,' he said, 'get three seahs of the finest flour and knead it and bake some bread.'
>
> Then he ran to the herd and selected a choice, tender calf and gave it to a servant, who hurried to prepare it. He then brought some curds and milk and the calf that had been prepared, and set these before them. While they ate, he stood near them under a tree. (Gen 18:1–8)

The story is exquisitely and expertly told. The narrator tells the reader in Genesis 18:1 that Yahweh appeared to Abraham, but of course

Abraham did not know this at first. So we have the gentle irony that we know more than the main character in the story knows—initially at least. This is similar to the beginning of Genesis 22, where the reader is told that the story to follow involved Yahweh testing Abraham—but Abraham does not know that it is only a test. God and the reader know that God will not go through with what he tells Abraham to do—but Abraham did not. If he had, it would not have been the test that it was. Similarly here, we watch as Abraham responds with customary but abnormally generous hospitality to three strangers who have unexpectedly disturbed his siesta. Part of the irony is that Abraham demonstrates his knowledge of God in behaving this way even when he does not actually know it is God he is entertaining—a point not lost as an incentive to hospitality by Hebrews 13:2.

However, as the story proceeds, there are hints as to the identity of at least one of these mysterious visitors, even though it is hard to say exactly when the penny dropped for Abraham. The fact that recognition of the Lord takes place in the course of a meal echoes a similar moment of recognition one Sunday evening in a home in Emmaus.

But what is happening here? God himself has come to dinner! As Kent Hughes points out,[1] this is the only occasion in the whole Bible, prior to the incarnation of God in Christ, where God eats with a human being. On other occasions when people made a meal for an angel of the Lord, it was consumed in flames as a burnt offering (Judg 6:18–24; 13:15–21). At the time of the making of the covenant at Mount Sinai, the elders of Israel went up the mountain with Moses and Aaron and his sons, where they had a vision of God, and then ate and drank without harm (Ex 24:9–11). On that occasion, the elders ate in the presence of God. But here, God eats in the presence of Abraham, standing attentively nearby in the shade of the tree. This is a moment of rare, indeed unique, intimacy.

When the meal was over, we read later 'Abraham walked along with them to see them on their way' (Gen 18:16). Abraham, who *eats* with God, now *walks* with God (as Enoch had done), and in a moment also *talks* with God. A friend indeed. Actually, 'to see them on their way' is literally 'to send them'. Abraham, who years before had obeyed God's sending, is now

---

[1] P. Kent Hughes, *Genesis: Beginning and Blessing* (Wheaton, IL: Crossway Books, 2004), 254–255.

the one sending God on his way! This storyteller has a fine eye for small ironies—but they all paint a picture of an intimate relationship.

The purpose of knowing and being known by God. The friendship had not started from Abraham's side, however. As we know from the narrative since Genesis 12, it was God who took the initiative in calling Abraham out of his homeland in Mesopotamia, with the twin command, 'Go . . . and . . . be a blessing' (Gen 12:1–3), and a suite of promises to accompany him. Abraham's response of obedience and trust had sealed the beginning of the relationship and characterized it ever more deeply, coming to a searing and soaring climax in Genesis 22.

At this point, then, it is God who recalls the relational truth that if Abraham has now come to know God it is because God first knew him. By this point in the story, readers are sure that both Abraham and Sarah have tumbled (embarrassingly, in Sarah's case) to the realization that one of these three hearty appetites belongs to none other than God (for reasons we shall see in a moment). But as the meal breaks up and the guests are about to resume their journey, God himself chooses to reveal more than just his true identity and to disclose his intentions also.

> Then the LORD said, 'Shall I hide from Abraham what I am about to do? Abraham will surely become a great and powerful nation, and all nations on earth will be blessed through him. For I have *known* him, *in order that* he will instruct his children and his household after him to keep the way of the LORD by doing righteousness and justice, *in order that* the LORD will bring about for Abraham what he has promised him.' (Gen 18:17–19, my translation)

'I have known him,' says God. This is usually and rightly translated, 'I have chosen him,' since that is exactly the meaning of God's knowledge in this case (as likewise of Israel as a whole, in Amos 3:2, where the same word is used). But it still important to feel the full flavour of the actual word in Hebrew. The intimate relationship between Abraham and God is, first and foremost, because God knows Abraham, not the other way around.

The point however is not merely chronological—who knew whom first. The point is profoundly purposeful. If Abraham has come to know God, it is because God knew him *for a purpose*. In fact, it was for a double purpose, which is clear from the repeated and emphatic 'in order that' in verse 19. The nearer purpose (in the middle of the verse) relates to the kind of community Abraham was to cultivate by his teaching. The longer-term purpose (in the final clause of the verse) relates to God's promise that through Abraham he would bless all nations on earth. These double purposes clearly mirror the dual content of the original promise that Abraham would himself become a great nation under God's blessing, and that all nations would be blessed through him.

(1) Blessing. Taking the longer vision first: God's choice of Abraham was for the purpose of blessing the nations. That was God's mission, God's long-term redemptive goal, and the launch pad of the whole of the rest of the Bible's story.[2] If Abraham had not got up and left his homeland in obedience to God, the Bible would have been a very thin book indeed. But because he did, the whole grand narrative of the Bible ran its course, and runs it still, for its climactic ending yet lies ahead of us. And that ending will see people from every tribe and language and people and nations, in fulfilment of God's promise to Abraham, gathered before the throne of God as his redeemed humanity in the new creation (Rev 7:9).

So then, the reciprocal 'knowing' between God and Abraham had a missional purpose: God's commitment to blessing humanity. Spoken against the backdrop of the actual reason for God's presence in this narrative—namely to act in judgement on the degraded wickedness of Sodom and Gomorrah, these words are a gospel life preserver in a sea of human sin. But they are also so typical of God. God on his way to judgement stops en route with Abraham. Not because he needed a meal, or because Sarah was a better baker than believer, but because it is God's way, in wrath to remember mercy. So God reminds himself of that wider, longer, and ultimately redemptive mission for all nations even at the point of proximate judgement in history. And because Abraham is key to that, God takes Abraham into his confidence. For Abraham, being known by God and knowing God in intimate collegiality, is inseparable from the mission of blessing that motivates the heart and plans of God.

If there is a lesson here for us, as there doubtless is in the narrator's mind in telling the story, it must be that knowing God is never an end in itself but must be pursued within the context of serving the mission of God in bringing blessing to the nations. Knowing God is missional, not merely

---

[2]This is the major theme of my book *The Mission of God* (Downers Grove, IL: InterVarsity, 2006).

devotional. Knowing God serves God's purpose of blessing others, not merely our personal enjoyment of being blessed.

(2) Teaching. Coming to the central phrase in Genesis 18:19, and the nearer of God's expressed purposes in 'knowing' (choosing) Abraham, we find a strongly ethical core to balance the missional thrust of the closing phrase. To be the means of blessing to the nations, as God had promised, Abraham must become a great nation. But what kind of nation, what kind of community must it then be?

The narrator is about to show us the kind of society it must *not* be— namely like Sodom and Gomorrah. The contrast at this point is very stark. Having spoken about his purpose in choosing Abraham, God immediately continues, presumably now speaking directly to Abraham,

> The outcry against Sodom and Gomorrah is so great and their sin so grievous that I will go down and see if what they have done is as bad as the outcry that has reached me. If not, I will know. (Gen 18:20–21)

The sin of Sodom is crying out to heaven. *Outcry* is the word that speaks of people crying out for help in the midst of cruelty, oppression and violence. It is the word repeatedly used of the Israelites crying out in Egypt. The rest of what we know about Sodom, from Genesis 19, Isaiah 1 and Ezekiel 16:49, tells us that it was a sink of the most appalling human wickedness, including violence, sexual perversion, inhospitality, bloodshed, injustice, arrogance, affluence and callous neglect of the poor (a rather modern-sounding list, when you compare it with the societies many of us live in).

In contrast to *that*, says God, I have chosen Abraham so that he will initiate and shape a community that will be utterly different: one that will walk in the way of the Lord, not in the way of Sodom; one that will be committed to righteousness and justice, not to perversion and oppression. Already in this text God anticipates the role that Moses will actually later play in giving commands to the people of Israel that would enable them to walk in the ways of the Lord and do righteousness and justice (cf. Deut 4:5–8; 10:12–19). But it all begins in the loins of Abraham (who, we recall with wry surprise, has not even had a son by Sarah yet, let alone a whole 'household after him' to instruct).

So a second major purpose of knowing and being known by God is the task of passing on the ethical requirements of God, so that his people can fulfil their missional function in the world. The remarkable logic of verse 19 contains three main elements: God's election of Abraham; God's ethical expectation from Abraham and his community; God's mission of bringing blessing to the world through Abraham. Election—Ethics—Mission. And each of the last two is expressed as the purpose of the first. 'I have chosen him so that . . . so that . . .' There is no biblical mission without biblical ethics. And there is no biblical election without the matching divine intention—a transformed and transforming community, and a blessed world of nations. And that, says God, is why I know Abraham and he knows me. As Calvin comments:

> Certainly God does not make his will known to us so that knowledge of him should die with us. He requires us to be his witnesses to the next generation, so that they in turn may hand on what they have received from us to their descendants. Therefore, it is a father's duty to teach his children what he himself has learned from God. In this way we must propagate God's truth. It was not given to us for our private enjoyment; we must mutually strengthen one another according to our calling and our faith.[3]

Challenging questions. The more intimate any friendship, the more liberty the friends feel to challenge one another within the bonds of understanding, affection and trust. We see something of this at two points in this rich narrative. Each side throws out a question to the other, which, by its rhetorical nature, presents a challenge and calls for a response. In this way also we see the profound confidence with which God knew Abraham and Abraham knew God.

(1) Challenge to faith. The first challenging question in the narrative is addressed to Abraham, but it is about Sarah, so it necessarily involved them both. The subtle narrative begins to disclose the identity of the feasting visitors.

'Where is your wife Sarah?' they asked him.

'There, in the tent,' he said.

Then one of them said, 'I will surely return to you about this time next year, and Sarah your wife will have a son.'

Now Sarah was listening at the entrance to the tent, which was behind him. Abraham and Sarah were already very old, and Sarah was past the age

---

[3]John Calvin, *Genesis* (Wheaton, IL and Nottingham, UK: Crossway Books, 2001), 177.

of childbearing. So Sarah laughed to herself as she thought, 'After I am worn out and my lord is old, will I now have this pleasure?'

Then the LORD said to Abraham, 'Why did Sarah laugh and say, "Will I really have a child, now that I am old?" Is anything too hard for the LORD? I will return to you at the appointed time next year and Sarah will have a son.'

Sarah was afraid, so she lied and said, 'I did not laugh.'

But he said, 'Yes, you did laugh.' (Gen 18:9–15)

It was at this point, if it had not happened already, that Abraham and Sarah become aware of whom they were entertaining. In asking after Abraham's wife, they not only used her name (how did they know it?), but used the new form of the name that God himself had only recently given to her (Sarah, instead of Sarai, see Gen 17:15–16). Then, one of the three speaks words that recall what God had said to Abraham on that same occasion and in almost the same words about the coming birth of a son.

Sarah's response, as she overhears the news (and she may be hearing it for the first time, since we are not told if Abraham had ever told her what God had told him in Genesis 17), is exactly the same as her husband's when he first heard it. She laughs (cf. Gen 17:17). In both cases it was the laughter of disbelief (not unbelief, but incredulity—the idea seemed impossible). Abraham laughed into the ground, to which he had fallen facedown. Sarah laughed 'inside herself' (literally), and ridiculed *in her thoughts* the idea that a one-hundred-year-old man and a long post-menopausal woman could enjoy sex let alone conceive a baby. Then came the next surprise that clinched the identity of the anonymous speaker. We read that Sarah was inside the tent door which was behind the 'man'. So she was behind his back. He could not see her, and he had not heard her, for she had laughed and spoken 'inside herself'. But he had heard the soundless laughter and read the unspoken thoughts and he asks two questions: 'Why did Sarah laugh?' and 'Is anything too hard for the LORD?'

Sarah was afraid—as well she might be—and her denial was partially true, she had not laughed out loud at least. Her consternation was not just because her inner thoughts had been (somewhat more delicately) repeated aloud—but because it really is a lot to ask of any woman to be confronted with two of the greatest attributes of God in quick succession, his omniscience and his omnipotence, when all she wanted was her siesta. So the episode ends with (I think) almost pantomime comedy over Sarah's laughing; perhaps it even ended with laughter all round. 'I didn't laugh.' 'Yes you did laugh.' 'No I didn't!' 'Yes you did!' And the narrator must be laughing as he tells the story for each occurrence of the word is a reminder that the son who is to be born will actually bear the name *Laughter*: Isaac—in Hebrew, *Yitzhaq*, 'He laughs' (which the narrator exploits to the fullest when he reaches that point in the story, see Gen 21:1–7).

But the question that God addresses to both Abraham and Sarah is the challenge to faith. '*Is anything too hard for the Lord?*' It is a very pointed question, for surely even God doesn't give babies to childless hundred-year-olds. Well, does he? Can he? One can imagine attempting to answer God's question with an oscillating conflict between head and heart. 'Well, no, of course . . . But yes, actually in this case . . . though not really, I suppose.' We recall the honesty of the man who said to Jesus, 'I believe; help my unbelief' (Mark 9:24 NRSV). Abraham and Sarah were obedient believers in God already, or else they wouldn't even be where they were, in the land of Canaan. But a son next spring? At this point their laughter shows that 'the powerful promise of God outdistances their ability to receive it.'[4] What we have here, then, is an encounter in which Abraham and Sarah's knowledge of God, which was considerable already, is stretched beyond the point of apparent possibility by the challenging question of the God of impossibilities. Brueggemann's reflection is worth quoting.

> Once again, this story shows what a scandal and difficulty faith is. Faith is not a reasonable act which fits into the normal scheme of life and perception. The promise of the gospel is not a conventional piece of wisdom that is easily accommodated to everything else. Embrace of this radical gospel requires shattering and discontinuity. Abraham and Sarah have by this time become accustomed to their barrenness. They are resigned to their closed future. They have accepted that hopelessness as 'normal.' The gospel promise does not meet them in receptive hopefulness but in resistant hopelessness . . . 'Is anything impossible for the LORD?' This question means to refute and dismiss the protests of the hopeless couple. The refutation is not stated as a proposition, assertion, or proclamation but as a question. It comes as a question because the gospel requires a decision. And that decision cannot be given from above. It must come from Abraham and Sarah.[5]

---

[4] Walter Brueggemann, *Genesis* (Atlanta, GA: John Knox Press, 1982), 158.
[5] Ibid.

Jesus posed the same challenge to the faith of his disciples, and called them to live in the light of the right answer (Mt 17:20; Mk 10:27).

To know God is to know there are possibilities that lie beyond the bounds of the possible.

(2) Challenge to intercession. The first challenging question in this encounter, then, is addressed by God to Abraham and Sarah as a challenge to faith. The second challenging question comes from Abraham and is addressed to God as an act of intercession. Actually, it is a series of questions, but they all revolve around the key one in Genesis 18:25: *'Will not the Judge of all the earth do right?'*

> Then the LORD said, 'The outcry against Sodom and Gomorrah is so great and their sin so grievous that I will go down and see if what they have done is as bad as the outcry that has reached me. If not, I will know.'
>
> The men turned away and went towards Sodom, but Abraham remained standing before the LORD. Then Abraham approached him and said: 'Will you sweep away the righteous with the wicked? What if there are fifty righteous people in the city? Will you really sweep it away and not spare the place for the sake of the fifty righteous people in it? Far be it from you to do such a thing—to kill the righteous with the wicked, treating the righteous and the wicked alike. Far be it from you! Will not the Judge of all the earth do right?'
>
> The LORD said, 'If I find fifty righteous people in the city of Sodom, I will spare the whole place for their sake.'
>
> Then Abraham spoke up again: 'Now that I have been so bold as to speak to the Lord, though I am nothing but dust and ashes, what if the number of the righteous is five less than fifty? Will you destroy the whole city for lack of five people?'
>
> 'If I find forty-five there,' he said, 'I will not destroy it.'
>
> Once again he spoke to him, 'What if only forty are found there?'
>
> He said, 'For the sake of forty, I will not do it.'
>
> Then he said, 'May the Lord not be angry, but let me speak. What if only thirty can be found there?'
>
> He answered, 'I will not do it if I find thirty there.'
>
> Abraham said, 'Now that I have been so bold as to speak to the Lord, what if only twenty can be found there?'
>
> He said, 'For the sake of twenty, I will not destroy it.'

> Then he said, 'May the Lord not be angry, but let me speak just once more.
> What if only ten can be found there?'
>
> He answered, 'For the sake of ten, I will not destroy it.'
>
> When the LORD had finished speaking with Abraham, he left, and
> Abraham returned home. (Gen 18:20–33)

God has honoured the intimacy that exists between himself and
Abraham by sharing his plans—to go down and see if the wickedness of
Sodom is as bad as the outcry against it. This knowledge leads Abraham to
initiate a remarkable dialogue with God, as they stand together overlooking
the very cities they are talking about. As Gordon Wenham points out, the
directness and intimacy of this conversation is all the more highlighted by
the fact that this is the very first time in the Bible that any human being
initiates a conversation with God—previously all divine-human encounters
have started with a question or statement by God.[6] And Abraham himself,
in his deferential forms of speech, shows that he is aware of the boldness of
what he is doing—a fact which in itself also points to the depth of his
confidence in his friendship with God. Nevertheless, though Abraham is
the first to break the silence of Genesis 18:22, God himself has created the
chink of opportunity which Abraham seizes. 'If not, I will know,' God had
said at the end of his speech about Sodom and Gomorrah. There was just
a possibility that things were not quite as bad as they sounded. Perhaps not
all the people were as wicked as the rumour that had reached heaven. In
allowing for that possibility, God waits to see what Abraham will do with
it. And, as God probably wanted and hoped for, Abraham steps into the
minimal hope that God has merely hinted at, with bold intercession around
the hypothetical possibility that it might be true.

Abraham's problem was focused on the character of God. If God were to
destroy the wicked cities totally, would he not then also destroy any righteous that might be there? And would that be consistent with his character?
If Yahweh is the universal God who defines what justice means, then surely
he must act according to his own justice. It is unthinkable that God should
do otherwise, is it not? The rhetorical question makes a categorical declaration: Whatever Yahweh does, will be done, and must necessarily be done,
in justice—his own divine, definitive justice. This is not (as sometimes

---

[6]Gordon J. Wenham, *Genesis 16—50* (Dallas, TX: Word Books, 1994), 52.

claimed) suggesting that God is himself subject to some higher power or 'principle' of justice (which would mean God is less than fully sovereign). Rather it accepts that God defines whatever is just and right, and so God will always act in consistency with his own character.

If that is granted, then what Abraham asks for, and the answers he receives each time from God, are both alike quite remarkable.

(3) A surprising kind of merciful justice. Take first of all the precise content of Abraham's request. His *premise* was that a just God would not kill the righteous *with* the wicked, as if making no distinction. But his *request* was not, as we might have expected, that God should therefore distinguish between the two in such a way as to spare or rescue the righteous and destroy the wicked. Rather, he asks that God should spare the whole city *including the wicked*, for the sake of any righteous who were there. In other words, Abraham's questioning seems to subvert the usual human calculus in these things. We tend to think that a few wicked people are all it takes for God to come slamming in with judgement, no matter how many relatively righteous folk are around. Abraham assumes the contrary, that a few righteous people would be all it takes for God to act mercifully toward a whole city full of the wicked. There is something here about Abraham's understanding of God's merciful character that transcends a more abstract calculus of 'blind justice' that 'gives each his due'.

It is hard to dig much deeper into the theological understanding of Abraham at this point, but I cannot help feeling this too has something to do with his knowing God. He has discerned in God a quality of righteousness that goes beyond numbers, scales and mechanical calculation of deserts. He has discerned that there is a *saving* and 'protective' power in righteousness that moves the heart and hand of God. God's willingness to spare the wicked for the sake of the righteous is a remarkably different kind of 'justice' for the judge of all the earth to be exercising. But there is a trajectory that leads from this insight into the saving potential of righteousness to the cross itself and the way Paul meditates on the perfect righteousness of the one man, Jesus (Rom 5:12–19). On a much later occasion, Ezekiel had to counterbalance this insight against those who wanted to presume upon it and protect themselves from the consequences of their own wickedness by pointing to a few righteous neighbours or family members. That's not the way it works, Ezekiel had to say. God *will* act to punish the wicked, even if the punishment is deferred, and do not try to imagine that you can claim vicarious credit out of somebody else's account (Ezek 14:12–23) and then go on being wicked.[7]

(4) *A surprising kind of bargaining.* But second, God's answers to each of Abraham's six queries demonstrate even more clearly something surprising about God's idea of righteousness—consistent with what has just been said.

It is often alleged that this exchange between Abraham and God is a typical piece of oriental bargaining. The context, it is said, is the bazaar, in which buyer and seller will haggle over the price of some object. The buyer offers the lowest price he can think of, to which the seller counters with something much higher. The buyer then makes slightly higher bids, and the seller makes slightly lower offers, until they eventually agree on a price somewhere in between, and shake hands on a satisfactory deal. But if this is the metaphorical background to this exchange between Abraham and God, then it is completely subverted and turned upside down.

Let us imagine that 'sparing Sodom' is the 'object' that Abraham is trying to 'buy.' He needs to discover what is the minimum 'price' in terms of righteous residents that God will be prepared to accept in exchange for the goods Abraham wants (which, we must remember, is that the whole of Sodom and Gomorrah be spared, not just that Abraham's relatives be rescued). So Abraham starts the bidding: 'Would you spare the whole city for the sake of fifty righteous people?' Now if this were a normal bargaining situation, then God would retort with something like, 'Oh no, I couldn't do it for only fifty; there would have to be at least a hundred.' After which Abraham might have haggled a bit more until some figure in between, such as seventy-five, would have been accepted. But on the contrary, and perhaps to Abraham's own surprise, his first offer is immediately and emphatically accepted with a very clear promise—Genesis 18:26.

Encouraged by this good news, Abraham proceeds to see if he can get the 'price' dropped still further—and every lower figure is equally quickly accepted by God. What is going on here? It is certainly not remotely like typical haggling. It is as if a would-be buyer says, 'Let me offer you fifty dollars for that piece of jewellery.' And the stallholder unexpectedly says with a smile, 'Sure, you can have it for fifty dollars.' So the surprised buyer

---

[7]Cf. Christopher J. H. Wright, *The Message of Ezekiel*, The Bible Speaks Today (Downers Grove: InterVarsity, 2001), 172–181.

says, 'Would you part with it for forty-five dollars, then?' And the seller says again, 'Sure, why not?' And so the buyer goes on offering a *lower and lower* price, gets the same accommodating answer each time, and eventually walks away with the thing for ten dollars. Not, it will be agreed, what normally happens in the marketplace.

But that's the point. This is not the marketplace. This is God, the judge of all the earth, and the impression we get is that, while he must act in punitive justice against the egregious wickedness of Sodom and Gomorrah, nothing would please him more than to be able to spare them if even a mere handful of righteous people were there—just as the impression one would get from the reverse haggling described above is that the seller was really just as keen to give the goods away as the buyer was in asking for them.

In other words, Abraham is learning more about God. Knowing God is taking on new and surprising depths, for he discovers in this intercessory encounter that God is far more compassionate than he ever thought possible. God will go a very long way to spare the wicked. It is almost as if he needs hardly any persuading at all to do so, if only he could. Abraham is already learning what Ezekiel would later put into words on behalf of God:

'For I take no pleasure in the death of anyone,' declares the Sovereign LORD. 'Repent and live!' (Ezek 18:32)

Say to them, 'As surely as I live, declares the Sovereign LORD, I take no pleasure in the death of the wicked, but rather that they turn from their ways and live. Turn! Turn from your evil ways! Why will you die, people of Israel?' (Ezek 33:11)

And in his intercession, Abraham is already mirroring back to God something of God's own compassion and generosity. Certainly he is 're-minding' God of the saving power of righteousness. To know God is to reflect God—even to reflect God back to God in intercession. If God grieved over Sodom, even as its wickedness angered him, because of the 'cry for help' that was coming up from the city (cf. Job 24:12), then God's emotions found a human heart to lodge in. For even Sodom had Abraham, a man who knew God, as its intercessor.

Remembering a friend. Things did not turn out quite as Abraham prayed for or expected. On the one hand, that is because even the rock-bottom 'price' that God accepted at the close of the intercession was not met. Not only were there not *ten* righteous people in Sodom, the narrative of Genesis 19 insists that there was not even *one*. The attack upon the house of Lot after the angelic guests had arrived there included all the men of the city, which is emphasized by the narrator:

> Before they lay down, the men of the city, the men of Sodom, both young and old, all the people to the last man, surrounded the house. (Gen 19:4 NRSV)

Even Lot, who we are told elsewhere had a righteous soul that was disturbed by his surroundings (though not enough to get out earlier; 2 Pet 2:7–8), was not actually a citizen of Sodom and was explicitly disowned by the rest of the inhabitants (Gen 19:9). So in the end, God fulfils his threat. The 'if not' clause on the clipboard of his angelic fact-finders remained inactivated. It really was as bad as the outcry. There were no righteous inhabitants to stay the execution, or at least postpone it. The judgement must fall.

So we cannot say that Abraham's intercession had been unsuccessful. The simple fact was that not even the minimum condition on which God and Abraham had finally agreed had been met.

However, although Abraham had not asked for it, God did act in merciful deliverance for the relatives of Abraham within the city—the family of Lot. The story need not detain us here, except for the way it concludes.

> So when God destroyed the cities of the plain, *he remembered Abraham*, and he brought Lot out of the catastrophe that overthrew the cities where Lot had lived. (Gen 19:29)

So the narrator makes a clear connection between the intercession of Genesis 18 and the rescue of Genesis 19. God acted. But as he acted, he 'remembered Abraham' as you do with your friends. Only this was not merely a casual memory. It implies that the *way* God acted and *the result* of God's action were both materially affected by Abraham's engagement in prayer with the God he knew so intimately. We may never plumb the depths of mystery that surrounds how God's sovereign action in history is connected to the prayers of God's people, but the Bible simply affirms that the link is there. 'God destroyed . . . God remembered . . . God brought out.'

Abraham knew his God, and God remembered his friend.

MOSES—GOD'S SERVANT

Abraham, as we saw, is called 'God's friend.' He is also once described as 'God's servant' (Gen 26:24). That is a term which is not nearly so common in the Old Testament as we have made it in popular Christian circles to describe almost any faithful Christian in any form of Christian ministry (and why not, of course?). It was, rather, a term of high honour reserved for a very select few of the great figures of the Old Testament story. It is most often used of David (e.g. 2 Sam 7:5; 1 Kings 11:13; Ezek 34:23), but also of Caleb (Num 14:24), Job (Job 1:8), Isaiah (Is 20:3), and Zerubbabel (Hag 2:23)—and of course the mysterious Servant of the Lord in Isaiah 40–55. The most outstanding, however, is undoubtedly Moses. Moses is called the servant of the LORD at the moment of his greatest triumph, the crossing of the Reed Sea (Ex 14:31), and at the moment of his mountain death and burial (Deut 34:5).

Moses's intimacy with God. It is not only from the sparing use of the term by the narrator, however, that we learn about Moses, the LORD's servant. God himself uses the term in a most illuminating divine testimony to the intimate relationship between God and Moses. Moses's sister and brother, Miriam and Aaron, had spoken against him, claiming equality with him in prophetic gifting and challenging the exclusiveness of Moses's right to be the sole spokesperson for God. God summoned the three siblings to his presence and then defended Moses (who had refused to defend himself) with these words:

> When there is a prophet among you,
>> I, the LORD, reveal myself to them in visions,
>> I speak to them in dreams.
> But this is not true of my servant Moses;
>> he is faithful in all my house.
> With him I speak face to face,
>> clearly and not in riddles;
>> he sees the form of the LORD.
> Why then were you not afraid
>> to speak against my servant Moses? (Num 12:6–8)

God acknowledges that there was an 'ordinary' level of genuine prophetic revelation that he mediated through dreams and visions to others.

But with Moses there was a direct revelatory encounter that took place 'mouth to mouth' (literally), in which Moses saw 'the form' of God (a term which suggests, not that Moses saw God directly—something denied elsewhere—but that he certainly had some kind of visual experience of the presence of God). Other texts describe how this direct intimacy between Moses and God was 'as a man speaks with his friend' (Ex 33:11), and even had physiological effects on Moses, noticeable to the people—his face shone with the reflected glory of God (Ex 34:29–35).

From Moses's side, it is made clear that this was something he sought and longed for. Indeed, though it's hard to believe—even after his encounter at the burning bush, his prolonged embodiment of the mighty power of God in the plagues and at the crossing of the sea, his forty days alone with God at the top of Mount Sinai, and his breathtakingly successful engagement with God on behalf of the people immediately afterwards—Moses still feels he does not know God well enough and wants more! In some ways, this is starting at the wrong end of our story, but it is a key point for our purpose of exploring what it means to know God.

Listen to Moses wrestling with God and asking to know him more. Some people are just never satisfied.

> Moses said to the Lord, 'You have been telling me, "Lead these people," but you have not let me know whom you will send with me. You have said, "I know you by name and you have found favour with me." If you are pleased with me, teach me your ways *so I may know you* and continue to find favour with you. Remember that this nation is your people.'
>
> The Lord replied, 'My Presence will go with you, and I will give you rest.'
>
> Then Moses said to him, 'If your Presence does not go with us, do not send us up from here. How will anyone know that you are pleased with me and with your people unless you go with us? What else will distinguish me and your people from all the other people on the face of the earth?'
>
> And the Lord said to Moses, 'I will do the very thing you have asked, because I am pleased with you and I know you by name.' Then Moses said, 'Now show me your glory.' (Ex 33:12–18)

The elements of Moses's desire are clear. He picks up God's affirmation that God is pleased with him and knows him by name, and says, in effect, 'Well, if that is so, teach me your ways. I want to know who you really are and how you operate' (as if he didn't know?). And when God promises to send his Presence (literally, his Face) to accompany the people, Moses retorts, in effect, 'You'd better; how else will the world know that we are any different from other nations if you are not among us?' And when God says, 'Fine, I'll do what you ask, because I am pleased with you and know you by name,' Moses fires his climactic request, 'Show me your glory, then!'

It is an amazing short interchange, displaying a great depth of familiarity and boldness, and yet still longing for more. Knowing God, for Moses, was not some static daze of mystical bliss. It was an ongoing, ever-deepening journey into the heart of God, with 'negotiations and love songs' along the way.

But we need to return to the start of the story to savour the encounter that has just preceded this intimate exchange.

Space for grace. As in Genesis 18–19, the context is one of gross sin and threatened judgement. The Israelites had rebelled against God immediately after the making of the covenant, while Moses was on Mount Sinai receiving the law from God. With Aaron's collusion they had made a golden image of a calf-bull, and then compounded their idolatry with immorality and revelry (Ex 32:1–6).

As Moses and Joshua come down the mountain, God speaks these terrifying words, threatening to destroy this whole people and start again with Moses.

> 'I have seen these people,' the LORD said to Moses, 'and they are a stiff-necked people. Now leave me alone so that my anger may burn against them and that I may destroy them. Then I will make you into a great nation.' (Ex 32:9–10)

In the encounter between God and Abraham in Genesis 18, we pondered the way God left a chink of opportunity, with the words, 'but if not, then I will know', about the evil report on Sodom. And that hint of an invitation was enough to set Abraham interceding. In a very similar way here, there is a mysterious quality about God's words to Moses, 'Now leave me alone . . .' Had Moses already started to interject to calm God's anger? Did God hope that he would? In any case, why did God need to say anything at all to Moses in this way, and declare his intention? Why did need to stop off for a meal with Abraham on his way to Sodom and chat about his intentions? The fact is, that God had no need whatsoever to pause in this way on either occasion. God could have poured out his anger from above on Sodom or on the

Israelites with no warning given to anybody. But on both occasions, God pauses to share his intention, and on both occasions God inserts a phrase that hints at an invitation for his human conversation partner to object or suggest other considerations. God leaves space for grace, scope for hope. Both Abraham and Moses know God well enough to pick up the hints and clues. Both jump to intercession. That's what people do who know God.

More challenging questions. The primary account of Moses's intercession is Exodus 32:11–14 (it is recalled again in Deut 9).

> But Moses sought the favour of the LORD his God. 'LORD,' he said, 'why should your anger burn against your people, whom you brought out of Egypt with great power and a mighty hand? Why should the Egyptians say, "It was with evil intent that he brought them out, to kill them in the mountains and to wipe them off the face of the earth"? Turn from your fierce anger; relent and do not bring disaster on your people. Remember your servants Abraham, Isaac and Israel, to whom you swore by your own self: "I will make your descendants as numerous as the stars in the sky and I will give your descendants all this land I promised them, and it will be their inheritance for ever."' Then the LORD relented and did not bring on his people the disaster he had threatened. (Ex 32:11–14)

There are three questions expressed or implied in Moses's prayer here. All of them are addressed to the heart of God, and what most matters to him.

(1) What about your covenant? 'Your people, whom you brought out of Egypt,' says Moses. This is the language of God's covenant commitment to Israel. In Deuteronomy the sharpness of this point is brought out more clearly, in Moses's reminiscence of this terrible moment. Listen to God virtually disowning the people, as if to say—'this is your lot, Moses, not mine.'

> Then the LORD told me, 'Go down from here at once, because *your* people whom *you* brought out of Egypt have become corrupt.' (Deut 9:12)

And then listen to Moses's riposte, as if to say, 'Sorry, God, but they are *your* people and it was you, not me, who brought them out of Egypt; I wasn't even very keen on the idea, as you may recall.'

> I prayed to the LORD and said, 'Sovereign LORD, do not destroy *your* people, *your own* inheritance that *you* redeemed by *your* great power and brought out of Egypt with a mighty hand.' (Deut 9:26)

All through the preceding months, God had been reaffirming his covenant commitment to Israel, and had just ratified it with a prolonged ceremony and celebration meal in Exodus 24. Moses was not about to let God back away from that commitment now. So he boldly reminds God of it.

(2) *What about your reputation?* We saw in chapters 2 and 3 that the exodus had been a massive demonstration, to Israel and Egypt alike, of the identity and power of Yahweh. They, and other nations, knew something about this incomparable God from what he had done in that great act of liberation of his people from slavery.

What would these other nations now think and say if Yahweh wiped the Israelites out in the wilderness? They would treat such news with utter mockery. Either Yahweh is malicious, they would scoff (he only got them out of slavery in order to kill them anyway!), or he is incompetent and can't complete the job (cf. Num 14:16, where Moses deploys the same argument on another occasion of threatened destruction). Malicious and/ or incompetent—is that the kind of reputation Yahweh wanted to be circulating around the Middle East? Moses knew what we know from the rest of the Old Testament, that God is passionately concerned for the honour of his own name. So here, he urges God to think twice before he acts precipitately and ruins his own reputation. Strong stuff, but powerfully effective. So effective in fact that Ezekiel later tells us that God thought a lot more than twice in restraining the full extent of his anger with Israel, precisely for the sake of his name (Ezek 20). And when he did finally pour it out in the exile, the result was such a massive degradation of his name among the nations, that he acted to restore them back to their land, for the same reason (Ezek 36:16–23).

(3) *What about Abraham?* Moses saves the most powerful argument to the end. God's promise to Abraham occurs many times in Genesis, but Moses picks out, through his choice of words in Exodus 32:13, the particular occasion that is recorded in Genesis 15. It was then that God had promised descendants as numerous as the stars in the sky. And more importantly, it was then that God had gone on oath, by a kind of 'self-curse' ritual of severed animals. This oath was confirmed explicitly as God swearing 'by myself' in Genesis 22:16. So God had, in effect, put his own life and existence 'on the line' in his promise to Abraham. His oath means, 'As surely as I am God, and will continue to be God, I will keep this promise; if I fail, I cease to be God.'

God had made an amazing alternative proposal to Moses: 'I will destroy *these* people, but I will not abandon the plan for which I brought them into existence—that is, to bring blessing to all nations, as I promised Abraham. So I will do it through *you and your descendants*. Abraham will be history. It will be the Children of Moses now. Turn the clock back to Genesis 11. We'll start all over again' (see Ex 32:10; cf. Num 14:12).

Far from being tempted by such a proposal, Moses shrinks in shock at the thought, and virtually rebukes God for even suggesting it. '*What about Abraham, and your promise to him?* You can't go back on that without breaking your own oath, sworn on your own life. God, this isn't even an option.'

This is an astounding piece of intercession. The paradox of it is that, in appealing to God to change the plan he has just announced, Moses is appealing to God to be consistent with the plan he had declared long ago. Intercession is not so much trying to change the mind of God as to engage with the deepest purpose of God and seek to align events and outcomes in the present to the known will of God. Above all, it shows how profoundly Moses knew God. He wasted no time trying to elicit divine sympathy for *Israel* ('they didn't really mean it'; 'I have been away a long time, it's not surprising'). Rather he went straight to the heart of the things that really matter *to God*—his covenant, his name, his mission to the nations. All these would be gravely endangered if God were to destroy the people completely in his anger.

Moses knew his God.

And God knew his Moses.

Perhaps he'd better think it through again.

Grace abundant. So we return to Moses, after the worst is over, virtually pestering God for a deeper knowledge and clearer vision of the very glory of God. What would God do in response for his resolute and persistent servant? We return to where we left off above, with Moses asking to see God's glory. Instead, God offers to show him his goodness, to proclaim his name, and to let Moses see 'his back'—all very mysterious, but a defining moment in Old Testament history and theology, when we hear God's self-identification.

> And the LORD said, 'I will cause all my goodness to pass in front of you, and
> I will proclaim my name, the LORD, in your presence. I will have mercy on
> whom I will have mercy, and I will have compassion on whom I will have

compassion. But,' he said, 'you cannot see my face, for no one may see me and live.'

Then the LORD said, 'There is a place near me where you may stand on a rock. When my glory passes by, I will put you in a cleft in the rock and cover you with my hand until I have passed by. Then I will remove my hand and you will see my back; but my face must not be seen.' (Ex 33:19–23)

Then the LORD came down in the cloud and stood there with him and proclaimed his name, the LORD. And he passed in front of Moses, proclaiming, 'Yahweh, Yahweh, the compassionate and gracious God, slow to anger, abounding in steadfast love and faithfulness, maintaining steadfast love to thousands, and bearing wickedness, rebellion and sin. But he will not neglect due punishment, visiting the wickedness of fathers on children and children's children to the third and fourth generation.'

Moses bowed to the ground at once and worshipped. (Ex 34:5–8, my translation)

Moses asked to know God, and God responds. When giving the Ten Commandments, he had sanctioned the second commandment (against idolatry) with the threat that God visits the sin of fathers on children to the third and fourth generation (which effectively confines the effect of sin and punishment within the living family of the perpetrator in a multigenerational family culture[8]), but followed by the promise of God's steadfast love to *thousands* [of generations] of those who love him (Ex 20:5). Now, in the wake of the great apostasy at Mount Sinai, God reverses the order of that combination. His limitless love (there have scarcely yet been a thousand generations in all human history) is put first, and the unavoidable realities of temporal punishments and their effect on connected generations within families is included as sad necessity. God cannot simply overlook sin indefinitely. But his choice is to 'bear' it—that is to 'carry' it in forgiving grace. And that in turn depends on what God puts at the very top of his identity card—words that entered into the definition of the character of Yahweh throughout the rest of the Old Testament.[9]

---

[8]That is to say most Israelite households included three or four living generations from grandfather to youngest sons. If the head of the household committed idolatry, the whole family would be sucked into it, and so the whole family 'to the third or fourth generation' would suffer the effects of it.

[9]The echoes, or direct quotations, of this verse can be seen all over the Old Testament, e.g. Num 14:18; Deut 5:9–10; 1 Kings 3:6; Neh 9:17; Ps 86:15; 103:8, 17; 145:8; Jer 32:18–19; Lam 3:32;

Yahweh, Yahweh, the compassionate and gracious God, slow to anger, abounding in steadfast love and faithfulness. (Ex 34:6, my translation)

Moses asked God to show him his *glory*. God said he would show him his *goodness*. Here is the definition of both. To know God is to know *this* God, the God of compassion, grace, love and faithfulness.

CONCLUSION

What, then, have we learned about knowing God from these two great Old Testament saints, Abraham and Moses?

In both cases, it is said that God knew them—that was the basis of whatever dimensions of knowing God they then enjoyed. To paraphrase John in a way he would probably approve, they knew God because he first knew them. In both cases, there was an intimacy with God that enabled an astonishing degree of forthright conversation, and meaningful dialogue. These were intensely personal relationships in which strong things could be said in the context of total trust.

In both cases, it is clear that God takes very seriously what his friend and his servant say to him. There is no sense that either conversation was all pre-scripted, or a big bluff. Knowing God means engaging in a relationship that has integrity and respect on both sides. In both cases, knowing God involved being taken into God's confidence as regards God's plans and purposes. There is a privilege and a responsibility in seeking to interpret the times in the light of the known word and will of God and with the mind of Christ, through his Spirit.

In both cases, the knowledge that God was about to act in judgement on the wicked brought not a flicker of gloating or anticipation of something long overdue. Rather it led to urgent intercession on behalf of those who stood, deservedly, in the blast-path of God's wrath. For those who know God, the knowledge of God's wrath is as distressing as the Scriptures say it is to God himself.

For Abraham, knowing God meant challenging him in relation to his justice, and learning that God was surprisingly willing to spare the wicked, while relentlessly powerful in his judgement on rampant, unrepentant and incorrigible evildoers.

Dan 9:4; Jonah 4:2; Nah 1:3.

For Moses, knowing God meant challenging him in relation to his covenant, his name and his promises, and finding that the way to stay God's hand was through God's heart, where those realities were eternally enthroned.

For us, the lesson most probably is that, in the adventure of knowing God, there are depths of prayer that we have scarcely begun to paddle in.

CHAPTER SIX

KNOWING GOD
THROUGH REFLECTING
HIS JUSTICE

Jeremiah's prophecy of the new covenant is familiar—perhaps mainly because it is quoted twice in the letter to the Hebrews.

> 'This is the covenant I will make with the people of Israel
>   after that time,' declares the LORD.
> 'I will put my law in their minds
>   and write it on their hearts.
> I will be their God,
>   and they will be my people.
> No longer will they teach their neighbour,
>   or say to one another, 'Know the LORD,'
> because they will all know me,
>   from the least of them to the greatest,'
>   declares the LORD.
> 'For I will forgive their wickedness
>   and will remember their sins no more.' (Jer 31:33–34)

'They will all know me, from the least of them to the greatest' (Jer 31:34). What does this mean? Most explanations and most sermons (including some of my own in the past) say that this promises a close personal relationship of every individual believer with the Lord, as part of the spiritual reality of the new covenant. In contrast to the alleged distance of the individual from God in the Old Testament, we are enabled in the New Testament, through the indwelling Holy Spirit, to know God personally and intimately, and without the mediating teaching of priests or leaders.

Now I will not for a moment deny that a close personal relationship with God is a very precious truth of Christian experience made possible for us through Christ's blood of the new covenant. But is this what Jeremiah was talking about when he spoke about knowing God? Supposing we could ask Jeremiah what he meant by this phrase 'then they will know me', I think the long-suffering prophet (or perhaps his faithful scribe Baruch) would have answered, 'Have you not been listening? I have explained *twice already* in my book what it means to know God. Try paying attention to my words.'

For indeed, in Jeremiah 9:23–24 and 22:13–17, we have passages in which 'knowing God' is not only referred to in a pivotal way, but virtually defined for us as well. In Jeremiah 9:23–24, knowing God is compared with the best gifts that God offers people and is found to surpass them. In Jeremiah 22:13–17, knowing God is contrasted with the worst wickedness that a recent king in Israel had embodied. And in both passages, we shall find the flavour is distinctly practical and ethical, and scarcely 'spiritual' or devotional at all. So apart from any other considerations, the following study is a small exercise in the importance of reading Bible texts in the light of their own immediate context, and not importing assumptions that are really from other parts of the Bible, or (more often) other vague and general aspects of Christian faith.

KNOWING GOD IN COMPARISON WITH
THE BEST GIFTS OF GOD

> 'Let not the wise boast of their wisdom
>> or the strong boast of their strength
>> or the rich boast of their riches,
> but let the one who boasts boast about this:
>> that they have the understanding to know me,
> that I am the LORD, who exercises kindness,
>> justice and righteousness on the earth,
>> for in these I delight,'
>>> declares the LORD. (Jer 9:23–24)

Jeremiah 9:23–24 is a beautifully crafted and balanced little poem. It is rather like a seesaw, or a pair of scales, with a central pivot and things balanced on either side. The central pivot, according to God who is speaking, is 'knowing me'.

Then on one side of that central pivot the prophet places three things that human beings value:

- wisdom
- strength
- riches

While on the other side, he places three things that God values:

- kindness
- justice
- righteousness

God's good gifts and their perversion. Jeremiah 9:23 is rather surprising— as much to us as doubtless to Jeremiah's hearers. All three things listed are highly valued good gifts of God. Elsewhere in the Old Testament these things are praised, commended, given thanks for. So Jeremiah is not talking here about some swaggering tycoon boasting of ill-gotten gains and throwing his muscle around. Wisdom, strength and wealth are all presented in the Old Testament as good gifts of God. They are not evil things in themselves, but can be signs of blessing.

(1) Wisdom. The word means 'applied knowledge'; the discernment that comes from experience of life; the combination of sharp insight and well-honed skills; the ability to understand deeply and to act accordingly. It is repeatedly commended in the book of Proverbs as the most valuable thing you can and should set your heart on. It is the fruit of a life lived in the fear of the LORD—that is, by taking God seriously and living according to his ways and standards. Biblical wisdom is not just intellectual, but also profoundly spiritual (it comes from relationship with God) and ethical (it is exercised in moral obedience to God). The young and newly appointed king Solomon, when he was given a chance to ask God for anything, asked for wisdom to do justice in his government, and was highly congratulated by God for doing so (even though the tragic irony of his reign shows that he squandered the gift and turned it into a nice little earner for his personal wealth and glory).

(2) Strength. This normally means simple physical vigour—whether the normal strength of able-bodied men (and it usually is men), or sometimes abnormal strength given by God. The remarkable vigor of Moses, which enabled him to climb mountains at the age of eighty and again at one hundred twenty and scan the horizon with undimmed eyesight, is noted with clear narrative pleasure. Samson of course is more ambiguous, but his great strength is certainly attributed to the Spirit of Yahweh. And in the Psalms, even if there is a bit of a moan that it all wears out for most of us around seventy or eighty, physical vigour is a thing to be prayed for and celebrated.

(3) Riches. Wealth can of course be the fruit of wickedness, oppression, theft and injustice. But it need not be. And there are clear cases of those we could call the righteous rich in the Old Testament, people like Abraham, Boaz and Job—as well as the anonymous figures whose righteous and generous use of wealth is commended in texts like Psalm 112 or Proverbs 31. God's will for his people was not perennial poverty, but abundance enjoyed with justice, compassion and generosity.[1]

So here is a little list of things that most Old Testament Israelites would have placed in a basket of positive goods. These were some of the ingredients of a life lived under the covenant blessing of God. Those who could be called wise, or strong, or rich, had nothing to be ashamed of—provided these qualities were acquired and exercised within the framework of covenant obedience.

But Jeremiah says—*Do not boast of these things.* For what happens when we do? Boasting means that we take credit for ourselves what are in reality gifts of God, and then turn them into matters of pride and self-glory. That in turn quickly perverts the good gifts themselves into cruel vices that usually issue in moral evils of all kinds. This is a temptation that Deuteronomy recognized very early on and warned Israel about even before they entered the land. The rich fertility of the land would give Israelites every opportunity to increase their wealth in crops, oil, wine, herds and flocks, etc. Then, says Moses,

> You may say to yourself, 'My power and the strength of my hands have produced this wealth for me.' (Deut 8:17)

---

[1] Jonathan J. Bonk, 'Righteous Rich,' in *Missions and Money: Affluence as a Missionary Problem—Revisited* (Maryknoll, NY: Orbis, 2006).

And that indeed is the self-made man's boast—claiming all he has accumulated as his own exclusive achievement and for his own exclusive benefit. There is no dispute that he has put in effort and strength. The question is where did *they* come from? Where did you get your strength, your abilities, your intelligence, your energy, the very breath you breathe?

But remember the LORD your God, for it is he who gives you the ability to produce wealth. (Deut 8:18)

But when people ignore this warning, then all three of the good gifts are corrupted into horrible parodies of what God intended them to be as blessings.

- Wisdom, as a matter of boasting, becomes intellectual arrogance, which is often characterized as 'folly' in the Wisdom literature.

- Strength, as a matter of pride, ends up as violence, aggression, grasping from others by the use of oppressive and unjust power. Bullying can be an individual or a national trait, and both are ugly abuses of strength.

- Riches, when accumulated out of covetous greed, turn to excess, extravagance and 'conspicuous consumption', and generate the horrendous injustice of exploitative wealth existing side by side with degrading poverty.

So then, these are good but dangerous gifts. And the main danger lies in the temptation to boast of them and thereby pervert them into terrible evils. And, says the prophet, a very powerful counterweight to that temptation is to understand that there is something far better than any or all of them by comparison. It is a good thing to enjoy the gifts of God. It is a far better thing to know the Giver himself. And so 'knowing God' becomes the pivot of the whole poem. If you are going to exult and glory in something—don't do it in relation to the lesser things that God gives. Do it on account of your relationship with God himself. But that will lead to a very different kind of 'boasting'.

For, to know God means to share in his concerns, understand his scale of values and priorities, and to take delight in what pleases him—as is true of any genuine human relationship as well.

God's delights and their practice.

'I am the LORD who exercises kindness,
     justice and righteousness on earth
     for in these I delight.' (Jer 9:24)

Here is the second group of three, this time not blessings of God that humans value, but actions of God that he values, and delights in when he sees them imitated.

(1) Kindness. The Hebrew word is *hesed*, and kindness is a slightly weak translation for it. It is a very strong word, speaking of committed faithfulness within a relationship, a commitment which is willing to take on costs or burdens for the sake of the other party, and to do so for the long haul. So it certainly includes the element of kindness, but exercised as an act of unselfish love, out of a strong sense of bonding. It is characteristic of God's faithfulness to his covenant promises—and therefore saturates the Psalms, where it is celebrated repeatedly. It is translated, 'unfailing love', 'lovingkindness', 'faithfulness', etc. As a human characteristic, it is modeled in the book of Ruth. Ruth is commended for her remarkable *hesed* to the family of her widowed mother-in-law Naomi, and her own deceased husband. Similarly, Boaz is commended for his *hesed* to Naomi's family by fulfilling the duties of a kinsman-redeemer, at cost to himself.

(2) Justice. The Hebrew word is *mishpat*. It is the act of putting things right for those who are wronged, whether (normally) through legal action on their behalf, or even through military action at times (as in the case of the 'judges'). It is an active word—not just a concept or ideal. It means taking up the case, or the cause, of those who are weak or vulnerable and acting to rectify their suffering.

(3) Righteousness. The Hebrew word is *tsedaqah*. It has at heart that which is straight and true, that which is truly what it ought to be. When used of human relationships it means when people behave to each other in the way that God wants—in fairness and compassion, in making sure that the weak are upheld and the strong restrained. Our translation 'righteousness' is somewhat too abstract and conceptual, and a bit moralistic. *Tsedaqah* in Hebrew is not a concept. It is what you do, or what governs what you do.[2]

These, then, are the things that God 'delights in' when they are done 'on earth' (not just in heaven), for they reflect his own character. He is the God of all faithfulness (Deut 32:4). Righteousness and justice are the foundations of his throne (Ps 97:2). So these things bring him the same pleasure

---

[2]On these ethical terms in the Old Testament, see Christopher J. H. Wright, *Old Testament Ethics for the People of God* (Downers Grove, IL: InterVarsity, 2004), esp. ch. 8 on justice and righteousness.

and joy that parents have when they see something of themselves in their children (at least the better traits).

We should savour that phrase, 'in these I *delight*'. This is not just a matter of a list of 'divine attributes' or 'ethical duties' that we can coolly list and contemplate. This verse uses the language of emotional response. What brings a smile to the face of God? To what circumstances does God respond with the exclamation, 'That's utterly delightful!'? What warms his heart? Answer: when he sees acts of committed love among people; when he sees people achieving justice for others; when he can affirm that a situation has been put right in his eyes—'On earth as it is in heaven'. Nothing is or remains perfect like this in a fallen world, of course. All our efforts are partial. But this verse encourages us to believe that God takes genuine pleasure in even faulty and provisional efforts that are truly characterized by these qualities. This must not be confused of course with the false idea that we can achieve or deserve our salvation through our own righteousness (which, Isaiah reminds us, is nothing more than filthy rags, if we place such saving expectations on it). Rather this is to say that the God of all justice and righteousness is pleased with the attitude and behaviour of those who share his commitment to such qualities and behaviour.

How did Israel know this? From where did they get the idea that Yahweh their God was passionately concerned about kindness, justice and righteousness, in doing them and delighting in them? From the very beginning of their own story as a nation. What else is the story of the exodus but a massive demonstration of God's faithfulness to his promise to Abraham, not only in rescuing Israel from Egypt but in persevering with them through their appalling behaviour in the wilderness? God's dealings with Pharaoh were an exercise in justice—putting down the oppressor and liberating the exploited. And God's law at Sinai provided Israel with a pattern of social righteousness which, had they observed it, would have made them the object of admiring questions to the surrounding nations (Deut 4:6–8).

But more than these historical demonstrations of God's character, there is the self-identification that God makes to Moses at Sinai. When Moses presses Yahweh to show himself, God does not provide an awesome visual cosmic show that might challenge the computer graphics of a Hollywood spectacular. No, he hides Moses, and allows him only to see 'his back' (whatever that mysterious phrase means). But God does speak. And what words he speaks—a proclamation of Yahweh's own name that resonates through the consciousness of Israel through all the generations of Old Testament history and literature.

> Yahweh, Yahweh, the compassionate and gracious God, slow to anger, abounding in love and unfailing commitment (*hesed*), maintaining love to thousands, and carrying wickedness, rebellion and sin, yet not failing to visit the guilty. (Ex 34:6–7, my translation)[3]

But even before that God had made a similar point to Abraham, about the kind of community he wanted, in line with his own character. After enjoying a meal with Abraham and Sarah, God (who was at that moment on his way with two angels to mete out judgement on Sodom and Gomorrah), reminds himself of the purpose for which he had called this man:

> Abraham will surely become a great and powerful nation, and all nations on earth will be blessed through him. For I have chosen him, so that he will direct his children and his household after him to keep the way of the LORD by doing what is right and just (*tsedaqah*, and *mishpat*), so that the LORD will bring about for Abraham what he has promised him. (Gen 18:18–19)

The mission of Israel then, as a people taught these things since Abraham, was to be a community of righteousness and justice, in the midst of a world like Sodom characterized by cruelty (note the 'outcry' of Gen 18:20–21), perversion, arrogant affluence and callous neglect of the poor (Ezek 16:49). Israel was to walk in the way of the LORD in a world walking in the way of Sodom. To be the people of this God, Yahweh, was to know what kind of life this God required and to walk in it. It still is.

So for us to claim to 'know God' means a lot more than a vague, or even an intense, subjective spiritual experience. It means to know *this* God, the God who calls for, who longs for, who delights in, the exercise of love, justice and righteousness. Are these things our delight also? If they are among his top priorities, are they also among ours? For if they are not, then it is not *this* God we know, but some other god more comfortable and congruous with our own predilections.

---

[3]See note 1 in chapter 1 and note 9 in chapter 5 for a list of references through the Old Testament that quote these verses.

What then do we learn from Jeremiah's exquisite mini-poem on knowing God in Jeremiah 9:23–24? First it reminds us of a point that is very familiar, but easily forgotten: that knowing God in personal relationship is more important and precious than enjoying any or all of his blessings in themselves. Wisdom, strength and riches can all be wonderful blessings, and whatever measure of them comes our way should be received with humble thanksgiving as gifts from our heavenly Father's hand.

Second, we are reminded that boasting in them is the fastest exit route from the personal joy of knowing God. Why is that? Mainly, I think, because all three of these things, when we take credit for them ourselves, generate pride, and pride is the number one poison, the impenetrable roadblock to knowing God. We easily puff up with pride in educational achievement and qualifications (and we don't make it easier when we identify and introduce other people with adulation for their stratospheric degrees, as if that was a measure of their spiritual stature as well). Our culture glories in sporting prowess, and the cult of the body-beautiful easily pollutes healthy Christian affirmation of the body into something much more deceptive and destructive. And of course greed, gluttony and avarice are still among the deadly sins, for this very reason—they are deadly to our relationship with God.

Perhaps that is why all three are subtly subverted in the New Testament, even as they are still affirmed as gifts. Not many, said Paul, among the Christians at Corinth, had been 'wise' in the world's eyes. Not many were among the powerful and wealthy. It was the weak, the poor and the apparently foolish that God had chosen and called to himself.

But third, we recall that when we obey the word of Jesus, and 'seek first the kingdom of God and his righteousness/justice', then these gifts of God can be ours as well—but on God's terms and for God's glory, not ours, and never as a matter of boasting.

You need wisdom?

> If any of you lacks wisdom, you should ask God, who gives generously to all without finding fault, and it will be given to you. (Jas 1:5)

You need strength?

> He said to me, 'My grace is sufficient for you, for my power is made perfect in weakness.' Therefore I will boast all the more gladly about my weaknesses

[was Paul thinking of Jeremiah 9:23 when he wrote this?], so that Christ's power may rest on me . . . For when I am weak, then I am strong. (2 Cor 12:9–10)

I can do all this through him who gives me strength. (Phil 4:13)

You need money?

I have learned to be content whatever the circumstances. I know what it is to be in need, and I know what it is to have plenty. I have learned the secret of being content in any and every situation, whether well fed or hungry, whether living in plenty or in want . . . And my God will meet all your needs according to the riches of his glory in Christ Jesus. (Phil 4:11–12, 19)

KNOWING GOD IN CONTRAST TO THE WORST EVIL OF HUMANITY

Jeremiah lived through the reigns of several kings. Two of them stood in stark contrast to each other. Josiah was a godly young king, only a little older than Jeremiah himself. But he died young in battle (that was a mystery of providence in itself, and Jeremiah grieved for him, it seems). Jehoiakim, who followed him, was the exact opposite, and yet had a long reign in which Jeremiah suffered increasing unpopularity and persecution for his critical outspokenness. Jeremiah 22:13–17, in the midst of a chapter that is an edited collection of several of Jeremiah's sayings in relation to the kings of Judah, is a powerful comparison of these two kings. And in it comes a sharp and uncompromising definition of what knowing God means. The words that follow were addressed to Jehoiakim.

'Woe to him who builds his palace by unrighteousness,
     his upper rooms by injustice,
making his own people work for nothing,
     not paying them for their labour.
He says, "I will build myself a great palace
     with spacious upper rooms."
So he makes large windows in it,
     panels it with cedar
     and decorates it in red.
Does it make you a king

to have more and more cedar?
Did not your father have food and drink?
   He did what was right and just,
   so all went well with him.
He defended the cause of the poor and needy,
   and so all went well.
Is that not what it means to know me?'
   declares the LORD.
'But your eyes and your heart
   are set only on dishonest gain,
on shedding innocent blood
   and on oppression and extortion.' (Jer 22:13–17)

The contrast. What a catalogue of wickedness we read in these verses. Jehoiakim stands accused by the prophet of

- exploitation of workers for low or no wages (something prohibited in the law Deut 24:14–15)

- conspicuous affluence and consumption (second storeys and windows were uncommon in normal homes; cedar was the most expensive kind of wood; red dye was the most expensive form of paint; and what was wrong with the palace of Solomon that Jehoiakim needed to build a new one?)

- fraud and greed

- bloodshed, violence and murder

- oppression and extortion

This is a picture of the abuse of governmental power and privilege that is all too familiar in the modern world too. And not just among notoriously corrupt regimes in the Majority World. All of the above can be laid on the charge sheet of some western governments and corporations in the way they deal with the poorer world.

By contrast, Jeremiah gives a very short and simple description of the reign of Josiah, in Jeremiah 22:15–16.

- He did righteousness and justice (which God delights in).

- He defended the poor and needy (whom God cares for).

And so, comments Jeremiah, 'It was *good* for him.' He was good. His reign was good. Things were good, under a king who put God's priorities above his own selfishness.

And then come the startling words at the end of Jeremiah 22:16.

'Is not this to know me?' saying of Yahweh. (Jer 22:16, my translation)

I find this a remarkable statement, and an infinitely challenging one. For in the midst of all our spiritualizing, pious, devotional, even mystical, verbosity over what 'knowing God' is all about, here is a stark four-word question (in Hebrew) that stands like a lighthouse on a rock in the middle of a tossing sea of words. We come wondering how to steer a course toward truly knowing God, and here we find a biblical, prophetic, inspired, luminous, *definition* of what knowing God is. It is simple and clear. Doing righteousness and justice; defending the poor and needy—*that* is to know God. Where does this leave our limp evangelical pietism, or our suspicion of all forms of social engagement, or the rationalizations by which we excuse ourselves from the ideological and practical battlefields of economics and politics? We do not all have Josiah's calling into political authority. But if we wish to be among those who know God and are worthy of his verdict—'good'—then we had better share Josiah's commitment to social justice and action for the poor and needy.

The source. How did Josiah come to know God in this essentially practical commitment to social justice? From God's law. The most notable event in the reign of Josiah was the rediscovery of the Book of the Law during the restoration of the temple (2 Kings 22). Josiah was already committed to the reformation of the faith of Judah, and this discovery accelerated his commitment and the reforms. Very probably the book that was discovered was, or included, what we now know as the book of Deuteronomy. Imagine listening to such words as these being read in your royal hearing. And notice how they link affirmations about what Yahweh is like and what he typically does, with what he wants his people to do.

For the Lord your God is God of gods and Lord of lords, the great God, mighty and awesome, who shows no partiality and accepts no bribes. He defends the cause of the fatherless and the widow, and loves the foreigner residing among, giving them food and clothing. And you are to love those who are foreigners, for you yourselves were foreigners in Egypt. (Deut 10:17–19)

So this is exactly what Josiah set out to do. He learned about the justice and compassion of Yahweh in the Scriptures, and then determined to imitate them in his own life, and to inculcate them in the social life of the nation. That's how, according to Jeremiah, he *knew* Yahweh—by doing what Yahweh did, and by implementing what Yahweh wanted to be done.

We are told very little about Josiah's inner spiritual life, other than that he had come to seek the God of his father David early in life (2 Chron 34:3)—possibly referring to a kind of personal conversion experience, in the wake of the whole generation of evil led by his grandfather Manasseh and his father Amon. But we *are* told about his intentional obedience to the law with its deep saturation with concern for the poor and needy, the marginalized and vulnerable—the widow, orphan and foreigner. As a result, Josiah goes down in the record as the only Israelite king in the whole Old Testament who gets an unsullied A+ on his ethical report card. This is the verdict of the historian (who was also imbued with the spirit of Deuteronomy).

> Neither before nor after Josiah was there a king like him who turned to the
> LORD as he did—with all his heart and with all his soul and with all his
> strength, in accordance with all the Law of Moses. (2 Kings 23:25)

Josiah, in short, knew the LORD. And the proof was practical and ethical. And the affirmation that he did know the LORD came not from his own boasting, but posthumously from God himself through his prophet.

CONCLUSION

In the light of both these texts, then, how can we claim to know God? Not on the basis of boasting of the things that we *have*—however good they may be, and however much they are in themselves the gifts and blessings of God.

Nor, indeed, on the basis of anything we might *say*, whether boasting or not. For we recall that Jesus warned us that, 'Not everyone who *says* to me, "Lord, Lord," will enter the kingdom of heaven' (Mt 7:21). Nor, either, on the basis of the great things we allege that we *do* in ministry. For not all such claims are authentic or demonstrate that those who profess them actually know God and are owned by Christ. Jesus added the following warning:

> Many will say to me on that day, 'Lord, Lord, did we not prophesy in your
> name, and in your name drive out demons and perform many miracles?'

Then I will tell them plainly, 'I never knew you. Away from me, you evil-doers!' (Mt 7:22–23)

These are sobering words. Who would you think has a better claim to know God than someone who has a prophetic ministry? Or someone who has a great deliverance ministry in the name of Christ? Or someone who performs miracles of healing (probably) in the name of Christ? Surely these great ministries are proof of knowing God? Not necessarily, says Jesus. There will be *many*, Jesus says, who do these things without knowing God at all. There will be many who appear to have the most spectacular minis-tries, but at the end of the day, Jesus will not own them, and will have to say: 'We don't know each other. I never knew you. So it follows that you never knew me.'

The only real test, according to Jesus is doing 'the will of my Father who is in heaven' (Mt 7:21). And what is that? Jesus endorsed, and modelled, all that the Old Testament said about Yahweh's care for the poor, his passion for justice and compassion. And if those things were the will of Yahweh, then they are certainly included among 'the will of my Father'. And so Jesus includes among the beatitudes a blessing on 'those who hunger and thirst for righteousness/justice'. The ones who will be owned and wel-comed by 'The King . . . my Father' will be those who fed the hungry, showed hospitality to the stranger, clothed the naked, cared for the sick and visited the prisoner (Mt 25:34–36).

James, whose letter possibly comes the closest in the New Testament to reflecting directly the ethos of the teaching of Jesus, asserts (and note the explicit relating of his point to God 'our Father'):

> Religion that God our Father accepts as pure and faultless is this: to look after orphans and widows in their distress and to keep oneself from being polluted by the world. (Jas 1:27)

Sadly, many of us are rather more keen on the latter (keeping ourselves unpolluted by the world) than on the former. Or we are very adamant on preserving the purity of the faith and sound doctrine. But James goes on:

> What good is it, my brothers and sisters, if someone claims to have faith but has no deeds? Can such faith save him? Suppose a brother or a sister is without clothes and daily food. If one of you says to them, 'Go in peace; keep warm and well fed,' but does nothing about their physical needs, what good

is it? In the same way, faith by itself, if it is not accompanied by action, is dead. (Jas 2:14–17)

John agrees.

> This is how we know what love is: Jesus Christ laid down his life for us. And we ought to lay down our lives for our brothers and sisters. If anyone has material possessions and sees a brother or sister in need but has no pity on them, how can the love of God be in that person? (1 John 3:16–17)

Or how, we might add, can the knowledge of God be in that person either.

All these are deeply challenging verses—to me as much as to any reader. And I have included these New Testament passages intentionally to show that the kind of sharp demands of practical social ethics we read in Jeremiah and Deuteronomy are not merely Old Testament obsessions that our more spiritual New Testament faith has left behind. The Bible speaks with one voice on this.

There is no true knowledge of God without the exercise of justice and compassion.

I have to ask myself, then, what is there in my life that shows any love for, and practical commitment to, the poor and the needy? God may not have called me to direct hands-on involvement in a social ministry, but whatever else I do for a living, can I see that God's concern for the weak and the poor is reflected at all in my praying, thinking, giving and doing? For according to the measure of my answer is the measure of my knowing God.

Josiah did righteousness and justice.

He defended the cause of the widow and orphan.

'Is that not what it means to know me?' declares the LORD. (Jer 22:16)

CHAPTER SEVEN

KNOWING GOD
THROUGH RETURNING
to HIS LOVE

I once saw a church poster that said:

'You can never get rid of love.
The more you give it away,
the more it keeps coming back.'

Hosea would have agreed. He is sometimes called 'the prophet of love', not only because he speaks about love a lot, but also because God demanded of him an amazing act of costly personal love in which the message of his book was fleshed out in his own suffering. And he also discovered something of the returns of love—the love that God commanded him to show by welcoming back an unfaithful but returning wife, and the love that God longed to show to an unfaithful people if only they would return to him.

But it would be equally accurate to describe Hosea as the prophet of the *knowledge of God,* for this is something he talks about even more often than love. In fact the Hebrew verb and noun for 'know' and 'knowledge' occur about a dozen times in this book of only fourteen chapters (English translations sometimes use different words to render the same Hebrew word, such as 'acknowledge', 'care for', 'realize' or 'recognize', but even so, the emphasis is clear). So Hosea certainly deserves his place in any book about knowing God. And more than that, he speaks about how God knew Israel as a son and wanted to relate to them as their Father, so Hosea doubly deserves his place in this book about knowing God the Father through the Old Testament. So we turn to his book, anticipating some rich and challenging teaching about what it means to know God.

If you list all the passages in Hosea that speak about knowing God, or the knowledge of God,[1] they fall roughly into three categories:

- the *historical* knowledge of God that Israel enjoyed through their experience of God's redemption (with some additional aspects to what we studied in chapter two above);

- the *lack* of the knowledge of God that Hosea observes among his contemporaries, manifested in spiritual rebellion and moral collapse throughout society; and

- the *restored* knowledge of God that Hosea looked forward to, if only the people would return to God in repentance that was genuine and not a superficial mouthing of the old litanies.

These, then, are the three main sections of our study in this chapter.

KNOWLEDGE OF GOD GAINED THROUGH REDEMPTION
Knowing God as Saviour

> Yet I have been the LORD your God
>   ever since the land of Egypt;
> you know no God but me,
>   and besides me there is no saviour. (Hos 13:4 NRSV)

This verse, like Hosea 2:15 and 12:9, takes us back to the exodus. That was when God had made himself so clearly known to the Israelites as Yahweh. That was when he had claimed them for his own and entered into exclusive covenant relationship with them. In chapter 2 we explored this in considerable depth and marvelled at the curriculum of knowledge of God that Israel gained through the experience of God's saving grace and

---

[1] If you want to read them all together (which is well worth pausing to do), they include Hos 2:8, 20; 4:1, 6; 5:4; 6:3, 6; 8:2; 9:7; 11:3; 13:4–5 (and cf. the last verse of the book, Hos 14:9). All the references in this chapter are to the verse numbering in English Bibles. The numeration in the Hebrew text is often somewhat different.

power. What we see again here is that, for Hosea too, the knowledge of God is not something mystical or esoteric. It is historical and experiential. Israel knew Yahweh because of his redeeming action, and they also knew that no other god had acted in that way. Accordingly, their unique experience generated unique knowledge of the unique God.

The language of this verse in Hosea has been strongly influenced, obviously, by the opening of the Ten Commandments.

> I am the LORD your God, who brought you out of Egypt, out of the land of slavery. You shall have no other gods before me. (Ex 20:2–3)

Israel was to *have* no other gods because they *knew* no other gods. This does not mean, of course, that the Israelites did not know that other nations had other gods—they had just been delivered from Egypt, a land of very powerful deities whose names they knew well. It means that Israel had covenant allegiance to Yahweh alone as their Saviour and Lord, and must not dissipate that loyalty by going after such other gods. The experience of God's salvation carries with it the immense privilege of knowing who the living God is, and the immense responsibility of living in complete loyalty to him alone. To know God in this sense is to be committed to him.

Hosea goes on in the following verse to make the knowledge between Israel and God a mutual thing:

> I *knew you* in the wilderness,
> > in the land of burning heat. (Hos 13:5, my translation)

Most English translations (but not the KJV) obscure Hosea's balanced phrasing by translating 'I knew you,' as 'I cared for you,' or 'I fed you'—which redundantly anticipates Hosea 13:6. Hosea's point is that Israel's knowledge of God is related to, and dependent on, God's knowledge of Israel (a point we saw earlier in the personal relationship between God and both Abraham and Moses). Those whom God calls to know him are those whom God himself knows—with all the personal, relational, pastoral and reassuring implications of that truth. Here the point is national; in Psalm 139 it is profoundly personal.

Israel, then, knew God as a privilege that resulted from the way God had rescued them from slavery and cared for them in the wilderness. Through these primary events and experiences Israel knew their God and

God knew his people. This is the essence of the covenant relationship—a relationship which, as we shall soon see, was being severely threatened by Israel's behaviour.

Hosea goes on to portray the redemptive covenant relationship between Israel and Yahweh by means of two powerful human metaphors: husband-wife, and father-son. Israel knew God (or should have done), as a wife knows her husband and as a son knows his father.

Knowing God as husband. We need to go right back to the beginning of the book of Hosea, and back to the personal experience out of which his whole message was shaped. Prophets in Israel were not unfamiliar with some very bizarre instructions from God in relation to the way they were to illustrate or act out their message, but this book opens with one of the most shocking things any prophet ever heard God tell him to do.

> When the LORD first spoke through Hosea, the LORD said to Hosea, 'Go, take for yourself a wife of whoredom and have children of whoredom, for the land commits great whoredom by forsaking the LORD.' So he went and took Gomer daughter of Diblaim, and she conceived and bore him a son. (Hos 1:2–3 NRSV)

The NRSV here preserves the shock of the triple repetition of the Hebrew word for the behaviour of a prostitute, which the NIV somewhat dissipates by its variation of 'adultery' and 'unfaithfulness'.

God's words here have caused commentators (and devout readers of all ages) considerable problems. Did God tell Hosea to do something that was, strictly speaking, contrary to the law of Moses? Prostitutes were not supposed to be tolerated in the land at all, let alone taken in marriage. If so, it must have been a terribly difficult and shaming thing for Hosea to be obedient to such a command.

Some people soften the matter by reading the verses 'proleptically'. That is to say, the editorial record of God's command to marry Gomer anticipates what actually happened later (that she was unfaithful to him and turned to prostitution) *as if* it had been part of the original instructions. Hosea didn't know at the time that this is how it would turn out—even if God did. Well, that is possible (we know that Hebrew sometimes expressed as a purpose something that we would more normally express as a result). But it seems better to me to take the words at face value. God told Hosea to go and take an unlawfully practising prostitute as his lawfully wedded wife. It may be shocking and hard to believe, but so was the behaviour of Israel that Hosea was called to address.

Now, in the rest of Hosea 2–3, it is clear that Gomer represents Israel and Hosea represents Yahweh, so that the human story of marriage, unfaithfulness and restoration becomes a living parable of the fraught but redeemable relationship between God and Israel. If Israel, then, were meant to know Yahweh because of what he had done for them, what should Gomer have known about Hosea from his action in taking her as his wife? That is an element in the analogy being presented to us in this prophetic combination of actions and words. Once again it is important to remind ourselves that whatever Gomer came to know about Hosea resulted from what Hosea actually *did*. Hosea did not join a society to debate the social evils of prostitution. Nor did he theorize about possible strategies for the uplift of fallen women. Nor did he simply complain about prostitutes, or even merely take pity on them.

He went and married one.

The same is true in any account of how we can come to know God. It is not through a process of speculation about what God may or may not be like. Nor is it a matter of merely checking off doctrinal check boxes about God's attributes. God the Son was not content either merely to discuss with his Father possible strategies for amelioration of the human condition, or to send a cosmic sympathy card telling us 'I share your pain'.

He came and died to save us.

Knowing God means knowing what *God* has done, knowing it was done *for me*, and knowing the *response* I should make.

Gomer would have known, from Hosea's action toward her, that he loved her (this is mentioned as something that he was told to do 'again' in Hosea 3:1, implying that it had been part of the original marriage); that he was willing to forgive her past life, or at least not let it stand in the way of their marriage; that he wished to rescue her from that past life; that he had chosen her in particular to marry in this way (since there were doubtless many others in similar circumstances); that he knew her by name (it is significant that she is named in the narrative); that he was prepared to trust her and provide for her (cf. Hos 2:8), up until her repeated unfaithfulness (evidenced in children that Hosea knew were not his own) led to a separation filled with grief and anger.

All of these mirrored the way Israel should have known Yahweh, in reflecting on what he had done for them in taking them to himself in covenant relationship. And indeed Hosea hints at the initial joy and delight of the relationship

> When I found Israel,
>> it was like finding grapes in the desert;
> when I saw your ancestors,
>> it was like seeing the early fruit on the fig tree. (Hos 9:10)

Jeremiah picked up this thought as he pictures Yahweh nostalgically thinking back to the wilderness period as a kind of honeymoon period:

> Go and proclaim in the hearing of Jerusalem:
> 'This is what the LORD says:
> "I remember the devotion of your youth,
>> how as a bride you loved me
> and followed me through the wilderness,
>> through a land not sown."' (Jer 2:2)

When you recall the actual stories of Israel's behaviour in the wilderness in the books of Exodus and Numbers, it is clearly a shocking comparison. Both these prophets are saying that the abysmal depravity of the nation in their own day made the wilderness era seem like a honeymoon by comparison!

Knowing God as Father. Hosea 11:1–4 is a sustained metaphor, comparing Israel's relationship to God with a son to his father. Since Hosea's prophecy is dominated by the initial marriage metaphor, this section is all the more interesting.

> When Israel was a child, I loved him,
>> and out of Egypt I called my son.
> The more I called them,
>> the more they went from me;
> they kept sacrificing to the Baals,
>> and offering incense to idols.
> Yet it was I who taught Ephraim to walk,
>> I took them up in my arms;
>> but they did not know that I healed them.
> I led them with cords of human kindness,

with bands of love.
I was to them like those
who lift infants to their cheeks.
I bent down to them and fed them.[2] (Hos 11:1–4 NRSV)

The theme of knowing God in this way is implied, even though only negatively, in Hosea 11:3. Sadly, Israel did not know what they should have known—namely that it was Yahweh who was caring for their interests as their fatherly God.

The themes we find built into Hosea's picture here are similar to the fatherly portraits of God we enjoyed in chapter 1 of this book in our trilogy. The historical reality that is being referred to yet again, of course, is the exodus and wilderness experience and all the events that fill that narrative. And these events are being here portrayed as the action of a father for a child in need. The strength of the father is made available in gentleness and love toward the child. As we also saw in chapter 5, the affirmation that Israel was Yahweh's firstborn son was made even before the exodus (Ex 4:22), as a reason for God's demand that Pharaoh should release him. But here the picture is not so much the issue of the rights of a firstborn and the claims of the divine Father over against the oppressor who is depriving the firstborn of his legitimate inheritance. Rather it is simply the picture of a loving and caring father that is to the fore.

What, then, were the fatherly actions of God that Israel should have known, as listed in this short parable of their history? Some very human and familiar parental actions are listed to illustrate God's relationship to his people:

---

[2]Hosea 11:4 is translated in different ways. I have chosen the NRSV here because it assumes that the metaphor of a father's relationship with a child continues through this verse, which I think is probably Hosea's intention. Some scholars (and cf. the NET) think that the metaphor has changed in this verse to Israel as an ox, being led gently by its owner with a leather rope, who lifts the yoke from its neck and bends down to feed it. The NIV mixes this metaphor into Hosea 11:4b. It is possible to translate 'cords of human kindness' and 'bands of love' as 'ropes of leather' (the Hebrew word *ahabah*, normally translated 'love' can mean 'leather' in a very few contexts; it is a homonym—i.e. a word that is spelled the same but can have completely different meanings, such as 'party' or 'match' in English). Hosea does compare Israel to a young ox elsewhere (Hos 4:16; 10:11). So the ox metaphor is possible here. However, in my view it seems more likely that the son-father metaphor is being continued.

I remember my Hebrew professor in Cambridge, commenting on the possibility that *ahabah* in Hosea 11:4 might mean leather rather than love and saying wryly that perhaps we should then translate Hosea 11:1 as 'When Israel was a child, I leathered him.'

- He loved them and called them to himself, as a father calls a child to his side. The tragedy was that his fatherly calling was met with incorrigible refusal and increasing distance.

- He taught them to walk. That is a patient parental process that involves a lot of falling down too, and Israel's multiple fallings tested the patience of God again and again.

- He took them up in his arms—the action of a father when a child is tired, or stumbling, or in some danger. The early history of Israel is replete with such actions by God on Israel's behalf.

- He healed them (cf. Ex 15:22–26)—even if they refused to acknowledge that it was Yahweh who did it. On occasion, by contrast, they hankered after the healthier diet, as they thought, that they had enjoyed in Egypt (Num 11:4–6).

- He led them, as a father leads a child to safety out of the murderous regime of Egypt.

- He lifted the yoke from their necks (if the NIV is to be preferred to the NRSV in Hos 11:4)—another clear allusion to the exodus; or (if NRSV is preferred), he lifted them into close intimacy with himself.

- He stooped down to feed them—literally at ground level in the case of the manna and quails.

These things are celebrated also in Deuteronomy 8, which is echoed by Hosea in several ways, and with the same perception of the fatherly nature of all that God did for Israel at that time of their history (Deut 8:5).

Here, then, as saviour, husband and father, is the God whom Israel knew, and these are the ways in which God had acted precisely so that they could know him. They were to know God through faithfulness as of a wife to a husband, and through obedience as of a son to a father. But the tragedy that Hosea observed was a people who should have known God in all these ways rejecting and suppressing that knowledge, and doing so to such an extent that Hosea could make the astonishingly absolute diagnosis, 'there is no . . . knowledge of God in the land' (Hos 4:1 NRSV).

KNOWLEDGE OF GOD LOST THROUGH REBELLION

Hosea gives us a number of clues as to how it was that a people who were unique among all the nations in being entrusted with the knowledge of

God (cf. Deut 4:32–39) came to be a people lacking not only the true knowledge of God but even any true insight into their own desperate plight (Hos 5:4; 7:9). The primary cause was the idolatrous seduction of the Canaanite fertility cults, likened to marital unfaithfulness, in which they refused to acknowledge the gifts they had received from Yahweh and even attributed them to other gods (Hos 2:5–8). A second cause was their refusal to live by the moral standards that God had established for their society in the Ten Commandments, and the infection of every area of social life with rampant evil (Hos 4:1–3). And a third cause was a total failure of moral leadership on the part of those who were supposed to be the teachers of the nation (Hos 4:4–6).

In other words, the knowledge of God was lost because the people persistently failed to acknowledge God's gifts, to walk in God's ways, and to teach God's laws. As we turn to consider each of these three failures, we will find that there are sharp lessons here for the people of God in any era.

Failure to acknowledge God's gifts. As far as we can tell, Hosea was the first to use the metaphor of marriage to portray the relationship between Yahweh and Israel. It was a remarkably bold step to take, in the context of the strongly sexual nature of the cult of Baal that he was opposing. It really is a case of stealing your enemy's guns. In the Canaanite fertility cult, the male god Baal had his female consort Asherah. Their sexual prowess mirrored and guaranteed the fertility of nature—of the soil, of your animals, and of your women. So the worship of these deities included the visible representations of standing stone pillars (the phallic symbol) and wooden poles or trees (as the female symbol). Israel had been told to destroy these things completely and have nothing to do with the religious practices that went along with them (Deut 7:5; 12:30–31). Those practices included sacralized sexual acts with religious prostitutes that were believed to foster fertility in the natural realm (described in Hos 4:10–14).

So Hosea was confronted with the Israelites falling into the Canaanite myth of the sacred marriage of the gods, in order to sustain their need for agricultural abundance and other natural blessings. They went after these other gods, thinking that it was the gods of the land and its Canaanite inhabitants who obviously were the custodians of material prosperity and family fortunes. These were the gods who needed a bit of persuasion and collaborative sexual prodding to get them to unload the good things of life.

Not only was this a denial of the fact that it was actually *Yahweh*, the Creator and controller of every natural process, who had always given them all good things richly to enjoy, it was also a terrible act of disloyalty to their covenant Lord. Hosea's boldness lies in the way he chose to counter this perversion—namely by taking over the sexual imagery of Canaanite fertility cults and transforming it into a vehicle to expose the horror of what Israel's sin was doing to them and to God.

Baal, the god of Canaan had his wife—Asherah. Yahweh too has a wife, announces Hosea. But the wife of Yahweh is not some goddess in the mythical world. No, Yahweh's wife is *his own people Israel*, in the real world of human history. Yahweh and Israel are bound together in a covenant relationship that was intended to be as lovingly exclusive as the human marriage bond. For that reason, Israel's behaviour in going after other gods (and also, as we read in the rest of the book, in going after political alliances with other nations, which involved religious deals with their gods also), was as grievous, hurtful and disloyal to Yahweh as was Gomer's behaviour in reverting to prostitution and bearing illegitimate children after accepting the status and benefits of being Hosea's wife. In both cases it was a shattering breach of trust that justified the baffled grief and anger of the offended partner.

In the transition from the narrative of Hosea 1 to the poetic form of God's address to Israel in Hosea 2, we move from the betrayed marriage of Hosea and Gomer to the broken covenant of God and Israel. The language sustains the metaphor, however, as Israel is addressed as a wife whose unfaithfulness has been exposed and denounced.

> Their mother has been unfaithful
>> and has conceived them in disgrace.
> She said, 'I will go after my lovers,
>> who give me my food and my water,
>> my wool and my linen, my oil and my drink.' . . .
> She has not acknowledged that I was the one
>> who gave her the grain, the new wine and oil,
> who lavished on her the silver and gold—
>> which they used for Baal.
> Therefore I will take away my corn when it ripens,
>> and my new wine when it is ready.

I will take back my wool and my linen,
>   intended to cover her naked body. (Hos 2:5, 8–9)

The accusation is clear. Israel went after her 'lovers'. This is a double entendre, since it refers of course to the gods of the Canaanites, but included the actual sexual rituals involved in their fertility cults. The sexual language is both metaphorical and literal. They did this in order to ensure agricultural fertility and sufficiency. Then, when they got those good things, they attributed them to the Canaanite gods, refusing to acknowledge the hand of Yahweh from whom in fact they received them. 'She has not *acknowledged*' is literally 'she did not *know*'. Again, we remember that this did not mean Israel no longer even knew the name of Yahweh. It means that they refused to acknowledge him in one of his most basic activities—the regularity and fruitfulness of the created order and the fertility of the land that he himself had given to them.

Ingratitude to God for all his good gifts leads to losing the knowledge of God. When we are tempted to attribute to other causes whatever measure of blessing comes our way in life, or even to claim credit for it ourselves, then we are on the dangerous road of forgetting the Lord.

> You may say to yourself, 'My power and the strength of my hands have produced this wealth for me.' But remember the LORD your God, for it is he who gives you the ability to produce wealth. (Deut 8:17–18)

Failure to walk in God's ways.

Hear the word of the LORD, O people of Israel;
>   for the LORD has an indictment against the inhabitants of the land.
There is no faithfulness or loyalty,
>   and no knowledge of God in the land.
Swearing, lying, and murder,
>   and stealing and adultery break out;
>   bloodshed follows bloodshed.
Therefore the land mourns,
>   and all who live in it languish;
together with the wild animals
>   and the birds of the air,
>   even the fish of the sea are perishing. (Hos 4:1–3 NRSV)

What happens when a whole people refuses to know the God who is their saviour, husband and father? What Hosea observes is a complete moral collapse of society and accompanying detrimental ecological effects. He brings this as 'an indictment'. The language is deliberately legal. The prophets often used the imagery of the law-court as a way of challenging Israel to face up to the serious consequences of their behaviour. And it is particularly appropriate here because the accusation includes the breaking of several of the central commandments of Israel's covenant law.

The phrase 'no knowledge of God' stands like a pivot between, on the one hand, two other things that were absent from the land, and six things that the land was filled with instead. Yahweh is the God of all truth, trustworthiness and faithfulness, and the God of unfailing covenant love. These things are summed up in two words by Hosea—*emeth* and *hesed*. But since the people had lost all effective knowledge of Yahweh, there was a corresponding loss of these essential characteristics in society as well. No knowledge of Yahweh leads to breakdown of all trust and commitment.

Modern echoes abound. It is not necessary for everybody in a society to be a Christian for there to be some level of truth and loyalty. But there does need to be some collective agreement on transcendent values that demand such qualities of behaviour between citizens and neighbours. In the case of the West, that transcendent role was filled for centuries with something akin to the biblical God, even if grossly distorted in the popular mind. Once even the caricature of deity loses any imperative grip on the social conscience, then the bonds of social truthfulness, trust, love, mutual commitment and kindness, all begin to dissolve under the acids of egocentric skepticism.

Instead of such godly characteristics, observes Hosea, the land is filled with the dismal fruit of moral disorder, the breaking of almost all the commandments in the second table of the Decalogue: abusive and violent language; public and private untruthfulness; crimes against life and property; a culture of rampant violence. No knowledge of God leads to no restraints on evil. Paul's searing commentary on this in Romans 1 and 2 expands Hosea's diagnosis of eighth-century Israel into a penetrating analysis of the human condition, once the suppression of the knowledge of God has worked like poison through human society.

Failure to teach God's laws. But who was really to blame? Well, of course, all the Israelites bore their share of blame for the social malaise to whatever extent they participated in it. But Hosea refuses to tolerate a frenzy of mutual accusation. He knows exactly where the primary responsibility lay and pointed his prophetic finger at the group within society to whom God had entrusted the task of teaching the people—the priests.

> Yet let no one contend,
>> and let none accuse,
>>> for with you is my contention, O priest.
> You shall stumble by day;
>> the prophet also shall stumble with you by night,
>> and I will destroy your mother.
> My people are destroyed for lack of knowledge;
>> because you have rejected knowledge,
>> I reject you from being a priest to me.
> And since you have forgotten the law of your God,
>> I also will forget your children. (Hos 4:4–6 NRSV)

We are familiar with the sacrificial work of the priests of Israel. They received the sacrifices of the people, performed appropriate rituals with the blood, and declared atonement. Not so well known, however, is the fact the priests were ordained to be teachers of God's law to the rest of the people. This was a vital part of the two-way direction of their ministry as mediators—middlemen who acted on behalf of the people before God, and on behalf of God before the people.

Through the priest's handling of the sacrifices, people could come into the presence of God. Through the priests teaching of the law, the knowledge of God would come to the people.

The commission to teach God's law was part of the ordination mandate given to Aaron and his sons in Leviticus. God said to them:

> You are to distinguish between the holy and the common, and between the unclean and the clean; *and you are to teach the people of Israel* all the statutes that the LORD has spoken to them through Moses. (Lev 10:10–11 NRSV)

This role is also seen as belonging to the whole tribe of Levi in the blessing that Moses spoke in relation to it.

> He teaches your precepts to Jacob
>> and your law to Israel.

He offers incense before you
> and whole burnt offerings on your altar. (Deut 33:10)

The fact that the Levites were commissioned and (in better times) trained to do this explains why they feature in programs of scriptural re-education at times of great reformation and renewal in the history of Israel. Jehoshaphat employed them, for example, in an overhaul of Israel's judicial system (2 Chr 19:8–10). Ezra used them to translate and explain the law to the ordinary people (Neh 8:7–8). Sadly, however, they seemed to have abdicated this responsibility more often than they fulfilled it. Hosea is not the only prophet who complains that the priests were not teaching the people. Centuries later Malachi makes the same accusation. Speaking of Levi, and thus of the priests as a class, Malachi says:

> True instruction was in his mouth and nothing false was found on his lips. He walked with me in peace and uprightness, and turned many from sin.

> 'For the lips of a priest ought to preserve knowledge, because he is the messenger of the LORD Almighty and people seek instruction from his mouth. But you have turned from the way and by your teaching have caused many to stumble; you have violated the covenant with Levi,' says the LORD Almighty. 'So I have caused you to be despised and humiliated before all the people, because you have not followed my ways but have shown partiality in matters of the law.' (Mal 2:6–9; see the whole section 2:1–9)

The clear implication of these texts is that, although nothing excuses people from their own responsibility in doing wickedness, there is an even higher level of responsibility and blame for those who are supposed to teach the Word of God to the people of God, but who fail to do so. And both Hosea and Malachi address devastatingly serious words from God to such failed teachers of the knowledge of God. Not surprisingly, James warned Christians not to be overkeen to take on the role of a teacher among God's people. It is an enormous calling, but it carries corresponding exposure to the potential judgement of God if our teaching leads people astray or fails to lead them in the ways of God (Jas 3:1).

The absence of good teaching and the danger of false teaching have been twin problems throughout the history of God's people, of course—not only in Old Testament Israel but all down the centuries of the church. In our day the failure of those who claim to be, or are commissioned to be, teachers of God's people seems to have reached epidemic proportions. In the West there are those who teach, practice and bless sexual lifestyles and relationships that are explicitly declared in the Bible to be displeasing to God. While all over the world, but especially in the Majority World, the so-called 'prosperity gospel' with all its 'sanctified' selfishness and covetousness, along with the arrogant affluence of those who presume to teach it from the Bible as 'what God wants', deceives millions and grieves the one who called us to self-denying humility and service.

Sex and money. Baal reloaded. The temptations of the Canaanite religion are alive and well today and just as infectious among God's people as in the Israel of Hosea's day. And Hosea's message is still as devastatingly relevant. Those whose false teaching or failure to teach the truth encourages Christians to indulge in ways of life that are ethically disobedient and displeasing to God must bear the greater guilt before God for the absence of the knowledge of God and the corresponding presence of so many moral and spiritual evils.

KNOWLEDGE OF GOD RESTORED THROUGH REPENTANCE

The root of Israel's problem, then, was that they had lost the knowledge of God, as saviour, as husband, as father—for all the reasons and in all the ways outlined above. Their only hope lay in recovering that knowledge, in coming back to the God they should have known, in being restored to the relationship they had so grievously betrayed. As God called on Hosea to rebuild the relationship with Gomer, so God intended to rebuild his relationship with his people, as a bridegroom wooing his bride once more. But before that happy restoration could be consummated, Israel had hard lessons to learn about what true repentance really meant. What was involved in returning to God and his love? Once again we need to look at some passages in the body of Hosea's prophecy before returning to the great message based on his marriage in Hosea 2.

The repentance that God wants. At first sight Hosea 6:1–3 sounds very promising—exactly what we longed to hear. Hosea is quoting what the people are saying, and it sounds like they want to come back to knowing God, in just the way Hosea has been saying they have failed.

> Come, let us return to the LORD.
> > for it is he who has torn, and he will heal us;
> > he has struck down, and he will bind us up.

> After two days he will REVIVE us;
>> on the third day he will raise us up,
>> that we may live before him.
> *Let us know, let us press on to know the* LORD;
>> his appearing is as sure as the dawn
> he will come to us like the showers,
>> like the spring rains that water the earth. (Hos 6:1–3 NRSV)

What the people say here clearly follows on from the concluding verses of chapter 5. There God had accused both the northern and southern kingdoms, Ephraim (meaning the northern kingdom of Israel) and Judah, of turning to Assyria for help. They had become aware of their social, moral and spiritual sickness, but they were turning to the wrong doctor. So God threatens to tear them to pieces until they return to him, admit their guilt, and seek his face. The language of 6:1–3 echoes this—mostly. Surely now at last they are singing the right tune?

Not yet, says God. To our surprise, God seems to dismiss these words of apparent repentance as shallow and fickle.[3]

> What shall I do with you, O Ephraim?
>> What shall I do with you, O Judah?
> Your love is like a morning cloud,
>> like the dew that goes away early. (Hos 6:4 NRSV)

The Israelites thought God would come back like refreshing rain. God ironically says that Israel's words of repentance are like mist and dew in the morning—very nice while they last but gone as soon as the day warms up. What is missing? Two things: specific confession of guilt and awareness of the need for forgiveness, on the one hand; and radical ethical change, on the other.

(1) Confession of guilt. The one thing that is lacking from the fine words in Hosea 6:1–3 is what God required in Hosea 5:15—'until they admit their

---

[3]The view of the majority of commentators is that Hosea 6:1–3 must be read, in the light of the immediately following verses, as an inadequate litany of repentance. Francis I. Andersen and David Noel Freedman, however, accept it at face value as a sincere expression of repentance. But this necessitates removing it from its present context between Hosea 5:15 and Hosea 6:4, and seeing it as a later response of the people: '5:12–15 and 6:4–6 together come before 6:1–3 logically, and in time' (Francis I. Andersen and David Noel Freedman, *Hosea: A New Translation with Introduction and Commentary*, Anchor Bible [New York: Doubleday, 1980], 426). But if one retains the present order of the text it is hard to avoid the impression that Hosea 6:4 is an implied rejection of the sincerity and efficacy of Hosea 6:1–3.

guilt'. There is no admission of guilt, no acknowledgement of specific wrongdoing in Hosea 6:1–3. Rather, it is simply assumed that God will restore the people and they will know him again—without dealing with the causes of the alienation.

Yet none of this (Hos 6:1–3) is enough. The crucial requirement of 'admitting their guilt' (Hos 5:15) has been omitted. They have faced their woundedness (Hos 6:2; cf. Hos 5:12–13) but not their waywardness. Healing is sought, even resurrection, but no specific sin is mentioned. This absence of repentance and failure to confess sins by name contrasts sharply with Hosea's closing song of penitence (Hos 14:1–3).[4]

There, in Hosea 14:1–3, Hosea frames words of repentance that explicitly acknowledge the guilt and sin of idolatry. And furthermore, he asks the people not only to repent of it, but to renounce it altogether; to stop idolizing military muscle (a very modern idolatry still) by recognizing that such 'gods' can never be stronger than the human hands that made them.

> Return, Israel, to the LORD your God.
>> Your sins have been your downfall!
> Take words with you
>> and return to the LORD.
> Say to him:
>> 'Forgive all our sins
> and receive us graciously,
>> that we may offer the fruit of our lips.
> Assyria cannot save us;
>> we will not mount war-horses.
> We will never again say "Our gods"
>> to what our own hands have made,
>> for in you the fatherless find compassion.' (Hos 14:1–3)

The repentance that God seeks, then, is one which clearly recognizes sin and renounces it, and on that basis asks for forgiveness. Anything else fails to grapple with the roots of our predicament. But when repentance meets God's criteria, then his response is immediate:

---

[4]David Allan Hubbard, *Hosea*, Tyndale Old Testament Commentaries (Downers Grove, IL: Inter-Varsity, 1989), 125.

I will heal their waywardness
 and love them freely,
  for my anger has turned away from them. (Hos 14:4)

(2) Radical ethical change. Ironically, the Israelites rejected Hosea's accusation that they no longer knew God. On the contrary, they protested, they were the people who *did* know God! Wasn't that what distinguished Israel from the surrounding nations? It should have been, but what Israel had forgotten was that to know God meant to walk in his ways. It meant reflecting his character. It meant an ethical commitment to do good. So Hosea starkly contrasts their claim and their practice—and depicts the inevitable judgement that such discrepancy would bring upon them.

Israel cries to me,
 'My God, *we—Israel—know you!'*
Israel has spurned the good;
 the enemy shall pursue him. (Hos 8:2–3 NRSV)

To claim to know God and simultaneously to reject the *good* is a blatant contradiction—verbal and existential. There is no knowledge of God without ethical commitment.

Furthermore, Hosea makes it crystal clear that such ethically transformative knowledge of God is far more important to God than any religious ritual—including even sacrifices that God himself had instituted. Hosea 6:6 is justly famous as a succinct summary of the priorities of God himself.

For I desire steadfast love and not sacrifice,
 the knowledge of God rather than burnt offerings. (Hos 6:6 NRSV)

Almost certainly there is an echo here of the ancient words of Samuel to disobedient Saul.

Does the Lord delight in burnt offerings and sacrifices
 as much as in obeying the Lord?
To obey is better than sacrifice,
 and to heed is better than the fat of rams. (1 Sam 15:22)

And they are quoted in turn, twice and with emphatic approval, by Jesus in his critique of his own contemporaries for their religious zeal that was heedless of the ethical priorities of God himself (Mt 9:13; 12:7).

Not surprisingly, then, as we read on in Hosea, this demand for radical ethical change—as definitive of what it means to know God through repentance—comes again and again. Two examples suffice:

> Sow righteousness for yourselves,
>> reap the fruit of unfailing love,
> and break up your unploughed ground;
>> for it is time to seek the LORD,
> until he comes
>> and showers his righteousness on you. (Hos 10:12)

> But you must return to your God;
>> maintain love and justice,
>> and wait for your God always. (Hos 12:6)

Notice the key ethical words, so typical not only of Hosea, but of the ethical teaching of the whole Old Testament: righteousness, faithfulness (*hesed*, 'unfailing love' or 'mercy'), love and justice. These are the qualities of life that God requires of those who would claim to know him, as we saw in our reflections on Jeremiah 9:23–24. And these will be the gift of God, the bridegroom, to his bride in the restored marriage to which we will turn in a moment.

But to conclude this section, Hosea reminds us that fine words are not enough. God seeks specific repentance over named sins, based on clear-eyed recognition and wholehearted renunciation of them. We have not begun to know God without that first step on the journey. And God makes clear that his priority is ethics over religion. Even those elements of religious practice that have biblical foundations are no substitute for practical obedience. And such biblical obedience is never merely a matter of private piety, but a commitment to social justice and compassion that mirrors the biblically revealed character of God.

We cannot claim to know God while colluding in injustice, cruelty and the idolizing of money, sex and power. By these standards, what might Hosea have to say to the deeply compromised Christianity of the western world?

The restoration that God promises. So, finally, we turn back to that marriage of Hosea and the profound message of love, betrayal and restoration that it embodied. In a sense Hosea 1–3 anticipates and summarizes the message of the rest of the book, and that is why we needed to explore some of the relevant sections from the later chapters before coming back to hear again the words of ultimate promise that are contained in Hosea 2.

And what wonderful words they are.

Take a moment to read again Hosea 2:2–13. It is a searing indictment of Israel, portrayed as an unfaithful, ungrateful and forgetful wife. The imagery is of divorce (v. 2), shame (v. 3), rejection (v. 4), promiscuity (v. 5), ingratitude (v. 8) and punishment (vv. 10–13).

'Therefore,' begins Hosea 2:14. Therefore what? Surely all prophetic precedent would lead us to expect a word of deserved judgement—the sentence ('guilty'), and the verdict ('destruction'). But the eyes of the prophet scan far beyond that inevitability. The reality of God's judgement on Israel lay in the immediate future and would be fulfilled in Hosea's own lifetime. But God's purposes in and through Israel went far beyond the present sinful generation. Accordingly, the prophet's vision sees far beyond the coming judgement to a future filled with hope, restoration and blessing. And to capture it for our imagination, he continues with the rich metaphor of love and marriage.

> Therefore, I will now allure her,
> > and bring her into the wilderness,
> > and speak tenderly to her.
> From there I will give her her vineyards,
> > and make the Valley of Achor a door of hope.
> There she shall respond as in the days of her youth,
> > as at the time when she came out of the land of Egypt.

On that day, says the LORD, you will call me, 'My husband,' and no longer will you call me, 'My Baal'. For I will remove the names of the Baals from her mouth, and they shall be mentioned by name no more. I will make for you a covenant on that day with the wild animals, the birds of the air, and the creeping things of the ground; and I will abolish the bow, the sword, and war from the land; and I will make you lie down in safety. And I will take you for my wife for ever; I will take you for my wife in righteousness and in justice, in steadfast love, and in mercy. I will take you for my wife in faithfulness; and you shall know the LORD. (Hos 2:14–20 NRSV)

We cannot dwell on each of the kaleidoscope images in this sparkling passage, but merely spin through them. It starts with the wooing, or alluring, by the heavenly suitor, longing to win back the love of his estranged wife. It moves on through a replay of the exodus, wilderness and conquest story, portrayed as a second honeymoon. It graphically insists on the daring sexual imagery of Yahweh as husband and Israel as wife, and uses that to exclude not only the blight of Israel's promiscuous attraction to the sexually degraded Baal worship, but even the names of the Baals themselves. It lifts our imagination even further with a vision of ecological renewal and international peace. Finally it invites us to witness the betrothal party, at which in Israelite custom gifts would be offered to the family of the bride. What gifts will the bridegroom bring to this marriage? Nothing less than the precious treasure of his own divine character, the five-fold list that summarizes the covenant identity of Yahweh himself: righteousness and justice, committed love and compassion, and trustworthiness. And these things will seal the marriage eternally.

But if these are the gifts that God brings to the marriage, what is expected of the bride? Nothing other than the same qualities reflected in her own life and relationships. The strongly ethical nature of God's character is the source of the ethical core of covenant relationship between God and his people.

And once again, we find that this is precisely what is meant by knowing God. For the climax of the whole scene is the final phrase of Hosea 2:20, '*and you shall know the Lord*'. Everything else in the whole dynamic sequence, from wooing to wedding, is for that purpose and is summed up in that experience.

The climactic position of this phrase in Hosea 2:20 mirrors the equally climactic position of the end of Hosea 2:13 (which in turn echoes Hos 2:8). The whole sequence of Israel's fickleness and failure could be summed up in two words in Hebrew: '*Me she forgot.*' Israel's covenant-breaking betrayal of Yahweh, their moral, social, political and spiritual breakdown, could all be attributed to this profound accusation—they had forgotten Yahweh. Now we have seen already that to say Israel 'did not know Yahweh' does not imply they had lost all awareness of God by that name. So also, to say that Israel had 'forgotten Yahweh' did not mean that they suffered collective amnesia about the name itself. To forget someone is relational, not just cognitive. If one person says of another, 'You've forgotten me,' it means that the other person has lost any sense of commitment or obligation; the

shared history no longer means anything; the love has died; the relationship holds no further personal investment. So it was between Israel and
God, in Hosea's accusation.

From that devastating word at the end of Hosea 2:13, then, to the ex-
hilarating promise in Hosea 2:20, we have leapt a mighty chasm, spanned
only by the breathtaking love and grace of God. We have been transported
from betrayal, adultery and marital breakdown (as Hosea's metaphor for
Israel's sin, in which is mirrored our own), to covenant intimacy, ethical
integrity and eternal security.

CONCLUSION

Of course, we understand that Hosea is describing a future that lies as yet
beyond us—in its ultimate fulfilment. His language and concepts here were
further developed by Jeremiah, who called the restoration of Israel what it
truly would be—a new covenant (Jer 31:31–34). The New Testament
teaches us that we already have the inauguration of this new covenant in
the crucified and risen Christ, and the bride of Christ awaits the bridegroom's return to consummate the relationship in the kind of perfection
that Hosea and other prophets glimpsed and stammered to express.

But although these are future realities to which we look forward with
eager anticipation, they are vitally relevant to how we live now. For we are
called to know God here and now. And in this chapter we have explored
Hosea's profound insights into what that means. God longs to be known
by us, as saviour, as father, as husband. We run terrible risks of forfeiting
the knowledge of God when we refuse to recognize his gifts, fail to live by
his standards, and neglect the teaching of his words and ways. But God in
his relentlessly persistent love longs to bring us to true repentance and
joyful restoration. There is, Hosea would say, a sweetness greater than even
the most loving human marriage when we return to the love that sought
us and bought us, woos us and wins us.

CHAPTER EIGHT

KNOWING GOD *in* EXPECTATION *of* HIS VICTORY

Of all the places you might think of looking for teaching on Gog and Magog, a book on 'Knowing God' is probably not one of them. They feature in plenty of 'end-times' potboilers—books purporting to give us a 'prophetic' timetable for the end of the world as we know it, in Armageddon almanacs, and the like. But what have Gog and Magog got to do with knowing God? It may come as a surprise to hear that when you study the text of Ezekiel 38–39 carefully, knowing God is the emphatic and repeated point of the whole prophecy. Not that you'd have guessed that from the way they are used (and abused) in much popular futuristic scaremongering.[1]

In our survey of biblical texts so far in this book we have observed that knowing God can indeed be an intensely personal experience—through prayer, for example, and certainly through repentance. But we have also seen that God is known in action—both his action and our own. We know God through the great things he has done and continues to do, and we know him by responding in practical imitation of his commitment to compassion and justice. In this chapter we move to a more future-orientated knowing of God.

One of the great phrases of Ezekiel is in the future tense: 'Then you will know' or 'then they will know' usually followed by 'that I am the LORD', or

---

[1] I have tried to provide a more balanced survey of these chapters in *The Message of Ezekiel*, The Bible Speaks Today (Downers Grove, IL: InterVarsity, 2001).

some other truth about who God is or what he has done. This phrase occurs more than eighty times in his book, so much so that it is like a kind of signature tune. Ezekiel is consumed by a passionate desire that people should come to know God for who God really is. Or to be more accurate, God is the one who passionately wills to be known—by his people and by the entire world—and Ezekiel is his mouthpiece. If any book of the Bible could be subtitled *Knowing God*, it would be the book of Ezekiel.

We could dip into it almost anywhere and find relevant texts for our theme in this book, but I have chosen the two chapters about Gog and Magog, Ezekiel 38–39, not only because they are so much misused and misunderstood, but also because they make crucial statements about the knowledge of God in relation to God's future victory over his enemies and protection of his people, and these need to be brought into close connection with New Testament teaching on those same themes. We need to know the God whom, according to these chapters, all nations will one day come to know in a shattering encounter with his reality. Before reading the chapters fully, take a moment to read the following key verses within them, so that you can see how prominent this theme is as a thread running through both chapters and bringing them to a grand climax: Ezekiel 38:16, 23; 39:6–7, 21–23, 27–29.

GOG AND MAGOG—THE MOVIE

The story in double outline. It would help to pause and read through Ezekiel 38–39 at this point, but just before you do, it is worth knowing in advance that each chapter is like a panel on which the same story is told, with slight variations and additions of detail. Basically, we have one story told twice over, rather like a cartoon movie. I use the word 'cartoon' because the language, imagery and pictures that are brought before the eyes of our imagination in these chapters are deliberately grotesque and horrific. There is a 'monster' quality about the whole scenario, and we need to take this form of writing into account before we attempt to interpret these chapters with wooden literalism.

The story can be fairly simply told.

Some mysterious character by the name of Gog, from the land of Magog, chief prince of Meshech and Tubal, will lead an alliance of other nations from the north to attack Israel. At the time (which is in some unspecified future) Israel will be living peacefully in her own land, without any military defences, and all unsuspecting of the plot being hatched against her. However, behind the scenes it is actually Yahweh who will be controlling events so that this hostile alliance of nations, far from carrying off plunder as they expected, will be massively defeated and slain by Yahweh himself, with accompanying cosmic phenomena (earthquake, plague, blood, fire, hail and brimstone). These enemy armies will be so big that, after their climactic defeat and destruction, it will take Israel seven months to bury the dead, during which time the scavenging birds and beasts will eat their fill. And the captured weapons of war will be so many that they will provide firewood for seven years. The end result will be that both Israel and all the nations will know conclusively that Yahweh is God and that the historical events of exile and restoration were all his doing. Thus, Yahweh's greatness, holiness and glory will finally be revealed and fully vindicated in the whole earth and to all nations—including his enemies.

A closer look. With that synopsis in mind, we can discern seven sections in the double account of the visionary attack and defeat. A brief run through these paragraphs will add some local (and rather lurid) colour to the outlines.

(1) Ezekiel 38:3–9. A grand alliance of 'many nations' musters to attack and invade the people of God. But already God's sovereignty can be seen at work behind all the human planning: 'I will turn you around . . . and bring you out' (Ezek 38:4). God is in charge even as implacable enemies plot their evil. The reader is given the hint that we are talking about some unspecified future, 'after many days . . . in future years' (Ezek 38:8), not a tight historical prediction.

(2) Ezekiel 38:10–13. The diabolical evil of Gog's intentions is now made clear. This is not a normal war between equally armed enemies, but a devastating attack upon 'a peaceful and unsuspecting people—all of them living without walls and without gates and bars' (Ezek 38:11) (i.e. a de-militarized community). This was certainly not the condition of the kingdoms of Israel and Judah before the exile, with their fortified cities and armies. Nor, thanks to Nehemiah, was it the condition of Judah after the exile. And equally certainly it could not by any stretch of imagination describe the modern state of Israel today, which is so often unhesitatingly read into this chapter by commentators convinced that these chapters describe some future attack on that country.

(3) Ezekiel 38:14–16. The invaders arrive in overwhelming numbers and force. But, just as previous prophets had said about previous invaders, the one who leads them is none other than Yahweh himself. But whereas in the past the purpose of God bringing enemies against Israel was to punish the Israelites, on this occasion it will be to destroy the enemies themselves, 'so that the nations may know me when I show myself holy through you before their eyes' (Ezek 38:16). As with Pharaoh (Ex 9:16), and Cyrus (Is 45:5–6), God supervises human plans and actions in such a way that in the end it is God's own name and glory that are made known in the world.

(4) Ezekiel 38:17–23. The first main panel of the narrative in Ezekiel 38 closes with the good news for Israel that Yahweh himself will intervene to defend his otherwise defenceless people. Gog and all his hordes will meet more than their match when they face the 'hot anger' of Yahweh. Not only is the future attack and defeat of Gog and his forces entirely under God's *control*, it was also within God's prophetic *foresight*. God's defenceless people may be taken by surprise, but God himself would not be. The fact that he warns his people of this impending attack means that, even if they may not know when it will actually happen, God himself has it covered.

The highly symbolic language that Ezekiel uses to describe how Yahweh will destroy these enemies of his people in Ezekiel 38:19–22 shows that we are not reading an account of history in advance, but a rhetorical vision of God in action. So there will be earthquake, environmental disaster, mountains trembling and crumbling, sword, plague, bloodshed, hail, fire and brimstone. A list like this immediately brings up memories of the flood, Sodom and Gomorrah, and the plagues of Egypt. We are being assured that, in every way possible, God will defeat and destroy his enemies. And the effect, we are reminded once again, will be the universal extension of the knowledge of God (Ezek 38:23).

(5) Ezekiel 39:1–16. As we begin Ezekiel 39, we are taken back to the beginning of the story, and we are reminded that everything is being choreographed by God himself. We are not told how Yahweh will disarm and defeat this enemy—but it is his direct action alone. This is not some great battle with the armies of Israel—they have none. Ezekiel uses seven different words for all the captured armour and weapons, says that this will keep Israel in firewood for seven years, and that the slaughter will be so great that it will take seven months to bury the dead. This triple use of

seven is also symbolic and helps us see that this is not a literal expectation but a figurative assurance of the climactic defeat of God's enemies.

(6) *Ezekiel 39:17–20*. Ezekiel knew how to shock his listeners and readers. Here he creates a grotesque mental picture with graphic detail, like some wild cartoon. Even if all the corpses of the defeated enemy were to be buried, the length of time it would take would give ample freedom to the scavenging birds and animals. Such is always the horrible reality of war in any age. But Ezekiel imagines these animals actually being invited as if to a sacrificial banquet. When we confront such a grisly image we must first of all recognize that this is deliberately exaggerated and caricatured language, not a literal prediction. And then second, we must be aware that such horrifying imagery conveys a horrifying reality: those who utterly and implacably remain enemies of God and his people, without repentance, will ultimately face utter destruction. Jesus's images of worms and smouldering fire may be more familiar, but are no less devastating in their effect. Knowing God is a serious matter.

(7) *Ezekiel 39:21–29*. With the armies of Gog comprehensively defeated, devoured and buried, there is nothing more to say about them. They disappear from the story as suddenly as they had entered it. But the learning goes on. And in this final section the theme of knowing God comes to a double climax. We are told what the nations will learn, and what Israel, as God's people will learn—and indeed what they need to learn even now before these things come to pass. We shall return to these lessons shortly.

Who or what is Gog? But first it is probably worth giving just some thought to the question that immediately arises in people's mind at this point—who or what is this mysterious 'Gog of the land of Magog'? Here is an extract from some comments I made on this in the Bible Speaks Today *Message of Ezekiel*.

> The honest answer is that nobody really knows, but not for want of trying. Certainly, there is no such person known within the rest of Old Testament history . . . Probably Daniel 11:40–45 has been influenced by the story of Gog . . . Early Christian eschatology also made use of Ezekiel's imagery to portray the great conflict between the forces of evil, both human and satanic, and the reign of God and Christ. Revelation 19:11–20:15 envisages a mighty attack by the massed forces of evil, led by Satan, but including 'Gog and Magog' (20:8), which is comprehensively defeated.[2]

---

[2] Wright, *Message of Ezekiel*, 324.

As the centuries of the Christian era passed, different generations have identified Gog with whatever fearsome foe of the day seemed to fit, or needed to be placed under the comforting prospect of God's terrible destruction. Augustine, for example, saw Gog in the faces of the terrible onslaughts of the Goths upon the Roman Empire, which seemed to signal the end of Christian civilization as then known. Luther identified Gog and Magog with the dreaded Turks of his day (with some geographical correspondence at least in his favour). In the twentieth century, a popular and influential brand of Christian fundamentalism confidently identified Gog and Magog with the communist Soviet empire. 'Rosh' (the Hebrew word meaning 'head' and translated as *chief prince* in the NIV, Ezek 38:2), was obviously Russia; *Meshech* must therefore be Moscow, and *Tubal* none other than Tobolsk.

On this flimsiest of word association (which has no etymological credibility whatever), the Christian world was warned of an impending invasion of the land of the modern state of Israel by the armies of the Soviet empire to the north, which would spark off the final great battle of Armageddon, and other events already plotted on a particular millennialist timechart. God, as well as Gog, had his marching orders. Those who were sceptical about the whole scenario were accused of not being prepared to take the Bible literally—to which a sufficient reply seemed to be that, if the foe from the north was to be literally equated with a Russian army invading modern Israel, then presumably we should expect them to be riding horses and fighting with bows and arrows. Even literalists have problems with consistency. And, we might add, literalism of this sort is not noted for its humility either. The collapse of the Soviet empire without a Russian soldier setting foot on the soil of Israel, let alone hordes of them being buried there, has not been marked by a chorus of the prophets of Armageddon-in-our-time saying, 'Thanks for all the money we made out of the books making that prediction, but actually, sorry, we seem to have got it wrong.'

My main problem with this kind of literalistic application of Ezekiel's vision to confident 'end-times' predictions is that it ends up totally distracting the consumers of the pulp-industry that produces them from the clear and intentional message that Ezekiel wanted us to hear. The primary and repeated point of the double chapter narrative is that Yahweh will be fully, finally and victoriously revealed in his true identity and in the justice of his ways. That revelation will be both to his people and to all nations on earth.

The defeat of God's enemies and the protection of God's people will lead both of them to *know God*. Not, we might add, to *know Gog*. For whoever, or whatever Gog may be, has been, or will be, his only reason for existence is that God will display his own glory through him. To spend our time in fascinated obsession speculating about the identity of Gog is to miss the whole point.

It doesn't matter who Gog is. It matters eternally who God is.

It seems tragically ironic that so many people, ancient and modern, devote endless energy trying to know who the legendary Gog might be, when the infinitely more important task is to know who the living God actually is.

Having said this, however, it seems to me, to quote once more from *The Message of Ezekiel*, that,

> we can see two levels of fulfilment. On the one hand, the symbolism speaks of an ever-present reality, namely human and satanic opposition to God and his people. History is littered with 'Gogs'—those who have thought they would eradicate the people of God. They have not triumphed so far, and this vision affirms that they never will. On the other hand, the extension and application of Ezekiel's vision by John in Revelation leads us to anticipate that the battle between God and his enemies will ultimately come to a climactic finale in which all the forces of Satan and those who have allied with him will be defeated by the power of Christ and then destroyed forever.[3] The defeat and destruction of Gog thus offers us prophetic assurance of the ultimate defeat and destruction of all that opposes God and endangers his people.[4]

So then, rather than any single identification, 'Gog' represents all those who oppose God, attack his people and seek to destroy them—of whom there have been many and doubtless many more to come. But these chapters give rock-solid assurance to God's people that God will ultimately defeat all such enemies. Here in Ezekiel, as in the book of Revelation, this is a necessary precursor to what follows. In Ezekiel 40–48 we have the

---

[3]In this double application (to continuing historical enemies of God's people, and to a climactic eschatological defeat of the ultimate enemy of God and his people), our interpretation is similar to that adopted by many in respect of the New Testament figure of 'antichrist'.

[4]Wright, *Message of Ezekiel*, 326.

picture of God once again dwelling in the midst of his people in the rebuilt temple. Such an idyllic picture needed the assurance that what had happened once would never happen again—namely an attack on God's city, people and temple. No, Ezekiel 38–39 declare in advance, that will never happen because those who would want to do that will have been eradicated. Similarly, in Revelation 21–22 we have the corresponding picture, consciously drawing from Ezekiel, of the dwelling place of God in the midst of the redeemed humanity in the new creation. And the eternal security of that state of affairs is guaranteed, because, just as Ezekiel 38–39 eliminates all that could threaten the restored Israel of God, so the preceding chapters of Revelation have described the ultimate purging of all that is satanic, wicked and anti-God from God's new creation.

> Just as the picture of comprehensive destruction of evil in Ezekiel 38–39 ushers in the prospect of Yahweh dwelling with Israel reconstituted in their land and worshipping him in the perfection of his restored sanctuary (Ezek 40–48), so the defeat of Satan in Revelation 19–20 ushers in the great vision of God dwelling with his people drawn from all nations in a new creation, worshipping the Lamb in the perfection of his presence that will need no temple (Rev 21–22).[5]

WHAT GOG AND THE NATIONS WILL KNOW

> You will advance against my people Israel like a cloud that covers the land. In days to come, Gog, I will bring you against my land, so that the nations may know me when I am proved *holy* through you before their eyes. (Ezek 38:16)

> And so I will show my *greatness* and my *holiness*, and I will make myself known in the sight of many nations. Then they will know that I am the Lord. (Ezek 38:23)

> I will display my *glory* among the nations, and all the nations will see the punishment I inflict and the hand I lay upon them. (Ezek 39:21)

The italicized words pinpoint the message for us. What the world will come to know, by one means or another, is the holiness, the greatness and the glory of Yahweh, the only living God.

---

[5]Ibid.

- *His holiness*, because he is utterly different from all other claimants to deity. He is above and beyond us and the universe, in his being, his moral character, and in his ways and actions.

- *His greatness*, because he is immeasurable and incomparable (Is 40). If the greatest things we can contemplate (the oceans, the mountains, the heavens) are tiny in comparison, how infinitely great must their Creator and sustainer be?

- *His glory*, because he is the only God with reality, substance, 'weight' (as the word literally means). His glory includes the vast fullness of the whole earth (Is 6) and yet transcends the heavens, for he has set his glory above the clouds.

Eventually the whole human race will know the truth about their Creator, in contrast to all the idolatries that we run after, which are unholy and dirty, pathetically insignificant, and futile in their emptiness. This is an awesome prospect, and yet it is also a hope-filled one. As we seek to live as the people of God in the midst of a hostile world (just as the Israel of Ezekiel's vision and indeed the Israelites of Ezekiel's ministry in exile), we are surrounded by peoples and their gods that give no allegiance to the God we know and love. In mission, we seek to engage with such people. Sometimes we find ourselves mocked by the gods of our culture: the idols of the rich and powerful in society; the symbols of affluence, arrogance and greed; the overwhelming machinery of economic and military domination; the threats and rivalry of some other faiths; the cynicism and pomposity of the media; the dazzling enticement of the prizes our society holds out for success or celebrity, etc. At times we, and the churches we serve, can feel weak, marginal, exposed, vulnerable to attack, defenceless against the powerful hostilities ranged against us. And in some parts of the world the hostility of the world against the church takes a literally violent form, and many of our sisters and brothers in Christ experience physical threats and assault, social disadvantage, immense psychological and spiritual pressures, imprisonment, torture and death. The language of Gog is not out of place in such circumstances.

But the Bible lifts up our eyes, our heads and our hearts. There will come a day, promises our Lord God, when the gods of the nations will be exposed for the empty sham that they really are, and when all the nations themselves will know who the only true and living God is, in all his holiness, greatness and glory. If this takes place within the context of searing judgement, as the narrative of the destruction of the armies of Gog and his allies portrays, it will nevertheless constitute unmistakable, undeniable and unavoidable knowledge of the living God.

Such a prospect of course gives us no joy, for it gives God no joy. This same prophet declares that God takes no pleasure in the death of the wicked, but rather that he should turn from his wickedness and live. But it does give us a perspective, an expectation and a hope. The wicked will not defy God forever. The false gods will not deceive the nations forever. As in the book of Revelation, the ultimate exposure and destruction of the enemies of God is an unavoidable corollary of the ultimate security of his people and redemption of his creation.

WHAT GOD'S PEOPLE WILL KNOW

These chapters were addressed originally to the exiles of Israel in Babylon, in the midst of precisely one of the Gogs that had tried to destroy their nation, their city, their temple and their God. So there is huge implicit encouragement in the message contained here. When Ezekiel says that Israel 'will know' something, it also implies that the learning should start here and now. We should begin now to know God in ways that anticipate the full knowledge of God that will come only when these great events reach their final fulfilment and are consigned to the old order that will forever be past.

So what was Israel to know, and what are we to know as we sit with them?

That all God's judgement was righteous.

> From that day forward the people of Israel will know that I am the LORD their God. And the nations will know that the people of Israel went into exile for their sin, because they were unfaithful to me. So I hid my face from them and handed them over to their enemies, and they all fell by the sword. I dealt with them according to their uncleanness and their offenses, and I hid my face from them. (Ezek 39:22–24)

Israel (and the nations) will come to know that there was nothing undeserved, unfair or excessive in what God had done. It was a key element of Israel's faith from the beginning that Yahweh the God of Israel was in his own self and character the definitive standard of justice. 'Will not the

Judge of all the earth do right?' asks Abraham (Gen 18:25). But Israel had often complained that it did not seem so, and Ezekiel particularly wrestled with people who were obsessed with that perverse perception of the ways of God. Nevertheless the day will come, Ezekiel insists through the graphic message of these two chapters, when everybody will know (whether part of God's covenant people or not) that God's punitive actions were utterly appropriate. He simply could not allow sin to go unpunished forever. He could no longer let his name be treated as 'profane'. He had acted out of the perfect justice of his own character.

Such knowledge of God, while it will be perfected in the future, ought to grasp us here and now in our consciousness. Yes, we know that in Christ we are spared the condemnation we deserve (Rom 8). Such is the glorious good news of the gospel. But let us always have in mind, with perennial gratitude, that it is only by the grace of God that we stand upright in that knowledge. Only because of the blood of Christ will it be true that the judgement that will ultimately fall on those who remain unrepentant enemies of God in their persistent wickedness will not fall on us.

That God's restoring grace is personal and unbelievably generous.

> Then they will know that I am the LORD their God, for though I sent them into exile among the nations, I will gather them to their own land, not leaving any behind. I will no longer hide my face from them, for I will pour out my Spirit on the house of Israel, declares the Sovereign LORD.
>
> (Ezek 39:28–29)

These words were spoken to people who had experienced precisely the opposite in their own history. They had known God turning his face away in grief and anger at their sin (Ezek 39:23). But now they will know the restoration of Aaronic blessing—God's face turned toward them in personal grace. The frown of judgement is replaced by the smile of love. They had known God pouring out his anger (Ezek 7:8; 9:8; 20:8, etc.), but now they will know the pouring out of his Spirit.

CONCLUSION

'Consider therefore the kindness and sternness of God,' says Paul in Romans 11:22. This chapter has opened our eyes to both. They go inseparably together. For the grace and kindness with which God will protect his people is an intrinsic part of the severity with which he will oppose and defeat all who seek to destroy them. Knowing God must therefore take the fullest account of the scope of these searing chapters—for that is their express purpose: 'then they will know'. The challenge to us is to ensure that we ourselves know God in his saving grace, and that we urgently seek to bring others to know him, others who as yet are strangers to his covenant mercy and in danger of being counted finally among his enemies.

CHAPTER NINE

KNOWING GOD THROUGH TRUSTING *in* HIS SOVEREIGNTY

I first preached a sermon on Psalm 46, combined with Habakkuk, on Wednesday 16 January 1991, at the weekly worship service at All Nations Christian College. That was the day the coalition forces, led by the USA, invaded Iraq in defence of Kuwait in the first Gulf War against Saddam Hussein. It was a harder message to prepare than any I had preached for a long time. There was a palpable fear among many people that this conflict could lead to a Third World War if Israel and then Russia were drawn into it. I shared that fear, but I remember many other mixed emotions as well, that I recorded in my notes.

I felt angry at the human madness that, on the western side of the Red Sea millions of poverty stricken people in Ethiopia were facing starvation, while on the eastern side of it, billions of dollars were feeding the machinery of war.

I felt confusion and despair at why this war was deemed necessary, what the real motivation for it was, why we had to be involved in it—and sick of the moral hypocrisy that surrounded it.

I felt some biblical déjà vu, seeing maps on the TV news bulletins that you normally associate only with the pages at the back of your Bible, maps which were now the scene of a modern replay of some biblical stories. There on the TV was what we call 'Mesopotamia', or in biblical scholarship, 'the Ancient

Near East'. It was the land of the tower of Babel, of Ur of the Chaldees and Abraham's migration. It was the land of Nineveh and Jonah, of Nebuchadnezzar and Babylon. And it was where the Bible locates the Garden of Eden. How short is human history! How small is human geography!

Most of all, as the father of two sons who were seventeen and eighteen at the time—the same age as some who would be fighting in yet another war—I felt the horror of yet more shattered families with grieving mothers, wives, orphans.

But what could I preach? What *can* you preach in the face of the brutal realities of war?

At All Nations in 1991, I was preaching to people who were training for cross-cultural mission. Single men and women, married folk with families, all heading into difficult situations, some into parts of the world that are endemically wracked with conflict and war. I have visited some of them in such locations since then, in Afghanistan for example, and most recently in Chad, where I preached from Psalm 46 and Habakkuk yet again, to people living in daily preparedness for an escalation of the internecine war in that land.

Psalm 46 and the prophecy of Habakkuk speak powerfully into times of war and international chaos—precisely because they speak from within such realities. Psalm 46 comes from some unspecified time of national emergency, when it seemed that the earth itself was dissolving in the maelstrom of violence and confusion being unleashed around the people of God.

What sort of song was a hymn-writer supposed to produce in the midst of such extreme danger?

Habakkuk lived in the dark days that preceded the Babylonian invasion, which brought about the destruction of Jerusalem and the exile of the people. The horror of anticipating those events was very real, since nobody in those days had any illusions about the mind-numbing brutality of what happened when cities were besieged and finally captured, when whole populations were decimated and enslaved.

What was a prophet supposed to think and preach in such days?

And we live now in a world that seems to become more dangerous and terrifying by the week. At the time of first writing this, more than a thousand people a month were being slaughtered in Iraq, and Lebanon was in ruins. At the time of revising it for this trilogy, millions have fled from the heartlands of ISIS, thousands have perished in the sea trying to find refuge in Europe, and Syria is in ruins. Britain and France, the two countries whose colonial ambitions and rivalries carved up the Middle East between them a hundred years ago, treacherously making and breaking promises to Arabs and Jews alike, have both felt the rebound of historical injustice in the slaughter of innocents on the streets. Nobody is counting the numbers killed in less publicized conflicts in some parts of Africa. The so-called 'War on Terror' terrifies us all, while violence often seems only just below the surface of some of the most sophisticated European cities, with its roots in ethnic and religious divisions and the fruit of ancient colonial injustices and contemporary economic inequalities.

What is a preacher supposed to hear from God's Word and declare through the spoken or written word for such a time?

And what does it mean to know God in such times? Both Psalm 46 and Habakkuk speak about knowing God. In fact the following two texts seemed essential to include in any book about the knowledge of God, and also seemed to fit together well as the foundation for this final chapter.

> Be still, and know that I am God;
>> I will be exalted among the nations,
>> I will be exalted in the earth. (Ps 46:10)

> For the earth will be filled with the knowledge of the glory of the LORD,
>> as the waters cover the sea. (Hab 2:14)

The psalmist and the prophet help us to remind ourselves of some of the central truths about our God, so that in knowing them (and knowing him), we may put our trust in God even in the extreme turbulence that surrounds us. And then, as we exercise that trust and grow in that knowledge, how are we to go on living? Let us then remember the God we know, and then choose to live as those who know God.

TRUSTING THE GOD WE KNOW

Bringing Psalm 46 and Habakkuk together, here are four things that they urge us to know:

- that God remains in control of the world;
- that God will act in just judgement within history;

- that God will defend his own people;

- and that God will finally be universally exalted.

God remains in control of the world. The lesson that Ezekiel taught us in the last chapter was well known to the song-writers of Israel. The world is not run by its human rulers, but by the living God. He is the God of all creation and equally Lord of all history. The psalmist looks at the earth, the sea and the mountains, and imagines all of them in turbulence—roaring, quaking, surging (Ps 46:2–3). But if you know who created them, you need not live in fear of even such frightening phenomena. He then extends the metaphor to the world of nations, similarly in turmoil. But if you know who is actually in charge, then behind all the human plotting and scheming, you are invited to see the hand of the Lord at work.

> Nations are in uproar, kingdoms fall;
>> *he* lifts his voice, the earth melts.
> The LORD Almighty is with us;
>> the God of Jacob is our fortress.
> Come and see *what the LORD has done*,
>> the desolations *he* has brought on the earth. (Ps 46:6–8)

Habakkuk was baffled and frightened by the national and international events of his day. His own nation seemed a chaotic mess of violence, conflict, breakdown of law and order, and absence of justice. He puts this problem to God in Habakkuk 1:2–4. And he gets an answer that seems even more puzzling. To solve the problem of his own sinful people, God is raising up a larger, and apparently even more sinful, nation to act as the agent of his judgement upon them—the Babylonians. This is not just an accident of history. It is the deliberate work of God.

> Look at the nations and watch—
>> and be utterly amazed.
> For *I am going to do something* in your days
>> that you would not believe,
>> even if you were told.
> *I am raising up* the Babylonians,
>> that ruthless and impetuous people,
> who sweep across the whole earth
>> to seize dwelling places not their own. (Hab 1:5–6)

This was not a new message of course. Isaiah had said the same thing a century before about the Assyrians, whom God had lifted up like a stick to beat Israel with (Is 7:18–20; 10:5–19). But it is not a message that is easy to hear and believe in the present. Looking back, we can easily talk with all the wisdom of theological hindsight about how God has been sovereign over the march of history. But when the world is falling apart around you, it is not such an obvious stance to adopt or truth to believe. And yet that is when it is even more vital that we *do* remember this truth.

When the axe actually did fall and Nebuchadnezzar finally attacked and destroyed Jerusalem and carried the bulk of the population of Judah off into two generations of demeaning exile, Jeremiah wrote a letter to the exiles in which he helped them to see things from this perspective.

At the human level, they were the people whom 'Nebuchadnezzar had carried into exile from Jerusalem to Babylon' (Jer 29:1). That is what you would have seen, with human eyes, at the ground level of human history: an invasion; a siege; suffering and death; defeat; capture; exile. And who was responsible? Nebuchadnezzar and his armies. But at the level of prophetic insight there was another hand involved. Jeremiah's letter begins with that higher perspective:

> This is what the LORD Almighty, the God of Israel, says to all those *I carried into exile* from Jerusalem to Babylon. (Jer 29:4)

For, as God had already told them years before, when Jeremiah had broken into an international Middle East diplomatic conference being held in Jerusalem, Nebuchadnezzar was merely a tool in the hands of the sovereign God of Israel.

> Give them a message for their masters and say, 'This is what the LORD Almighty, the God of Israel, says: "Tell this to your masters: with my great power and outstretched arm I made the earth and its people and the animals that are on it, and I give it to anyone I please. Now I will give all your countries into the hands of *my servant Nebuchadnezzar* king of Babylon; I will make even the wild animals subject to him. All nations will serve him and his son and his grandson until the time for his land comes; then many nations and great kings will subjugate him."' (Jer 27:4–7)

God remained in control right through the darkest days of Israel's Old Testament history. In fact, the surprising thing is that the Israelites held on to this affirmation when everything seemed to deny it. From a Babylonian perspective the matter was much simpler: the gods of Babylon had defeated the god of Israel. Yahweh was no better or stronger than the other gods of the pathetic little nations that had been trampled by the armies of the new empire. But Israel's faith was at its most amazing when, in such times, the worst and weakest times, they could still affirm, 'Our God reigns'. The language of Psalm 47 already flavours the confidence of Psalm 46. The assurance that Habakkuk draws from his knowledge of God's sovereignty in Israel's past sustains his hope in the fearful prospect of the present and future (Hab 3).

Knowing God, then, means knowing the God who is in charge of current affairs—and trusting him when the world goes mad.

God works out his judgement in history. When wars happen the issue of justice is invariably raised. Does either party in the conflict have 'right on its side'? If a country is attacked, is it justified in fighting back to defend itself? If one country attacks another, is a third country justified in intervening to defend the weaker country against the attacker? For many centuries, Christians have sought to define a 'just war' ethic, setting out strict criteria (which are almost impossible to satisfy in most conflicts, especially as the momentum and brutality of war gather pace), by which a war might be deemed just, so that those waging it may salvage some sense of their actions in the war being 'justified'. These are issues that Christians rightly struggle with and there are agonies of conscience down whatever road is followed.

From a biblical perspective, we have to affirm that human justice ultimately depends upon and flows from the justice of God. So any justice that is claimed by or for a country engaged in warfare can only be evaluated, from a Christian point of view, in relation to the judgement or justice of God within history. But that too is a far from easy task. There is no doubt, biblically, that God 'reserves the right', so to speak, to use any nation as the agent of his judgement or justice on any other nation. That is what he did in using the Israelites in judgement on the wickedness of the Canaanites in the generation of the conquest. And it is what he did many more times in judgement on the Israelites through successive generations in which they suffered divine wrath at the hands of their enemies. So the principle is established in the Old Testament. God can use one nation as an agent of justice against another.[1]

---

[1] For a much fuller discussion of the Old Testament's theology of God and the nations—in history and the future, see Christopher J. H. Wright, *The Mission of God*, ch. 14. (Downers Grove, IL: InterVarsity, 2006).

But that doesn't make it any easier to accept, Habakkuk must have thought. Habakkuk had complained to God about the injustice that was going on in his own society (Hab 1:1–4). How much longer could God put up with it and not act? God's answer shocked him (though actually, in the light of all Israel's history to this point, it shouldn't have). God was raising up the Babylonians as the agent of his judgement upon Israel, precisely because of the wickedness Habakkuk was pointing out (Hab 1:5–11).

But how could that be fair? Surely that was even worse! Could God punish the wicked who were his own people by means of even more wicked people who were not?

> Your eyes are too pure to look on evil;
>> you cannot tolerate wrongdoing.
> Why then do you tolerate the treacherous?
>> Why are you silent while the wicked
>> swallow up those more righteous than themselves? (Hab 1:13)

But, yes, that was exactly what God was about to do—but it was not by any means the end of the story. Babylon's time would come.

The utterly crucial point to grasp here is that, just because God uses one nation as the agent of his judgement on another does not make that first nation more righteous than the latter. God does not rule the world by the conventions of Hollywood, nor is he restricted to using only the 'good guys' to accomplish his purposes. And this applied just as much to Israel as anybody else, as Deuteronomy 9 had made devastatingly clear.

Before the conquest of Canaan, God warned Israel not to fall into a simplistic, binary, logic: 'The defeat of our enemies is the result of their wickedness and our righteousness. So God is on our side against them.' 'Not so, says God; not remotely so' (see Deut 9:4–6). Israel was right about the wickedness of the Canaanites, for which God would indeed drive them out. But they were utterly wrong about their own righteousness. For, as the list of Israel's rebellions showed, if anybody deserved to be destroyed it was the Israelites themselves. They had only the grace of God and the intercession of Moses to thank that it had not happened long ago. So God could use wicked, judgement-deserving Israelites as the agent of his judgement on Canaan. He could just as consistently use wicked, judgement-deserving Babylonians as the agent of his judgement on Israel. The outworking of

God's justice in history is not a matter of siding with the good guys against the bad guys, because the reality of human behaviour and relationships is far more complex and ambiguous than Hollywood endings. The stick in the hand of God by which he uses one nation as the agent of his judgement against another may be a very bent stick indeed.

Coming back to Habakkuk, then, God moves seamlessly from the fact that he is raising up the Babylonians to judge Israel, to the fact that Babylon itself stands under his judgement for a catalogue of wickedness that fills the rest of Habakkuk 2. This is very similar to Jeremiah. Having written to the exiles that Nebuchadnezzar had merely carried out the will of God in carrying off the exiles to Babylon, he puts into the next diplomatic mailbag a ferocious and sustained declaration of the judgement of God that awaits Babylon itself (Jer 50–51).

And so it must also be in our day. If we choose to believe that in some of our contemporary conflicts God may use one powerful nation (or a coalition of powerful nations) as the agent of judgement on tyrannous regimes, then this says nothing, in and of itself, about the moral righteousness of the nation or nations so used. Yet, sadly, the rhetoric of self-righteousness that tends to get wrapped around the geo-political posturing of western leaders falls into exactly that presumption.

But look at the condemnation of Babylon in Habakkuk 2. This is the nation God will use as his rod of justice. Yet its catalogue of wickedness strikes me as eerily modern in its relevance to western culture. Of course these words were originally aimed at Babylon, but 'Babylon', as we know, becomes a universal symbol in the Bible for human societies standing in arrogant rebellion against God—ancient and modern. Where might the prophet's words be addressed today, when he highlights the following?

- Economic imperialism and plundering greed (Hab 2:6–8)
- Profiting from unjust trading (Hab 2:9)
- Secret undermining of the stability of other nations (Hab 2:10)
- Building cities at the cost of human lives (Hab 2:12)
- Ecological destructiveness ('Lebanon' probably here stands for forests; Hab 2:17)
- Rampant national idolatry, trusting in one's own resources and products (Hab 2:18–20)

So if that is God's assessment of the nation he was using as his agent of judgement, how could we have evaluated those events by the criteria of 'just war'? Not without considerable ambiguity. All we can do, with Abraham, is to ask the rhetorical question that embodies its own answer, 'Will not the Judge of all the earth do right?' (Gen 18:25). And then, we recall with a shudder that the question was first asked just before the judgement of God fell upon Sodom and Gomorrah, and drove Abraham to intercession—a point to which we will return below.

Knowing God means trusting God's sovereign judgement. It does not mean knowing all the answers to the ambiguities of history, or knowing the whole script in advance. And it certainly does not mean handing out medals for righteousness for those God may choose to use as agents of his own justice in world affairs.

God will defend his people. We return to Psalm 46. This psalm is astonishingly relevant to our day, because it faces up to the two terrifying realities that seem to dominate our anxieties: on the one hand, within the natural order, the known dangers of natural disasters such as earthquakes and unknown dangers of climate change; and on the other hand, within the international order, the escalating dangers of war in so many places. Psalm 46 is for such a time as this. And it opens with a resounding assertion of God's constant protection.

> God is our refuge and strength,
>> an ever-present help in trouble. (Ps 46:1)

Psalm 46:2–3 then goes on to envisage the first kind of catastrophe (natural disaster), while Psalm 46:4–7 envisages the second (war). In both cases, says the psalm, God will defend his people.

In Psalm 46:2–3 the psalmist imagines the collapse of the natural world. The language he uses pictures a kind of 'uncreation'. In our contemporary world, some of the doomsday scenarios used to warn us about the long-term effects of climate change, global warming, rising sea levels, environmental catastrophe and so on, would fit the language of the psalm. It is possible he is thinking of literal earthquakes and the devastating turbulence of the sea that sometimes accompanies them. Lying along the great fault that stretches through Palestine and on down to the Great Rift Valley, the land of Israel was familiar with such things.

But it is equally likely that he is using the language also in a symbolic, or apocalyptic way (as it is used, for example, in Is 24:19–20; 54:10; Hag 2:6), in which case his affirmation of God's sovereignty recalls God's conquest of chaos in creation. The mountains may slip and slide (Ps 46:2), but the God who created them is a better place of safety than they ever were anyway.

In Psalm 46:4–7 the psalmist turns to the international scene. If, in Psalm 46:2, it was the sea that was in turmoil and the mountains that were slipping and falling, in Psalm 46:6 it is the nations that 'are in uproar', and kingdoms that slip and fall (the verb 'fall' is the same in both verses, for the mountains and the kingdoms). The world of nations and kingdoms seems as unstable as nature in an earthquake. Everything shifts. The earth itself, where everything seemed so unmovable, has melted into a mud-patch at the voice of God (Ps 46:6). No wonder the nations are in a skid.

Where then is security to be found? Not in some mountain fortress, nor in some national security programme. If mountains and men both melt before God, then the only place of safety is in God himself—which is where Psalm 46:1, 5, 7 and 10–11 place it. In Psalm 46:1, God is described in two ways: as a shelter or refuge, and as a strength or fortification. This gives both a passive and active dimension. God is a place to hide and be safe. But God is also the warrior who defends his people 'at break of day' (Ps 46:5), just as he did on the night of the exodus, or in the deliverance from Sennacherib (2 Kings 19:35–36).

So the place to be when the world falls apart is in 'the city of God' (Ps 46:4). For it is the only thing in this psalm that 'will not fall' (Ps 46:5). This is the third time the same verb is used. Mountains—bastions of solid rock can slip and fall (Ps 46:2). Kingdoms—even great fortified empires, slip and fall (Ps 46:6). But the city of God stands firm (Ps 46:5)—for as we know from the rest of the Bible, it is eternal, and stands ultimately for the new creation, where God himself dwells with his people. It is the presence of God within the city that guarantees its security against all that nature or nations can throw against it.

For who is this God in the midst?

> The LORD Almighty is with us;
>> the God of Jacob is our fortress. (Ps 46:7)

'The Lᴏʀᴅ Almighty' is literally Yahweh of Hosts (i.e. the Lord of all armies) earthly or heavenly. And 'the God of Jacob' was especially remembered for his protection. Jacob himself speaks of him as 'God, who answered me in the day of my distress and who has been with me wherever I have gone' (Gen 35:3). And Jacob's beautiful blessing of his two grandsons majors particularly on this note of protection:

> May the God before whom my fathers
>   Abraham and Isaac walked faithfully,
> the God who has been my shepherd
>   all my life to this day,
> the Angel who has delivered me from all harm
>   —may he bless these boys. (Gen 48:15–16)

Habakkuk, in similar circumstances, but knowing even beyond the perspective of the psalm that the catastrophe that was about to engulf Israel was in fact the judgement of God, nevertheless looked to God for final deliverance.

> Lᴏʀᴅ, are you not from everlasting?
>   My God, my Holy One, we will not die.
> You, Lᴏʀᴅ, have appointed them to execute judgement;
>   you, my Rock, have ordained them to punish. (Hab 1:12)

Habakkuk gathers up all his trust in God into that one ancient title: 'Rock.' Israel had used this term to celebrate the delivering, protecting power of Yahweh, and the security of belonging to him, from very early on (cf. Deut 32:4, 30–31). Jesus used the same imagery in his famous parable of the wise and foolish builders, which a children's chorus has turned into song.

> Build on the rock, the rock that ever stands;
> Oh, build on the rock, and not upon the sands;
> You need not fear the storm, or the earthquake's shock;
> You're safe for evermore if you build on the rock.

This does not mean that believers will be immune from pain or suffering, that they will never face danger or death, or that believers will never get killed in times of natural catastrophe or armed attack. That was not true in Israel's day nor is it true in ours. Christians suffer and lose their lives along with others in such times. So the declaration of God's protection here is not some talisman or mantra that protects its wearer or chanter from any physical harm whatsoever. What is promised is *ultimate* security. Whatever happens, the believer's life is in God's hands. And for the believer, of course, physical death is never ultimate—death does not have the last word. The key message of this psalm, as for Habakkuk, is that God's people will survive. They will never be obliterated. The Lord knows those who are his. And those who are in Christ are in the only totally safe place. Eternally.

God will be exalted among the nations. The final verses of Psalm 46 invite us to come and see both aspects of God's power at work—over nature and over the nations. It is a curious thing that whereas many modern people look at the awesome power of nature, when it wreaks desolation, and conclude that there is no God, the biblical writers saw in such natural forces one of the great demonstrations of God's power. These things are 'the works of the LORD' (Ps 46:8). But beyond the natural order, the psalmist thinks of the international order (or rather, disorder) that pervades history. And he looks forward to the end of history and anticipates the shalom of God that God alone will have created from the debris and exhaustion of all the wars of history (Ps 46:9). He sees the grim legacy of battle: broken bows, shattered spears and burnt shields—as we might scan the burnt out tanks, the shattered homes and broken lives. And out of it all, he hears the great climactic command of God himself:

'Be still, and know that I am God.' (Ps 46:10)

The word does not mean 'please be nice and quiet', as if addressed to people on a silent retreat, or to readers in a library. It is an abrupt and authoritative order: 'Stop fighting!' 'Cease fire!' It is spoken in the midst of the conflict, to bring it to a peremptory end, just as the command of Jesus, hurled at the raging wind and waves, 'Peace, be still!' brought the storm to a sudden calm.

This then is the final whistle of history. The match is over. And who has finally won? Who stands alone on the battlefield? No human army. No human nation or empire claiming to have right on its side. No crooked cop posturing as the world's policeman. Only the living God will be finally exalted on that day. The world is commanded to listen up and acknowledge him for who he truly is.

So this is God's final word. He calls us to know who he is *now*, because of what he will be acknowledged to be *then*. He will be exalted. And he will be exalted in both the spheres we have been considering—'among the *nations*' and 'in the *earth*'. That is to say, in the international arena and in the world of nature. He is Lord of history and Lord of creation, and he will one day be exalted supremely in both.

Furthermore, if God's exaltation is to be among the nations and in the earth, it clearly means that it will be *public* and it will be *here*. This is not just some pietistic hope that God will be exalted in our hearts or up in heaven. We have already seen in earlier chapters that 'knowing God' cannot be confined to private devotion or spiritual aspirations. It is something rather that God intends to fill all the earth, not just the hearts of his people.

And that is how Habakkuk gives expression to the same confident hope that brings Psalm 46 to an end.

> For the earth will be filled with the knowledge of the glory of the LORD,
>> as the waters cover the sea. (Hab 2:14)

This ray of light and hope comes (as in Psalm 46) in the midst of talk of God's judgement on human violence. And it echoes the promise associated with the universal and peaceful rule of God's Messiah in Isaiah 11:9.

It is rather a pity that the last line of each verse of the wonderful hymn, 'God Is Working His Purpose Out', shortens Habakkuk's prophecy by omitting the word 'knowledge', (doubtless to make the line fit the rhythm of the poetry). The hymn repeats:

> The earth shall be filled with the glory of God as the waters cover the sea.[2]

But Habakkuk's point is not that the *glory* of God will fill the earth at some time in the future; it already does. 'The whole earth is the fullness of his glory,' sing the seraphim in Isaiah 6:3 (my translation). Rather, his point is that all people will come to *know* the God whose glory they see every day simply by living in his creation. It will be the *knowledge* of God that will be universal and all-pervasive. Indeed, in this wonderful vision of our future habitation, in the new creation, the knowledge of God will be *definitive* of our new reality. It will be as impossible for there to be anywhere on earth where God is *not known*, as it is impossible for there to be a sea that is not

---

[2]Words written by Arthur Campbell Ainger, 1894.

full of water. Being covered with water is what constitutes and defines a sea. Being filled with the knowledge of God's glory is what will constitute and define the earth in the new creation.

The God who will be universally exalted will be the God who will be universally known. This is God's mission and goal: to vindicate his own glory, to bring peace to his creation, and to be known for who he truly is by all his creatures.

LIVING AS THOSE WHO KNOW GOD

> Are You not from everlasting,
> O LORD, my God, my Holy One?
> We will not die. (Hab 1:12 NASB)

We will not die, *we will live*. But how? How shall we then live, we who already know this God? If we know God, then we must live as those who do. We must live in the light of what we know. And from these two Scriptures, as we have seen, we know four things:

- that God remains in control of the world;
- that God will act in just judgement within history;
- that God will defend his own people;
- and that God will finally be universally exalted.

What, then, are the matching commitments that we are called to make in response to these great affirmations?

Because we know God remains in control, we will live by faith. Habakkuk, we have seen, was desperately baffled by the events that were unfolding in his own day. The wickedness of his own people was bad enough; the news that God intended to punish them through the Babylonians who were more wicked still, seemed even worse. Yet he remains convinced that God knows what he is doing and remains in sovereign control. So how was he to live with the tension between the present realities and the expectation of God's eventual judgement on the wickedness of Babylon too? By sustaining a firm trust in God. That was the right thing to do. That was what a person who was in a right relationship with God should do. In the midst of all the turmoil—national, international, moral and spiritual—the righteous person goes on trusting God and living in the strength of that faith.

And so Habakkuk framed a three-word sentence (in Hebrew) that came to define the very essence of the biblical gospel—for Paul, and for Christian faith ever since.

The-righteous-person   by-his-faith   shall-live.[3] (Hab 2:4, my translation)

The contrast with the first half of the verse is with the ungodly person (or nation, since Babylon is already in view), who is puffed up with arrogance and greed, and whose life is not upright at all. Such a person has no place for God, feels no need of God, does not live by God's ways, and is certainly not right with God. The righteous person, on the other hand, such as Habakkuk was striving to be, knows that the key to life is firm trust in God.

The word 'faith' here is the word that means firm, strong, committed trust. It can also mean faithfulness—that is, the kind of faithfulness to God that springs from faith in God's promises. It includes dependability, loyalty to God's covenant. Such qualities are the mark of the righteous person, and they are the way to life and living.

And it is precisely in the times of extreme danger, of natural or national catastrophe, that such faith and faithfulness are proved. It is when life is baffling that we affirm the sovereign reign of God *by faith*, and live accordingly. So this verse is not just defining the *starting point* of the life of a believer—through justification by faith. It is describing the *life* of faith, the habitual stance of the one who is in a right relationship with God. Such a life of faith, of unwavering trust in God when all around seems to contradict it, is a deliberate choice and calls for constant renewal. It is in knowing God that we choose to go on trusting God. The only alternative is not to trust, which is effectively to deny our faith.

> Either we view our lives in terms of our belief in God, and the conclusions which we are entitled to draw from that; or our outlook is based upon a rejection of God and the corresponding denials. We may either 'withdraw' ourselves from the way of faith in God [Heb 10:38], or else we may live by faith in God. The very terms suggest corresponding ways of life. As a man believes so is he. A man's belief determines his conduct. The just, the righteous, shall live by faith; or, in other words, the man who lives by faith is righteous. On the other hand the man who 'draws back' is unrighteous because he is not living by faith. Here is the great watershed of life, and all of us are on one side

---

[3]The hyphens indicate each of the three words in Hebrew

of it or the other. . . . Either my life is based on faith or it is not. If it is not, it does not much matter what my views may be, or whether I am controlled by political, social, economic, or any other considerations. What matters is whether I am accepting God's rule or not.[4]

Islamic rhetoric refers to Christians as 'infidels'—unbelievers. Perhaps that is truer than we might like to admit. Where is our trust placed when life gets tough and the world (or our world) falls to pieces?

Because we know God will act in judgement, we will live by prayer. Habakkuk had received some shattering news. His own people were about to fall under the sword of Babylon, though the hand that wielded that sword would be none other than Yahweh their God. Yes, Babylon too would eventually face the wrath of God for their arrogant, destructive, oppressive greed. That was the theme of the bulk of Habakkuk 2. So the future looked bleak indeed. The judgement of God would fall on Israel and their enemies alike. What is the response of those who know God?

For Habakkuk it was to turn to prayer. It is a remarkable feature of the book that Habakkuk 1 is a conversation in prayer between Habakkuk and God—setting out Habakkuk's problems. Then Habakkuk 2 is a declaration of God's coming judgement. This is then followed immediately in Habakkuk 3 by another lengthy prayer, which comes to a remarkable and triumphant conclusion.

It begins in a remarkable way too, as we see in Habakkuk 3:2.

> LORD, I have heard of your fame;
> > I stand in awe of your deeds, O LORD.
> Repeat them in our day,
> > in our time make them known;
> > in wrath remember mercy. (Hab 3:2)

Like so many of the great prayers of the Old Testament (as we saw in chapter 5) this one makes three key moves. Habakkuk recalls God's great acts in the past, with appropriate awe; he then asks God to do again what he had so marvellously done before; and he asks God to remember mercy even in the midst of deserved judgement.

This is the prayer of one who knows God. He knows the awesome history of God; he knows the contemporary power of God; and he knows the

---

[4]D. Martin Lloyd-Jones, *From Fear to Faith* (Leicester: IVP, 1953), 50.

merciful character of God. And he brings all that knowledge of God to bear on the problem he is facing.

For us, likewise, to recognize that events in our world today may involve elements of God's judgement does not paralyze prayer. We do not just say, 'If that's how God is going to act, then there is no point in us praying.' On the contrary, such knowledge motivates and energizes prayer.

That's what we see in other similar cases in the Bible. Think of Abraham, again, praying for Sodom in the wake of God's declared judgement. Think of Jeremiah, praying for the people of Judah, until God told him to stop because they were past praying for (Jer 14:11). Think of Jeremiah telling the exiles to pray even for Babylon (Jer 29:7)! Think of Daniel praying three times a day, in the midst of his career in the government service of Nebuchadnezzar (Dan 6).

Our enemies may indeed stand under the judgement of God. All the more reason to pray for them, according to Jesus (Mt 5:44). Judgement lies in the hand of God. Prayer is the weapon of love that he puts into our hands.

Because God will defend his people, we will live without fear (Ps 46:2; Hab 3:16–19).

> God is our refuge and strength,
>> an ever-present help in trouble.
> *Therefore we will not fear.* (Ps 46:1–2)

This is not sheer bravado. Nor is it a complete absence of natural physical fear in the face of suffering and death. Habakkuk was clearly very frightened indeed and he doesn't deny the physiological dimensions of it.

> I heard and my heart pounded,
>> my lips quivered at the sound;
> decay crept into my bones,
>> and my legs trembled. (Hab 3:16)

Paul urged Christians not to 'grieve like the rest of mankind, who have no hope' (1 Thess 4:13). He did not mean that Christians should not experience the normal grief of bereavement—but that their grief should be transformed by hope. So should fear. The common biblical command, 'Do not be afraid' (it is said to be the statistically most repeated command in the Bible) does not mean that believers should never experience the normal feelings of being afraid in dangerous circumstances. But it certainly does mean that natural fear is transformed by faith in the living God and his eternal protection.

Nor is this refusal to give way to fear merely a failure to face up to the real facts of the situation and all its dangers. Habakkuk knew exactly what enemy invasion would mean: the systematic destruction of the country's agricultural supplies and all the horror of siege, starvation and death. But even as he faces such a prospect, he refuses to give up his trust in God. The concluding words of his book are deservedly famous, for their resolute trust in God even in the face of impending calamity. Here is a man who knows his God.

> Yet I will wait patiently for the day of calamity
>   to come on the nation invading us.
> Though the fig tree does not bud
>   and there are no grapes on the vines,
> though the olive crop fails
>   and the fields produce no food,
> though there are no sheep in the sheepfold
>   and no cattle in the stalls,
> yet I will rejoice in the LORD,
>   I will be joyful in God my Saviour. (Hab 3:16–18)

Because God will be exalted, we will live for God's mission. The final verse of Habakkuk (apart from his instruction to the orchestra!) is surprisingly upbeat. In the wake of the section just quoted, you might have expected something along the lines of keeping one's head down until the storm has passed. If the world is in such a mess, and God's judgement is on the way, best keep a low profile, stay out of harm's way, and hold onto your faith. Not Habakkuk. God had given him a revelation that was to be read while running like a messenger (Hab 2:2). So Habakkuk would run, and not just on the flat. With God's strength, he would stride over the mountains.

> The Sovereign LORD is my strength;
>   he makes my feet like the feet of a deer,
>   he enables me to tread on the heights. (Hab 3:19)

So the closing picture of Habakkuk is of joy, strength, speed and climbing, not sitting back or opting out. Here is a man who knows God, and knows where his strength comes from. And he knows that he has a message from God to deliver.

We live in dangerous times, but God's mission goes on, as it has done through all the dangerous times and darkest eras of history. The first Christian century that gave birth to the New Testament was no picnic for the messengers of the gospel. That didn't stop them. They responded to the mission of God as it was entrusted to them by Jesus and took the dangers in their stride. After all, Jesus did not say, 'Go and make disciples of all the *safe* nations.'

Christian mission has never depended on favourable circumstances, peace and tranquillity. We pray for such circumstances, of course, as Paul told us to, since they do facilitate the spread of the gospel and growth of the church (1 Tim 2:1–4). But we are not dependent on them.

What motivates and drives our mission is *God's* ultimate goal to be known and exalted in all the earth. That is the focus of God's reign, the purpose of God's sovereignty within history. If we claim to know this God, then we had better be found obedient to his call to share his mission, and face even the extreme challenges of our dangerous world in his strength and with his protection.

CONCLUSION

Faith, prayer, courage, mission. All are active, dynamic words. Once again we see how far removed 'knowing God' is from mere pietism or the cultivation of some mystical dimension of our inner selves. Habakkuk and the author of Psalm 46 doubtless did have a close personal knowledge of their God. But what they affirm here is no subjective emotion. They build their confidence on strong affirmations about God's rule in nature and history, over creation and over the nations. It cannot have been any easier to do that in their day than in ours (just because they are 'in the Bible'). Rather, their tough commitment and confidence against all visible odds, stem from a radical understanding of who this living God, the LORD God of Hosts, truly is, and what it means to say that he is 'with us'.

HOW DO YOU KNOW
THAT YOU KNOW GOD?

Some of the chapters on our journey of biblical discovery have focused on the more personal ways in which some biblical characters knew God, like Abraham and Moses. Others have reflected on the personal implications for faith and worship that we find when the psalmists talk about knowing God. But much of our journey has explored what it meant for the people of God as a whole to know their God, or for other peoples to come to know Israel's God. In the process we have discovered enormous truths about God, about his character and action, and of course about his nature as our heavenly Father. But you may still be left wondering, 'Do I really know this God? How can I *know* that I know him?'

Someone spoke to me during the conference that I mentioned in the preface, after I had given several Bible addresses on the theme of knowing God. 'I want to know God,' he said, 'but I don't seem to, or at least I can't claim to.' This was a mature Christian—not someone on the edge of faith and conversion. It sounded like he was unsure what the experience of knowing God was supposed to be like, and longed for some clarity or reassurance. This is not surprising, since people's subjective and personal experience of God varies a lot. It varies according to what we've been taught. It varies according to what we therefore come to expect. It varies according to the latest testimony we may have heard. And it certainly seems to vary according to different personality and temperament types.

There are some who are very ready with expressions like, 'God just spoke to me'; 'I just know God wants me to do this, or that'; 'I really felt God's presence in the room.' It's hard to doubt their sincerity, though one sometimes might request further clarification of exactly what such claims actually mean. I have no doubt that some people do indeed have a direct and physiological consciousness of God, especially when they pray. One of my friends, when we would be praying together, would physically tremble as she 'felt God' (as she put it), and I know her to be a godly and sensible woman, spiritually mature and seasoned in Christian ministry. And in view of the biblical precedents for the impact of God's presence, it would be foolish to deny such elemental ways of 'knowing God' quite directly. Indeed, I sometimes envied the simplicity and directness of my friend's testimony to her awareness of God's presence.

On the other hand, there are many people, including myself most of the time, for whom knowing God is much more matter-of-fact and down-to-earth. We don't hear voices or feel shivers. We don't get transported, or 'slain', or ecstatic. We don't 'feel the wind of the Spirit', or any of the other common expressions in certain Christian groups and cultures. And yet we are constantly aware of the reality of God. God is simply 'there' as the whole foundation, background, foreground and ambience of our daily lives. Knowing God is simply a dimension of living. We slightly modify the words of a popular song:

> Father God I wonder how *I'd manage* to exist
> Without the knowledge of your parenthood and your loving care . . .[5]

I sometimes think it is a bit like marriage. 'Knowing your spouse', in a happy and positive married relationship does not always mean being physically close together, always talking or touching, always having intense feelings of being 'in love' (however wonderful, essential and assuring such times are). And yet, being married and knowing him or her is part of the bedrock of daily existence. It is a condition of life, consciously or subconsciously, not something you have to 'feel' or 'experience' every moment in order to know its reality. Maybe we could learn more from the depths of our human relationships about what it means to be in a 'knowing' relationship with God.

---

[5]Words by Ian Stuart Smale.

And yet, and yet . . . however much our doctrinal heads tell us that we do know God, our hearts still long for the assurance to go along with the faith. We want to be sure. We want to *know* that we know God. Can we have that assurance?

Absolutely yes, says John!

> Now by this we may be sure that we know him, if we obey his command-
> ments. Whoever says, 'I have come to know him,' but does not obey his
> commandments, is a liar, and in such a person the truth does not exist; but
> whoever obeys his word, truly in this person the love of God has reached
> perfection. By this we may be sure that we are in him: whoever says, 'I abide
> in him,' ought to walk just as he walked. (1 John 2:3–6 NRSV)

The test and the proof are practical. One of the passionate concerns that the first letter of John addresses is precisely that of assurance. John longs for his readers not only to have the right doctrine (to believe the truth), and not only to have the right ethics (to live in the right way), but also to have full assurance of their standing in relation to God and to other children of God within the fellowship of other believers. So he wants us not only to know God, but also *to know that we know him*.

First John 2:3 is actually a quite remarkable epistemological claim. Epistemology is concerned not only with knowledge in itself, but with *how* we come to know what we know, and *by what criteria* we can evaluate various claims to know anything. So here, John does not simply say, 'This is how we know him, by obeying him.' That in itself would be true, of course. We have seen that most clearly in chapter 6 above, in the words of Jeremiah 22:15–16: to do righteousness and justice—that is to know God. But John goes further than that. Not only do we know God through obeying him, but also we know that we know God through obeying him. Our obedience is the means of assurance as well as the source of the knowledge itself. Or to put it in more technical language, the epistemological foundation for our knowledge of God lies in the practical realm of obeying him.

And for our encouragement, this is how it was for Jesus also. There is no question but that Jesus knew God. We began this book observing the astonishing intimacy of his daily communion with his Father in prayer. But even for him, this knowledge of God was both expressed and assured in obedience, in doing his Father's will (as he so often put it). Indeed, as

Hebrews observed, part of the very purpose of his incarnate life as a real human being was that he learned through the experience of earthly suffering what obedience means for humans like us (Heb 5:8). There was a dimension of knowing God as Father that, even for Jesus God's Son, could only come through obedience and the suffering it involved.

So then, returning to 1 John, if you want to be sure that you know God, then walk as Jesus walked, live as Jesus lived (1 John 2:6)—in obedience to your heavenly Father. Then, *by doing that and in the process of doing that,* you will know that you know him.

> The friendship of the LORD is for those who fear him,
>   and he makes his covenant known to them. (Ps 25:14 NRSV)

> You are my friends if you do what I command you. I do not call you servants
> any longer, because the servant does not know what the master is doing; but
> I have called you friends, because I have made known to you everything that
> I have heard from my Father. (John 15:14–15 NRSV)

The psalmist and Jesus together make the point very clear: intimacy with God flows from reverence and obedience toward him. As he makes himself known to us, we assuredly come to know him.

So let us not be discouraged by stories of people who speak of mysterious experiences of knowing God, or the testimonies of those who sound so much more spiritual than ourselves. We can only look on the outside of such claims; the Lord looks on the inside and sees the heart. What does he see in your own? If he sees a heart that is set on obeying him in daily practical life—faithfully, humbly, with patience, perseverance, courage and joy—then he says, 'I know you, and you know me!'

> But if anyone obeys his word, love for God is truly made complete in them.
> This is how we know we are in him. (1 John 2:5)

BOOK THREE

KNOWING *the* HOLY SPIRIT *through* *the* OLD TESTAMENT

PREFACE

When I told people that I had been invited by the organizers of the New Horizon convention in Northern Ireland in August 2004 to deliver a series of five Bible expositions on the theme of 'The Spirit of God in the Old Testament', some wondered if I could find enough to fill one talk, never mind five—such is the widespread lack of awareness among many Christian people of the identity, presence and impact of the Spirit of God in the Bible before Pentecost. It's not that they don't believe he existed before Pentecost. They believe in the Trinity, after all. It's just that they have never noticed how extensive a role the Spirit actually plays in those centuries before Christ. Of course, it could be that they just never read the Old Testament, but let's be charitable.

Even for myself, however, when I got down to the preparation of those five addresses, I discovered there was far more than my first impressions. Some research in concordances and Bible software quickly brought up references I had never noticed before, and as the list grew to fill several pages, it was clear I could not confine the series to just five texts. So I grouped my findings into five major themes, under the titles that now form the chapters of this book. As I came to the end of the series that summer in Northern Ireland, many people came up to share their surprise that they had never realized just how much there was about the Holy Spirit in the Old Testament, and the idea for this book was born. Some years ago I wrote a book called *Knowing Jesus through the Old Testament*. It was born out of the conviction that Jesus only makes sense in the light of the Scriptures that shaped his identity and mission, just as the Old Testament itself only makes sense in the light of the Christ who fulfils it. This book reflects a comparable conviction. The Holy Spirit whom we meet in such power in the New Testament—whether in the ministry of Jesus, or the narrative of Acts, or the theology of Paul—is none other than the Spirit of the Lord God of Israel in the Old Testament. So if we want to have a fully biblical understanding of the Holy Spirit, as well as a biblically informed and biblically evaluated experience of his presence and power in our lives, then we need the Old Testament too.

These chapters, then, do not offer another manual on what it means to be sanctified by the Holy Spirit, or how to be filled with the Holy Spirit, or how to exercise the gifts of the Spirit, or how to bear the fruit of the Spirit— all vitally important topics in the teaching of the New Testament on Christian discipleship. What this book does is to ask us to consider that if these are the things we truly seek, do we really know the one from whom we expect to receive them? He is the Spirit who breathed in creation and sustains all life on earth. He is the Spirit who empowered the mighty acts of those who served God over many generations. He is the Spirit who spoke through the prophets, inspiring their commitment to speak the truth and to stand for justice. He is the Spirit who anointed the kings, and ultimately anointed Christ the Servant-King. And he is the Spirit through whom the whole creation will finally be renewed in, through and for Christ. Do we know him? Do we know what we ask for when we ask to receive him? We could not know him clearly apart from Christ and the New Testament. But we can know him in all his mighty, biblical, divine fullness only through the Old Testament also.

I would like to thank Norman Sinclair and all the rest of the New Horizon team for the invitation to deliver those five addresses on such a subject. The preparation was a blessing to me, just as I pray that this book, which follows the content of the addresses much as they were delivered, with some modification and expansion, especially in the last two chapters, will be one to its readers.

Each new generation is a testimony to the Holy Spirit as 'the Lord and giver of life', so this book is dedicated to the next generation of our family in the lives of our first two grandchildren.

Chris Wright

CHAPTER ONE

THE CREATING SPIRIT

The Spirit of God, relegated by some people to his grand entrance on the day of Pentecost, actually appears in the second verse of the Bible:

> In the beginning God created the heavens and the earth. Now the earth was formless and empty, darkness was over the surface of the deep, and the Spirit of God was hovering over the waters. (Gen 1:1–2)

Beginning here, rightly, at the beginning, we shall think first of the Spirit and the universe—hovering and speaking. Second, we shall observe the Spirit and the earth—sustaining and renewing. Third, we shall consider the Spirit and human beings—breathing and leaving. And finally we shall look forward to the Spirit and the new creation—groaning and birthing.

HOVERING AND SPEAKING: THE SPIRIT AND THE UNIVERSE

Genesis 1:1, the opening verse of the Bible, makes the fundamental affirmation on which our whole biblical worldview is built. The one living God created everything that we see around, above and beneath us. The whole universe exists because God made it.

The second verse goes on to give us our first picture of creation in its earliest stage—a picture of chaos and darkness. That indeed is how one Bible translation puts it. So does an old Christian hymn:

> Thou, whose almighty Word
> Chaos and darkness heard
> And took their flight.[1]

---

[1]John Marriott, 'Thou, Whose Almighty Word,' 1813.

The stuff of creation is there, but it has not yet been shaped to the world we now know. But the Spirit of God is there too. Here for the first time also we meet the suggestive range of meaning that the Hebrew word *ruakh* can have. Some translations speak of 'the wind of God', or 'a mighty wind', blowing over the waters. *Ruakh* can indeed mean wind, and also breath— things that are unseen, but very powerful in their effects. However, almost certainly the writer is speaking of the Spirit of God, in the more personal sense, for he speaks of the Spirit 'hovering over the waters' (not 'hoovering over the waters,' as an international student who was reading the lesson at a service at All Nations Christian College some years ago earnestly asserted). Wind blows; it does not 'hover'. So we are not just being told that it was a bit windy back at the beginning. Rather we are being told that the powerful Spirit of God was hovering, poised for action. The word 'hovering' in Hebrew is used of an eagle hovering in the sky, poised, alert and watchful, ready for instant action to catch its fledglings. In Deuteronomy 32:11 it is a metaphor for God watching over his people.

The action comes in Genesis 1:3, when God spoke into the darkness. There is a close link throughout the Bible between the Spirit and the word of God. It is closest when the word *ruakh* is used alongside the word *neshama*, which also means breath. Either or both together can speak of the powerful, creating, breathing word of God. That is what comes into action in this verse.

Job links together God's power, wisdom, breath, hand and 'whisper' in all the great works of creation. These words are all used in a great parallel cooperation:

> By his power he churned up the sea;
>> by his wisdom he cut Rahab[2] to pieces.
> By his breath the skies became fair;
>> his hand pierced the gliding serpent.
> And these are but the outer fringe of his works;
>> how faint the whisper we hear of him!
> Who then can understand the thunder of his power? (Job 26:12–14)

---

[2]'Rahab' was an ancient mythological name for the great serpent that was thought to inhabit the ocean. Job is here using pictorial language to speak of God's power over the seas and his ability to subdue all forces that might oppose him.

The Israelites of the Old Testament thought about God as Creator, not only in the teaching of Genesis but also in their worship. Psalm 33 includes a powerful reflection on God as Creator, and the role of his word and his breath in creation. It does not use the word *ruakh*, but comes very close in speaking of God's breath and word together, for these are certainly connected with God's Spirit.

The psalm begins by celebrating the transforming power of the word of God. In Psalm 33:4–5 we hear language that comes from the great exodus deliverance, when God had brought Israel out of the injustice and oppression of their slavery in Egypt, and proved his faithful love to them.

> For the word of the Lord is right and true;
>   he is faithful in all he does.
> The Lord loves righteousness and justice;
>   the earth is full of his unfailing love. (Ps 33:4–5)

The psalmist affirms that God's word is always like that. It deals in what is right and true, faithful and just, and ultimately fills the earth (not just Israel) with God's love. We need to notice that the psalmist is not just talking about 'God' in a general sense, but specifically about the Lord. When this word appears in capital letters as it does in our English Bibles, it is translating the Hebrew personal name of God—Yahweh (or Jehovah in older translations). It is the word of Yahweh (not the word of any other god) that is right and true. It is the faithfulness, justice and love of Yahweh (not any other god) that will fill the earth.

This is a great vision of the transforming power of the word of this God, embracing the whole earth in its scope. But is it not also grandiose and idealistic? How can the word of the God of a little nation like Israel be a word for the whole earth? The answer comes from Psalm 33:6–9. It is because Yahweh, whom Israel knew as their national redeemer, is also the universal Creator. He is the God of Genesis as well as the God of Exodus. The God of Israel is able to transform the world because he is the Creator of the world. So our anticipation of what he will be able to do in the future is firmly based on our knowledge of what he has already done through his word in the past.

So, in Psalm 33:6–9 the psalmist echoes the great creation narrative by combining the word of the Lord with the breath of his mouth (which as

we have seen is closely linked to his Spirit, as in Psalm 104:29–30) and also
by combining the great created realities in the same order as Genesis 1—the
heavens, the waters and the earth. The psalmist is almost certainly reflecting
on that creation narrative and the role of Spirit and word of God in it.

> By the word of the LORD were the heavens made,
>> their starry host by the breath of his mouth.
> He gathers the waters of the sea into jars;
>> he puts the deep into storehouses.
> Let all the earth fear the LORD;
>> let all the people of the world revere him.
> For he spoke, and it came to be;
>> he commanded, and it stood firm. (Ps 33:6–9)

By including all these three great orders of creation—the sky, the sea and
the earth—the psalmist challenges our fallen human tendency to turn any
or all of them into things we worship in place of their Creator. By implication he also challenges whole worldviews that spring from such idolatries.

- **The heavens (Ps 33:6).** The heavens and all the stars were made by
  God. But in the surrounding nations the heavenly bodies were very
  powerful gods. The sun was a major god in Babylon and Egypt. In stark
  contrast, the account of creation in Genesis 1 did not even name the
  sun, but simply describes it as the greater of the two big lights that God
  made and put in the sky! Likewise, the stars were commonly considered deities that controlled human destinies. But Genesis lists them
  almost as if they were just a divine afterthought: 'he also made the
  stars' (Gen 1:16). The stars? They are not gods! They are just something else that God 'also made'. Isaiah 40:26 engages in the same kind
  of unmasking of any divine claims that others might submit for the
  starry hosts. So there is no place, then, in the thinking of this psalm
  for astrology—that very ancient practice that amazingly survives to
  this day. The heavenly bodies, far from being deities from which you
  can get some clue about the present or future, are themselves only
  created objects that were called into existence by the word of the Lord.

- **The sea (Ps 33:7).** In Canaanite mythology the sea was also a powerful god (called *Yamm*). The sea was associated with chaotic power
  and evil. As we saw above, this myth is reflected in Job and elsewhere

with the concept of Yahweh's victory over the great deep. But in Genesis the great deep is itself the creation of the Lord God. And here in this psalm, far from something to be afraid of, the sea is put in a very diminutive perspective. The oceans? God's got them in a jam jar. They are just another of the great storehouse of wonders that he made by his creative word. So there is no place in this psalmist's thinking for the kind of dualism that pits a good god against an evil one or sees an endless cosmic struggle between chaos and order. The living God has all things, including the oceans, under his control.

- **The earth (Ps 33:8–9).** Canaanites also had a god for the earth. It was especially the role of Baal, the son of El, to provide the fertility of the soil and the animals. So they invested greatly in the so-called fertility cults to ensure health and wealth, through sympathetic religious placation of the gods of the earth. Today various kinds of new spirituality often involve attributing divine status to the earth, as a mother goddess figure, or simply as a cosmic divine life force, with which we need to establish harmony. On the contrary, says our psalmist, the earth itself is the creation of God. He simply spoke it into existence with a word of command. So, far from us needing to pay any homage to the earth, the earth itself and all its inhabitants are summoned to pay proper honour to their Creator.

All of these great realities, then, are the effect of the divine word, the work of the same Creator Spirit of God, the product of the breath of his mouth. Our worldview must take this into account. We may (or we may not) like to have a strong emphasis on the Holy Spirit in our ministry or in our particular Christian tradition or in our own personal devotion. But have we included this dimension within our biblical understanding of who the Holy Spirit is and what he has done? The Spirit is the one through whom the living God spoke the universe into existence and brought light, order and fullness to the world we now inhabit. He is, as the Nicene Creed puts it, 'the Holy Spirit, the Lord and giver of life'.

SUSTAINING AND RENEWING: THE SPIRIT AND THE EARTH

Old Testament Israelites did not spend a lot of time wondering about how the world *began*, except that it began by God's say-so. Once they had affirmed that in Genesis 1–2, enough seemed to have been said. But they did reflect often, and with great wonder, on how the world is continuously *sustained*, restored and rejuvenated. Every day you wake up—it is still there! Which is very reassuring. And just as importantly, the seasons come and go, year in and year out. There is a vast regularity about the whole system of the earth, which the human race has observed for countless generations. And again, the Israelites recognized the hand of their God in that amazing process. So did other nations, of course. All great civilizations have attributed natural processes to whatever gods they worship. The Canaanites had a rich mythology of gods and goddesses through which they explained the cycle of seasons and the annual need for rain and sun and fertility. One major Canaanite myth told of the great battle between Baal (god of life and fertility) and Moth (god of death). Initially Baal is slain (just as the season of growth and fertility comes to an end). But then, with the help of his consort, Asherah, he is brought back from the grave to life again and so the seasonal cycle can continue.

But for the Israelites, life could not be parcelled out to different gods in that way. All life on earth is sustained by the Spirit of God—from the lowliest fish to the most powerful human being. They not only worshipped one God only—their covenant God, Yahweh; they also affirmed that Yahweh alone was God. 'You were shown these things,' said Moses to the Israelites, speaking of the exodus and their encounter with God at Sinai, 'so that you might know that Yahweh is God . . . in heaven above and on the earth beneath; there is no other' (Deut 4:35, 39, my translation). For that reason, therefore, they understood that all life on earth is sustained and renewed by the Spirit of the one living God—from grass-roots level (literally) to the human pinnacle of creation. If it were not for the life-sustaining Spirit of God, life would be instantly extinct, dead in the dust.

> If it were his [God's] intention
>   and he withdrew his spirit and breath,
> all humanity would perish together
>   and mankind would return to the dust. (Job 34:14–15)

Psalm 104 is a beautiful psalm of creation, celebrating the sheer magnificence of all that God has made. After listing the many wonders, climaxing in human life itself, the psalmist pauses in amazement:

> How many are your works, LORD!
>> In wisdom you made them all;
>>> the earth is full of your creatures. (Ps 104:24)

Then he goes on from considering the work of God as Creator, to the way God sustains and provides for all he has made. There is no place here for Deism—the belief that once God had created the cosmos, he stepped back and let it run without any personal involvement on his part, like an unwinding clock. God, in the Hebrew world of thought and worship, is not distant and remote from the natural world. On the contrary, God is actively present in sustaining everything that lives and breathes on his planet. And it is precisely through his Spirit that he does this:

> All creatures look to you
>> to give them their food at the proper time.
> When you give it to them,
>> they gather it up;
> when you open your hand,
>> they are satisfied with good things.
> When you hide your face,
>> they are terrified;
> when you take away their breath,
>> they die and return to the dust.
> When you send your Spirit,
>> they are created,
>>> and you renew the face of the ground. (Ps 104:27–30)

So the Creator Spirit is also the provider Spirit. Or, to put it more formally, in this psalm we have moved from the doctrine of creation to the doctrine of providence. God not only brings all things into existence, he also sustains all things by his power. Day by day, season by season, year by year, from age to age, the Spirit of God is there, sustaining and renewing the earth. God the Creator, God the provider—both are truths that the Bible links with the Holy Spirit.

This great truth was also affirmed by Jesus, not about the Holy Spirit directly, but about our heavenly Father. It is God himself, Jesus reminded us, who clothes the grass of the field, and adorns the lilies with their beauty. It is God who feeds the ravens, and knows when a sparrow falls to earth

(Mt 6:25–34). Jesus saw in these truths (which he learned from his Scriptures—what we call the Old Testament) a great encouragement to personal faith. If your Father God cares so much about even the smallest items in his vast creation, how much more does he care for you—so trust him! Like the psalmist, Jesus knew that if God is everywhere present through his Spirit in the whole of creation, you can never get lost from God (Ps 139:7). So the truth of the universal sustaining, providing, caring role of the Spirit of God in creation is a heart-warming reassurance of our personal security and of provision for our practical needs. If God's Spirit cares in this way for the whole creation, he can certainly manage to care for you. That is a wonderful thought, and we need to hold on to it in faith and confidence.

But although the Old Testament believers could draw the same personal conclusions, it is still very important to note that they affirmed this truth for *its own sake*. God, through his Spirit, has created and continuously sustains all that exists. And he does so for creation's own sake and for God's own glory. And we are part of that. It's not that we say 'God cares for me, oh, and by the way he also cares for the rest of creation', but, 'God cares for creation, and amazingly, he cares for me too'. Similarly, although we often talk about how we are to 'care for the environment', it is actually the other way round. It is the environment that cares for us! The 'environment', as we lamely call it, is God's creation into which he has put us. And if he did not continuously sustain and renew it, we would not long survive within it. The world we live in, then, is not only the product of the Spirit of God through his almighty word in creation, but it is also the arena of his constant presence, surveillance and sustenance.

And furthermore, God actively loves all that he has made. Psalm 145 echoes the creational language of Psalm 104. It moves from the observation of God's providence in nature to the affirmation of his universal love for all that he has made. The word *all* or *every* (the same word in Hebrew) occurs sixteen times in this one psalm—stressing the limitless universality of God's love as Creator and provider. Not just all the *people*, but *everything* he has made.

> The eyes of all look to you,
> > and you give them their food at the proper time.
> You open your hand
> > and satisfy the desires of every living thing.

> The LORD is righteous in all his ways
>   and faithful in all he does.[3] (Ps 145:15–17)

So far we have seen that the living God whom Israel knew as Yahweh, their Lord God, is the Creator, sustainer, provider and lover of the whole of creation. And in all these roles, the Spirit of God was and is active. Where does this lead us?

If we long for a deeper experience of the Spirit of God, what exactly are we looking for? It will not mean merely enjoying more spectacular exhibitions of his alleged presence, or exercising more and more of the gifts associated with the Spirit in the New Testament. There are many ways, of course, in which such deeper experience of God's Spirit will affect us (not least in bearing more of the fruit of the Spirit in more Christlike character). But one thing it will certainly do, if we take these Scriptures seriously, is to drive us to a more balanced biblical worldview in which we stand in awe and wonder at the relationship between God and the whole of creation, and take it seriously. It is sad that so many Christians, though claiming to know God and to be filled with his Spirit, pay so little attention to this foundational biblical truth. Or perhaps they treat it as no more than that—a kind of invisible foundation that they take for granted and think no more about. 'God made the world? Great, what's next?' Whereas, both in ancient times and today, this is a startlingly aggressive affirmation, in the context of all kinds of rival claims—religious or secular.

Or they may be under the sway of a peculiarly negative attitude to the physical world, thinking that only that which is 'spiritual' really counts at all (which is usually further confined to getting your soul to heaven when you die, along with as many others as you can take with you through evangelism). The physical world is either just the dispensable stage on which that spiritual drama takes place for the moment; or worse, it is under some kind of cosmic demolition order just waiting to be carried out before we can all relocate gratefully to heaven.

Against all such minimizing and trivializing popular viewpoints, the Bible affirms creation, affirms the whole of creation, and affirms that the whole of God, including his Spirit, is involved in its origin, sustenance and future. Our God is the God of the whole creation. He made it, he sustains

---

[3]Or, 'loving towards all he has made'—the translation I prefer.

it, and he loves it. Such a holistic worldview affects many things, but at least the following two:

Science

Science is another of God's great gifts to humanity. Science had its origin in the biblical worldview that the universe is a rational unity that can be understood because the consistency of its laws and processes comes from the mind of the one who created it. However, as modern western science has developed, it tends now toward a dogmatic naturalism—the view that the material realm is all there is. Thus, any idea of a divine intelligence behind the origin and structure of the universe or of a divine purpose for which it exists and to which history is leading is ruled out as fanciful or wishful dreaming.

Against such a mindset, the biblical teaching on creation and providence affirms that the universe is not just a meaningless product of expanding energy. The earth is not just a self-sustaining biosystem. Nature is not just there for human use and exploitation. No, in all that happens, including what we (rightly but insufficiently) call 'natural processes', God is actively involved through his Spirit. Indeed the whole of creation in all its fullness is intimately linked to the glory of God—that is, to his reality, his substance, his intrinsic 'God-ness'. For as Isaiah heard the heavenly creatures proclaiming, 'The whole earth is full of his glory'—or as it could be more literally translated, 'The fullness of the earth is his glory.' That is, it is not that the earth is like some kind of empty bucket which gets filled up with God's glory. No, the fullness of the earth is that glory. The glory of the living God is (at least in part) constituted by the incredible diversity and plenitude of this great living organism we call planet Earth. So also the psalmist, having affirmed the renewing power of the Spirit of God, goes on,

> May the glory of the LORD endure for ever;
>   may the LORD rejoice in his works. (Ps 104:31)

Ecology

If all life on earth is sustained by God, and loved by God, then there are more ways of grieving the Holy Spirit than just lack of personal sanctification. Of course we are aware of all kinds of personal ways in which we can grieve or quench the Holy Spirit in our lives. But here is another way that we have never perhaps thought of as we should. I am constantly surprised at how many Christians have no interest in ecological issues or even in Christian efforts to care for creation through dedicated and scientifically well-accredited conservation work. They know about such things as destruction of habitats, draining of wetlands, burning of forests, pollution of the atmosphere, rivers, and oceans, global warming, loss of species, etc. But they care little, or only in a perfunctory way. Worse, some Christians manage so to distort their view of the future that they have a kind of theology of obliteration. If the whole earth is destined to destruction, they argue, why bother caring for it now. Use it up as fast as we can, before it all goes up in smoke.

And yet they say they believe the Bible, the same Bible that tells us that the earth was made by God the Father, is sustained by God the Spirit and will be the inheritance of God the Son; the same Bible that tells us that God loves all he has made, that the Spirit gives life to all and that God has reconciled all things to himself through the blood of Christ on the cross. And yet they manage to treat this marvellous creation of God with callous contempt—in practice if not in their conscious attitudes.

Surely, we have to protest against such attitudes, especially when they are held by Christians, and challenge ourselves and others to recognize that wilful or careless destruction of any part of the good earth God has given us grieves the Holy Spirit who is its Creator and sustainer.

BREATHING AND LEAVING: THE SPIRIT AND HUMANITY

So far we have considered Genesis 1:1–2, along with Psalm 33, relating the Spirit of God to the whole universe. Then we narrowed our focus to the earth itself and enjoyed Psalm 104's portrait of the sustaining and renewing power of the Spirit in all of nature. Now we come to the work of the Spirit of God as Creator particularly in relation to human beings:

> The LORD God formed the human from the dust of the ground[4] and breathed into his nostrils the breath of life, and the human became a living creature. (Gen 2:7, my translation)

---

[4]The first Hebrew word here is *ha'adam*; the second, translated 'ground', is *ha'adamah*. It is clear that the two are related. The human creature is an earth creature—the same connection that can be seen in the way the word human is derived from the Latin word humus, which means 'soil'. This is why I have translated *ha'adam* as 'the human', rather than 'man' or even 'Adam'. The text is not referring here either to the distinct masculine gender (the distinction of genders is the focus of the latter part of the story), nor to the named individual, but to the human being as a distinct species and the unique relationship that God establishes as they are formed.

This is a famous verse, but greatly misunderstood, so we have to deal with that misunderstanding before we can grasp its positive message. Traditionally and popularly it has been assumed to be a description of God breathing an immortal soul into Adam, as that which distinguishes people from animals. The soul, then, is thought to be something that humans have that animals do not possess, and this verse describes how and when we got it. This view owed a lot to the older KJV translation of the final phrase, 'man became a living soul'. However, this will not stand up to careful examination of the text. We must look at the two phrases—'breath of life' and 'living creature'.

'Breath of life' cannot mean an immortal human soul that is distinct from the animals, because the exact same words have already been used in Genesis 1:30 to describe all animals and birds that live and breathe on the ground or in the air. The phrase is used again with the same inclusive sense in Genesis 6:17. It refers simply to the common life of all animals (like mammals) that breathe.

Similarly, the phrase 'living creature' is not at all unique to human beings. It has already been used three times in chapter 1 (Gen 1:20, 24, 28) to describe the rest of the animal creation, and will be used again in that way in the flood narrative (Gen 7:4). All humans and animals have this in common: that they are 'living creatures'. In fact, the word here translated 'creature' is indeed the same word that is sometimes translated 'soul' (*nephesh*), but it is not something that human beings uniquely possess. In fact, it is not something that is 'possessed' at all. It is what we are, along with other living creatures made by God. God made all living creatures, including us human ones.

So Genesis 2:7 is not telling us how man got his soul. But it is certainly saying something very significant and positive about human life in relation to God. In fact, the point of the verse is not to distinguish us from animals, but to connect us with God. For the words 'God breathed into his nostrils' speak of tender, personal intimacy. It is of course a figure of speech (since God does not have literal physical breath). But it is a phrase which, from other contexts, would certainly indicate the presence of the Spirit of God, who can also be called the breath of God (e.g. in Ezek 37:9–10, 14).

As human beings, we are creatures who, like all other mammals, have the breath of life. But we are also uniquely created in God's own image and with special tender intimacy, enlivened with the breath of God. And it is this work of the Spirit in human life that generates all that makes human life so special. Job reflects on this connection between God's Spirit (or breath) and human life and capacity in several places.

> As long as I have life within me,
>   the breath of God in my nostrils,
> my lips will not say anything wicked. (Job 27:3–4)

> But it is the spirit in a person,
>   the breath of the Almighty, that gives them understanding. (Job 32:8)

> The Spirit of God has made me;
>   the breath of the Almighty gives me life. (Job 33:4)

But, as the Genesis story proceeds from this tender creation of human life in intimate relation to God, we come to the horror story of Genesis 3. We sinned. We rebelled. We disobeyed God, choosing to believe a lie, trust ourselves and reject the moral authority of our Creator. And the result was the sentence of death.

Genesis 6:3 makes an interesting comment on the state of affairs that exists because of human sin, and connects it with God's Spirit. We needn't go into detail on Genesis 6:1–2, since there are many different views on what it is describing, except to say that it seems to be talking about some serious transgression of the boundaries between the realms of heaven and earth. But the effect was that God acts to curtail the length of normal human life.

> My Spirit will not remain in the human being for ever, for he is flesh. His days
> shall be limited to a hundred and twenty years. (Gen 6:3, my translation)

Flesh here, in contrast to *spirit*, means 'mortal'. The point is that human beings do not possess 'natural immortality'. We live as long as we are given life by God's Spirit. So, yes, all human life is energized by the Spirit of God, in the sense that we are alive and breathing in God's world. But all human life is also mortal. We live only as long as that Spirit remains. When God withdraws that Spirit, we revert to what we are—flesh; and we return to what we are made from—dust. This is the same reality that Psalm 104:29–30 affirms about all animate life on earth, and it is echoed even more bluntly in Ecclesiastes' poetic reflection on human death as the moment when,

the dust returns to the ground it came from,
> and the spirit returns to God who gave it. (Eccl 12:7)

So the paradox of the relationship between the Spirit of God and human life on earth in the Old Testament is this. On the one hand we have the breath of life—physical life, the gift of God, which we share with all other living creatures on the planet. But on the other hand we are spiritually dead in our rebellion against God and destined to die in the end when that life-giving Spirit leaves—as destined to die physically as we are already dead spiritually. Hence the paradoxical title of this section—'breathing and leaving'. Life and breath are the gift of God's Spirit. But when the Spirit leaves, breathing stops and our mortality asserts itself.

Is there then any hope for us? Is there any hope for creatures like us who have the gift of life through the Spirit of God and yet live under the sentence of death, knowing that the Spirit of God will not remain in us forever in our mortality? Yes indeed, as we shall see in later chapters, and especially when we come to the New Testament. God promised, even in the Old Testament, to give us new life, new hearts and a new spirit. The New Testament picks this up and gives us fuller teaching on regeneration through God's Spirit, and the eternal life that is ours in Christ. So yes, there is hope for us through the life-giving Spirit of Christ.

The New Testament focuses mainly on the hope for *human beings* that comes through the work of Christ and the Holy Spirit. But it does not overlook the role of the Spirit in the wider creation, which is so prominent in the Old Testament, though of course the New Testament has more to say about Jesus Christ as the Word of God, as the agent and heir of creation. Let's conclude this chapter, however, by looking on to the role of the Spirit in the new creation. At this point we do need to turn to the New Testament, to its fuller vision of the future in the plan of God. But all that it says is built upon the foundation already laid in the Old Testament—including the teaching we have surveyed about the action of God's Spirit in creation. We turn to Romans 8:19–27, a key passage which links the Spirit and the new creation through the metaphor of labour pains and childbirth.

GROANING AND BIRTHING: THE SPIRIT AND NEW CREATION

The creation waits in eager expectation for the children of God to be revealed. For the creation was subjected to frustration, not by its own choice,

but by the will of the one who subjected it, in hope that the creation itself will be liberated from its bondage to decay and brought into the freedom and glory of the children of God.

We know that the whole creation has been groaning as in the pains of childbirth right up to the present time. Not only so, but we ourselves, who have the firstfruits of the Spirit, groan inwardly as we wait eagerly for our adoption to sonship, the redemption of our bodies. . . .

In the same way, the Spirit helps us in our weakness. We do not know what we ought to pray for, but the Spirit himself intercedes for us through wordless groans. And he who searches our hearts knows the mind of the Spirit, because the Spirit intercedes for God's people in accordance with the will of God. (Rom 8:19–23, 26–27)

This wonderful passage links together the resurrection of Christ with our own bodily resurrection and the redemption of the whole creation, and links them all with the Spirit. You might have thought that the word *joy* would be the dominant note in contemplating such a scenario. But the keyword in Paul's description is *groaning*. However, it is the groaning of labour pains, so the joy of birth lies ahead. These are the groans of gestation and birth. Yes, we live in this old world of sin and rebellion. But that old world is, in Paul's picture, the womb of the new creation, which is being brought to birth through Christ and the Spirit. And as Paul also says, if anyone is in Christ—new creation is already there (2 Cor 5:17)! We who are born again by God's Spirit through faith in Christ are part of the new creation that is being brought to birth.

There are actually three 'groanings' in the passage:

Creation is groaning (Rom 8:22)
Creation is groaning because of our sin, as a result of which it has been subject to frustration in its prime purpose of giving glory to its Creator. And, as Hosea put it, even the land mourns and grieves because of the accumulated weight of human wickedness perpetrated on it and against it (Hos 4:1–3). But the groaning Paul is thinking of specifically is the groaning of childbirth. For the new creation is already gestating in the womb of the old. So the pain of creation *now* is in eager anticipation of the joy to come. Indeed, such pain is actually a guarantee of the joys ahead. For, as every mother and midwife knows, once labour pains have begun a birth is unstoppable.

We are groaning (Rom 8:23)

We too should groan because of our sin, but again Paul has a different groaning in mind. We groan in eager longing for that new creation which will mean the redemption of our bodies. It is so important in this passage to see that Paul does not talk about 'the salvation of our souls', but the redemption of our bodies. Paul's expectation for the future is wholly creational. That is, he never sees salvation as a matter of *escaping out of* creation into some ethereal spiritual state. He rejected the kind of dualism that was prevalent in the Greek philosophical and religious culture of his day. No, God's redemption *embraces* his whole creation, and the resurrection of Jesus was the firstfruits of that great project. We human beings, therefore, will need new bodies to inhabit that new creation—and that is indeed what we look forward to. For, as he says elsewhere, we shall be transformed into the likeness of the risen Christ. His resurrection body is the prototype for the redemption of our bodies also (cf. Phil 3:21). This is why the Apostles' Creed so carefully says, *not*, 'I believe in the immortality of the soul' (which the ancient Greeks readily believed in), *but,* 'I believe in the resurrection of the body' (which they certainly did not).

The Spirit is groaning (Rom 8:26)

He is groaning within us as we live and pray—still living in the midst of this old creation with all its confusion and struggle, yet living also as the firstfruits, the advance guard of the new creation. For we too, if we are in Christ, are already participating in a reality that is still awaiting its full birthing in the future. For, as Paul also exclaims, 'If anyone is in Christ, new creation!' (2 Cor 5:17, my translation).

So the whole metaphor is one of pain here and now but joy later. That is the essence of birth pains: hard labour followed by supreme joy as a new life bursts forth into the world. So the New Testament concept of our present suffering (which Paul has been talking about in Romans 8) is not just a matter of 'stick it out here for a while, but soon you'll go to heaven when you die.' Rather it is to recognize that God is bringing forth a whole new creation, redeemed by Christ and birthed by the Holy Spirit. And if we are in Christ and indwelt by the same Spirit, then we are already part of that new creation. And along with this wonderful old creation, we wait with impatient eagerness for that glorious birthday.

CONCLUSION

'Did you receive the Holy Spirit when you believed?' Paul asked the new believers at Ephesus (Acts 19:2). They had not even heard of him. We certainly have, so a more appropriate question for us might be, 'Are you aware of what you have received when you received the Holy Spirit?' For we have now surveyed the scale and scope of what it is, or rather who it is, that you are asking to receive when you do.

The Holy Spirit, who lives in you if you are a child of God through faith in his Son Jesus Christ, is the Spirit of God who hovered over the very beginning of God's creation as it was spoken into existence. The universe itself owes its being to the Spirit of God.

The Holy Spirit is the one who has been constantly sustaining and renewing the creation ever since, so that the sun rose this morning for another new day and there was breakfast on your table.

The Holy Spirit is the one who gives life to every mortal creature that breathes on the planet, and who is the energy behind every breath you take in this life. And he is the one who gives life eternal to your mortal self, if you have put your faith in the crucified and risen Christ.

The Holy Spirit is the midwife of God's new creation, in which you will live in a resurrection body as part of God's new, redeemed humanity, and in which you will serve him and his creation as you were intended to.

This is the Holy Spirit, the Spirit of the God of the Bible. Do you know him?

CHAPTER TWO

THE EMPOWERING SPIRIT

*P*ower. The word, like the thing itself, is much abused. Recently I heard a current affairs discussion on the radio in which someone said, 'Power is the ability to make other people suffer.' That is a rather cynical view, but it is probably quite close to popular feelings about people who wield 'power'. It implies that all power is evil and oppressive. But this is a false and dangerous misconception.

Power, basically, is neutral. It simply means the ability to do things. Power is needed if you are going to do anything good, as well as if it is used for evil. Power is the capacity to accomplish goals, or to influence the outcome of events and processes. That is why, when you find that you are unable do either of these things (accomplish your goals or influence events), you feel literally 'power-less'.

In one analysis of human motivation[1] (that is, theory about what motivates us to do what we do most of the time), power is one of three dominant motivations that, according to the theory, govern all we do. These are the things that get us up in the morning and make us feel that another day is worth living. These are the things that 'make us tick'. These are the things, conversely, that will leave us very frustrated if we cannot fulfil them over long periods of time. Each of us has a motivational profile in which these three prime motivators are differently configured. Some of us are almost entirely motivated by one, and very little by the other two; others of us have

---

[1]George New and David Cormack, *Why Did I Do That? Understanding and Mastering Your Motives* (London: Hodder & Stoughton, 1997).

more evenly distributed motivational drives. But in all of us, one of these three is relatively predominant: (1) *achievement*—the desire to get things done and accumulate a satisfying list of accomplished goals; (2) *affiliation*— the desire for good relationships with others, and enjoyment of company for its own sake, regardless of what gets achieved; and (3) *power*—the desire to have an influence, make an impact, change things in some way through our involvement.

Power, then, is effective action, making a difference, influencing events, changing the way things are or will be. It is not surprising, then, that the Spirit of God in the Old Testament is commonly linked with power, for the biblical God is nothing if not effective in action and in bringing about change! Indeed, when the Israelites spoke of the Spirit of Yahweh, it was often simply a way of saying that God himself was exercising his power on the earth, either directly or, more commonly, through human agents. The Spirit of God is God's power at work—either in direct action or in empowering people to do what God wants to be done.

Empowering *people*. That's when the trouble starts. For human beings are not machines or robots. We are people to whom God has given the very risky capacity for making up our own minds about things and exercising our own choices. That was the power God gave us when he created us, and sadly we abused it right up front. We took power into our own hands by rebelling against God's authority, rejecting his instructions and choosing to decide for ourselves what we will consider good and evil. The result of this tragic exercise of our own power, which is usually called the Fall and is described in Genesis 3, is the terrible mess that we now live in. Every aspect of human life (spiritual, physical, intellectual, emotional and social), has been corrupted by sin. So all our boasted power is, spiritually speaking, our weakness—the weakness of sinful human nature.

And yet, it is human beings like us that God chooses to empower through his Spirit. The men and women in the Bible whom God empowered were just as much fallen sinners as you or I. With the single exception of Jesus Christ, to say that somebody was filled with, or empowered by, God's Spirit did not mean they were sinless, or that everything they subsequently did was morally perfect or precisely what God wanted in every respect. For when God's power and human weakness were combined in a single sinful human being, the results were not always predictable and were sometimes downright ambiguous. The reason is that the person in question, even when empowered by the Spirit of God, was still a fallen, sinful human being like you or me. If that was true in the Bible, how much more is it still true today? We shall need to come back to this point.

Let us then look first at some examples of people in whom the Spirit of God generated power and ability. Then we shall focus on the example of Moses in whom the Spirit of God produced a wonderful combination of power and humility.

POWER AND ABILITY

When some people in the Old Testament were said to have the Spirit of God, it simply meant that they had a God-given ability or competence or strength to do certain things for God or for his people. God's Spirit empowered and enabled them to do what had to be done.

Bezalel and Oholiab. Now it's very possible that you have never heard of the two gentlemen named Bezalel and Oholiab. But if you are interested in the Holy Spirit, you should have. For these are the first people in the Bible who are described as 'filled with the Spirit of God'. Being filled with the Spirit is something many Christians aspire to, though not many Christians expect the experience to do for them what it did for Bezalel and Oholiab. What did the filling of God's Spirit do in their lives? It enabled them to be craftsmen, working in metal and wood and precious stones, and all kinds of artistic design—and to be able to teach others the same skills. Here's the account:

> Then Moses said to the Israelites, 'See, the Lord has chosen Bezalel son of Uri, the son of Hur, of the tribe of Judah, and *he has filled him with the Spirit of God*, with wisdom, with understanding, with knowledge and with all kinds of skill—to make artistic designs for work in gold, silver and bronze, to cut and set stones, to work in wood and to engage in all kinds of artistic crafts. And he has given both him and Oholiab son of Ahisamak, of the tribe of Dan, the ability to teach others. He has filled them with skill to do all kinds of work as engravers, designers, embroiderers in blue, purple and scarlet yarn and fine linen, and weavers—all of them skilled workers and designers. So Bezalel, Oholiab and every skilled person to whom the Lord has given skill and ability to know how to carry out all the work of constructing the sanctuary are to do the work just as the Lord has commanded.' (Ex 35:30–36:1)

Putting these things together like this gives great dignity to such skills. I love the fact that on this first occasion when the Spirit of God, which had been so active in all the wonderful craftsmanship of creation itself, is said to fill a human being, it is to enable that person to exercise the same kinds of delegated skills. There is something so wonderfully creative (and therefore God-like) in what this passage describes: craftsmanship, artistic design, embroidery with rich colours, carving wood and stone. I fondly wish I had some of these skills and greatly admire the work of artists who do. We should take seriously that these things are said to be marks of the filling of God's Spirit. Of course, Bezalel and Oholiab were so filled for the purpose of working on the tabernacle—the holy tent of God's presence among his people. But I don't think we need to limit the action of God's Spirit in this gifting only to 'sacred' purposes. Presumably Bezalel and Oholiab had these skills as gifts from God's Spirit and exercised them in ordinary life before and after they were employed in constructing the tabernacle.

The creation narrative, as we saw in the last chapter, portrays God himself as the universal master craftsman who rejoices in the goodness and beauty of all he has so wonderfully designed and executed. This text encourages us to believe that the same Spirit of God who was at work in creation is also at work in that same wider sense, in all those who, as human beings made in God's image, enrich our world with all kinds of creativity in art, music, colourful design, beautiful craftsmanship and (adding this to console myself in at least one area of creative endeavour), skilful speech and writing. When we honour and admire such art, we give glory to the Spirit who empowers it.

The judges. The judges were the men and women who were leaders among the tribes of Israel before they established a monarchy. They got a book named after them in the Old Testament. The word *judges* is not very helpful since it suggests stern patriarchs sitting behind large benches in stuffy courtrooms dealing with successions of criminals. In Hebrew the title meant simply someone who puts things right, by whatever means. This might include acting in a judicial or legal way to sort out disputes between people, or giving judgements on difficult local problems. But it could also include leading the people in battle against oppressive enemies, or calling the people to united action against some sudden threat. Some of them seem to have been fairly local heroes, whereas others rose to more national prominence and leadership.

One thing that is said quite often about these 'judges' is that the Spirit of the Lord (Yahweh) would come upon them. When this happened it was a signal for action. Empowered by the Spirit of the Lord, they could exercise charismatic leadership and do valiant exploits that were recited around the campfires of Israel for generations to come. Here are some examples, all from the book of Judges:

> The Spirit of the LORD came upon [Othniel], so that he became Israel's judge and went to war. (Judg 3:10)

> Then the Spirit of the LORD came on Gideon [literally it says, 'clothed himself with Gideon'—God's Spirit put Gideon on like a coat!], and he blew a trumpet, summoning the Abiezrites to follow him. (Judg 6:34)

> Then the Spirit of the LORD came upon Jephthah. . . . He advanced against the Ammonites. (Judg 11:29)

> [Samson] grew and the LORD blessed him, and the Spirit of the LORD began to stir him while he was in Mahaneh Dan. (Judg 13:24–25)

> The Spirit of the LORD came powerfully upon [Samson] so that he tore the lion apart with his bare hands as he might have torn a young goat. (Judg 14:6)

> Then the Spirit of the LORD came powerfully upon [Samson]. He went down to Ashkelon, struck down thirty of their men, stripped them of everything and gave their clothes to those who had explained the riddle. Burning with anger, he returned to his father's home. (Judg 14:19)

> The Spirit of the LORD came powerfully upon [Samson]. The ropes on his arms became like charred flax, and the bindings dropped from his hands. Finding a fresh jawbone of a donkey, he grabbed it and struck down a thousand men. (Judg 15:14–15)

It is very clear that the Spirit of God is synonymous with power. People do great things when the Spirit of Yahweh comes upon them. But with Samson, something is very disturbing. In his case, power means enormous physical strength. It starts innocently enough under the sign of God's blessing. But as the story proceeds, that strength gets more and more out of control. Samson's human weakness is all too visible under his superhuman strength.

In Uganda there is an advertisement for Pirelli tyres that appears on many large billboards along some roads. On the advertisement there is a huge black fist with the knuckles pointing downward, looking as if it's coming out of the picture at you. The base of each knuckle takes the form of a massive tyre with patterned tread, such as you see on giant trucks. Beneath the image is the message 'Power is nothing without control'. It has a point—spiritually too. It's no good having superhuman powers if you lose control, lose the plot and in the end lose the whole point of having the power in the first place.

So here with Samson it seems that even Spirit-given power, power that had been promised and given by God, can be misused and exploited for very questionable behaviour. I don't think the narrator of these stories means us to assume that God necessarily approved of all that was done in the power of his Spirit. There is a growing excess in Samson's raging violence. Not every manifestation of spiritual power is unambiguously holy or wholesome. We will come back to that point too.

Saul. Saul was the first king in Israel, but in many ways he was also the last of the line of judges. In his early days, he acted very much like the previous judges, and there is a kind of overlap between that era and the full-blown monarchy that really got going with David. So, just like the other judges, we read that 'When Saul heard their words [about the threats of the Ammonites], the Spirit of God came upon him in power, and he burned with anger' (1 Sam 11:6). He then went out to win a great victory, as a result of which he was confirmed as king.

The initial role of the Spirit in the story of Saul is to authenticate Samuel's anointing him as king and to authorize his leadership. So we read,

> Then Samuel took a flask of olive oil and poured it on Saul's head and kissed him, saying, 'Has not the LORD anointed you ruler over his inheritance?' (1 Sam 10:1)

This is followed by a number of predicted signs that will confirm to Saul what Samuel has said and done, including:

> The Spirit of the LORD will come powerfully upon you, and you will prophesy with them, and you will be changed into a different person. (1 Sam 10:6)

Sure enough,

> As Saul turned to leave Samuel, God changed Saul's heart, and all these signs were fulfilled that day. When he and his servant arrived at Gibeah, a procession

of prophets met him; the Spirit of God came powerfully upon him, and he joined in their prophesying.[2] (1 Sam 10:9–10)

But this initial authorization was later withdrawn by God in the wake of Saul's increasing disobedience and folly. So we are told that 'the Spirit of the Lord had departed from Saul' (1 Sam 16:14) and in its place a very different kind of spirit afflicted Saul with God's permission—a spirit that took the form of dark moods, depression and murderous jealousy, and could also be linked to the strange phenomenon of 'prophesying' (1 Sam 18:10–11).

So then, surveying this material, there is something mysterious about the manifestations of the Spirit of God at this earlier period of Israel's life. The Spirit of God, it seems, can be very good, positive and enriching, giving people ability, competence and power, or filling people for skilful and creative tasks. The Spirit can give people great powers of leadership and courage. The Spirit can also be unpredictable, sudden and surprising. The Spirit can be abused by those who run wild and wilful, indulging in excess, out of control. And the Spirit can be withdrawn from those who persist in disobedience or folly.

There is something of a caution here for us. The power of the Spirit of God can be tied up with the very ambiguous powers of men. Not all so-called manifestations of the Spirit are in and of themselves welcome signs of the wholesome activity of God. They can be mixed up with the unwelcome manifestations of self-serving human ambition. And sometimes they can be deployed in ways that are out of control and potentially devastating.

We need wisdom and discernment. 'Test the spirits,' says John, 'to see whether they are from God' (1 John 4:1). Not everyone, says Jesus, who claims to do miraculous wonders—often associated with the Spirit of God—is necessarily in the kingdom of God (Mt 7:21–23). We shall return to this warning again in the next chapter when we look more closely at the question of false prophets.

POWER WITH HUMILITY

The text for this section is really the whole story that we read in Numbers 11–14. It is a particular period in the turbulent life of Moses. You might find

---

[2]'Prophesying' at this early stage in Israel's life seems to have been a charismatic outpouring in a state of trance. Later it involved Saul stripping and lying prostrate on the ground with such prophets (1 Sam 19:19–24). It was not yet the clear and articulate delivery of a specific message from God that characterized later prophets.

it helpful to pause and read through those chapters now. As you do so, you
will notice the references to God's Spirit. There are not many, of course,
and the narratives of Moses's life do not often refer to the Spirit of God.
However, later Israelites were in no doubt at all that God had been very
powerfully active through his Spirit in the life and work of Moses. Here, for
example, is how a later prophet referred back to that era:

> Then his people recalled the days of old,
>   the days of Moses and his people—
> where is he who brought them through the sea,
>   with the shepherd of his flock?
> Where is he who set
>   his Holy Spirit among them,
> who sent his glorious arm of power
>   to be at Moses' right hand,
> who divided the waters before them,
>   to gain for himself everlasting renown,
> who led them through the depths?
> Like a horse in open country,
>   they did not stumble;
> like cattle that go down to the plain,
>   they were given rest by the Spirit of the LORD.
> This is how you guided your people
>   to make for yourself a glorious name. (Is 63:11–14)

The same passage, a little earlier, says that the people of Israel 'rebelled
and grieved his Holy Spirit' (Is 63:10). These are two of the very few
occasions when the Spirit of God in the Old Testament is actually called
his *Holy Spirit*. It is clear, of course, that the main focus of the Spirit's
presence in this recollection is on the powerful acts of deliverance that
Israel experienced—especially the exodus and the gift of the land. But it
is equally important that the Spirit is linked to the role of Moses himself
as the leader of Israel at that time. The power of God was exercised
through the person of Moses. He was the human agent of God's Spirit.
Moses, then, gives us a model of Spirit-filled leadership. He was clearly a
leader of great power, given by God. And yet he served God faithfully—
as Hebrews also testifies, 'Moses was faithful as a servant in all God's
house' (Heb 3:5).

What were some of the marks of the Spirit of God in the leadership of Moses that we can find in this section of narrative? Moses exercised great power, but, as we shall now see, it was power without personal pride, power without personal jealousy and power without personal ambition. Let's think of each of those three characteristics.

Power without pride

> Now Moses was a very humble man, more humble than anyone else on the face of the earth. (Num 12:3)

This is a remarkable testimonial. The word here translated 'humble' is *'anaw*, and indeed it can mean meek and humble (e.g. in Prov 3:34 and Prov 16:19 where it is contrasted with 'proud'). But most often it means, not so much a subjective virtue or an inward personal characteristic as an objective state inflicted by others. The word describes people who are lowly because of some affliction, people who suffer by being put down and demeaned by others—more humiliated than humble (which was true enough of Moses a lot of the time, even as a leader):

> The vast bulk of the occurrences of this and related words denote the position of people who have been humbled or afflicted in one way or another. It suggests people who are weak in some respect. They lack resources or power. . . . To say Moses was the lowliest person on earth [means that he] was just the most ordinary of men, one of whom Yhwh made extraordinary demands, and on whom his people put extraordinary pressures.[3]

Is this not very ironic? Those who are lowly by definition 'lack resources or power'. Yet Moses was a man of incredible power. Even secular historians would agree that Moses has to be included among the greatest of all human leaders and nation builders. He was, after Abraham, the 'father of the nation'—the one who consolidated the Israelites from a bunch of escaped slaves into a nation and led them to the brink of their settlement in the land of Canaan. Moses was a leader, and a very great one. Yet Moses was a servant, and a very lowly one. A leader and a servant. A servant leader or a leading servant. Is it possible to be both? According to our text the answer is yes, because the Bible affirms both of these paradoxical truths about him.

---

[3]John Goldingay, *Old Testament Theology, Volume One: Israel's Gospel* (Downers Grove, IL: InterVarsity, 2003), 311.

The secret of Moses's power lay in the Spirit of God, and the secret of his humility lay in his lack of self-sufficiency.

Let's turn to our text. Numbers 11 describes just one more of the many crises that Moses had to face. Like many human conflicts, it revolved around our most basic human need—food. God had provided the people with manna. Their catering budget was a miracle a day. But it was not enough. 'The rabble with them began to crave other food' (Num 11:4), as they remembered the menus of Egypt—fish, cucumbers, melons, leeks, onions and garlic (a healthy diet indeed, even if they were being whipped as slaves in the meantime). So they complained that they had lost their appetite and demanded meat. Moses, as usual, becomes the focus of their discontent. Here is the next challenge to his leadership, the next demand on his competence. What emergency plan can he come up with to solve this problem? Here is how the record describes his response. It is not flattering.

> Moses heard the people of every family wailing at the entrance to their tents. The LORD became exceedingly angry, and Moses was troubled. He asked the LORD, 'Why have you brought this trouble on your servant? What have I done to displease you that you put the burden of all these people on me? Did I conceive all these people? Did I give them birth? Why do you tell me to carry them in my arms, as a nurse carries an infant, to the land you promised on oath to their ancestors? Where can I get meat for all these people? They keep wailing to me, "Give us meat to eat!" I cannot carry all these people by myself; the burden is too heavy for me. If this is how you are going to treat me, please go ahead and kill me right now—if I have found favour in your eyes—and do not let me face my own ruin.' (Num 11:10–15)

What a litany of accusing questions! What a sarcastic ending ('if you love me, kill me now')! This is not 'alpha male' leadership. This is not the calm assurance of a man who always knows exactly what he's going to do next, like James Bond. This is the panic of a man who has no clue where sufficient resources for the problem can be found. Self-sufficiency? Not an ounce.

Now this had not always been true of Moses. Think of him in his prime as the young prince of Egypt. Presented with a situation of obvious injustice, he knew exactly what to do. Summary justice. Instant execution of the offender. Two verses are all it takes to describe the whole incident: one for the problem, one for the solution (Ex 2:11–12). Problem spotted. Problem buried. Except that it wasn't, and Moses learned the hard way that quick reliance on his own solutions could result in long-term evacuation from any connection with the problem at all.

Meet Moses again, however, with his shoes off at the burning bush and he is a different man, much chastened by forty years with his father-in-law's sheep and daughters. This time his sense of inadequacy is desperate and embarrassing. 'Anyone but me, Lord', is the gist of his answer when God tells him it is time to return to Egypt and put *God's* solution into action.

Meet him on many occasions later when there is a problem. Where will you find him? Not setting up a committee to draft strategic plans and emergency rapid response tactics. Often you will find him flat on his face. So often we read the words, 'Moses fell on his face before the LORD' (Num 14:5; 16:4, 22; 20:6). That is not the posture of the self-sufficient, though it suits the lowliest man on earth very nicely. Moses was a free man, and his greatest freedom was freedom from pride and self-sufficiency.

It was not because Moses had no gifts, no abilities of his own. We are not told anything explicitly about his upbringing at the court of Pharaoh by the Old Testament narrative, but Stephen draws the very probable inference that 'Moses was educated in all the wisdom of the Egyptians and was powerful in speech and action' (Acts 7:22). Hebrews also imagines the life of Moses in the court of Pharaoh and talks about pleasures and treasures (Heb 11:25–26). So this was a man who probably spoke and wrote several languages, may well have been involved in international diplomacy and treaties, and had almost certainly been trained in the political and military arts of government. Not to mention the sheer physical vigour of the man that he was able to confront the might of an empire at the age of eighty, and climb a mountain to scan the whole horizon with undimmed eye-sight at one hundred twenty. No doubt about it, Moses was a man of remarkable natural resilience.

But whatever his gifts and strengths, he did not depend on them. He found no reassurance in his own resources. Rather, he turned to God. And that was the best thing to do, for as the narrative tells us, God had the next step already worked out.

> The LORD said to Moses: 'Bring me seventy of Israel's elders who are known to you as leaders and officials among the people. Make them come to the tent of meeting, that they may stand there with you. I will come down and speak with you there, and I will take some of the power of the Spirit that is

on you and put it on them. They will share the burden of the people with you so that you will not have to carry it alone.' (Num 11:16–17)

This gives us two insights into Moses's humility:

(1) Dependence on God's Spirit. We might not have known it from the earlier part of the story in this chapter, but the Spirit of God was 'on Moses'. Even Moses seems to have forgotten this. Perhaps it's easy to overlook your spiritual gifts when several hundred thousand people are demanding that you serve them up hot dinners (non-vegetarian, please). But this was indeed the answer, and the only one. Whatever might or might not happen next, only the power of God's Spirit could achieve it, for it was beyond the power of Moses to make anything happen at all.

But that is exactly the lesson that we learn here. Personal powerlessness is precisely the opportunity for God's power. Paul had learned this lesson very thoroughly also in his own battered career as a missionary.

> Such confidence we have through Christ before God. Not that we are competent in ourselves to claim anything for ourselves, but our competence [or sufficiency] comes from God. . . . We have this treasure in jars of clay to show that this all-surpassing power is from God and not from us. (2 Cor 3:4–5; 4:7)

> He said to me, 'My grace is sufficient for you, for my power is made perfect in weakness.' Therefore I will boast all the more gladly about my weaknesses, so that Christ's power may rest on me. That is why, for Christ's sake, I delight in weaknesses, in insults, in hardships, in persecutions, in difficulties. For when I am weak, then I am strong. (2 Cor 12:9–10)

This idea has been well expressed in our own time through the words of a familiar worship song:

> He turns our weaknesses into his opportunities, so that the glory goes to him.[4]

(2) Acceptance of God's Spirit in others. Moses needed to be willing at this point, not only to depend on God for himself personally, but also to depend on the help of others, to whom God would give a share of the same Spirit that Moses had. Spirit-filled leadership becomes shared leadership. Actually, this takes more humility than dependence on God alone. Some of

---

[4]Graham Kendrick, 'Rejoice', Kingsway's Thankyou Music, 1983.

us are very willing to trust God. Trusting *others*, who (we are asked to believe) also have the Spirit of God, feels like a much more dubious proposal. But it is one of the marks of the Holy Spirit in anyone who is a servant-leader like Moses that they are humble enough to recognize God's gifts in others, and share leadership with them. *Pride* says, 'If it can't be me and my power, then at least let it be my exclusive franchise of God's power. If I can't do it on my own, then let God do it, but make sure it's through me and nobody else.' *Humility* says, 'If God knows as well as I do that I can't do this alone, then let God provide Spirit-filled helpers for me—the more the better. I need them as much as I need God.'

Power without jealousy

The story proceeds from one problem to another.

> So Moses went out and told the people what the LORD had said. He brought together seventy of their elders and had them stand around the tent. Then the LORD came down in the cloud and spoke with him, and he took some of the power of the Spirit that was on him and put it on the seventy elders. When the Spirit rested on them, they prophesied, but did not do so again.
>
> However, two men, whose names were Eldad and Medad, had remained in the camp. They were listed among the elders, but did not go out to the tent. Yet the Spirit also rested on them, and they prophesied in the camp. A young man ran and told Moses, 'Eldad and Medad are prophesying in the camp.'
>
> Joshua, son of Nun, who had been Moses' assistant since youth, spoke up and said, 'Moses, my lord, stop them!' (Num 11:24–28)

Delegated leadership is all very well in theory. In practice it may lead to apparent chaos. Or at least to what are euphemistically called 'circumstances beyond our control'. Moses was willing to share the source of his leadership, the Spirit of God, and therefore also the practical outworking of his leadership. And that in itself, as we have just said, is a mark of his servant spirit and mature humility.

But then there is a sudden outburst of unscripted charismatic activity! It's a bit unclear exactly what was happening and why it was a problem. But if Moses and the other sixty-eight elders received the Spirit at the Tent of Meeting, which was outside the regular camp, then whatever Eldad and Medad were up to in the camp was beyond Moses's immediate observation or control. Things could easily get out of hand here. All this Spirit sharing is fine, provided it's kept under strict surveillance, right here where we can keep an eye on what's going on. But unauthorized, unsupervised, unofficial outbursts right in the midst of all the people in the camp could lead to, well, who knows where it might lead? And, perhaps with such thoughts, the voice of loud objection is raised by the number-two leader, Joshua: 'Moses, my lord, stop them!'

What lies behind Joshua's rude interruption and urgent advice to Moses? We are not told, but the narrator may be giving us a small clue in his reminder that Joshua had been Moses's assistant more or less all his life. Joshua's identity and status were entirely wrapped up with Moses. So perhaps Joshua felt that his own standing and authority were being threatened, if others were now going to be allowed to do what only Moses should do. Why, even he, Joshua (as far as we know), had not been privileged with such manifestations of the Spirit. So it was hardly fair that these outer ranks of leadership should suddenly enjoy them—especially if they hadn't even bothered to turn up in person!

It is an interesting and common phenomenon that 'big people' are often surrounded by their acolytes and groupies (whether deliberately or not). These latter—the special assistants, the minders and fixers—have a vested interest in keeping the big leader firmly on his pedestal. Anything that might diminish or dilute the authority of the number one is felt as an even bigger threat to the number two. So Joshua tells Moses to stop this dangerous development, right now, with respect, sir.

Moses's reply is a classic:

> Are you jealous for my sake? I wish that all the LORD's people were prophets and that the LORD would put his Spirit on them! (Num 11:29)

I can't help thinking that there was a twinkle in Moses's eye as he put Joshua in his place. 'Is it me you're really concerned about, or yourself? What is happening here is no problem for me; why is it a problem for you?' Moses had no personal jealousy, for his status, office or privilege—or even for a monopoly of God's Spirit and his gifts. If God wanted others to enjoy (if that's the right word) the experience of his Spirit and all the manifestations that went with it, that's fine by Moses. They'll find out soon enough that it isn't all standing about prophesying, by any means. There is a lot of work to be done, not to mention all the hungry people out there. For the moment, whatever power God's Spirit would give Moses was power without jealousy. He would gladly share it. In fact, if God wanted to share the Spirit more widely still, he would welcome that too.

Again, I ponder what lay behind Moses's wish here. What led Moses to wish that God would democratize his Spirit in a strange anticipation of those later prophets who said God planned to do exactly that (as we shall see in chapter 5 below) and of the day of Pentecost when it actually happened?

Possibly it is evidence of Moses's reluctance to be a leader at all. This was not a job he had asked for, and he had done his best to decline it when it was first proposed. Was that an underlying attitude that never really left him? Yes, he was faithfully obeying God's call and leading this people, with the power of God's Spirit. But not because it was something he enjoyed or because he secretly relished being the 'top guy'. On the contrary, he would far rather have slipped back into the ranks and let others take over the leadership. So is his wish here a rather tongue-in-cheek comment that being the one with the Spirit of the LORD is not all it's made out to be? If everybody could have the Spirit, then maybe Moses's own life would not be so unbearable as the butt of everybody else's problems. They could do their own prophesying and sort out their own mess. Even if this is all it means, it is a worthwhile point to ponder. The best leaders are often the most reluctant leaders, while those who hanker after all the power and status of leadership are usually the worst.

More likely, and more deeply, I think Moses's reply to Joshua is evidence of Moses's own profound security in his personal relationship with God. He had no personal jealousy as regards the Spirit of God, because he had no need to. Nothing could threaten or diminish what he and God shared in the intimacy of their relationship. God himself comments on this in the next chapter. He speaks warmly of Moses as

> my servant Moses;
>   he is faithful in all my house.
> With him I speak face to face,
>   clearly and not in riddles;
>   he sees the form of the LORD. (Num 12:7–8)

Whatever the last mysterious line means, it undoubtedly speaks of a very close personal relationship between Moses and God. Moses knew who he was in himself, and he knew whose servant he was. In fact that *was* his identity—servant of the LORD. That was his status. Nothing could threaten or diminish that. He was utterly secure in that knowledge. Even when he was angrily protesting to God and ruefully suggesting that shooting him would be the most merciful option, he was living out the intimacy of that relationship. Only the closest friend of God would speak to him like that, eyeball-to-eyeball indeed (as the expression 'face to face' literally reads in Hebrew). And Moses will do it again in Numbers 14 as we shall see.

So, with such deep and unshakable security in his relationship with God, Moses had no need for jealousy of others. He had no need to stand on his own authority or status or prerogatives. He had no need to monopolize the Spirit of God or the power it conferred. He could wield power *with humility* because he held power *without jealousy*.

There is a well-known paradox that bossiness is often a sign of insecurity. Those who are not secure in their own identity and relationships compensate for the inner inadequacy with excessive outer authoritarianism. Power-hungry control freaks deform human communities at all levels, sadly including Christian ones. Underneath the façade is often the attempt to prove something to themselves, the world, the church or God. 'This is who I am because this is what I can do', or 'This is how great I am because this is what I can make you do.'

True humility, by contrast, is the sign of a person at ease with him- or herself and God. When you know that your own life is securely bound up with Christ in God and that nothing and nobody can rob you of it; when you know that your identity and security lie in God's grace, not in anything you can do to prove or earn either of them; when you can rest in the assurance that all things in heaven and earth are yours, and you are Christ's and Christ is God's (1 Cor 3:21–23); when these things fill your conscious and subconscious mind, what is there to be proud of? Who is there to be jealous of? What is there to be threatened by? What is there to worry about losing, when you cannot lose all this?

It has always seemed to me that the best way to learn humility is not to try. The paradox is that genuine, unselfconscious humility is the fruit of exalting and glorying in the status we have in Christ as children and servants of God. The more you revel in that status before God, the less you are bothered about preserving petty status before others. This is exactly the lesson that Jesus modeled and taught in washing his disciples' feet (John 13:3–15). John very carefully says that 'Jesus knew that the Father had put all things under his power, and that he had come from God and was returning to God' (John 13:3). And the logic of his sentence is very clear. John does not say that *in spite of* knowing this, *nevertheless* Jesus washed their feet, but rather that *because* he knew these things he did so. It was because Jesus was so utterly secure in his relationship with his Father, so fully aware of his identity and his destiny, that he was the only person in the room who was inwardly free enough to do the work of a slave. The disciples were arguing jealously about who was the greatest. But because Jesus knew himself to be the Son of God, he was free to be the servant of men. That is power without jealousy, power to be the servant of others.

You want to be humble like Moses? You want to have the power that comes from God's Spirit, but to exercise it without pride and jealousy? Then fill your mind often with the knowledge that the Holy Spirit has made you a child of the living God. You are a son or daughter of the King of the universe. What more status do you need? Glory in that—and humility will bloom quietly, unconsciously and fragrantly as the fruit of the same Spirit.

Power without ambition

The story moves forward yet again. The people reach the borders of the Promised Land. Spies are sent out in Numbers 13. But the majority report is filled with such alarm that the people refuse to go any further. So in Numbers 14 we find the people of Israel giving vent again to their endemic grumbling against Moses. At first they propose to choose another leader and return to Egypt. But when Moses and Aaron, along with Joshua and Caleb, try to persuade them not to rebel against the LORD and to go forward into the land, things get decidedly more ugly.

> The whole assembly talked about stoning them. Then the glory of the LORD appeared at the tent of meeting to all the Israelites. The LORD said to Moses, 'How long will these people treat me with contempt? How long will they refuse to believe in me, in spite of all the signs I have performed among them? I will strike them down with a plague and destroy them, but I will make you into a nation greater and stronger than they.' (Num 14:10–12)

Not for the first time, God proposed destroying these people and starting all over again with Moses. In Exodus 32–34, on the occasion of Israel's horrendous apostasy with the golden calf, right at the foot of Mount Sinai while Moses was up there getting the Ten Commandments, the same thing had happened. God in anger suggested getting rid of this nation of rebels and making a fresh start with Moses himself. These terrible occasions—at Sinai and here at Kadesh Barnea—burned themselves into Moses's memory. He recalls them both and the desperate intercessory response he had to make in Deuteronomy 9 when he reminds Israel, on the verge of going in to conquer the nations of Canaan, that if anybody deserved to be wiped out, it was they. It is worth reading Deuteronomy 9 to feel the passion of Moses's memories and the amazing grace of God's continued patience with this people.

It was an incredible temptation, if we can look at it like that. What was God proposing? He was offering to transfer to Moses the promise that he had made to Abraham (that he would be a great nation) and its implications. God still had his ultimate purpose in mind. But he would carry it out by a different route. Forget the tribes of Israel. From now on, it will be the children of Moses. He will be known as the God of Moses. Moses will be the patriarch of a new nation, his own descendants. Just God and Moses and his seed forever. And wouldn't they get on so well together, if only *these* people were finally out of the way? Such thoughts could easily have fed Moses's ambitions—if he'd had any. He could step away from the burdens of leadership of this rancorous mob, and step into the limelight of history.

How did Moses respond to God's combination of threat and offer? Numbers 14:13–19 gives his immediate answer. But the remembered version in Deuteronomy 9 is more structured, and ties it in with his similar prayer at Sinai, from Exodus 32. It shows how Moses answered God on both occasions.

> I lay prostrate before the Lord those forty days and forty nights because the Lord had said he would destroy you. I prayed to the Lord and said, 'Sovereign Lord, do not destroy your people, your own inheritance that you redeemed by your great power and brought out of Egypt with a mighty hand. Remember your servants Abraham, Isaac and Jacob. Overlook the stubbornness of this people, their wickedness and their sin. Otherwise, the country from which you brought us will say, "Because the Lord was not able to take them into the land he had promised them, and because he hated

them, he brought them out to put them to death in the wilderness." But they are your people, your inheritance that you brought out by your great power and your outstretched arm.' (Deut 9:25–29)

Moses not only refused God's offer, he virtually rebukes God for even making it. God had spoken of destroying 'these people' (Num 14:11). Moses reminds God of just who 'these people' actually are. Actually, Moses does a lot of reminding, which is not to suggest that God was suffering an attack of amnesia, but rather that Moses is doing what all intercessory prayer does—it appeals to those things we know are of supreme importance to God himself. So Moses says, 'Remember Abraham'—the one to whom you swore on oath to bless his descendants and through them bless the world. You can't go back on that promise without denying your own self as God. 'Remember the Egyptians'—in other words, God had a reputation to think of. The exodus had happened in the glare of international awareness (cf. Ex 15:14–15). If Yahweh God now turns and destroys the very people he had rescued, how will that look to the rest of the world? They will think that Yahweh is either incompetent or malicious. Is that the kind of reputation God wants? And above all, 'Remember that these are *your* people.' This is the clinching argument, emphasized again in Moses's final appeal: *your people, your inheritance*. Destroy these people, cautions Moses, and you will destroy your own future, for this is what you yourself have called your own special personal possession (Ex 19:5–6).

Moses had been called by God to serve God by serving *these* people. And he was not going to be deflected away from that calling—not even by God himself! He had no personal ambitions to be the father of a great nation in his own right. His job was to be the servant of God and the servant of *these* people—no matter what. But what people they were! Moses probably had the most critical, rebellious, awkward, ungrateful, unreasonable congregation of grumpy old men that any leader or pastor could ever have. Think of some of the things he has had to cope with in these narratives in the book of Numbers alone:

- Administrative overload
- Catering problems
- Charismatic outbursts
- Family feuds and disapproval of his own marriage

- Refusal to follow the vision God had given through him
- Rejection of his authority to speak for God
- Attacks from outside the community
- Sexual immorality within the community

And God suggests, 'Let's get rid of all of that and all of them, and you can be the head of a new community altogether.' Tragically, apart from actually killing people, that seems to be what some leaders do—whether leaders of churches or mission organizations. In fact that's how some of them became leaders in the first place—by jumping out of a church or organization they didn't like or one that caused them too many problems and just starting up a new one, preferably named after themselves (with 'international' or 'incorporated' tacked on to add importance). Any such temptation, any such ambition, is precisely what Moses flatly refuses here. The power of his leadership, and certainly the power of his intercession at this precise moment, was that it was power without selfish ambition. So Moses says to God, in effect, 'Not interested. These are your people. You called me to serve them and lead them, and that is what I will do. So please don't dangle alternative scenarios before me.'

I am reminded of the example of Jesus, who also had to put up with a lot of grief from his followers. In the end, one of them betrayed him, one of them denied him, and all the rest ran away at the crucial moment. And yet Jesus remained utterly committed to them, so that in his final hours he could affirm to his Father that he had lost not one of them, except Judas, who had excluded himself (John 17:12). Or we might recall the similar example of the apostle Paul. It was to the Christians at Corinth, who had caused him endless problems (including some that involved misunderstanding and abuse of the gifts of the Spirit and some that were very similar to those faced by Moses) that Paul nevertheless wrote the astonishing words, 'We [preach] . . . ourselves as your servants for Jesus's sake' (2 Cor 4:5). He was appalled at the thought that some of them even wanted to use his name as a slogan for their faction. 'What, after all, is Apollos? And what is Paul? Only servants . . .' (1 Cor 3:5).

You may perhaps be in some form of Christian leadership. You are certainly in some form of ministry, for all disciples of Jesus are. This is a good point to do a motivational profile on yourself. What drives your work?

What are your ambitions? To serve God and his people? That sounds great, but is it a concealed ego booster, or is it a total dedication to *these* people— the real, gritty, grainy people whom God has entrusted to you? Is your leadership a life of very particular servanthood to a very particular people— like Moses?

CONCLUSION

The paradox of the power of Moses, then, is this. The greatest evidence of the *presence* of the Holy Spirit in his life was precisely the *absence* of those things that are commonly linked with great and powerful people: pride in one's own self-sufficiency, jealous defence of one's own prerogatives, driving ambition for one's own legacy. This is the power of the Holy Spirit in a human life. This is power *with* humility.

The church needs leaders. And leaders need power, if they are ever to get anything done (or, more properly, if God is ever to get anything done through them). But the kind of power they need is not the kind of power by which the world generally assesses leadership—'Not by might nor by power, but by my Spirit,' says the LORD (Zech 4:6).

Pray for those whom God has called into positions of leadership among his people, including yourself if appropriate, that there will be much greater evidence of the empowering Spirit of God, and much less evidence of the ambiguous and dangerous power of our fallen human weaknesses. May we be filled with the power of God's Spirit, in the likeness of Moses, and of Jesus.

CHAPTER THREE

THE PROPHETIC SPIRIT

Above all, you must understand that no prophecy of Scripture came about by the prophet's own interpretation of things. For prophecy never had its origin in the human will, but prophets, though human, spoke from God as they were carried along by the Holy Spirit. (2 Pet 1:20–21)

Peter tells us here that the prophets of the Old Testament did not make up their own messages out of their heads or imaginations. Rather, he affirms the double authorship of the Scriptures: 'Men and women moved by the Holy Spirit spoke from God' (NRSV). It was human beings who did the speaking, but it was God who provided the message. The words they spoke and wrote were therefore their own freely chosen words, but those words conveyed what God wanted to be said. And the means by which this happened, Peter adds, was the power of the Holy Spirit, carrying these prophetic speakers and writers along.

The New Testament, then, affirms the work of the Spirit of God in the Old Testament, not only in creation (chapter 1), not only in works of power and leadership (chapter 2), but also in the revelation of God's word. Paul tells us that the Spirit searches the deep things of God. For 'no one knows the thoughts of God except the Spirit of God' (1 Cor 2:10–11). God's Spirit, then, is the agent of communication from God's mind, with God's word, through God's prophets, to God's people.

In the Old Testament the prophets were key transmitters of this communication. Of course, they were not the only ones through whom the

Holy Spirit communicated God's revelation. God's Spirit was at work in those who wrote the narratives, those who framed the law, those who composed the psalms, those who gathered words of wisdom, and so on. All Scripture is breathed out by God through his Holy Spirit (2 Tim 3:16). However, the distinctive mark of the prophets is that they made the direct verbal claim, 'Thus says the Lord'—meaning that the words which then followed from their mouth or pen constituted the direct message of God himself. So in this chapter we shall look at the work of the Spirit in the ministry of the prophets.

> As for me, I am filled with power,
>   with the Spirit of the LORD. (Mic 3:8)

Micah here makes exactly the claim that 2 Peter 1:21 refers to. He has been commissioned to speak to Israel, and he is filled with the Spirit of the LORD to do so. Remarkably, however, such a direct claim on the lips of a prophet is quite rare. The only other example is Isaiah 48:16, where the prophet says, 'Now the Sovereign LORD has sent me, with his Spirit.' Isaiah 61:1 is another possibility, but it is most likely that the prophet is there speaking with the voice of the coming Servant of God, rather than directly of himself (which is most likely the case in Isaiah 48:16). Why is this? Why is it that the prophets of the Old Testament, especially the early ones, hardly ever actually claim to be speaking by the Spirit of God, even though the New Testament affirms that they were? Why is this claim so rare in the Old Testament itself?

One probable reason is the problem that all the genuine prophets of God faced, namely the presence of false prophets among the people. Micah, in the same context as his own claim, refers to them scathingly:

> As for the prophets
>   who lead my people astray,
> they proclaim 'peace'
>   if they have something to eat,
> but prepare to wage war against anyone
>   who refuses to feed them.
> Therefore night will come over you, without visions,
>   and darkness, without divination.
> The sun will set for the prophets,
>   and the day will go dark for them.

The seers will be ashamed
    and the diviners disgraced.
They will all cover their faces
    because there is no answer from God. (Mic 3:5–7)

These were people who claimed to speak from God, and very probably claimed the Spirit of God when doing so (e.g. 1 Kings 22:24), but who did not bring the true word of God at all—on the contrary, they undermined and perverted it. Possibly for this reason, most of the prophets whose words we now have in our Bible preferred to talk about 'the word of the LORD' as an objective reality, rather than claim the more subjective experience of the Spirit of the LORD.

So then, in order to see this contrast clearly and therefore appreciate what the true prophetic Spirit was like, we need to look first of all at the phenomenon of false prophecy. It will be a rather grim task, but exposing falsehood is always a necessary part of exalting the truth. We shall find that the problem of false prophecy did not end with the Old Testament, and there are good lessons for us to learn here to help us be discerning in our own response to prophetic claims today.

FALSE PROPHETS AND THEIR OWN SPIRIT

'Woe to the foolish prophets who follow *their own spirit* and have seen nothing!' declares God through Ezekiel (Ezek 13:3). There are many texts denouncing false prophets. You may find it helpful (though probably depressing) to read through the following primary passages before we come to a thematic analysis of what they (and others) have to say about the false prophets in Israel: Jeremiah 23:9–32, Ezekiel 13 and Micah 2:6–11.

We can identify three major features that marked out these prophets as false, as not having come from God, as dangerously misleading to the people. All of them are worth reflecting on today.

Lack of personal moral integrity. The lives of these people who claimed so much were actually sensual and ill-disciplined. By the standards of God's law they were not even good Israelites, let alone good prophets. For example, they were guilty of:

- *Drunkenness.* The only spirit they knew was the trio of wines, beers and spirits.

Priests and prophets stagger from beer
and are befuddled with wine;
they reel from beer,
they stagger when seeing visions,
they stumble when rendering decisions.
All the tables are covered with vomit
and there is not a spot without filth. (Is 28:7–8; cf. Mic 2:11)

- *Sexual immorality.* They made public pronouncements, but lived in private sin.

Among the prophets of Jerusalem
I have seen something horrible:
They commit adultery and live a lie. (Jer 23:14)

- *Greed.* They were prepared to sell their clever words to the highest bidder. They claimed to have the word of God, and yet they had no shame in offering to 'sell' it, like street-vendors or prostitutes.

Her leaders judge for a bribe,
her priests teach for a price,
and her prophets tell fortunes for money. (Mic 3:11; cf. Jer 6:13)

So they lacked personal moral integrity. How then could they dare to speak on behalf of the God of all truth and integrity? How could they live in immorality and yet presume to represent the Holy One of Israel? How could they live in grasping greed and have any contact with the heart of the God who cared for the poor and needy?

'By their fruit you will recognize them,' said Jesus (Mt 7:16). We also need to be watchful and discerning regarding those who claim to have, or are paraded as having, great 'prophetic ministries'. We are right to inquire whether there is personal moral integrity along with the great public persona. We are right to be suspicious if there are hints of questionable behaviour, the whiff of fraud or corruption, or evidence of a greedy, opulent lifestyle. The Holy Spirit is not at all honoured by, or even present in, those who use his name to feed their own lusts or line their own pockets.

Now it is important not to say this simply as a blanket condemnation. I am not saying we should expose other people's false claims in order to point with smug relief to our own superiority. That is the Pharisees' attitude, and Jesus condemned such self-righteousness mercilessly. Nor am I claiming for a moment that only those who are morally perfect can engage in any Spirit-filled ministry. If that were the case, the ranks of those who could do so would be very thin indeed. In fact there would be no ranks at all, for all of us are sinners and all of us fall short of God's standards of personal integrity. I am a sinner saved by grace, as much as you are, or any other person in ministry. In fact, if being morally blameless were the criterion, none of the Bible would have been written, because it too was written by people who were sinners.

The question is, however, are we *repentant* sinners? Are we *forgiven* sinners? Do we know what it is to have been on our face before the Lord, begging for his mercy and restoration? Are we seeking to walk in the light? Are we daily conscious of our sin, but daily striving to please our Lord? The test then, is whether there is a clear *determination* to walk in integrity, to live by the moral standards of God's word, to repent humbly and quickly when we fail, and to put things right in the sight of God and the church. That is what is lacking in these false prophets, ancient and modern. We need to know that the words that are claimed to be words from God are coming from the mouths of those who know their own unclean lips and unclean hearts and have had both cleansed by the grace of God. We need to know that whatever ministries people have or claim, they are being exercised by those who know themselves to be forgiven failures and who live with a sense of grateful astonishment that God should use them at all.

Lack of public moral courage. These prophets caught the mood of the public at any given time and then simply reflected it, echoing it back to willing listeners who were only too pleased to have their opinions endorsed by apparent spokespeople for the Almighty. They never challenged or rebuked that public mood or that dominant social consensus, even when it was clearly in breach of the known laws and will of God.

During the era of the great Old Testament prophets, the nation of Israel (including both kingdoms—Israel in the north and Judah in the south) stood in great danger of God's imminent judgement. All kinds of social rottenness were devouring their society. There was economic oppression and exploitation of the poor. There was a succession of appalling governments that ranged from incompetent to vicious. There was blatant corruption of the judicial system by the wealthy. There was degrading sexual immorality under religious pretexts and the accompanying horror of child sacrifice. And underlying it all there was rampant spiritual apostasy as Israelites at every level broke faith with the LORD, their covenant God and Redeemer, to go after other gods and idols. The nation was an absolute mess and in very great danger.

But these alleged prophets, when asked to comment, were not at all alarmed. 'It's OK,' they chorused. 'God is not bothered. All is well' (cf. Jer 5:12). It was as if their nation was bleeding to death from a gaping wound and all they could offer was a strip of sticking plaster.

> They dress the wound of my people
>> as though it were not serious.
> 'Peace, peace,' they say,
>> when there is no peace.
> Are they ashamed of their detestable conduct?
>> No, they have no shame at all;
>> they do not even know how to blush. (Jer 6:14–15)

Far from offering any radical solution to the festering problems of their society, they themselves were part of the problem, for they acquiesced in its evil by condoning it.

> They keep saying to those who despise me,
>> 'The LORD says: You will have peace.'
> And to all who follow the stubbornness of their hearts
>> they say, 'No harm will come to you.' (Jer 23:17)

Ezekiel says that all the efforts of these prophets to reassure the people in spite of their wickedness were like building a wall that is so flimsy it is bound to collapse (the sin of the nation), and then just whitewashing over the cracks in the hope nobody will notice (the words of the prophets). A shower of rain will wash off the whitewash and reduce the whole thing to rubble. Then those who built it and those who whitewashed it will both be crushed in the devastation (Ezek 13:10–16).

We too live in a society that turns moral values upside down. Certainly that is true of contemporary Western society. It has become a society where basic human goodness is mocked and God's standards for family and community life are attacked and vilified. It is a society where all kinds of practices that are contrary to God's best will for human life and human relationship are advocated and encouraged. It is a society that manages to live in obscene wealth and luxury while fully conscious of the poverty and suffering of the majority of the human race. It is a society in bondage to massive public idolatries to the false gods of mammon (consumerism), military security and national pride.

And we too have religious figures who engage in the same double deception that false prophets inflicted on Israel: those who *discourage* the righteous with lies and threats and *encourage* the wicked in their ways while failing to warn them of the consequences. This is exactly what Ezekiel observed as so sickening to God, and as something that only God could rescue his people from.

> Because you *disheartened the righteous* with your lies, when I had brought them no grief, and because you *encouraged the wicked* not to turn from their evil ways and so save their lives, therefore . . . I will save my people from you hands. And then you will know that I am the LORD. (Ezek 13:22–23)

Lack of any prophetic mandate from God. There is a gaping credibility gap in relation to these prophets, between the claims and the truth, between the charade and the reality. They claim to have come from God, but God has never seen them in his presence. They announce that they speak in God's name, but God has never sent them. They wear the prophetic mantle, but they have no prophetic mandate.

> Which of them has stood in the council of the LORD
>> to see or to hear his word?
>> Who has listened and heard his word? . . .
> I did not send these prophets,
>> yet they have run with their message;
> I did not speak to them,
>> yet they have prophesied.
> But if they had stood in my council,
>> they would have proclaimed my words to my people
> and would have turned them from their evil ways
>> and from their evil deeds. (Jer 23:18, 21–22)

> Their visions are false and their divinations a lie. Even though the LORD has not sent them, they say, 'The LORD declares,' and expect him to fulfil their words. Have you not seen false visions and uttered lying divinations when you say, 'The LORD declares,' though I have not spoken? (Ezek 13:6–7)

Here, then, are people who are not sent by God, and yet they have a great deal to say. They never stop talking. They have the public ear and

dominate the national media. They are not short on content. But if God
didn't send them, where does it all come from? Whatever spirit they claim
is certainly not the Holy Spirit of God. If any spirit is involved, it is 'their
own spirit' (i.e. their own imaginings, their dreams, their weird and wonderful ideas). They sound most impressive, but there is no substance, only
wind (Jer 5:13) and self-delusion. Worse, much of what they say is not even
original, but swapped and stolen from one another. The only thing worse
than nonsense is second-hand nonsense. Unlike recycled garbage that can
at least be made productive, this recycling of so-called prophetic messages
remains useless no matter how many times you hear it.

> 'I have heard what the prophets say who prophesy lies in my name. They say,
> "I had a dream! I had a dream!" How long will this continue in the hearts of
> these lying prophets, who prophesy the delusions of their own minds? . . . Let
> the prophet who has a dream recount the dream, but let the one who has my
> word speak it faithfully. For what has straw to do with grain? . . . I am against
> the prophets who steal from one another words supposedly from me. . . . I am
> against those who prophesy false dreams,' declares the LORD. 'They tell them
> and lead my people astray with their reckless lies, yet I did not send or ap-
> point them. They do not benefit these people in the least,' declares the LORD.
> (Jer 23:25–26, 28, 30, 32)

What a catalogue. What an indictment. But this is religion without the
Spirit of God. This is religion that endorses the social status quo without
challenge, and leaves the people without the living word of God. This kind
of so-called prophetic activity is not pleasing to God—he is against it. It is
not owned by God—he neither called them nor sent them. Rather, those
who indulge in it are called to repent or else be judged along with those
they have so cruelly deceived.

These Old Testament warnings about false prophets are still very relevant today. We are assailed by falsehoods masquerading as some new revelation from God. I am not thinking only of speculative books and theories
that reach incredible levels of popularity in the secular arena, such as *The
Da Vinci Code*. Far more damaging are books, films and websites from
Christian sources that distort the Bible at a fundamental level and then
build fantasy on that distortion to feed our fascination with the future. And
they do this in spite of Jesus's warning not to waste time speculating about

his return, but simply to be prepared for it by getting on with the job he entrusted to us. These books, backed up by all the power of consumerist merchandising, sell by the millions, like fast food, and make their authors and publishers millionaires. But they distract and mislead God's people into obsessions with so-called prophetic signs and end-time scenarios, while at the same time doing little to address the screaming suffering and injustices of our world, or the rampant evil in the very societies where such 'prophetic' books and ministries proliferate.

Then there are the televangelists and purveyors of prosperity 'gospel' (an abuse of the term, since it is far from good news), appealing to, and exploiting for profit, people's innate material greed in the name of God's blessing. Add to that the inflated claims and grossly insensitive publicity of some of the great 'healing miracle' merchants. And even at the lowly level of ordinary local churches there are those who abuse the Holy Spirit by claiming his authority for their latest 'revelation' or for the latest fashionable theory, style, song or method.

We should remember the sobering warning of Jesus that not all who claim his name are what they seem:

> 'Not everyone who says to me, "Lord, Lord," will enter the kingdom of heaven, but only the one who does the will of my Father who is in heaven. Many will say to me on that day, "Lord, Lord, did we not prophesy in your name, and in your name drive out demons and perform many miracles?" Then I will tell them plainly, "I never knew you. Away from me, you evildoers!"' (Mt 7:21–23)

I find this one of the most sobering, even frightening, parts of the Bible. Jesus says it is possible to have a great so-called prophetic ministry—ostensibly in the name of Christ—and yet not belong to the kingdom of God. Jesus says it is possible to have a great deliverance ministry and yet not be owned by Jesus. Jesus says it is possible to do great miracles and yet not be doing the will of our Father in heaven. Jesus says it is possible to claim to be doing ministry in his name and yet to be disowned and dismissed by him as an evildoer.

I doubt if I would have the courage to say such things in the face of so much that is claimed today as 'mighty ministries'. So I am glad Jesus said these words, not me. They are terribly scary words. Jesus says this will not be just a minor irritation, but a common problem: 'Many will say to me. . . . And I will tell them, "I never knew you."' And if Jesus does not know them, then they certainly do not know him.

What does this call for? It means we simply must be discerning about all ministry claims and the alleged statistics that so often go along with them. We should ask, 'Where is the fruit? Where are the changed lives? Where is the evidence of the work of the *Holy* Spirit? Where are the people who are now more like Jesus, more committed to the love, compassion, justice and integrity of God and God's kingdom?' And of course it means that we must also be ruthlessly honest with our own motives and ambitions in ministry. There is a rather old-fashioned saying that talks about someone being 'mightily used by God for his glory.' Well, it can be wonderfully true. But there are times when I look at some great and prominent people for whom this claim is made, and I wonder just who is being used by whom—and for whose glory.

GOD'S PROPHETS AND GOD'S SPIRIT

At last, and with some relief, we can turn from our doleful survey of false prophets and their own spirit, to the more cheerful side of our theme—the fact that there were true prophets of God who did indeed perform their ministry through the Holy Spirit of God. At the beginning of the last chapter we saw that later prophets looked back and saw the work of the Holy Spirit in the life and leadership of Moses (Is 63:10–14). In relation to the prophets themselves, it is interesting that although they hardly ever claimed the Spirit of God for themselves, it was recognized in the later Old Testament that it was indeed through God's Spirit that true prophets had spoken.

This is a point that Nehemiah makes in his great prayer of confession with reference to both Moses and the prophets. Speaking of the time of Moses and the years in the wilderness Nehemiah says, 'You gave *your good Spirit* to instruct them' (Neh 9:20). The reference is undoubtedly to the role of Moses in teaching Israel the law. Nehemiah says he did it by God's 'good Spirit'—which connects with what we saw in the last chapter about the Spirit on Moses in Numbers. Speaking of the later centuries of Israel's history, Nehemiah laments the fact that

> for many years you were patient with them. *By your Spirit* you warned them
> through your prophets. Yet they paid no attention. (Neh 9:30)

Moses of course was himself a prophet—the first great prophet indeed in the long line that led eventually to Jesus. So in both verses Nehemiah is describing prophetic ministry—as *teaching* (from Moses in Neh 9:20) and *warning* (from the prophets in Neh 9:30). And he sees both these tasks as essentially the work of God's Spirit. Here, then, we have the true source of the ministry and message of those who were true spokespersons for God.

We have just seen some of the ugly marks of the *false* prophets who lacked God's Spirit. They lacked personal moral integrity, public moral courage and a prophetic mandate from God. What then were the marks of the *true* prophets who were filled with the Spirit? A long list might be drawn up of the finer points of Old Testament prophets, but I want to focus on texts where a connection is specifically made between prophets and the Spirit of God. And in that regard, I think two points are outstanding. Because they were speaking by the Spirit of the LORD God, true prophets had (1) a compulsion to speak the truth and (2) the courage to stand for justice.

Compulsion to speak the truth. Our example for this point may seem somewhat surprising. The person we have in mind was not even an Israelite. Yet in the story of his encounter with Israel from a safe distance, we are explicitly told that he was filled with the Spirit of God (Num 24:2)—the God of Israel. His name was Balaam, and he was a prophet of sorts—a seer or diviner who lived far to the east in Mesopotamia. You can read his whole story in Numbers 22–24. When the Israelites camped in the plains of Moab on their way toward the land of Canaan, the local king of Moab, Balak, 'was terrified because there were so many people' (Num 22:2-3). As it turned out, he need not have feared, since Israel had instructions not to conquer Moab but to pass through it on their journey (Deut 2:9). However, Balak in his fear turned to sorcery and hired Balaam to put a curse on Israel. Balaam's reputation in such matters was apparently gold standard (Num 22:6). Balak had obviously not heard of the boomerang danger of such a tactic, for God had promised Abraham that 'whoever curses you I will curse' (Gen 12:3).

Balaam makes three attempts to curse Israel, while Balak promises to pay ever-higher fees in ever increasing frustration. All three attempts are abortive since Balaam finds he can do nothing but bless Israel. In the end he gives up, forfeits his fee, delivers a few final oracles and sets off for home a wiser, and perhaps humbler, man.

The interesting point for our purpose here is that Balaam was instructed in advance to be careful to say only what God told him. And then, when he is filled with the Spirit of God, he finds that he cannot do anything else but speak the truth from God. His altercations with Balak make the point with some humour, as Balak gets angrier with every failed attempt to get what he had paid for.

> Balak said to Balaam, 'What have you done to me? I brought you to curse my enemies, but you have done nothing but bless them!' He answered, 'Must I not speak what the LORD puts in my mouth?' (Num 23:11–12)

> Then Balak said to Balaam, 'Neither curse them at all nor bless them at all!'
> Balaam answered, 'Did I not tell you I must do whatever the LORD says?' (Num 23:25–26)

> Then Balak's anger burned against Balaam. He struck his hands together and said to him, 'I summoned you to curse my enemies, but you have blessed them these three times. Now leave at once and go home! I said I would reward you handsomely, but the LORD has kept you from being rewarded.'
> Balaam answered Balak, 'Did I not tell the messengers you sent me, "Even if Balak gave me all the silver and gold in his palace, I could not do anything of my own accord, good or bad, to go beyond the command of the LORD— and I must say only what the LORD says"?' (Num 24:10–13)

That is the mark of someone truly filled by the Spirit of God. Balaam, then, though a non-Israelite, can be seen here as a model for every true Israelite prophet (and we could certainly wish that the limits Balaam articulated for himself were true of every Christian preacher as well). Micaiah said exactly the same thing when he was hauled before Ahab and Jehoshaphat for a pre-battle blessing (1 Kings 22:14). The irony in that story is that Ahab insisted on hearing the truth and then deliberately (and fatally) chose to ignore it. But by ignoring it he brought about its fulfilment.

Also interesting is what Balaam says in his oracles, when the Spirit of God came upon him (Num 24:2):

> How can I curse
>   those whom God has not cursed?
> How can I denounce
>   those whom the LORD has not denounced? (Num 23:8)

God is not human, that he should lie,

    not a human being, that he should change his mind.

Does he speak and then not act?

    Does he promise and not fulfil?

I have received a command to bless;

    he has blessed, and I cannot change it. (Num 23:19–20)

Balaam, speaking by the Spirit, cannot curse those whom God has blessed. Sadly today we have religious leaders who feel free to bless what God has condemned and claim the enlightenment of the Spirit in doing so.

So then, as early as the time of Israel in the wilderness we find a lesson in what happens when someone exercises prophetic gifts under the control of the Spirit of God. They have a compulsion to speak the truth—even if they come out of a pagan background.

A far greater body of truth, however, had already been communicated through that other, much greater, Spirit-filled prophet in these narratives—Moses himself. That is, the Torah—the law of God, given at Sinai. Paul calls the law 'the embodiment of knowledge and truth' (Rom 2:20). No wonder, for Nehemiah says the law was taught by the Spirit (Neh 9:20), and he is the Spirit of truth.

This great legacy of God's law in the Old Testament—unprecedented and unparalleled (Deut 4:32–33; Ps 147:19–20)—underlies all the rest of the Old Testament. The law formed the foundation for the preaching of the prophets, provided the evaluating criteria for the history writers and watered the roots of Israel's worship. And all of this has been bound together within the Scriptures we now hold in our hands. The Scripture comes to us as the word of God, through the Spirit of God. And because those who spoke and wrote by the Spirit were under the compulsion of the truth of God himself, this word is truth. As truth, the word of God in the Scriptures is trustworthy and is given in order to form the foundation of all our thinking, believing and behaving. It is this word of truth that shapes our worldview as believers and thus governs how we see everything else in life. The Word of God is the platform on which we build the whole of our lives.

The truth and trustworthiness of God's word is one of the most precious things the writer of Psalm 119 celebrated in his great poem.

The statutes you have laid down are righteous;
> they are fully trustworthy. . . .
Your righteousness is everlasting
> and your law is true. . . .
All your words are true;
> all your righteous laws are eternal. (Ps 119:138, 142, 160)

For this reason the psalmist confidently builds his whole life upon it. Jesus held the same belief as the psalmist about God's word. 'Your word is truth,' said Jesus to his Father (John 17:17), having already acknowledged the work of the Spirit of God in the delivery of truth (John 16:13).

Is that what you believe? That God's word, which we now have in Scripture, is true and trustworthy? It's what Jesus believed. It's what the psalmists, the prophets, Moses and even Balaam believed (not to mention his donkey). It is a fundamental part of the Christian faith that God has not left us in the darkness of ignorance or error. Rather, as Peter reminded us at the beginning of this chapter, God has spoken through human beings who were carried along by the Spirit as they spoke and wrote. And the essential mark of that Spirit-controlled utterance is truth and trustworthiness. But it is not enough just to give mental assent to it, merely by repeating after me, 'I believe the Bible is true'. At least two further steps need to be taken.

First of all, are you building your whole life, in all its dimensions, on the truth of the Word of God? Is your worldview shaped by the Bible? Is the Bible not merely the object, but the subject, of your thinking? That is to say, the Bible should be not only something we *think about*, but something we *think with*. It is to provide the foundations for how we think about everything else and is to be the guide to how we act in all circumstances.

Second, are you testing all the claims and teachings you encounter—in books, tapes or other media, from the pulpit or from celebrity Christian communicators—*by the truth of the Bible*? The best example to follow is that of the Bereans. When they had heard the apostle Paul preaching, sure, 'they received the message with great eagerness'. But even though it was from Paul, they still 'examined the Scriptures every day to see if what Paul said was true' (Acts 17:11). For only the Scriptures would prove the truth or otherwise of his words—even the words of an apostle. Is that what you do? Scripture is the reality checkpoint to which you should invite all claims for your allegiance to accompany you. You read an intriguing Christian book with highly persuasive praise on its cover. Yes, but, you should be asking yourself, is that what the Bible really says? And if the book builds its case on a few Bible passages, is that what the Bible, taken as a whole in context, really means? Is it true to the whole message of Scripture or is it a distortion achieved by twisting one part of the Bible out of context and out of proportion?

I don't mean to turn us all into cynics who can *never* accept or believe anything. The problem is, it seems to me, that too many Christians are only *too quick* to accept and believe anything and everything. My plea is simply for a greater discernment, remembering the words of Jesus: not everything that claims his name is necessarily owned by him. Not everything that claims the Spirit comes from the Spirit of truth. Fortunately, the same Spirit of truth who spoke through the prophets and inspired the Scriptures also takes up residence in every believer. So it is one of the marks of the work of the Holy Spirit in our lives that he convinces us of the truth of his own word and leads us into truth. But he is not the Spirit of contradiction. That is why it is proper to weigh up all prophetic words that claim to be given by the Spirit and to test them against the Scriptures.

The courage to stand for justice. God sent his prophets to expose the wickedness of his people and to warn them of its dire consequences. Such a task was unpopular and costly. Far easier to be one of those cheerful prophets of peace and prosperity. Nobody likes to be exposed or challenged. And nobody likes to be the whistle-blower when others are doing wrong. And yet, under that Spirit-filled compulsion to speak the truth, the prophets had to do it and did it with courage. Of the prophets who lived before the exile, Amos suffered ecclesiastical anger and deportation; Hosea suffered intense marital pain as the cost of the message his broken marriage symbolized; Jeremiah suffered family hostility and death threats, political ostracism, physical abuse and life-threatening incarceration; one of Jeremiah's contemporaries, Uriah, was put to death for the same message (Jer 26:20–23).

Looking back on that era of prophecy before the exile, Zechariah sums up both the message they brought and the rejection they experienced:

> Are these not the words the LORD proclaimed through the earlier prophets when Jerusalem and its surrounding towns were at rest and prosperous, and the Negev and the western foothills were settled?

And the word of the LORD came again to Zechariah: 'This is what the
LORD Almighty says: "Administer true justice; show mercy and compassion
to one another. Do not oppress the widow or the fatherless, the foreigner or
the poor. Do not plot evil against each other."'

But they refused to pay attention; stubbornly they turned their backs and
covered their ears. They made their hearts as hard as flint and would not listen
to the law or to *the words that the LORD Almighty had sent by his Spirit* through
the earlier prophets. So the LORD Almighty was very angry. (Zech 7:7–12)

Here again, we notice that it is a later prophet who can speak of the role
of the Spirit in the ministry of the earlier ones (a claim they so rarely made
for themselves). And we also notice that the major features of the message
of those earlier prophets, sent by God's Spirit, were the fundamental requirements of God's law: to do justice, to show mercy and compassion, and
to reject the exploitation of the needy. This is not really very surprising. We
are told that these are the very things God is most concerned about. So
naturally, if the Spirit of Yahweh, the God who cares passionately about
justice and compassion gets hold of somebody and compels them to speak
out, what else will they speak about? The prophetic Spirit of *truth* is also
the Spirit of *justice*. Truth and justice are of the very essence of the character
of the God of the Bible (Is 5:16). His Spirit inevitably highlights truth and
justice whenever he speaks. He could not be the Spirit of the LORD God
and not speak of what the LORD God delights in and longs for. So any
person who claims to speak in the name of the LORD but whose message
lacks truth or is unconcerned for justice is not speaking by the LORD's Spirit.

And so we come back to the prophetic text where we began this chapter,
Micah 3:8, and quote it this time in full. Micah is contrasting himself with
the false prophets and their congenial message.

> But as for me, I am filled with power,
>   with the Spirit of the LORD,
>   and with justice and might,
> to declare to Jacob his transgression,
>   to Israel his sin.

This verse is all the more significant precisely because, as we have seen,
it is so unusual for a pre-exilic prophet to speak of the Spirit of God in relation to his own words. But when this prophet does, the connection he

instantly makes is with justice. In fact the parallel structure of the second and third lines in the verse virtually equate the two. For Micah, to be filled with the *Spirit* is to be filled with *justice*, which in this context probably means 'with passion for the just cause of the poor and exploited.'

Why is this connection so natural that it can be stated in this directly parallel form? Because the Spirit in the Old Testament is the Spirit *of Yahweh—the Lord*, not just of any god, not just of some abstract divine impulse. And the rest of the Old Testament shows beyond all possible doubt that Yahweh, the God of Israel, is the God whose very character is the foundation of all justice, righteousness, truth and integrity. This Yahweh is on the throne of the universe, and 'righteousness and justice are the foundation of his throne' (Ps 97:2). Anyone, then, who truly has the Spirit of *this* God will love what he loves, will value what he values, will care for those he cares for. In fact, nobody can even claim to know God who is not concerned for justice.

'Let not the wise boast of their wisdom
  or the strong boast of their strength
  or the rich boast of their riches,
but let the one who boasts boast about this:
  that they have the understanding to know me,
that I am the Lord, who exercises kindness,
  justice and righteousness on earth,
  for in these I delight,'
    declares the Lord. (Jer 9:23–24)

'[Josiah] did righteousness and justice,
  so it went well for him.
He defended the cause of the poor and needy,
  so it went well.
Is not this what it means to know me?'
    declares the Lord. (Jer 22:15–16, my translation)

Here, then, is another test of whether or not some of these great, so-called prophetic ministries are truly from the Spirit of *this* God. Are they concerned about justice for the poor and needy? Or do they avoid all such issues on the grounds of 'staying out of politics' (and therefore in fact endorsing the political status quo that keeps such people poor and needy)?

'Staying out of politics' is precisely something the Spirit-led prophets of the Old Testament never did. It would never have occurred to them, even though they would have had a far more comfortable life if they had. But then, a comfortable life was not what a prophet expected. If the Spirit of Yahweh called you, it called for the courage to stand for justice.

CONCLUSION

What, then, have we learned in this chapter about the prophetic Spirit? We began with 2 Peter 1:20–21, and we saw that it tells us that true prophecy in the Old Testament was inspired by the Holy Spirit as 'men and women moved by the Holy Spirit spoke from God' (NRSV). That is why we believe in the inspiration of the Bible and in its double authorship— words of human beings and Word of God. But that conviction then drove us back to see *exactly what kind of word* it was that the Holy Spirit inspired the prophets to speak. And we have seen that, in contrast to the false prophets who deceived people with lies of their own devising and never challenged them about the rampant injustice in society, Spirit-filled prophets spoke the truth and stood for justice.

The same Micah who claimed the power and justice of the Spirit of the Lord also threw out the following classic challenge:

> He has shown you, O man, what is good.
>   And what does the Lord require of you?
> To do justice, to love faithfulness,
>   and to walk humbly with your God. (Mic 6:8, my translation)

As we seek to discern the presence or absence of the Spirit in ministries that claim to be prophetic today, we should listen to those who bring that kind of message, and whose personal and organizational lives embody it. And we should beware of false prophets who have no concern for doing justice, who love only themselves and who walk in arrogant defiance of God, no matter how much they claim the name of his Son or his Spirit.

CHAPTER FOUR

THE ANOINTING SPIRIT

In the last two chapters we saw the work of the Spirit of God in the Old Testament in empowering leaders, in giving the law and in enabling people to stand up for justice. Kings in Israel were supposed to embody all three of these. Kings were expected to be strong leaders in order to defend their people (like the judges), in battle if necessary. Kings were expected to know and serve the law and to give wise decisions when cases were brought before them. And most of all kings were ideally expected to provide justice for the weak and poor—especially those who lacked the natural protection of strong families to care for them, such as widows and orphans. Here are some texts that express these ideals. You will notice that they come from all over the Old Testament—the Law, the Prophets, the narratives, the psalms and the wisdom literature. The mandate and expectations on Israelite kings was extensive and well known.

> When [the king] takes the throne of his kingdom, he is to write for himself on a scroll a copy of this law, taken from that of the Levitical priests. It is to be with him, and he is to read it all the days of his life so that he may learn to revere the LORD his God and follow carefully all the words of this law and these decrees and not consider himself better than his fellow Israelites and turn from the law to the right or to the left. (Deut 17:18-20)

> Endow the king with your justice, O God,
>   the royal son with your righteousness.
> May he judge your people in righteousness,

your afflicted ones with justice. . . .
May he defend the afflicted among the people
and save the children of the needy; . . .
For he will deliver the needy who cry out,
the afflicted who have no one to help.
He will take pity on the weak and the needy
and save the needy from death. (Ps 72:1, 2, 4, 12–13)

It is not for kings, Lemuel—
it is not for kings to drink wine,
not for rulers to crave beer,
lest they drink and forget what has been decreed,
and deprive all the oppressed of their rights. . . .
Speak up for those who cannot speak for themselves,
for the rights of all who are destitute.
Speak up and judge fairly;
defend the rights of the poor and needy. (Prov 31:4–5, 8–9)

Hear the word of the LORD to you, king of Judah, you who sit on David's throne. . . . Do what is just and right. Rescue from the hand of the oppressor the one who has been robbed. Do no wrong or violence to the foreigner, the fatherless or the widow, and do not shed innocent blood in this place. (Jer 22:2–3)

When all Israel heard the verdict the king [Solomon] had given, they held the king in awe, because they saw that he had wisdom from God to administer justice. (1 Kings 3:28)

Praise be to the LORD your God, who has delighted in you and placed you on the throne of Israel. Because of the LORD's eternal love for Israel, he has made you [Solomon] king, to maintain justice and righteousness. (1 Kings 10:9)

Such high expectations could not be met with human strength alone. That is why for all these responsibilities, kings needed the Spirit of the LORD God. And that is what their 'anointing' symbolized. Kings in Israel were anointed with oil, speaking of the commissioning and empowering that Yahweh (the LORD) gave them through his Spirit for the tasks he laid upon them.

Anointing, then, is a sign of 'office'—not in the sense of status and privilege, but rather in the sense of task and responsibility. An 'anointed one' simply meant somebody chosen and commissioned by God to do a job that God wanted to be done, and then enabled by the power of God's Spirit to get on and do it. In that sense it could even apply to a non-Israelite king. Remarkably (and probably surprisingly for those who first heard it), Isaiah speaks of God referring to Cyrus, the king of Persia, in this way:

> [He] says of Cyrus, 'He is my shepherd
>   and will accomplish all that I please;
> he will say of Jerusalem, "Let it be rebuilt,"
>   and of the temple, "Let its foundations be laid."'
> This is what the LORD says to his anointed,
>   to Cyrus, whose right hand I take hold of . . . (Is 44:28–45:1)

Cyrus could be called 'the LORD's anointed one' because, as the text says, he was going to carry out what God wanted to be done, and God would strengthen and enable him to do it.

So in this chapter we shall look first of all at the anointing of the historical kings of Israel and what that meant. Then, second, we shall look at the anointing of the one whom the Old Testament anticipated as the coming servant-king. That will mean we have to look also at the whole mission of God through Israel, which the servant-king would be anointed to carry out in the power of God's Spirit. Naturally enough, that will lead us on, third, to the anointing and mission of Jesus, the Christ (which of course means 'anointed one'), who fulfilled the mission of the servant-king. And from there it is but one more step, finally, to consider the anointing and mission of those whom Christ himself commissioned—namely the church, including ourselves. The continuity in all this great sweep of biblical teaching is provided by the one we are focusing on throughout this book—the Holy Spirit of God.

ANOINTING AND THE HISTORICAL KINGS

Saul. Saul was the first anointed king of Israel. You can read the story in 1 Samuel 9–10. The relevant verses that refer to his anointing and the role of the Spirit are as follows:

> Then Samuel took a flask of olive oil and poured it on Saul's head and kissed him, saying, 'Has not the LORD anointed you leader over his inheritance?' . . .
>   'The Spirit of the LORD will come powerfully upon you, and you will prophesy with them; and you will be changed into a different person.' . . .

> When he and his servant arrived at Gibeah, a procession of prophets met
> him; the Spirit of God came powerfully upon him, and he joined in their
> prophesying. (1 Sam 10:1, 6, 10)

The anointing was, on the one hand, a simple physical act. A flask of
olive oil was actually poured over Saul's head as a symbolic and very visible
gesture. But it was then followed, on the other hand, by a spiritual
anointing—an experience of the mysterious power of the Spirit of Yahweh
that clearly affected Saul very deeply and visibly. This combination of symbolic action and internal effect had two implications in this instance. On
the one hand, it authenticated the word of Samuel as a prophet—for what
he had told Saul to expect actually did happen (not to mention the fact
that his lost donkeys were found). And on the other hand, it initially au-
thorized Saul himself for the leadership role into which he was about to be
thrust. His early actions were clear demonstrations of the power of the
Spirit of Yahweh at work in his leadership.

However, as we saw in chapter 2, in Saul's case, as with some of those
who had been judges before him, this anointing did not guarantee his
success as a leader or his faithfulness or his long-term effectiveness. Because
of folly and disobedience, his career went from early hope to mid-term
squandering to final self-destruction. Nevertheless, it is interesting that his
status as 'the LORD's anointed' was respected, even by David who had also
been anointed to be the next king (1 Sam 16:13). Clearly, the act of
anointing and the power of the Yahweh's Spirit that went along with it was
not something to be lightly disregarded, even when the one who bore it
was becoming increasingly unworthy of it.

David. In the wake of Saul's failure, and even while he was grieving over
it, Samuel was asked to anoint David instead.

> The LORD said to Samuel, 'How long will you mourn for Saul, since I have
> rejected him as king over Israel? Fill your horn with oil and be on your way;
> I am sending you to Jesse of Bethlehem. I have chosen one of his sons to be
> king.' (1 Sam 16:1)

After some formalities and an unexpected delay, the right son is finally
found and the ceremony is completed.

> Then the LORD said, 'Rise and anoint him; this is the one.'
> So Samuel took the horn of oil and anointed him in the presence of his

brothers, and from that day on the Spirit of the LORD came powerfully upon David. (1 Sam 16:12–13)

In David's case, as distinct from Saul's, the anointing is met with a more wholehearted obedience to God (though not by any means with moral perfection, as we well know from the rest of his story; David was still capable of great sin). God speaks of David as 'a man after my own heart' (1 Sam 13:14). This phrase almost certainly does not mean in Hebrew what it has come to sound like in English. As an idiom in English, the phrase 'a man after my own heart' has come to mean someone I am particularly fond of, who shares my likings, perhaps even my favourite person. But we know that God has no special favourites in that sense. We must remember that the Hebrew word *heart* was not so much the seat of the emotions as of the will. Your emotions were located somewhat lower down the body—in your bowels. The heart, in Hebrew idiom, is where you do your thinking, weighing up, deciding and planning. So 'a man after God's *heart*' means one who will think and do as God chooses, one who will carry out the plans that God has in his mind. When the phrase is first used in 1 Samuel 13:14, it stands in contrast to Saul who had failed to carry out God's commands. David is neither morally perfect nor God's special favourite. He is simply the one who will obey and accomplish where Saul had disobeyed and failed.

Saul and David, then, were both anointed as kings. But their stories show clearly that anointing by itself is no guarantee of faithfulness or even of long-term legitimacy in the service of God. Anointing must be met with obedience to God, with trust in God, with serving God and doing his will. Even for the foreign king Cyrus (who was never of course literally anointed as an Israelite king), this was the point. As the text above shows, whether he was ever aware of it or not, he was chosen by God to accomplish God's purpose within history, and he did so. In contrast, most of the kings of Israel, though physically anointed and fully aware of what it meant, actually failed to do what their anointing symbolized. They were anointed on their head with oil, but they were not obedient in their lives. They failed to fulfil the significance of their anointing.

It was this continuing failure of the historical kings of Israel (both in the northern kingdom of Israel and the southern kingdom of Judah) that led to increasing hopes of a coming anointed one, a coming king in the line of

David, a man truly 'after God's heart', who *would* be fully obedient, who would fully carry out the saving work of God in the power of God's Spirit. So we turn now to consider that figure of prophetic hope and vision.

ANOINTING AND THE COMING SERVANT-KING

Here are some of the key texts regarding the anticipated king. As you read them, consider what elements they all have in common.

> A shoot will come up from the stump of Jesse;
>> from his roots a Branch will bear fruit.
> The Spirit of the LORD will rest on him—
>> the Spirit of wisdom and of understanding,
>> the Spirit of counsel and of might,
>> the Spirit of knowledge and fear of the LORD—
> and he will delight in the fear of the LORD.
> He will not judge by what he sees with his eyes,
>> or decide by what he hears with his ears;
> but with righteousness he will judge the needy,
>> with justice he will give decisions for the poor of the earth.
> He will strike the earth with the rod of his mouth;
>> with the breath of his lips he will slay the wicked.
> Righteousness will be his belt
>> and faithfulness the sash around his waist. (Is 11:1–5)

> Here is my servant, whom I uphold,
>> my chosen one in whom I delight;
> I will put my Spirit on him
>> and he will bring justice to the nations.
> He will not shout or cry out,
>> or raise his voice in the streets.
> A bruised reed he will not break,
>> and a smouldering wick he will not snuff out.
> In faithfulness he will bring forth justice;
>> he will not falter or be discouraged
> till he establishes justice on earth.
>> In his teaching the islands will put their hope.
> This is what God the LORD says—
> The Creator of the heavens, who stretches them out,

who spreads out the earth with all that springs from it,
>who gives breath to its people,
>and life to those who walk on it:
I, the LORD, have called you in righteousness;
>I will take hold of your hand.
I will keep you and will make you
>to be a covenant for the people
>and a light for the Gentiles,
to open eyes that are blind,
>to free captives from prison
>and to release from the dungeon those who sit in darkness. (Is 42:1–7)

The Spirit of the Sovereign LORD is on me,
>because the LORD has anointed me
>to proclaim good news to the poor.
He has sent me to bind up the broken-hearted,
>to proclaim freedom for the captives
>and release from darkness for the prisoners,
to proclaim the year of the LORD's favour
>and the day of vengeance of our God,
to comfort all who mourn,
>and provide for those who grieve in Zion—
to bestow on them a crown of beauty
>instead of ashes,
the oil of joy
>instead of mourning,
and a garment of praise
>instead of a spirit of despair. (Is 61:1–3)

I trust you noticed at least three things that these great passages from Isaiah all have in common:

- They all speak of a coming one—sometimes in the language of kingship (son of David), coronation and rule; sometimes in terms of a servant.

- They all speak of the role of the Spirit of Yahweh (the LORD) in relation to that person and the tasks he will carry out. He will manifestly be filled with the power of God's Spirit.

- They all speak of God achieving his own mission or purpose through this servant-king—this figure who will come.

Here, then, is clearly an 'anointed one' par excellence. Like the historical kings, he too will be anointed, but there is a mystery in that his kingship will be unlike most human kings we've ever known. He will be characterized by the humility and gentleness of a servant. Like the kings, his anointing will symbolize the power and presence of God's Spirit, but in his case there is detailed description of what that will include. And above all, his anointing is essentially his commissioning to carry out God's ultimate mission and purpose for the world—not just for Israel but 'to the ends of the earth.'

Now this is a lot to grasp all at once, even though as Christians we know it leads ultimately to Jesus Christ, our servant-king. But before we look at Jesus, we need to put all of this prophetic picture that points to him in its wider context. We need to see it in the light of the whole sweep of God's mission in the Bible. Paul speaks about 'the whole counsel of God' (Acts 20:27, RSV) by which he means the whole revealed plan, purpose or mission of God that we know from the Scriptures. Paul spent three long years teaching that to the Christians in Ephesus—and now we're going to take a whirlwind tour through it in three short subheadings! We shall look at the mission of God, the mission of Israel and the mission of the Servant. Only then can we fully understand the mission of Jesus and the mission of the church. And of course we will be linking the role of the Spirit of God to all of these dimensions. And we need to start right at the beginning.

The mission of God. The Bible presents to us a God with a mission. Even in its opening pages we meet God setting about his work of creation as a dynamic mission to be accomplished. There we see God systematically thinking, planning, deciding, commanding, acting, accomplishing and evaluating. Creation is the opening mission statement of our biblical God.

When human beings appear in this story, a clear mission is also expressed. God's purpose was that these human creatures should be made in his own image, and that they should rule the earth (Gen 1:26–28). But if they were to be like God (in his image), then they would exercise that rule through care and service (Gen 2:15). Kingship exercised through servanthood is the very nature of human relationship to creation as described in Genesis 1–2. This was God's intended pattern for life on earth.

That's why he made the earth. That's why he put us in it. That was the creational mission of God.

But we blew it. We rebelled against God's authority, distrusted God's word and disobeyed God's commands (Gen 3). As a result we plunged ourselves and the earth into the chaos of sin and evil, violence and corruption, strife and suffering, that we find ourselves in still. The story of the accumulating grip of sin in the human race runs through Genesis 3–11, climaxing in the story of the tower and city of Babel in Genesis 11. There God deals with humanity as they try to act in unified arrogance. Instead, the nations now find themselves scattered in confusion over the face of the earth, which we already know stands under God's curse. It is a bleak picture indeed. What hope is there now for the mission of God in creation?

But God decided not to abandon nor to destroy his creation, but rather to redeem it. So he called Abraham, and with Abraham we enter the next major phase of the mission of God—God as redeemer.

Genesis 12 records God's call, command and promise to Abraham:

> Go from your country, your people and your father's household and go to
>   the land I will show you.
> I will make you into a great nation,
>   and I will bless you;
> I will make your name great,
>   and you will be a blessing.
> I will bless those who bless you,
>   and whoever curses you I will curse;
> and all peoples on earth
>   will be blessed through you. (Gen 12:1–3)

God promised three things to Abraham himself: (1) that he would have descendants and become a great people; (2) that God would bless this people in a special relationship which is later called a covenant; and (3) that God would give them a land to live in. These promises provide a framework for the following major sections of the Old Testament story, as bit-by-bit God fulfilled them. But the bottom line of the covenant with Abraham widens the scope of the promise out far beyond Israel as a nation: 'through you all nations on the earth will find blessing.' The vision is universal. In fact, this promise to Abraham in Genesis 12 is God's answer to the problems posed by human sin in Genesis 3–11. In Genesis 11 we found the nations scattered under God's curse. Now we hear that God's intention is that the nations should once again be blessed, as the earth and humanity were at creation.

So Abraham is actually a fresh start for the world. This promise is God's great manifesto. This text is God's declaration of his mission, which is nothing less than the blessing of all nations. So important is this promise to Abraham in the Bible that Paul actually calls it the gospel. We may have thought that the gospel begins with Matthew, but Paul says it begins in Genesis.

> So also Abraham: 'believed God, and it was credited to him as righteousness.'
>
> Understand, then, that those who have faith are children of Abraham. Scripture foresaw that God would justify the Gentiles by faith, and announced *the gospel in advance* to Abraham: 'All nations will be blessed through you.' So those who have faith are blessed along with Abraham, the man of faith. (Gal 3:6–9)

The mission of God, then, is to bless all nations on earth. But how? Well, we need the whole of the rest of the Bible to answer that, including of course the New Testament. But the first part of the answer lies in Genesis also—the promise of a people. Out of Abraham's descendants, at first physical, and then also his spiritual seed, God would create a whole community of people through whom his blessing would come to the nations.

But this would need to be a different kind of people from the sinful nations already rampant on the earth. In a world that was characterized by Sodom and Gomorrah, God wanted there to be a people who would be different, people who would be committed to his ways and his values. That, God reminded himself in a conversation with Abraham, was the very reason for which he had chosen Abraham in the first place. God spoke these words at the very point when he was on his way to judge Sodom and Gomorrah:

> Abraham will surely become a great and powerful nation, and all nations on earth will be blessed through him. For I have chosen him, so that he will direct his children and his household after him to keep the way of the LORD by doing what is right and just, so that the LORD will bring about for Abraham what he has promised him. (Gen 18:18–19)

Do you see how these verses bind together some very important things? At the beginning (Gen 18:18) and at the end (last line of Gen 18:19) God reminds himself of his ultimate mission, which is blessing for all nations. But then in the middle he speaks of his choice of Abraham ('I have chosen him') and his ethical expectation on Abraham's people, Israel ('to keep the way of the LORD by doing righteousness and justice'). The whole statement is tightly bound together as a declaration of intent. God had called Abraham. Why? So that he would teach his descendants to live in the way God wanted. Why? So that God could fulfil his promise of blessing all the nations. The mission of God, then, includes God's people and God's standards. God was not going to bless the nations just straight out of heaven; he would do it through a people on earth. But that community of God's mission on earth were not just to be the physical and historical means by which God would eventually send his Son to be our Saviour; they had a part to play by being different, by living in the ways of the LORD. That was their mission.

The mission of Israel. The people of Israel in the Old Testament knew that God had chosen them. They were a chosen people—that was one of their most fundamental beliefs. But they were not chosen for a unique and exclusive privilege that would forever belong to them alone. No, they were chosen for a unique and inclusive responsibility which would ultimately extend to all nations on earth. Their mission was to fulfil God's mission by being the vehicle of his blessing to the nations, or—to use the language of Isaiah—to be a light to the nations that God's salvation should go to the ends of the earth. Israel in the Old Testament was not chosen *over against* the rest of the nations, but *for the sake of* the rest of the nations.

This identity and mission was given to Israel right at the start of their pilgrimage as a nation, the moment they reached Mount Sinai after the exodus. Right there, before they went any further, and before he even gave them the Ten Commandments or the rest of the law, God makes this very important statement to Israel:

> You yourselves have seen what I did to Egypt, and how I carried you on eagles' wings and brought you to myself. Now if you obey me fully and keep my covenant, then out of all nations you will be my treasured possession. Although the whole earth is mine, you will be for me a kingdom of priests and a holy nation. (Ex 19:4–6)

The two phrases at the end of this passage express what God had in mind for Israel. They were to be a *priestly* people and a *holy* nation. In order to understand this, we need to remember what the priests were in Israel. The priest stood in the middle between God and the rest of the people. In that position he operated in both directions. On the one hand, it was the job of the priest to teach God's law to the people (see, e.g. Lev 10:10–11; Deut 33:10; Jer 18:18; Mal 2:7–9). So through the priests, God would come to the people and make his way known to them. On the other hand, it was the job of the priest to bring the sacrifices of the people to God so that through the blood sprinkled on the altar, their sins would be atoned for and they could come back into fellowship with God and one another. So through the priests, the people could come to God. The priests, then, brought God and people together by bringing God's law to the people and bringing the people's sacrifices to God. And then they were also entrusted with pronouncing God's blessing upon the people (Num 6:22–27).

So it is wonderfully significant that God here in Exodus 19 says to his whole people, 'You will be my priesthood among all the nations on the earth.' That is, as a whole people, you will be for the nations what your priests are for you. You will be the people through whom God will make himself known to the nations through the revelation that he will give to you in his law and all the other words and Scriptures. And you will be the people through whom eventually God will draw the nations to himself, into a forgiven, reconciled, covenant relationship. Thus, just as your priests bless you, so you will be a blessing to the nations. Now that role and identity of Israel as a 'priesthood' for God among the nations was therefore a 'missionary' task.

How was Israel to fulfil this mission? Did it mean that they were supposed to set off on missionary journeys to the other nations? I don't think so. I do not find evidence in the Old Testament itself that God ever intended Israel to *go to* the rest of the nations during that era. Occasionally an individual might be sent—as, for example, Jonah was sent to Nineveh. But on the whole, the mission of Israel was a matter of *being* rather than *going*. There was something fresh and unprecedented when Jesus after his resurrection told his disciples to go and make disciples of the nations. That was the dawn of a new era. So mission in the New Testament is mainly 'centrifugal'—that is, going out from the centre toward the edges—an expanding mission. This certainly involved sending people, as the church at

Antioch sent Paul and Barnabas. But in the Old Testament, mission is more 'centripetal'—that is, attraction toward a central point. That is part of the meaning of Israel being a light to the nations: nations would be attracted to that light, for light is by its nature attractive (cf. Is 62:1–3).

So if Israel were not meant to *go* but to *be*, what exactly were they to be? The same verse gives the answer. They were to be *holy*. Being holy fundamentally means being different or distinctive. God wanted Israel to be a model of how human life ought to be. He wanted Israel to be a society that was visibly, socially, economically, politically and religiously different from the nations around. They would be as different from the other nations in their quality of life as Yahweh, the God of Israel, was different from the gods of the other nations in his moral character. So Israel's mission was to reflect Yahweh their God in the midst of the nations—to be holy as he is holy; to be light as he is light. In practical terms, this sense of Israel's distinctiveness was expressed often in their law. For example:

> You must not do as they do in Egypt, where you used to live, and you must not do as they do in the land of Canaan, where I am bringing you. Do not follow their practices. You must obey my laws and be careful to follow my decrees. I am the LORD your God. (Lev 18:3–4)

> Be holy because I, the LORD your God, am holy. (Lev 19:2)

> Observe [these laws] carefully, for this will show your wisdom and understanding to the nations, who will hear about all these decrees and say, 'Surely this great nation is a wise and understanding people.' What other nation is so great as to have their gods near them the way the LORD our God is near us whenever we pray to him? And what other nation is so great as to have such righteous decrees and laws as this body of laws I am setting before you today? (Deut 4:6–8)

Well, it all started off with great hopes and good intentions. 'Everything the LORD says, we will do,' chorused the Israelites, twice over (Ex 24:3, 7; Deut 5:27). And then they went off and did everything except what the LORD said, and did many things that the LORD had specifically said they should not do. So the whole history of Israel, as it is told in the great history books of Joshua, Judges, Samuel and Kings, is one of disobedience, rebellion and failure. In fact, Israel simply replicates the story of the fall of humanity. The people who were to be the carriers of God's healing and blessing to sinful humanity were infected by the same virus of sin as the rest of the human race. The story of Israel is a recapitulation of the story of Genesis 1–11. Blessing, promise and command, followed by sin and rebellion. Perhaps we should not be very surprised.

So the history of Israel finally ran into the buffers of God's judgement and into the sands of exile. The northern kingdom of Israel was destroyed by Assyria and the people scattered in 721 BC. And in 587 BC, Nebuchadnezzar came down on Jerusalem with his Babylonian armies. The city was besieged and destroyed after terrible suffering. The temple was burned down and the king was carried off into exile along with most of the population of Judah. And all the prophets of the time interpreted these events clearly as the judgement of God.

So was it 'The End'? Was their history at a full stop? Had Israel finally stepped off the stage into the graveyard of oblivion, never to rise again? Many in Israel thought so and sank into despair. But not God. Certainly it was the end for that generation, but it was not the end of God's covenant promise to his people as a whole. And it was certainly not the end of God's mission to bless the nations through this people.

The great prophecies that we sampled earlier from Isaiah were addressed to the exiles, and they spoke of hope beyond judgement. Yes, Israel was suffering God's punishment for their sin, but the time of punishment would end and God's word would be 'Comfort, comfort my people' (Is 40:1). And the heart of that note of comfort and reassurance was that Israel was still God's servant, still called and chosen in Abraham, still intended to be for the blessing of 'all flesh', who would ultimately see God's glory.

> But you, Israel, my servant,
>> Jacob, whom I have chosen,
>> you descendants of Abraham my friend,
> I took you from the ends of the earth,
>> from its farthest corners I called you.
> I said, 'You are my servant';
>> I have chosen you and have not rejected you.
> So do not fear, for I am with you;
>> do not be dismayed for I am your God.
> I will strengthen you and help you;
>> I will uphold you with my righteous right hand. (Is 41:8–10)

So there is a future for God's people. God's mission for Israel still goes on. The promise to Abraham is not dead. The nations will still be blessed.

But the massive question was, how could Israel fulfil such a mission now, given their situation? In exile, Israel was a failed servant. They were disabled and disqualified by their sin and rebellion. They were historically paralysed. This is the utterly realistic assessment of their condition. Here is the same prophet's dire description of Israel in exile:

> Hear, you deaf;
>> look, you blind, and see!
> Who is blind but my servant,
>> and deaf like the messenger I send?
> Who is blind like the one in covenant with me,
>> blind like the servant of the LORD?
> You have seen many things, but you pay no attention;
>> your ears are open, but you do not listen.
> It pleased the LORD
>> for the sake of his righteousness
>> to make his law great and glorious.
> But this is a people plundered and looted,
>> all of them trapped in pits
>> or hidden away in prisons.
> They have become plunder,
>> with no one to rescue them;
> they have been made loot,
>> with no one to say, 'Send them back.' (Is 42:18–22)

The mission of God's Servant. And so, in this context of Israel as God's failing servant, God announces a new beginning, a new arrival—one who would come and embody the mission of Israel by taking it on himself. He is announced as 'my Servant' or 'the Servant of the LORD'. The Servant of the LORD in Isaiah would have a mission *to* Israel—to restore Israel again to God—and would also embody the mission *of* Israel by bringing God's blessing to the nations. This was a task that only the unique Servant of the LORD could accomplish.

Of course, these chapters of Isaiah also prophesy the return of the exiles to Jerusalem and remarkably foretell that it will be Cyrus, king of Persia, who would achieve this by allowing them to go free (Is 44:28). And indeed that is what happened in 538 BC when Cyrus, after conquering Babylon, passed an edict that all the small populations in captivity in Babylon, including the Jews, were free to return to their homelands (2 Chron 36:22–23; Ezra 1:1–4). However, the political level was one thing, but the spiritual condition of Israel and the long-term purpose of God through them was quite another. Cyrus would send Israel back to Jerusalem. But only the Servant could bring Israel back to God. Cyrus would restore the fortunes of physical Israel as a nation in their own land. Only the Servant could fulfil the mission of Israel to be a light to all the nations and take God's salvation to the ends of the earth.

So we need to look carefully at this Servant figure in the prophecies of Isaiah, this anointed Servant of the LORD. For in him we will find crucial clues in our quest for knowing the Holy Spirit through the Old Testament. This Servant is said to be endowed with God's Spirit. So by looking closely at him, we will see the work of the Spirit at its most profound and transforming.

He is introduced as an individual (as distinct from the reference to Israel as God's servant in Is 41:8) for the first time in Isaiah 42:1–7, one of the texts quoted above (it would be worth reading it again at this point). Immediately we are reminded that he will have the Spirit of God upon him in order to carry out the mission entrusted to him. So the anointing power of Yahweh's Spirit, which readers of this prophecy would have associated with the power of God in the lives of the judges and kings like David, will be the hallmark of this Servant. Whatever the Servant does, God will be the one working through him. Whatever mission he has, he has received from God. Whatever he will accomplish, God will be accomplishing it through him. That is the point of being anointed with God's Spirit. It is a commitment and commissioning to do the will and purpose of God. We saw that so many of the historically anointed judges and kings lost sight of the purpose of their own anointing and went off to do their own thing, with disastrous results. *This* anointed Servant, however, will be the perfectly obedient one. By the Spirit of God he will fully accomplish what God intends. So what is that?

There are four main dimensions to the Spirit-filled mission of the Servant that we can see in Isaiah 42:1–7. Each of them deserves a chapter on its own because they are all major biblical themes, but we can only summarize them here.

Justice (Is 42:1, 3, 4)

Justice is the most repeated word in the passage—it occurs three times. The mission of the Servant is, above all, a mission to bring justice. In Old Testament terms, to do justice means putting things right. It includes putting an end to situations that are unfair, situations of exploitation and violence, and restoring those who are the victims of such behaviour. It includes what we mean when we speak of 'human rights'. God says that the work of his Servant will ultimately bring about these things for the nations. So the mission of the Servant is very much in the public arena and ultimately international in scope. It is not just a matter of putting people right with God, or even only of putting things right for Israel. The text speaks rather of a comprehensive and universal achievement of God's justice on earth.

Compassion (Is 42:2–3)

Isaiah 42:2–3 stands in sharp contrast to what has been said about Cyrus, the king who would conquer and crush nations beneath his feet (Is 41). The Servant will be equally effective but without noise and violence. His will be justice with gentleness, strength with compassion. He will be filled with *my* Spirit, promises the LORD, so he will share the LORD's tenderness for the weak and vulnerable. The Servant's mission will be successful, but not coercive. His method will not be to solve the problem of the weak and poor by eliminating them but by restoring them in compassionate justice.

Enlightenment (Is 42:7)

The Servant will bring light and sight to the eyes of those in darkness and blindness. In the immediate context, this was a word of hope for Israel, who were 'blind' and in the darkness of exile. But in the wider horizon of this Servant's global mission, it must include bringing enlightenment to all who live in the darkness of sin without the light of the revelation of God's saving love.

Liberation (Is 42:7)

Again, this would originally have brought joy to the exiles, to know that their Babylonian prison would finally be opened to set them free. But it is the language used of God's liberating intention for human beings in all forms of oppression and bondage, not least to the sin and rebellion that lies at the root of all human suffering.

All of these were important and resonant words for the exiles, to whom the prophet's words were first addressed. But the scope of the Servant's Spirit-filled mission, we have been told, goes beyond Israel to the nations. The Servant will bring the blessing of God's justice to the nations—which echoes the Abrahamic mission of Israel itself.

So, in Isaiah 49:1–6 the Servant speaks and addresses the nations in his own right. He tells how God has given him a mission which has two clear parts.

> Listen to me, you islands;
>> hear this, you distant nations:
> Before I was born the LORD called me;
>> from my mother's womb he has spoken my name. . . .
> He said to me, 'You are my servant,
>> Israel, in whom I will display my splendour.'
> But I said, 'I have laboured in vain;
>> I have spent my strength for nothing at all.
> Yet what is due me is in the LORD's hand,
>> and my reward is with my God.'
> And now the LORD says—
>> he who formed me in the womb to be his servant
> to bring Jacob back to him
>> and gather Israel to himself,
> for I am honoured in the eyes of the LORD
>> and my God has been my strength—
> he says:
> 'It is too small a thing for you to be my servant
>> to restore the tribes of Jacob
>> and bring back those of Israel I have kept.
> I will also make you a light for the Gentiles,
>> that my salvation may reach to the ends of the earth.' (Is 49:1, 3–6)

Notice the transition that takes place between Isaiah 49:5 and Isaiah 49:6. The Servant's mission is to restore Israel to God. But, God says, that is not all. That is not nearly enough. In addition to his mission to Israel, God's long-range purpose for his Servant is to bring God's salvation to the ends of the earth! Also notice carefully that this mission of the Servant to the nations is *in addition to*, not *instead of*, his mission of restoring Israel.

Mission to the nations is an extension of the mission to Israel, not a replacement of it. So the Servant, then, has a mission *to Israel*. And yet, he also embodies the mission *of Israel* by being commissioned to take the blessing of God's salvation to the nations.

But this mission of the Servant will be costly. The verses we have just read in Isaiah 49 speak of frustration and struggle. The next time the Servant speaks, it is to describe his experience of rejection, contempt and physical abuse (Is 50:6). And the climactic Servant passage, Isaiah 52:13–53:12 describes how the Servant will suffer a travesty of justice in which he is finally executed with great violence. Yet through that death, as a self-sacrifice, God's saving purpose will be accomplished. For God will lay on his Servant the sin of us all, and by his death he will enable many to be counted righteous. The Servant, says our prophet, *will accomplish* all God's purpose, but it will be at the cost of his own life. Yet through paying that ultimate price, the Servant will experience victory and vindication from God, and finally be glorified.

> See my servant will act wisely;
>> he will be raised and lifted up and highly exalted. . . .
> But he was pierced for our transgressions,
>> he was crushed for our iniquities;
> the punishment that brought us peace was on him,
>> and by his wounds we are healed.
> We all, like sheep, have gone astray,
>> each of us has turned to our own way;
> and the LORD has laid on him
>> the iniquity of us all. . . .
> After he has suffered
>> he will see the light of life and be satisfied;
> by his knowledge my righteous servant will justify many,
>> and he will bear their iniquities. (Is 52:13; 53:5–6, 11)

Finally, in Isaiah 61:1–2 this Servant (for almost certainly these are the Servant's own words) speaks again, in language that echoes our first passage (Is 42). 'Here I am,' he says. 'This is what I came to do. This is what the Spirit of the LORD has anointed me to do.'

> The Spirit of the Sovereign LORD is on me,
>> because the LORD has anointed me

> to proclaim good news to the poor.
> He has sent me to bind up the broken-hearted,
>   to proclaim freedom for the captives
>   and release from darkness for the prisoners,
> to proclaim the year of the LORD's favour
>   and the day of vengeance of our God,
> to comfort all who mourn. (Is 61:1–2)

Did you notice again the same claim to the anointing of the Spirit of God? And the same multitasking description of his mission? And did you recognize here a word that brings us very close to our next step—namely to Jesus himself with these words on his lips in a synagogue in Nazareth one Sabbath morning?

But just before we jump the centuries to Jesus, let's pause to look back over what we have discovered so far. We have seen the *mission of God*— which is to bless all nations on earth. We have seen the *mission of Israel*— which was to be the vehicle of that blessing to the nations, as promised to Abraham. But in the context of Israel's historical failure, we have seen the *mission of the Servant of the Lord*—a dual mission of restoring Israel and also bringing justice, compassion, enlightenment and liberation to the ends of the earth. All this was prophesied with Israel still in exile.

Well, the exile came to an end in 538 BC. Or did it? Yes, many (though by no means all) Jews returned from Babylon to Judah, rebuilt Jerusalem and eventually the temple also. But the centuries passed and Israel seemed to be still under the heel of foreign oppressors—initially the Persians, then the Greeks and finally the Romans. In heart and spirit they felt like exiles even in their own land. They felt unforgiven, un-liberated and oppressed, as though they were still in captivity. And so they continued to long for deliverance, for true liberation. They took up these prophecies again, knowing that of course they had been partially fulfilled in the remarkable release from Babylon and return to their own land, and yet knowing also that they spoke of something greater and more magnificent yet to come. They longed for the One who would come and achieve all that God had promised. They longed for the Anointed One, the one on whom God's Spirit would rest, the one who would bring in the longed for age of God's unhindered rule and the end of the domination of their enemies.

ANOINTING AND THE MISSION OF JESUS, THE CHRIST

And so it was, then, that on a Sabbath morning in a dusty synagogue in Nazareth, in the backwaters of despised Galilee, a thirty-year-old local villager took his turn to read from the scroll of the Prophets. Jesus read these words that we have since numbered and labelled as Isaiah 61:1–2. Then he sat down. That was the customary posture for explaining the Scriptures. What might the people have expected in a 'sermon' on that text? Probably they would have expected Jesus to comment on the text in the way it had always been expounded. They would have expected to hear it in the way they had always heard it, that is, with the longing ears of a patiently suffering and long awaiting people. 'What we have just read is what God has promised us,' they might have expected to hear Jesus reaffirm. 'The prophet tells us that this is the one we pray for. This is the one we hope for. This is the one who will come to our rescue in the power of God's Spirit like the judges of old. May your anointed one come soon, O LORD! May he even come tomorrow.'

But Jesus shatters that weary assumption with words that must have electrified them all. 'Today,' he quietly begins, 'TODAY this Scripture is being fulfilled! Right here among you, as you listen to *me!*' Jesus claims the prophetic text as his own. Jesus makes himself the embodied sermon. And in doing so, Jesus makes the mission of God, the mission of Israel and the mission of the Servant his own mission. As the astonished people listen, the emphatic scriptural word '*me*' is no longer merely the unidentified voice of an expected One, speaking out of the ancient text of a dusty scroll. It has now become the living and very identifiable voice of one of their own young adults from their own town, speaking out of the preacher's chair in their own synagogue. Jesus ben-Joseph, son of the village carpenter, dares to claim, 'The Spirit of the LORD is upon *me*; the LORD has anointed *me*.'

Through this text Jesus sets out the manifesto of his own mission. Through this text Jesus answers in advance the questions that became more and more insistent as his ministry gathered pace. Who are you? What do you think you are doing? Why do you feel compelled to act in this way? Why are you no longer minding your own business in your father's carpenter's shop? What is the power by which you do these things? And Jesus answers: 'I have been anointed by no less than the Spirit of the LORD God himself, and this text sets out the contours of the mission of God that I am to fulfil.'

But if Jesus is the one anointed by the Spirit of God, what should we expect to find in his life and ministry? Knowing the Holy Spirit through the Old Testament, we should find exactly what we do find—namely that those same four key marks of the anointed Servant of the LORD spelled out in the Old Testament are combined also in the ministry of Jesus.

There was *justice*. That was implicit in his announcement of the reign of God, which all Jesus's contemporaries knew from their Scriptures would bring God's justice to the world. Justice would mean God putting things right, and that is what Jesus went about doing in his personal relationships and teaching. It did not happen in the form of a violent revolution such as some of his supporters wanted. And it did not happen all at once, for the kingdom of God is like a seed growing secretly, or like yeast slowly permeating the dough. But it was a key element in what he taught his disciples to seek. 'Blessed are those who hunger and thirst for justice,' he said. 'Seek first the kingdom of God and his justice' (Mt 5:6; 6:33, my translation).

There was *compassion*. Jesus sought out all those whom society rejected and marginalized, and ministered especially to them: the sick, women, children, the morally and politically compromised (prostitutes and tax collectors), Gentiles, 'sinners'. He even gained a reputation for such behaviour. 'Friend of sinners,' they called him. They meant it as an insult, but Jesus took it as a compliment, for it summarized exactly why he came.

There was *enlightenment*. Teaching, teaching, always teaching—that's the picture of Jesus we see in the Gospels. Jesus certainly opened the eyes of the physically blind, but on an even greater scale he opened the eyes of the spiritually blind to the truth about God, about sin, judgement and forgiveness, about himself and the significance of his coming in relation to the story of Israel, about how life was to be lived by those who submitted to the reign of God.

There was *liberation*. Jesus went about delivering people: from sickness, from the chains of paralysis, from the burden of sin, from the loneliness of ritual exclusion, from demonic oppression, from the prison of remorse. And of course, as he put it himself, he came ultimately to give his life 'as a ransom for many', thus achieving ultimate liberation for sinners.

But the Gospels show us that Jesus not only fulfilled the task of the Servant in the power of the Spirit, he also accepted the fate of the Servant, as prophesied in Isaiah. And that was to suffer rejection, contempt, unjust trial and bloody execution. And in doing all this, he took upon himself the deepest cause of all injustice, cruelty, blindness and bondage—namely our sinful rebellion against God. So Jesus went to the cross, and the cross was the cost of all those dimensions of God's mission as itemized in the mission of the Servant. And yet, although this Servant-mission led him finally to the cross, the process began even on that Sabbath in Nazareth when the people, offended by his claims and his unfavourable contrast between their hard refusal to accept him and the blessing God had brought to Gentile outsiders in the Old Testament (the widow of Zarephath and Naaman the Syrian), hustled him off for an abortive lynching.

ANOINTING AND THE MISSION OF THE CHURCH

So at last we come to our final step. We are those who claim to follow Jesus. We claim to be filled with the same Holy Spirit. And these are not arrogant claims, for they stand upon clear New Testament statements and promises. But if so, what kind of effect should the presence of the Holy Spirit have in our lives and ministry?

To put it more simply, what is 'the anointing'? This is a phrase that is much used in some Christian circles. In itself it is a curious abbreviation and easily misunderstood. We ought to talk more fully of 'the anointing of the Holy Spirit', since the term 'the anointing', when it is used on its own these days, sometimes seems to mean little more than a powerful personality or a particularly spectacular way of speaking and ministering. As applied to preachers in some Christian cultures, it seems to be equated with plenty of noise. The greater the volume of shouting, the more proof there is that the preacher has 'the anointing'. This seems a long way from the anointing of the Servant of the Lord, for whom the proof of the Spirit of God was precisely that he achieved his mission but did not 'shout or cry out or raise his voice in the streets'. In Uganda, during a preaching seminar there, I preached several expositions of the Bible as models that were then evaluated by the participants. One participant's written comment is my favourite. 'I could feel the sweet flow of the Spirit without noising up.' This encouraged me, not only to be reminded that I didn't have to shout and jump around just to prove the Holy Spirit was speaking through the message, but also that the participant had realized (as an apparent surprise) that anointing is not a matter of decibels.

No, anointing by the Spirit, we have now clearly seen from the Bible, is not primarily an external thing that proves its presence by noise (though of course the Spirit of God can make a great deal of noise on occasion, as on the day of Pentecost). Rather, spiritual anointing is primarily an equipping for mission, a commissioning for service. Anointing by God's Spirit is what enables people to do what God wants to get done. And for us who follow Jesus, anointing is enabling us to do what the Scriptures have shown so clearly that God wants to get done. Mission for us has to be *mission in Christ's way*, and that means following the pattern of Spirit-filled servanthood that characterized him.

Now of course Jesus was unique. His life was unique. He was *the* Servant of the LORD—the only perfectly obedient one. His death was unique, for he was the only perfect embodiment of the living God in a human life—the unique God-man. And so he alone could take our sin upon himself in such a way that 'God was in Christ reconciling the world to himself'. Nobody else ever has done, ever could do, or ever needs to do what Jesus alone has done as the Son and Servant of the living God in the power of God's Spirit. In all these ways Jesus uniquely and perfectly fulfilled the mission of God for the salvation of the world.

Yes, but in another sense, Jesus passed on that mission of God to his disciples. The risen Jesus proclaimed his own universal Lordship as the foundation for mandating his disciples to replicate themselves by spreading communities of obedient discipleship throughout all the nations (Mt 28:18–20). For that task he specifically empowers them by the Holy Spirit (Luke 24:45).

> You will receive power when the Holy Spirit comes on you; and you will be my witnesses in Jerusalem, and in all Judea and Samaria, and to the ends of the earth. (Acts 1:8)

So Jesus entrusts to us, to us who stand at the end of the line of this great survey of the biblical story, the mission of God (to bless the nations of humanity), the mission of Israel (to be a light to the nations and the agent of blessing), the mission of the Servant (to bring salvation to the ends of the earth), and his own mission (that repentance and forgiveness of sins should be preached in his name—see Luke 24:47). The church is now the inheritor and agent of all these dimensions of the great biblical mission— and especially the servant mission.

This is how Paul saw his own mission. He was called to be the apostle to the nations (Gentiles), but in that task Paul saw simply the continuation of the mission of God's anointed Servant. So in Romans 15:8–9 he describes how the Messiah (Christ) became a servant of *Israel* so that the gospel could go to *the nations*. And in Acts 13:47, he explicitly quotes the Isaiah texts and applies that servant task and responsibility to himself and his small band of church-planting missionaries.

So, in line with Paul, we need to see that the mission of the Spirit-anointed Servant to the nations becomes ours too. We too need to be committed to the same holistic mission as the Servant of Isaiah 42, Isaiah 61 and Luke 4. For it is clear that in his own earthly lifetime Jesus did not 'complete' the tasks of bringing justice, enlightenment and liberation to the ends of the earth. These same tasks are ours. And they call for the same combination of spiritual and physical, personal and social, historical and eternal dimensions as they did in his own ministry. For it is in *all* of these that the good news of the gospel is to be heard, applied and lived out.

Historically the church has indeed seen its mission in these broad terms. It is not a matter of engaging in *both* the gospel *and* social action, as if Christian social action was something separate from the gospel itself. The gospel has to be demonstrated in word and deed. Biblically, the gospel includes the totality of all that is good news from God for all that is bad news in human life—in every sphere. So, like Jesus, authentic Christian mission has included good news for the poor, compassion for the sick and suffering, justice for the oppressed, liberation for the enslaved. The gospel of the Servant of God in the power of the Spirit of God addresses every area of human need and every area that has been broken and twisted by sin and evil. And the heart of the gospel, in all of these areas, is the cross of Christ.

CONCLUSION

What then is anointed mission? If it is anointed by the Spirit of God, then it will be mission that reflects the one who quoted the Old Testament and said 'The Spirit of the Lord is upon me, because the Lord has anointed me . . .' If it is to be mission in the way of Christ, then it will be mission in the way of the One who unquestionably knew the Holy Spirit through the Old Testament.

There is a bracelet that carries the letters WWJD. It is meant to remind its wearers of the slogan 'What Would Jesus Do?' as a way of facing everything in life from the perspective of that question. I think if you had given one to Luke, he would have changed the letters to WDJD—'What *Did* Jesus Do?' and then asked you to read the rest of his Gospel.

Filled with the Holy Spirit (as Luke stresses often), Jesus ate and drank with the poor and the marginalized, fed the hungry, talked with children, taught the crowds, comforted the bereaved, restored the ostracized, released the demon-oppressed, challenged the rich and the authorities, brought people forgiveness of sins, healed relationships as well as bodies, and in all of this declared that God reigns—here and now, and still to come. And all of this was part of *his* anointed mission. 'The Spirit of the Lord is upon *me*,' he said, 'for the Lord has anointed *me*' (Luke 4:18). Yes, but he also said, 'As the Father has sent me, I am sending *you*.' And with that he breathed on them and said, 'Receive the Holy Spirit' (John 20:21–22).

Mission in the way of Christ, then, is mission that is empowered by the anointing Spirit of God, committed to the justice and compassion of God, characterized by the Servant of God, including even suffering and the way of the cross. Before we pray so glibly (for ourselves or others) for the anointing of the Spirit, perhaps it would be good to remind ourselves what the Bible says that will mean.

CHAPTER FIVE

THE COMING SPIRIT

O ur exploration of the work of the Holy Spirit in the Old Testament has opened up some very broad horizons so far. We have seen how the Israelites recognized the Spirit of Yahweh, their God:

- in creating the universe and sustaining all life on earth

- in powerful leadership, yet exercised humbly in Moses

- in the words of the prophets who courageously stood for truth and justice

- in the anointing of their kings and in the expectation of a truly anointed one to come

But as Old Testament believers looked forward through the eyes of their prophets and indeed through the hopes of their worship songs, they longed for a new era of the unhindered, unchallenged reign of Yahweh, the LORD God of Israel. That is, they wanted to see as a reality what they affirmed by faith—the kingdom of God (as the New Testament calls it). And a very significant part of that expectation was that when God fully established his reign over his people and over the earth, there would be a fresh and un-precedented outpouring of God's Spirit. This, they believed, would be one of the clearest signs of the arrival of the new age of salvation and blessing—it would be the era of God's Spirit. This did not mean of course that they thought the Spirit of God was not present already. Our study so far has shown just how much the Israelites did indeed know about the Spirit of God and exactly how they thought of his activities. But this future coming of the Spirit would be more than anything hitherto known, and would have some life-changing, history-changing, earth-changing effects. The creating, empowering, prophetic, anointing Spirit whom they already knew was also the coming Spirit for whom they longed. And it is this future longing for the coming of the Spirit of God (sometimes called the 'eschatological' vision of the Old Testament) that leads directly on to its fulfilment at Pentecost and the great teaching of the New Testament about the Holy Spirit in relation to Jesus Christ.

So let us look at three passages in the prophets that describe the coming Spirit and the amazing effects that they anticipate—one from Isaiah, one from Ezekiel and one from Joel.

RE-CREATION AND RIGHTEOUSNESS: ISAIAH 32

Like so many of the chapters in Isaiah, this one mixes words of imminent judgement on the people of the prophet's own day in Jerusalem with words of future hope. It begins with the bold affirmation that one day there will be a truly righteous king reigning over the people (in contrast to the degenerate dynasty that occupied the throne of David at the time).

> See a king will reign in righteousness and rulers will rule with justice.
> (Is 32:1)

This, as we have seen, is an essential part of Israel's hope and faith—that an ideal king would do what their historical kings were anointed, but lamentably failed, to do.

Later in the chapter, that age of righteous rule is further described as an outpouring of God's Spirit in such a way that everything is transformed by it. Remember that the Spirit of God in Old Testament thought is connected with creation, with justice and with the exercise of power for the benefit of society. In this passage all three realms are affected, as they are flooded and washed by the outpoured Spirit.

> Till the Spirit is poured on us from on high,
>   and the desert becomes a fertile field,
>   and the fertile field seems like a forest.
> The LORD's justice will dwell in the desert
>   his righteousness live in the fertile field.
> The fruit of that righteousness will be peace;

its effect will be quietness and confidence for ever.
My people will live in peaceful dwelling places,
  in secure homes,
  in undisturbed places of rest. (Is 32:15–18)

The *created order* (Is 32:15) will be renewed and restored to its full fertility and growth. The Spirit who is already constantly at work sustaining and renewing creation (Ps 104; see ch. 1), will then do so in full abundance and all nature will be transformed by his power and presence. The picture given here of the effects on creation of the outpouring of the Spirit are a condensed form of longer and more graphic descriptions of the new creation later in the book of Isaiah. Read especially Isaiah 65:17–25. Perhaps only poetry can express what lies beyond our imagination. William Cowper, the author of some familiar Christian hymns, composed a lengthy poem, of which the following lines catch something of Isaiah's vision:

Rivers of gladness water all the earth,
And clothe all climes with beauty; the reproach
Of barrenness is past. The fruitful field
Laughs with abundance; and the land, once lean,
Or fertile only in its own disgrace,
Exults to see its thistly curse repeal'd.
The various seasons woven into one,
And that one season an eternal spring,
The garden fears no blight, and needs no fence,
For there is none to covet, all are full.
The lion, and the libbard, and the bear,
Graze with the fearless flocks. . . .
One song employs all nations; and all cry,
'Worthy the Lamb, for he was slain for us!'
The dwellers in the vales and on the rocks
Shout to each other, and the mountain tops
From distant mountains catch the flying joy;
Till, nation after nation taught the strain,
Earth rolls the rapturous Hosanna round.[1]

---

[1]William Cowper, 'The Task,' book 6, lines 763–774, 791–797, in *The Complete Poetical Works of William Cowper, Esq,* ed. Rev. A. M. H. Stebbing (New York: D. Appleton, 1856), pp. 344–345. 'Libbard' probably means leopard.

The *moral order* (Is 32:16) will be set right once again. The outpouring of the Spirit—who is, as we saw in chapter 3, the Spirit of justice—will inevitably mean that the very character of God will pervade the universe. Righteousness and justice are two of the biggest words in the whole ethical vocabulary of the Old Testament. They are not merely things that we are supposed to do in human life (though they certainly are that, of course). They define the order of the universe under God's rule, for, as Psalm 97:2 puts it, they are the foundation of God's throne. So when the Spirit is poured out, then God's own moral character will prevail, and will once again flood the whole of creation.

It is worth noting that Isaiah 32:16 sets justice and righteousness in the desert and in the fertile field. Righteousness and justice apply not only to the social world of human relationships (that is what immediately follows in Is 32:17), but also to the created environment in which we live—whether the uncultivated wilderness or the cultivated lands of human occupation. These too are places where justice is needed, for they are both the victims of vast and vicious injustice at human hands. The Spirit who created and sustains the earth also longs for it to be treated with justice and righteousness. And this vision looks forward to the day when it finally will be.

The *social order* (Is 32:17–18) will be restored to *shalom*. This beautiful word in Isaiah 32:17 speaks of human society enjoying the fruit of justice, which means the end of all violence, fear and dislocation because of the absence of all the things that produce them. In their place comes rest, security, confidence and wellbeing. All this too the prophet sees as the result of the outpouring of the Spirit.

So then, in the long gaze of the prophet, all these things will come about when the Spirit is poured out from on high. As with so many of the words of the prophets, we have to allow for the 'telescopic' nature of a vision like this. Yes, we know that the Spirit was poured out on the day of Pentecost. But all these full effects of the Spirit's flood lie ahead of us yet. It is similar to what the New Testament teaches about the kingdom of God. It was indeed inaugurated by Jesus in his earthly lifetime. And yet we still look for its complete realization at his return. We still pray, 'Your kingdom come, your will be done on earth as it is in heaven.' There is an 'already but not yet' about the kingdom of God. In the same way, we have received the firstfruits of the Holy Spirit or in Paul's metaphor, the 'down-payment' or guarantee (Eph 1:13–14). But we still long and pray, as Romans 8:18–27 reminds us, for the completion of God's work of cosmic renewal, the new creation and the ultimate reign of God in righteousness and peace.

RENEWAL AND RESURRECTION: EZEKIEL 36–37

Ezekiel knew a thing or two about the Spirit of God. It was the Spirit, he tells us, that on several occasions had literally lifted him up and carried him around the place—sometimes (it would seem) in physical reality and sometimes in his visions—once even by the hair of his head (see Ezek 2:2; 3:12, 14, 24; 8:3; 11:24; 37:1).

Ezekiel lived among the exiles in Babylon. He was among those who had been deported by Nebuchadnezzar in 597 BC. Ten years later, Nebuchadnezzar went on to destroy the city and burn the temple in 587 BC, and a whole new flood of captives from Judah joined Ezekiel and the other exiles languishing in their 'grave' (for that is what they called it, as we shall see). They thought it was all over. But was it? God had apparently become the enemy of his own people. By his graphic acted prophecies, Ezekiel made it clear that it was the hand of their own God, Yahweh, who was wielding the sword of Nebuchadnezzar. Was it really the end for the nation of Israel? Could there be any hope for the future? It seems that for the first few years, the first group of exiles with Ezekiel were optimistic about going home soon, since the city and temple were still standing. But once the Babylonian armies stormed the walls of Jerusalem, the hopes of the people lay buried in the smouldering rubble of the city and the temple. 'We might as well be dead,' they said. 'We are nothing more than dry bones here in exile, with no life, no hope, no future.' And they were right. There was no hope at all—from their side. Israel had sinned itself to the graveyard of history.

But they reckoned without God. The message of the prophets, especially Jeremiah and Ezekiel (who both witnessed the exile) and the great chapters of Isaiah 40–55 that address the exiles, was that the same God who had driven them from his land in anger at their persistent sin and rebellion for generations would eventually bring them back from exile to their own land again. And he did in 538 BC when Babylon itself fell to the Persians and King Cyrus passed a decree that released small captive communities like the people of Judah to return to their homelands. The return from exile was the immediate historical fulfilment of so many of the prophetic predictions that God would gather his scattered people and restore them to their own land again.

But Ezekiel sees beyond the physical restoration of the people of Judah to their little territory round Jerusalem. Like the other prophets, he saw an even greater restoration of the people to God himself and also that this required an even deeper work of grace in the hearts and wills of the people. They needed not merely political liberation and geographical relocation. They needed a radical heart transplant. In fact, they needed nothing short of resurrection. And both would be the work of the coming Spirit of God. We need to look at two passages where Ezekiel describes the work of the Spirit in these breathtaking (or perhaps better, breath-giving) transformations.

Ezekiel 36:25–27

> I will sprinkle clean water on you, and you will be clean; I will cleanse you
> from all your impurities and from all your idols. I will give you a new heart
> and put a new spirit in you; I will remove from you your heart of stone and
> give you a heart of flesh. And I will put my Spirit in you and move you to
> follow my decrees and be careful to keep my laws.

This is one of my favourite passages in the book of Ezekiel, and indeed in the Bible. It presents the gospel of God's grace in such graphic categories and is the nearest you get in the Old Testament to regeneration by the Spirit. It begins (in Ezek 36:24), as the prophets habitually do, on the plane of anticipated history—the return of Israel to the land at the end of the exile. But it moves quickly beyond anything that ever perfectly characterized the returned exiles in their postexilic history. It speaks of spiritual reality with ethical results. It speaks of cleansing and moral transformation, of radical inward change and radical outward obedience. It is, in short, a very rich word about what God alone can do through his Spirit. Knowing the Holy Spirit through the Old Testament could not be more profound, or more prophetic of Christ's work, than this.

It can only begin, of course, with the cleansing and forgiving work of God. That is a matter of pure grace and has to be an act of God. We cannot cleanse ourselves, but God promises to do so in Ezekiel 36:25. However, that is only the start. Ezekiel saw that Israel's sin (and ours) lies much deeper than either ritual uncleanness or even merely external actions. And so he goes on to describe the work of the Spirit of God in the very depths of our being.

The problem lay not just in Israel's behaviour, but in the source of their behaviour—the attitudes and mentality that characterized them. In short, the problem was in their 'heart' and 'spirit'. The two terms *heart (leb)*, and *spirit (rûah)* describe the inner human person. In Hebrew idiom, the heart is the locus of the mind, not primarily of the emotions. It is in or with the heart that a person thinks, decides and wills. The spirit reflects the inner feelings and aspirations of the person—again, not merely in the sense of emotions, but in terms of the attitude, disposition and motivation which one brings to choices and actions. The two terms are closely related, but not identical. Israel will have to *think* differently, and *feel* differently. Their whole inner world needs to be transformed.

No longer was it enough to expect God to 'circumcise their hearts' in the graphic metaphor of Deuteronomy 30:6 (cf. Jer 4:4). Much more radical surgery is needed now. So . . . God proposes a heart transplant. He will remove the *heart of stone*, which has made Israel hard, cold, unresponsive and dead to God's words of command or of appeal. And he will implant in its place *a heart of flesh*—flesh which is living, warm and soft, and which, in Hebrew idiom, speaks of close kinship and intimate relationship. God will transform Israel's whole mindset and fundamental orientation of will, desire and purpose.

The purpose of such transformation is wholehearted obedience. But that requires a further action of God upon Israel. '*I will put my Spirit in you.*' . . . And the effect of that will be that Israel will at last be obedient. . . . The paradox here is that God himself, by the gift of his Spirit, will see to it that his renewed people actually will fulfil the condition that he himself sets.[2]

God demands obedience. The Spirit of God enables the obedience that God demands. This is the wonderful promise of this text.

A similar paradox is found in Deuteronomy 30:1–10 (on which Ezekiel may well be reflecting here). There, in verses 2 and 10 (cf. 6:5), the fundamental command that Israel should love God with all their heart and soul is echoed in the condition that they must turn to him and obey him with all their heart and soul. Yet in the very centre of the passage (v. 6), God will do in and for Israel what Israel's history so gloomily demonstrated they could not do for themselves. God's grace will give what God's law requires. The gospel is already breathing through such texts in the law—as it is here in Ezekiel's prophecy.

---

[2]Christopher J. H. Wright, *The Message of Ezekiel*, The Bible Speaks Today (Downers Grove, IL: InterVarsity, 2003), 296–297.

There is, of course, a tension here (as throughout the Bible) between the role of human will and choice and the role of divine causation. God commands obedience and we must make our free choice to respond and obey—or not. But at the same time, God gives his Spirit and 'makes' that obedience happen. One pole of the tension affirms human freedom. The other affirms divine sovereignty. No amount of theology will ever be able to provide a complete correlation of both truths which does not leave us still conscious of mysteries somewhere beyond our grasp. Ultimately, the proof and the test come through experience.[3]

And that seems to be what Paul comes down to when reflecting on the role of the Spirit in relation to the law in actual practical experience of Christian living in Romans 8. The Spirit (which he significantly calls 'the Spirit of life') sets us free from the law at one level—in relation to sin and death and the inability of our fallen human nature to obey God. Yet the very purpose for which Christ died, and for which we are granted the indwelling Spirit, is 'in order that the righteous requirements of the law might be fully met in us, who do not live according to the sinful human nature ['flesh'] but according to the Spirit' (Rom 8:1–4).

Paul almost certainly had Ezekiel in mind as he wrote this, proving that the Spirit Paul knew through the risen Christ was the same Spirit whom he knew from his Old Testament Scriptures—and the same Spirit whom we can know in the same twofold way, through Christ and the Scriptures.

Ezekiel 37:1–14

Thorough washing and a heart transplant—such are the wonderful promises connected with the coming of the Spirit in the section we have just read. But such actions, though possibly cosmetic, are not particularly helpful if performed on a corpse. And that is how the exiles felt—dead. As dead as dry bones. Look at what they were saying about themselves: 'Our bones are dried up and our hope is gone; we are cut off' (Ezek 37:11). So God has to come up with an even more powerful solution. Nothing short of bringing the people back from the grave will be enough. Can God really do that? Can the Spirit of God give life to the dead? 'Can these bones live?'

Ezekiel is given the answer in a vision that is probably the one thing most people remember about him—the valley of dry bones and the

---

[3]Ibid., 297.

mesmerizing mental picture of them all coming together, bone to bone, growing back their soft tissues, and then rising in unison to life as a great army of soldiers. No horror movie could produce more graphic and startling special effects than the way Ezekiel tells his vision. And no passage of Scripture, short of the actual resurrection of Jesus himself, more powerfully portrays the sovereign Holy Spirit of God—'the Lord and Giver of life'. Here again we are privileged to learn something of the power of the Holy Spirit through the Old Testament.

Ezekiel's graphic vision of dry bones is a picture of how the exiles thought of themselves—that is, as good as dead. Ezekiel first of all hears God's astounding questions, 'Can these bones live?' Ezekiel would not have doubted God's power to revive the dead (there were stories in the Scriptures to that effect), but surely only when there was a body to revive soon after death, not when all that was left were bleached bones. But then, in remarkably courageous obedience, Ezekiel, in his vision, 'preached' to the bones, so that the flesh came back upon them. That is itself was an amazing miracle of reversal, but what advantage has a lifeless corpse over a lifeless skeleton? No breath, no life, no hope. It is at that crucial point in the vision that the Spirit-breath of God arrives on the scene.

> Then suddenly, into the continuing silence of death, the divine voice speaks for the third time, to initiate the second and final part of the momentous revival: *'Prophecy to the breath . . . "Come from the four winds, O breath, and breathe into these slain, that they may live"'* (9). At this point it is worth noting the dominance of this whole scene by the Hebrew word here translated *breath*. It is the word *rûah*, and it is used ten times in this single section (37:1–14), but with a wonderful variety of significance. At the beginning and end of the section it refers unmistakably to the Spirit of Yahweh which had lifted Ezekiel and *set* him in the valley (1), and would eventually also lift the whole people and *settle* (same word) them back in their own land (14). But the word also means 'breath' in a literal, straightforward sense, and this is its meaning in verses 5, 6, 8 and 10. *Rûah* also means 'wind'— powerfully moving air—and this too is found in verse 9, where *from the four winds* means, 'from all directions of the earth'. The central use, in verse 9, *O breath*, which Ezekiel is commanded to summon by prophetic word, has the ambiguity that it doubtless means the Spirit of the living God, but also accomplishes the miraculous act of artificial respiration by which the corpses

begin literally to breathe again and stand up alive and vigorous as an army. So the whole scene, then, is permeated by the various activities of *rûah*— human, natural and divine: breath, wind and Spirit. And the single total effect of all this activity of *rûah* is life, life out of utter deadness.

There is another event being mirrored here. The picture of the divine breath breathing into inanimate bodies so that they come to life undoubtedly recalls the original creation of humanity as recorded in Genesis 2:7. In that account also there is a two-stage process of divine activity. First God fashioned the human creature out of the lifeless dust of the earth. At a biological level we share the same stuff and substance as the rest of creation, animal, vegetable and mineral. But then, in an act of tender intimacy, God breathed into human nostrils the breath of life[4] so that the human became a living being—living because breathing. So here in Ezekiel's vision, the unique, life-giving power of the creator God once more breathes life into inert human flesh and brings forth a miracle of new existence. The revival of Israel will be nothing less than the re-creation of humanity—a thought we must return to. . . .

When we seek to understand Ezekiel's message in its own context, it is vital to remember that his main point was to bring hope *to Israel as a people*. His vision and its interpretation was not intended to teach a doctrine of individual bodily resurrection, but to compare the restoration of Israel to the imaginary bringing back to life of the bones of a massive army of slain soldiers. The language is symbolic and metaphorical, and its application was for the still living, not the already dead. That is, Ezekiel's vision promised the exiles still alive in Babylon that there would be a living future for Israel in the return from exile; it did not promise that those who had died [in the siege of Jerusalem] in 587 or those who would die during the exile itself, would literally come back to life to share in that return. . . .

Nevertheless, there is no doubt that Ezekiel's vision of the dry bones and their revival functions is a very important link in a theological chain to which the full biblical hope of resurrection is anchored. At one end is the connection we have already noted between Ezekiel's vision of God breathing life into the lifeless bodies of Israel's defunct army and the Genesis tradition of God breathing the breath of life into the human-shaped pile of dust that then became a living human being [Gen 2:7]. God's renewal of Israel was like a rerun of creation. Or, to put it the other way around, what God was about to do for Israel would be like the first act in the renewal of humanity

---

[4]See the discussion of this text, and what it does and does not mean, in chapter 1 above.

as a whole. . . . Just as [Israel's] sin and punishment mirrored the fallenness of the whole human race, so too their restoration would prefigure God's gracious purpose of redemption for humanity. Resurrection for Israel anticipated resurrection for all.

And at the centre of the chain, of course, stands the risen Jesus himself. The most significant echo of Ezekiel 37 comes in a locked room on the very evening of his resurrection, when, we read, '[Jesus] breathed on them and said, "Receive the Holy Spirit"' [John 20:22]. The Lord of life himself, freshly risen to his feet from where he had lain among the bones of the dead,[5] adopts simultaneously the posture of Ezekiel in summoning the breath of God, and the posture of God himself in commanding the breath of the Spirit to come upon the disciples.

But this risen Jesus was the Messiah. And slowly the disciples came to realize that in the resurrection of the Messiah God had done, through Jesus, what they were hoping and expecting that God would do for Israel [Luke 24:19–27, 45–49]. The redemption, revival and resurrection of Israel were embodied in the resurrection of Jesus the Messiah. As James would later affirm the Davidic monarchy was also restored [Acts 15:16–17], and as Hebrews would argue in detail, all the great realities of Israel's faith and covenantal security are now embodied in Jesus and inherited by those who believe in him—believing Jews and Gentiles alike.

So the resurrection of Jesus *did* fulfil the vision of Ezekiel through [Christ's] personal embodiment of the restoration of Israel. But, in line with the thrust of our earlier point, the restoration of Israel through Jesus was also the first stage of God's wider project of the redemption of the human race. The breath that breathed life into the dead came from *the four winds*—that is, from the Spirit of God who is at work everywhere in the world, in all directions. That which was focused with tremendous resurrection power on Ezekiel's dead bodies, and then on the dead Messiah, is the same power that is available to the ends of the earth to bring life, salvation and the hope of bodily resurrection to all who trust in the one who sends it. For 'if the Spirit of him who raised Jesus from the dead is living in you, he who raised Christ from the dead will also give life to your mortal bodies through his Spirit, who lives in you' (Rom 8:11).[6]

---

[5]I am speaking figuratively here of the tomb in general as the place of dry bones; we know that Jesus was laid in a new tomb in which nobody had previously been interred.
[6]Wright, *Message of Ezekiel*, 306–311. Used by permission.

Once again, then, we find that the great teachings, prophecies and pictures of the Old Testament about the Spirit enrich our personal experience of life in Christ. Of course we say that we believe in the Holy Spirit. But, as we have seen from the very first chapter of this book, are we fully aware of all that he is, of all he has done, still does and will do? He is the Spirit of the God who spoke creation into existence and breathed life into humanity. He is the Spirit whom Ezekiel saw raising God's people from the dead. He is the Spirit who raised Jesus from the dead. He is the Spirit who now gives life to his people and to every individual in whom he dwells by faith in Christ. This—we gasp when we realize—is none other than 'the Spirit who lives in you'.

REPENTANCE AND RESTORATION: JOEL 2

At last we come to the passage which some people might have expected us to tackle right at the start of our study since it is the Old Testament text quoted by Peter on the day of Pentecost. And for some people (though not readers of this book by now), that is about all they know of the Holy Spirit in the Old Testament—namely that Joel foretold that the Spirit would be poured out, and since that happened at Pentecost, what more needs to be said?

> And afterwards,
>   I will pour out my Spirit on all people.
> Your sons and daughters will prophesy,
>   your old men will dream dreams,
>   your young men will see visions.
> Even on my servants, both men and women,
>   I will pour out my Spirit in those days.
> I will show wonders in the heavens
>   and on the earth,
>   blood and fire and billows of smoke.
> The sun will be turned to darkness
>   and the moon to blood
>   before the coming of the great and dreadful day of the LORD.
> And everyone who calls
>   on the name of the LORD will be saved;
> for on Mount Zion and in Jerusalem
>   there will be deliverance,

as the LORD has said,
even among the survivors
whom the LORD calls. (Joel 2:28–32)

As always, we need to set this text in its wider context in the book of Joel, and especially in the remarkable second chapter.

Joel prophesied in the midst of a national disaster which he sees as the judgement of God. It is described as an invasion of locusts in Joel 1, and either it was simply that (locust invasions were, and still are, utterly devastating) or it was an invasion by some enemy army that is described metaphorically in this way. Most likely, it was in fact a plague of locusts. Joel 2 continues this theme for its first eleven verses. These verses are a mixture of simple description and frightening images, which those who have ever witnessed a locust attack say is very accurate. There is the devouring devastation (Joel 2:3), their frightening appearance and noise (Joel 2:4–5), the panic they cause (Joel 2:6), their invasion of cities and even houses (Joel 2:7–9), the way they make the ground seem to shiver and ripple and the sky turn dark (Joel 2:10).

But Joel mixes with these literal descriptions some other phrases that see behind it all the judgement of God. This is the 'day of the LORD' (Joel 2:1, 11); it is like the fall of humanity in the garden of Eden (Joel 2:3); it is like the earthquake and darkness that symbolize the dread presence of God's wrath (Joel 2:10). And finally, quite explicitly, the army of locusts is nothing less than the LORD's own army, with him at the head—utterly frightening stuff.

The LORD thunders
at the head of his army;
his forces are beyond number,
and mighty is the army that obeys his command.
The day of the LORD is great;
it is dreadful.
Who can endure it? (Joel 2:11)

But then suddenly and surprisingly, there is a complete change of tone at Joel 2:12. The God who is at the head of the devouring army of locusts in Joel 2:11 suddenly appeals to the people in the next verse to turn to him in repentance, 'even now'.

'Even now,' declares the LORD, 'return to me with all your heart, with fasting
and weeping and mourning.'

Joel then jumps into the space created by what God has just said in Joel
2:12, with some added motivation and reasons to do what God says (Joel
2:13–14), with some practical instructions (Joel 2:15–17a) and with a
ready-made liturgy of repentance (Joel 2:17b).

This, then, is the context that is leading us on eventually to the great
promise of the outpouring of the Spirit later in the chapter. Before we get
there, however, we need to see what this chapter says about genuine repentance and total forgiveness. For only then will we appreciate its promise of
universal blessing. This, after all, was how Peter applied it on the day of
Pentecost. On that occasion, Peter called for repentance and promised
forgiveness and blessing to all who would respond to the outpouring of the
Spirit and the message about Jesus. Peter himself knew the Holy Spirit
through the Old Testament, so we must follow his example. Let's look, then,
at what Joel has to say about repentance and forgiveness, to prepare ourselves for what he says about the coming of the Spirit.

Genuine repentance (Joel 2:12–17)

How can we tell that the repentance described in these verses is genuine?
Fundamentally because it is based upon *truth*. The motivation, the methods,
and even the format, of the repentance Joel calls for are all founded on
essential biblical truths about God and about God's people. At least three
great realities stand out in these verses:

(1) *God's grace (Joel 2:13)*

Rend your heart
    and not your garments.
Return to the LORD your God,
    for he is gracious and compassionate,
slow to anger and abounding in love,
    and he relents from sending calamity.

The last three lines of this wonderful verse are like a refrain in the Old
Testament. In fact, they are God's name-badge. It is God's own self-
description when Moses asked to know his identity. This is who Yahweh is.
This is the personal character that is to be understood every time that name
is used. It comes for the first time in Exodus 34:6, and remarkably, there

also it is in the context of terrible sin and the threat of total destruction. But (as we saw in chapter 2 of this book in our trilogy) because of the selfless intercession of Moses, God's wrath was averted and his amazing grace and forgiveness were demonstrated. From then on, the phrases of this great self-affirmation by God echo through the Old Testament at least eight times. You can check it out (it will make an encouraging read) in Numbers 14:18; Nehemiah 9:17; Psalms 86:15; 103:8; 145:8; Jonah 4:2; Nahum 1:3; and of course here in Joel 2:13.

In fact, these phrases (the last three lines of Joel 2:13) are the nearest the Old Testament comes to what we might call 'propositional theology'— that is, defining the attributes of God. Deuteronomy 6:4 would be another such text—categorically affirming that the LORD God is one. These verses define that one God as fundamentally the God of grace and compassion.

But how can we cope with putting Joel 2:11 (God's anger) and Joel 2:13 (God's grace) together? They are both affirmed. And of course Israel knew Yahweh as the God of wrath against all human wickedness, pride and idolatry. But they also knew that this same God was the God of grace, of infinite love and mercy, who longed for nothing more than to have sinners turn to him in repentance so that he could meet them with mercy and blessing. For of course Joel 2:11 and Joel 2:13 do not actually stand together. Joel 2:12 comes in between, and what makes the difference is genuine repentance. Ultimately, we can hold these great Old Testament truths together only at the foot of the cross. For there we see the total outpouring of God's judgement along-side the ultimate demonstration of God's grace, as the wrath of God was borne by God himself in the willing person of his own Son.

(2) God's covenant (Joel 2:17a) 'Return to the LORD *your* God,' urges Joel 2:13. 'Spare *your people*, LORD,' prays Joel 2:17. This is the language of the covenant relationship in which God had repeatedly said, 'I will be your God and you will be my people.' It is amplified by the phrase 'your inheritance', also in Joel 2:17—which could refer to the people or the land or both together.

So here is repentance which appeals to the great fact of the covenant relationship between God and his people in the Old Testament. The people of Israel at that time were God's people in God's land, and God had made his commitment to them (as they had to him, of course, and then broken it). So they appeal to God not to break his commitment, not to destroy them, but rather to remember his own promises. The Israelites had been unfaithful to God, but they appeal to God to be faithful to himself. That is a firm foundation for all prayer, but especially repentance.

This is exactly the basis on which Moses, as we saw, appealed to God to spare the Israelites after the great apostasy of the golden calf in Exodus 32–34, which we considered in chapter two above. We looked at the prayer of Moses as he recalls it in Deuteronomy 9:25–29. It would be worth reading that prayer again and comparing it with what Joel puts in the mouths of the people here. In fact, you will find that this appeal to God's covenant marks all the great prayers of repentance and intercession in the Old Testament. Perhaps the most notable are those of Moses, Nehemiah and Daniel, respectively recorded in Deuteronomy 9, Nehemiah 9 and Daniel 9. That makes it easy to remember. Dial 999[7] for repentance and intercession.

(3) God's honour (Joel 2:17b) If God's people suffer shame and disgrace, then so does the God they call their own. The watching nations would not only mock Israel, they would jeer at Israel's God as well. 'Where is their God?' they will taunt. And so, in their repentance and appeal to God to be merciful to them, they make this point to God. Is this what he wants to see happen? How can God allow his honour and glory to be trampled on and ridiculed in the world? Remember Moses saying to God, 'What will the Egyptians think if you destroy these people in the wilderness after delivering them out of slavery?'

One of the marks of genuine repentance is that you find yourself more concerned for God's honour than your own. Coming to an awareness of your own sin can (should) produce deep shame. That is especially so if it is the kind of sin that involves other people and can bring embarrassment at the very least and complete ruin of one's reputation at the worst. But what makes it far worse is when you suddenly realize: 'I am a Christian. I bear the name of Christ. What I have done is a disgrace to *his* name, not just mine. What damage this is doing, or could do, to the honour of the Lord and the good name of his people.' At that point, you begin to cry out to the Lord, 'Lord, have mercy. Spare me and forgive me, please, but do it not just for my sake, but for the sake of *your* name. I can't bear the thought of what people will say about you and all the others who carry your name.

---

[7] 999 is the telephone number for the emergency services in the UK, the equivalent of 911 in the USA.

Lord, protect the honour of your own name. Don't let *my* sin and folly be the cause of mockery and slander against *you*.' When we begin to think and pray like that, it is evidence of the work of the Holy Spirit.

Here then are the foundations for real prayer, and genuine repentance that moves the heart of God. These foundations are simple, but massive, biblical truths: God's identity and character is to be gracious; God is committed to his covenant promises; God's greatest concern is for the glory of his own name in the world. So when we are turning to God in repentance, or seeking to lead others to do so, let's get to the heart of God. Let our focus be not on my need, my fears and my reputation, but on God's character, God's covenant and God's honour. Then we can turn the 'may' of Joel 2:14 into a confident, 'He will turn . . .'

Total forgiveness (Joel 2:18–27)

Try to imagine the scene. A massive act of national repentance is taking place, publicly announced (Joel 2:15), supported by every level of society (Joel 2:16), and led by the religious leaders (Joel 2:17). That is what Joel calls for, and what may well have happened.

At the end of Joel 2:17 there is silence. Waiting for God.

The words of scorn put into the mouths of the nations—'Where is their God?'—are echoed as words of longing in the hearts of the people, 'Where is our God? What is his reply?' When you need a word from the Lord, you need a prophet, and that is where Joel once again steps into the situation with exactly that. He has a word from God, and it is almost beyond belief. The God who was thundering in judgement (Joel 2:11), now speaks words of utterly incredible grace and mercy, beginning with the one they most needed to hear: 'the LORD took pity on his people' (Joel 2:18).

The message that follows in Joel 2:19–27 is one of immediate and total forgiveness, demonstrated in restoration and blessing. The grace they had appealed to in Joel 2:13 will now pour itself out in overwhelming physical beneficence. Take a moment to read and savour those verses, remembering that you are hearing them in the context of a devastating plague of locusts that has brought the whole land and its agricultural survival to the brink of extinction. Here are just the opening and closing notes.

> Then the LORD was jealous for his land
>   and took pity on his people.

The LORD replied to them:
'I am sending you grain, new wine and olive oil,
     enough to satisfy you fully;
never again will I make you
     an object of scorn to the nations.' . . .
'You will have plenty to eat, until you are full,
     and you will praise the name of the LORD your God,
     who has worked wonders for you;
never again will my people be shamed.
Then you will know that I am in Israel,
     that I am the LORD your God,
     and that there is no other;
never again will my people be shamed.' (Joel 2:18–19, 26–27)

What stands out in this joyful passage, as much as in the description of the people's repentance in Joel 2:12–17, are the same three elements: God's covenant, God's grace, and God's honour, though with the strongest emphasis undoubtedly on the central one—grace.

(1) God's covenant. We find here the same possessive relationships that were central to the covenant between God and Israel. They frame the whole section: 'his land . . . his people' in Joel 2:18; 'your God . . . my people' in Joel 2:27. That is the only framework for the saving work of God and experience of his mercy and forgiveness.

(2) God's grace. God promises to restore all the damage done by the locusts, to give fresh growth and abundant harvests once again. It is a vivid and beautiful picture of the end of the locust invasion (Joel 2:20), of lovely sweet rain (Joel 2:23), of greenery and fruit (Joel 2:22) and of an overflowing plenitude of the blessings of life—grain, wine and olive oil (Joel 2:24).

At a deeper level it resonates with the language of judgement lifted, the curse driven back and blessing released. So although the text describes a historical recovery from a particularly bad locust attack in ancient Israel, it speaks also with overtones of God's ultimate purposes for the redemption of creation. When we read the Old Testament, we need to remember that Israel was called for the sake of all nations and their land often stands as a microcosm for the whole earth. This being so, it is striking that the song of rejoicing in Joel 2:21–23 is so comprehensive in those who are summoned to respond to what God is doing.

Do not be afraid, *land of Judah;*
　　be glad and rejoice.
Surely the LORD has done great things!
　　Do not be afraid, *you wild animals,*
　　For the pastures in the wilderness are becoming green.
The trees are bearing their fruit;
　　the fig tree and the vine yield their riches.
Be glad, *people of Zion,*
　　rejoice in the LORD your God,
for he has given you the autumn rains
　　because he is faithful.
He sends you abundant showers,
　　both autumn and spring rains, as before. (Joel 2:21–23)

Land, animals and humans are all included in the effects of God's saving purpose. God's blessing is for his whole creation—a truth and a joyful anticipation that is of ecological relevance today. No wonder that on other occasions the worshippers of Israel orchestrated a massive ode to joy among the whole of creation in anticipation of God coming to put things right in his world. Set Psalm 96:11–13 along side these words of Joel and you will see what I mean.

But for the people, the words of greatest comfort and purest grace must surely be Joel 2:25:

I will repay you for the years the locusts have eaten—
　　the great locust and the young locust,
　　the other locusts and the locust swarm—
my great army that I sent among you.

'Repay you'? What a startling way to make the point. The word is a technical word for legal compensation. It means to make good some loss you have caused somebody else to suffer. God is offering to pay Israel back for the damage caused—as if it was all God's fault, as if God were taking the blame, as if God were the one in the wrong, as if God owed them anything. In fact, as Joel and all the prophets made so clear, the fault lies with Israel and their congenital rebellion and wickedness. Here was a people who, as so often before, deserved nothing at the hand of God other than destruction, and yet God is the one offering to pay them compensation!

It is wonderful enough to know, negatively, that

He [God] does not treat us as our sins deserve or repay us according to our iniquities,

as Psalm 103:10 puts it (though only the cross reveals what it cost God himself to be able to act in this way). That is amazing grace in itself, and not one of us would be here writing or reading this if it were not true that God does not treat us as we *do* deserve. But that God should repay us what we *don't* deserve, what we lost because of our own sin (which is what Joel is talking about)—that is an even more amazingly positive act of sheer grace. Indeed, putting the two together produces that classic twin definition of God's mercy and God's grace. God's mercy is God *not* giving us what we *do* deserve. God's grace is God *giving* us what we *do not* deserve.

This verse, Joel 2:25, has been a favourite of many people for generations —understandably so. It speaks of God's power to renew and restore what has been lost in the devastation of our sinfulness. God can turn waste and loss into profit and growth. We should be careful to remember, though, that 'the locusts' of this promise were in fact the agents of God's own judgement. We are not talking here merely about the 'slings and arrows of outrageous fortune'—the accidents and lost opportunities, the failures and regrets, that are part of our everyday lives. It is of course another part of biblical truth that God is active within all the circumstances of our lives, that 'in all things God works for the good of those who love him', and that nothing can separate us from the love of God in Christ (Rom 8:28–39). But this verse in Joel holds out the transformative, redemptive power of God, even over those things that have been the mark of judgement.

Sin has consequences—in this life as well as in eternity. Sin devastates and destroys. It wastes and ruins. And not all those consequences can be undone in this life. The murder victim does not come back to life because the murderer becomes a Christian. The family wrecked by adultery and divorce is not necessarily restored when the adulterer comes to Christ. But, nevertheless, the testimony of many people is not only that genuine repentance *purges* the past (as Ezek 18:21–22 so explicitly declares), but that God's grace can *redeem* the past, and often does so in stunning ways.

So there is a terribly serious and terribly attractive word here for Christians who may be tempted, as I once was, to go on living in a state of life, or in a relationship, or in habits of behaviour that they know to be sinful and displeasing to God. Stay there and the locusts will do their vicious work, robbing your life of greenery—joy, growth and fruitfulness. But turn in genuine repentance to God and not only will you sink into the warm cleansing waters of his mercy and grace, but you will discover his power to restore even those things you may have feared you had lost forever. I write as one who, by God's mercy, has learned the profound and humbling truth of this in experience—even in the midst of a lifetime of personal Christian profession and public Christian ministry. How many more years will you let the locusts eat before you turn back to the Lord and prove his promise?

3) *God's honour.* God heard the prayer of his people, not just that they should be spared the dreadful judgement but also that he, God himself, should not be slandered among the nations. Rather, they should know who the true and living God really is. But that knowledge has to start with the people of Israel themselves. How can the world come to know who God is, if his own people do not acknowledge him as they ought? So the climax of Joel's word of promise to the waiting people comes in Joel 2:27:

> Then you will know that I am in Israel,
>> that I am the LORD your God,
>> and that there is no other;
> never again will my people be shamed.

As a result of God's saving action, things will be known about him. The living presence of the one and only unique God would be known and would be so visible that the people he lives among would have no need for shame. On the contrary, they will rejoice to be known as his as much as he will be pleased to be known as theirs.

A missional vision is implicit here, at least in principle. For when God is known in Israel, then ultimately the nations too will come to know him. That, after all, was the reason why God had called and created Israel in the first place—to be a light to the nations, to be the means through which he would reveal himself and his saving purpose to the ends of the earth. And so the goal of God's acts of judgement as well as his acts of redemption is that ultimately the whole world will know him.

And that is what leads us, finally, to the climax of the whole chapter, as Joel's vision broadens out beyond the removal of the immediate danger (the

plague of locusts), and even beyond the prospect of rapid recovery of the
national economy, to what it all points toward in God's ultimate purpose.
'And afterward,' Joel adds (Joel 2:28), not specifying a time or date, but indicating a future prospect. And that brings us back to our main theme—the
coming Spirit. For what a coming it is that Joel now portrays! In the context
of genuine repentance and total forgiveness, we are now ready to picture that
outpouring of the Spirit of God that Peter affirms took place at Pentecost.

Universal blessing (Joel 2:28–32)

'*You* will know,' says Joel 2:27. And the echo of so many other texts of the
Old Testament is 'and *the nations* will know.' But how? How will the knowledge
of God be spread? The answer in this immediate context is, by the overwhelming communicating power of the Spirit of God being poured out on
his people in such a way that the prophetic word will be on everyone's lips.

In the previous verses God promised to pour out rain—sweet irrigating
rain on thirsty ground and on vegetation devastated and devoured by the
locusts of his judgement. But now it is not just rain, but his own Spirit that
God promises to pour out. And we now know something of what this Spirit
of God would have meant to Old Testament believers. This is the Spirit who
birthed and sustains all creation. This is the Spirit who equips people for
craftsmanship and empowers them for leadership. This is the Spirit who
inspired the prophets to speak the truth and stand for justice. This is the
Spirit who anointed kings and who will anoint the coming righteous Servant-
king. This is the Spirit God says he is going to pour out 'on all people'!

In these verses Joel tells us that the coming of the Spirit will be marked
by effects that are universal, cosmic and saving.

(*1*) *Universal.* Do you remember the longing of Moses, possibly expressed
with ironic weariness, 'I wish that all the LORD's people were prophets and
that the LORD would put his Spirit on them!' (Num 11:29)? 'He will,' answers Joel, 'He will!' The outpouring of God's Spirit will make what must
have seemed like a dream to Moses into a real possibility. The Spirit will
be available for all.

> And afterwards,
>   I will pour out my Spirit on all people.
> Your sons and daughters will prophesy,
>   your old men will dream dreams,

> your young men will see visions.
> Even on my servants, both men and women,
>> I will pour out my Spirit in those days. (Joel 2:28–29)

We can't miss the note of universality in this outpouring, for Joel expands his initial phrase 'all people' in three remarkable ways. It will be on men and women (sons *and* daughters). It will be on old and young. And it will even be on slaves, male and female. In other words, there will be no privileged distinctions among God's people as regards who gets the Spirit— no distinctions of gender, age or class. All will have equal access to sharing in the outpouring that is promised. There is something very similar here to what Paul affirms has taken place in Christ:

> There is neither Jew nor Gentile, neither slave nor free, nor is there male and female, for you are all one in Christ Jesus. (Gal 3:28)

And Paul says this in the same context as telling the Galatians that, as the spiritual seed of Abraham in Christ, they have also received the 'promise of the Spirit' (Gal 3:14), the Spirit who witnesses in our hearts that we are children of God (Gal 4:6). And this is what Peter told his listeners on the day of Pentecost also.

(2) Cosmic. But it is not just that the Spirit will have his effect horizontally on all people, at the human level. Joel goes on to use language that implies a cosmic effect.

> I will show wonders in the heavens
>> and on the earth,
>> blood and fire and billows of smoke.
> The sun will be turned to darkness
>> and the moon to blood
>> before the coming of the great and dreadful day of the LORD. (Joel 2:30)

This is the kind of language that biblical writers used when they wanted to intensify the significance of some event they were describing or anticipating. Sometimes there may have been quite literal events that could be described in such terms—as for example the earthquake and apparently volcanic fire and smoke that terrified the Israelites at Mount Sinai. But more often this kind of language is intended figuratively as a way of expressing something that is, as we might say, 'earth-shaking'—that is, of tremendous, or ultimate, power and effectiveness. The psalmists used it a lot (cf. Ps 18:7–15; 97:5). We still use such language in somewhat modified ways when we describe some political event as 'cataclysmic', or some historical event or battle as 'a watershed', or some serious threat as 'facing the abyss'.

So, on the one hand, Joel, speaking in familiar prophetic language, probably did not mean us to take his words literally, and Peter certainly did not. For if on the day of Pentecost Jerusalem had actually been filled with blood, fire and smoke in the midst of a combined solar and lunar eclipse, we can be sure that the crowds would have had more to get excited about than a bunch of jabbering disciples whom they thought were drunk.

Yet, on the other hand, we cannot just dismiss Joel's imagery as purely rhetorical exaggeration. First of all, we should remember that the creation itself did respond to the climactic events of the death and resurrection of Jesus. The sun was darkened in the final hours of his crucifixion, and the earth quaked to mark both his death and his resurrection. And second, we should remember that the whole Bible teaches that the redeeming work of God (including of course the outpouring of the Spirit) encompasses the whole cosmic order. Paul tells us that through the cross God will bring about the reconciliation of the whole creation ('all things . . . in heaven and on earth') to himself (Col 1:20). And the outpouring of the Spirit was, after the resurrection itself, the first anticipation of the new creation. A whole new world was born on Easter Sunday, and a whole new era of the outpoured Spirit began at Pentecost. And, as Peter recognized, these things were of cosmic importance. The whole creation is affected. That is why he could point to what seemed so puzzling to the onlookers (the manifestation of the Spirit on the disciples), and boldly make an equation between 'this' event and 'that' Scripture. '*This*,' he says, '(though it may not look like it) is *that* which was spoken by the prophet Joel' (Acts 2:16)—and then goes on to quote our text in full. After that he tells the story of Jesus, climaxing with the cosmic affirmation of Jesus's resurrection and ascension:

> Exalted to the right hand of God, he has received from the Father the promised Holy Spirit and has poured out what you now see and hear. (Acts 2:33)

Paul takes the same theology to its cosmic conclusion when he speaks of the whole creation straining forward to that full redemption that will include us and it together and of how the Spirit is given to us as the 'firstfruits', or guarantee, of this grand prospect (Rom 8:18–24). Joel's language of 'wonders in the heavens and on the earth' seems almost restrained by comparison.

(3) *Salvation.* We reach at last the climactic words of this chapter, the climactic words of Joel's sermon and of Peter's, and what must also be the climax of this book:

> And everyone who calls
>   on the name of the LORD will be saved;
> for on Mount Zion and in Jerusalem
>   there will be deliverance,
>   as the LORD has said,
> even among the survivors
>   whom the LORD calls. (Joel 2:32)

Could you ever imagine that a chapter that begins as this one does—with words of sheer terror—could end with words of such promise? Listen again to the words of 'alarm' in Joel 2:1–2:

> Let all who live in the land tremble,
>   for the day of the LORD is coming.
> It is close at hand—
>   a day of darkness and gloom,
>   a day of clouds and blackness.

The chapter ends with another reference to the day of the LORD (at the end of Joel 2:31), but this time it is transformed into a day of opportunity and hope. There is salvation for anyone who wants it—all they have to do is call on the name of the LORD. That is, they must turn to Yahweh in the genuine repentance that is based on his grace, his covenant and his honour, as was carefully laid down in Joel 2:12–17. And so in the astonishing transformation that we have witnessed in this chapter, Yahweh, the LORD God who is Judge and executioner from the start of the book of Joel right through until Joel 2:11, has become the LORD God who is Saviour of all who call on his name.

Peter holds out this verse from Joel to the Jews from around the Mediterranean who had gathered in Jerusalem, offering them salvation literally in the place where it had once been promised by Joel and where it had now been accomplished by Jesus. They are those who can now not only call on God, but whom God is actually calling to himself (as the last line of Joel 2 puts it and Peter echoes in Acts 2:39). All that is required is true repentance and baptism in the name of Jesus, through whose death forgiveness of sins is now possible. And if they do those things, then 'you will receive the gift of the Holy Spirit' (Acts 2:38).

Paul, however, goes further still, for he sees even more clearly the universal implications of all that God had said and done in Israel. The salvation offered to Israel was the salvation offered to the world. For it was for the world's sake that God had chosen Israel, just as it was for the world's sake that he had sent his only Son. So Paul affirms,

> If you declare with your mouth, 'Jesus is Lord,' and believe in your heart that God raised him from the dead, you will be saved. For it is with your heart that you believe and are justified, and it is with your mouth that you profess your faith and are saved. As Scripture says, 'Anyone who believes in him will never be put to shame.' For there is no difference between Jew and Gentile—the same Lord is Lord of all and richly blesses all who call on him, for 'Everyone who calls on the name of the Lord will be saved.' (Rom 10:9–13)

'*The name of the Lord.*' Clearly, when Joel wrote these words, he meant the name of the LORD, Yahweh, the God of Israel. Equally clearly, when Paul quotes them, he means the Lord Jesus, for he has just said that confessing 'Jesus is Lord' is an essential criterion of salvation. In fact it was the earliest and shortest Christian creed. So we have here one of the many places in the New Testament where words of the Old Testament written by or about Yahweh, the God of Israel, are calmly taken up and used about Jesus of Nazareth. Jesus is indeed Immanuel, God with us. Jesus shares the identity of the true and living God of Israel's faith and worship and hope.

But what will lead people to say such words—in their hearts and on their lips? None other than the Holy Spirit of God. For it is the Spirit, as Jesus said, who 'will convict the world of guilt in regard to sin and righteousness and judgement' (John 16:8). So it will be the Spirit who will thus lead people to see their need of the salvation God offers through Christ. And it is only through the Holy Spirit, as Paul said, that anyone can come to confess, 'Jesus is Lord' (1 Cor 12:3). Joel would have thoroughly agreed.

CONCLUSION

When the Spirit came at Pentecost, then, he came with a great deal of expectation hanging on his coming. In this chapter we have seen how the prophets of Israel looked forward to transformation at every level when the Spirit would come, according to God's promise. There would be change at cosmic, ecological, international, moral, spiritual and personal levels. We have to acknowledge, in relation to all this, that there is an 'already . . . but not yet' about the fulfilment of these Spirit prophecies, just as there is about the kingdom of God as preached and inaugurated by Jesus. The kingdom has come, but not yet in all its fullness. The Spirit has come, but not yet with all that was promised. What we do see, most certainly, is the work of the Spirit in drawing people to repentance, forgiveness and restoration, just as Joel (and indeed Jesus) said he would.

And so, as we disembark from our long voyage of discovery of the Spirit of God in the Scriptures, and especially the Old Testament, our final picture of the Spirit must be one of him doing his favourite work—leading people to salvation in Christ. Yes, we now have grasped something of the vast scale of the work of the Spirit of God—in creation, in empowerment, in prophecy, in anointing for mission, in new creation. Perhaps the Holy Spirit will no longer be the neglected person of the Trinity that we have allowed him to be before. Or perhaps we will have a far richer appreciation of his person and activity than the limited role we normally allow him in certain kinds of worship or times of 'ministry'. But most of all, because God is the saving Father, and because Jesus is the saving Son, we will rejoice to see the saving Spirit, sent by both Father and Son to point men and women, sons and daughters, old and young, to the one in whom alone they can be saved.

BIBLIOGRAPHY

There is a vast amount of literature on Jesus (in general) and on his relation to the Old Testament (in particular) – infinitely more than on the topic of the Spirit of God or the fatherhood of God in the Old Testament. So the book list below relates predominantly to the first volume in this trilogy, without making any claim to be a complete guide to its subject matter. It does, however, seek to include some of the more significant recent works, many of which I found helpful in my own preparation, as well as works cited in the footnotes of the second and third volume. In the absence of footnotes in the text of the first volume, this bibliography therefore also stands as an acknowledgement of the debt I owe to the work of others in the field of Jesus research. It is confined to books; to have included articles in journals would have made it almost endless. Many of the works cited here include detailed bibliographies of wider relevant literature for those who wish to explore topics more extensively.

Andersen, Francis I., and David Noel Freedman. *Hosea: A New Translation with Introduction and Commentary*. Anchor Bible. New York: Doubleday, 1980.

Bammel Ernst, and C. F. D. Moule, eds. *Jesus and the Politics of His Day*. Cambridge: Cambridge University Press, 1984.

Blomberg, Craig L. *Interpreting the Parables*. Leicester: Apollos, 1990.

Bock, Darrell L. *Jesus according to Scripture: Restoring the Portrait from the Gospels*. Baker: Grand Rapids; Apollos: Leicester, 2002.

———. *Studying the Historical Jesus: A Guide to Sources and Methods*. Baker: Grand Rapids; Apollos: Leicester, 2002.

Boers, Hendrikus. *Who Was Jesus? The Historical Jesus and the Synoptic Gospels*. San Francisco, CA: Harper & Row, 1989.

Bonk, Jonathan J. 'Righteous Rich.' In *Missions and Money: Affluence as a Missionary Problem – Revisited*. Maryknoll, NY: Orbis, 2006.

Borg, Marcus J. *Conflict, Holiness and Politics in the Teaching of Jesus*. New York: Edwin Mellin, 1984.

Bowker, John. *Jesus and the Pharisees.* Cambridge: Cambridge University Press, 1973.

Brandon, S. G. F. *Jesus and the Zealots.* Manchester: Manchester University Press, 1967.

Bruce, F. F. *Paul and Jesus.* Grand Rapids: Baker, 1974; London: SPCK, 1977.

Brueggemann, Walter. *Genesis.* Atlanta, GA: John Knox Press, 1982.

———. *The Land: Place as Gift, Promise and Challenge in Biblical Faith.* Philadelphia, PA: Fortress, 1977.

———. *The Prophetic Imagination.* Philadelphia, PA: Fortress, 1978.

Calvin, John. *Genesis.* Wheaton, IL and Nottingham, UK: Crossway Books, 2001.

Charlesworth, James. H. *Jesus within Judaism.* New York: Doubleday, 1988; London: SPCK, 1989.

Chilton, Bruce D. *A Galilean Rabbi and His Bible: Jesus' Use of the Interpreted Scripture of His Day.* Wilmington: Michael Glazier, 1984.

Chilton, Bruce D., and James I. H. McDonald. *Jesus and the Ethics of the Kingdom.* Grand Rapids: Eerdmans, 1987.

Clowney, Edmund P. *The Unfolding Mystery: Discovering Christ in the Old Testament.* Leicester: IVP, 1988.

Dunn, James D. G. *Jesus and the Spirit: A Study of the Religious and Charismatic Experience of Jesus and the First Christians as Reflected in the New Testament.* London: SCM, 1975.

———. *Jesus, Paul and the Law.* London: SCM, 1989.

———. *The Partings of the Ways: Between Christianity and Judaism and Their Significance for the Character of Christianity.* London: SCM; Philadelphia, PA: Trinity Press, 1991.

Evans, Craig A. *Life of Jesus Research: An Annotated Bibliography.* Leiden: Brill, 1989.

France, R. T. *Divine Government: God's Kingship in the Gospel of Mark.* London: SPCK, 1990.

———. *The Gospel according to Matthew: An Introduction and Commentary.* Leicester: IVP; Grand Rapids: Eerdmans, 1985.

———. *Jesus and the Old Testament: His Application of Old Testament Passages to Himself and His Mission.* London: Tyndale, 1971.

———. *Jesus the Radical.* Leicester: IVP, 1975, 1989.

———. *Matthew: Evangelist and Teacher.* Exeter: Paternoster, 1989.

Goldingay, John. *Approaches to Old Testament Interpretation.* Leicester: Apollos, updated edition 1990.

————. *Isaiah*. New International Biblical Commentary. Peabody, MA: Hendrickson; Carlisle: Paternoster, 2001.

————. *Old Testament Theology, Volume One: Israel's Gospel*. Downers Grove, IL: InterVarsity, 2003.

Green, Joel B., and Max Turner, eds. *Jesus of Nazareth Lord and Christ: Essays on the Historical Jesus and New Testament Christology*. Grand Rapids: Eerdmans; Carlisle: Paternoster, 1994.

Harvey, Anthony E. *Jesus and the Constraints of History*. Philadelphia, PA: Westminster, 1982.

————. *Strenuous Commands: The Ethics of Jesus*. London: SCM, 1990.

Hengel, Martin. *Christ and Power*. Belfast and Dublin: Christian Journals, 1977.

————. *Was Jesus a Revolutionist?* Philadelphia, PA: Fortress, 1971.

Hooker, Morna D. *Continuity and Discontinuity: Early Christianity in Its Jewish Setting*. London: Epworth, 1986.

Horsley, Richard A., and John S. Hanson. *Bandits, Prophets and Messiahs: Popular Movements in the Time of Jesus*. Minneapolis, MN: Winston, 1985.

Hubbard, David Allan. *Hosea*. Tyndale Old Testament Commentaries. Downers Grove, IL: InterVarsity, 1989.

Hughes, R. Kent. *Genesis: Beginning and Blessing*. Wheaton, IL: Crossway Books, 2004.

Keck, Leander E. *Who Is Jesus? History in Perfect Tense*. Columbia: University of South Carolina Press, 2000.

Kim, Seyoon. *The Son of Man as the Son of God*. Grand Rapids, MI: Eerdmans, 1985.

Leivestad, Ragnar. *Jesus in His Own Perspective: An Examination of the Sayings, Actions and Eschatological Titles*. Minneapolis, MN: Augsburg, 1987.

Lloyd-Jones, D. Martin. *From Fear to Faith*. Leicester: IVP, 1953.

Marshall, I. Howard. *I Believe in the Historical Jesus*. London: Hodder & Stoughton, 1977.

————. *Jesus the Saviour: Studies in New Testament Theology*. London: SPCK, 1990.

————. *The Origins of New Testament Christology*. Updated edition. Leicester: Apollos, 1990.

Meyer, Ben F. *The Aims of Jesus*. London: SCM, 1979.

Mott, Stephen C. *Jesus and Social Ethics*. Grove Booklet on Ethics No. 55. Nottingham: Grove Books, 1984.

Motyer, Alec. *Look to the Rock: An Old Testament Background to Our Understanding of Christ*. Leicester: IVP, 1996.

Moule, Charles F. D. *The Birth of the New Testament*. 3rd ed. London: A & C Black, 1981.

———. *The Origin of Christology*. Cambridge: Cambridge University Press, 1977.

New, George, and David Cormack. *Why Did I Do That? Understanding and Mastering Your Motives*. London: Hodder & Stoughton, 1997.

Newman, Carey C. ed. *Jesus and the Restoration of Israel: A Critical Assessment of N. T. Wright's Jesus and the Victory of God*. Downers Grove, IL: Inter-Varsity; Carlisle: Paternoster, 1999.

Oakman, Douglas E. *Jesus and the Economic Questions of His Day*. Studies in the Bible and Early Christianity Vol. 8. New York: Edwin Mellin, 1986.

Pate, C. Marvin et. al. *The Story of Israel: A Biblical Theology*. Downers Grove, IL: InterVarsity; Leicester: Apollos, 2004.

Richardson, Alan. *The Political Christ*. London: SCM, 1973.

Riches, John Kenneth. *Jesus and the Transformation of Judaism*. New York: Seabury, 1982.

Ringe, Sharon H. *Jesus, Liberation and the Biblical Jubilee*. Philadelphia, PA: Fortress, 1985.

Rosenberg, Roy A. *Who Was Jesus?* Lanham, NY, and London: University Press of America, 1986.

Rowland, Christopher. *Christian Origins: An Account of the Setting and Character of the Most Important Messianic Sect of Judaism*. London: SPCK, 1985.

Sanders, Ed Parish. *Jesus and Judaism*. Philadelphia, PA: Fortress, 1985.

Stott, John R. W. *Christ the Controversialist*. London: Tyndale, 1970.

Theissen, Gerd. *The Shadow of the Galilean*. London: SCM, 1987.

Thompson, William M. *The Jesus Debate: A Survey and Synthesis*. New York: Paulist Press, 1985.

Tomasino, Anthony J. *Judaism before Jesus: The Events and Ideas That Shaped the New Testament World*. Leicester: IVP, 2003.

Vermès, Géza. *Jesus the Jew: A Historian's Reading of the Gospels*. London: Collins, 1973, and SCM Press, 1985.

Wenham, David. *The Parables of Jesus*. London: Hodder & Stoughton; Downers Grove, IL: InterVarsity, 1989.

Wenham, Gordon J. *Genesis 16 – 50*. Dallas, TX: Word Books, 1994.

Westermann, Claus. *The Parables of Jesus in the Light of the Old Testament*. Edinburgh: T & T Clarke, 1990.

Wilkins, Michael J., and James P. Moreland. *Jesus under Fire: Modern Scholarship Reinvents the Historical Jesus*. Grand Rapids: Zondervan; Carlisle: Paternoster, 1996.

Wilson, Marvin R. *Our Father Abraham: Jewish Roots of the Christian Faith.* Grand Rapids, MI: Eerdmans, 1989.

Witherington, Ben, III. *The Christology of Jesus.* Minneapolis, MN: Fortress, 1990.

————. *The Jesus Quest: The Third Search for the Jew of Nazareth.* Downers Grove, IL: InterVarsity; Carlisle: Paternoster, 1995.

Wright, Christopher. J. H. *God's People in God's Land: Family, Land and Property in the Old Testament.* Grand Rapids, MI: Eerdmans; Carlisle: Paternoster, 1990.

————. *Living as the People of God: The Relevance of Old Testament Ethics.* Leicester: IVP. In the USA, *An Eye for an Eye.* Downers Grove, IL: InterVarsity, 1983.

————. *The Message of Ezekiel.* The Bible Speaks Today series. Downers Grove, IL: InterVarsity, 2001.

————. *The Mission of God: Unlocking the Bible's Grand Narrative.* Downers Grove, IL: InterVarsity; Nottingham: IVP, 2006.

————. *Old Testament Ethics for the People of God.* Downers Grove, IL: InterVarsity, 2004.

Wright, N. T. *The Challenge of Jesus.* London: SPCK, 2000.

————. *The New Testament and the People of God.* London: SPCK, 1992.

————. *Jesus and the Victory of God.* London: SPCK, 1996.

————. *The Resurrection and the Son of God.* London: SPCK, 2003.

Yoder, John Howard. *The Politics of Jesus.* Grand Rapids, MI: Eerdmans, 1972.

Young, Brad H. *Jesus and His Jewish Parables.* New York: Paulist Press, 1989.

Zeitlin, Irving M. *Jesus and the Judaism of His Time.* Oxford: Polity Press, Blackwell, 1988.

SCRIPTURE INDEX

OLD TESTAMENT

Genesis
1, *176, 416*
1–2, *418, 476*
1–11, *15, 36, 100, 482*
1:1, *413*
1:1-2, *413, 423*
1:3, *414*
1:16, *416*
1:20, *424*
1:24, *424*
1:26-28, *476*
1:28, *424*
1:30, *424*
2, *87*
2:4, *14*
2:7, *261, 423, 424, 504*
2:15, *476*
3, *425, 431, 477*
3–11, *477, 478*
3:15, *72*
4–11, *31*
5:1, *14*
5:28-29, *88*
6:1-2, *425*
6:2, *104*
6:3, *425*
6:4, *104*
6:17, *424*
6:18-21, *72*
7:4, *424*
8:21–9:17, *72*
9:3-6, *73*
10, *11*
11, *11, 15, 332, 477, 478*
12, *11, 15, 36, 315, 477*
12:1-3, *74, 315, 477*
12:2-3, *13*
12:3, *36, 37, 113, 461*
13:16, *116*
15, *331*

15:1-21, *74*
15:5, *116*
15:6, *99*
16–50, *322*
17, *74, 319*
17:1-27, *74*
17:15-16, *319*
17:17, *319*
18, *59, 313, 326, 329*
18–19, *329*
18:1, *313*
18:1-8, *313*
18:9-15, *319*
18:16, *314*
18:17, *313*
18:17-19, *315*
18:18, *113, 479*
18:18-19, *37, 343, 478*
18:18-20, *114*
18:19, *39, 59, 74, 81, 170, 317, 479*
18:20-21, *317, 343*
18:20-33, *322*
18:22, *322*
18:25, *230, 321, 383, 393*
18:26, *324*
19, *317, 326*
19:4, *326*
19:9, *326*
19:29, *313, 326*
21:1-7, *320*
22, *102, 314, 315*
22:2, *93, 94, 308*
22:16, *331*
26:24, *327*
35:3, *395*
38, *12*
48:15-16, *395*

Exodus
1, *273*
1–15, *284*
1:7, *65*
2:11-12, *439*

2:23-25, *292*
2:24, *57*
3:12, *66*
3:13, *289*
3:16-17, *57*
4:19-31, *57*
4:22, *56, 80, 107, 111, 113, 160, 295, 300, 357*
4:22-23, *294, 296*
5, *285*
5:1-2, *284*
6:2-8, *285*
6:5-8, *57*
6:6-8, *76, 272, 290*
6:9, *290*
6:12, *285*
7, *285*
7–11, *285*
7:3-4, *289*
7:5, *285*
7:17, *285*
8:10-11, *286*
8:19, *286*
8:22, *206*
8:22-23, *286*
9:13-16, *43, 287*
9:14, *36, 206*
9:16, *36, 206, 376*
9:20, *288*
9:29, *36, 206*
10:2, *285*
11:3, *288*
11:7, *285*
11:9-10, *289*
12:12, *287, 290*
14, *285, 288, 289*
14:4, *288*
14:18, *288*
14:25, *288*
14:31, *327*
15, *205, 273, 290*
15:2, *232*
15:6, *228*
15:11, *290*
15:12, *228*

15:13, *273*
15:14-15, *448*
15:14-16, *43*
15:18, *205, 206, 291*
15:22-26, *358*
19, *270, 480*
19:3-6, *75, 76*
19:4, *255*
19:4-5, *165*
19:4-6, *16, 66, 113, 479*
19:5, *36, 76*
19:5-6, *173, 448*
19:6, *39*
19:24, *75*
20, *164*
20:2, *165*
20:2-3, *353*
20:5, *333*
20:8-11, *176*
20:12, *106*
21:15, *106*
21:16, *181*
21:17, *106*
21:26-27, *181*
22:21, *168*
23:1-12, *177*
23:9, *168*
24, *135, 331*
24:3, *481*
24:7, *481*
24:9-11, *314*
32, *447*
32–34, *71, 259, 261, 447, 510*
32:1-6, *329*
32:9-10, *329*
32:10, *332*
32:11-12, *43*
32:11-14, *330*
32:13, *331*
33:11, *328*
33:12-18, *328*
33:19-23, *333*
34, *82*
34:5-8, *333*

34:6, *259, 260, 334,*
  508
34:6-7, *259, 270,*
  343
34:7, *260*
34:29-35, *328*

Leviticus
10:10-11, *363, 480*
18:3, *173*
18:3-4, *481*
18:5, *186*
19, *171*
19:2, *171, 172, 481*
19:9-10, *171, 183*
19:13, *171*
19:14, *171*
19:15, *171*
19:16, *171*
19:18, *77, 171*
19:23-25, *171*
19:32, *171*
19:33-34, *171*
19:33-36, *168*
19:34, *171*
19:35-36, *171*
20:26, *174*
25, *192*
25:23, *184, 190*
25:35, *168*
25:37-38, *168*
25:42, *168*
26:3-13, *87*

Numbers
6:22-27, *480*
11, *439*
11–14, *436*
11:4, *439*
11:4-6, *358*
11:10-15, *439*
11:16-17, *441*
11:24-28, *442*
11:29, *443, 516*
12:3, *438*
12:6-8, *327*
12:7-8, *444*
13, *446*
13–14, *255*
14, *445, 446*
14:5, *440*
14:10-12, *446*

14:11, *448*
14:12, *332*
14:13-19, *447*
14:16, *331*
14:18, *259, 333, 509*
14:24, *327*
16:4, *440*
16:5, *224*
16:22, *440*
20:6, *440*
22–24, *461*
22:2-3, *461*
22:6, *461*
23:8, *462*
23:9, *174*
23:11-12, *462*
23:19-20, *463*
23:21-23, *206*
23:25-26, *462*
24:2, *461, 462*
24:10-13, *462*
35:31-34, *181*

Deuteronomy
1–3, *254*
1:2-3, *254*
1:19-46, *255*
1:30-31, *254*
1:31, *105*
1:32, *255*
2, *269*
2:5, *269*
2:9, *269, 461*
2:10-12, *42, 269*
2:19, *269*
2:20-23, *42, 269*
4, *219, 270*
4–11, *160, 161, 213*
4:5-8, *76, 317*
4:6-8, *44, 174, 306,*
  342, 481
4:9, *276*
4:12, *270*
4:32, *268*
4:32-33, *463*
4:32-34, *38, 268*
4:32-38, *79*
4:32-39, *77, 359*
4:32-40, *161, 267*
4:33, *269*
4:34, *268, 269, 273,*
  274

4:35, *38, 245, 267,*
  280, 418
4:36, *269, 270*
4:37, *269, 274*
4:37-38, *38*
4:38, *269*
4:39, *219, 245, 267,*
  281, 418
4:39-40, *39*
4:40, *175, 282*
5, *270*
5:1-22, *161*
5:6, *270*
5:9-10, *259, 333*
5:12-15, *176*
5:27, *481*
5:33, *175*
6, *213*
6:4, *225, 245, 509*
6:4-5, *160, 281*
6:5, *77, 108*
6:10-12, *161*
6:13, *157*
6:13-14, *160*
6:16, *157, 159, 161*
6:20-25, *165*
6:21, *279*
6:24, *175*
7:5, *359*
7:6-7, *297*
7:6-8, *107*
7:7-8, *16, 162*
7:7-9, *108*
7:9-10, *162*
8, *77, 258, 358*
8:1-5, *161*
8:2-5, *158, 256*
8:3, *157*
8:5, *106, 358*
8:6-18, *161*
8:17, *339*
8:17-18, *161, 162,*
  361
8:18, *340*
9, *330, 391, 447,*
  510
9:4-6, *16, 162, 391*
9:7-29, *162*
9:12, *330*
9:25-29, *448, 510*
9:26, *330*
10:12, *108, 170*

10:12-13, *164*
10:12-19, *317*
10:12-22, *75*
10:14, *219, 246*
10:17, *219, 246*
10:17-19, *170, 347*
12:30-31, *359*
13, *178*
13:1-5, *179*
13:6-11, *179*
14:1, *106, 107, 108,*
  295
14:1-2, *297*
14:28-29, *176, 184*
15:1-2, *194*
15:7-8, *168*
15:12-18, *181*
15:13-15, *168*
16:18-20, *171*
17, *306*
17:14-20, *81*
17:18-20, *305, 469*
18:15, *99*
18:18, *99*
20:19-20, *171*
21:10-14, *182*
21:18-21, *106*
22:8, *171*
23:15-16, *181*
24:6, *183*
24:10-13, *183*
24:14, *171*
24:14-15, *346*
24:17, *171*
24:19, *171*
24:19-22, *183*
25:13-16, *171*
27:16, *106*
27:18, *171*
28:1-14, *87*
29, *271*
29:22-28, *44*
29:29, *271*
30:1-10, *501*
30:6, *501*
30:15-16, *163*
30:15-20, *175*
30:16, *186*
30:19-20, *163*
31:9-13, *277*
32, *104, 113, 290,*
  295

32:4, *341, 395*
32:6, *104, 107, 295,
   296*
32:11, *414*
32:15, *232*
32:15-18, *104*
32:18, *107, 249, 296*
32:18-19, *295*
32:19, *107*
32:19-20, *104*
32:30-31, *395*
32:39, *104*
33:3-5, *207*
33:10, *364, 480*
34:5, *327*

Joshua
2, *12*
23–24, *82*

Judges
3:10, *434*
6, *106*
6:18-24, *314*
6:34, *434*
9:1, *253*
11:29, *434*
13:15-21, *314*
13:24-25, *434*
14:6, *434*
14:19, *434*
15:14-15, *434*

Ruth
1, *12*

1 Samuel
8–12, *17*
8:10-18, *18*
9–10, *471*
9:1, *253*
10:1, *435, 472*
10:6, *435, 472*
10:9-10, *436*
10:10, *472*
11:6, *435*
12, *82*
12:13-15, *305*
12:25, *305*
13:14, *473*
15:22, *23, 368*
16:1, *472*

16:6, *253*
16:12-13, *473*
16:13, *472*
16:14, *436*
18:10-11, *436*
19:19-24, *436*

2 Samuel
1, *12*
6, *78*
7, *17, 78*
7:5, *327*
7:10-16, *79*
7:12-16, *304*
7:14, *80, 106*
7:14-16, *97*
7:22, *291*
7:22-24, *79*
8:16, *253*
23:1-7, *78*

1 Kings
3:6, *259, 333*
3:28, *470*
8:41-43, *202*
10:9, *470*
11:13, *327*
18, *19, 188*
21, *19, 189*
22:14, *462*
22:24, *453*

2 Kings
17:15, *170*
19:35-36, *394*
21, *21*
22, *347*
22–23, *82, 277*
23:25, *348*

2 Chronicles
20:7, *313*
29–31, *82*
29:1, *253*
33, *21*
34:3, *348*
36:22-23, *484*

Ezra
1:1-4, *484*
2, *10*

Nehemiah
5, *194*
8, *277*
8:7-8, *364*
9, *510*
9:17, *259, 333, 509*
9:20, *460, 461, 463*
9:30, *460, 461*

Job
1:6, *104*
1:8, *327*
2:1, *104*
24:12, *325*
26:12-14, *414*
27:3-4, *425*
29–30, *106*
29:12-16, *263*
31:13-15, *181*
32:8, *425*
33:4, *425*
34:14-15, *418*

Psalms
1, *306*
1:1, *170*
2, *80, 102, 124, 206,
   306, 308*
2:7, *80, 93, 159, 306,
   308*
2:7-8, *13*
2:8, *159*
2:8-11, *80*
8:2, *227*
8:4, *129, 130*
15, *207*
17:7, *228*
18:2, *232*
18:7-15, *518*
20:7, *228*
22:1, *248*
24, *205, 207, 226*
24:4, *207*
25:14, *407*
27, *263*
27:7-9, *263*
27:9-10, *262*
27:10, *249, 263*
29, *205*
33, *227, 415, 423*
33:4-5, *415*
33:6, *416*

33:6-9, *415, 416*
33:7, *416*
33:8-9, *417*
33:13-15, *246*
36:6, *232*
42:5, *232*
46, *385, 386, 387,
   390, 393, 396, 397,
   403*
46:1, *393, 394*
46:1-2, *401*
46:2, *394, 401*
46:2-3, *388, 393*
46:4, *394*
46:4-7, *393, 394*
46:5, *394*
46:6, *394*
46:6-8, *388*
46:7, *394*
46:8, *396*
46:9, *396*
46:10, *387, 396*
47, *44, 45, 205, 390*
47:1-4, *44*
47:7-9, *113*
47:8-9, *45*
60:5, *228*
62:7, *232*
65:7, *227*
68, *263*
68:4-6, *262*
68:5-6, *263*
68:8, *270*
68:20, *232*
72, *13, 80, 81, 208,
   306, 307*
72:1, *470*
72:1-2, *306*
72:2, *470*
72:4, *81, 470*
72:8-11, *80*
72:10, *55*
72:12-13, *470*
72:17, *13, 80*
80:17, *129*
82, *304*
82:6, *104*
82:6-7, *304*
86:8-9, *291*
86:15, *259, 333, 509*
88:1, *232*
89, *78, 307*

89:6, *104*
89:6-8, *291*
89:9, *227*
89:26, *244, 252, 262*
89:26-37, *80, 307*
89:38-39, *308*
91, *159*
91:11-12, *159*
93, *205*
93–99, *213*
95, *205*
95:1, *232*
96, *49, 113, 205, 212*
96:1-3, *44, 45, 278*
96:4-9, *291*
96:11-13, *230, 513*
97, *205*
97:2, *207, 341, 467, 498*
97:5, *518*
98, *113, 205, 212*
98:1-3, *44*
98:6-9, *210*
99, *205*
99:4, *207*
102:13-22, *122*
103, *260, 261*
103:1-2, *262*
103:8, *259, 333, 509*
103:8-14, *259*
103:10, *260, 514*
103:12, *260*
103:13, *106, 261*
103:14, *262*
103:17, *259, 333*
104, *418, 420, 423, 497*
104:24, *419*
104:27-30, *419*
104:29-30, *416, 425*
104:31, *422*
105–107, *50*
107, *50*
107:3, *142*
110, *228, 229, 230*
110:1, *133, 228, 229*
110:6, *80*
112, *339*
118:15-16, *228*
119, *166, 463*
119:57-60, *167*
119:64, *167*

119:138, *464*
119:142, *464*
119:160, *464*
132, *78*
139, *353*
139:7, *420*
145, *205, 420*
145:8, *259, 333, 509*
145:8-9, *207*
145:11-13, *206*
145:15-17, *421*
146, *208*
146:7-10, *208*
147:19-20, *269, 463*

Proverbs
3:11-12, *257*
3:12, *106*
3:34, *438*
14:31, *169*
16:19, *438*
17:5, *169*
19:17, *169*
21:13, *170*
29:7, *170*
30:17, *106*
31, *339*
31:4-5, *470*
31:8-9, *470*

Isaiah
1, *317*
1:2, *107, 295*
1:2-4, *298*
1:11-16, *24*
1:11-20, *189*
2:2-5, *154, 210*
5, *189*
5:16, *466*
6, *381*
6:3, *397*
7, *90*
7:14, *51*
7:18-20, *389*
9:1-2, *54*
9:1-7, *54, 308*
9:6-7, *309*
9:7, *87*
10:5-19, *43, 389*
11:1-5, *87, 474*
11:9, *397*
19, *46, 289*

19:18-25, *289*
19:19-25, *46*
19:23-25, *55*
20:3, *327*
23:18, *48*
24, *122*
24:19-20, *394*
26:9, *122*
28:7-8, *454*
30:1, *295, 299*
30:9, *107, 295, 299*
32:1, *496*
32:15, *497*
32:15-18, *497*
32:16, *498*
32:17, *498*
32:17-18, *498*
33:20-24, *210*
34, *122*
35, *122, 216*
35:3-6, *216*
35:5-6, *136*
40, *381*
40–45, *61*
40–48, *43*
40–55, *25, 57, 61, 83, 85, 94, 110, 113, 121, 138, 223, 228, 327, 499*
40:1, *482*
40:3, *123, 215*
40:8, *227*
40:13, *224*
40:26, *416*
40:27, *24*
41, *485*
41:2-4, *125*
41:8, *84, 313, 484*
41:8-10, *137, 482*
41:25, *125*
42, *102, 154, 487, 493*
42:1, *47, 93, 94, 134, 136, 137, 308, 485*
42:1-4, *87, 136*
42:1-7, *475, 484*
42:1-9, *94, 139, 154*
42:2-3, *485*
42:3, *139, 485*
42:4, *47, 485*
42:4-6, *113*
42:5, *84*

42:6, *84, 135, 137*
42:7, *136, 139, 485*
42:14, *249*
42:18-22, *139, 483*
42:19, *84*
42:24, *139*
43, *143*
43:1-7, *143*
43:3, *232*
43:5, *142*
43:6, *295*
43:6-7, *115, 300*
43:10, *137, 143*
43:12, *143*
43:16-17, *288*
43:18-19, *101*
43:21, *137*
43:22-28, *139*
44:1-2, *137*
44:5, *46*
44:28, *125, 483*
44:28–45:1, *471*
44:28–45:13, *43*
45:1, *125*
45:1-4, *125*
45:1-5, *125*
45:4, *60, 137*
45:5-6, *376*
45:13, *125*
45:18-19, *272*
45:20-23, *122*
45:21-22, *234*
45:21-24, *223*
45:21-25, *126*
45:22, *47*
45:22-23, *223*
45:23, *224*
46, *255*
46:3-4, *256*
48:1, *115*
48:13, *228*
48:16, *452*
48:17-19, *78*
48:18-19, *115*
49, *140, 143, 487*
49:1, *140, 486*
49:1-6, *94, 486*
49:3, *137*
49:3-6, *486*
49:4, *140, 148*
49:5, *139, 486*
49:5-6, *122*

49:6, 47, 84, 137,
    140, 148, 486
49:8, 84
49:14, 24
49:15, 249
50:4-10, 94
50:5-9, 140
50:6, 487
51:4-5, 47, 113
51:4-8, 87
51:12, 129
52:7, 209
52:7-10, 209
52:12, 110
52:13, 487
52:13–53:12, 94, 487
53, 134, 135, 136,
    154, 260, 261
53:4, 136
53:4-6, 261
53:5-6, 487
53:6, 170
53:10-11, 134
53:10-12, 110
53:11, 487
53:12, 134, 135, 261
54:5-10, 85
54:9, 84
54:9-10, 84
54:10, 394
55, 84
55:3-4, 85, 87
55:3-5, 13, 84
55:6-9, 85
56:1-8, 122
56:7, 202
58:1-7, 189
58:6-10, 174
60:1-6, 55
60:10-14, 122
61, 126, 192, 208,
    248, 493
61:1, 136, 216, 452
61:1-2, 136, 192,
    487, 488, 489
61:1-3, 475
62:1-3, 481
63–64, 111
63:10, 437
63:10-14, 460
63:11-14, 437
63:15-16, 107, 301

63:16, 111, 294, 295
64:4, 291
64:7-9, 301
64:8, 107, 111, 295
65:17-25, 497
66:18-24, 122
66:19-24, 122

Jeremiah
2, 82
2:2, 356
2:3, 36
2:27, 252
3–4, 114
3:4, 114, 295
3:4-5, 298
3:5, 114
3:19, 106, 114, 295
3:19-20, 298
3:22, 107
4:1-2, 78, 114
4:2, 37
4:4, 501
4:5-9, 197
4:22, 295
5, 82
5:12, 456
5:13, 458
6:13, 86, 454
6:14-15, 456
7, 202
7:1-11, 189
7:1-15, 62
7:12-15, 99
7:15, 197
7:21-26, 24
8:10, 86
9:23, 338, 345
9:23-24, 24, 337,
    338, 344, 369, 467
9:24, 86, 224, 340
10:6-7, 291
10:11-12, 246, 291
11, 82
12:15-16, 46
14:11, 401
16, 122
18:18, 480
19:1-15, 197
20:1-2, 198
22, 209
22:1-5, 97

22:2-3, 81, 470
22:13-17, 337, 345,
    346
22:15-16, 86, 346,
    406, 467
22:15-17, 24
22:16, 347, 350
23:1-6, 85, 209
23:5-6, 87
23:9-32, 453
23:13, 81
23:14, 454
23:17, 81, 456
23:18, 457
23:21-22, 457
23:25-26, 458
23:28, 458
23:30, 458
23:32, 458
25:15-33, 122
26, 198
26:20-23, 465
27, 197
27:4-7, 389
27:5-7, 43
29:1, 389
29:4, 389
29:7, 401
30–31, 83
30–34, 121
31, 56, 296
31:9, 107, 113, 294,
    295, 296
31:9-10, 300
31:11-14, 88
31:15, 52, 53, 56
31:16-17, 56
31:18-20, 111
31:20, 295, 296, 300
31:31-34, 24, 82,
    135, 372
31:33, 85, 86
31:33-34, 336
31:34, 85, 86, 336
31:35-37, 85
32:2, 99
32:18-19, 259, 333
32:38-40, 85
33:15-18, 85
33:15-26, 87
33:19-26, 85
37:11-15, 198

40:1, 56
49:19, 291
50–51, 392
50:44, 291

Lamentations
3:32, 259, 333

Ezekiel
2:2, 499
3:12, 499
3:14, 499
3:24, 499
7:8, 383
8:3, 499
9:8, 383
11:24, 499
13, 453
13:3, 453
13:6-7, 457
13:10-16, 456
13:22-23, 457
14:12-23, 324
16:49, 317, 343
18:21-22, 514
18:32, 325
20, 331
20:8, 383
33:11, 325
34, 83, 85, 209
34:11-24, 83
34:23, 327
34:23-24, 87
34:25-27, 84
34:26-29, 88
34:29, 84
36, 83
36–37, 83
36:8-12, 88
36:16-23, 44, 331
36:24, 500
36:25, 85, 500
36:25-27, 500
36:26-32, 87
36:30, 84
36:33-35, 84
37, 24, 505
37:1, 499
37:1-14, 87, 502
37:9-10, 424
37:11, 502
37:14, 424

37:15-28, 83
37:23, 85
37:27, 85
38, 376
38–39, 373, 374, 380
38:2, 378
38:3-9, 375
38:4, 375
38:8, 375
38:10-13, 375
38:11, 375
38:14-16, 376
38:16, 374, 376, 380
38:17-23, 376
38:19-22, 376
38:23, 374, 376, 380
39, 376
39:1-16, 376
39:6-7, 374
39:17-20, 377
39:21, 380
39:21-23, 374
39:21-29, 377
39:22-24, 382
39:23, 383
39:27-29, 374
39:28-29, 383
40–48, 24, 121, 379, 380

Daniel
2:37-38, 43
3:25, 104
4:3, 206
4:17, 43, 206
4:24-25, 54
4:25, 43, 206
4:26-27, 208
4:32, 43, 206
4:34-35, 206
6, 401
7, 67, 110, 131, 132, 133, 134
7:9-10, 132
7:13, 130, 132
7:13-14, 228
7:14, 132
7:18, 132
9, 510
9:4, 259, 334
9:24, 125
9:25-26, 124

10:13, 132
10:20-21, 132
11:40-45, 377

Hosea
1, 360
1–3, 369
1:2-3, 354
1:10, 116, 142
2, 360, 365, 370
2–3, 355
2:2-13, 370
2:5, 361
2:5-8, 359
2:8, 352, 355, 371
2:8-9, 361
2:13, 371, 372
2:14, 370
2:14-20, 370
2:15, 352
2:16-23, 99
2:20, 352, 371, 372
3:1, 355
4:1, 352, 358
4:1-3, 359, 361, 427
4:2-3, 74
4:4-6, 359, 363
4:6, 352
4:10-14, 359
4:16, 357
5:4, 352, 359
5:12-13, 367
5:15, 366, 367
6:1-2, 112
6:1-3, 365, 366, 367
6:2, 367
6:3, 352
6:4, 366
6:6, 184, 189, 352, 368
7:9, 359
8:2, 352
8:2-3, 368
9:7, 352
9:10, 356
10:11, 357
10:12, 369
11:1, 51, 53, 56, 107, 112, 295, 296, 357
11:1-4, 106, 356, 357
11:3, 352, 357
11:4, 357, 358

12:6, 369
13:4, 352
13:4-5, 352
13:5, 353
13:6, 353
14:1-3, 367
14:4, 368
14:9, 352

Joel
1, 507
2, 507, 520
2:1, 507
2:1-2, 519
2:3, 507
2:4-5, 507
2:6, 507
2:7-9, 507
2:10, 507
2:11, 507, 509, 511, 519
2:12, 507, 508, 509
2:12-17, 508, 512, 519
2:13, 508, 509, 511
2:13-14, 508
2:14, 511
2:15, 511
2:15-17, 508
2:16, 511
2:17, 508, 509, 510, 511
2:18, 511, 512
2:18-19, 512
2:18-27, 511
2:19-27, 511
2:20, 512
2:21-23, 512, 513
2:22, 512
2:23, 512
2:24, 512
2:25, 513, 514
2:26-27, 512
2:27, 512, 515, 516
2:28, 516
2:28-29, 517
2:28-32, 100, 507, 516
2:30, 517
2:31, 519
2:32, 224, 235, 519
3, 122

Amos
1:2–2:3, 41
2:6, 194
2:6-16, 39
2:10-16, 62
3:1-2, 40, 269
3:2, 39, 62, 315
5:2, 62
5:11-12, 194
5:21-24, 24, 189
9, 122
9:7, 40, 42, 62
9:11-12, 46, 146

Jonah
4:2, 259, 334, 509

Micah
2–3, 122
2:6-11, 453
2:11, 454
3:5-7, 453
3:8, 452, 466
3:11, 454
4, 122
4:2-5, 210
4:6-9, 210
5:1-5, 210
5:2, 51, 53
6:8, 468
7:18, 291

Nahum
1:3, 259, 509

Habakkuk
1, 43, 400
1:1-4, 391
1:2-4, 388
1:5-6, 388
1:5-11, 391
1:12, 395, 398
1:13, 391
2, 392, 400
2:2, 402
2:4, 399
2:6-8, 392
2:9, 392
2:10, 392
2:12, 392
2:14, 387, 397
2:17, 392

2:18-20, 392
3, 390, 400
3:2, 400
3:16, 401
3:16-18, 402
3:16-19, 401
3:19, 402

Zephaniah
3, 122
3:9, 122
3:14-17, 122

Haggai
2:6, 394
2:6-9, 48
2:23, 327

Zechariah
4:6, 450
7:7-12, 466
9:9, 202, 233
9:9-10, 141
9:9-13, 121
9:10, 202
14:16-19, 122

Malachi
1:6, 106, 295, 299
2:6-9, 364
2:7-9, 480
2:10, 295
3:1, 123, 217
3:1-3, 202
4:5, 218

NEW TESTAMENT

Matthew
1, 29, 89
1–2, 51
1–5, 6
1:1-17, 49, 54
1:3-6, 12
1:6-11, 12
1:17, 13
1:18, 9, 35
1:18-25, 51
1:21, 233
2, 92
2–4, 54
2:1-12, 51

2:13-15, 51
2:15, 56
2:16-18, 52
2:19-23, 52
3, 92, 156
3:3, 215
3:17, 92, 156
4, 156
4:1-3, 156
4:1-11, 213
4:13-16, 54
5–7, 166
5:3-12, 166
5:6, 490
5:14-16, 174
5:16, 166
5:17, 185
5:17-20, 164
5:20, 175
5:38-48, 185
5:40-45, 198
5:44, 401
5:45, 74, 172
5:46-48, 174
5:48, 173
6:1-8, 175
6:12, 195
6:19-34, 196
6:24, 196
6:25-34, 159, 420
6:31-34, 174
6:33, 166, 490
7:16, 454
7:21, 348, 349
7:21-23, 436, 459
7:22-23, 349
7:24-27, 186
7:28-29, 186
8:5-13, 142
8:11-12, 142
8:17, 136
8:21-22, 179
9:10-13, 185
9:13, 368
10:5-6, 142
11, 215
11:4-5, 136, 216
11:10, 217
11:29, 186
12:1-14, 177
12:7, 184, 368
12:9-14, 185

12:15-21, 136
12:46-50, 179
13:41-42, 131
15:24, 142
16:21, 110, 112
17:1-13, 218
17:20, 321
18:12-35, 194
18:21-35, 168
19:17, 186
19:28, 131, 141
20:1-16, 196
21:12-13, 201
21:16, 227
21:45, 194
22:15-22, 194
22:34-40, 177
22:41-46, 124
23, 189
23:2-3, 176
23:4, 177
23:13-14, 177
23:23, 176
23:37-39, 203
25:31-32, 231
25:31-46, 170, 185
25:34-36, 349
26:28, 135
26:63-64, 132
28:16-20, 219
28:18-20, 492
28:19, 142
28:20, 278

Mark
1:2-3, 123
1:11, 308
1:24, 91
1:27, 91
2:7, 91, 233
2:10, 130
2:16, 91
2:23-28, 177
2:24, 91
2:27, 177
2:28, 130
3:6, 187
4:41, 92
5:25-34, 185
6:2, 91
6:3, 91
7:9-13, 176

8:31, 110, 112, 130
9:24, 320
9:31, 130
10:21, 186
10:23-31, 197
10:27, 321
10:45, 134
11:15-17, 201
11:17, 202
11:27, 194
12:1-9, 193
12:7, 109
12:32-33, 178
12:35-37, 228
13:2, 203
13:31, 227
14:24, 135
14:36, 109
14:58, 203
14:61-62, 126, 228
14:62, 131
15:29, 203

Luke
1–2, 149
1:16-17, 123, 149
1:32, 149
1:47, 233
1:52-55, 149
1:68-79, 149
1:69, 233
1:71, 233
1:77, 233
1:80, 95
2:11, 233
2:29-32, 144, 149
2:30, 233
2:36-38, 149
2:49, 92, 119
2:52, 95
3:8-9, 123
3:23, 93
3:23-38, 12
4, 493
4:14-21, 213
4:16-21, 216
4:18, 494
4:18-19, 136, 192
4:18-21, 126, 154
4:21, 192
4:24-30, 142
6:27-32, 173

6:34-36, *173*
7:34, *196*
7:36-50, *166, 185, 200*
7:41-43, *194*
8:25, *227*
9:22, *112, 133*
9:28-36, *50*
9:31, *30, 273*
9:44, *130*
11:1, *243*
11:4, *195*
12:13-21, *194*
12:15-21, *178, 196*
12:32, *141*
12:32-34, *197*
13:14, *201*
13:34-35, *203*
14:1-24, *200*
14:12-14, *197*
14:16-24, *197*
14:26, *179*
16:1-8, *194*
16:13, *196*
16:29-31, *184*
19:1-9, *195*
19:42-44, *203*
19:45-46, *201*
21:20-24, *203*
22:20, *135*
22:25-30, *174*
22:27, *135*
22:36, *134*
22:37, *134*
24, *103*
24:19-27, *505*
24:26, *129*
24:44-47, *149*
24:45, *492*
24:45-49, *505*
24:46, *112*
24:46-48, *143*
24:47, *492*

John
1, *100*
1:3, *227*
1:6, *123*
1:14, *218, 236, 272*
1:46, *54*
2:3, *406*
2:19, *203*

4:25-26, *126*
4:34, *97, 119*
6, *158*
7:41-43, *54*
8:31-41, *62*
8:58, *220*
10:30, *310*
12:34, *129*
13:3, *446*
13:3-15, *446*
14:15, *166*
14:15-18, *275*
14:25-26, *275*
14:31, *166*
15:1-8, *109*
15:9-17, *166*
15:14-15, *313, 407*
16:8, *520*
16:12-16, *275*
16:13, *464*
17:12, *449*
17:17, *464*
17:20, *275*
20:21-22, *494*
20:22, *505*
20:29, *275*

Acts
1:1, *49*
1:1-8, *149*
1:6, *144*
1:8, *143, 492*
2:16, *518*
2:16-21, *100*
2:24-26, *111*
2:24-28, *112*
2:32-36, *229*
2:33, *518*
2:38, *234, 520*
2:39, *520*
3, *145*
3:13, *136*
3:25-26, *145*
3:26, *136*
4:12, *234*
4:27, *136*
4:30, *136*
5:31, *234*
6:14, *203*
7:22, *440*
7:56, *130*
9:5, *221*

9:17, *221*
10, *145*
10:44-48, *145*
11, *145*
11:15-18, *145*
11:21, *145*
12:21, *145*
12:23, *145*
13:13-52, *90, 155*
13:16-41, *155*
13:32-33, *67, 129, 148*
13:38, *234*
13:46-47, *148*
13:47, *84, 493*
15:11, *234*
15:12-18, *146*
15:13-19, *46*
15:16-17, *505*
17:11, *464*
19:2, *429*
20:27, *476*
20:35, *197*
28:23-28, *150*

Romans
1, *362*
1–8, *147*
1:1-5, *118*
1:2-5, *116*
2:16, *231*
2:20, *463*
2:25-29, *75*
4, *100*
4–5, *42*
5:8, *275*
5:12-19, *323*
5:14, *98*
8, *302, 383, 428, 502*
8:1-4, *502*
8:11, *505*
8:15-17, *302*
8:18-24, *519*
8:18-27, *499*
8:19-21, *303*
8:19-23, *427*
8:19-25, *210*
8:19-27, *426*
8:22, *427*
8:23, *428*
8:26, *428*

8:26-27, *427*
8:28-30, *303*
8:28-39, *514*
8:31-39, *303*
8:32, *94*
8:34, *229*
8:38-39, *303*
9–11, *48, 147, 152*
9:5, *49*
9:6, *147*
9:24-26, *142*
9:26, *116*
10:9, *222, 235*
10:9-13, *520*
10:13, *224, 235*
11, *151*
11:1-2, *147*
11:22, *383*
11:26, *147*
14:9-12, *231*
14:10, *231*
14:11, *224*
15:7-9, *153*
15:8-9, *493*

1 Corinthians
1:31, *224*
2:10-11, *451*
2:16, *224*
3:5, *449*
3:21-23, *445*
8–10, *225*
8:4-6, *225, 237*
8:6, *225, 247*
10:6, *98*
10:11, *98*
10:25-26, *225*
10:26, *226*
11:25, *135*
12:3, *222, 520*
15:3-4, *112*
15:24-28, *229*
16:21, *220*
16:22, *220*

2 Corinthians
1:20, *29, 67*
3:4-5, *441*
4:5, *449*
4:7, *441*
5:10, *231*
5:17, *427, 428*

10:17, *224*
12:9-10, *345, 441*

Galatians
2:20, *275*
3, *42, 48, 60*
3–4, *100*
3:6-9, *478*
3:8, *60*
3:14, *60, 123, 517*
3:16, *65*
3:16-22, *62*
3:19, *65*
3:26-29, *117*
3:28, *49, 517*
3:29, *49, 60*
4:4-7, *117*
4:6, *517*

Ephesians
1:13-14, *499*
1:19-23, *230*
1:20-23, *229*
2–3, *48, 152*
2:11-22, *100*
2:15-16, *152*
3:6, *152*
3:14-19, *105*
5:5, *178*

Philippians
2, *224*
2:5-11, *237*
2:6-11, *223*
2:9, *223*
2:10-11, *223*

2:11, *222*
2:16, *231*
3:17, *98*
3:21, *428*
4:11-12, *345*
4:13, *345*
4:19, *345*

Colossians
1:15-20, *226, 237*
1:20, *518*
2:15, *274*
3:1, *229*
3:5, *178*

1 Thessalonians
1:7, *98*
4:13, *401*

2 Thessalonians
1:5-10, *231*
3:9, *98*

1 Timothy
2:1-4, *403*

2 Timothy
2:19, *224*
3:14-16, *277*
3:16, *276, 452*
3:16-17, *102*

Titus
2:7, *98*
2:13, *234, 235*

Hebrews
1:1-2, *272*
1:2, *29, 109, 227*
2:6, *130*
2:10, *234*
2:10-18, *115*
3:5, *437*
3:7–4:11, *63*
5:8, *109, 257, 407*
5:8-9, *115*
5:9, *234*
7:25, *234*
8:5, *29*
8:9-13, *82*
10:15-18, *82*
10:19-39, *63*
10:38, *399*
11:25-26, *440*
12:4-11, *258*
13:2, *314*

James
1:5, *344*
1:27, *349*
2:14-17, *350*
2:19, *281*
2:23, *313*
3:1, *364*

1 Peter
1:21-25, *136*
2:4-12, *100*
2:12, *174*
2:24, *261*
3:21, *98*

5:3, *98*
5:8, *293*

2 Peter
1:16-18, *218*
1:20-21, *451, 468*
1:21, *452*
2:7-8, *326*
3:3-7, *73*

1 John
2:3-6, *406*
2:5, *407*
2:6, *407*
3:16-17, *350*
4:1, *436*
4:17-21, *167*

Revelation
1, *270*
1:5, *230*
1:7, *132*
1:12-16, *132*
1:13, *130*
3:14, *230*
5:13, *230*
7:9, *316*
7:10, *232*
19–20, *380*
19:11–20:15, *377*
21–22, *90, 380*
21:1-3, *88*
21:24, *48*
22, *15*

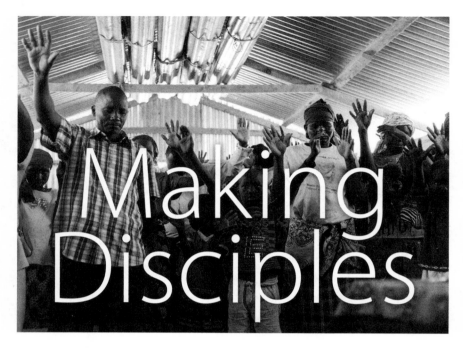

Around the World — Christianity is exploding
with growth in numbers

Yet — Believers are struggling to grow in Christ

That's Why Langham Exists

Our Vision

To see churches in the Majority World equipped for mission
and growing to maturity in Christ through the ministry of pastors
and leaders who believe, teach and live by the Word of God.

www.langham.org

FOUNDED BY JOHN STOTT